Essential Principles of Business for CSEC

3rd Edition

Dr. Alan Whitcomb
with Macpherson Barnes

CSEC® is a registered trade mark of the **Caribbean Examinations Council (CXC)**. **Essential Principles of Business for CSEC®** is an independent publication and has not been authorised, sponsored, or otherwise approved by CXC.

Longman
Part of Pearson

Contents

Profile 1: Organisational Principles

Background to business
1.1	The development of economic activity	1
1.2	Scarcity and choice in modern society	4
1.3	Economic systems	6
1.4	Types of production	8
1.5	Interdependence of industry	11
1.6	Things to do	12

Types of business
2.1	Reasons for establishing a business	15
2.2	Private and public enterprise	15
2.3	Limited liability	16
2.4	Private ownership	16
2.5	Special business relationships	20
2.6	Business growth	23
2.7	Government-owned businesses	26
2.8	The role of government agencies	28
2.9	Things to do	32

Business organisation
3.1	The role and functions of a business	37
3.2	Management	39
3.3	Organisational structure	44
3.4	Small and large businesses	50
3.5	Management and industrial relations	53
3.6	Motivation theories	53
3.7	Management information systems (MIS)	55
3.8	Things to do	57

Recruitment, selection and training
4.1	Recruiting employees	61
4.2	The human resources department	63
4.3	Staff orientation and training	64
4.4	Welfare of employees	65
4.5	Staff records	65
4.6	Dismissal and redundancy	65
4.7	Things to do	67

Motivation of employees
5.1	Job satisfaction	70
5.2	Wages	71
5.3	Working conditions	74
5.4	Things to do	77

Industrial relations
6.1	The importance of industrial relations	82
6.2	Trade unions	82
6.3	Collective bargaining	83
6.4	Industrial legislation	84
6.5	Restrictive practices	84
6.6	Pressure groups	85
6.7	Things to do	86

Establishing a business
7.1	The role of the entrepreneur	90
7.2	Evaluating the prospects	90
7.3	Planning	91
7.4	Obtaining capital equipment	94
7.5	Forming a limited company	95
7.6	The stakeholders of a business	98
7.7	Things to do	100

The legal aspects of business
8.1	Business and the law	104
8.2	Contract formation	104
8.3	Termination and discharge	110
8.4	Mistakes and misrepresentation	110
8.5	Things to do	111

Business documentation
9.1	Transactions	115
9.2	Making enquiries	115
9.3	Purchasing	117
9.4	Despatch	119
9.5	Charging	119
9.6	Foreign trade documents	125
9.7	Stock records	127
9.8	Things to do	129

Instruments of payment
10.1	Cash and near cash	133
10.2	Bank accounts	134
10.3	Electronic banking	138
10.4	Bank cards	141
10.5	Things to do	143

Insurance
11.1	The insurance industry	148
11.2	The purpose of insurance	148
11.3	Uninsurable risks	150
11.4	The principles of insurance	151
11.5	Types of insurance	152
11.6	The insurance contract	154
11.7	Things to do	156

Profile 2: Production, Marketing and Finance

Chapter 12 — Production
- 12.1 The factors of production — 160
- 12.2 Production levels — 166
- 12.3 The chain of production — 167
- 12.4 Techniques of production — 169
- 12.5 Business size — 171
- 12.6 Location of business — 177
- 12.7 Business expansion — 177
- 12.8 Labour versus technology — 181
- 12.9 Things to do — 183

Chapter 13 — Marketing
- 13.1 The market — 188
- 13.2 What is marketing? — 190
- 13.3 The marketing department — 191
- 13.4 Marketing mix — 192
- 13.5 Product life cycle — 195
- 13.6 Merchandising — 197
- 13.7 Price determination — 198
- 13.8 Competition — 201
- 13.9 Things to do — 203

Chapter 14 — Market research and advertising
- 14.1 Aims of market research — 209
- 14.2 Types of market research — 211
- 14.3 Market research in action — 212
- 14.4 Functions of advertising — 215
- 14.5 Forms of advertising — 217
- 14.6 The advertising campaign — 218
- 14.7 Promotion — 219
- 14.8 Consumerism — 222
- 14.9 Things to do — 225

Chapter 15 — Distribution
- 15.1 What is distribution? — 231
- 15.2 The channels of distribution — 232
- 15.3 Wholesalers — 232
- 15.4 Retailers — 234
- 15.5 The international market — 241
- 15.6 Transportation — 241
- 15.7 Things to do — 248

Chapter 16 — The financial sector
- 16.1 Caribbean banking — 257
- 16.2 Commercial banks — 257
- 16.3 The central bank — 258
- 16.4 Specialist banks — 260
- 16.5 Personal budgeting — 261
- 16.6 Sources of finance — 263
- 16.7 Savings and investment — 266
- 16.8 The stock market — 267
- 16.9 Things to do — 273

Chapter 17 — Business finances
- 17.1 The balance sheet — 279
- 17.2 Cash flow — 280
- 17.3 Costs and revenues — 281
- 17.4 Break-even — 282
- 17.5 Capital — 283
- 17.6 Turnover — 284
- 17.7 Profit — 286
- 17.8 Return on capital invested — 287
- 17.9 Things to do — 288

Profile 3: The Business Environment

Chapter 18 — The role of governments
- 18.1 The responsibilities of governments — 293
- 18.2 Government assistance to entrepreneurs — 296
- 18.3 Government intervention in business — 297
- 18.4 Social services — 299
- 18.5 The role of government agencies — 300
- 18.6 Governments and the labour force — 301
- 18.7 Things to do — 304

Chapter 19 — Taxation
- 19.1 Principles of taxation — 309
- 19.2 Functions of taxation — 310
- 19.3 Methods of taxation — 310
- 19.4 Economic effects of taxation — 312
- 19.5 Inflation — 313
- 19.6 Things to do — 315

Chapter 20 — Social accounting
- 20.1 The standard of living — 319
- 20.2 National income — 321
- 20.3 Gross national product (GNP) — 324
- 20.4 National expenditure — 326
- 20.5 National debt — 327
- 20.6 Growth and development — 327
- 20.7 Things to do — 330

Chapter 21 — Global trade
- 21.1 The importance of international trade — 334
- 21.2 Balance of trade — 336
- 21.3 Balance of payments — 336
- 21.4 Methods of selling abroad — 338
- 21.5 Difficulties faced by exporters — 339
- 21.6 Free trade restrictions — 339
- 21.7 Seeking assistance — 341
- 21.8 Things to do — 342

Chapter 22 — Regional and global business environment
- 22.1 Caribbean economic institutions — 346
- 22.2 International organisations involved in trade — 351
- 22.3 Caribbean economic problems — 354
- 22.4 The impact of local and foreign investment — 359
- 22.5 Things to do — 360

Chapter 23 — The school-based assessment
- 23.1 The basis of assessment — 364
- 23.2 The SBA requirements — 364
- 23.3 Starting off the project — 365
- 23.4 Carrying out your research — 366
- 23.5 Data collection — 366
- 23.6 Accounting for the '3 Profiles' — 372
- 23.7 Analysing the data collected — 374
- 23.8 The report — 375
- 23.9 Alternative to the SBA — 377

Index — 378

Preface

This book is intended for use as a basic text for students preparing for the CSEC examinations in Principles of Business and other related examinations. The book will also be useful for those who may not be taking examinations but have an interest in learning about the world of business.

The aim of the book has been to present comprehensive coverage of the syllabus in a readable and interesting style that will appeal to the full range of abilities. Wide and constructive use of illustrations is an important feature of the book.

Each chapter of text is supported by a variety of activities, containing varied degrees of difficulty, that will help the student to form revision notes and practise objective tests and stepped structured questions. Also included are exercises that encourage independent research.

The activities at the end of each chapter give a variety of opportunities for 'differentiation', allowing the learning material to be directed at varying degrees of student ability. The **Search and find** work could be tackled by all students, perhaps with the teacher deleting questions related to topics that are considered unnecessary or which some students will find too difficult. This type of activity helps the student produce revision notes. The **What do you know?** exercise is a relatively simple objective recap test that most students will enjoy completing. The other objective test takes the form of the classic multiple choice test. There is also a collection of **Structured questions** at the end of each chapter. These are '*stepped*', that is, each sub-part becomes progressively more difficult, thus allowing all students to achieve introductory questions whilst stretching the more able person in later sub-sections. The weighting of these questions is indicated by the mark allocation suggested. Many of these questions are related to data which adds interest and aids learning. A **Key words** exercise requires the student to show their understanding of important business-related words used within the chapter. The final activity consists of a variety of **Research assignments**. These are intended to be tackled by the more able student as investigative learning, often giving the opportunity for research and providing evidence of independent thought. They provide a useful selection of ideas to encourage individual research and contribute to **School-Based Assessment**.

The answers to the objective tests are available on the Longman Caribbean website.

How to use this book

Each chapter of this book is written in a clear, direct style.

Within each chapter you will see some activities called 'Key Words'. Within this exercise you are required to find out the business-related meaning of a collection of words from the section that are important to your learning. You are required to include each term in a separate sentence to show that you understand their appropriate use in a business context. You can use these activities to create your own glossary of relevant terms.

When a complete chapter has been carefully studied, the 'Things to Do' section at the end of the chapter can be tackled. This section contains a variety of activities aimed at reinforcing and testing the learning that has taken place. Your teacher may decide to specify which elements of these they want you to do, but you may also want to do others as additional practice for your personal satisfaction. This important part of each chapter contains the following elements:

 Search and find. You are required to write out a series of questions and their answers to formulate revision notes on the theme of the chapter.

 What do you know? This simple exercise consists of ten sentences with key words omitted. You are required to write out the sentences and insert the missing word which can be chosen from a list at the end of the test.

 Structured questions. These are a very important and unique feature of this book because they are excellent preparation for exams. The questions are weighted for progressive difficulty, in a similar way that exam questions are weighted. The weighting for each part of the question is shown in brackets, thus indicating the level of difficulty of each part. Many of these questions are data response questions, that is, they are based on some given information that you are required to study before tackling the questions.

 Research assignments. Each chapter ends with this, the most challenging section, which consists of a selection of assignments that can be used as a basis for individual research and practice for the SBA component.

On the accompanying interactive CD-ROM, you will find a series of multiple-choice questions, requiring the selection of one appropriate answer from four alternatives. There are ten multiple-choice questions for each chapter. You (or your teacher) can choose to tackle these after completing a chapter, a profile, or the whole book, depending on what you want to revise.

Background to business

1.1 The development of economic activity

Direct production

All people have three basic **NEEDS** – food, clothing and shelter, and many of the activities we engage in are aimed at satisfying those needs. Activity which results in the satisfaction of our needs is often referred to as 'economic activity', therefore, people are sometimes called 'economic animals'.

Early people had a simple way of life. They would provide all of their needs themselves without the aid of others. This is called **direct production**. They would hunt animals and gather plants and berries. They were living in a **subsistence economy** – providing just sufficient to survive, but not to improve their way of life.

In time people learnt to plant seeds to grow what they wanted, and to pen animals. This resulted in less time having to be spent in searching for food. Early people were now able to improve their way of life by building a permanent home, and by making tools to improve ways of satisfying their needs. One of the results of these improvements was that people found they were producing more goods than required. They were producing a **surplus**. They began to exchange goods for the surplus of others.

Barter

The exchange of one thing for another without the use of money is called **barter**, and this was the way the earliest form of trade took place. An important advantage of the barter system of trading was that it made it possible for people to dispose of any surplus they had, and at the same time obtain a wider variety of things they needed. This helped people to improve their way of life and it also allowed them to **specialise** in producing the things they could do best. This increased their **productivity** and resulted in more surplus and further **wealth**. It may seem that the barter system of trading was a simple way to trade but there were a number of disadvantages caused by problems of the system.

Fig. 1.1 *Exchange by barter*

Problems associated with the barter system

- *A double coincidence of wants.* People not only had to find someone who wanted their surplus, but the person they found had to offer what they wanted.
- *An exchange rate.* Having found others who wanted what they had to offer, early traders still had to agree on the quantities of each other's goods that were to be exchanged. Imagine the difficulty in deciding how many chickens to exchange for an axehead.

1

Principles of Business – Profile 1

- *Divisibility of goods.* Some rates of exchange did not make it possible to trade because some goods could not be split into smaller parts. For example, if one axehead was worth half a live pig, then it was not possible to trade with only one axehead because you cannot have half a pig and also keep it alive.
- *Storage of wealth.* Many goods which had been exchanged could not be saved for use at a future date because such items as food could not be stored for a long period of time.

Money

The development of money solved many of the problems of barter. When we talk of money today we cannot help but think of coins and notes, but money was not available in this form to early man. Other things were used instead. These included such things as shells, dogs' teeth, beads, grain, spearheads, hides, arrowheads, fishhooks and animals. They were used as we would now use money. Even today many things are used instead of money in some parts of the world, and when a country's economy collapses people tend to change back to using goods instead of money because they do not trust money any more.

Fig. 1.2 *Goods used instead of money*

The characteristics of money

For something to be considered as money, or in place of money, it must have the following qualities.

- It must be *durable*   It must be hard-wearing
- It must be *acceptable*   People must agree to its use
- It must be *divisible*   Possible to divide it into smaller units if necessary
- It must be *portable*   It must be convenient to carry

The use of money meant that people could sell their surplus of goods in exchange for money and use the money to buy their needs. Money acted as a **medium of exchange**. Trade became much simpler.

Eventually metal became a popular choice for money in any part of the world where it was common. Metal was:

- long-lasting
- able to be divided into smaller units and sizes
- scarce.

Some metals such as gold and silver were scarcer than others, and money made from these was of greater value.

The functions of money

- A medium of exchange   *Money makes the exchange of goods easier and makes barter unnecessary*
- A measure of value   *Money can be used to state prices for goods*
- A store of value   *Money can be saved, whereas to save goods may be inconvenient or impossible*
- A standard for postponed payments   *Money can be earned at one time and spent at another*

The way that money as we know it today developed is interesting. After experimenting for hundreds of years with the kind of things that you learnt about earlier, most communities decided to use precious metals as the most satisfactory kind of money. Eventually they created coins in various sizes

Chapter 1 – **Background to business**

which made it easier to carry and to divide into smaller sections.

Goldsmiths, who were the people who had safes and strong-rooms, began keeping safe the money of other people. They noticed that people were frequently coming to collect some of the money to pay their debts to others. The goldsmiths created promissory notes that their customers could give to others so that they could come and get the money from the goldsmiths themselves. These promissory notes were acceptable to everyone because the goldsmiths were well trusted. Paper money had been created.

As the use of paper money grew, the goldsmiths noticed that the money and precious metals in their safes and strong-rooms was rarely required, so they began to loan some of it out for a fee. They also developed little slips of paper, that we now call cheques, to enable their customers to transfer some of their wealth to others without the need to carry cash around with them. They were now acting as bankers.

Since these early times, money and banking has continually developed into many other forms, including bills of exchange, credit cards, electronic transfer, tele-banking and e-commerce. All of these are examined later in this book (see Chapters 9 and 10), and you will find them listed in the index.

Indirect production

When early people exchanged their surplus by barter with others they were engaging in indirect production: satisfying their needs in co-operation with other people.

A result of co-operating in this way was that people's basic needs were more easily satisfied. They now found that it was also possible to obtain things they wanted which are not essential to life. Further improvement in their way of life took place. In modern society, people's needs and wants have changed. Today we need a variety of products and we want things such as music and fine arts.

In modern industrial society most people satisfy their needs by co-operating with others to produce (indirectly) the needs of everyone. Sharing work in this way is known as the *division of labour* or *specialisation*, since people are specialising in doing a part of the whole process and dividing the labour (the human input into work activity) between many, which benefits everyone.

You will have realised that entrepreneurship (management of a business enterprise) plays an important part in enabling indirect production to take place. Entrepreneurs take the risk of setting up a business, thus enabling people to participate in indirect production. (See also Chapter 7.)

There are two ways of looking at division of labour:

Division of labour by product

This refers to people doing what they do best in exchange for money, and then using the money earned to buy the goods and services of others. In this way people become consumers: the buyers of a final good (sometimes referred to as a commodity) or service. We can see examples of this aspect of division of labour in all the working people we know. All workers are specialists.

Fig. 1.3 *Division of labour*

Principles of Business – Profile 1

Division of labour by process

By organising production into many stages or processes, workers become more specialised in their work, and consequently they produce more. For example, in a car production factory we can see a complete production line attended by many workers, each making their own contribution to the end product.

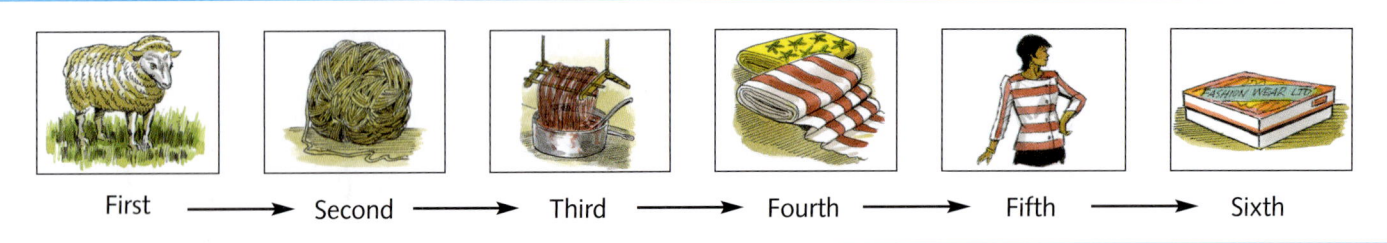

Fig. 1.4 *Example of division of labour*

Advantages of specialisation
▶ Workers become more expert in their jobs.
▶ Jobs become simpler and easier to learn.
▶ Output per person increases.
▶ Machinery and automation can be used.
▶ Workers can more easily change jobs.
▶ Unit costs are reduced.

Disadvantages of specialisation
▶ Repeating a single task can become boring.
▶ Individual crafts and skills are lost through mechanisation.
▶ Greater use of machinery can cause unemployment.
▶ Production can easily be stopped by strikes.
▶ Slow workers may be unable to keep up with others.

KEY WORDS
Find out the business-related meaning of each of the following terms. Write a separate sentence for each term to show your understanding.

direct production   indirect production   surplus   barter   needs
wants   promissory note   goods   enterprise   entrepreneur
labour   specialisation   commodity   entrepreneurship

1.2 Scarcity and choice in modern society

Today, specialisation has spread world-wide, with not only individuals but whole communities concentrating on doing what they do best. But in order to specialise in this way, *exchange* must take place if everyone's wants are to be satisfied. The bus driver works for wages, but needs food, so the wages are exchanged in order to satisfy his needs. The term 'market' is often used to refer to any exchange mechanism that brings together the sellers and buyers of a product.

The process of exchange involves making choices. In other words, the bus driver has to choose between keeping his wages, or putting them in the bank, and buying food. Or he might have wished to purchase a luxury item, but just had to choose between buying that item and buying food.

Chapter 1 – **Background to business**

Whenever we go shopping we are involved in the basic economic activity of making **choices** because we have scarce resources. We may have to choose between buying a T-shirt and a cassette which we want. Or we may have to choose between a cassette player and a camera. We have **unlimited wants**, but we have **limited resources** (money) available. Consequently, we not only have to make a choice, but we also have to form a **scale of preference**. We have to put what we want into some order of priority.

Fig. 1.5 *Our resources are limited but our wants are unlimited. We have to make choices.*

Scarcity and choice are not only problems that have to be faced by individuals. All **organisations** that are formed to achieve certain goals face these difficulties. Businesses have to decide how to use their limited resources to best effect for the benefit of the shareholders. For example, a business may have to decide between **ploughing back** most or all of its **profit** (when a firm's revenue is greater than its total costs) into the business, and paying its shareholders large dividends (or any dividends at all) for a particular year. Conversely, the business may make a **loss** (a shortfall in its trading activities), in which case its resources will be even further limited, and the firm will have to decide what choices to make in order to restore financial stability.

Governments also have to decide what use to make of the limited resources they have available to the best benefit of the community. For example, some of our Caribbean countries have limited supplies of foreign currency, yet a large amount of goods must be imported in order to support the various sectors of the communities. The governments have to choose between buying basic food items such as wheat and corn which are important staples, and caviar, which is a luxury item. Or the governments have to decide whether to invest the scarce foreign money in the buying of raw materials for the manufacturing sector, or to invest the money in the buying of **consumer products**.

The success with which individuals, businesses and governments make choices and use their scarce resources has a considerable influence on the quality of life of us all. This is sometimes referred to as the basic **economic problem** – how to use available resources in a community to the best benefit of society.

Principles of Business – Profile 1

1.3 Economic systems

The term **economy**, as we are using it here, is used to define a country in terms of the total composition of its economic activities.

The processes of production, exchange, scarcity and choice that we have looked at so far all take place in a political framework. The decision of what to produce or what choices to make from the limited resources available is influenced by the political situation within which the decision is made. No two countries are organised in the same way, but they all have to solve three basic problems, as follows.

- *What should be produced?* For example, what quantities of food, machinery or services should be produced?
- *How should production be organised?* What is the best way to combine the factors of production? Should automated or manual methods be used? What technological equipment (e.g. computers) is required? Where should the production take place?
- *For whom should production take place?* Should everyone be entitled to an equal share of production, or should some receive more than others?

Economists distinguish between four different economic systems which answer the foregoing questions. The first of these described here is a subsistence economy.

Subsistence economy

A subsistence economy is one where there is little specialisation and little trade. In such an economy people tend to live in family groups and grow most of their own food. It is called a 'subsistence economy' because people do little more than subsist – they can provide only the basic necessities to live. This was the form of economy that was a feature of the life of early people. Today more advanced forms of economy exist.

Other economic systems differ according to the extent to which the government interferes with the economy. There are three basic approaches adopted by governments in dealing with the economic problem: free market economy, controlled economy and mixed economy.

Free market economy

In a free market economy there is little or no government interference in the economy. It is based on the private ownership of the factors (means) of production and the means of distributing goods and services. **Market forces** are allowed to determine how resources are allocated. Sometimes such economies are referred to as market economies, unplanned economies, free enterprise, laissez-faire or capitalist systems.

There is no example of a 'pure' free market economy because governments play an important part in the running of all countries. The nearest to a true free market is probably the USA, although the UK has recently moved considerably in this direction. Some Caribbean countries have been moving towards the free enterprise system. Such countries, for example Jamaica and Trinidad and Tobago, have taken steps to sell state-owned enterprises, remove subsidies, and allow the exchange rate to float.

Fig. 1.6 *These three basic questions must be answered by every society*

Advantages of free market economy
- Free competition stimulates innovation and keeps prices down.
- Individuals are completely free to use their income and labour to their best advantage.
- Consumers decide what will be produced by influencing market forces.

Disadvantages of free market economy
- It encourages inequalities of wealth.
- Advertising can be used to create an artificially high demand for products.
- The more powerful businesses may buy out the smaller ones, thus reducing competition.
- Wealthy people are more able to purchase and influence the market than the poor.
- Companies may be tempted to restrict supplies to keep prices artificially high.

Controlled economy

In a controlled (or command) economy all the economic decisions are made by the government. The state decides what to produce, how it is to be produced and how it should be allocated to consumers. In other words, unlike in the free economy, it is the state that decides what the community needs and, therefore, demand is not influenced by the consumer. China and Cuba are examples of controlled economies.

Advantages of controlled economy
- The state ensures that the needs of the whole community are met, and not just the needs of those with the most wealth.
- State control eliminates wasteful competition.
- The state will provide goods and services that private enterprise would be unwilling to provide.
- It is not possible for a private monopoly to develop.

Disadvantages of controlled economy
- Free enterprise and competition are discouraged.
- Too many non-productive government officials are required to administer the system.
- Centralised production may not respond quickly enough to changing conditions and needs.
- Creativeness and efficiency are not encouraged.

Mixed economy

A mixed economy is a combination of elements from a free economy and a controlled economy. There is a public sector controlled by the government which provides goods and services that the state feels it can manage most efficiently, and a private sector in which individuals risk capital in producing goods and services for profit. Most Caribbean countries have mixed economies.

Globalisation

'Globalisation' does not really, as yet, have a precise definition. However, it can be seen as the intensification and spread of world-wide social, economic, cultural and political relationships among countries. Globalisation began with the development of international trade and has continued to grow. Cane sugar, an agricultural product of the Caribbean for many centuries, brought many peoples, cultures and systems of operation together. Thus, globalisation can be seen as the linking of distant localities in such a way that local activities are shaped by events occurring thousands of miles away.

A major benefit of globalisation is the provision of high quality goods and services at a cheaper rate. This is achieved through the **economies of scale** which firms contributing to globalisation enjoy. In contributing to the process of globalisation, firms not only provide goods and services economically, but they also provide employment for people who may have otherwise been unemployed.

The impact of globalisation has had some adverse effects on small economies of the Caribbean. Large international firms that can produce high quality goods and services at a cheaper cost set a challenge to small firms that are producing similar goods and services. For example, international firms in the area of clothing and textiles have made great inroads into the Caribbean market. Thus small firms are finding it difficult to compete.

From the foregoing it will have been seen that globalisation has opened the way for greater co-operation between countries, but it has also challenged Caribbean countries to examine the contribution they can make to the global market place.

1.4 Types of production

Earlier in this chapter we compared direct and indirect production. With direct production we said that individuals or small groups satisfy their wants entirely by their own efforts, unaided by others. However, indirect production, which is a feature of developed societies, involves specialisation, working for wages, and using the money earned to buy goods and services provided by others. Indirect production can be divided into three categories: primary production, secondary production and tertiary production.

Primary production is concerned with the extractive industries, secondary production with the manufacturing and constructive industries, and tertiary production with the provision of services.

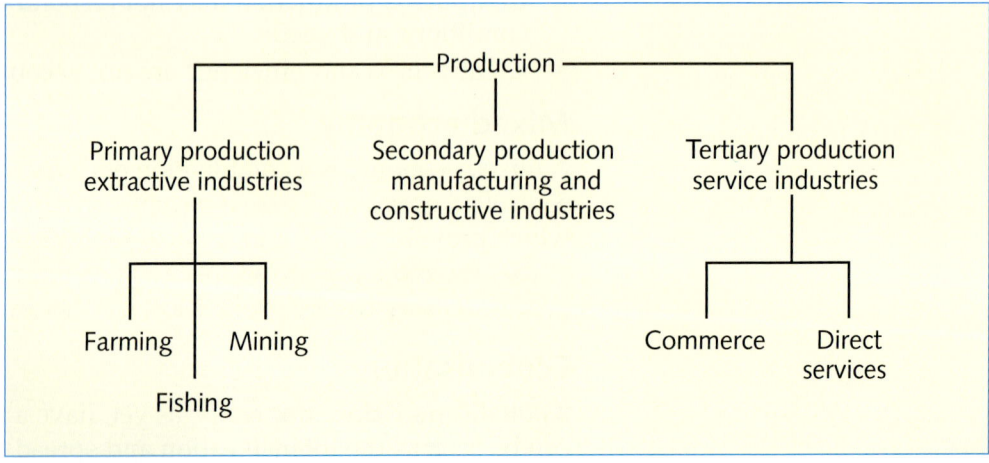

Fig. 1.7 *Family tree of production*

Chapter 1 – **Background to business**

Primary production

Primary production is concerned with the extraction of basic materials provided by nature, which are either above or below the earth's surface. The extractive industries are farming, fishing and mining. Without these much subsequent production would not take place.

Agriculture is an important primary production in most Caribbean territories. Sugar cane as well as many tropical fruits are grown. The following are other examples of primary production in the region:

Anguilla	fish	Guyana	timber, bauxite, rice
Barbados	fish oil	Jamaica	bauxite, coffee
Belize	timber	Leeward Islands	cotton, vegetables
Grenada	spices	Trinidad	oil, pitch
		Windward Islands	spices, cotton, arrowroot

Secondary production

Secondary production consists of the manufacturing and constructive industries. These industries take raw materials (obtained by the extractive industries) and change them into finished goods.

Manufacturers may make the whole finished product or make a part or parts which will be put together and made into a completed article, for example, aluminium converted into pots and pans.

The construction industry takes raw materials and partly finished products and changes them to an end product, for example buildings, roads and bridges.

Fig. 1.8 *Extractive industries*

Principles of Business – Profile 1

Types of production	Caribbean	Nigeria	Brazil	Chile	Canada	UK	USA
			Other countries				
PRIMARY PRODUCTION (extractive)	Agriculture *sugar cane, cotton, timber, rice, arrow-root, spices, coffee, bananas, citrus* Fishing Mining *bauxite, ore, oil, pitch*	Agriculture *nuts, rubber gum, timber, cotton, coal, peanuts* Mining *tin, coal, oil*	Agriculture *coffee, tobacco, corn, cotton, sugar cane, cocoa* Mining *iron ore, bauxite, ore, salt, lead*	Agriculture *grapes, citrus, rice, corn, peas, beans* Mining *copper, iron ore, nitrate, silver, coal*	Agriculture *wheat, oats, barley, tobacco, timber, vegetables* Mining *gold, natural gas, copper, nickel, iron, zinc, lead*	Agriculture *barley, oats, wheat, potatoes, vegetables, fruit, hops* Mining *natural gas, coal*	Agriculture *barley, wheat, corn, cotton, tobacco, soya beans, potatoes, vegetables* Mining *coal, oil, natural gas, copper, iron ore*
SECONDARY PRODUCTION (changing primary goods into finished goods)	Manufacturing *rum, molasses, fish oil, processed coffee, processed foods, milk, garments, asphalt, furniture, sugar* Construction *buildings, bridges, roadways*	Manufacturing *textiles, leather goods and hides, pottery* Construction *buildings, bridges, roadways*	Manufacturing *sugar, processed coffee, textiles, processed foods, pharmaceuticals, chemicals, electrical equipment* Construction *buildings, bridges, roadways*	Manufacturing *wines, processed foods, leather goods, copper ingots* Construction *buildings, bridges, roadways*	Manufacturing *machinery & equipment, paper & paper pulp, petroleum refining, wood products* Construction *buildings, bridges, roadways*	Manufacturing *iron & steel, motor vehicles, transportation equipment, food processing, brewing & distilling, leather goods, textiles* Construction *buildings, bridges, roadways*	Manufacturing *iron & steel, processed foods, machinery & equipment, motor vehicles* Construction *buildings, bridges, roadways*
TERTIARY PRODUCTION (direct services)	Commerce	Commerce	Commerce	Commerce	Commerce	Commerce	Commerce

Table 1.1 *Comparison of types of production in the region with types of production in other parts of the world*

Fig. 1.9 *The Red House, Trinidad: seat of parliament*

Tertiary production

When goods leave the producer (those who make consumer goods) they do not usually pass directly to the consumer (the ultimate purchaser). They have to be transported, stored, insured, advertised and sold by traders on the open market. These and the many other commercial activities make up tertiary production, and make change of ownership from producer to consumer possible. Tertiary production is sometimes called the service industry, but more often it is referred to as commerce and direct services.

Commerce can be divided into two clear areas: trade and services to trade.

- *Trade* is the buying and selling of goods in order to change the ownership. This can be divided into local trade and foreign trade.
- *Services* assist the buying and selling of goods, for example banking, finance, insurance, transport, communications and advertising.

Direct services are the activities provided by people that do not change the ownership of goods but which are essential to the well-being of the community, for example tourism, nursing, teaching, dentistry and acting.

1.5 Interdependence of industry

Industries depend on each other for goods and services. The tourist industry, for example, depends on the agricultural industry for supplies of food, and so some farmers sell their products – vegetables, citrus, among other products – directly to the hotels. The tourist industry is a large earner of foreign currency, and so the banks (including the central banks) depend on the earnings from tourism in order to meet the needs of individuals who, like businesses, require foreign currency to purchase raw materials from overseas. The raw materials are usually needed for the production of craft goods, hence the productive or manufacturing sectors also depend on the foreign currency earnings from tourism to an extent.

Let us now briefly summarise what we have learnt in this chapter.

- *Direct production* is characteristic of underdeveloped countries. It involves a considerable degree of self-sufficiency, and people live at subsistence level.
- *Indirect production* is a feature of all advanced economies, and this form of production is most common today. It involves people co-operating with others to obtain their needs.
- *Specialisation* is an essential part of indirect production and it involves people doing what they do best. Facilities for exchange must exist for specialisation to take place.
- *Tertiary production* or commerce describes the activities that are positioned between the producer and the consumer. These provide the means of buying and selling goods and services. They play a vital part in enabling people to specialise, earn wages and then buy their wants. They also play a major role in co-ordinating and promoting the activities of producers. We will now examine some of the ways in which this is done.

Traders, such as retailers, help producers by distributing their products. Exporters sell locally produced goods overseas. This not only provides work for producers, but also brings in foreign money (through their **profit**) that is needed to pay for the import of raw materials and finished goods that we cannot economically produce at home. In this way, home producers are able to specialise in manufacturing products for which they are best suited.

The services to trade also play an important part in co-ordinating the work of producers and distributing their products. For example, finance provides the **capital** necessary for a business to buy the assets it needs and also for consumers and businesses who wish to buy on credit. Banking makes transfer of payments between buyers and sellers possible. Banks also provide a variety of other services that make it easy for payments to be made, and therefore encourage production and trade to take place. Insurance solves some of the risks involved in producing and trading, such as the danger of loss or damage to goods or equipment. Transport provides the physical link between producers, traders and consumers, and gets goods to the market in good condition. Advertising helps producers and traders to make consumers aware of the availability of goods and services. Various communication facilities enable businessmen to communicate with each other and their customers at the various stages of production and distribution.

From the foregoing we can see that commercial activities are essential for production to take place, but also that commercial activities would not be

Principles of Business – Profile 1

KEY WORDS

Find out the business-related meaning of each of the following terms. Write a separate sentence for each term to show your understanding.

stakeholder   consumer
market   profit   loss
service   exchange   wants
consumer   product
capital   economy
producer   trade
scale of preference
subsistence economy
free market economy

needed if it were not for specialisation making exchange necessary. In other words, primary, secondary and tertiary production are independent.

You will have also realised from the last section of this chapter, that business has an effect on a wide range of people and other businesses and organisations. Any individual, group or organisation that is affected by the activity of a business is often referred to as a stakeholder, because they have an interest in what the business does. For example, your school has an interest in local businesses because they:

- may cause local pollution
- provide employment
- bring prosperity to the area
- provide some of the things you want.

Others will also be affected by a business. For example, shareholders will depend on it for income, the local council for taxes, customers for supplies, employees for wages, suppliers for trade, and many others. The relationship between these many stakeholders can be very complex, and they can lead to conflicts, for example, with pressure groups. You can read more about stakeholders in Chapter 7 of this book.

1.6 Things to do

This section contains a variety of exercises to help you create revision notes, to test your understanding and to prepare you for examinations.

Search and find

1. What is direct production and why does it limit the quality of life?
2. Why is the production of a surplus important?
3. What is barter and what are the problems of trading in this manner?
4. How does money solve the problems of barter?
5. What qualities are necessary for something to be used as money?
6. What are the functions of money?
7. In what way does indirect production require people to co-operate?
8. How does specialisation help to create a surplus?
9. Explain the difference between division of labour by product and division of labour by process.
10. List the advantages and disadvantages of division of labour.

Chapter 1 – **Background to business**

11 Why is exchange so important for specialisation to take place?

12 Why are we all required to make choices and form a scale of preference?

13 Why is making wise choices important to individuals, businesses and whole countries?

14 State the four basic problems that economic systems have to attempt to solve.

15 What is a subsistence economy and why is it not a satisfactory way of life?

16 'The free market economy and a controlled economy are very different.' Explain this statement.

17 What is a mixed economy?

18 What do you understand by the term 'globalisation'?

19 In what ways does 'globalisation' present a challenge to the Caribbean region?

20 Why is primary production also referred to as the extractive industries?

21 How does secondary production rely upon primary production?

22 Why is tertiary production so important to the other forms of production?

23 Distinguish between trade and the services to trade.

24 What are direct services? Give four examples of occupations that provide a direct service and say how they contribute to the quality of life.

25 In what ways are primary, secondary and tertiary production interdependent?

26 Give examples of primary industries in the Caribbean territories.

27 What are the basic economic problems that face the Caribbean region?

28 'Your school is a stakeholder in local business, but others are stakeholders in your school.' Explain this statement.

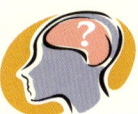

What do you know?

Write out the complete sentence and insert the missing word, which can be chosen from the list at the end of the questions.

1 ..... production means producing all of your needs without the help of others.
2 In a subsistence economy, just enough is provided in order to .....
3 One of the difficulties of barter was that of agreeing an ..... rate.
4 ..... makes the exchange of goods easy and barter unnecessary.
5 A problem of specialisation is that repeating a task can become .....
6 One of the advantages of division of labour is that workers become more ..... in their job.
7 We are all involved in the basic economic activity of making a ..... because of scarce resources.
8 Forming a scale of preference involves putting things we want in order of .....
9 In a free market economy there is no ..... interference.
10 Free competition stimulates innovation and can help to keep ..... down.

Choose the missing words from the following:

priority   expert   survive   money   choice   boring   direct   government   prices   exchange

13

Principles of Business – Profile 1

Structured questions

Q1 Primary production is sometimes referred to as the extractive industries.

(a) Why is this? — 2

(b) Name the three extractive industries. — 3

(c) What is secondary production? Name the two main categories into which this form of production can be divided. — 4

(d) Name five of the elements of tertiary production. — 5

(e) 'Tertiary production is very different from the other forms of production, but it is just as important.' Explain this statement. — 6

Q2

(a) Define barter. — 2

(b) Briefly explain three of the problems of barter. — 2

(c) Explain how money solves most of the problems of barter. — 2

(d) Spearheads, teeth and shells have all been used as money in the past. What common features do they all have that made them suitable for this purpose? — 3

(e) Why did metal become a popular substance for use as money? — 3

(f) Clearly describe the basic functions of money. — 8

Q3

(a) Describe each of the following economic systems:
  (i) subsistence economy   3   (iii) controlled economy   3
  (ii) free market economy   3   (iv) mixed economy   3

(b) Give examples of countries of the Caribbean region which utilise two of the economic systems described in (a) above. — 8

Research assignments

1 Explain to an imaginary visitor from China the main differences between the economic system that exists in his or her own country and that existing in a Caribbean country of your choice. Include evidence that supports your report.

2 a) Imagine yourself to be a manufacturer of furniture. Describe how you would use division of labour in the production of a specific item of furniture.

  b) One of the disadvantages of specialisation is that work can become boring for the worker. Suggest ways that you would try to overcome this problem.

  c) What evidence can you give that proves that division of labour operates successfully in your locality?

3 What is division of labour? Show how this must lead to commercial activities, using specific examples and evidence from local businesses to illustrate your answer.

4 Explain why the success of industry is influenced by the effectiveness of commerce. Use specific examples from local businesses to illustrate your answer.

Types of business

2.1 Reasons for establishing a business

A **business** (sometimes referred to as a **firm**) is a producer or distributor of goods or services. The most obvious reason for starting a business is to make a **profit**, which is the result when a firm's sales revenue is greater than its total costs. Profit is important because it enables the business to survive and grow, and it also provides the owner(s) – the **entrepreneur(s)** – with a return for taking the risk of losing the money they have invested.

However, there are other reasons why someone may want to start a business; a person may have a good idea that they realise will meet a public need, and, therefore, they feel they have an opportunity to do well. Another reason could be that someone has lost their job, and perhaps received a redundancy payment and they wish to become self-sufficient. Alternatively, someone may just not like working for someone else and just want to be their own boss.

Although we have said that profit can be the most important reason for establishing a business, this is not always the case. For example, some charities are set up on business lines but profit is not their main concern. Many organisations operate as businesses but can pay their operating costs, such as the wages of staff, through fund-raising activities, donations, and receipt of grants from government bodies.

Similarly, some public services are not operated on the same profit-related concept of private businesses. Public services are provided by organisations such as the police, fire services, schools and hospitals, and many others. The money to operate them is raised by the government, through taxation, so that the services can be provided free to all. Sometimes the service may raise some income, for example a library service may sell some products, or charge for special services, thus bringing in some revenue. But these types of service are very different from the private services provided a bank, for example.

2.2 Private and public enterprise

In most Caribbean countries we say there is a **mixed economy**, because some businesses are privately owned and others are owned by the state. The private businesses or enterprises are those that are owned by private individuals (that is, by *some* of the public). The main types of private enterprise are:

- sole proprietors
- partnerships
- private limited companies
- public limited companies.

There are also some organisations in which a special relationship can be observed. These businesses include co-operatives, holding companies and building societies. These special relationships are examined later in this chapter.

Public enterprise refers to industries and services owned by the state (that is, by *all* of the public) and run by either local or central government, for example, public utilities.

Principles of Business – Profile 1

2.3 Limited liability

People who invest in businesses (**entrepreneurs**) face many risks. The obvious risk they face is that the firm does not make a **profit**, or, even worse, that it makes a **loss**. The most serious risk is that the business may go **bankrupt**, i.e. it cannot pay the money it owes to its creditors. Under such circumstances, if the business has unlimited liability, the owners of the business are not only liable to lose the money they have invested in the firm, but they can also have their personal assets (such as home and car) taken in order to pay off their debts. Although many small businesses have unlimited liability, larger companies would not be able to attract sufficient investors if everyone faced the risk of unlimited liability. For this reason, the status of limited liability exists.

The status of **limited liability** allows people to invest in a business without having to face the risks of unlimited liability which have already been outlined. When a business has limited liability the investor is only liable to lose the amount of money he or she has put into the business, and his or her private possessions cannot be taken if the firm fails. Thus a limited liability company is said to have a separate corporate identity, an identity all of its own and separate from the identity of the owners of the business. It can sue and be sued in its title name, which must include the word **Limited** (Ltd.) (or PLC if it is a public company).

2.4 Private ownership

The sole proprietor

This type of business may be operated by the proprietor (owner) alone or may employ several people, but the main feature of it is that it is owned by one person and tends to be a small business. A sole proprietor business is often also referred to as a **sole trader**. There are many examples of sole proprietorships in the Caribbean.

Do not fall into the trap of thinking of the sole proprietor only as a retailer. Any business, be it a small factory, window cleaner, removal firm, gardener or decorator, is a sole proprietor if it is owned by one person.

Sole proprietors tend to have only a few employees, and less machinery or capital than larger businesses. They also have less plant and fewer opportunities for economies of scale. Their market tends to be less diversified than larger businesses because their level of operations limits their output.

Figure 2.2 shows the advantages and disadvantages of the sole proprietor.

Not surprisingly, the sole proprietor is more likely to fail than any other form of business and is particularly open to pressure from the larger types of business.

Most businesses try to expand in a natural attempt to make the business more stable and to give it greater continuity. One of the ways in which a sole trader may expand is by taking one or more persons into part ownership of the business to form a partnership.

Partnership

The law allows this type of business to have between two and twenty persons

Fig. 2.1 *Business titles set in distinctive styles*

Chapter 2 – **Types of business**

as members, although there are exceptions. A bank is not allowed to have more than ten partners, and certain professional firms such as accountants, solicitors and stockbrokers are allowed to have more than twenty partners.

This type of firm solves some of the problems faced by the sole proprietor. For example, because there are more people in a partnership there is more experience and knowledge available when making decisions, and sometimes one or more partners have specialist knowledge, such as accountancy, to look after the financial side of the business. The partnership still has, however, some disadvantages.

Like the sole proprietor, the partnership generally has unlimited liability and each partner is fully liable for the debts of the business. By this we mean that should the business go bankrupt, the partners do not necessarily have to face the debts equally. For example, if a two-person business goes bankrupt and one partner has no personal possessions whilst the other has many, the creditors can claim the total debt from the wealthy partner. On the other hand, if both partners have sufficient personal possessions to meet the debts they will make equal contributions.

A **partnership deed** sets out the rights of each partner as to the division of the profits and so on. If such a deed does not exist then it is assumed that the profits or debts of the partnership are shared equally.

A partner may be willing to introduce capital into a business but may not wish to take an active part in the running of the business. Such a person is known as a **sleeping partner**. However, the sleeping partner will still have to meet his or her share of the debts should the business go bankrupt.

It is possible to have a limited partnership, but at least one partner must accept unlimited liability. Consequently, limited partnerships are relatively rare.

Some professional bodies do not allow their members to form limited companies. These include solicitors, doctors and accountants.

> A small business like mine needs less capital
>
> *but* I have to provide all the capital myself. It can be difficult to get a loan because I'm a bigger risk than a large company.
>
> When I make a profit it's all mine
>
> *but* I have unlimited liability if the business goes bankrupt. If I am unable to pay my creditors, they can take everything I own.
>
> I'm my own boss, make all my own decisions, and I'm involved with every aspect of the business and all my clients.

Fig. 2.2 *Sole proprietor advantages and disadvantages*

Advantages of a partnership
- Easily formed.
- More people to contribute capital than sole proprietor.
- Greater continuity than sole proprietor.
- Expenses and management of business are shared.

Disadvantages of a partnership
- Generally unlimited liability.
- Possible disagreements between partners.
- Each partner is liable for the debts of the business.
- Membership limit of twenty restricts resources of business.

Private limited companies

Any company which is not registered as a public company is a private limited company. This type of company must include the word 'Limited' (or Ltd.) in its title.

A private limited company is allowed to have a minimum of two members (**shareholders**). There is no upper limit. The capital of the business is divided into shares, but the shares cannot be sold on the Stock Exchange and they cannot be advertised for sale publicly. Therefore, new shareholders must be found privately; hence the term 'private'. The shareholders may or may not take part in the running of the business. If the company makes a profit it pays a 'dividend' on each share.

Principles of Business – Profile 1

Some private companies may wish to keep control over the transfer of ownership of their shares. For example, a family concern might wish to ensure that ownership or control remains within the family. The private company may, if it wishes, write a rule into its articles of association requiring its members to offer shares for sale to existing members before attempting to sell them to non-members.

Carefully audited accounts have to be kept for annual inspection. This can cause considerable expense.

Public limited companies

Private and public limited liability companies are sometimes called **joint stock companies** because each is an association of people who join together to contribute money to a joint or common stock, which is used in some form of business, and the profit or loss is shared among the contributors.

The public limited company must indicate its public status by including the letters PLC (or plc) in its title.

It takes a minimum of two persons to form a public company, and there is no maximum membership. Such companies are allowed to sell shares to the public. The transfer of share ownership is simple, and therefore the number of owners or shareholders can become very considerable. Consequently, this type of business can raise almost limitless funds.

Obviously, it would not be practicable for all the shareholders to take part in the running of the business, and therefore the shareholders elect a small committee called a **board of directors** to take decisions on their behalf, and this board elects a **chairman** to regulate their meetings.

Even the board of directors would consist of too many people for them all to take part in the day-to-day running of the business, so they appoint a person to carry out this task, and the appointed person is known as the **managing**

We have more people to invest capital

but we are not allowed to sell shares to the public on the Stock Exchange. This may limit the capital we can raise. We may decide to restrict share transfer which would further limit capital raised.

The burden of work and responsibility is shared rather than falling on one person or partnership

but it can take a lot longer to reach decisions and take action when many people are involved.

Our liability is limited

but we must keep audited accounts.

Fig. 2.3 *Advantages and disadvantages of a private limited company*

Chapter 2 – Types of business

director. Private limited liability companies also set up a board of directors, a chairman and a managing director.

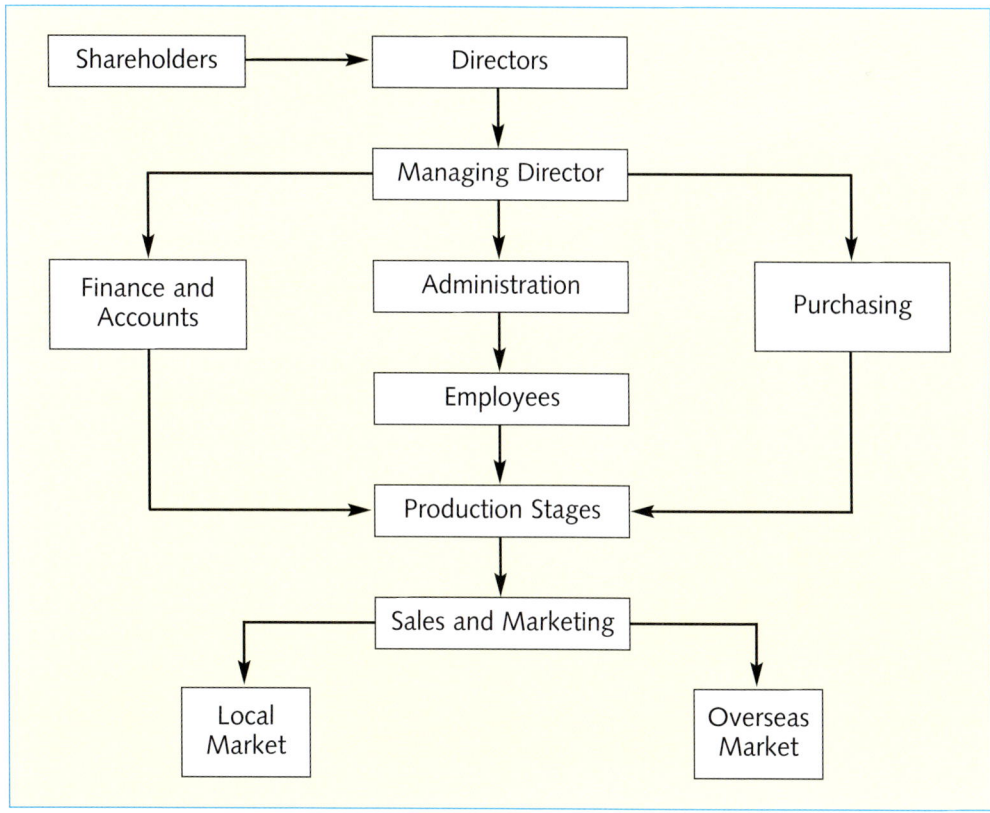

Fig. 2.4 *Typical structure of joint stock company*

Look at figure 2.4, a diagram of one possible structure of a joint stock company. The business of this particular company involves the production and sale of goods. You will observe that the diagram indicates the election of the board of directors by the shareholders, and they in turn have elected a chairman and appointed a managing director. It can also be seen that three lines of activity emerge from the position of managing director, leading to the sections of the firm that control administration, finance and purchasing.

The administration department co-ordinates and supervises the activities of other sections of the firm, whose function it is to put into effect the policies determined by the board of directors. The finance and accounts department has a dual role to play. It monitors the debts owed to the firm by its customers and by the firm to its suppliers, and at the same time it closely watches the overall financial status of the company. The purchasing department buys supplies and raw materials to be converted into manufactured goods through the production stages of the firm.

The disposal of the finished products is the responsibility of the sales and marketing departments which may be divided into separate sections to deal with various target markets.

The public company has limited liability, and it obviously enjoys greater continuity than the other forms of business we have examined so far, but it also has several other advantages. As already explained, the public company can sell its shares to the public, and when this has been done, ownership of the shares can easily be transferred to new owners via the market provided

Fig. 2.5 *Some examples of public companies in the Caribbean*

by the Stock Exchange. This ease of transfer of share ownership encourages investors to provide capital to businesses, which they would have been reluctant to do were it not so simple to regain at least some of the capital invested.

Advantages of public companies

Because they can advertise for inputs of capital from the public in the form of shares and debentures, public companies can obtain large quantities of capital and resources which can make them into large, strong business units. This is the main advantage of this type of business.

Their size enables them to enjoy economies of scale (advantages of size) such as:

- being able to purchase supplies in bulk, thus obtaining the most favourable terms, particularly in relation to price
- purchasing equipment which will save labour and expense
- finding it easier to borrow money and obtain credit.

Disadvantages of public companies

The main disadvantage of this type of business unit stems from its size. When a company is large it can become burdened by too much paperwork or red tape, employees and shareholders can feel too detached from the day-to-day activities of the business, and decisions made can take too long to be put into practice.

The public company, like the private company, has to send a copy of its audited accounts to the Registrar of Companies and to each of its shareholders. Therefore it is difficult for this type of company to keep its affairs secret.

The fact that shares can easily be transferred can also be a disadvantage to the business, because it allows the possibility of the firm being taken over by another company that has managed to obtain a controlling number of shares.

In addition, the management of large companies can become too impersonal and inflexible. It can also become inefficient and overstaffed, and therefore wasteful of resources.

KEY WORDS

Find out the business-related meaning of each of the following terms. Write a separate sentence for each term to show your understanding.

firm   profit   loss
private enterprise
public enterprise
bankrupt   partnership
sole proprietor
limited liability
private company
public company
director   shareholder

2.5 Special business relationships

There are some businesses which, although they fall within the types of business we have already looked at, have some special relationship within their organisation.

Co-operatives

Co-operatives are special types of business organisations. They are incorporated financial institutions or other types of institutions owned and controlled by groups with specific interests, and thus have common goals and objectives. They aim to improve the economic well-being of their members.

The characteristics of a co-operative are determined by its type and purpose. There are four basic types of co-operative: consumers' co-operatives, marketing co-operatives, workers' co-operatives and producers' co-operatives.

- *Consumers' co-operatives* are stores which share the net profits of the business among members. Britain was a world leader in the development of co-operatives, with the earliest consumer co-operative established by a group of Rochdale weavers in the UK in 1844. They became known as the 'Rochdale Pioneers'. Some co-operatives have formed their own manufacturing and wholesaling businesses, but they have come under increasing pressure from other chain stores. Only a limited number of consumer co-operatives are found in the Caribbean.

- *Marketing co-operatives* are businesses where several individuals or small businesses combine to sell their goods or services. For example, a group of small farmers may establish a co-operative to sell their produce. They could also co-operate in this way to buy their supplies (e.g. seeds) in bulk, or to combine the use of some equipment. An example of this form of co-operation is the Christiana Potato Growers Co-operative.
- *Workers' co-operatives* are businesses that are owned and run by their own workforces. For example, the crews of a bus company may actually own the company. In such cases the workers are highly motivated because it is in their personal interest to work as effectively and as efficiently as possible. These types of business are sometimes referred to as people's co-operatives.
- *Producers' co-operatives* are involved in producing certain products. Farmers in a community may form a producers' **credit union**. They share workloads and often equipment also, take decisions about productive activity, and share profits.

Co-operatives are **financed** by their members. The co-operative sells shares to its members. Members can buy as many shares as they wish, but this does not mean that a member with a large number of shares will have more voting rights than someone with fewer. The democratic principle of 'one person, one vote' applies, that is, one vote to each member.

Shareholders receive a **dividend** if the co-operative makes a profit from its operations. The amount of dividend is related to the number of shares held. In other words, a larger shareholding will receive a greater dividend than a smaller shareholding. Dividends are generally small, since the major goal of a co-operative is not to make a profit but to provide a service to its members. Dividends are shared out in proportions determined by the members who vote on the proposals at their annual meeting.

Earnings from a co-operative are not totally consumed in the payment of dividends. Most of these are ploughed back into the co-operatives to finance operational needs identified by the members.

Membership of some co-operatives is open to all members of the public who are of age. However, membership in certain types of co-operatives is restricted to people who have **common goals**. For example, the Teachers' Co-operative Society is open to teachers and not to the public at large; the service is designed specifically for teachers. Similarly, a producers' credit union would only be open to the producers it is established to serve (e.g. farmers).

A co-operative society is **controlled** by its members through the shares they have purchased and the **voting rights** mentioned earlier. The society is **governed** by a general meeting. At the annual meeting, members appoint a committee to deal with the operational activities. Committee members are drawn from the general membership. Some co-operatives employ professionals to manage their affairs.

Principles of Business – Profile 1

Members, individually, contribute to the share capital of the co-operative society by purchasing shares. Additional amounts saved in the co-operative are used to buy shares. From the pool of these additional funds, loans are provided to members.

The profits or earnings generated by a co-operative require a fair system of distribution. However, members may do the following:

- Reserve the profits for use in the co-operative.
- Share the profit among members in the portions they have agreed.
- Establish a fund into which profits are kept for the benefit of members.

Advantages of a co-operative society

- Members benefit from the pooling of funds for the purpose of lending to other members.
- Even though the returns on investments are low, members have an opportunity to build the financial base of their co-operative society.
- Members have a say in what goes on in their society.

Disadvantages of a co-operative society

- Because the profit motive is not the major aim of a co-operative society, as is the case in other types of business, they tend to suffer from lack of resources.
- Limited resources reduce opportunities to undertake major economic activities for the benefit of members.

The Co-operative Credit Union League is the governing body for local co-operatives and credit unions. The League monitors the activities in co-operative societies. Thus, co-operative bodies are registered with this body. The following are some of the ways in which the League assists co-operatives:

- structure and management of co-operatives
- advertising and promotional activities
- planning and delivery of workshops and seminars
- publication of newsletters
- accounts and audit services
- insurance facilities
- financial services.

The Credit Union League is a member of the Caribbean Confederation of Credit Unions and also the World Confederation of Credit Unions.

Franchises

Franchising is another form of co-operation. It is co-operation between a big firm and a sole proprietor. In franchising, a well-known company allows someone to buy the right to use their products or techniques under their trade names. This is a fast-growing sector of the economy. In the Caribbean and many other parts of the world franchising is becoming particularly popular in the 'fast food' trade.

Franchising offers a 'ready made' business opportunity for those with some capital who are willing to work hard. The potential entrepreneur (franchisee) pays to use the name, products or services of the major company (franchisor), which receives a lump sum and a share of the profits of the business (sometimes called royalties).

Fig. 2.6 *Well-known franchises operating in the Caribbean*

The franchisee receives the majority of the profits, but must also meet most of any losses. In addition to allowing use of their name, products, techniques or services, franchisors usually provide an extensive marketing back-up in return for the money they receive.

Fast food giants such as Wimpy, Kentucky Fried Chicken, Popeye's, Pizza Hut and Burger King are particularly well known in the franchising sector, but the range of franchise activities is much wider than just fast food, and the following are just a few examples of this type of business:

- developing and printing of photographic films
- home tuning of car engines
- drain clearing
- car wash centres
- door-to-door ice cream sales
- bakeries.

Building societies

Building societies are also an example of a special business relationship. They act as intermediaries between 'small' savers who wish to invest funds and people who wish to borrow money to purchase or improve property.

Building societies lend by means of a **mortgage**, which is a long-term loan, often repayable over a period of twenty years or more. Most of the deposits of building societies are lent out in this way, but some of their funds have to be kept to meet demands for cash withdrawals.

It is usual for the deeds of the property purchased by the borrower to be held by the building society until the loan has been repaid. If the borrower defaults on the repayment, the society can sell the property to recover the debt.

Building societies have always competed with the commercial banks to obtain deposits from savers. In recent years they have begun to compete with banks also by offering many of the financial services that have traditionally only been provided by the banks.

Holding companies

For a variety of reasons, businesses sometimes form a temporary or a permanent combination to achieve a certain aim. For example, the combination of three or four businesses might usefully bring together several separate processes into one production or marketing unit.

This kind of partnership of companies is usually incorporated as a holding company. Each member company retains its legal entity but overall control lies with the holding company.

2.6 Business growth

Reasons for growth

Most of the large firms that exist today started as a small business and have grown. Many of today's small firms are tomorrow's big businesses. Businesses grow and expand for a variety of reasons.

- They are successful, and expansion is necessary to meet the demand for their product.

Principles of Business – Profile 1

Fig. 2.7 *How many times have I got to tell you? I'm not interested in a merger.*

- They wish to make a greater level of profit.
- They are trying to gain economies of scale.
- They wish to reduce competition and become market leaders, maybe even gain a monopoly.
- They wish to secure their sources of supply or outlets for their products.

Expansion will only take place if the business can benefit and make extra profits.

Methods of growth

Basically firms can grow in four ways.

- By working existing plant and machinery harder, pushing it towards full capacity.
- By extending existing capacity or moving to a new, bigger site.
- By a **merger** with another company. A merger is where two or more companies voluntarily join together to form a single organisation. A **vertical merger** refers to two or more companies at *different* stages of the production process joining together, e.g. a bakery chain might buy a wheat farm. A **horizontal merger** is where two or more companies at the *same* stage of production join together, e.g. one grocery store joining with another grocery store.
- By a **takeover**. A takeover is different from a merger in that the company being taken over has not agreed to the two companies joining together.

Where a firm has acquired a number of other companies which retain their original names, it is known as a **holding company** (described earlier).

Directions of growth

Businesses need not expand simply by doing more of what they are already doing. Depending on the motives for expansion they can grow or integrate in a number of directions.

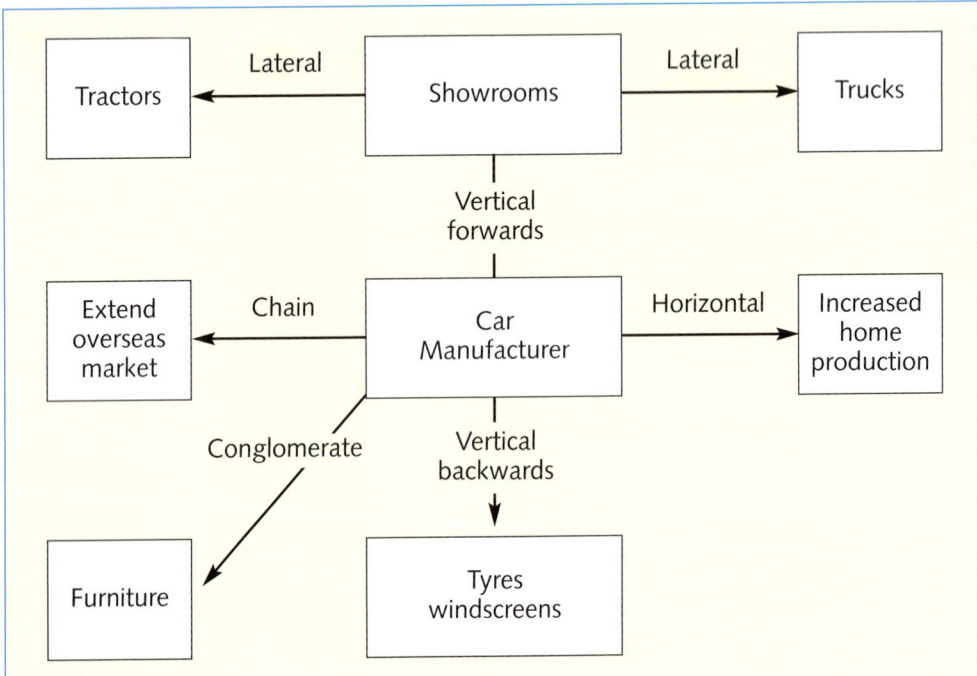

Fig. 2.8 *Integration*

24

- *Horizontal integration.* This is when a business extends its current operations, doing more of what it already does. It expands at the same level in the chain of production (e.g. a car manufacturer expands and builds another plant to produce more cars).
- *Chain integration* is expansion to produce the same product, but for a different market (e.g. a car manufacturer producing more cars to sell in a new overseas market).
- *Lateral integration* is expansion into a similar area of production, using similar techniques and processes but making something different (e.g. a car manufacturer expands to produce tractors or trucks).
- *Vertical integration.* Vertical integration may be 'backwards' or 'forwards', or in both directions.
  - Expansion backwards along the chain of distribution occurs when a business begins to produce the components and raw materials the business needs (e.g. a car manufacturer begins to produce tyres or windscreens for use in its cars).
  - Expansion forwards involves extending along the chain of production, taking on the selling of the products (e.g. a car manufacturer opens up its own car showrooms).

A conglomerate is a very large company made up of a variety of businesses producing different goods or services. Conglomerate integration refers to expansion into an area that has nothing to do with the current operations of the business, e.g. a car manufacturer begins to produce furniture as well as cars.

Multinationals

It is not unusual for expansion to take place across international borders. In other words, companies sited in different countries may combine to form a multinational company. The multinational is an enterprise that has subsidiaries or branches in more than one country.

The main objective of a multinational is to expand its operations into other profitable areas. It will do this in order to gain as large a share of the world market as possible, and to use its expertise and skills to the benefit of all the companies in the group.

The decision-making process is controlled by the parent company and implemented through its foreign subsidiaries. These subsidiary companies are either firms that have been set up by the parent company or they are foreign businesses which have been taken over. The parent company may own the subsidiaries completely, it may have a controlling interest (own majority of the shares), or it may just own a large and influential number of shares in the subsidiary.

Multinationals can bring benefits to an economy. Many of these benefits are gained from the multinational's wide experience across several countries.

- Reduced unemployment
- Introduction of new technology
- Improved training in latest skills
- Additional work for other companies.

The disadvantages of multinationals to an economy are that they:
- may import overseas personnel rather than recruit locally.
- may want to use working practices of another country, possibly resulting in industrial relations problems.

- may take their profits out of the country.
- can be difficult for governments to control because of their size and power.

Monopoly

Business in most democratic societies is based on the concept of free competition. Firms do not have the right to compete unfairly with rivals.

A possible result of the expansion of organisations is that they may end up in a monopolistic position. A monopoly exists when a company has so much control over the supply of a commodity or service that it is able to also control the price. In law, a monopoly exists when a company controls 25% or more of the total supply of a product. Whilst such a situation is beneficial to the firm, it can be against the interests of the consumer if the company abuses its power.

2.7 Government-owned businesses

State corporations

In Caribbean countries there are a few state-owned organisations, commonly referred to as **state corporations**. They are formed, out of necessity, by an Act of Parliament, mainly because the services required are not usually undertaken by private investors, even though everyone benefits in the long run. They have limited liability and, by an Act of Parliament, they can be dissolved. State-owned corporations are legal entities.

Types of state-owned corporations include public utility organisations such as the telephone, telegraphic and telecommunications, light and power, transportation, public broadcasting agencies, bureaux of standards, scientific research and environmental organisations.

State-owned corporations fall under the umbrella of the Central Government system, and thus under a Ministry of Government which is managed by an

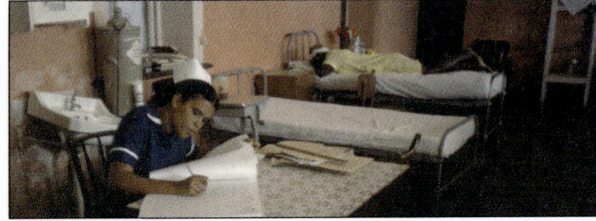

Fig. 2.9 *State enterprises are run by central government*

elected government minister. The government appoints a board of directors that oversees the day-to-day operations of the corporation. They are free to make their own business decisions, but these must be done within the context of the legal framework by which they are guided.

State-owned corporations do not exist to make profits as such, but to provide a vital service to the community or the country as a whole.

Advantages of state corporations
- The service or good is provided at a cheaper price.
- They provide employment for many persons and thus contribute to the economic life of the country.
- The community receives services which would otherwise not be provided, or would be provided at a higher cost to the consumer.

Disadvantages of state corporations
- A state-owned corporation usually provides a single, vital service to the country. Therefore, they have a monopoly on the services provided.
- Because of the lack of competition, the organisations do not always provide the high quality of service that is desirable. Consumers sometimes have to accept mediocre service because they have no alternative choice.
- State-owned corporations often run into financial difficulties, because of the lack of entrepreneurial thrust of profit-making. Governments often have to inject large amounts of money into these organisations to keep them operational.
- Because of the inputs from governments into these organisations, political inputs have to be taken into consideration when decisions are being made. The political overtures interfere with the overall management of state-owned corporations.

Statutory bodies

A statutory body is an organisation formed by the government for a particular purpose. The organisation is a type of state-owned corporation, and thus has similar formation procedures, objectives, management structure, and advantages and disadvantages.

Nationalised industries

These are government-owned industries which are established to provide a particular service or to provide a particular good. Sometimes, too, the state takes over a private sector industry in order to ensure that the community is not deprived of an essential good or service. Often the industry taken over is a fledgling industry.

The government owns most, if not all of the shares in a nationalised industry. Usually, a chief executive officer is appointed by the state. This person reports to the appropriate minister of government under whose portfolio the organisation falls. The government usually begins by injecting into the organisation the required funds and other resources needed. However, the organisation is required to work towards economic viability in the long term.

Public and private sector motives

The main aim of firms in the private sector is to make a profit, which is the reward to the owners for taking the risk of investing money in the business.

Traditionally, public sector organisations have not been profit-motivated to the same extent as private sector enterprises. Many people argue that some goods and services are essential and should be provided by the State either at a subsidised price or without charge. Others argue that the public sector is inefficient because it does not have the same profit motive as the private sector.

In recent years public sector organisations have been forced to adopt many of the profit-related features of successful private sector businesses operating in the same field of business as them. They have also been obliged to acknowledge political and public pressure to become more profit-conscious.

Regulatory practices governing establishment of a business

The regulatory practices governing the establishment of businesses refers to the rules and regulations by which persons who wish to establish a business should be guided.

Certain business operations must be duly registered with the **Registrar of Companies** and in some cases with government departments. A **certificate of registration** is issued, which must be appropriately displayed in the place of the business.

Different groups of business operators need different types of treatment.

- Professionals such as doctors, lawyers, accountants, pharmacists and some engineers register with their professional associations. The governments permit such bodies to play a major role in overseeing the professional conduct of their members.
- Trades persons, such as electricians, by the very nature of their trades, have to be duly licensed. Electricians, for example, must sit and pass qualifying examinations before they receive their licence to practise unsupervised.
- Food handlers are required to obtain the food handlers' permits. These persons are required to take a medical examination to satisfy the authorities that they are in good health, especially related to situations in which there could be a serious spread of disease through the handling of food.

2.8 The role of government agencies

Caribbean governments operate within two broad structures. These are the **central government structure** and the **local government structure**. The central government structure is designed to reflect the higher levels of administration within the government, while the local government structure is designed to reflect the municipal or community affairs section of government.

Government departments

Because of the nature of some of the tasks needed to be carried out by governments, specialised areas such as departments, divisions and agencies have to be established to handle them. For example, the Services Commission Division is responsible for matters related to staffing in the Civil Service as a whole, even though individual ministries have their personnel departments.

Another important department is the Department of Statistics. This department handles statistics for the whole country. All government offices need to submit the required statistics to this department so that the government can undertake informed planning.

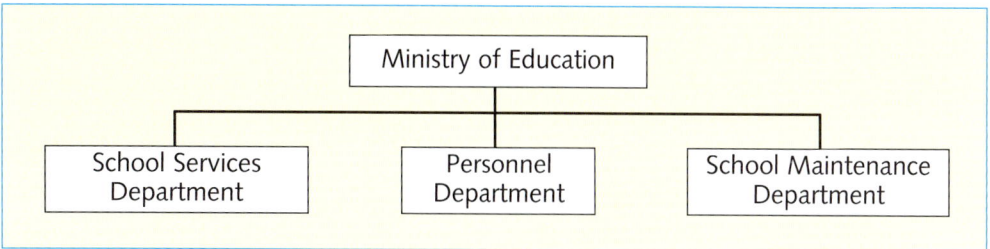

Fig. 2.10

Central government

Within this structure are the government ministries and departments and agencies to which the ministers of government are assigned. Figure 2.10 shows the basic structure of a ministry.

Each ministry has a permanent secretary who is a senior civil servant who handles the administration of the ministry as well as some departments, but who works closely with the elected and assigned minister of government. The permanent secretary is a servant of the people of the country and, therefore, is required to deliver a service for the benefit of the people.

A team of officers and other administrative staff are employed by government ministries to carry out the operational and management activities. The typical basic structure showing their position in the hierarchy can be seen in figure 2.11.

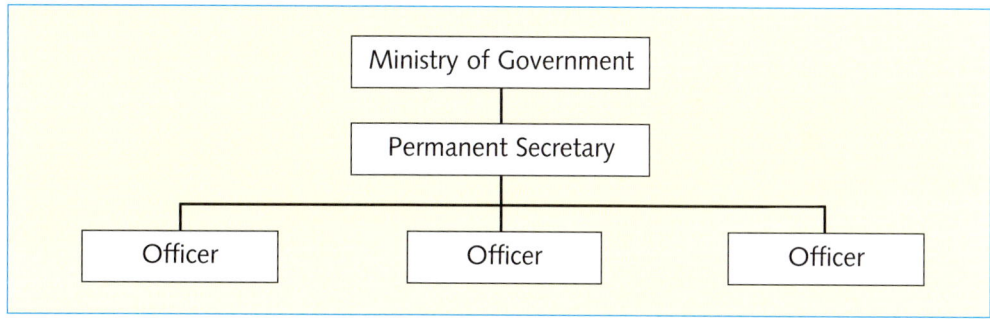

Fig. 2.11

The major goal of a ministry is to carry out the function that it has been assigned. This is done mainly through the implementation of the policies of government that are laid down for that ministry. It is the government ministry that is responsible for the implementation of government policies. Often, an advisory committee, a task force or consultants may be appointed to assist with specific assignments or projects being undertaken by a ministry.

The funding of costs associated with the operations of a ministry are provided through budget allocations approved by the finance ministry. Sometimes projects are funded by funding agencies.

From the foregoing it can be seen that government departments are not established to make profits, but to offer services in the area in which it has been assigned, for example, health, education, works and construction, social welfare and finance.

Advantages of ministries and government departments
- They organise the implementation of government policies.
- They monitor activities in society to ensure they are within the legal framework.
- They assist the government to meet the needs of people.
- They make it possible to break down the major task of managing the country into manageable portions that can be assigned to departments, sections, divisions and individuals.

Disadvantages of government departments
- Government ministries and departments are subjected to change of government, even before a government's term of office has expired. Consequently, many policies, projects, assignments and other tasks are abandoned before they come to fruition.
- Government ministries and departments are constrained by resources and, therefore, so many well-deserving projects are designed but not implemented because of the limited resource allocation situation.
- Often, government ministries and departments lack the expertise necessary for their general and specific functioning because of the low salaries and wages that governments can afford to offer. This affects the quality of service that can be provided.

The local government or municipal authority

Local government is involved with **community affairs**. Municipality is concerned with local self-government. Thus, the people who live in towns, districts, parishes and cities have a say in how community activities are carried out, and even participate in the debate at the community level on how legislations are drafted and implemented. These functions are carried out by councillors and citizens invited to sit on committees.

Local government is part of the **public enterprise system** (see earlier). Members of the community with **voting rights** (those who are of voting age and are duly registered) elect their representatives through the local government election process.

The municipality is governed by a **Council**. The Council consists of all the people who were successfully voted into office in **Local Government Elections**; those elected become known as Councillors. From among the Councillors, a **Mayor** and **Deputy Mayor** are elected. The Councillors and the relevant central government ministers participate in the selection of people to hold these positions.

The Mayor chairs the **Parish Council meetings** and represents the community at various civic and other functions. The most important job of the Mayor is to present the people's concerns to the appropriate authorities. The **Ministry of Local Government**, and thus the minister in charge of the ministry, are directly associated with the municipal authority.

The council is assigned a **secretary**. The secretary provides services to the meetings as well as handling much of the administrative duties of the Council Office.

The councillors represent their communities at meetings. They also see to their overall maintenance. Since there are usually large numbers of councillors to effectively handle the various community activities, committees are established to undertake specific tasks. These committees consist of the people who operate at the 'grass-roots' of council activity and aim to ensure that the community's needs are clearly identified, that cases are well represented at council level, and that appropriate steps are taken, where possible, to deal with each case, and thus satisfy the identified needs of the community in the long run.

The municipal authority has responsibility for road maintenance, fire service, public health, garbage collection and disposal, poor relief, civic amenities such as parks and gardens, public cemeteries, the cleaning of water tables, gullies, culverts and the provision of water for domestic and other purposes.

Major funding for the municipal authorities comes from budgetary allocations channelled through the Ministry of Local Government. Other sources of funds include grants from the government for projects, receipts from rates and taxes levied on the public for certain services, for example, the use of public parking facilities, recreational facilities such as beaches, zoos, museums, the use of public markets for vending, and the provision of services which attract government stamp duty. The sums generated can be used as backing for loans needed by the municipality to finance its activities.

Advantages of municipal authorities

- Members of communities have a say in the decision-making process.
- Members of the community can contribute to policy decisions.
- Government policies are not just imposed on the community.
- Local needs are addressed at local levels.

Disadvantages of municipal authorities

- Resources are limited, therefore much of what needs to be done for the betterment of a community cannot be carried out.
- Central government is the main provider of funds to municipal authorities. Because central governments are elected for five-year periods, many longer term objectives cannot be fully realised. Many projects have to be aborted after a change of central government, because the new government may not wish to pursue the policies of the out-going government. Often a new administration will decide they want resources channelled into other areas of need.

KEY WORDS

Find out the business-related meaning of each of the following terms.
Write a separate sentence for each term to show your understanding.

co-operative   franchise   comglomerate   integration   merger   takeover
multinational   monopoly   state corporation   local government
central government   nationalised

Principles of Business – Profile 1

2.9 Things to do

This section contains a variety of exercises to help you create revision notes, to test your understanding and to prepare you for examinations.

Search and find

Write out the question and the answer by referring back through the text to form revision notes.

1. Why might an individual want to take the risk of starting their own business?
2. Why is it said that in most Caribbean countries there is a 'mixed economy'?
3. How does private enterprise differ from public enterprise?
4. Explain the meaning of limited liability.
5. Why is the sole proprietor the most common type of business? What are the advantages and disadvantages of this type of business?
6. What advantages would a sole proprietor gain by going into partnership?
7. Why are limited partnerships relatively rare?
8. Make a detailed comparison between private and public limited companies. Include a list of the advantages and disadvantages of each of these forms of business ownership.
9. Give a brief description of the various forms that co-operatives may take.
10. Why can a franchise be said to be a 'ready made business'?
11. Why are building societies an example of a special business relationship?
12. What is a holding company?
13. What are the reasons for business growth?
14. Explain the difference between a merger and a takeover.
15. Describe the different forms of integration.
16. What is a multinational company?
17. Why are monopolies generally not in the public interest?
18. What is a state corporation? How does it basically differ from businesses in the 'private sector'?
19. What are the arguments for and against state ownership of business?
20. How do the motives of private sector businesses differ from those in the public sector?
21. In what basic ways would you say that the responsibilities of local government differ from those of central government?
22. What, if any, similarities can you see between central or local government and private sector businesses?

Chapter 2 – Types of business

What do you know?

Write out the complete sentence and insert the missing word, which can be chosen from the list at the end of the test.

1. In most Caribbean countries there is a ..... economy.
2. The sole proprietor business is more likely to ..... than any other type of business.
3. The partnership ..... sets out the rights of each partner.
4. The ..... company must include the word Limited or Ltd. in its title.
5. The owners of a public limited company are called .....
6. A ..... has subsidiaries in more than one country.
7. A ..... co-operative is owned and run by its own workforce.
8. In ....., a well-known company allows someone the right to use their products or techniques.
9. ..... integration refers to expansion into an area that has nothing to do with the current operations of the business.
10. ..... enterprise refers to industries and services owned and operated by government.

Choose the missing word from the following:

conglomerate   fail   franchising   private   mixed   public   worker   deed   shareholders   multinational

Structured questions

Q1 Figure 2.12 shows the letter heading of a limited company. Answer the following questions related to it.

— ESC —

ELECTRONICS SERVICES COMPANY LIMITED
St. John's, Antigua
Telephone: 694609

Directors: Al Simon, Priscilla Douglas (Managing)
Mark Kirwan.

Fig. 2.12 *Letter heading*

(a) How can you tell from the letter heading whether this is a private or a public company? **1**

(b) Who is the managing director of this company? **1**

(c) How does the function of a managing director differ from that of the other directors? **2**

(d) What do you understand by it being said that this company has 'limited liability'? **4**

(e) Give three advantages and three disadvantages of this type of business organisation. **6**

(f) If the firm that uses the letter heading were to expand, which type of organisation would it change to? What would be the advantages and disadvantages of making such a change? **6**

Principles of Business – Profile 1

Q2 Examine the diagram of a company's structure (figure 2.13) and answer these questions related to it.

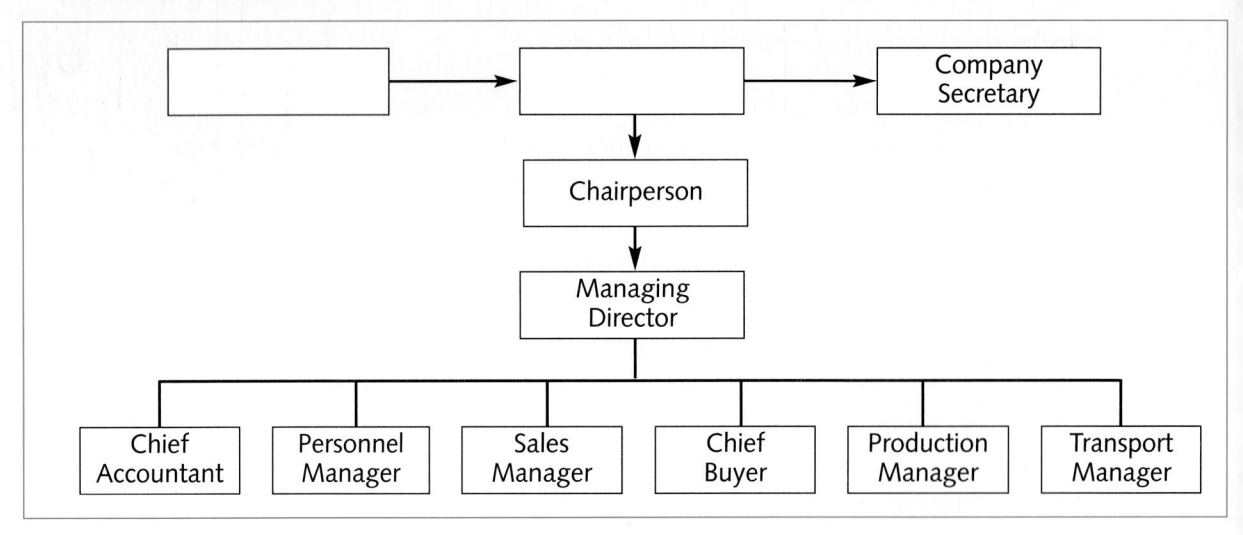

```
[          ] → [          ] → [Company Secretary]
                    ↓
              [Chairperson]
                    ↓
              [Managing Director]
                    |
   ┌──────┬──────┬──────┬──────┬──────┐
[Chief   [Personnel [Sales  [Chief  [Production [Transport
Accountant] Manager] Manager] Buyer] Manager]   Manager]
```

Fig. 2.13

(a) There are two main forms of business organisation to which this diagram could be said to apply. What are they? **2**

(b) Name the groups of people in the labels missing from this diagram. **2**

(c) Explain the function of the two groups of people you have identified in part (b). **4**

(d) 'The chairperson is higher up in the company hierarchy, but has less day-to-day involvement in the running of the business than the managing director.' Explain this statement. **4**

(e) Briefly but clearly explain the function of four positions in the above diagram which have not already been dealt with in this question. One of those chosen should be the company secretary. **8**

Q3 'Franchising is one of the fastest-growing sectors of the economy; over 20% of retail sales are accounted for by this form of trading, and the trend is growing each year.'

(a) Give a brief description of what you understand by franchising. **2**

(b) Franchising is particularly evident in the 'fast food' trade. What do you understand by 'fast food'? **2**

(c) Name three major franchising companies. **3**

(d) Give three examples (other than in the food trade) of services which are frequently provided by franchise companies. **3**

(e) What are the benefits of franchise arrangements from the point of view of:
  (i) the franchisor **2**
  (ii) the franchisee? **2**

(f) Give a clear explanation of the difference in the organisation of a normal sole proprietor business and that of a business with a franchise arrangement. Include mention of differences with regard to capital formation and the distribution of profits. **6**

Chapter 2 – Types of business

Q4

(a) What is a sole proprietor business? — 2

(b) State two advantages of this type of business when compared with larger organisations. — 2

(c) Two of the disadvantages of this type of business are that it has 'unlimited liability' and that it can suffer from 'lack of continuity'. Explain these two terms. — 4

(d) Clearly explain two other disadvantages this type of business faces. — 4

(e) How far would change from sole proprietor to partnership status help to solve the problems stated in parts (c) and (d) of this question? — 8

Q5 Diane Evans holds a majority shareholding in Easy Electronics plc, a company that owns a large chain of shops that sell a wide range of household electrical goods. Hightec Electrical plc produces a range of hairdryers etc. Hightec have been trying to take over Easy Electronics for some time. They have been openly buying ordinary shares on the Stock Exchange over the last year, but they have not managed to obtain sufficient shares in order to make a bid for the company. They have now offered to buy Diane Evans' shares at a price above the current market price.

(a) What do the letters plc stand for? — 1

(b) What implications do the letters plc have for companies? — 2

(c) What is meant by the wording 'Diane Evans holds a majority shareholding'? — 2

(d) What do you understand by the term 'takeover' as used here? — 2

(e) State at least three ways in which the takeover could affect the workers of Easy Electronics if it were to take place. — 3

(f) What factors might Diane Evans take into account before agreeing to sell her shares? — 4

(g) Suggest reasons why Hightec would want to take over Easy Electronics. — 6

Q6 The flow diagram of the basic structure of a parish council in figure 2.14 shows the various personnel involved in its operation. Answer the question related to the diagram.

(a) What is a council? — 1

(b) How do councillors obtain their positions? — 2

(c) How does the work of a mayor differ from that of other councillors? — 2

(d) What is the purpose of a committee? Give an example of a task that a committee might carry out. — 3

(e) Describe two contrasting examples of the responsibilities of a parish council. — 4

(f) In what ways does a parish council meet the needs of the local community? — 4

(g) Why can the activities of a parish council be said to be just as important as those of central government? — 4

Mayor
|
Deputy Mayor
|
Secretary
|
Councillors
|
Committees

Fig. 2.14

Principles of Business – Profile 1

Research assignments

1. What is a nationalised industry and how does it differ from a business in private ownership? What are the arguments for privatisation of state-owned businesses? Which of these arguments do you support? What evidence is there to say your view is right?

2. Explain why a sole proprietor might decide to become a private limited company. How would such a change be financed? Give descriptive examples of local businesses that have changed in this way.

3. What is a limited company? Why has the limited type of company become the major form of business in existence today? What evidence exists that limited companies are the 'major form of business' in your locality?

4. Mrs Latter is the sole proprietor of a small factory producing soft toys. She is considering expanding her business by taking in some partners.

    a) Describe as fully as possible the advantages and the disadvantages of expanding the business in this way.

    b) Put forward a case supporting the view that Mrs Latter might also consider changing her business into a private limited company.

    c) Investigate some local businesses that have changed their status in some way. How could Mrs Latter learn from the experiences of the businesses you have investigated?

5. Locate a well-established local entrepreneur who started his or her business from 'scratch'. What factors can you identify as making important contributions to its apparent success?

6. Make a diagrammatic 'map' of the organisation structure of a small and a medium-sized local firm with which you are familiar. Comment on the differences observed.

7. Select two competing businesses situated within your locality and show:

    a) how they compete

    b) why they are both able to survive in spite of the competition they are part of.

8. Make a survey of all the businesses within a clearly defined area in your locality and identify the legal structure (legal identity) of each. Present the information collected in some appropriate diagrammatic form (with a 'key' if necessary). To what extent are the firms investigated reliant upon the local transport network?

Chapter 3: Business organisation

3.1 The role and functions of a business

The main aim of any business is to make profits in order to give the best possible return to the owners for the money they have invested in the company. Businesses achieve this aim mainly through their major functional areas of production, finance, marketing and personnel.

Production

The broad function of production is to satisfy human wants. In order to do this through the production of goods and services the firm will have to co-ordinate several areas.

- The purchase of stocks and raw materials.
- The design of goods.
- Research, development and experimental work.
- The manufacture of the company's products.
- The control of quality of production.
- The storage of the raw materials and finished goods.

We can see this reflected in the production of furniture. Consider a firm designing prototype furniture from raw materials it has purchased. It will research the market to investigate the best ways to market such items. This research will also reveal what need there may be to amend the design of the prototypes, and to produce samples to show prospective customers and obtain orders. Only then will full-scale production take place, during which

Marketing	Production
Personnel	Finance

Fig. 3.1 *The functional areas of a business*

quality control will be maintained to ensure that what is produced is of the required standard, and workers called progress chasers will make sure that goods are produced within the timescale required. The finished products will then be stored until they are required for the intended market.

Finance

Finance is required to form a business and to fund its operations. It is required, for example, to purchase plant machinery and raw materials, and to pay wages to workers. A business also needs finance to meet day-to-day running expenses and to meet maintenance costs.

There are four main sources of business finance (capital):

- savings of the entrepreneur(s)
- capital borrowed from a bank or some other financial institution
- capital raised by the sale of shares in the business
- profits of the business reinvested (plough back).

The finance of businesses is examined in more detail in Chapters 16 and 17.

Marketing

The marketing function of business aims to anticipate consumers' demand in order that the right products are manufactured. Once the commodities have been produced it is the function of marketing to promote sales to the consumer. Marketing is not confined to goods alone; labour, capital, land and buildings must also be marketed as well as the many services that are needed. Chapters 13 and 14 examine marketing in detail.

Personnel

The personnel function of a business is to provide employment. Theoretically, the more businesses that exist, and the more successful they are, the greater is the number of personnel needed. However, in reality the provision of employment is far more complex than this simple view. For example, technological developments which lead to increased efficiency and business growth can also result in a reduction of the number of employees needed in a particular industry.

The integration of the two broad technologies of computers and telecommunications has led to increased efficiency and business growth. The revolution in electronics has transformed many of the traditional areas of employment. For example, many of the functions of office workers have been bypassed by computers and word processors. Methods of communication have also rapidly changed, with telecommunication making an even greater contribution, and the automated factory is now becoming more commonplace.

Part of the personnel function of business is the management of personnel: to recruit people with appropriate skills, care for their welfare, and ensure that where necessary in-service training is provided to update their skills. The personnel function is examined in Chapters 4, 5 and 6.

3.2 Management

Management functions

The functions of management can be grouped into eight areas.

- *Planning:* involves looking ahead: making decisions and formulating policy on the intentions and objectives of the organisation, and the methods to be used to achieve the objectives. Planning assists the efficient utilisation of the firm's resources, and it emphasises preventative rather than corrective measures.
- *Organising:* ensuring that workers can get on with their job by making sure that people, materials and machinery are available in the right place at the right time. Good organisation involves planning what is to be done, who is to supervise it, time frames and the most efficient method of doing it.
- *Directing:* giving instructions to workers so that they are clear as to how their work should be done to best benefit the organisation.
- *Controlling:* supervising and checking the activities and performance of subordinates to ensure that instructions are being carried out properly and plans and methods are being followed.
- *Co-ordinating:* directing and integrating the activities of the team under management's direct supervision, and contributing to the overall co-ordination of the activities within the organisation in order to form a united strategy of operations to achieve the organisation's objectives.
- *Delegating:* involves assigning tasks or goals to subordinates whilst at the same time granting them the necessary authority to carry out the tasks. The subordinates must recognise their responsibility and accept their accountability for the expected performance.
- *Motivating:* encouraging other members of the organisation to carry out their tasks properly and effectively. Although extrinsic incentives such as wages help to motivate people, the ability to motivate others is very much dependent upon leadership qualities which are discussed later. Intrinsic incentives such as job enlargement and job satisfaction also help to motivate people. Motivation is examined in greater detail in Chapter 5.
- *Industrial relations* (the relationship between employees and employers) make an important contribution to the motivation of employees. Industrial relations is dealt with in Chapter 6.

Responsibilities of management

The foregoing functional areas of a business have to be co-ordinated and managed to ensure that the resources of the business are used to the best advantage.

All members of an organisation have some responsibility, even if it is only to have regard for their own safety and that of their work colleagues. But the higher in the hierarchy of the organisation that a person is, the greater will be that person's responsibility. Consequently, the greater degree of responsibility lies with the managers of an organisation, whether they are managing directors or managers of departments. Managers, in this respect, are those who have the responsibility to direct, control and co-ordinate others.

The management of an organisation is responsible to the firm's owners, customers and employees.

Principles of Business – Profile 1

- *Owners and shareholders:* to achieve the best possible return for the capital they have invested and to reinvest or 'plough back' sufficient capital in order to ensure sound future growth and development of the business.

  Managers will realise this ideal by maximising efficiency and creating a surplus (profit). Maximising **efficiency** involves 'doing things right' and being **effective** ('doing the right things'), which usually results in improved **productivity** (creating greater output) and a bigger profit. Producing a profit is evidence of being efficient.

- *Customers:* to provide goods or services of good quality, within the agreed period of time, and at a fair and economic price.

  Although legislation aimed at protecting customers exists (see Chapter 14), good managers recognise that considering their responsibilities to customers is good for **public relations** (improving public image).

- *Employees:* to provide the safest and most comfortable working conditions possible, to pay a fair wage and to secure future employment as far as possible.

  Provision of **training** for employees is a further responsibility of managers. Appropriate training is important because it helps the employees to achieve self-improvement, and this results in them becoming more effective as employees.

  It is also important that managers **communicate** effectively with employees – keeping them informed of the aims of the business and how it intends to achieve them. Communication also entails managers recognising and taking into account what the employee needs, not only to do their job well, but also for their personal development.

  Human relations are a further important tool in the management of employees. This refers to knowledge of the way in which groups work together, the needs of individual workers and the effect of different forms of supervision on employees. Teamwork is an important feature of this. **Teamwork** can have the beneficial effect of encouraging the development of a team spirit and a sense of common purpose.

The management also has some responsibility to the government, and to society. It fulfils its responsibility to the government by ensuring that the company is abiding by the law and behaving in a manner that is compatible with the country's trading practices both at home and overseas. Its responsibility to society is to ensure that the firm's operations do not cause harm to the general public, for example being environmentally aware.

In order to meet these responsibilities the management must organise and co-ordinate the work of others. The manager will, therefore, at times be required to:

- appoint and train new staff
- communicate company policy
- give instructions and set tasks
- assess performance
- discipline and dismiss staff.

Superiors are expected to be responsible for the actions of their subordinates. Although they can delegate the power or authority to carry out tasks to subordinates, the responsibility for actions cannot be delegated and ultimate responsibility always remains with the manager.

KEY WORDS

Find out the business-related meaning of each of the following terms. Write a separate sentence for each term to show your understanding.

marketing   production
finance   personnel
motivating   delegating
progress chasers
human relations
plough back

Leadership

People who are in a supervisory position in business need to have some understanding of group dynamics; that is, the way that people interact in a group situation. The extent to which people work effectively (or not) together affects the overall success potential of the business. In the business sense there are four basic elements of group behaviour: the group, an objective, the individual and the leader.

The group

Groups can be divided into two categories.

Informal groups have usually come together voluntarily (e.g. a music group), and the purpose of the group is not defined too specifically. There are no set rules (although an informal group may have an objective, such as to raise money for charity), and the leader will be chosen by the members of the group.

Formal groups are usually created for a specific purpose, such as a department in a firm. This type of group has a formal structure, a specific objective and an appointed leader. In fact, the leader may be the one who chooses the members of the group, and consequently enjoys the power of authority. People in businesses and factories generally work in formal groups, with expected standards of production and behaviour.

An objective

Because most groups in business are formal ones, they require a clear objective, for instance to formulate a marketing campaign for a new product. Unless the objectives are clearly defined (i.e. by the leader) the group will lose direction; the objectives will be liable to be misinterpreted.

The individual

Even though he or she is part of a group, each person still has to work as an individual in order to contribute to the group objective. However, this can result in a problem if the views of the individual, or his or her attitude or behaviour, are not in harmony with the rest of the group. Under such circumstances the importance of the objective may be sufficient to solve the conflict. Alternatively, it may be the skill of the group leader that will be the deciding factor.

The leader

Whereas the leader of an informal group may be chosen by the group members, with formal groups the leader is often appointed, as with a manager or chairperson. Such a leader may have the power to regulate the group's behaviour (e.g. they may be in a position to be able to direct someone to do something), but to use their authority in this way may adversely affect the group morale and attitudes. For this reason a good leader will try to identify the parameters within which the group can operate, often delegating some responsibility to members of the group.

Earlier in this chapter we saw that it is important that workers feel motivated. Wages are often assumed to be a motivating factor, but an unlimited amount of capital to provide wages cannot be guaranteed, and wages alone are limited in the extent to which they can be relied upon to encourage people to work hard and effectively.

The success of management and the ability to motivate others is very much dependent upon the ability to lead. But leadership qualities are difficult to identify and to define. Firstly, this is because they depend on the manager's own attitude towards the responsibilities delegated to him or her and to his or her subordinates. Secondly, the ability to lead is considerably influenced by the attitude of the manager towards the problems of his or her subordinates. Thirdly, some of the qualities required to lead others differ from one occupation to another.

To be able to motivate others, managers must also be inspired. They need to be committed to their organisation and must have an interest and pride in the products or services which they produce or sell. Leadership qualities are particularly revealed by the willingness of superiors to listen to, and understand, problems from their subordinates' point of view.

Styles of leadership

There are four basic styles of leadership and a leader may combine any of these.

Authoritarian or autocratic

The leader is the absolute authority on all matters, deciding what to do, and whatever others may think, it is done. It is often the case that this type of leader frequently uses his or her position in authority to exert his or her will on others.

Such an approach to leadership is often effective, but it is not necessarily the most efficient approach. Although work may be completed in the way that the leader has specified, at the same time employee input and innovation is discouraged.

Participative or democratic

The leader will consult with those likely to be affected before making a decision, although the leader will reserve the right not to act on a majority view.

This style of leadership is popular because it enables workers lower down in the hierarchy to participate in the decision-making process. Consequently, they are more highly motivated and need less supervision.

Laissez-faire or free-rein

In this style of leadership the leader gives limited direction to workers. They are given general directions on the tasks to be tackled and then left to achieve them in the way they think is best.

There are circumstances where this style of leadership is appropriate (e.g. where the employee acts in a consultancy capacity), but generally, most employees prefer to work under some degree of authority from a superior.

Charismatic

A charismatic leader is one who influences and motivates others because she or he has outstanding personality or character. This type of leader is relatively rare. Those that do exist can be very successful in the extent to which they can motivate others to do things to support them.

Chapter 3 – Business organisation

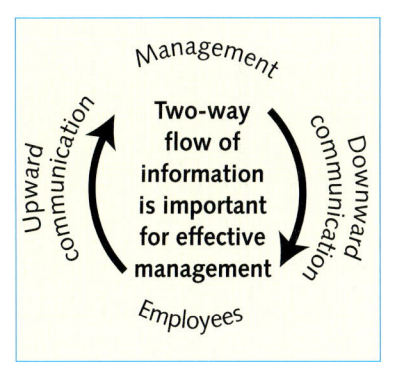

Fig. 3.2 *Two-way communication flow*

Management communication

The success of any organisation is greatly influenced by the participation of all its members in its activities. We have seen earlier in this chapter that managers have an important part to play in co-ordinating and motivating all workers to achieve a common goal. But for all the workers to make a contribution, they need to know what goals they are expected to achieve. Experience has shown that people are more committed to involvement in an organisation where they are well informed of policies, and even more so when they have participated in making decisions.

Good communication is important in involving all members of an organisation in its activities. The most effective management communications require a two-way flow of information – downwards from management and upwards from employees.

Downward communication is initiated by management and is used to inform employees of the company's proposals, policies, decisions and progress. There are two main methods of downward communication, oral and written.

- *Oral:* direct command, discussions, meetings, loudspeaker, intercom, closed-circuit television, telephone.
- *Written:* letters, memoranda, noticeboards, reports, company magazine, handbooks.

Upward communication may be initiated by employees but it is often 'collected' by management. For example, management may well require specific information from employees. This feeds back to management the views, suggestions, proposals and problems of employees. Upward communication can be 'collected' by direct and indirect methods.

- *Direct:* by managers talking to employees and elected representatives.
- *Indirect:* suggestion schemes, attitude surveys.

Teamwork

An effective tool of management is grouping people into teams. In a business, members of the organisation have a specific job to do, but they will also be a member of a group or team. For example, a sales representative will be a member of a group of people such as a marketing team.

The ability of a team to work together is important for two reasons:

1. When people work in a pleasant and co-operative atmosphere, they tend to work harder and more effectively.
2. A good team can achieve more in a shorter period of time than individuals or a weak team.

Managers need to choose team members carefully. A good team member will:

- listen to others and seriously consider their ideas, views and beliefs
- think carefully before speaking
- offer help and support and make suggestions when they are needed
- be prepared to accept constructive criticism from others
- put their own views in a calm and responsible manner
- act as a 'peacemaker' whenever possible.

Principles of Business – Profile 1

Teamwork benefits employees because:

- it gives them a sense of common purpose and a feeling of 'belonging'
- they can consult experienced colleagues if they are unsure of something
- working as part of a group is easier than working alone.

Employers benefit from teamwork because:

- it enables workers to specialise which results in 'economies of scale'
- groups make 'top to bottom' communication better
- co-ordination of groups is easier than managing individuals
- the output of groups is greater than that of individuals.

3.3 Organisational structure

Chain of command

Many companies are organised in the form of a pyramid. The person at the top of the pyramid has the most authority, and the steps down the pyramid indicate less authority. Each person in the pyramid is responsible to the person immediately above. The sections of the pyramid below the person in the managing position make up the chain of command. This shows the lines of communication between the person in the supervisory position and his or her subordinates. Each manager delegates work to the people below him or her in the chain.

Span of control

The number of subordinates a manager supervises, or the effective limit to the number of others that a manager can supervise efficiently, is sometimes referred to as the 'span of control' or the 'span of management'. There are a number of factors that influence the span of control, and they include the following.

- *The complexity of the work.* Some work is easy to check whilst other work demands closer supervision by the manager.
- *Self-discipline of workers.* Where workers are well motivated and have a professional approach a greater number can be supervised.
- *Method of communication.* Some methods of communication (e.g. face-to-face) are more demanding than others (e.g. electronic methods).
- *Frequency of supervision.* The more frequently that a manager needs to see subordinates, the more limited will be the span of control.
- *Capability of the manager.* Some managers have more ability to lead and motivate than others, and this will extend their span of control.

If workers do not need close supervision then the span of control can be wide and flat. Where there is a need for closer supervision the span of control will be narrow and contain more people in sub-supervisory positions.

Organisational structure

To be able to achieve its objectives satisfactorily, a firm relies on two types of relationship between personnel. These relationships are called the 'organisational structure' of a firm. One type is 'formal' and the other 'informal'.

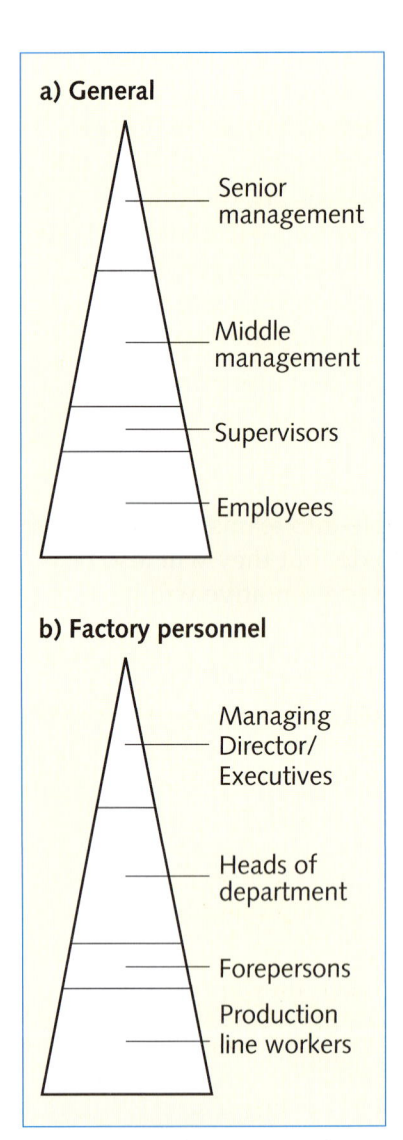

Fig. 3.3 *Pyramid organisation charts*

a) General
- Senior management
- Middle management
- Supervisors
- Employees

b) Factory personnel
- Managing Director/Executives
- Heads of department
- Forepersons
- Production line workers

Chapter 3 – **Business organisation**

Formal organisation is concerned with the official lines of communication followed by employees in carrying out management decisions. It allows those in charge to define objectives for each section or department to enable the organisation to achieve its corporate aims. Formal organisation helps to define responsibilities and to ensure that tasks are not duplicated but are co-ordinated between functions within an organisation, so that each department blends its activities with those of other departments to form a corporate strategy.

The functions found in organisations will vary depending on their type or size, and this will affect the organisational structure used. There are basically four types of formal organisational structure, and a business might incorporate more than one of these.

- Line organisation
- Line and staff organisation
- Functional organisation
- Committee organisation.

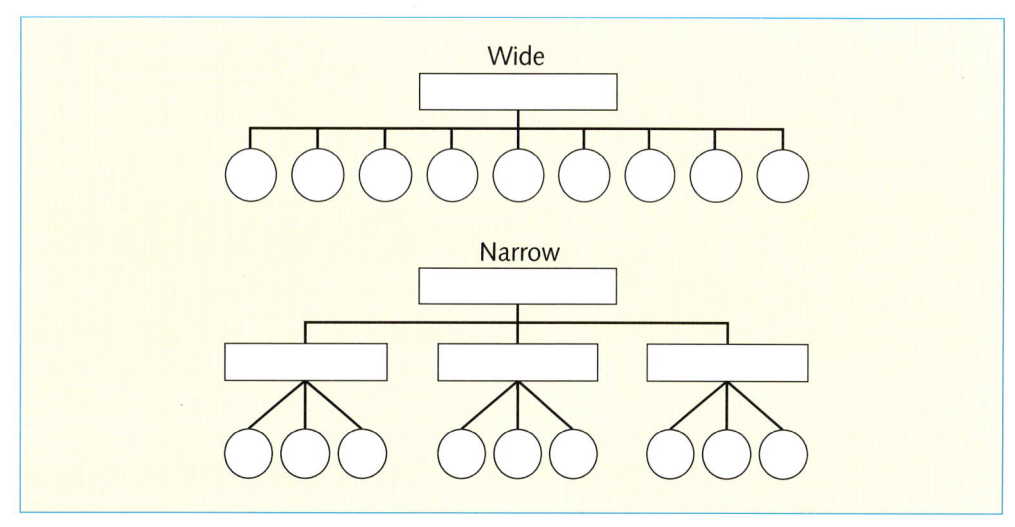

Fig. 3.4 *Wide and narrow spans of control*

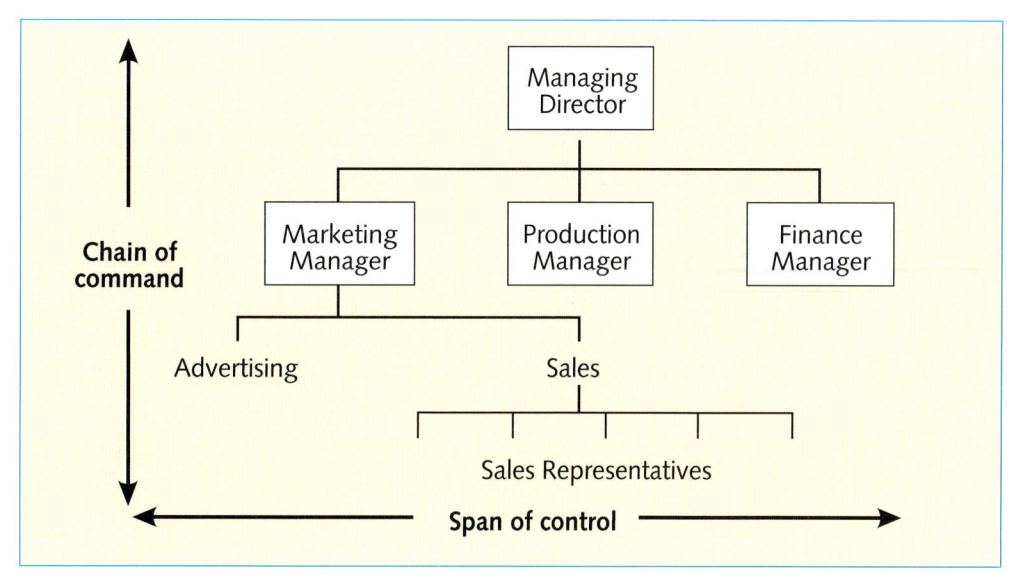

Fig. 3.5 *Combined chain of command and span of control*

45

Line organisation

This is a traditional form of organisation which involves a direct flow of authority, and responsibility is dispersed and delegated from top to bottom. The owner or chief executive will instruct those below her/him, such as departmental managers (sometimes referred to as *line managers*). They in turn will instruct the less senior employees who comply with the instructions (this is regarded as a *narrow span of control*).

Within this hierarchical form of organisation everyone has some responsibility. The higher the position in the hierarchy the greater is the responsibility, and this responsibility cannot be delegated. Tasks or objectives can be delegated, and so can authority or the right to use power. This right is defined by the hierarchy, and should correspond with position in the hierarchy.

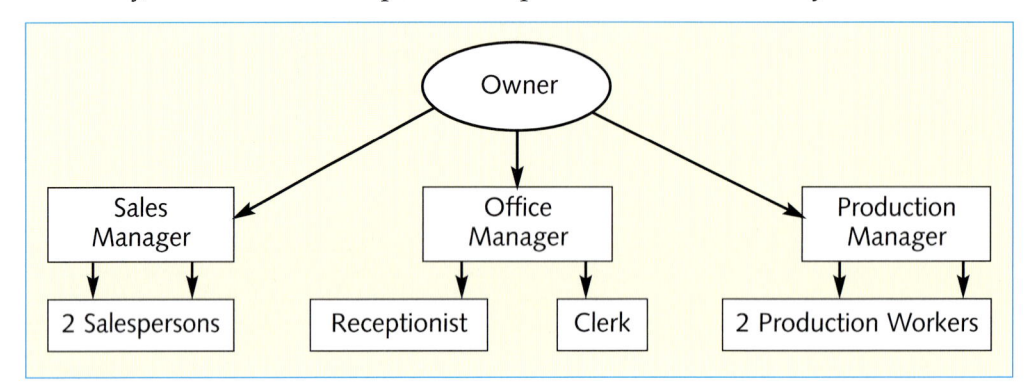

Fig. 3.6 *Line organisation in a small business*

The benefit of this method of organisation is that it is easy to understand, since it has an uncomplicated chain of command. Decisions can be reached quickly. It is particularly suited to a small business. However, this type of structure ties up the owner or chief executive with administration, leaving little time for policy making and planning. At the lower levels, some employees may be over-aware, under this structure, of the 'lowliness' of their position, and they may therefore feel less 'job satisfaction'. It also restricts the inclusion of specialist personnel services which would be required by more than one department. A small firm could buy in specialist services such as legal advice and services offered by research agencies, but this would be uneconomical for a large firm justified in employing its own specialists. For this reason the line organisation tends to be less suited to a large firm, and mostly is seen in the small firms just described.

Line and staff organisation

Staff organisation is a development of a line organisation. Some activities of a business cut across the departments of its linear structure because they offer a service facility (such as legal or research activities) to several if not all departments. As mentioned earlier when examining line organisation, a large firm would find it more economical to employ specialist staff to offer these services and advice to other departments. With line and staff organisation a specialist is allocated to advise each department of their specialism. Staff of these 'back-up' services can advise but generally not direct or control the other departments.

Chapter 3 – Business organisation

A major advantage of this system is that it allows the employment of specialist workers. The main disadvantage is that the lines of responsibility and authority are less clear and this can result in disputes between specialist personnel and heads of departments.

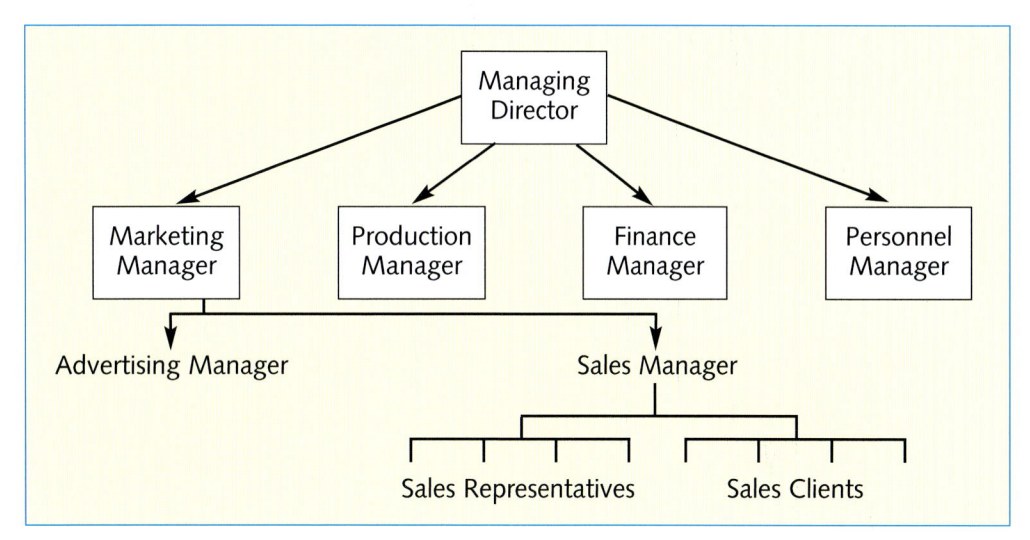

Fig. 3.7 *Line organisation in a larger firm*

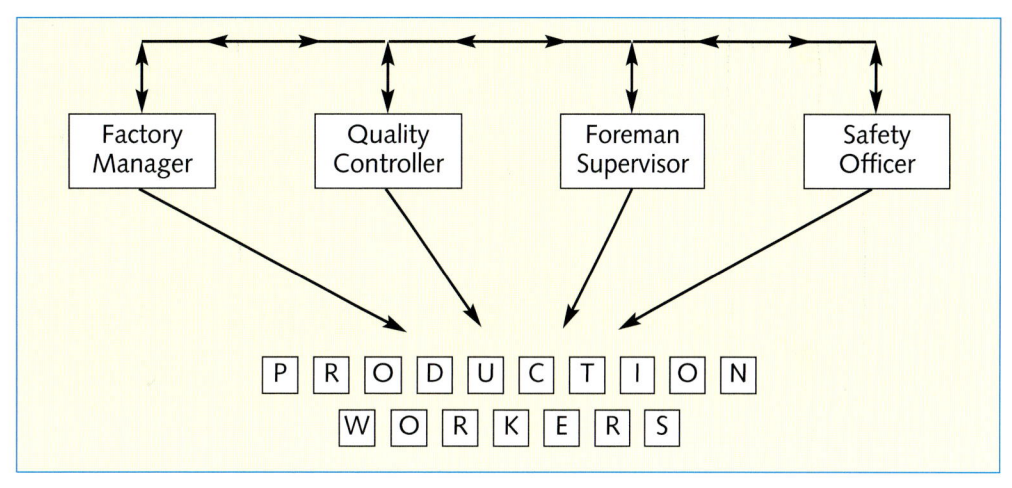

Fig. 3.8 *Line and staff organisation*

Functional organisation

This type of organisation divides the business into departments to carry out basic functions such as finance, production, sales, warehouse/delivery, etc. This is a **wide span of control**.

The head of each specialist department supervises, controls and is responsible for just the one function with which it is involved throughout the organisation. This can sometimes cause friction and this type of organisation requires a lot of co-operation and common sense to avoid confusion and conflict within the workforce.

This method of organisation does have its place in a business which has branches located in scattered places around the Caribbean, or in a situation in which there is a need to have specialist functions based away from the head office, for example a shipping office or warehouses positioned near docks.

In the former case, the specialist departments would probably be based at the head office, and control of the branches would emanate from there, although the branch managers would retain a certain amount of autonomy whilst being able to draw on the functions and expertise at headquarters.

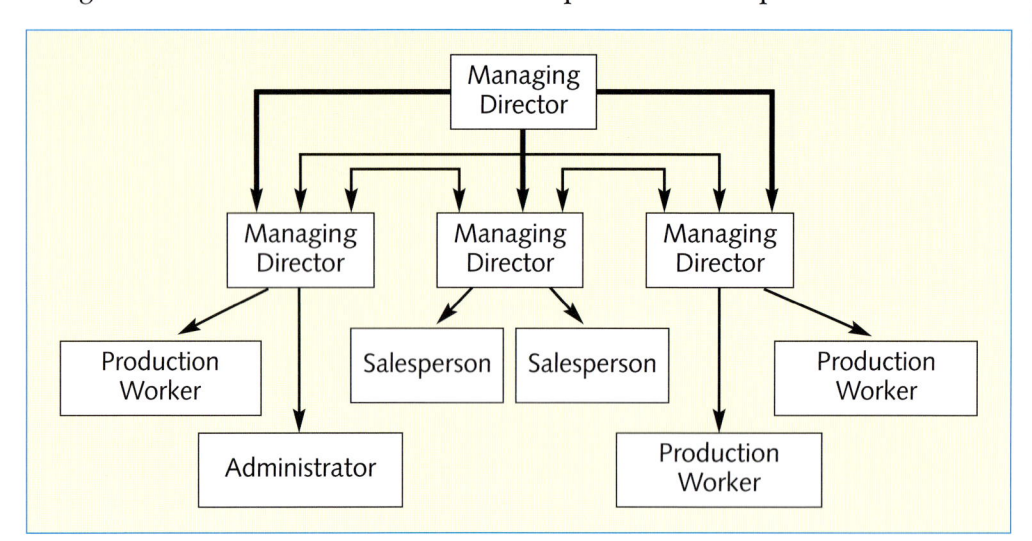

Fig. 3.9 *Functional organisation*

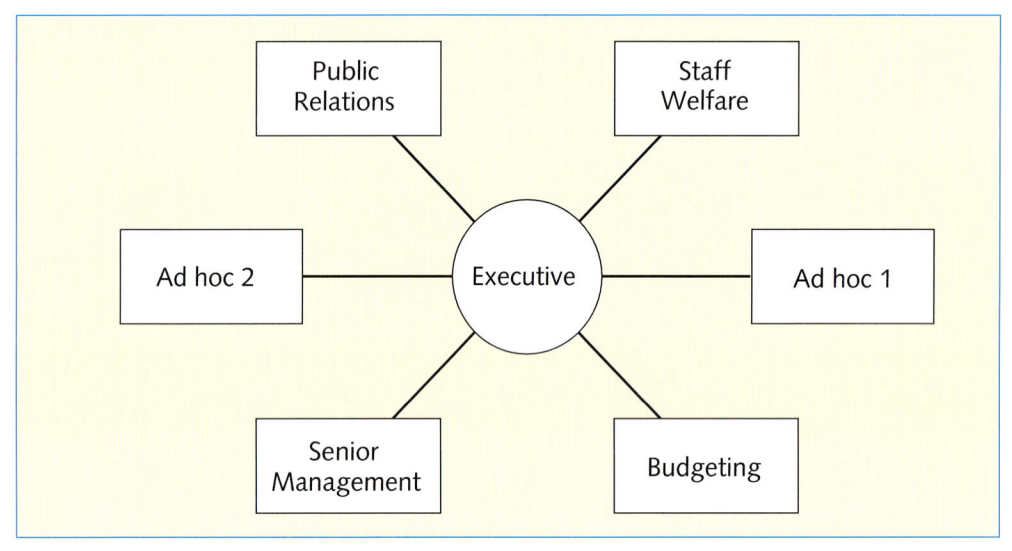

Fig. 3.10 *Committee organisation*

Committee organisation

The committee organisation is based on the management principle of grouping specialists in committees to advise the executive and to assist it in developing policies and procedures. Some committees have authority to make recommendations to supervisors (**upward communication**), others are formed purely to receive information (**downward communication**), and some undertake management functions such as **policy making**. Some will be permanent working groups whilst others will be 'ad hoc' – set up to examine a particular problem and dissolved once they have achieved their goal.

Committees invariably slow up the decision-making process, but they improve morale by allowing employees to participate in it. The combined judgement of several specialists in similar or diverse areas promotes sound decisions.

Chapter 3 – Business organisation

Informal organisation

Some groups have an influence on an organisation, but their actions are not necessarily directed by interests of the business. Workers tend to form into informal groups based on their interests or skills. For example, a group of workers might get together to organise a social function. The reason for this grouping is not intended to benefit the organisation, although it may well have a good influence on morale, something in the firm's interest. In another example, workers might group together to express an adverse opinion about a new development the firm wants to undertake.

It is important for management to recognise the way in which informal groups work if they are to minimise the damage they can cause, or maximise the benefits to be gained by utilising such groups wherever possible.

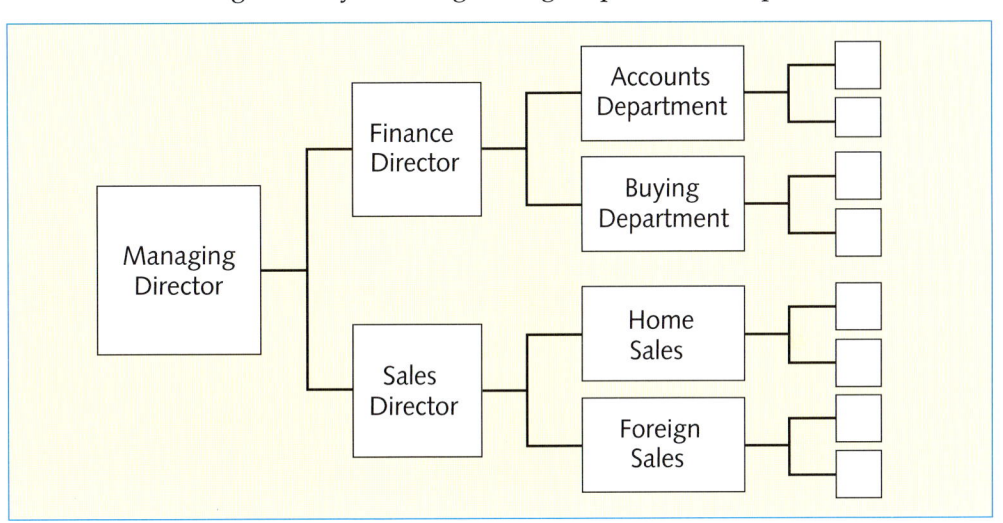

Fig. 3.11 *A horizontal organisation chart*

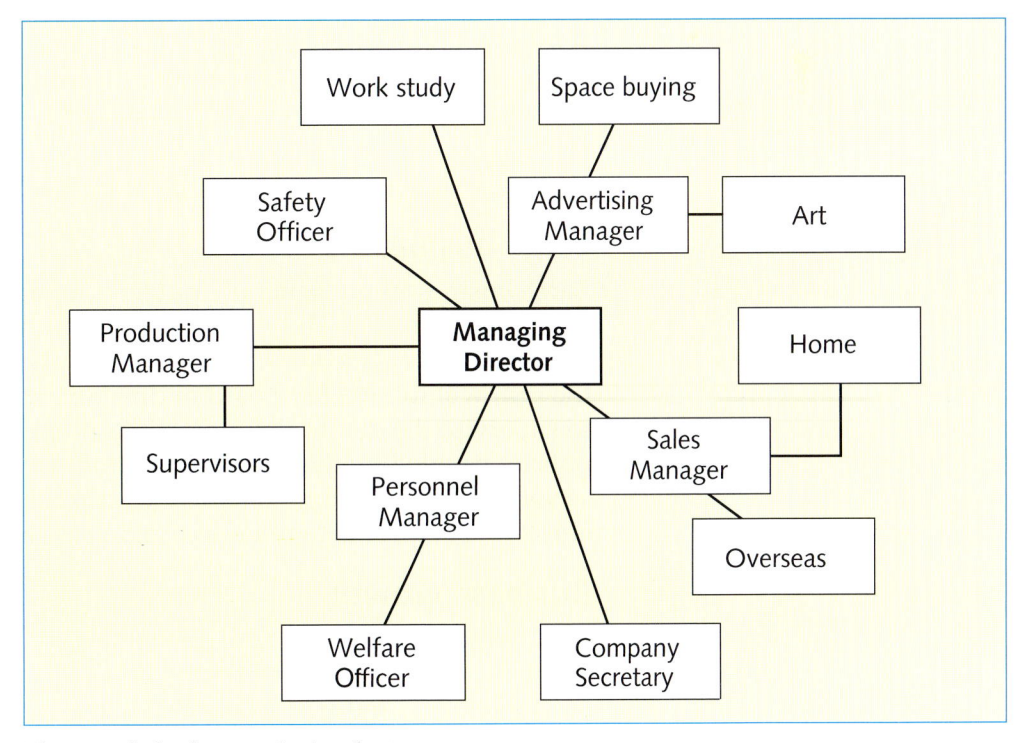

Fig. 3.12 *A circular organisation chart*

49

Organisation charts

Organisation charts are illustrations which show the formal structure of an organisation. The chart shows the different positions in the business and indicates what is done by each part, or shows the links between various parts of the organisation.

The size of a business will obviously influence the structure and complexity of the chart. There are a variety of ways of presenting organisation charts. The method shown in figure 3.7 is a vertical organisation chart. This is the most popular, but there are others. For example, a pyramid organisation chart is shown in figure 3.3, and others in figures 3.12 and 3.13.

KEY WORDS

Find out the business-related meaning of each of the following terms. Write a separate sentence for each term to show your understanding.

informal group   formal group   leader   teamwork   communication   leadership   organisation   organisational chart   span of control   chain of command

3.4 Small and large businesses

The internal structure of a firm is influenced by its size. The small business is organised fairly simply, whereas the larger company has a more complex structure and more divisions.

Small businesses

Small businesses cannot easily be divided into departments because they do not have the people or floor space to organise in this way. Consequently, workers in small firms tend to specialise less and they are required to have a wider range of skills and a broader knowledge of the way that the business is organised. This is because the workers need to be able to carry out a wider variety of tasks, whereas in a large organisation they would have more opportunity to specialise in a particular activity. However, the variety of the work in a small organisation is considered to be an advantage by some workers.

Large businesses

Large businesses are generally public companies, which were dealt with earlier in Chapter 2. These types of organisation are owned by shareholders. The shareholders elect a board of directors to decide the general policies that the firm will follow. The board of directors will appoint a managing director to supervise the day-to-day operations of the business, and to ensure that the policies decided by the board of directors are carried out. A company secretary is also appointed to deal with legal matters such as contracts of employment, product guarantees and government legislation.

Business growth

As a business grows, it usually generates economies of scale. This means that as the business's size increases, its unit costs fall: the cost of each item the business sells is reduced because unit costs are more widely spread. Thus, it is cheaper to produce goods or services on a larger scale.

Internal economies of scale occur as a result of various factors within the business, and these factors are related to its size. For example, a larger business can afford to buy and use more expensive equipment (e.g. computers and robotics), and these reduce operational costs. Other internal economies of scale include being able to employ specialist workers, being able to buy in bulk, and finding it easier to raise finance and borrow money.

External economies of scale refer to the benefits gained by all the businesses in a particular industry. Sometimes, for example, businesses with similar interests locate in a particular area. This can benefit all such related businesses because other supporting businesses (e.g. those providing support services) will also locate in the region, making access to them easier. Similarly, skilled labour will move into the area to the benefit of all the businesses. In addition, such businesses may co-operate to create joint research facilities which again benefit them all.

Increased share of the market

When a business is becoming more successful it will be obtaining an increased share of the market, and it will be achieving this increase at the expense of its competitors. In order to satisfy the increased numbers of customers, it will have to expand the business to meet the increased demand it is creating.

Securing sources of supply

When a business has to rely on others to supply it with materials or services, it can be at a disadvantage. For example, if the supplier receives a better offer from other buyers, they may bargain for a better price. Similarly, when a supplier is finding that demand for its goods or services is particularly good, they will be more choosy who they will supply them to. A business may become large enough through expansion to create its own sources of supply and avoid having to rely too much on other businesses. For example, a manufacturer of canned food may expand into farming, thus becoming its own supplier (backward integration).

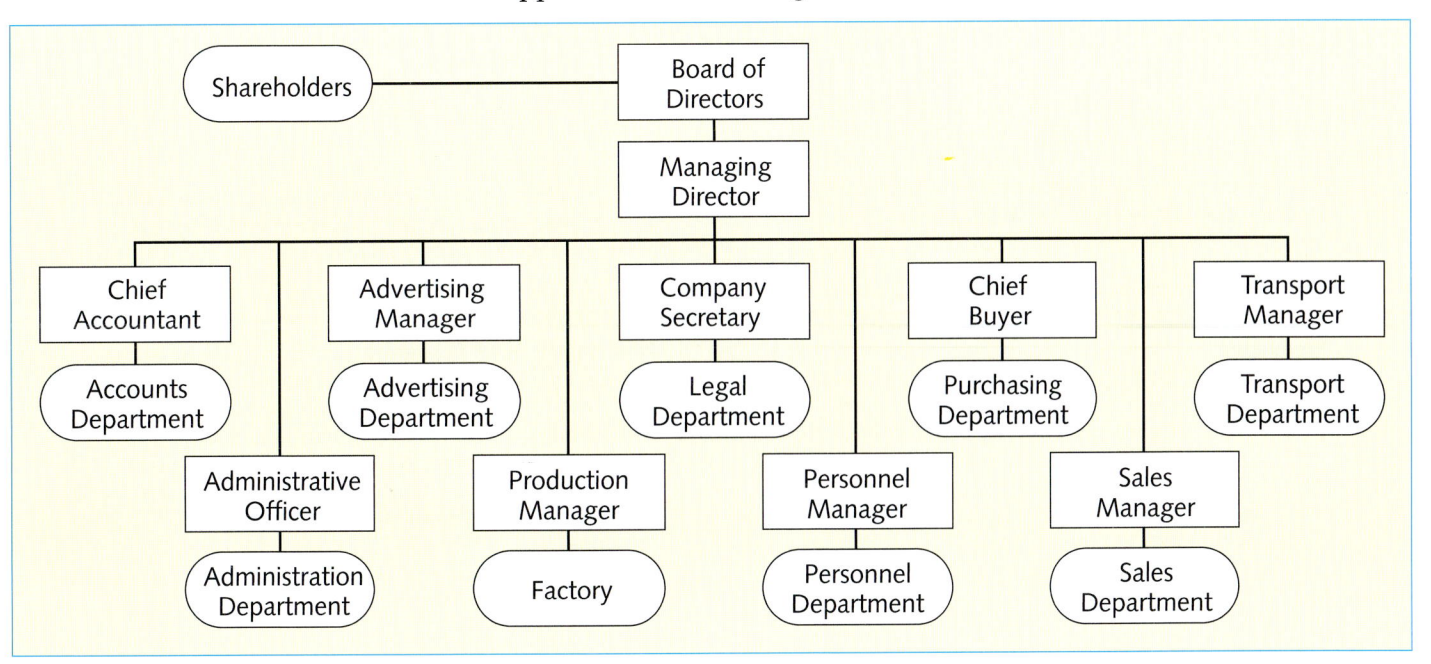

Fig. 3.13 *Company structure. A large business can be divided into separate departments, each with its own management and internal structure.*

Principles of Business – Profile 1

Accounts
Records all payments in and out of the firm. It is particularly concerned with incoming and outgoing invoices, and maintaining the firm's money flow. Payment of wages is frequently included in the responsibilities of this department. The modern accounts department has an extensive data processing system backed up by computers.

Legal
Most legal matters are dealt with by the company secretary, although a very large organisation might have a legal department. The department's activities include legal matters such as contracts, guarantees, insurance, compensation, etc.

Purchasing
The purchasing or buying department is responsible for all items bought by the firm. It obtains quotations from suppliers and issues orders, ensuring delivery is made on time. It also checks that prices, quality and quantity delivered correspond with the quotation and order. This department also deals with 'requisitions' which are written requests for supplies from other departments in the firm.

Sales
To plan and organise the selling of goods or services offered by the firm. This department is one of the most essential because without it other departments would not be needed. Sales representatives provide an important link between the company and potential customers.

Advertising
May be a separate department or it can be incorporated into the sales department. The aim of this department is to make potential customers aware of the goods or services the company offers and to encourage custom. Smaller firms may employ the services of an advertising agency to carry out this work for them.

Transport
May operate the company's own fleet of vehicles, or alternatively it organises other forms of transport using agencies outside the firm. The function of this department is to arrange for delivery of goods to customers on time, in good condition, at home or overseas, and by the most economical method and route applicable.

Administration
Many firms have a general office concerned with co-ordinating the activities of the various departments of the firm. The administration department may include back-up facilities such as centralised filing, typing pool, mail room, reprographics and data processing. The administration department is frequently closely related to the managing director.

Production
Where the company is involved in production of some commodity, a production department may be used to co-ordinate the work of the factory unit. 'Progress chasers' may be employed to ensure that delivery schedules are adhered to, and 'quality controllers' can be used to maintain production standards and investigate complaints or deal with goods returned as faulty.

Personnel/Human Resources
Concerned with finding the right person for vacant jobs, dismissing unsuitable workers, dealing with resignations and providing references. It is involved directly in any induction training or staff training school the company operates. It maintains personal records of all employees and is involved in the welfare and happiness of all personnel.

Fig. 3.14 *The departments of a large company*

Securing outlets

Growth can enable a business to create its own outlets for its products. For example, a shoe manufacturer could expand to set up its own retail shops or mail order company.

Business growth and organisational structure

As a business grows in size it has various effects on the organisational structure. For example, whilst the growing company can employ more people, this can have implications for the organisational structure. It affects the chain of command and span of control examined earlier in this chapter. The possible problems this could create will influence the type of organisational structure the business will choose.

3.5 Management and industrial relations

Managers of all sizes of business have a responsibility to motivate employees, and to promote good working relationships with them. This is essential in order to promote goodwill and to avoid industrial disputes. The basic way that these two ideals can be realised is by:

- Maintaining good two-way communication between management and employees. In this way misunderstandings can be reduced because employees will be familiar with what the management are trying to achieve, and the management will be fully aware of the employees' views.
- Establishing clear grievance guidelines and procedures. Both the management and the employees must be fully aware of these procedures and actively participate in using them. In other words, the rules are laid down and the correct procedures followed. Everyone knows where they stand!
- Practising the good leadership skills described earlier in this chapter. These can do much to motivate employees and help to reduce internal conflicts. Whichever style of leadership is used within the organisation, most employees respond well to encouragement, praise and consideration.
- Providing good working conditions that illustrate that management recognise that their employees deserve good surroundings, and that these will help to raise their sense of worth.
- Taking steps to make the employees' work more interesting and varied, through job enlargement or job enrichment.
- Ensuring that employees are paid a fair and commensurate wage, and can see there are incentives to work well, e.g. bonuses, raises, etc. In this way the employee can see that the increased prosperity of the business is related to their income.

Motivation of employees and industrial relations are examined in greater depth in Chapters 5 and 6

3.6 Motivation theories

Motivation refers to the force or process which influences people to behave in the way that they do. In a work situation, motivation can be seen as the ways that people are influenced to achieve required task objectives. There are many

Principles of Business – Profile 1

theories of motivation and we will examine two important ones here. The first is the '**hierarchy of needs**' theory, and the other one we will examine is '**hygiene-motivation**' theory. Theories such as these are important for business because they indicate how workers can be less productive if their needs are not recognised and satisfied. For example, we might think that pay (and material prosperity) is the most important factor in job satisfaction, but when that has been satisfied other factors are seen to be equally as important.

5 Self-fulfilment needs
4 Self-esteem or ego needs
3 Social needs
2 Safety needs
1 Basic needs

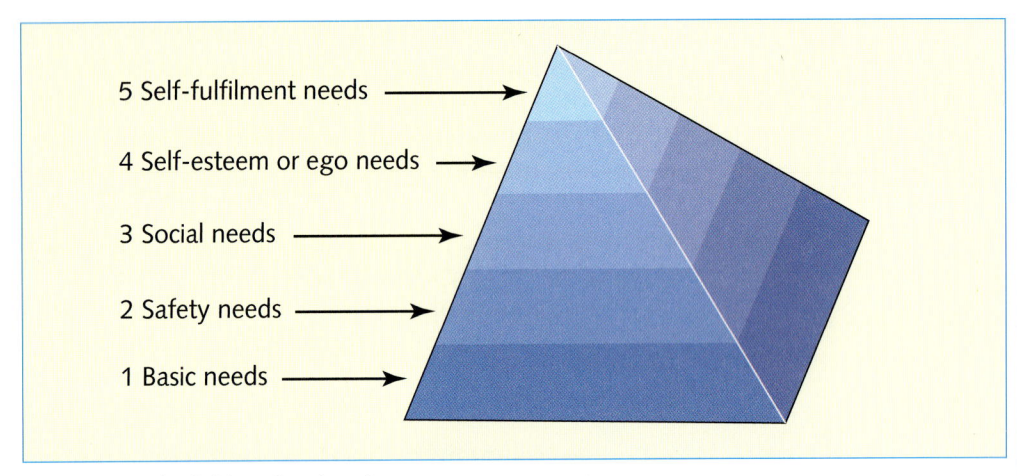

Fig. 3.15 *Maslow's hierarchy of needs*

Abraham Maslow formulated a now famous 'hierarchy of needs'. These needs, which are ordered in a hierarchy (see figure 3.15), can be summarised as follows in relation to the working situation:

1. *Basic needs.* Survival requirements – need for food, drink, shelter, warmth, ventilation, rest breaks and payment.
2. *Safety needs.* Protection from danger – need for job security and a safe working environment, i.e. sound health and safety provisions.
3. *Social needs.* Friendship – companionable relationships with other employees.
4. *Self-esteem needs.* Ego needs – recognition of a 'job well done'.
5. *Self-fulfilment needs.* Personal ambition – realisation of individual potential, complete job satisfaction.

Initially, the lower order of needs such as 1 and 2 above determine behaviour, but once these are satisfied, the higher needs become more dominant.

Hygiene factor	Motivating factors
• Organisation aims recognised by staff • Competent management • Pay seen as 'fair' • Interpersonal relationships satisfactory • Working conditions have to be acceptable	• Achievement – job satisfaction • Recognition – appreciation of efforts • The work – interesting and pleasurable • Responsibility – people respond to responsibility • Advancement – self improvement

Figure 3.16 *Two factor Theory of Motivation*

Frederick Herzberg formulated another theory of needs that is summed up as a 'hygiene-motivation theory'. He argued that people are motivated by two kinds of need, *hygiene needs* and *motivation needs*. **Hygiene needs** are the physical working conditions and the relations that exist between management and staff. If the hygiene needs are neglected in the work place, workers will be dissatisfied and their performance will suffer. **Motivation needs**, such as the need to feel a sense of achievement and responsibility, are also important if the best performance is to be obtained from the workforce. Herzberg's *Two factor Theory of Motivation* is typically summarised by the table in figure 3.16 on the previous page.

The importance of this theory in the work situation is that it is important for managers to ensure that both hygiene factors (e.g. pay and working conditions) and 'motivators' (e.g. self fulfilment and job satisfaction) are provided for the workforce to be contented and motivated. Not surprisingly this theory has been referred to as aimed at **'job enrichment'**.

3.7 Management information systems (MIS)

What is MIS?

MIS is a modern concept that is rooted in **information technology** and **information systems**. A management information system is enhanced with computer technology and telecommunications technology. MIS can be said to be the development and use of effective information systems in organisations to support decision-making by management. Because of its link to the computer, the systems concept of **input-process-output** is an integral part of management information systems. Storage and retrieval complement input-process-output and thus makes the MIS more 'user friendly'.

The aim of a management information system is to provide accurate and timely information whenever and wherever it is needed in an organisation. This is to facilitate the decision-making process.

The major functions of an MIS include systems planning, organising, designing, overseeing and monitoring. The MIS team plans the system, organises the system to facilitate the day-to-day operations, designs the system to meet the needs of the organisation, oversees the total MIS system and monitors MIS centres within the organisation.

Characteristics of an MIS

Management information systems have the following main characteristics:

- *Provide reports* These are mainly standardised reports such as sales, financial and other reports as stipulated and required by organisations. They are regular recurring reports which are presented in summary form.
- *Static structure* The structure of an MIS is relatively static, mainly because the reports needed by organisations are standardised, and require limited change from week to week or month to month.
- *Stable technology* The MIS technology is stable. Procedures and methods may change mainly due to the updating of the system, but the basic technology remains the same.

Types of management information systems

Transaction processing systems

These are in common use today in supermarkets, stores, petrol stations and other similar sales outlets to handle point-of-sale transactions. Additionally, the processing of orders, especially those that are received electronically, is greatly enhanced by the transaction processing system. The automatic teller machine is part of the transactions processing system. Quick response of the system, reliability of the system, and stability of the technology are not just a few features of the system, but also major requirements of the system.

Decision-making support system

This is a support system to enhance decision-making in organisations. This system operates in a less structured MIS environment. Therefore, in terms of its characteristics, it responds to ad hoc instructions since varied needs are to be satisfied, is more flexible and adaptable, and thus requires more facilities than the standard MIS system.

Office automation system

This system is designed to support office communication systems. It features a multi-media system that facilitates data processing, text editing, graphics, illustrations, voice and video communications for teleconferencing. Additionally, the system is structured and standardised. It requires flexible, adaptable and stable technology.

Office automation system applications include electronic mail, electronic bulletin boards, voice mail, image processing collaborative document processing and video-conferencing. A major requirement is a network system – local area network (LAN) to facilitate its operations.

Executive support system

This system supports management decision-making. Senior executives who need to make decisions on a regular basis utilise this system. The major characteristics are: high-level, aggregated and standardised information and data in areas such as sales and finance, among other types of reports that support decision-making. Often data must be taken from different sources in order to generate the required report. Important to this system, as is the case with other systems, is timeliness and accuracy of the data and information provided by the system.

Benefits of MIS to organisations

A number of benefits are obtained from a management information system. These include the following:

- It enhances communication and decision-making in organisations.
- It provides a good data base which enhances the timeliness and accuracy of information.
- It can contribute to the improvement of productivity since the 'turn round time' on tasks can be lessened considerably, providing of course, that persons are trained to use the system.
- It reduces the cost of labour since routine tasks can be carried out by a computer, thus requiring less labour-intensive inputs into production and services.
- It assists in the development of organisation policies.

Departments within an organisation benefit from the following:

- Standardised procedures in carrying out various tasks, or completing various assignments.

- Saving of space.
- Reduction in the cost of technology, thus funds from budget allocation can be used for other tasks.
- Improvement in the monitoring and maintenance tasks.
- Provision of staff training and updating.

KEY WORDS

Find out the business-related meaning of each of the following terms. Write a separate sentence for each term to show your understanding.

hygiene needs   motivation needs   business growth   motivation
industrial relations   economies of scale   information technology
hierarchy of needs   management information system   industrial dispute

3.8 Things to do

This section contains a variety of exercises to help you create revision notes, to test your understanding and to prepare you for examinations.

Search and find

Write out the question and the answer by referring back through the text to form revision notes.

1. What is the main aim of a business?
2. How do the four functional areas of a business help it achieve its general aim?
3. Why is management an important aspect of a business?
4. Briefly describe the responsibilities of management.
5. Why do managers have more responsibilities than their subordinates?
6. Give at least three examples of the responsibilities you think a manager has to the government and society.
7. In what ways does management meet its responsibilities?
8. Describe the main functions of management.
9. Why is it important for a manager to have an understanding of group dynamics?
10. Explain the difference between informal groups and formal groups.
11. Why is it important that a firm's objectives are clearly understood by its employees?
12. Why is it that wage levels are limited in the extent to which they can be relied on to encourage people to work hard and effectively?
13. Why is it difficult to define the qualities needed to lead others?
14. List in your order of priority ten qualities you would look for in a potential manager of a medium-sized manufacturing company.
15. Briefly describe each of the four styles of leadership.

Principles of Business – Profile 1

16 Why is communication an important factor in management?

17 'Effective management requires a two-way flow of communication.' Explain this statement.

18 Why are there so many variations in the span of control?

19 How does chain of command differ from span of control?

20 Describe the four types of formal organisational structure.

21 Produce simple diagrams to illustrate the four types of organisation charts in this chapter.

22 Make an outline comparison between the organisational structure of a small business and that of a large business.

23 How does the function of a managing director differ from that of other directors?

24 Describe the functions of six departments in a large company.

25 Briefly describe the benefits of business growth.

26 Give two examples each of internal and external economies of scale.

27 Why does business growth affect organisational structure?

28 Critics of Maslow's theory of a 'hierarchy of needs' say that not everyone has all the needs or the hierarchy he assumed. Do you think this criticism is valid?

29 In what ways do you think that Herzberg's 'hygiene-motivation theory' could help managers to get the best out of their workers?

30 Describe how you believe managers can motivate workers, apart from giving them more money.

31 Define the term 'management information system'.

32 Give examples of the application of MIS.

33 How can MIS benefit an organisation?

What do you know?

Write out the complete sentence and the missing word, which can be chosen from the list at the end of the questions.

1 A major aim of a business is to make a ..... for the owners.
2 The broad function of production is to satisfy human ......
3 ..... is required to form a business and to fund its operations.
4 The ..... function of a business aims to promote sales of a company's products or services.
5 The ..... function of a business is to provide employment.
6 A greater degree of responsibility lies with the ..... of an organisation.
7 The managers of a business will organise and ..... the work of others.
8 There is an effective ..... to the number of workers a manager can supervise efficiently.
9 ..... groups have usually come together voluntarily.
10 ..... groups are usually created for a specific purpose.

Choose the missing words from the following:

formal   wants   marketing   personnel   finance   limit   co-ordinate   managers   profit   informal

Chapter 3 – **Business organisation**

Structured questions

Q1 Look at the illustration of a company organisation structure (figure 3.13) and answer the following questions.

(a) Which of the labels in the diagram refers to the owners of the business? **1**

(b) Only one of the labels in the diagram is an elected position. Name the elected position. **1**

(c) Which of the departments in the diagram would be responsible for issuing contracts of employment? State two other functions of this department. **3**

(d) Name the department that would carry out the following work and state the manager who would be responsible for the work of the department:
  (i) planning routes for company delivery trucks
  (ii) interviewing prospective employees
  (iii) sending out invoices. **6**

(e) Describe the work of three workers from the following list:
  (i) progress chaser   (iii) sales representative   (v) quality controller.
  (ii) wages clerk   (iv) goods inwards clerk **9**

Q2

(a) Name the department likely to be responsible for:
  (i) carrying out market research **1**
  (ii) ordering new stock. **1**

(b) Name the personnel likely to be responsible for:
  (i) deciding main company policy **1**
  (ii) preparation of a balance sheet. **1**

(c) Why is a company's transport department particularly important both to its sales department and to its factory? **4**

(d) Rose Petal is the Production Manager of a medium-sized manufacturing company. She recently carried out a study of the way her department operates, with a view to identifying areas for improvement. Her main findings were:
  • There is *insufficient delegation* of decisions.
  • The supervisors in the factory workshops have *too wide a span of control*.
  (i) Explain the statements in italic. **4**
  (ii) How might Rose Petal's company be affected by these problems and what might she do to improve the situation? **8**

Q3

(a) Why is management necessary, particularly in a large organisation? **2**

(b) In what way would you say that management differs from leadership? **4**

Principles of Business – Profile 1

(c) The following list includes management personnel, other workers and documents associated with their work. Copy out the headings, and place each under the appropriate heading (the italicised items have already been put under their correct headings).

Management personnel	Other workers	Documents
sales manager	representative	quotation
personnel manager	legal clerk	
quotation	requisition	
transport manager	*representative*	
chief buyer	welfare officer	
delivery note	chief accountant	
routeing clerk	guarantee	
sales manager	order clerk	
pay advice	company secretary	
wages clerk	staff records	

4

(d) Describe the work of each of the following business occupations:
- (i) company secretary
- (ii) welfare officer
- (iii) routeing clerk
- (iv) personnel manager
- (v) representative

10

Q4 The following questions are all related to motivation theories.

(a) Why do workers have 'needs' other than payment? **1**

(b) In what way can Maslow's theory be said to be a 'hierarchy'? **2**

(c) Where would you say that the provision of a suggestion box by management fits into Maslow's theory? **3**

(d) Maslow's theory identified five needs. Briefly describe any two of these. **4**

(e) Frederick Herzberg identified a 'hygiene-motivation theory'. Explain clearly the difference between the two main factors that he identified. **4**

(f) Describe three contrasting ways that could draw on theories to motivate the workers. **6**

Research assignments

1. Carry out an investigation into two local companies, one large and one small. Compare the advantages and disadvantages of their forms of internal organisation.

2. Give a detailed description of the functions of four departments of a large company you have access to and show how any one of them is dependent upon the other three.

3. Make a diagrammatic 'map' of the organisational structures of a small and a medium-sized local firm with which you are familiar. Comment on the differences observed.

4. What evidence can you find of the existence of MIS in businesses? Does the size of the business have any relevance?

Chapter 4: Recruitment, selection and training

4.1 Recruiting employees

Publicising vacancies

When a firm wishes to attract applications for a vacant position there are a variety of avenues open to it:

- school/college careers advisers
- job centres run by the government's training agency
- employment agencies run by private firms
- local careers officers
- newspaper advertisements
- friends and relatives.

Advertisements are the most common way of publicising a job vacancy and inviting applications. These advertisements are important to the firm; they must therefore be carefully formulated so that they attract the right sort of applicant. They must clearly state what is required, otherwise valuable time will be wasted investigating the suitability of applicants. They are also important to job hunters because they help to ensure that they only apply for the kind of job they really want.

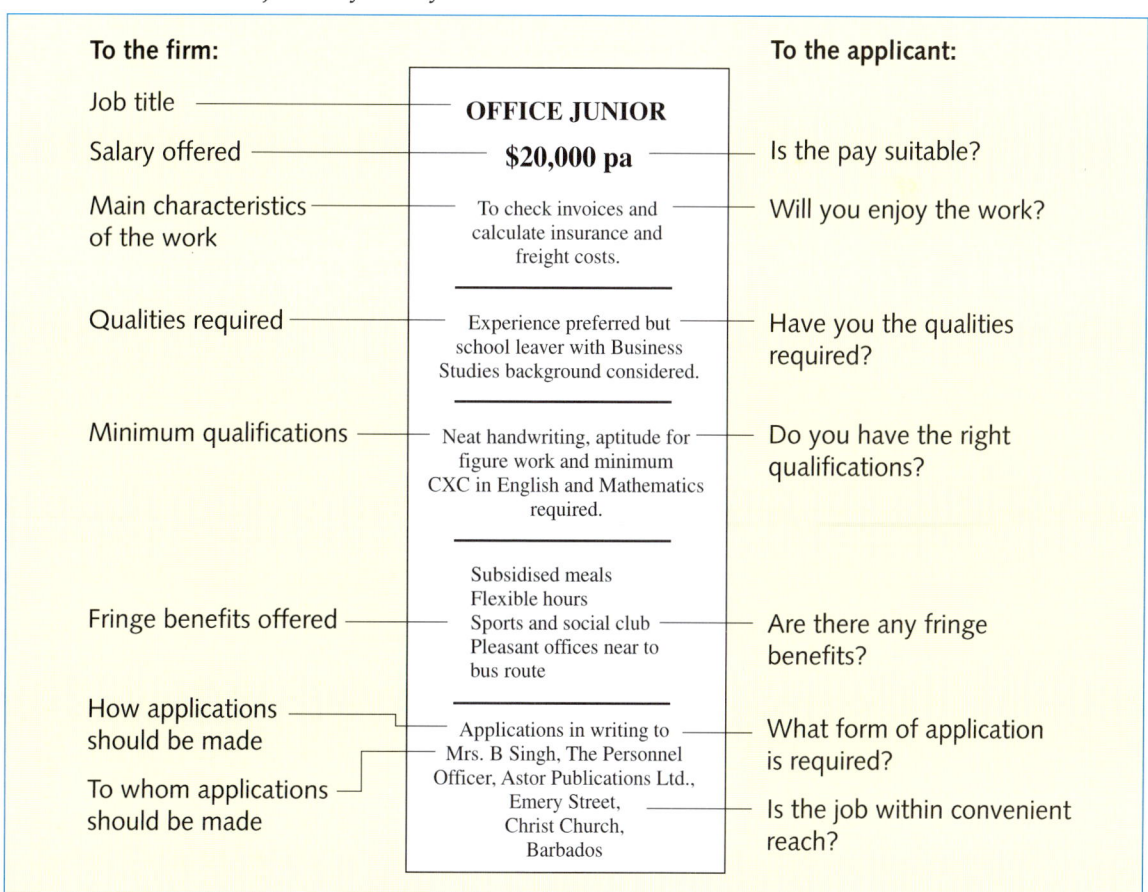

To the firm:		To the applicant:
Job title	**OFFICE JUNIOR**	
Salary offered	**$20,000 pa**	Is the pay suitable?
Main characteristics of the work	To check invoices and calculate insurance and freight costs.	Will you enjoy the work?
Qualities required	Experience preferred but school leaver with Business Studies background considered.	Have you the qualities required?
Minimum qualifications	Neat handwriting, aptitude for figure work and minimum CXC in English and Mathematics required.	Do you have the right qualifications?
Fringe benefits offered	Subsidised meals Flexible hours Sports and social club Pleasant offices near to bus route	Are there any fringe benefits?
How applications should be made	Applications in writing to Mrs. B Singh, The Personnel Officer, Astor Publications Ltd., Emery Street, Christ Church, Barbados	What form of application is required?
To whom applications should be made		Is the job within convenient reach?

Fig. 4.1 *Job advertisements must be clearly worded and carefully read by applicants*

Principles of Business – Profile 1

```
Telephone 268 6949                          4 Hill Walk
                                            ANCHOVY
Mr. P. Daley                                St. James
Daley Designs plc
16 Market Street
Montego Bay
St. James


Dear Mr. Daley,                             12 May 2007

I refer to your advertisement in the 'Evening Post' inviting applications
for the position of general sales clerk, and I would like to apply for
the vacancy.

I am 16 years of age and I leave school at the end of this month.
I have completed examinations in the following subjects, for which I
am awaiting results: English, Mathematics, Business Studies,
Technology, Computer Studies and Art and Design.

I enjoy sport and I have represented the school in both hockey and
basketball. My other main interest is reading, particularly historical
novels.

For the past two years I have worked as an assistant in a local
hardware store, and I believe that this experience could make me a
suitable applicant for the vacancy you have available.

I hope you find my application of interest and I would be pleased to
attend an interview at your convenience. References are available
from my school and from my part-time job if you require me to
obtain them.

Yours sincerely
Kirsty Davies
KIRSTY DAVIES
```

Annotations:
- ← Your home address – note home town in capitals
- ← Name and address of the person you are writing to
- ← Date
- ← Say which job you are applying for
- ← Qualifications or examinations taken
- ← Personal interests
- ← Relevant past experience and why you think you are suitable
- ← Print your name under your signature

Fig. 4.2 *Letters of application for employment should be carefully written, following the correct format*

Letters of application

Prospective applicants should read the advertisement carefully. Not only will it give important information about the job and the firm, but it may also offer clues about what should be included in the letter of application.

In some cases it may be acceptable to type or word process a letter, in others the advertisement may state that the application should be in *first hand*, in which case the letter should be handwritten, preferably on plain paper. It is sensible to make a rough draft of the proposed letter before writing it out in an acceptable form. If the instructions do not tell you to write it, type it.

Curriculum vitae

Job advertisements today frequently ask for a curriculum vitae (cv) from applicants. A cv is a brief history of the applicant, including school attended, qualifications, relevant experience, etc. This should be typed to accompany the letter of application, thus making it possible to make the letter shorter and more concise. Sometimes names, addresses and telephone numbers of the **referees** are included at the end of the cv.

Chapter 4 – **Recruitment, selection and training**

CURRICULUM VITAE	June Simon
ADDRESS	21 Court Street St. John's, Antigua
DATE OF BIRTH	12 October 1991
SEX	Female
PLACE OF BIRTH	St. John's
NATIONALITY	Antiguan
EDUCATION	Princess Margaret High School St. John's, Antigua 2002 to 2007
CXC	English Language Mathematics French Biology History Business Studies
INTERESTS	Reading Outdoor sports Music
WORK EXPERIENCE	Saturday job in family general store

Fig. 4.3 *Example of a curriculum vitae*

Application form

An application form is a standard printed form sent out by firms for applicants to fill out, providing specific information to support their application. The form may be sent to the applicant for completion prior to the interview, or it may have to be completed under supervision at the interview. There are two main reasons why firms use an application form as part of the recruitment and selection process. Firstly, it acts as a check on personal details, qualifications and experience, and it ensures that key information is included in the minimum space. Secondly, it allows selection panel members to make comparisons between candidates easily.

References

Most employers will require applicants to provide the names of persons (**referees**) willing to attest the character of the candidate. Written declarations (**testimonials**) from reliable persons testifying to the good character of the applicant may also be required. Referees should be contacted by the applicant for permission before their names are used on the cv.

4.2 The human resources department

The human resources department (sometimes called the personnel department) is concerned with finding the right person for each job, and if necessary giving him or her induction training. This department also deals with resignations, providing testimonials and dismissing unsuitable workers. It maintains personal records of all employees and is involved in the welfare and happiness of all personnel.

Applications for employment are received and considered by the personnel department. This department is headed by the personnel manager.

Short list of applicants

From the many applications received in response to the advertisement, the personnel department lists a few of the most promising applicants and invites them to attend an interview. For this reason, the written application is very important if the applicant is to reach the next stage on the way to getting the job.

Interviews

Short-listed applicants for employment are interviewed (usually in the personnel department) before any job offer is made. The aim of the interview is not only to assess the suitability of the candidate for the vacant position, but also to give the applicant the opportunity to seek further information about the job. During the interview the applicant may be required to complete an **aptitude test** designed to assess his/her suitability for the job.

The interview is crucial for the applicant because it is at this time that the interviewer assesses the candidate's appearance, ability to communicate and

Principles of Business – Profile 1

general manner. Consequently, it is important to be thoroughly prepared for the interview. The following are tips for people who are called for interview.

Preparation for the interview
- Do a little homework about the job for which you have applied.
- Use your common sense about your appearance, and dress carefully.
- Take the letter inviting you for interview.
- Remember the name of the person you have to see.
- Know exactly where the interview will take place.
- Plan the route to get there so that you arrive promptly for the interview.

During the interview
- Only sit down when invited to.
- Do not smoke.
- Try to be relaxed and confident, but not flippant or over-familiar.
- Concentrate fully on the interviewer.
- Be prepared to answer questions.
- Try to ask some sensible questions when you are invited to do so.

Questions to be prepared for
- Why do you want the job?
- What qualities do you have to offer?
- What are your ambitions?
- What do you do in your spare time?
- What do you read?

Questions you could ask
- What does the job involve?
- What hours are involved?
- What is the salary?
- What are the opportunities for promotion?
- What are the holiday arrangements?
- What fringe benefits are available?

4.3 Staff orientation and training

All new members of staff need to become acquainted with other members of the firm, as well as becoming familiar with the organisation of the business. Many firms organise an induction or orientation programme to introduce new employees to their workplace and colleagues. The induction programme will often be managed by the personnel department.

Staff training is often an important part of the introduction of staff to a new job. This will aim to help new employees quickly to become a useful part of the organisation by familiarising them with any new skills they need.

Staff training does not only apply to new employees. Sometimes existing staff will be transferred to other departments or other jobs which may require training in new skills. A large firm may operate its own internal training school, or alternatively staff may be encouraged to attend college courses to learn new skills.

4.4 Welfare of employees

Welfare refers to the concern for people's physical well-being. Social facilities, lighting and cooling or air-conditioning, hygiene and canteen services are all examples of things that contribute to the welfare of employees. These all come within the functions of the personnel department.

The personnel department may be responsible for the operation of the company's sports and social club, organising activities and events which encourage employees to socialise. A member of this department may also visit sick or retired employees.

The firm may have its own *in-house newspaper* or magazine which is used to keep the workers up to date with events in which the company is involved, as well as providing a means of general communication.

Most firms recognise that good *working conditions* not only keep the employees happy, but also help to make them more productive and efficient. For this reason, firms try to provide good working conditions, but there are four Acts which are particularly concerned with staff welfare. These are dealt with, together with other aspects of working conditions, in the next chapter.

1. Factories Act
2. Contract of Employment Act
3. Health and Safety at Work Act
4. Employment Act

Find out when these Acts were passed in your island, and what are their main aims.

4.5 Staff records

The letter of application for employment, the curriculum vitae or the completed application form, together with the results of any aptitude test taken when the new employee joins the firm, form the basis of the employee's record. This information is held by the employer on a confidential file, usually in the personnel department.

Over the years the record is periodically updated with other information. For example, people in supervisory positions will occasionally write progress reports on their subordinates. These reports and other records of the employee's progress in the firm will include the following:

- punctuality
- health
- academic progress
- promotions and salary increases
- suitability for further promotion
- misdemeanours.

From the foregoing it should be obvious that the contents of personnel records are *highly confidential*. For this reason, people who work in the personnel department are expected to be discreet. In addition, the security of personnel records is of the utmost importance.

4.6 Dismissal and redundancy

Dismissal

In Chapter 6, reference is made to the *Contract of Employment Act*, which requires all employees to be given details of the terms of their employment. The Contract of Employment includes the length of *notice* (length of time as

Principles of Business – Profile 1

notification of ceasing employment) to be given by the employer and the employee. When a worker wishes to work elsewhere he or she is required to give a period of notice which allows the employer to look for a new employee. Similarly, if the employer wishes to dismiss the worker, a period of notice is generally observed, although there are exceptions to this, such as when the employee has been guilty of a serious misdemeanour. In such circumstances it is usual that certain steps are followed:

1 oral warning
2 written warning
3 suspension
4 dismissal.

Obviously, the employee may get instant dismissal for breaking important rules of the organisation, for example for stealing.

Today workers are protected against unfair dismissal by the **Employment Protection Act**, which requires an employer to show that there are good reasons for terminating the employment. An employee who feels that he or she has been unfairly dismissed can complain to his or her union or to the appropriate section of the labour ministry. If, upon investigation, it is found that the employer acted unfairly or unreasonably, an order of reinstatement of the employee will be issued to the employer. If the employer refuses to comply, then the matter will be referred to the **Industrial Disputes Tribunal** which will make the final decision.

Grievance procedure

An employee has a grievance in the following situations.
- An existing employer/employee agreement has been broken.
- A labour law has been violated by the employer.
- The employer has acted in an unfair manner.
- The health or safety of the employee has been put at risk.

The first point of contact for the employee is the **work supervisor**, who may be willing and able to offer a remedy for the grievance. In any case, the supervisor is likely to be the source of contact between the aggrieved person and the firm's management.

Should representation through the supervisor be inappropriate or unsatisfactory, the worker will contact his or her union representative, often another employee of the company. This person will be familiar with the rights of the worker and will act on his or her behalf, or direct the grievance to the union for advice and guidance. The union may even decide that the employee does not have a real grievance, and it will advise the worker of this.

Redundancy

Redundancy refers to a situation when an employee loses his or her job because it no longer exists. This may occur because the business has been forced to cease trading, or because the firm no longer has the capacity to employ the same number of workers.

When an employee loses his or her job as a result of redundancy, he or she needs financial help to make the transition to new employment.

The **Redundancy Payments Act** requires employers to make a lump sum payment to employees being made redundant (as long as they have served for a minimum period of time). The amount of redundancy compensation depends upon the age, length of service and pay of the employee.

KEY WORDS

Find out the business-related meaning of each of the following terms. Write a separate sentence for each term to show your understanding.

aptitude   reference
short-list   interview
employer   employee
referee   fringe benefits
grievance   redundancy
notice   interview

4.7 Things to do

This section contains a variety of exercises to help you create revision notes, to test your understanding and to prepare you for examinations.

Search and find

Write out the question and the answer by referring back through the text to form revision notes.

1. List five sources of information about job vacancies.
2. Why are job advertisements important to both the firm and the applicant?
3. List four specific pieces of information that the job applicant can obtain from the advertisement.
4. What does it mean when an advertisement states that applications must be in 'first hand'?
5. Make a list of six suggestions you would give someone to help him or her to write a letter of application for a job.
6. What is a curriculum vitae? What information does it contain?
7. In what way does an application form differ from a cv?
8. What is the function of 'referees' and 'testimonials' in relation to applications for employment?
9. Give a brief summary of the main functions of the personnel department of a firm.
10. What is a short list?
11. What is the main purpose of the interview?
12. Why might a job applicant be required to complete an aptitude test?
13. In what way can someone usefully prepare for a job interview?
14. List six points the candidate should observe during the interview.
15. Give four examples of questions that might be asked of an applicant at the interview.
16. Suggest four questions the job applicant could ask when invited to do so.
17. Why would a firm be interested in the welfare of its employees?
18. In what way might a firm show its care for the welfare of its employees?
19. How would the personnel department in particular be involved in the welfare of employees?
20. Briefly describe the kind of information likely to be found in personnel records. Why is the security and confidentiality of personnel records important?
21. What regulations exist to protect an employee from unfair dismissal?
22. Explain the purpose of redundancy payments.

Principles of Business – Profile 1

What do you know?

Write out the complete sentence and insert the missing word, which can be chosen from the list at the end of the test.

1. If job applicants are told to write in 'first hand', the letter should be .....
2. A cv is a brief ..... of the applicant for a job.
3. The ..... department is concerned with finding the right person for a vacant job.
4. Short-listed applicants for employment are usually ..... before any job offer is made.
5. All new members of staff need to be ..... with other members of the firm.
6. A staff ..... programme introduces new employees to their workplace and colleagues.
7. Sometimes staff being transferred to other departments will require training in new .....
8. A firm may have its own in-house ..... which is used to keep workers up to date with the company's activities.
9. Personnel records are kept ..... by the personnel department.
10. Today, workers are protected against ..... dismissal.

Choose the missing words from the following:

history   skills   personnel   unfair   handwritten   newspaper   acquainted   confidential   interviewed   orientation

Structured questions

Q1 Refer to the advertisement for an office junior (figure 4.1), and answer these questions.

(a)	Name the company that has advertised this vacant position.	1
(b)	To whom in particular should applications be sent?	1
(c)	What qualities are required of applicants for this job?	2
(d)	What will be the yearly salary to be paid and, assuming that wages are paid monthly, what would be the gross monthly income?	2
(e)	Why do you think that the job advertised requires an 'aptitude for figure work'?	2
(f)	Explain what the four 'fringe benefits' listed involve.	4
(g)	Write a suitable letter of application for this position using the correct method of letter layout.	8

Q2 You have left school and are looking for employment.

(a)	Give two reasons why you should read a job advertisement carefully.	2
(b)	List three tips that you would suggest people might take into account when writing letters of job application.	3
(c)	Advertisements for jobs frequently ask applicants to provide a curriculum vitae (cv). Give three examples of information that would be included in a cv.	3
(d)	Briefly describe four ways you and other school leavers could find employment, and list the various people who could help you.	4
(e)	Give an outline of the different sorts of induction and training you might receive, either within a business or through some organisation outside of your employment.	8

Chapter 4 – **Recruitment, selection and training**

Q3 Read again the letter of application in figure 4.2, and answer these questions.

(a) Name the person who is applying and the name of the company they are approaching. **1**

(b) The job being applied for is that of General Sales Clerk. What kind of duties could this type of occupation include? **2**

(c) Why is a prospective employer interested in an applicant's personal interests? **3**

(d) If you were considering this application, what aspects of past experience would you consider important? Give reasons for your choice. **4**

(e) Letters of application are often used to form a 'short list'. What is the purpose of a short list and what factors influence its formulation? **4**

(f) List three questions that might be asked at an interview by the interviewer, and three that the interviewee might ask. **6**

Q4

(a) State two of the main functions of a personnel department. **2**

(b) Briefly describe one form that staff training might take within a firm. **2**

(c) State two methods that a company could use to keep its employees informed of events that the business is involved in. **2**

(d) A firm received 40 letters of application in response to a job advertisement placed in the local press. List four points the firm might take into account to decide a short list of people to be invited for interview. **4**

(e) Why is the interview crucial for both the job applicant and the employer? **4**

(f) Most firms consider that staff welfare is important. Briefly describe three ways that a firm might be involved in the welfare of its employees. **6**

Research assignments

1 Your friend has been short-listed for a job that she has applied for. Explain the advice you would give your friend to help her to be successful at the interview. In what ways might your advice vary depending on the type of job involved?

2 Fizzy Pop Ltd. is a manufacturer of soft drinks, and you are employed in the public relations department. The company is to have a visit from a number of young people from the local school who are to do three weeks of work experience prior to leaving school. You have been asked to talk to them about various aspects of business work. Write notes for your talk about four different occupations in business, including an explanation of the qualities needed for each of the positions you have chosen.

3 Collect at least five advertisements for varied jobs in different types of businesses. What differences do you think exist in the way each business recruits employees, and how far do you think these differences are reflected in the advertisements you have collected?

4 Give a detailed description of the various ways that businesses recruit employees. How do these differ in relation to the size of the firm? Include evidence to support your answer.

5 a) Describe what you would consider would be a suitable orientation programme for your school/college for: i) new students   ii) new teaching staff.

b) Present some evidence from new students and teaching staff showing how some of them view your ideas.

Motivation of employees

5.1 Job satisfaction

People spend a large percentage of their life at work. Therefore, it is important that they get some satisfaction from their job. Not all jobs can give satisfaction, and people have different ideas of what constitutes a good job. For some people pay is the most important factor; others will have some other priority. Often it is a combination of many factors which makes a job satisfying. The following are just some of these factors. What others would you include? What would be your own order of priority?

- Pay and opportunity for wage increases
- Promotion prospects
- Working hours and times of attendance
- Holiday arrangements
- Job security
- Friendship and relationships between employees
- Conditions in which the work is carried out
- The nature of the duties to be performed.

Some of these factors are within the influence of the employee, but the employer has by far the greater effect on working conditions. However, there are laws which ensure that working conditions do not fall below an agreed minimum standard. Some of these laws are examined later in this chapter.

In Chapter 3 of this book, we examined two of the main motivation theories. One of the theories we looked at was that of the psychologist Abraham Maslow. He formulated a 'hierarchy of needs' in the 1940s, which is still relevant today and has an important link to job satisfaction. A hierarchy means that the more important things are at the top, and less important things are at the bottom. You will probably recall that Maslow identified the following five levels in the hierarchy of needs, with number one indicating the most important and ultimate goal:

1 **Basic** Physiological requirements for survival; in the work situation these include food, drink and a tolerable level of comfort, e.g. ventilation, rest, shelter and, of course, payment.
2 **Safety** A safe working environment incorporating protection against danger, including job security.
3 **Social** Friendship and companionship of fellow employees, a sense of belonging and being part of a team.
4 **Self-esteem** Recognition of a job well done; status and recognition of achievement, promotion and possibly independence.
5 **Self-fulfilment** Achieving personal ambitions; reaching full potential; complete job satisfaction.

At any given moment in time, one of these needs is dominant, and the needs in this group have to be met in order for the individual to be able to move on to the next level in the hierarchy. In the work environment, employees must be provided with the opportunity to fulfill these needs.

5.2 Wages

Wage differentials

Wages are the reward paid for labour. Not surprisingly, wages are considered more important to most people than many other things in life. This is because the level of earnings has such a considerable effect on the quality of life. The amount of income received influences the type of house and furnishings one can have, the quality of car owned, and where and for how long holidays are taken. The poorly paid person cannot hope to compete with the highly paid person with regard to standard of living and leisure facilities. But for a variety of reasons, some people are better paid than others, and it is important to understand why this is so.

The key to the reason for *wage differentials* is demand and supply. For the purpose of comparison, we can take the wages of doctors and bus drivers as examples of where differences in wage levels exist. Both of these occupations are important to the community, but the doctor's wage is considerably higher than that of a bus driver. In other words, the cost of the doctor's services is far higher than the cost of the bus driver's services. Alternatively, we could say that the supply of doctors is smaller than the supply of bus drivers, forcing up the price of the doctor's services.

The supply of doctors is smaller than that of bus drivers for the following reasons. These same reasons can also be applied to many other examples of occupations where wage differences exist.

- Being a doctor requires a high degree of skill and academic ability.
- The medical training period is too long for many people.
- There is a degree of risk involved in medicine (e.g. infection).
- Medical work requires a special aptitude.

What other reasons can you think of for wage differentials?

Rates of pay

There are several ways by which wages may be calculated, and sometimes a wage payment may combine more than one of these.

Flat rate

A set rate of pay per week or month based on a standard number of hours. Many workers are paid by this system, but it does not always provide incentive to give extra time or effort.

Time rate

The worker is paid a set amount for each hour worked. The worker is paid overtime at a higher rate of pay for additional hours worked.

Piece rate

This is not as common today as it was in manufacturing in the past. A payment is made for each good quality item produced to encourage the production worker to give maximum effort.

Bonus

Paid to employees as a share of additional profits gained by the employer due to increased effort or efficiency of the work group.

Principles of Business – Profile 1

Commission
A payment made additional to a flat or time rate as a percentage of the value of sales or business promoted.

Deductions from pay

Gross pay is the total amount earned by the employee before any deductions have been made.

Net pay is the amount received by the employee after any deductions have been taken away. This figure is particularly important because it represents the actual income the worker receives.

Statutory deductions
These are compulsory deductions enforced by law:

- *Income tax:* deducted from each wage payment through the PAYE (Pay As You Earn) system.
- *National insurance:* weekly contributions to the state welfare scheme (for health services, etc.), taken from each payment of wages.

What other types of statutory deductions are you aware of that you could add to this list?

Voluntary deductions
Wage earners can decide whether or not they want further deductions to be taken automatically from their wages. Examples of such voluntary deductions include the following.

- Union membership fees
- Contribution to company social club fund
- Payments to private pension schemes
- Insurance premiums
- Private medical scheme payments
- Credit union savings payments.

Payment of wages/salaries

The responsibility for the payment of wages varies depending on the size of the business and the way its structure is organised. In a very small business, it may be the person who looks after the accounts who will also deal with wages; in a larger business there may a completely separate department called the Wages (or Payroll) Department. Whatever the case, people involved with payment of wages need an aptitude for working with figures, and they are often required to be familiar with the use of a computer.

When an employee is paid at a time rate, he or she will have a time card (clock card) which is kept in a rack near a time clock. As the employee arrives and leaves work he or she 'clocks' on and off by inserting the card into the time clock. The times printed on to the time card are used by the payroll department to establish how much the employee should be paid.

Whether payment of wages is made by cash, cheque or credit transfer, the employee receives a pay advice. This is usually a slip of paper that is filled in by the payroll department, often by computer, so that the employees can see how their net pay has been calculated. The pay advice will contain the following information:

Chapter 5 – **Motivation of employees**

- employee's name and work number
- tax code
- national insurance number
- gross pay
- bonus, commission, overtime
- compulsory deductions
- voluntary deductions
- net pay.

Much of the payroll department's work of calculating wages and producing pay advices can be assigned to computers. When the worker clocks in and out, the time data can be recorded on the time card by punched holes or magnetic ink characters. The data can be read by computer and used to calculate net pay automatically; then the pay advice is printed out.

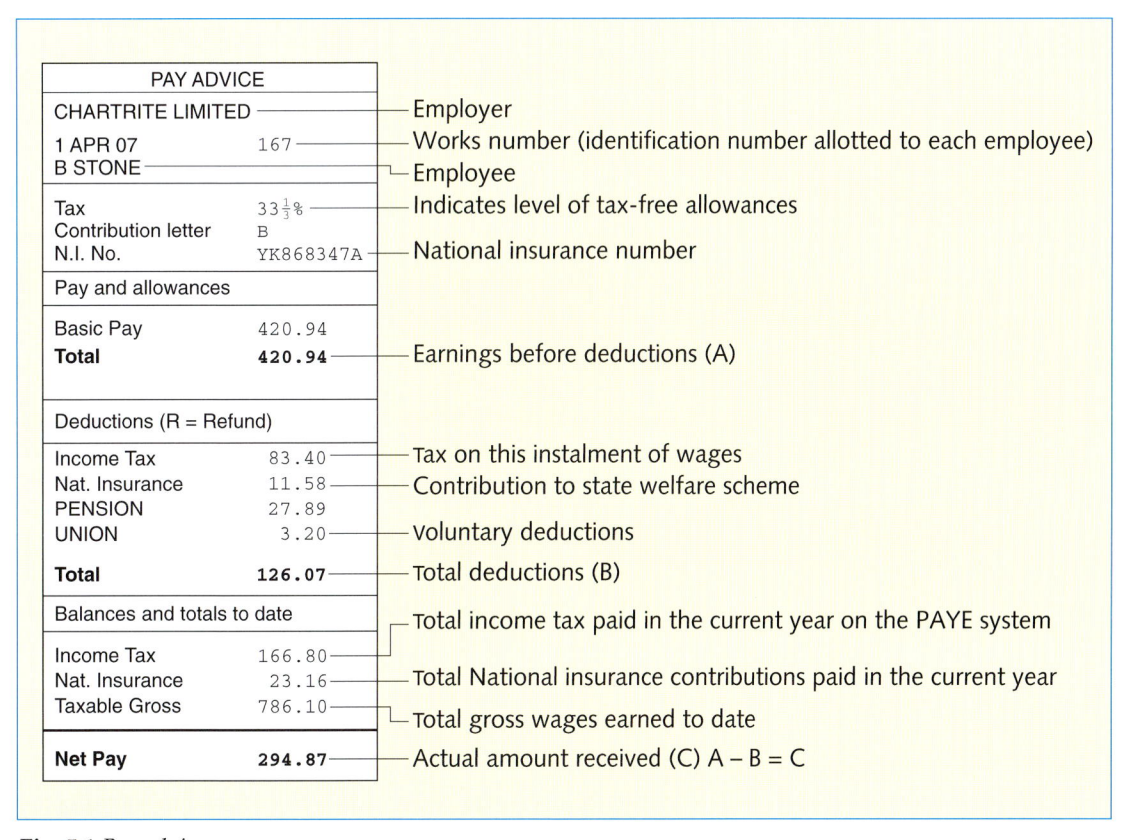

PAY ADVICE		
CHARTRITE LIMITED		— Employer
1 APR 07	167	— Works number (identification number allotted to each employee)
B STONE		— Employee
Tax	$33\frac{1}{3}$%	— Indicates level of tax-free allowances
Contribution letter	B	
N.I. No.	YK868347A	— National insurance number
Pay and allowances		
Basic Pay	420.94	
Total	**420.94**	— Earnings before deductions (A)
Deductions (R = Refund)		
Income Tax	83.40	— Tax on this instalment of wages
Nat. Insurance	11.58	— Contribution to state welfare scheme
PENSION	27.89	
UNION	3.20	— Voluntary deductions
Total	**126.07**	— Total deductions (B)
Balances and totals to date		— Total income tax paid in the current year on the PAYE system
Income Tax	166.80	
Nat. Insurance	23.16	— Total National insurance contributions paid in the current year
Taxable Gross	786.10	— Total gross wages earned to date
Net Pay	**294.87**	— Actual amount received (C) A – B = C

Fig. 5.1 *Pay advice*

Fringe benefits

Some firms offer 'invisible' additions to the wages of their employees. These are called **fringe benefits** or **perks**. The following are examples of the kinds of benefits given by employers in addition to wages.

- Free or subsidised meals
- Company car
- Free membership of private health schemes
- Low interest-rate loans for house or car purchase, etc.
- Reduced prices for company products or services
- Assistance with expenses in removal to a new abode
- Help with payment of private education fees.

5.3 Working conditions

Although wages are important in motivating people to work hard and effectively, we have recognised in this chapter that other factors, such as job satisfaction, are also important. Obviously, what our job involves affects the way we respond to work, and the content of a job is summarised in a job description and a job specification. The number of hours that we are required to work and the times of the day we have to do the hours also influences how we feel about our job.

Most employers recognise that working conditions are important in motivating people to work hard, but there are certain laws and rules that have been established to ensure that minimum standards of comfort and safety are adhered to by employers.

The nature of the job

Job description

This is a broad general statement which may include:

- job title
- details of duties and responsibilities
- place or department where work is to be carried out
- special features or skills and qualifications related to the job
- supervision and assessment arrangements.

Job specification

This is a detailed statement drawn up from the job description, and it contains references to the qualities required of candidates for the job. It includes:

- responsibilities involved
- qualifications and past experience needed
- skills of initiative or judgement necessary
- physical fitness required
- personal characteristics considered important.

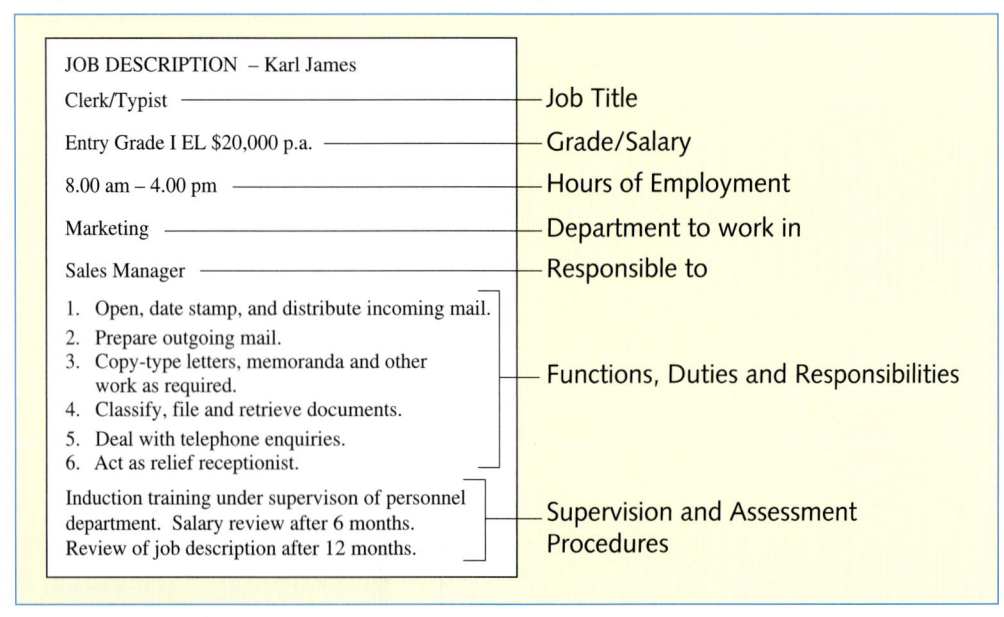

```
JOB DESCRIPTION  – Karl James
Clerk/Typist ─────────────────────────── Job Title
Entry Grade I EL $20,000 p.a. ─────────── Grade/Salary
8.00 am – 4.00 pm ─────────────────────── Hours of Employment
Marketing ─────────────────────────────── Department to work in
Sales Manager ─────────────────────────── Responsible to
 1. Open, date stamp, and distribute incoming mail.
 2. Prepare outgoing mail.
 3. Copy-type letters, memoranda and other
    work as required.                              ── Functions, Duties and Responsibilities
 4. Classify, file and retrieve documents.
 5. Deal with telephone enquiries.
 6. Act as relief receptionist.

 Induction training under supervison of personnel
 department.  Salary review after 6 months.      ── Supervision and Assessment
 Review of job description after 12 months.         Procedures
```

Fig. 5.2 *Job description*

Chapter 5 – **Motivation of employees**

Contract of Employment Act

This act requires employers to give employees particulars of their terms of employment in the form of a contract, which must either be given to the employee or kept where they have access to it. The contract includes:

- job title
- hours of work
- holiday arrangements
- rate of pay and how frequently paid
- period of notice to be given by either side
- person to contact in event of a grievance
- legal rights such as belonging (or not belonging) to a union.

Hours of employment

One of the most important terms of employment is the hours of work. This refers not only to the total number of hours to be worked, but also to what times of the day or night the hours have to be worked.

Although some people do '**shift work**', most people work fixed hours. Consequently, most people are travelling to and from work at similar times. This results in traffic jams and congestion on public transport, and discomfort for travellers. It also means that public transport is not being used economically.

Not everyone finds it convenient to work the same hours as others. Workers sometimes need periods of time when they are not required to be at work. In addition, many businesses have periods of the day when not all members of staff are required to be present. At other busy 'core' times, everyone is needed.

Flexible working time (FWT)

Flexitime or **flexible working time (FWT)** is a system of arranging working hours so that at **peak** or **core** times all members of staff are at work, but their other hours are flexible, as long as they complete the required total number of hours per week.

The working day of the firm is defined in three ways:

1 *Band time:* this is the total period of time the business operates, for example, 8.00 am to 6.00 pm.
2 *Core time:* this is the period of time when all members of the firm are expected to be at work.
3 *Flexible time:* this is the period outside the core time when employees can choose whether they work or not, as long as they complete the total number of weekly hours they are paid for.

To choose their working hours, employees first calculate core time. Core time in the above example is 5 days × 3 hours (11.00 am to 2.00 pm) = 15 hours. This leaves 20 hours (35 – 15 = 20) of working which can be chosen from FWT. Before choosing the hours of flexitime, employees will have to take into account the time they wish to use for lunch breaks. Most firms will insist that the employee takes at least a 30-minute lunch break.

Health and safety

The health and safety of employees is a major aspect of working conditions. Both the employer and the employee have responsibilities in this respect. These can be summarised as follows.

Principles of Business – Profile 1

KEY WORDS

Find out the business-related meaning of each of the following terms. Write a separate sentence for each term to show your understanding.

wage differentials
job satisfaction
piece rate   commission
bonus
job specification
core time   gross pay
net pay   deductions
job description
flexible working time
overtime   flat rate

- The employer's duty can be summed up as the responsibility to provide a safe workplace, including arrangements for hazards such as fire, and the maintenance and safety of machinery and equipment.
- Employees have the duty to take reasonable care for the safety of themselves and other working colleagues at all times, and to co-operate with the employer on all matters of safety.

The duty of employers to provide safe working conditions is backed up by a range of laws, although most employers recognise that it is in their interests to secure the health and safety of their employees.

The Factories Acts

The various Factories Acts, such as those of Barbados and Trinidad and Tobago, deal with health and safety in the workplace. These Acts include the following rules.

- Workplaces must be properly lit and well ventilated.
- Sufficient toilet and washing facilities must be provided.
- Moving machinery must have a fence around it.
- Hoists, lifts, etc. must be properly constructed and maintained.
- Floors, passages and stairs must be kept unobstructed.
- Floors must not have slippery surfaces.
- Fire escapes must be provided and maintained.
- Rooms must not be overcrowded (a minimum of 8.5 cubic metres per person).
- Temperatures must not fall below 16°C (after the first hour of working).
- There must be adequate supplies of fresh or artificially purified air.
- There must be suitable natural or artificial lighting.
- Suitable and sufficient sanitary conveniences must be conveniently accessible and must be clean and properly maintained.
- Accessible washing facilities with running hot and cold water, soap and clean towels, must be provided.
- Accidents must be reported.

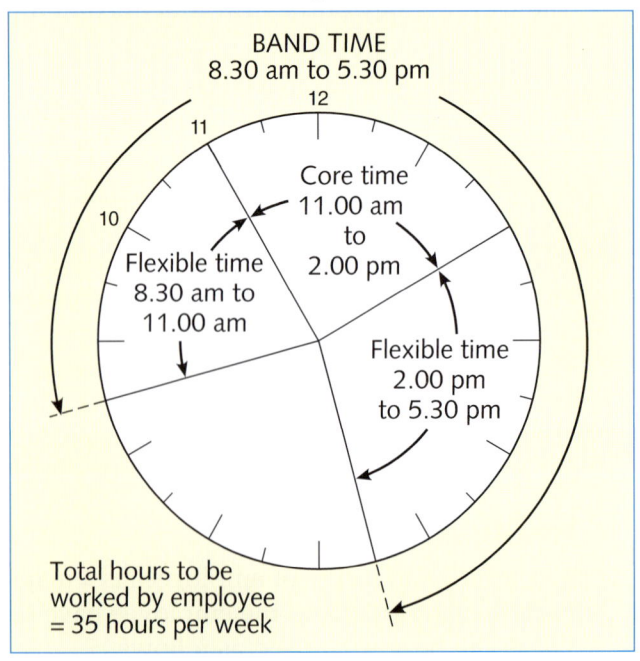

```
BAND TIME
8.30 am to 5.30 pm

Flexible time      Core time
8.30 am to         11.00 am
11.00 am           to
                   2.00 pm

                   Flexible time
                   2.00 pm
                   to 5.30 pm

Total hours to be worked by employee
= 35 hours per week
```

Fig. 5.3 *Flexible working time*

5.4 Things to do

This section contains a variety of exercises to help you create revision notes, to test your understanding and to prepare you for examinations.

Search and find

Write out the question and the answer by referring back through the text to form revision notes.

1. Why is it important that people gain satisfaction from their jobs?
2. Why are Maslow's 'hierarchy of needs' important in business?
3. Why are wage differentials often the source of envy and discontent between workers?
4. List five factors which influence the supply of people suitable for a particular form of employment.
5. Briefly describe each of the following ways of calculating wages: flat rate, time rate, piece rate, bonus, commission.
6. Explain the differences between gross pay and net pay.
7. If you have earned a gross wage of $110.28 and must pay deductions totalling $27.36, what will be your net pay?
8. Give examples, and explain the difference between statutory deductions and voluntary deductions.
9. Cash is one way of paying wages. Name two others.
10. What is the purpose of a time card system? How can this system be of help to the payroll department of a firm?
11. List at least six items of information likely to be found on a pay advice.
12. Briefly describe the way that a computer could be employed in the payroll department.
13. What are fringe benefits? Give six examples.
14. List the kind of information that is contained in the contract of employment.
15. How does a job description differ from a job specification?
16. Why are hours of employment important to the working conditions of an employee?
17. What is flexible working time? Why is it possible to operate this system for people working in a restaurant, but very difficult to adopt for a school?
18. 'Employees as well as employers have a responsibility for safety in the workplace.' Explain this statement.
19. What aspects of health and safety in the workplace are contained in the Factories Acts?

Principles of Business – Profile 1

What do you know?

Write out the complete sentence and insert the missing word, which can be chosen from the list at the end of the test.

1. It is important that people get some ..... from their job.
2. ..... are the reward paid for labour.
3. Some occupations command a high wage because they require a high degree of skill and ..... ability.
4. Sometimes a ..... is paid to workers as a share of additional profits achieved due to increased efficiency.
5. ..... pay is the total amount earned by the employee before deductions have been made.
6. The worker receives ..... pay after any deductions have been taken away.
7. A pay ..... is issued with a wage payment so that the employee can see how their net pay has been calculated.
8. Much of the work of a wages department can be assigned to .....
9. A job ..... is a broad general statement about an area of work responsibility.
10. All employees should have access to their ..... of employment.

Choose the missing words from the following:

net   computers   bonus   satisfaction   gross   wages   advice   academic   description   contract

Structured questions

Q1 The following questions are related to the time card shown in figure 5.4. Ronald Latter is paid at a time rate of $12 per hour. Overtime is paid at the rate of time-and-a-half and Saturday work is paid double-time.
If employees are five minutes or more late for work, a 30-minute pay penalty is imposed. Pay is calculated to the nearest full 15 minutes.

TIME CARD

Works No. 323	Department Sales	Employee's Name Ronald Latter	Week Commencing Mon. 5 May

Day	Ordinary Time				Overtime		Hours		
	In	Out	In	Out	In	Out	Basic	Overtime	Saturday
Monday	0807	1201	1300	1700			7½		
Tuesday	0800	1202	1301	1701	1730	2030	8	3	
Wednesday	0759	1200	1259	1701	1731	1932	8	2	
Thursday	0801	1201	1301	1700			8		
Friday	0758	1200	1303	1701			8		
Saturday					0900	1201			3
					Total Hours				

..........hours at £......... = ...
..........hours at £......... = ...
..........hours at £......... = ...
Total gross pay £

Fig. 5.4 *Time card*

(a) Briefly explain the purpose of a time card. **1**

(b) What is meant by the terms 'time-and-a-half' and 'double-time'? **2**

(c) What is the firm hoping to achieve by imposing a '30-minute pay penalty'? Where can the penalty be seen imposed on this time card? **3**

(d) How can the use of time cards help to make it possible to operate a 'flexitime' system? **4**

Chapter 5 – **Motivation of employees**

(e) Calculate the following aspects of Ronald's pay:
- (i) flat rate earnings
- (ii) overtime pay
- (iii) Saturday pay
- (iv) total gross pay **4**

(f) 'Although wages can motivate workers they do not necessarily give job satisfaction.' Discuss this statement. **6**

Q2 Refer to the job description in figure 5.2 and answer these questions.

(a) Why is it important for an employee to have a job description? **2**

(b) The job description refers to 'induction', which is sometimes called 'orientation'. Why is this important for new employees? **2**

(c) Why would existing employees possibly need training as well as new recruits? **3**

(d) List three functions of the personnel department other than induction and training. **3**

(e) How does a job specification differ from a job description? **4**

(f) Another document that is issued to all employees is the Contract of Employment. List six different items of information contained in this document. **6**

Q3 The following questions are all related to the pay advice in figure 5.1.

(a) What is the purpose of a pay advice? **1**

(b) Explain how this employee's net pay has been calculated. **2**

(c) This pay advice relates to just one calendar month of employment. Assuming that the employee's rate of pay and monthly deductions do not change, what would be the figure for gross pay and net pay for a 12-month period? **2**

(d) How can allocating an employee a works number assist computerised handling of payroll management? **2**

(e) State three functions the union is likely to carry out on this worker's behalf in return for the payment being made to it. **3**

(f) Identify the two compulsory and two voluntary deductions from pay shown on this pay advice. **4**

(g) Clearly explain the similarities and also the differences between income tax and national insurance. **6**

Q4 Table 5.1 shows the sales record of a team of sales representatives over a six-month period. Each representative is paid a basic wage, plus a commission of 10% which is paid at the end of each six-month period.

(a) On which month was the total sales of the six representatives highest? **1**

(b) Which salesperson has achieved the highest overall total sales? **1**

(c) What work does a sales representative do? **2**

(d) What is the total sales figure achieved by representative P. Chantrey for the six-month period, and how much commission will that person receive? **3**

79

Principles of Business – Profile 1

Name	Jan $	Feb $	Mar $	Apr $	May $	June $	Total sales	Commission due $
B Carter	11,500	12,500	14,000	11,000	13,000	15,000	77,000	7,700
J Brady	9,400	10,000	11,000	9,000	9,000	11,000	59,400	5,940
P Daly	12,500	12,000	13,000	11,000	12,000	13,000	73,500	7,350
P Chantrey	9,000	9,500	9,500	10,000	11,000	10,500		
M Perry	10,000	10,500	11,000	11,000	12,000	13,000	67,500	6,750
C Stone	9,600	9,500	11,500	11,000	11,000	11,500	64,100	6,410
Total $	62,000	64,000	70,000	63,000	68,000	74,000		

Table 5.1 *Sales record*

(e) What do we mean when we say that 'each representative is paid a basic wage, plus a commission of 10%'? **3**

(f) What was the total sales of the whole sales team for the six-month period, and how much in total will be paid by the company in commission? Show all calculations. **4**

(g) Draw a line graph to plot the total combined sales of all the representatives month by month over the period covered by the record. Write a brief summary report of what your graph shows. **6**

Q5

(a) Name two methods of wage payment other than by cash. **2**

(b) Why does the receipt of wages monthly make it more important to budget carefully than when payment is made weekly? **2**

(c) Norma Robinson receives a basic pay of $320.80 plus a bonus payment of $60.40, and she pays the following deductions:

Income tax	$74.60
National insurance	$14.50
Private medical scheme	$20.00

  (i) How much will Norma's gross pay be? **1**
  (ii) How much net pay will she receive? **2**
  (iii) How much will Norma pay in compulsory deductions and how much will she pay by voluntary payments? **3**

(d) Explain each of the following terms related to earnings:
  (i) overtime **2**
  (ii) commission **2**
  (iii) piece rate. **2**

(e) Give four reasons why there are differences between the rates of pay people receive. **4**

Q6 Although some people work shift work, most people work fixed hours. This question is about hours of employment.

(a) Some people have to work shift work. What is shift work? **1**

(b) State two problems that are caused by the majority of people working the same hours. **2**

(c) What is flexible working time (FWT)? **2**

(d) In what way can FWT help to reduce the problems caused by most people working similar hours? **3**

(e) In relation to FWT, explain each of the following terms:
   (i) band time
   (ii) core time
   (iii) flexible time. **6**

(f) 'Both a restaurant and a bus company may have two core times, but their core times will often be at different times of the day.' Explain this statement in relation to flexible working time. **6**

Research assignments

1 A top-class sportsman could well earn $500,000 in a year, while a truck driver might earn $20,000 a year. Give a detailed explanation of the reasons for wage differentials using examples to illustrate your answer. Present documented evidence of other examples of wage differentials.

2 Carry out a survey to establish what percentage of people in your sample have a job description. Ask four people in your sample to let you have a copy of their job description. What observations can you make about the information you have collected?

3 Collect a variety (at least five) of advertisements for contrasting occupations that include details of wages to be paid. With reference to specific advertisements in your samples explain the differences in wage levels that you can observe.

4 What evidence would you offer that supports the view that job satisfaction is just as important as wages?

Industrial relations

6.1 The importance of industrial relations

The employees of an organisation are the most important and also the most costly of its resources. They are important because they are so essential at all levels of business operations. But most people work for a livelihood, and the role they play in the organisation is of less importance to them. This can be a source of conflict between the employer and the employee.

Employees will want to obtain the highest wage they can, so that they can buy the material things they want. The employer, however, will want to keep the firm's wage bill as low as possible, and this can result in a kind of continual tug-of-war between the employer and employee.

The term '**industrial relations**' is generally used to refer to the degree of conflict or peace in industry and between employers and employees.

6.2 Trade unions

Trade unions are associations of workers in an industry or group of industries who join together in their common interest to regulate the relations between employees and employers. By co-operating together in this way, members of a union hope to win concessions from their employers, and this reflects the motto of the trade union movement: 'In unity is strength'.

Trade unions are organised nationally with '**shop stewards**' located within the workplaces. These people provide the link between the members and the union committee, and they act as spokespersons between the workers and the firm's management.

Trade unionism developed in the Caribbean region after the First World War as a reaction against the owners of factories accompanying an upsurge in demand for improvement in the conditions of working class people. Today, it is generally agreed that trade unions play a controversial but important role in industry. They are important to employers because they enable them to negotiate with a small number of people rather than many.

There are different types of union, classified according to the types of worker they represent. In many countries, the trade unions have joined together to form congresses or councils. In the Caribbean, for example, the Caribbean Congress of Labour (CCL) is an example of this type of union of unions. It has affiliate members in most West Indian territories.

The Caribbean Congress of Labour (CCL)

The CCL is a regional body to which unions in the thirteen nations of CARICOM belong. It is the umbrella body of the labour movement in the English-speaking Caribbean.

The CCL is a member of the International Labour Organisation (ILO), the American Federation of Labour-Congress of Industrial Organisations

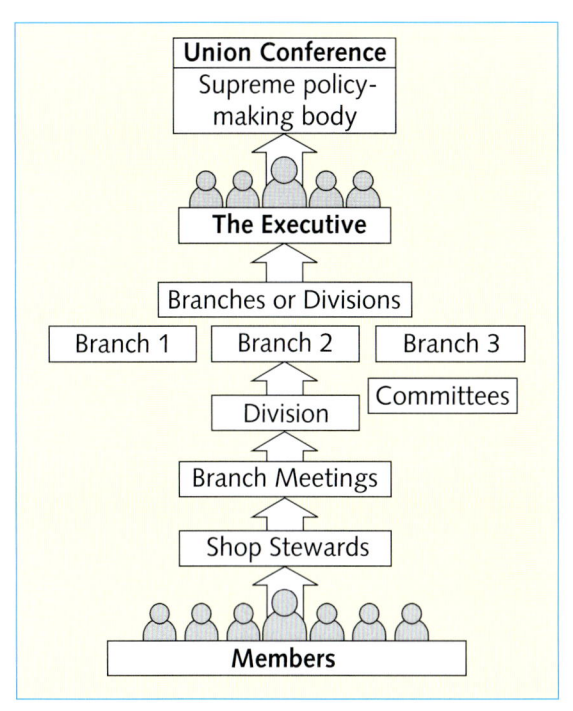

Fig. 6.1 *A typical union structure*

(AFL-CIO), and the International Confederation of Free Trade Unions (ICFTU) among others.

Individual unions also have direct affiliations with some international unions. For example, those unions with a socialist philosophy tend to belong to international unions with similar ideologies. However, with the unification of Eastern Europe this situation may well change.

Trade union aims

Trade unions aim to secure for workers:

- participation in company decision-making processes
- improved wages and reduced working hours
- better working conditions
- full employment and national prosperity
- job security
- benefits for members who are sick, retired or on strike
- improved social security payments such as unemployment and sickness benefit and pensions
- an influence on government
- a reasonable share in the wealth of the country
- improved public and social services.

6.3 Collective bargaining

The main function of trade unions is to obtain improved wages and working conditions for their members. Sometimes the employer reaches a satisfactory wage agreement with individual employees, but wage settlements are often the result of *collective bargaining*. This refers to talks between representatives of employers and trade unions to decide pay rates and other terms and conditions of employment.

The union represents a group of workers and negotiates a settlement on their behalf with an employer or a group of employers. It is just as much in the interest of the unions as it is in the interest of the employer to reach a speedy settlement, because both sides can only benefit if there is continuity in working.

Although pay is one of the main subjects of collective bargaining, many others can be involved, including:

- hours of work
- holiday entitlement
- sick pay
- pensions
- maternity leave
- working conditions
- training
- promotion
- redundancies
- recruitment.

Although negotiations between employers and employees may not reach an agreement, there are other means of solving the deadlock.

- *Conciliation* is where a third party is appointed to try to help find a solution that is acceptable to both sides.
- *Arbitration* is where both sides of a dispute request that it goes before an arbiter, whose verdict both sides agree to accept. The Industrial Disputes Tribunal is the arbiter in most of these cases.

6.4 Industrial legislation

In the Caribbean region certain laws have been implemented which specify forms of behaviour considered reasonable for both the employers and the unions. Rules covering actions that should be avoided by management and the union are often set out in union brochures, and sometimes on membership cards. The following are typical of these rules.

The union must not:

- coerce anyone to join or not to join a union
- coerce employees in their choice of the parties to bargain on their behalf
- charge unfair membership fees
- refuse to bargain collectively with an employer
- cause the employer to pay for services not rendered
- influence an employer to discriminate against an employee.

The employer must not:

- interfere with or restrain employees who wish to join a union
- discriminate against people because of union membership
- refuse to bargain collectively with employees' representatives
- discriminate against employees who testify before tribunals.

6.5 Restrictive practices

The term **restrictive practices** or **industrial action** refers to measures taken by workers either to put pressure on their employers during the course of an **industrial dispute**, or as a response to their working conditions. The following are some of the ones most commonly used.

Strike

If wage negotiations break down completely, or some other dispute arises, workers may cease work (withdraw their labour). There are two main types of strike.

- *Official strike:* workers withdraw their labour on advice, in consultation, and with union approval and backing. Under these circumstances the union may provide strike pay from the funds contributed by members.
- *Unofficial strike:* sometimes called a 'wildcat' strike. The workers cease work without union backing.

Demarcation dispute

A demarcation dispute is one where who does what is in question; a dispute between unions may be involved. This is a situation where one group of workers objects to another group doing particular work. Often this kind of dispute is the result of differences in rates of pay between one group of workers and another. It may be that one group of workers is doing work that another group thinks 'belongs' to them.

Overtime ban

Overtime provides a convenient way for employers to get extra working hours from employees without having to take on extra workers. When an overtime ban is in force the workers refuse to work additional hours.

Chapter 6 – **Industrial relations**

Work-to-rule
Work is carried out in accordance with every minor rule, with workers following all the rules and regulations of the company exactly. By sticking strictly to the rules in this way, work is slowed down and productivity is reduced.

Go slow
This has similarities to a work-to-rule. The workers do their job thoroughly, but at a slower pace than normal, thus causing a fall in output.

Closed shop
A closed shop means that all workers in a firm belong to one union, and they refuse to work with anyone who is not a member of that union.

Picketing
In order to ensure maximum effect from their industrial action, a group of workers on strike may stand outside the firm's entrance and try to persuade other workers not to 'cross the picket line', that is not to enter the premises.

Sit-in
Workers occupy the premises, ensuring that no goods enter or leave, and preventing the operation of the firm. Sometimes, such as when a factory is threatened with closure, the sit-in becomes a 'work-in'. Workers occupy the factory and keep it in operation without the presence of the management.

Union busting
Union members may refuse to work on or move certain machines or equipment, or refuse to work with other people or groups. Someone who goes against the union's wishes by working during a stoppage is sometimes called a **union buster**. Similarly, a worker who reports for work normally whilst the majority of his or her colleagues are on strike is sometimes referred to as a '**blackleg**' or a '**scab**'.

Employer action
Although attention is generally focussed on workers during industrial action, sometimes employers also take industrial action. For example, they may **lock out** the employees (i.e. prevent the workers from entering the workplace) in an attempt to gain concessions during a dispute, or to prevent possible damage to equipment and machinery.

6.6 Pressure groups

Pressure groups are organisations (sometimes voluntary) which seek to persuade the government, local council, or some other organisation to recognise their views and respond to them. They try to influence the decision-making process by demonstrating the strength of their feelings.

The trade unions are an example of a pressure group. They not only try to influence employers on behalf of their members, but they also present the views of their members on 'social issues'.

Principles of Business – Profile 1

Fig. 6.2 Pressure groups

Pressure groups are not all formal ones. Sometimes an informal group will develop spontaneously, perhaps due to a passing situation, for example the planned development of an industrial estate in a predominantly residential area.

Although pressure groups are often portrayed in the media as trying to influence the authorities, they do at times try to influence business also. Apart from workers trying to influence pay awards, the general public pressurise businesses by protesting about issues such as advertising techniques, sexual inequality and environmental conflicts.

Governments and businesses are subject to pressure from groups both within and outside the organisation. Inside the business, pressure may come from groups of shareholders trying to influence company policy. But the main pressure on firms tends to be external pressure, that is, consumer pressure.

The most obvious pressure that consumers can put on a firm is to take their business elsewhere, although if the firm is very powerful or has a monopoly this may be difficult. Consumers are also assisted in their attempts to put pressure on businesses by various consumer protection facilities.

Some television and radio programmes act as watchdogs to expose firms who are guilty of malpractice, and many newspapers and magazines run 'consumer watchdog' articles which attempt to protect consumer interests.

KEY WORDS

Find out the business-related meaning of each of the following terms. Write a separate sentence for each term to show your understanding.

shop steward   strike   lockout   union buster   union picketing
industrial action   arbitration   work-to-rule   industrial dispute

6.7 Things to do

This section contains a variety of exercises to help you create revision notes, to test your understanding and to prepare you for examinations.

Search and find

Write out the question and the answer by referring back through the text to form revision notes.

1. What do you understand by the term 'industrial relations'?
2. Why would you say that employers and employees are bound to come into conflict?
3. What is a trade union?
4. Briefly describe the main specialist types of union that exist.
5. What are the aims of trade unions?
6. What do you understand by the term 'collective bargaining'?

Chapter 6 – Industrial relations

7 List the kind of issues other than pay that a trade union might take up through collective bargaining.

8 Say what you understand by the terms 'conciliation' and 'arbitration'.

9 Briefly outline the basic rules which unions and employers must observe during negotiations.

10 What are restrictive practices? What do they aim to achieve?

11 Explain the difference between an 'official' strike and an 'unofficial' strike.

12 Trade unions use a variety of methods to try to persuade employers to agree to wage claims. Explain how each of the following methods operates:
   (a) overtime ban
   (b) work-to-rule
   (c) go slow

13 In what way is a demarcation dispute one where 'who does what' is in question?

14 What are pressure groups?

15 In what way do pressure groups influence businesses?

What do you know?

Write out the complete sentence and insert the missing word, which can be chosen from the list at the end of the test.

1 The ..... of an organisation are the most important and also the most costly of its resources.
2 The term 'industrial relations' refers to the extent to which peace or ..... exists between employers and employees.
3 Unions are important to ..... because they allow them to negotiate with a small number of people.
4 One of the aims of trade unions is to secure improved working ..... for workers.
5 Wage settlements are often the result of .....
6 ..... is where a third party is appointed to try to find an acceptable solution to a dispute.
7 ..... is where both sides of a dispute request that it goes before an arbiter.
8 A ..... dispute is one about 'who does what'.
9 ..... groups are voluntary organisations which seek to persuade the authorities.
10 When workers ..... they withdraw their labour.

Choose the missing words from the following:

pressure   conditions   arbitration   employees   conciliation   employers   strike   negotiations   demarcation   conflict

Principles of Business – Profile 1

Structured questions

Q1 Look at the newspaper article in figure 6.3.

CARTER STRIKE SOLUTION

It looks as if the long-running dispute at the Carter electronics plant may finally be coming to an end, with the unions and management yesterday agreeing upon a pay award of 12.5% linked to a productivity agreement worked out between the management and shop stewards.

Rose Webber, the union spokesperson, said, 'I am delighted at the agreement and will be putting it to our members in a ballot tomorrow with a recommendation for acceptance'. For the management, Peter Stewart commented that the productivity deal was vital to enable the company to fund the wage rise, which is twice the current rate of inflation, without any compulsory redundancies.

Provided the agreement is accepted by the workforce, the plant could be back in full production next week after six months of disruption. One picket said, 'I'll be glad to get back to work, but I won't work with any union busters'.

Fig 6.3 *Industrial dispute*

(a) How long has the dispute referred to in this article been going on?	1
(b) What information in this article indicates that the settlement that was reached was a result of negotiations?	2
(c) What is the function of a shop steward?	2
(d) What is a productivity deal?	3
(e) Why might the negotiations have resulted in redundancies were it not for the productivity deal?	4
(f) Explain each of the following terms used in this article: (i) picket (ii) union busters.	4
(g) There is some evidence in the article of the kind of restrictive practices that have been used during the dispute. (i) List the methods used. (ii) Describe two other methods that the workers could have used.	4

Q2

(a) What is a trade union?	2
(b) Explain the basic difference between a white collar union and other types of union.	4
(c) Describe two functions of a trade union.	4
(d) Explain three possible advantages of being a member of a trade union.	4
(e) Describe two possible disadvantages of being a member of a trade union.	6

Q3

(a) What are restrictive practices?	2
(b) One of the people who plays an important part in organising restrictive practices is the shop steward. What are shop stewards?	2

(c) What is a 'closed shop'? **2**

(d) Describe two forms of restrictive practice. **4**

(e) Briefly explain the terms 'conciliation' and 'arbitration'. **4**

(f) In what way does collective bargaining benefit both the worker and the employer? **6**

Q4

(a) What do you understand by the term 'industrial relations'? **2**

(b) Briefly describe one way in which trade unions can help to avoid industrial conflict. **2**

(c) In what ways can industrial unrest be seen to be damaging to both employees and employer? **3**

(d) Name three different types of union from the Caribbean region and explain the types of worker they represent. **3**

(e) Identify *two* advantages and *two* disadvantages of being a member of a trade union. **4**

(f) 'If the main aim of workers is to obtain the highest wage and best working conditions, and employers seek to keep costs down, conflict between the two is inevitable.' Discuss this statement. **6**

Research assignments

1 Your best friend has just started work in a local factory and has been asked by the shop steward if he would like to join the trade union. Some workers are members and others are not. Advise your friend of all the implications of taking up or turning down the offer. Back up your advice with information from reliable published sources.

2 Describe the work of trade unions. Considering that they all have similar aims, why are there sometimes disputes between unions? Obtain some information from major unions and the press to complement your answers.

3 Collect at least four newspaper articles containing reports of industrial problems. In each case describe the influence that trade unions might have on the event in question. Comment on whether their involvement is likely to improve or worsen the situation.

4 What contribution do you feel trade unions make to the economy of your country? What evidence can you present to support your answers?

5 You have been selected by your school to attend the Youth Congress on trade unionism in the English-speaking Caribbean. Apart from being in attendance you have been asked to give a 15 minute presentation on collective bargaining. Prepare the paper you will read at the meeting using the following guidelines:
   a) introduce the topic
   b) explain the broad meaning of collective bargaining
   c) describe collective bargaining objectively
   d) give any additional information you think important
   e) produce a collection of appropriate overhead projector transparencies and indicate

Chapter 7

Establishing a business

Earlier in this book, in Chapter 2, we examined the reasons why someone would want to establish their own business. In this chapter we will study the kind of things the budding entrepreneur must be aware of and do when setting up a business.

7.1 The role of the entrepreneur

Enterprise is one of the **factors of production**. Participating in enterprise is a unique form of labour; you have to be able to organise the other factors of production to produce goods or services and make a **profit** (or a **loss**).

An **entrepreneur** is a person who undertakes the risks involved in establishing and running a new business, and the act or process of managing a business enterprise is referred to as **entrepreneurship**. Entrepreneurs are characterised by the role they play in enterprise, such as:

- Inventing and commercialising new goods and services
- Planning, developing and marketing their ideas
- Accessing sufficient funds to operate the business
- Seeking out new business opportunities
- Looking for ways to improve the production of goods or services.

One of the earliest decisions a new entrepreneur will have to take is what **type of business** they are going to establish. Are they going to be a sole trader, a partnership or a limited company? You studied the form each of these takes earlier, in Chapter 2. You also learnt the advantages and disadvantages of each of them. Although most people would like to own a large limited company, the new entrepreneur usually has to start more modestly and become a sole trader or form a partnership, perhaps waiting until the business is well established before even taking on the costs of becoming a limited company.

The new business person will also have to take into account local, regional and global rules and **regulations** that may affect their profitability. For example, there may be limits on importing or exporting certain products or raw materials, and there will certainly be local planning rules related to building and building use. If they are going to employ others, they will also have to take into account the many laws and regulations related to employment, dismissal, safety and working conditions that you learnt about in Chapters 4 and 5 of this book.

7.2 Evaluating the prospects

Entrepreneurs attempt to earn a **profit** by taking the risk of operating a business enterprise, but also face the **risk** that they may make no profit, or even make a loss. There are two important questions that a budding entrepreneur needs to be able to answer before embarking on a business venture:

Chapter 7 – Establishing a business

1. Have you got the necessary qualities (personal traits)?
2. Have you got what others want?

Anyone wanting to start their own business needs to research these questions very carefully if they are to hope to be successful in business.

To be successful in business an entrepreneur must have the following qualities:

- *Initiative.* The entrepreneur needs to be self-motivated. They should not need others to tell them what to do.
- *Determination.* Someone who is likely to give up easily is not likely to be successful in business. All entrepreneurs suffer setbacks from time to time, but it is important that they have the perseverance to fight back.
- *Responsibility.* A good entrepreneur will not blame others when things go wrong. They will recognise the cause of the failure and accept the responsibility to do something about it.
- *Imagination.* The entrepreneur needs to be innovative and creative, thinking of and developing new ideas.
- *Flexibility.* Entrepreneurs need to be able to see themselves as others do, e.g. their customers or other business people. The successful businessperson can adapt their ways to make them more acceptable to others.
- *Independence.* Entrepreneurs must be goal-orientated and willing to work long hours, often alone after others have gone home.
- *Willing to take risks.* An entrepreneur has to risk their own money to run a business. A successful businessperson develops a flair for business opportunities and continues to take calculated risks when necessary.

The entrepreneur also must be sure that they have an idea, skill, service or a product that others want, and that they can provide it at a competitive price. This can partly be explored through market research, which is investigated in depth later in Chapter 14.

A firm's success is largely decided by the decisions of its customers (those who buy their goods or services), in particular the decision to buy or not. Customers will not buy just because the business has a good advertising campaign. They will be interested in the quality and unique features of the product or service that is being offered. And even this will be shunned if the price is not competitive. In other words, the firm must show some competitive advantage that others cannot match.

7.3 Planning

In order to achieve its objectives, a business needs a plan. Planning greatly improves a firm's survival prospects. Of course, it is easy enough for a business to say it is planning to do something, but it is a different matter to actually prove that what is planned can or will be done. A feasibility study provides an investigation, backed by data, to demonstrate that what is planned is really possible. Planning needs to take into account both short-term and long-term factors.

Long-term planning

This requires considerable skill as it incorporates developments that are expected within a period of up to ten years ahead. Many business developments can take several years to complete, and even longer before they show any return on the investment. For this reason, long-term planning is often about what the business intends to do rather than what it is currently doing.

Short-term planning

This generally refers to any developments likely to come into effect within the next three years. Short-term is generally easier than long-term planning because fewer changes are likely to occur, but is also usually more precisely formulated. A business plan is a typical example of short-term planning.

The business plan

A business plan is an explanation of who is responsible for the business, what the business is intended to do, how it is going to get the money to do it, and what profit it hopes to make. It can help the entrepreneur to clarify what they are expecting to achieve, and to monitor **success levels** against those expectations. Business plans are often presented to a bank or some other financial institution when applying for a loan, or some other form of borrowing.

The business plan helps the entrepreneur by:

- providing a blueprint for the operation of the business
- identifying the income and expenditure likely to occur
- giving the entrepreneur a medium with which to monitor progress of the business
- providing a guide to the goals of the business for those financing the firm
- enabling professional advisers to monitor the progress of the business.

The content of the business plan

The business plan will give an executive summary (details of the owners). It will also state the aims and objectives of the business, and it will explain how these are to be achieved. There is no set formula for a business plan, but it will typically contain the following details:

- *Executive summary.* Details of the owners, name and address of the business, aims and objectives of the business
- *Operational analysis.* Production, purchasing, selling, e.g. products/services to be sold, costs, and prices to be charged
- *Market analysis.* Who the intended customers are, customer needs, competition, size of market, etc., and proposed marketing strategy, e.g. the way that customers will learn about what is being marketed, and how the competition will be beaten
- *Financial analysis.* How the business will be financed, profit and loss forecasts, cash flow forecasts, capital expenditure requirements
- *Management controls.* Ways in which the business is expected to grow, recording procedures, and methods for monitoring progress.

The potential market

An important part of the business plan is the explanation of the **marketing potential**. There are five aspects to be stated in the business plan in relation to the potential market:

1 *The business.* What market is the business trying to enter? What is the actual nature of the business? It is not sufficient to state that the nature of

the business is 'retailing' or 'selling a service'. It is necessary to be more specific, e.g. 'renovation of antique furniture'.

2 *Identifying the market.* Who are the potential customers? Where are they located? Is the market big enough to take another business?

3 *Defining the competition.* What competition exists, and in what way is the new venture going to be competitive in the market?

4 *Defining the opportunity.* What are the strengths and weaknesses of the firm and its competitors? What is the likelihood of the firm gaining a share of the market? Is the firm going to be selling something that will be different or innovative?

5 *Defining the market approach.* What strategies will the firm adopt to:
   - Contact potential customers
   - Encourage customers to buy
   - Satisfy their customers
   - Maintain customers' loyalty?

More detailed information related to marketing and market research is given in Chapters 13 and 14.

Financial implications

The entrepreneur needs to assess whether or not the new venture will be financially viable. What are the capital requirements? How much money is required to 'start up' the business? What further injections of capital will be needed to sustain the firm's activities? Will the provision of such capital result in profits and so make the venture worthwhile? Some of the financial issues the entrepreneur will need to consider include:

1 Capital requirements

Capital is the term used to describe the money invested in a business, and the entrepreneur needs to give a lot of thought to the money they will need to get their business started. One of the major difficulties faced by a new business is start-up crisis, which is usually caused by trying to operate without enough funds. To avoid this, the business plan should include:

- a clear statement of what the entrepreneur needs to start the business (e.g. plant, machinery, stocks)
- an estimate of the costs involved in obtaining these items
- an estimate of the extra funds needed in the first 6 months (at least) for ongoing costs (e.g. rent of premises, further purchase of stock, and interest on any loans).

The business plan should show that the estimates are realistic and also indicate where the money will come from.

2 Sources of capital

There are two basic sources of start-up capital for the new entrepreneur: their own money, or someone else's. In practice, most new businesses are set up using a mixture of sources. Venture capital refers to money subscribed in the form of share capital and loan capital to finance new firms and activities considered to be of a risky nature and, therefore, unable to attract finance from more conventional sources.

Principles of Business – Profile 1

3 Assessing financial viability

Two of the most common items included in a business plan to help assess financial viability are the cash-flow forecast and the break-even forecast.

A cash-flow forecast, as the name implies, forecasts likely changes in the cash resources available to the business, i.e. the size of the firm's bank balance or overdraft. It shows the actual movement of money into and out of the firm's bank balance or overdraft. It takes full account of the fact that the firm may not be paid immediately for work done, and that the firm may not have to pay immediately for things purchased.

The break-even forecast is an estimate of the level of sales at a given price that the firm needs to achieve in order to cover its total costs. In drawing up a break-even chart, the entrepreneur needs to take into account all the costs involved in providing the firm's goods or services, and the effect on possible sales of them. All sales above the break-even point add to the firm's profits. It is important that the proposed selling price is realistic otherwise the forecast level of sales will not be achieved. (See also figure 17.4 and the explanation in Chapter 17 – Business finances.)

> **KEY WORDS**
>
> Write a separate sentence for each of the following key terms used in this chapter to show you understand them in the business context.
>
> entrepreneur   competitive advantage   business plan   start-up capital
> start-up crisis   cash-flow forecast   break-even forecast

7.4 Obtaining capital equipment

Firms have a number of choices when purchasing major equipment.

- They can buy what they need with cash, which includes payment by cheque. This is the most straightforward method of purchasing. Some suppliers require cash with order (CWO), whilst some require cash on delivery (COD); and some may offer a certain percentage reduction in the selling price for prompt payment (cash discount). One of the problems of paying immediately for purchases is that it reduces the amount of capital the firm has available (cash flow) to make other purchases.
- They could also buy through hire purchase. In this case the business hires the equipment or goods by making a deposit and paying the remaining amount in regular instalments over a period of time. The goods do not become the property of the 'hirer' until the last payment is paid. The total of the repayments is usually considerably more than the cash price, although sometimes the seller may offer 'interest free' credit.
- Another alternative is to lease the equipment. This refers to an arrangement whereby the business (the lessee) pays for the use of the equipment over a period of time, but where it remains the property of the owner (the lessor). The lessee often has the option to purchase the leased item at a favourable price at the end of the lease period. There are various leasing systems, e.g. with service costs met by the lessee, or alternatively with these costs met by the lessor.

Chapter 7 – Establishing a business

> ➤ **Trade credit** is another method that allows the purchaser to have the use of equipment before paying for it. In this case, the supplier gives the purchaser a period of time to pay for the goods after receiving them. This gives a purchaser, such as a retailer or wholesaler, the opportunity to perhaps actually sell the items on before they have to pay for them. This helps to improve their cash-flow situation.

Interest is usually charged for credit arrangements, so the purchaser needs to know the cash price, and how much interest will be charged for purchasing on credit. These interest charges must be taken into account in any costing to be sure that the purchases being made are cost effective. However, these various arrangements are useful if a business lacks the finance necessary to purchase property or equipment, or if it needs the finance for other activities. They are also useful if the business only needs to use expensive equipment very occasionally, or if it needs specialist service back-up.

We can say that interest is the cost of borrowing but there can be another cost of using someone else's money. Most lenders ask for some form of security against non-repayment of loans. The security the business can offer against non-repayment will typically be things that it owns, e.g. property deeds, buildings, machinery, vehicles, etc. Typically a bank or some other financial organisation may ask a new sole trader entrepreneur to hand over the deeds to his house as security against a loan to the business. Or an established business may issue **debenture stock** as a means of securing capital. This means that the company's business assets act as security. If the business defaults on the loan, the lender will take these items and sell them to regain as much of the loan as possible. The things that the business identifies as security against a loan are referred to as collateral. (See also Chapter 17 – Business finances.)

KEY WORDS
Find out the business-related meaning of each of the following terms. Write a separate sentence for each term to show your understanding.

cash with order
cash on delivery
cash flow   collateral
hire purchase
lease   lessee   lessor
trade credit   interest

7.5 Forming a limited company

All forms of private business, including sole traders, partnerships and private and public companies, must register with the Registrar of Business Names if they operate a business in a name other than that of the owner. Even a sole trader, say John Jones trading as John Jones Enterprises, must register.

When a company is being formed, it must register with the **Registrar of Companies**. This registration is carried out mainly by the presentation of two completed documents, the **Memorandum of Association** and the **Articles of Association**, by the promoters of the company.

Memorandum of Association

This document states the external relationship of the company, that is, its relationship with other organisations.

The Memorandum of Association consists of six main clauses:

- *Name clause*. This states the name of the company, for example 'Carter Electrical Engineering Company Ltd.' (The Registrar of Companies will ensure that two companies are not formed bearing the same name.) The memorandum of a public company has to state in a separate clause (clause 2) that 'The company is to be a public company.' The public company will indicate its status by the letters PLC at the end of its title, whereas the private company will end its title with Limited (Ltd.).

- *Situation clause.* This states the domicile (home) of the company; only the country where the registered office is situated is needed, for example 'Barbados'. The company can move its registered office within the stated country.
- *Objects clause.* This states the object for which the company is established, for example 'to undertake the installation of domestic and industrial electrical appliances'.
- *Liability clause.* This is a straightforward statement that the liability of members is limited by the amount invested in shares in the company.
- *Capital clause.* This states the amount of capital with which the company is to be registered and the manner in which the capital is divided into shares, for example $200,000 divided into $1 shares.
- *Association clause.* This is a declaration by the signatories, stating that they wish to form the said company and that they are prepared to take up and pay for the number of shares shown on the form beside their names. The minimum number of signatories is two.

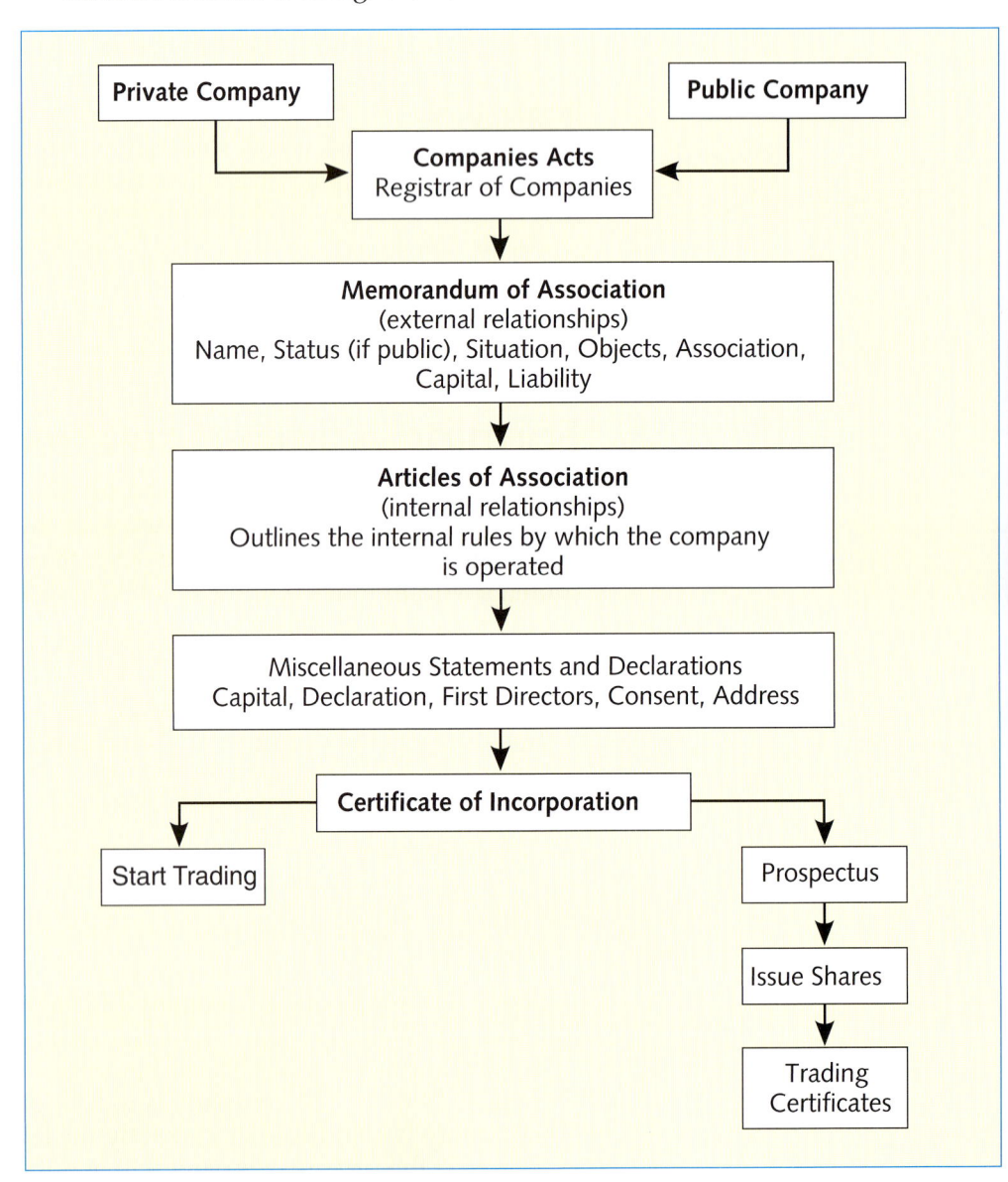

Fig. 7.1 *Forming a limited liability company*

Articles of Association

This document outlines the internal relationships of the company, that is, the broad way in which the internal organisation will operate. It must be signed by the same people who sign the Memorandum of Association.

The contents of this document are more flexible that those of the Memorandum of Association, and they can be easily changed by the shareholders. However, any alterations to the Articles of Association must not conflict with the Memorandum of Association. Among other things, the Articles of Association show:

- The rights of shareholders
- The method of election of directors
- The way in which meetings are to be conducted
- The division of profits.

Miscellaneous statements and declarations

In addition to the Memorandum of Association and the Articles of Association, those forming a company must also make the following statements and declarations:

- *Statement of Nominal Capital.* This statement reflects the capital clause of the Memorandum of Association in that it shows the amount of registered capital and the manner of its division into shares.
- *Declaration.* Usually made under oath, through a solicitor, by the company secretary or a director confirming that all the requirements of the Companies Act have been met.
- *List of First Directors.* The names of the first directors are listed. The minimum number for a private company is one and for a public company the minimum is two (not to be confused with the membership minimum of two for a private company).
- *Statement of Consent.* Written by each of the proposed directors confirming that they are willing to act in that capacity.
- *Address of Registered Office.* States the specific registered address of the company (the situation clause of the Memorandum of Association only states the country). Any change in this address must be registered within 28 days of the change.

If the Registrar of Companies is satisfied that all the foregoing have been carried out correctly, she/he will issue a Certificate of Incorporation.
A private company can now commence business and a public company can now proceed to raise capital.

Raising capital

The directors of the public company now attempt to raise the capital stated in the capital clause of the Memorandum of Association. This is done by issuing a prospectus. A prospectus is a private circular or an advertisement giving a frank outline of what the company hopes to do, and detailing the amount of capital needed in order to begin trading.

When the Registrar of Companies is satisfied that the company has met all the legal requirements, a trading certificate (also called a Certificate of Incorporation, as with a private company) is issued, allowing the company to begin trading.

Principles of Business – Profile 1

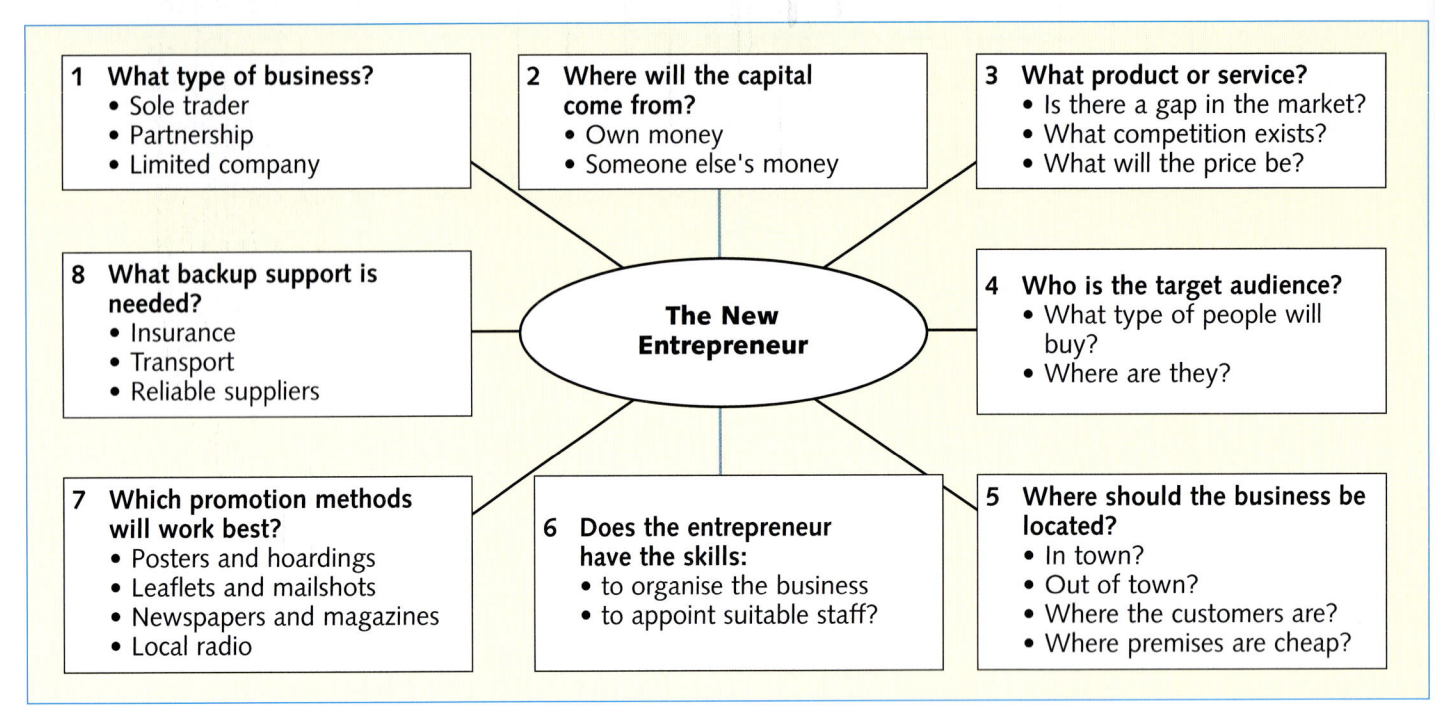

1 What type of business? • Sole trader • Partnership • Limited company	2 Where will the capital come from? • Own money • Someone else's money	3 What product or service? • Is there a gap in the market? • What competition exists? • What will the price be?
8 What backup support is needed? • Insurance • Transport • Reliable suppliers	**The New Entrepreneur**	4 Who is the target audience? • What type of people will buy? • Where are they?
7 Which promotion methods will work best? • Posters and hoardings • Leaflets and mailshots • Newspapers and magazines • Local radio	6 Does the entrepreneur have the skills: • to organise the business • to appoint suitable staff?	5 Where should the business be located? • In town? • Out of town? • Where the customers are? • Where premises are cheap?

Fig 7.2 *Considerations in setting up a business*

Having learnt about the steps involved in setting up a business you might want to look again at a few elements of Chapter 3, and figures 3.13 and 3.14. These show the typical departments of a business, once it is established, and the key personnel involved in them. In particular, you may want to look at the departments of production, marketing and finance, which play a key role in any business. You will learn more about these departments later in this book; production in Chapter 12, marketing in Chapters 13 and 14, and finance in Chapters 16 and 17.

7.6 The stakeholders of a business

Although the main aim of the managers of a business is to run the firm to make a profit for its owners, today they are expected to have regard for all the stakeholders. A **stakeholder** is any person, group of people, or organisation that has an interest in the business. Although the owners are the obvious stakeholders, many others have an interest in the firm:

- *Owners or shareholders* are the main stakeholders. They have invested their money in the firm and look for a return on their investment in the form of dividends and an increase in the value (appreciation) of their shares in the business.
- *Customers of the business* are dependent on the firm for their supplies and so rely on them for raw materials, finished goods and services.
- *Suppliers to the business* will want the business to be successful because this increases their own potential development.
- *Employees* are dependent on the business for their jobs and incomes. When spending their wages they are contributing to the economy, and so their stake holding has wider implications.
- *Local community* has several interests in businesses; it sees the firm as a local employer, a contributor to the economy both locally and nationally.

Chapter 7 – Establishing a business

The community also hopes that businesses will help to develop and protect the environment.

- *Government* are stakeholders as businesses pay taxes to both local and central government. The fact that firms employ workers, and they pay taxes also further supports government aims. Many businesses also sell goods and services to other countries (exports). This contributes to the whole country's balance of payments.
- *Pressure groups* have an interest in what a business does and may want to influence it in some way. For example, a union will want to influence the firm to gain the best wages and working conditions for its members. Other pressure groups may want to influence the business in relation to protection of the environment or on animal welfare issues.
- *Schools* may be supported or sponsored by local businesses. They may send their pupils to local businesses for work experience, and they would hope that in due course their pupils will be rewarded for their studies by obtaining employment.

KEY WORDS

Find out the business-related meaning of each of the following terms. Write a separate sentence for each term to show your understanding.

- name clause
- status clause
- situation clause
- articles of association
- objects clause
- capital clause
- association clause
- stakeholders
- liability clause
- memorandum of association

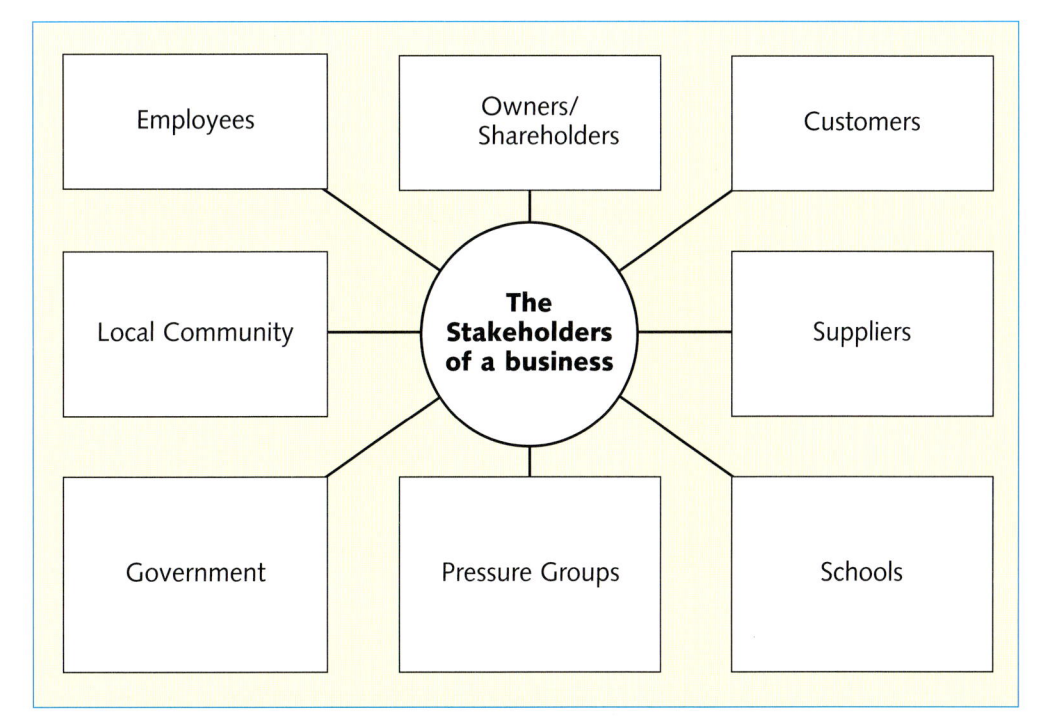

Fig. 7.3 *Many groups are stakeholders of a business*

The Stakeholders of a business:
- Employees
- Owners/Shareholders
- Customers
- Local Community
- Suppliers
- Government
- Pressure Groups
- Schools

Principles of Business – Profile 1

7.7 Things to do

This section contains a variety of exercises to help you create revision notes, to test your understanding and to prepare you for examinations.

Search and find

1. Enterprise, entrepreneur and entrepreneurship are all terms that are used in relation to business ownership. What is the meaning of each of these terms?
2. Why do potential entrepreneurs need to question whether they have the right qualities to run their own business?
3. Briefly describe the three most important qualities you feel someone setting up their own business needs. Put these in your order of priority and justify the order you have chosen.
4. How would a budding entrepreneur know if they have a competitive advantage?
5. How does a business plan help an entrepreneur, and also encourage support from others?
6. Summarise the main elements that should be included in a business plan.
7. In what ways does the 'market potential' part of the business plan help to give confidence in the prospects of a new business?
8. How can careful consideration of the financial implications of a new business avoid a 'start-up crisis'?
9. Describe at least four of the possible ways of obtaining capital equipment.
10. Give a summary description of the process followed in forming a limited company.
11. Why are there so many stakeholders in a business?

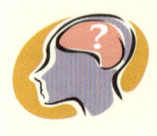

What do you know?

Write out the complete sentence and insert the missing word, which can be chosen from the list at the end of the test.

1 An entrepreneur needs to be ….. .
2 ….. greatly improves a firm's survival prospects.
3 One of the major difficulties faced by a new business is ….. crisis.
4 A new entrepreneur can use their own ….. or someone else's.
5 Some suppliers may offer a ….. for prompt payment.
6 ….. is usually charged for credit arrangements.
7 All ….. businesses must register with the Registrar of Business Names.
8 ….. offers a 'ready-made' opportunity for the entrepreneur.
9 A ….. is where two or more companies voluntarily join together.
10 A ….. is a company with subsidiaries in more than one country.

Choose the missing word from the following:

interest   merger   franchising   planning   capital   discount   self-motivated
start-up   multinational   private

Chapter 7 – Establishing a business

Structured questions

Q1 Look at the newspaper article shown here in figure 7.4 and answer these questions.

Going it Alone

There has never been a better time to start a business of your own, but our Business Correspondent Amira Shah reports, it's a rocky road before you can hit the big time.

Instant sucess is rare in business and budding entrepreneurs need to be aware of the five stages of growth of a business:

Existence At the existence stage the founder is technically orientated and using all the energy to design and manufacture a product (or provide a service). The business is run by the owner who often performs all the managerial functions.

Survival At the survival stage the business becomes more aggressive in seeking new customers and a small standardised product line appealing to a wider set of customers is developed. The number of employees starts to expand and the owner becomes much more burdened with management responsibilities.

Success At the success stage the business credibility and technical feasibility has been established. Economies of scale are introduced into the production process. The owner has to make a decision, either to concentrate all his or her energies on expanding the company with the consequent risks or to keep the company stable and profitable and provide a basis for alternative interests.

Take off If the owner decides on the expansion route and is successful then he or she should reach the take off stage. At this stage there are multiple product lines and a divisionalised organisation structure to cope with the increasing complexity of the business.

Resource maturity At the resource maturity stage, the business is now very well established. It is successful and the owner and the business have become quite separate financially and operationally. However, it can become very bureaucratic and stifle innovation.

One of the major challenges for independent business people is that both the problems faced and the skills necessary to deal with them change as the business grows. You need to anticipate these changing factors based on the stage of development of your business. Similarly at the success stage, you have to decide whether or not to commit all your time and risk everything you have worked for to date in order to grow further.

Fig 7.4 *Going it Alone*

(a) Explain the words 'founder' and 'entrepreneur' used in the newspaper article. **2**

(b) Why does the owner of the business tend to be carrying out all the managerial functions at the 'existence' stage of business development? **2**

(c) Advertising tends to become an important feature of a business at the 'survival' stage. Why is this so? **3**

(d) What does it mean in the article when it says that the business 'credibility and technical feasibility has been established' at the 'success' stage? **3**

(e) What 'economies of scale' are likely to be introduced during the success stage of development? Why are these not likely to be introduced earlier in the development of the business? **4**

(f) In what ways do the skills required of a businessperson change as the business grows? **6**

Q2 Refer to the diagram shown earlier in this chapter as figure 7.1 showing the process of forming a limited liability company and answer the questions given here.

(a) At which of the stages in the flow diagram shown is a business given an identity separate from its owners? **1**

(b) How can the general public readily tell whether a business is a private or a public company? **2**

(c) If two limited companies were formed with the same name this could cause confusion. How is this avoided? **2**

(d) What are the implications of a business having limited liability? **2**

(e) The diagram shows that a public company raises its capital eventually by issue of shares. How does a private company raise its capital? **3**

101

Principles of Business – Profile 1

(f) Briefly state the differences in function of the Memorandum of Association and the Articles of Association, giving a separate example of a item unique to each. **4**

(g) Explain the differences between a private limited company and a public limited company. **6**

Q3 Refer to the diagram shown earlier in this chapter as figure 7.2 and answer these questions related to it.

(a) What is an entrepreneur? **2**

(b) The section of the diagram that refers to sources of capital identifies two basic places where this can be obtained by someone getting started:

   (i) State two ways, other than their own savings, in which an entrepreneur might get sufficient money to start a business without borrowing. **2**

   (ii) Name two different sources of 'other people's money' that an entrepreneur might have access to in order to start up a business. **2**

(c) Give two reasons why an entrepreneur could prefer to set up a business as a sole trader rather than with one partner or more. **4**

(d) What advantages could someone setting up a new business gain by going into partnership? **4**

(e) What kind of skills, other than those needed to recruit suitable staff, does an entrepreneur need to be able to organise their own business? **6**

Q4 The following questions are also related to figure 7.2.

(a) Why do new entrepreneurs need to carefully identify the 'target audience'? **2**

(b) State two specific different ways in which a firm could identify the appropriate target audience for its goods or services. **2**

(c) What is meant by the word 'promotion' in the way it is implied in the diagram? **2**

(d) State three factors that will influence the choice of methods of promotion that will be used by an entrepreneur. **3**

(e) Why is it important for an entrepreneur to establish where there is a 'gap' in the market? **3**

(f) Briefly describe four ways in which an entrepreneur could find out what competition exists. **4**

(g) Why would a firm need 'reliable suppliers' in order to successfully influence its target audience? **4**

Q5 Lucy Lastic has trained as a 'fast food' chef. She works for Burnt Burger Ltd., a national chain of restaurants that has steadily expanded, and Lucy's wages have risen as the company has increased in size.

During her employment with Burnt Burger, Lucy has been promoted several times and is now manager of five branches of Burnt Burger in an area about 100 miles from her home town of Silver Sands. She lives near her work during the week and travels home to visit her family at weekends.

Lucy is considering setting up her own business in Silver Sands. She is thinking of providing a catering service for weddings. Lucy discussed her ideas with some friends who have already set up their own catering business. They advised Lucy to investigate her idea more carefully and to formulate a business plan.

(a) Considering the responsible job Lucy already has, give two reasons why she might want to start her own business. **2**

(b) Give one advantage and one disadvantage of Lucy considering forming a partnership with one other person. **2**

(c) What are the risks Lucy faces in running her own business that do not exist when working for someone else. **3**

(d) Why is a business plan likely to be particularly useful in Lucy's case? **3**

(e) Write a list of information you think should be in Lucy's business plan? **4**

(f) Describe three contrasting possible sources of start-up finance for Lucy's business, and explain the cost implications of each. **6**

Research assignments

1 Use the local telephone directory business pages to find the addresses of government agencies in your area that assist businesses. Find out what support they provide for people who want to start their own business. Interview some owners of small businesses to find out whether they are aware of the facilities available, and if they feel they are helpful. Write a report of your findings and suggest how the government could improve the help it provides.

2 Decide on a sole-proprietor type of business you would like to set up. Formulate a business plan that is realistic for the size and type of business you have in mind. Write a letter to a local bank manager setting out your proposal and asking, if you were really going to undertake this development, whether your request for a loan would be likely to be successful.

3 Take any six different small businesses in your area and find out the main business objectives of each of them. What conclusions can you draw from the differences that exist between them?

4 What market potential do you consider exists in your area for a new restaurant? In what ways would you organise the business and where would you locate it?

5 What kinds of small retail business would you feel it would be worthwhile to start up in your locality? Where would you suggest the business should be located? Produce evidence to support your suggestions.

6 If you were someone who has recently been made redundant with $60,000 as redundancy pay, what entrepreneurial opportunities exist in your area that you feel would be a sensible way to use the money.

7 Imagine that you work for your local council, who intend to set up a business park in your area. You have been asked to investigate the best way to proceed.

   a) Carry out a survey of local businesses to find out what facilities they would want provided to persuade them to move to a business park.

   b) Write a report to the council leader suggesting the type of business park that should be built.

   c) In your report explain the type of business that would be attracted to the business park, and those for whom it would not be appropriate.

The legal aspects of business

8.1 Business and the law

By now you will have realised that being in business is not a simple matter; there are legal constraints, and ignorance of the law is no excuse or defence. There are many laws that aim to control and protect businesses, and they are continually increasing. Their main purposes are:

- To ensure there is free competition between businesses (see Chapter 1)
- To maintain a good level of safety and improve working conditions (see Chapters 4 & 5)
- To protect consumers (see Chapter 14).

There are quite clear requirements for the registration of business names, and you learnt in Chapter 2 that there are regulations regarding the structure of the business; is it to be a sole proprietor (sole trader), a partnership, a private limited company, or a public limited company, or some other form of organisation? Whatever the case, there are laws that apply.

There are laws of product protection, to prevent others from stealing the intellectual creation of people (copyright), and also to prevent imitation of original invention of products (patent). Patent and copyright laws are provided by government to reward and protect creative efforts. At the beginning of this book you will see that the copyright holder of this book is indicated by the sign ©.

Another form of protection available to business is a trademark. Trademarks are words, letters or symbols that are associated with a particular company or product. Company names, team emblems and label designs are typical examples of the use trademarks. A trademark can be a valuable tool in the marketing of products because many become famous throughout the world. Once a trademark is well established it is a simple matter to just display the trademark to cause the public to make the association between it and the company's products or services.

The law of contract is particularly important to business and many thousands of contracts are made each day in the business world. Indeed, even in private life we are often involved in contracts, even if in a simple format.

8.2 Contract formation

What is a contract?

A contract is a legally enforceable, binding agreement between two or more parties whereby something is done, or promised to be done, or given or promised to be given. It is more than an agreement because it is enforceable by law. In other words, if any of the parties do not abide by the contract, the other parties can take legal action against them.

A contract involves an obligation on the part of the contractors. This obligation may be expressed verbally or in writing, but there must be an apparent intention to create legal relations and not just a mutual exchange of promises (which would be an agreement). A contract may be written or unwritten, depending on its type. A written contract takes a particular format. In other words, the wording, phraseology and terms used follow an accepted format that is recognised as legally significant. Such written contracts may be formalised by a seal or by a witnessed signature. An advantage of a signed contract is that the parties concerned cannot dispute the contents.

Types of contract

Speciality contracts (contracts by deed) are also called 'deeds' or contracts under seal. They tend to be a more formal type of contract, often written on a special form, and they have three requirements:

1. *Signing* – the contract is signed by the parties involved
2. *Sealing* – the contract is attached with some form of raised seal
3. *Delivery* – the contract is placed (or touched) by the person to whom it is delivered. All parties involved must have a copy.

A speciality contract does not have legal significance unless all three of the above procedures have been carried out. Sometimes such contracts will have an attestation by one or more witnesses, but this is not always necessary. Some examples of speciality contracts are: mortgage agreements, insurance contracts, land or property sales, hire purchase agreements, and some sales of goods.

A contract of record refers to an order imposed by a court requiring a party to abide by a ruling set down by the Court. The ruling may require a person to do, or not do, something. For example, a businessperson may be told they must cease trading, or that they must pay compensation to some aggrieved party.

A simple contract, as its name implies, is a 'simple' agreement between two parties. It needs no special form; it may be by word of mouth (orally), or sometimes in writing (*some* simple contracts must be in writing) or they may be implied by conduct (indicated by actions). Simple contracts are the most frequent form of contract undertaken. For example, a business person may engage in simple contracts every day while travelling, dining in a restaurant, buying stationery from nearby shop, etc. When you get on a bus, the driver has offered you a ride, you have accepted the offer and you are expected to pay for the journey. A contract has been carried through from start to finish.

The parties of a contract

We have said that a contract is a legally binding agreement between parties. It is possible to have two or three parties, and these are:

- *the offeror* – the person who makes the offer
- *the offeree* – the person to whom the offer is made
- *the acceptor* – the offeree, having accepted the offer.

Although this is a relatively simple structure, it can become more complicated if these roles blur. Sometimes the offeror can end up becoming the offeree and acceptor. For example, if A (offeror) offers to sell something to B (offeree) and B makes a counter offer (such as, 'You are asking me to pay too much, I offer to pay less'), then, if A accepts the counter-offer, A now becomes the offeree and acceptor.

Principles of Business – Profile 1

Fig. 8.1 Negotiating a contract

The contract process

The formation of a simple contract involves one party (the **offeror**) making an **offer** to the other party (the **offeree**) that must then be **accepted** by the latter party. For example, one firm (e.g. a **seller**) may offer to produce a product for another company at some future date and on specified terms (e.g. in three weeks time, and at a given delivered price). In return, the other company (the **buyer**) would agree to pay a specified sum of money (a **consideration**) for the goods to be supplied.

Fig. 8.2 There are three elements to the contract process

Having made the contract, both parties would then be legally bound to honour the agreement. In the event of either party failing to comply with the terms of the contract, the other party could seek damages for **breach of contract** through the courts.

To be a party to a contract there must be **intent** to enter into the agreement. If you are very young, drunk, or similarly limited when you make an agreement, a court may hold that you did not intend to make it and the agreement will, therefore, be held to be invalid. This means that the agreement cannot be enforced. Similarly, if someone was forced into an agreement (e.g. by threat), the agreement would be **invalid**. It is also important to realise that a supplier has no obligation to accept an offer to buy from a purchaser.

Fig. 8.3 A contract would be invalid if there was any threat involved

Chapter 8 – **The legal aspects of business**

> **KEY WORDS**
>
> Find out the business-related meaning of each of the following terms. Write a separate sentence for each of the following key terms used in this chapter to show you understand them in the business context.
>
> agreement   offeror   invalid   deed   trademark   patent   contract
>
> intent   simple contract   offeree   speciality contract   copyright

The offer

An *offer* is a bid or a proposal made by one person to another. A contract has not been made until an offer has been *unconditionally* accepted. The offer made must be *certain*; to say, 'I may be interested in buying the trainers' is not a specific offer. The offer made must also be actually communicated to *the person* the offer is intended to be made to. For example, if you placed an advertisement in a newspaper saying that you would like to buy some trainers, you are not making a *specific offer* because you have not specified the person to whom you are making the offer. So, you would not be obliged to buy all (or any) of the trainers that readers of the advertisement want to sell to you. Neither are you making a specific offer if the person to whom you are making the offer doesn't receive it (e.g. if you send a written offer in the post and it isn't received).

An *invitation to treat* is an invitation to make an offer. It is a statement which is intended to persuade *someone else* to make an offer. The price label put on by a shop is an invitation to treat. If the shop assistant tells you that the price shown is wrong, and that the real price is higher, there is nothing you can do about it. In this case, your offer (in response to the price shown) has been *rejected*. However, there are some instances where you may be protected by consumer protection law. Some examples of invitation to treat are shown in figure 8.4.

An offer can be *express* (orally or written) or *implied* from the conduct of the person making the offer. An example of an express offer would be if you placed an advert in the newspaper offering a reward for the return of your lost wallet. A case of implied offer would occur if you accepted the offer of a ride on a bus and handed the correct fare to the driver. No words need to be spoken, but the offer is made and accepted by implication.

The acceptance

A party to a contract can be said to accept an offer when she/he willingly accepts or agrees to it. An acceptance of an offer can be made in several ways. It can be made by a *written statement*. If the written acceptance is sent by post it is effective from the *time of posting*. This applies even if the letter is delayed or lost in the post. However, it will of course make matters simpler if some recorded method of postage is used. The acceptance can be made by a *verbal statement* (e.g. the sales assistant says 'I agree to sell you the trainers', or similar such wording). Acceptance can also be *by conduct* (e.g. the sales assistant puts the trainers in a bag and puts your money in the till).

If the offeror wishes to *revoke* (cancel) the offer, this must be done before acceptance. In the case of post, this means before the acceptance is posted.

Fig. 8.4 *Examples of invitations to treat*

Today, of course, we have a range of **electronic** methods of communication via which we use to immediately pass information to each other. For example, we use the telephone, fax machine, email, etc. In such cases the acceptance is effective when it is received by the recipient.

The acceptance of an offer must be **unqualified**. In other words, it must correspond exactly with the offer. The acceptance must not introduce new terms. For example, if you offer to buy the trainers for $50 but the shop assistant says that the price is really $60, there is not complete acceptance. The assistant has introduced a new term and in doing so has created a **counter offer**.

The acceptance of the offer must not be **uncertain** either. If the shop assistant says that your offer will *probably* be accepted, then the acceptance is not complete, because the outcome is not **certain**.

The consideration

Consideration is the name given to the price or benefit that the parties to a contract receive. A contract must involve some kind of payment or other consideration to be valid. Obviously, it is usual for both the offeror and the acceptor to benefit, and the consideration is the item of value (e.g. goods, services, money) that each gains.

A court will not necessarily look too closely at the **adequacy** of the consideration, but it must exist. For example, if you agreed to buy the trainers for the outrageous price of $500, although the value is only $50, the court will not question your decision. Or, if the assistant decided to sell them to you for just $1, that is a matter of agreement between the two of you. However, it may be that in some circumstances a court will question whether some undue pressure has been put on either of the parties of a contract if the consideration is extremely inadequate.

Capacity

In the legal environment, the term '**capacity**' is used to identify who is eligible to enter into a contract. Generally speaking, all persons are eligible to enter into a contract. However, anyone who enters into a contract must be able to take responsibility for his/her action associated with the contract. They must have **contractual capacity** to be **eligible** to enter into a contract. To ensure that persons are not exploited or taken advantage of by virtue of their particular circumstances at any point in time, the law makes certain provisions. Thus, the following persons are not normally considered to have full capacity.

- **Minors** (people below the age of 18) have some restrictions on the type of contract that is binding on them. If a minor enters into a contract where they are not eligible to do so, the agreement is said to be **void**. For example, a minor can contract for the purchase of **necessaries** – essential goods and services (e.g. food and clothing) but not luxury items, such as a car. A minor cannot enter into agreements that will result in them owing money.
- Persons who are **under the influence** of alcohol or drugs are in a state that suggests temporary loss of full consciousness and, therefore, are unable to undertake any binding legal decision. Sobriety must be proven in order for full capacity to be accorded to such persons.

- Persons who are diagnosed as being mentally ill are not normally accorded full capacity. The argument is that such a person would be unable to make informed decisions and thus take responsibility for the outcomes of the contract entered into during that state of insanity. However, if it can be proven that such a persons are, without doubt, capable of entering into contracts, then they would be granted full capacity.
- An alien is a person who lives in a country other than his/her own, and who is not a naturalised citizen of that country. An alien would not be granted full capacity if his or her country is at war with the country in which he or she is living. When peace returns between the two countries, the alien could be accorded capacity.

There are two exceptions to capacity law regarding minors:

- A minor could be permitted to enter into a contract if it can be proven that what is required by the minor is a necessity. According to the provisions of the law of capacity, a necessity is an article that is deemed 'reasonably necessary to the minor, having regard to the minor's station in life'. 'Having regard to the minor's station in life' is the important phrase here. According to the law, the article must be deemed a necessity at the 'time of delivery'.
- Minors may also be permitted to enter into contracts of educational value, for example, a contract for a student educational loan.

Legality

All contracts must conform to the law. If a contract involves any illegal acts it is deemed to promote civil wrongs, crime or immorality and becomes illegal and void.

Possibility

This means that within the context of consideration, the parties to a contract must be in a position to deliver the requirements of the contract. However, from time to time 'impossibility' arises, and thus interferes with the possibility of meeting the obligations of the contract. For example, a contract may have been drawn up between two parties to use a venue for an event. However, if the facility is destroyed by a freak storm just before the event, then the party responsible for that part of the contract can use the best possible method to carry out his/her part of the contract. For example, if the other party has another venue, the party's side of the contract can be fulfilled.

Good faith

Good faith refers to the genuineness of the parties involved to stick to a contract. In any contract, all parties must enter of their own free will (threat and persuasion should not be involved), so good faith is assumed.

Case law

Often, cases that appear in court related to breaches of contract, etc., are very similar to ones that have been aired in courts previously. Obviously, it would be an awful waste of time to hear exactly the same kind of cases repeated many times. And it would be a travesty of justice if one court came to a particular decision whilst another came to a different one when the issues involved are the same. Case law helps to reduce this possibility.

Case law or common law is based upon the outcome of previous court cases (case studies), which serve as a precedent in guiding the judgement of

---

KEY WORDS

Find out the business-related meaning of each of the following terms. Write a separate sentence for each term to show your understanding.

good faith   minor
consideration offer
specific offer
rejected
unconditionally
counter offer
invitation to treat
acceptance   contractual
capacity   eligible
revoke   unqualified

subsequent court cases. In other words, where a previously held court case is recorded as resulting in a particular judgement, in a subsequent case where similarity of circumstances can be proven, the judgement should be the same. Where important legal principles are involved the *plaintiff* or *defendant* may appeal against the judgement to a higher court.

8.3 Termination and discharge

Termination of the offer

An offer does not last for an indefinite period. An offer lapses:

- if either the person making the offer or the person to whom the offer is made dies (by *death*)
- if it is not accepted within a specified period of time or, if no particular time has been specified, within a reasonable period of time (by *time lapse*)
- if one of the parties becomes bankrupt (by *bankruptcy*)
- if one contract is substituted for another (e.g. improved or amended), in which case the original contract ceases to exist (by *merger*)
- if one party only completes part of the contract (by *renunciation*)
- if the original contract was illegal (by *legislature*)
- if the contract had a clause where one party has the right to end the contract by warning in advance (by *notice*).

We can see an example of time lapse in a situation where, for example, you find that there is a scuffmark on the trainers referred to earlier, but offer to buy them if the assistant removes the mark, your offer will lapse if the assistant is unable to remove the mark.

Discharge of the contract

To *discharge* someone is to release them from their legal obligation. There are four main ways that a contract is terminated or discharged:

1. **By performance** – this is the most usual way that a contract is terminated. The contract is fulfilled and completed, e.g. a job is completed or the purchaser agrees to buy something, pays for it and leaves the shop.
2. **By agreement** – when both parties agree to cancel out the agreement before it is completely performed by either party, e.g. the purchaser takes an item back to the shop and is given their money back.
3. **By breach of contract** – if one party does not carry out his or her part of the agreement, e.g. a seller agrees to deliver goods in three weeks but fails to do so. Under some such circumstances the *injured party* can sue for *damages*.
4. **By frustration** – when circumstances beyond the control of the parties make it impossible to complete the contract in the manner that was intended, e.g. irreparable damage occurs to an object that forms the main part of the contract. However, frustration is not a release for people who try to avoid their obligations with excuses.

8.4 Mistakes and misrepresentation

Sometimes mistakes occur in contract procedure making the agreement *void* (not valid).

Common mistake

A common mistake occurs when the parties of a contract agree relating to the subject of the contract but both parties are equally mistaken about some aspect of the contract, e.g. the object of the contract does not exist.

Mutual mistake

Sometimes the parties of a contract have both misunderstood each other. The classic example often used to explain this is when a person offers two cars for sale: one is black; the other is white. The offeror believes they are selling the black car, but the offeree is intending to buy the white car. Neither party is misleading the other. The error is only recognised when change of ownership takes place.

Misrepresentation

A *misrepresentation* is a statement that is untrue. A misrepresentation can be a mistake, in other words, an *innocent misrepresentation*; a statement that has been made in the belief that it is true. A *fraudulent misrepresentation* is an untrue statement that is made knowing it to be untrue. In relation to contract, fraudulent misrepresentation refers to a statement used by someone to get another person to enter into a contract with them. In this case it can be said that it is a statement of inducement. In such circumstances the contract would be void, and the injured party can sue for damages.

KEY WORDS

Find out the business-related meaning of each of the following terms. Write a separate sentence for each term to show your understanding.

legality   void
defendant   renunciation
fraud   plaintiff
case law   revoked
breach   acceptance
bankruptcy
misrepresentation

8.5 Things to do

This section contains a variety of exercises to help you create revision notes, to test your understanding and to prepare you for examinations.

Search and find

Write out the question and the answer by referring back through the text to form revision notes.

1. How would you say that the law both supports and restricts business?
2. How does an informal agreement differ from a contract agreement?
3. 'An invitation to treat is not the same thing as an offer.' Explain this statement.
4. In what way is a contract a 'binding agreement' between two or more parties?
5. What is 'simple' about simple contracts?
6. Simple contracts are the most frequently used. Why is this?
7. How does a speciality contract differ from a simple contract?
8. Describe the three main elements of the contract process.
9. Why is it important that someone has the 'capacity' to participate in a contract?
10. Who is not considered to have 'capacity'? Give reasons for your answer.
11. In what ways are the rules for posting an acceptance different from that of using electronic methods of communication?

Principles of Business – Profile 1

12 How do case studies help court cases to be concluded more speedily?

13 In what ways can a contract be 'discharged'?

What do you know?

Write out the complete sentence and insert the missing word, which can be chosen from the list at the end of the test.

1 Copyright laws exist to protect people's ….. creation.
2 A contract is a ….. binding agreement.
3 ….. contracts are also called 'deeds'.
4 A ….. may impose a contract of record.
5 Failing to comply with the terms of a contract could result in being sued for …..
6 An offer is a bid or ….. made by one person to another.
7 The acceptance of an offer must be …..
8 A minor has ….. on the contracts the may enter into.
9 Persons involved in making a contract must have an ability to act …..
10 A contract must ….. to the laws.

Choose the missing words from the following

*responsibly   proposal   court   legally   conform   restrictions   intellectual
unqualified   speciality   damages*

Structured questions

Q1 If you are a *minor* when you make an agreement, a court may hold that you did not intend to make the agreement because you do not have the *capacity* to do so.

(a) What does the word *minor* mean in the way it is used here? **1**

(b) Give two reasons why a minor is not allowed to enter into formal contracts. **2**

(c) What is meant by the term 'capacity'? **2**

(d) Who else may be affected by capacity in relation to contracts? **2**

(e) To be a party to a contract you must intend to enter into the agreement. How could it be proven that you did or did not intend to enter into a contract? **3**

(f) Describe *four* features of a contract. **4**

(g) Explain the difference between a simple contract and a speciality contract. What connections are there between these contracts and the terms 'minor' and 'capacity'? **6**

Q2 You see a jacket for sale in a shop window with a price sign of $150. Your uncle tells you that, as it is your birthday, he will give you the money to buy the jacket. You decide to go to the shop and buy the jacket.

(a) What represents the 'invitation to treat' in this situation? **1**

(b) Who is the *offeror* and who is the *offeree* in this example? **2**

Chapter 8 – The legal aspects of business

(c) What will be your uncle's legal position in this matter? Give a reason for your answer. **2**

(d) If you are a minor at the time you make the purchase, what would your legal position be? **3**

(e) If when you get to the shop the assistant tells you the price shown in the window is wrong, and the real price is higher, what action can you take? Give reasons for your answer. **3**

(f) You decide to buy the jacket. When you get it home you discover a seam in the lining is torn. Your uncle offers to take the jacket back to the shop as he provided the money for the purchase. What is the contractual position in this situation? Give reasons for your answer. **4**

(g) Has your trading in this example been within a simple contract or a speciality contract situation? Within your answer demonstrate that you understand the difference between these two aspects of contract. **5**

Q3 'Most of us are involved in making agreement contracts many times in a week, but business contracts are frequently more formal.'

(a) How does a contract differ from an agreement? **2**

(b) What is a simple contract? **2**

(c) Distinguish between offer, acceptance and consideration in contracts. **3**

(d) How do speciality contracts differ from simple contracts? **3**

(e) Briefly describe four ways that a contract can become invalid. **4**

(f) Why are business contracts often more formal than simple contracts? Give three examples to illustrate your answer. **6**

Q4 **You and your friend Shelly are both 16 years of age. You have been friends for many years. You have both worked in the same busy travel agency since you left school. You promised Shelly to give her a lift to work every day on your motorcycle, and you have done this each working day for three months. Once a week, Shelly pays for your lunch in the local delicatessen. Yesterday, you were sick and couldn't take Shelly to work, and you didn't phone to tell her you wouldn't be coming. Shelly was three hours late for work. The manager was very angry and is deducting money from her wages. Shelly is very upset because she can't afford to lose the money. She has told you that she expects you to give her the money she has lost in wages or she is going to take you to court for breach of contract.**

(a) What is meant by the term 'breach of contract'? **1**

(b) In what ways may a breach of contract arise? **2**

(c) If a breach of contract does occur, what remedies are available to the injured party? **3**

(d) Have you committed a breach of contract? Justify your answer. **3**

(e) Did you have any form of contract with Shelly? Give reasons. **3**

(f) 'All contracts are agreements, but not all agreements are contracts.' How does this statement relate to your situation with Shelly? **4**

(g) Shelly is possibly just a bit upset at present and probably won't take you to court, but in what ways could you put your arrangements with her on a more formal basis? **4**

Principles of Business – Profile 1

Q5

(a) Polly Darton allowed Mary Banilow to keep her horse free of charge in the field Polly owns. What could be said to be the consideration involved here? **2**

(b) Sally Burton placed an advertisement to sell her car for $3000. David Tew bought the car and paid the full price but he borrowed the money from Caribbean Bank Ltd. Name (i) the offeror, (ii) the offeree, and (iii) the acceptor in this situation. **3**

(c) Ian Legon paid $100 deposit to Selene Robbins against purchase of her car on the understanding that Selene will keep the offer open for one month while Ian raises the rest of the money. Before the month is up Selene accepts an offer of more money for the car than she was originally asking. What is Ian's position? **4**

(d) Sima Paxman offered to sell her house to James Roberts at a certain price. James said he would think it over and let Sima know. One month later James contacted Sima to say he had decided to buy the house, but Sima has now promised to sell it to someone else. Is Sima in breach of an agreement? Give reasons for your answer. **4**

(e) Tim Osler owns a milk bar. He purchased a second-hand pinball machine from Future Technical Ltd. for $1000, for which he signed a sales contract. Later he discovered that some of the functions on the machine did not work properly. When Tim asked Future Technical for a refund of his money the company drew his attention to a clause in the sales contract that disclaimed any liability for defects. Clearly explain how you see Tim's position if he were to sue Future Technical in court, and advise him concerning future contract negotiations. **7**

Research assignments

1. Assume you want to go on holiday with four of your friends. Go to a travel agent and obtain a travel brochure for a foreign destination that you would like to visit. Read all the literature you are given very carefully, particularly the booking conditions. Explain clearly:

   a) When does your contract with the company accepting your book actually come into effect?

   What would happen if:

   b) The outbound or return flight is delayed for more than 12 hours.
   c) One of your friends no longer wanted to go on the holiday, but another friend would take their place if the booking could be changed to their name.
   d) The company say they want to increase the price of the holiday due to an unexpected rise in aircraft fuel costs.
   e) The hotel you are due to stay at has been destroyed by fire.
   f) The airline that you are due to fly with has gone bankrupt.
   g) The travel company cancelled your holiday just two weeks before you were due to travel due to terrorism activity at your holiday destination.
   h) Five weeks before the holiday you decide not to go.

2. Organisations frequently display notices that read such as: 'Cars are parked at owners' risk'; and, 'Articles are left in this building at owners' risk'; or, 'Please examine your change before leaving the cash till as we cannot be held responsible for errors after you have left the store'. What is the legal validity of these statements? Discuss the same thing for two other notices you have seen.

3. a) Carry out a survey of adult relatives and friends who are minors and form a summary of the kinds or agreements and contracts they have entered into over a period of one month. What conclusions can you draw from your findings?

   b) Make a survey of two different types of local businesses to find out the kind of contracts they have been involved in over the same period as your friends and relatives. Compare these findings with those in part (a) and explain what legal implications are involved.

Chapter 9

Business documentation

In this chapter we shall focus particularly on trading documents, that is, documentation that is raised during the buying, selling and transporting of goods. However, you should be aware that these are only a part of the wide-ranging documents that businesses use. For example, in Chapter 11 you will learn about the documentation involved in insurance, and at many other places in this book you will learn about many other forms of business documentation.

9.1 Transactions

The complete process of supplying goods or services from the initial enquiry to eventual payment is called a *transaction*. At various stages in a transaction, documents are raised.

When trading, both the buyers and the sellers of goods need to use certain documents to make sure there is no confusion about what has taken place between them, and to provide a record or proof of activity. Within this chapter we shall study the style and the use of the main business documents.

In a similar way that each house owner decorates his or her house in the manner that appeals to him or her, so each business designs its documents in the manner that it feels is most attractive or most workable for its requirements. Therefore, you may find that the same document may have a different style of layout for different companies. We shall follow a typical business transaction from start to finish and study the documents that are used at each stage, in the order in which they appear in trading.

It will be of help to your study of this topic if you bear in mind that the documents are moving in two directions: to and from the buyers and sellers of goods or services. We shall assume that the buyer is female and the seller male.

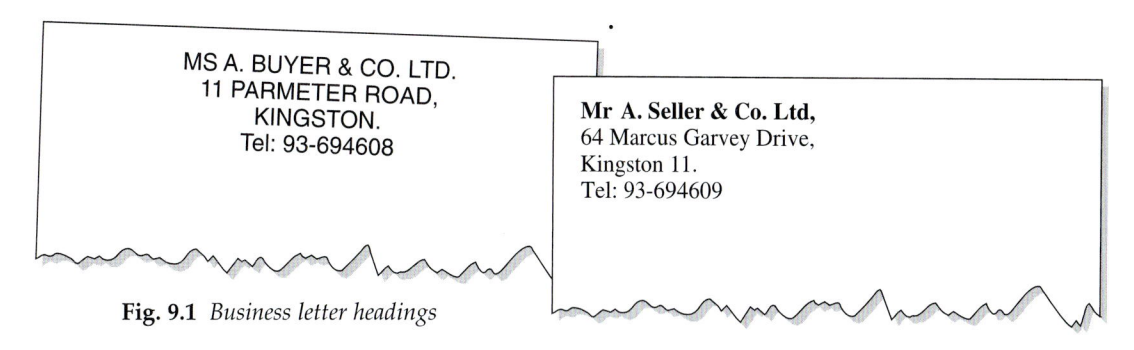

```
MS A. BUYER & CO. LTD.
   11 PARMETER ROAD,
        KINGSTON.
     Tel: 93-694608
```

Mr A. Seller & Co. Ltd,
64 Marcus Garvey Drive,
Kingston 11.
Tel: 93-694609

Fig. 9.1 *Business letter headings*

9.2 Making enquiries

Letter of enquiry

A person wishing to buy goods will try to find out information about them. She will send a letter of enquiry to a seller (or many sellers), requesting information such as:

115

Principles of Business – Profile 1

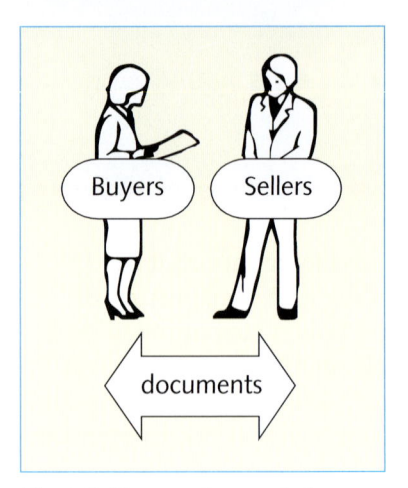

Fig. 9.2 *Documents move in two directions*

- specifications (details of the goods)
- prices
- delivery period
- payment procedures.

The enquiry may be a letter or it may be a standard printed form on which the information required is to be filled in.

Sometimes, rather than send enquiries direct to prospective suppliers, an intending buyer may invite, perhaps by advertisement, any number of people to make an offer (or tender) for supply of the goods or services required. A *tender* is a competitive quotation, one submitted in competition with other tenders.

The supplier who submits the tender which appeals most to the buyer will usually be sent a *contract* which states exactly what has been agreed. (For more on contracts see Chapter 8.)

Quotation

Having received the enquiry, the seller will send a quotation that says what he can offer. This can take many forms. He might send a price list which gives a description and price, or he might send an illustrated leaflet or catalogue with prices indicated.

The seller may send a letter which gives details of prices as well as descriptions of the items to which the enquiry relates. Again, such a letter may be a basic printed type of form which can be used for a whole range of products or quotations.

In the following example (figure 9.4), note how the seller uses a separate catalogue reference number to identify each item he offers. This helps to avoid confusion where two particular descriptions are so similar that a mistake can be made.

Where the seller is unable to quote a precise price, he quotes an *estimated* or expected cost.

Apart from prices and specifications, the quotation also give details of discounts offered.

- *Trade discount:* given to people in the same trade as the seller to enable them to make a profit on resale.
- *Quantity discount:* given to encourage the buyer to place a large order.
- *Cash discount:* this is shown as 'terms' on many documents; it is given to encourage prompt payment.

The quotation also includes details of the arrangements for carriage (transport) of the goods. In other words it states who is required to pay for transport costs.

- *Carriage paid* (carriage outwards): The cost of transport of goods is included in the price, in other words the seller pays transport costs.
- *Carriage forward* (carriage inwards): The cost of transport is not included in the price and must be paid by the buyer of the goods.
- *Ex works:* This is similar to carriage forward in that when a price is quoted 'ex works', the price refers to the goods at the factory, i.e. carriage is additional to the price.

The foregoing are the main terms that are used in quoting and trading, but there are some others that are used (usually in abbreviated form) that you should be aware of.

Chapter 9 – **Business documentation**

- *C/F (cost and freight):* cost includes freight charges.
- *CIF (cost, insurance and freight):* same as above, but also includes cost of insurance whilst goods are in transit.
- *FOB (free on board):* cost includes freight charges, including loading on to a ship.
- *FOR (free on rail):* as above, but includes loading on to a rail wagon.

9.3 Purchasing

Order

If the buyer finds the quotation satisfactory, she will send the seller an official order, which advises him of the:

- goods that are required
- place to be delivered
- date delivery is required
- agreed price.

In the example of an order in figure 9.6, you will note that the order has a number in the top right-hand corner. This makes it easy to refer to a particular order and also easier to find it in a filing system.

You will note that the delivery address is different from the address from which the order has come. This could occur where a business has an office at one address, and a warehouse or factory at another.

Even when an order has been placed by telephone, it is customary to send a confirming order in writing, and in fact many sellers will not actually

---

MS A. BUYER & CO. LTD,
11 PARMETER ROAD,
KINGSTON.
Tel: 93-694608

Mr A. Seller & Co. Ltd,   1 June 2007
64 Marcus Garvey Drive,
Kingston 11.

Dear Sirs,

We would be pleased to receive at your earliest convenience your best quotation for the supply of the following items.

Your quotation should indicate delivery period, carriage terms, prices and cash discounts.

20 Reams   A4 Bond Typewriting Paper White
20 Reams   A4 Bank Typewriting Paper Yellow
10 Reams   A5 Bond Typewriting Paper White
10 Reams   A5 Bank Typewriting Paper Yellow

Yours faithfully,
for MS A. BUYER & CO. LTD.,

S. Webber

S. Webber
Chief Buyer

Fig. 9.3 *Letter of enquiry*

QUOTATION

Mr A. Seller & Co. Ltd,
64 Marcus Garvey Drive, Kingston 11.
Tel: 93-694609

Ms A. Buyer & Co. Ltd.,   4 June 2007
11 Parmeter Road,
Kingston.

Dear Sirs,

We thank you for your letter of enquiry dated 1st June 2007 and we are pleased to offer the following quotation to supply the mentioned items.

Please note that the prices, terms and delivery periods are those current at the time of writing, and are only valid for a period of three months from the date of this letter, after which time a new quotation should be requested.

20 Reams   A4 Bond Typewriting Paper White.
Cat.No. 3498 $1.30 per ream

20 Reams   A4 Bank Typewriting Paper Yellow.
Cat.No. 3100 $0.90 per ream

10 Reams   A5 Bond Typewriting Paper White.
Cat.No. 3499 $0.85 per ream

10 Reams   A5 Bank Typewriting Paper Yellow.
Cat.No. 3101 $0.60 per ream

Delivery is carriage paid 6 weeks from receipt of order.
Terms: 5% 7 days, $2\frac{1}{2}$% 28 days, otherwise net.

Yours faithfully,
for MR. A. SELLER & CO. LTD.

B. Henry

B. Henry
Sales Manager

Fig. 9.4 *Quotation*

Principles of Business – Profile 1

Stationery Requisition		
From	Marketing Dept.	
To	Stationery Store	
QUANTITY	DESCRIPTION	
50	C6 Envelopes	
2	A4 Lever Arch Files	
1	Box A4 Carbon Paper	
1	Box small paper clips	
4	Reams A4 blank paper	
Signed *Justin Time*	Date 24 June 2007	

Fig. 9.5 *Stationery requisition*

despatch goods by telephone request only. In such an event the word 'confirmation' will be typed in capitals on the order.

Sometimes there is a need to order items within an organisation as opposed to from an outside supplier. For example, the government may establish a 'department of supplies' from which other government departments or ministries purchase their supplies. In some business organisations departments and sections also have to obtain their stationery from some form of central supplies division.

To call the document requesting internal supplies an 'order' could be confusing, so to differentiate between an internal and an external order an internal request for supplies is called a *requisition*.

Acknowledgement of order

Having received the order from the customer, the seller sends an acknowledgement stating:

➤ that he has received the order
➤ that he is willing to supply the goods required
➤ when he expects to carry out delivery.

ORDER   No. 013448

MS A. BUYER & CO. LTD.
11 PARMETER ROAD,
KINGSTON.
Tel: 93-694608

Mr A. Seller & Co. Ltd,   10 June 2007
64 Marcus Garvey Drive,
Kingston 11.

Quantity	Description		Price
20 Reams	A4 Bond Typewriting Paper White.	Cat.No. 3498	1.30 per ream
20 Reams	A4 Bank Typewriting Paper Yellow.	Cat.No. 3100	0.90 per ream
10 Reams	A5 Bond Typewriting Paper White.	Cat.No. 3499	0.85 per ream
10 Reams	A5 Bank Typewriting Paper Yellow.	Cat.No. 3101	0.60 per ream

Deliver to Ms A. Buyer & Co. Ltd,
Shop 21,
Spanish Court,
New Kingston.

S.Webber
Signed Head Buyer

Delivery 6 weeks from date of order

Please note this company will only honour official orders signed by an authorised member of this company, and will only accept goods of the standard, style and price indicated on this order.

Fig. 9.6 *Order*

Chapter 9 – **Business documentation**

The acknowledgement may be in the form of a letter or a printed form. If looks similar to the order because it is sending back the same information as the order supplies. When the buyer receives the acknowledgement, she will check it thoroughly to see that it agrees with the order.

9.4 Despatch

Advice note

The advice note is sent ahead of the goods to advise the buyer ('**consignee**') that the goods are on the way to her and that she should expect their arrival. If the goods do not arrive within a reasonable period of time (dependent upon how far the goods must travel), then the buyer will notify the seller ('**consignor**') so that he can make enquiries with the carrier of the goods.

The advice note is sent to the buyer's office and may show prices as well as details of the goods being sent.

Delivery note

The delivery note is usually packed in with the goods, and when the buyer unpacks the parcels she will check that she has received the items stated on the delivery note. Where a company uses its own vehicles to deliver goods the driver will be given a carbon copy of the delivery note which he will get the receiver of the goods to sign to confirm delivery. Note that the delivery note does not reveal the seller's prices.

If the goods are delivered by transport other than the seller's own, then a document, very much the same as the delivery note but called a **consignment note**, is given to the carrier to obtain a signature.

Later in this chapter you will also learn about the many documents that are involved when goods are **transported** to foreign countries.

> **KEY WORDS**
>
> Find out the business-related meaning of each of the following terms. Write a separate sentence for each term to show your understanding.
>
> **consignment note   buyer**
> **tender   transaction**
> **requisition   order**
> **consignor   seller**
> **quotation   consignee**
> **estimate**

9.5 Charging

The invoice

This is one of the most important and probably the most well known of trading documents. It is sent from the seller to the buyer to advise her how much she owes the seller for a particular delivery of goods.

The invoice states:

- the quantity of goods supplied
- the individual prices
- the total amount owed.

It need not necessarily be regarded as a demand for payment, because many invoices may be sent by a seller to a buyer, and it may be that the buyer will pay for all the invoices in one payment at the end of the month.

Where the buyer's office is separate from the warehouse or factory, the invoice is sent to the office.

Look at the invoice in figure 9.9 and you will see that it shows:

- the individual invoice number
- the buyer's order number.

The buyer then knows which order the invoice refers to.

Principles of Business – Profile 1

```
                           ADVICE NOTE                    No. AN.137892

                        Mr A. Seller & Co. Ltd,
                        64 Marcus Garvey Drive,
                             Kingston 11.
                            Tel: 93-694609

Ms A. Buyer & Co. Ltd.,                          Date    15 June 2007
11 Parmeter Road,
Kingston.                                        Dated   10 June 2007

              Order No.         0.13448
              Despatch details  one carton - rail         Terms:
                                14/6/2007                 5% 7 days
                                                          2½% 28 days
                                                          otherwise net
```

Quantity	Description	Amount	Price
20 Reams	A4 Bond Typewriting Paper White. Cat.No. 3498	1.30 per ream	26.00
20 Reams	A4 Bank Typewriting Paper Yellow. Cat.No. 3100	0.90 per ream	18.00
10 Reams	A5 Bond Typewriting Paper White. Cat.No. 3499	0.85 per ream	8.50
10 Reams	A5 Bank Typewriting Paper Yellow. Cat.No. 3101	0.60 per ream	6.00

Deliver to Ms A. Buyer & Co. Ltd,
Shop 21, Spanish Court,
New Kingston.

Fig. 9.7 *Advice note*

```
                           DELIVERY NOTE                  No. DN.137892

                        Mr A. Seller & Co. Ltd,
                        64 Marcus Garvey Drive,
                             Kingston 11.
                            Tel: 93-694609

Ms A. Buyer & Co. Ltd.,                          Date    14 June 2007
11 Parmeter Road,
Kingston.                                        Dated   10 June 2007

              Order No.         0.13448
              Despatch details  one carton - rail         Terms:
                                14/6/2007                 5% 7 days
                                                          2½% 28 days
                                                          otherwise net
```

Quantity	Description	Amount	Price
20 Reams	A4 Bond Typewriting Paper White. Cat.No. 3498		
20 Reams	A4 Bank Typewriting Paper Yellow. Cat.No. 3100		
10 Reams	A5 Bond Typewriting Paper White. Cat.No. 3499		
10 Reams	A5 Bank Typewriting Paper Yellow. Cat.No. 3101		

Deliver to Ms A. Buyer & Co. Ltd,
Shop 21, Spanish Court,
New Kingston.   E & OE

Fig. 9.8 *Delivery note*

Chapter 9 – **Business documentation**

Can you spot the following terms on the invoice? Take note of what each means.

- *E & OE.* You will see these letters in the bottom left-hand corner of the example invoice, and they stand for the words 'errors and omissions excepted'. By this the seller is telling the buyer that he reserves the right to correct any error made on the invoice at some later date. For example, our invoice reads $58.50, but had the person preparing the invoice keyed in $8.50 by mistake the seller has reserved the right to correct the error when he discovers it.

- *Terms – 5% 7 days, $2\frac{1}{2}\%$ 28 days, otherwise net.* This wording on the invoice refers to a cash discount which the seller offers to encourage the buyer to pay the debt quickly. If the amount owed is paid within seven days, the seller will allow 5% off the invoice price. If the buyer takes more than seven days, but less than twenty-eight days to pay, the seller will allow $2\frac{1}{2}\%$ off the invoice price. Where the buyer takes more than twenty-eight days to pay the terms are net, in other words no discount will be allowed.

INVOICE		No. I. 137892 — • Serial number of seller's invoice
Mr A. Seller & Co. Ltd,		
64 Marcus Garvey Drive,		— • Name and address of seller
Kingston 11.		
Tel: 93-694609		

Ms A. Buyer & Co. Ltd., Date   16 June 2007 — • Date of invoice
11 Parmeter Road,   Dated 10 June 2007 — • Details of buyer's order
Kingston.

Order No.   013448
Despatch details one carton - rail — • Method of despatch
                 14/6/2007

Terms: — • Cash discounts offered for prompt payment
5% 7 days
$2^1/_2$% 28 days
otherwise net

Quantity	Description	Amount	Price
20 Reams	A4 Bond Typewriting Paper White. Cat.No. 3498	1.30 per ream	26.00
20 Reams	A4 Bank Typewriting Paper Yellow. Cat.No. 3100	0.90 per ream	18.00
10 Reams	A5 Bond Typewriting Paper White. Cat.No. 3499	0.85 per ream	8.50
10 Reams	A5 Bank Typewriting Paper Yellow. Cat.No. 3101	0.60 per ream	6.00
	Gross invoice		$ 58.50 — • Before deduction of discounts
	Less 20% Trade discount		11.70 — • Discount given to other traders
	Net invoice		**$ 46.80** — • Amount to be paid by buyer

Deliver to Ms A. Buyer & Co. Ltd, — • Delivery address can be different from invoice address
Shop 21, Spanish Court,
New Kingston.

E & OE — • E & OE – Errors & omissions excepted – seller reserves the right to correct errors at later date

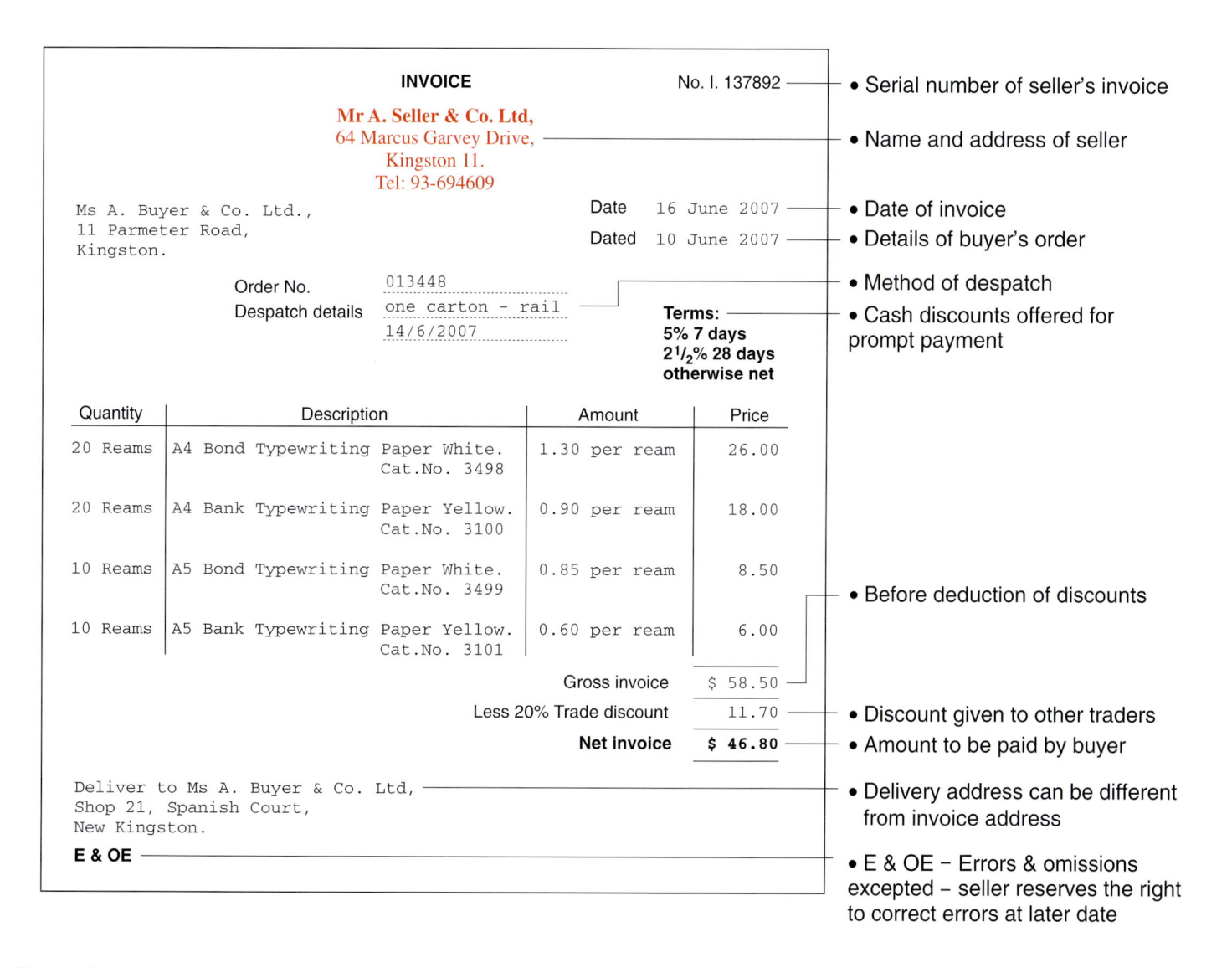

Fig. 9.9 *Invoice*

Pro forma invoice

In appearance this is exactly the same as the invoice except that it has 'pro forma invoice' as its title.

Where a seller does not know a buyer, he may be unsure whether he will receive payment in due course if he sends the goods, but at the same time will not want to miss the opportunity of supplying an order.

To get around this problem, before despatching the goods the seller will send the buyer a pro forma invoice which will charge for the goods in advance. When payment has been received he will then deliver the items ordered.

Credit note and debit note

It may arise that a customer is sent an invoice, and before the invoice is paid it is discovered that the customer is entitled to some reduction in the amount charged. The document which shows the reduction is called the credit note. It is sent by the seller to the buyer.

There are many reasons why the customer may be entitled to a reduction of the invoice value. For example:

- the price charged on the invoice may be too high
- some of the goods sent may be faulty or too few sent
- discounts omitted or too small
- errors in charging for transportation.

Whatever the reason, the credit note has the effect of reducing the debt that the buyer owes to the seller. The credit note is usually printed in red, and shows:

- the reason the credit note is issued
- the goods involved, their price and value
- reference numbers of documents involved in the sale and supply.

The debit note (sometimes called a supplementary invoice) has the reverse effect of the credit note, in that it makes an additional charge. For example:

- the original charge on the invoice was insufficient
- more goods were sent than invoiced and the buyer agrees to keep them.

Note: The debit note and credit note are both sent by the seller. They both have a similar appearance except for their colour and the word 'debit' or 'credit' as a title.

Tax on purchases

Indirect taxes are taxes paid on goods and services and are only paid when the purchases are made. There are many examples of this kind of tax and different names are used such as 'purchase tax', 'value added tax', 'sales tax', 'customs and excise duties', and others. Jamaica has a General Consumption Tax (GMT) that is levied on a number of different items and services. Other Caribbean islands have their own method of taxing goods and services and you should familiarise yourself with the system applied in your area, and the manner of calculating it into trading documents.

```
                              CREDIT NOTE                              CN3478

                           Mr A. Seller & Co. Ltd,
                           64 Marcus Garvey Drive,
                                Kingston 11.
                                Tel: 93-694609              21 June 2007
Ms A. Buyer & Co. Ltd.,                              Date  16 June 2007
11 Parmeter Road,
Kingston.                                            Dated 10 June 2007

                    Credit against  013448
                    Order No.       .................

                    Invoice No.     I137892
                                    .................

Quantity                                             Price     Amount

20 Reams by allowance in respect of overcharge       0.10      $ 2.00
         on item A4 Bond Typewriting Paper
         Cat. No. 3498

         Charged @ $ 1.20 per ream
         Price     $ 1.20 per ream

E & OE
```

Fig. 9.10 *Credit note*

Statement of account

Rather than expect a customer to pay for each individual invoice that has been sent, which could mean that she would have to write out several cheques during the month, the seller will send a statement of account at the end of the month to sum up all the business that has taken place during the month. Thus, the statement of account is used only for credit transactions. The statement of account shows:

> - any amounts outstanding and unpaid from previous statements – shown by the words 'to account rendered'
> - amounts which increase the debt the buyer owes to the seller (invoices and debit notes)
> - amounts which decrease the debt (credit notes issued and payments made).

Look at the statement of account in figure 9.11. Note that it shows all business between a buyer and seller for a month. Where the debt is increased it is shown under 'debit'. Anything that reduces the figure in the amount column is shown under 'amount'.

Payment arrangements

The arrangement between the seller and the buyer for payment of goods and services supplied will depend on how well the seller knows the buyer. The following are the most common arrangements.

- *Payment in advance:* the seller may require payment prior to supply by cash with order (CWO) or in response to a pro forma invoice.
- *Cash on delivery (COD):* the buyer is required to pay the carrier the value of the goods on delivery.

Principles of Business – Profile 1

- *On receipt of invoice:* to gain the benefit of cash discounts offered for prompt payment.
- *Against statement of account:* where the buyer has been granted trade credit, payment can be delayed until the end of the month.

Payment of debts

By cheque

There are many ways to pay a debt, but the most popular in business is for payment to be made by cheque. It is possible to obtain a receipt stating that payment has been made, but usually this is unnecessary unless payment is made by cash.

Where the buyer sends a cheque covering only some of the invoices listed on the statement a **remittance advice note** will also be sent listing the invoices which the cheque is intended to pay.

By cash

For small amounts, cash in the form of coins and bank notes may be used. These are **legal tender**. This term refers to the universal acceptance of certain methods of payment where there is no doubt about their worth. In this respect a cheque is not legal tender, even though it is one of the frequently used methods of payment.

STATEMENT OF ACCOUNT

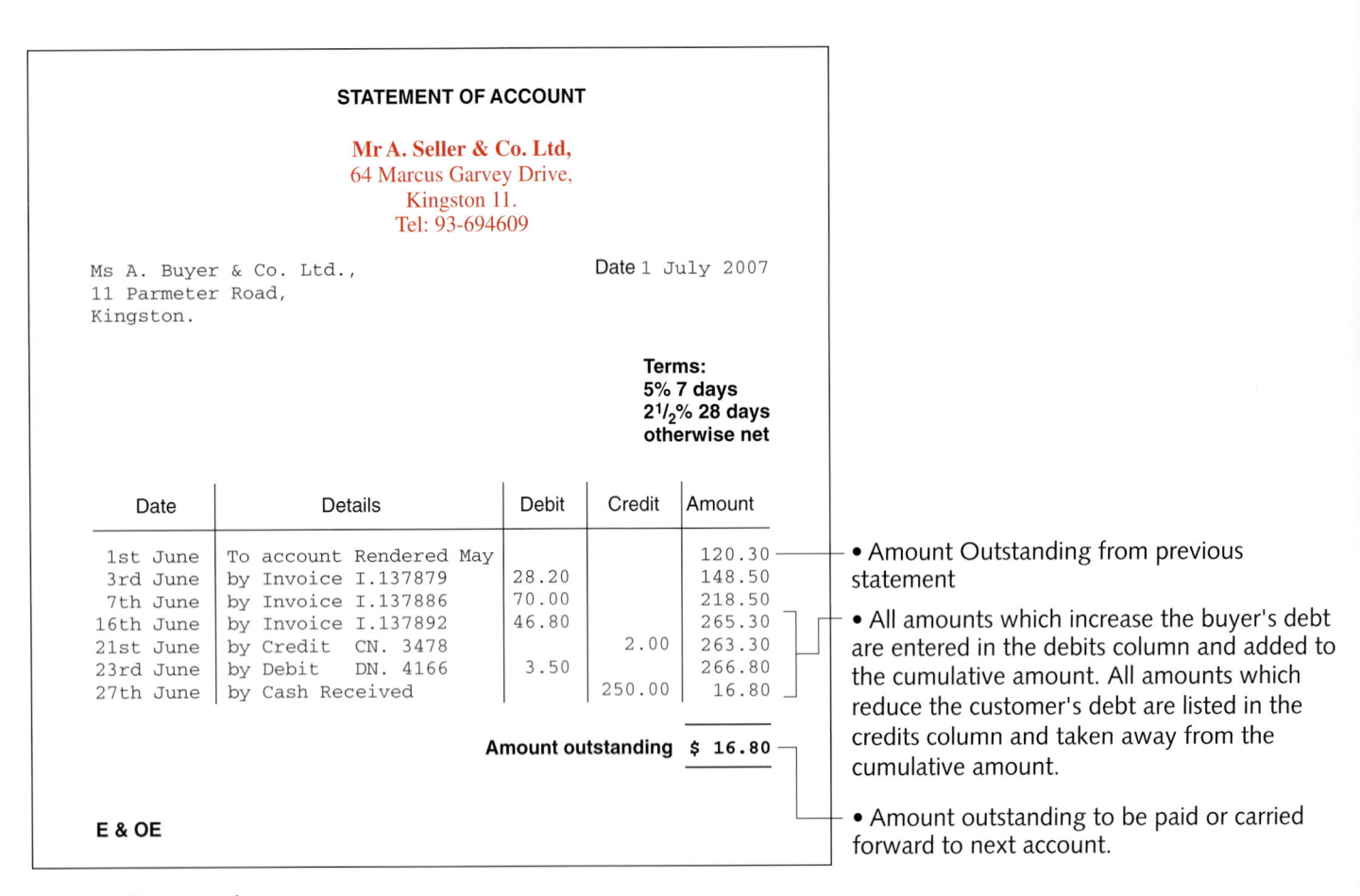

Mr A. Seller & Co. Ltd,
64 Marcus Garvey Drive,
Kingston 11.
Tel: 93-694609

Ms A. Buyer & Co. Ltd.,
11 Parmeter Road,
Kingston.

Date 1 July 2007

Terms:
5% 7 days
2½% 28 days
otherwise net

Date	Details	Debit	Credit	Amount
1st June	To account Rendered May			120.30
3rd June	by Invoice I.137879	28.20		148.50
7th June	by Invoice I.137886	70.00		218.50
16th June	by Invoice I.137892	46.80		265.30
21st June	by Credit CN. 3478		2.00	263.30
23rd June	by Debit DN. 4166	3.50		266.80
27th June	by Cash Received		250.00	16.80

Amount outstanding $ 16.80

E & OE

- Amount Outstanding from previous statement
- All amounts which increase the buyer's debt are entered in the debits column and added to the cumulative amount. All amounts which reduce the customer's debt are listed in the credits column and taken away from the cumulative amount.
- Amount outstanding to be paid or carried forward to next account.

Fig. 9.11 *Statement of account*

Banker's draft

This is a cheque drawn on a bank instead of a person's bank account. A banker's draft is guaranteed by the bank. This makes the draft as good as cash because the bank has guaranteed it for the customer, who has paid the value of the draft to the bank in advance. The bill of exchange discussed in the following section is another form of banker's draft.

> **KEY WORDS**
>
> Find out the business-related meaning of each of the following terms. Write a separate sentence for each of the following key terms used in this chapter to show you understand them in the business context.
>
> cheque   debit note   discount   legal tender   credit note   remittance terms
> invoice   advice note   debit note   indirect tax

9.6 Foreign trade documents

Most of the documents referred to so far in this chapter may also be used in foreign trade, but there are also some documents which apply particularly to that purpose. The following are the main documents used in foreign trade.

Payment documents

Bill of exchange

The bill of exchange is a document that is sometimes used in home trade, but it is most commonly used in foreign trade. It is particularly used in the settlement of international debts.

The bill of exchange is made out by the seller/exporter (the *creditor*) of goods requiring that the buyer/importer (the *debtor*) pays a sum of money on demand, or on an agreed future date (usually after three months).

Both the buyer and the seller benefit from the use of a bill of exchange. The buyer (importer) obtains *credit* on the transaction, and the seller benefits because instead of waiting for payment he can either sell the bill at a 'discount', or 'negotiate' it by using it to pay off his own debts, or use it as collateral against a bank loan.

Documentary bill

This is a bill of exchange with all related documents of title attached, including the invoice and insurance policy. This can be used to give a bank the right to take possession of the goods if the bill of exchange is not honoured when it *matures* (when payment is due).

Documentary credit

An exporter can request that a customer (the importer) makes payment for goods by 'documentary credit'. This enables the exporter to obtain payment before the documents of title/ownership are released to the importer. The importer arranges for her bank to guarantee that the payment will be made when the documents of title are handed over.

Letter of credit

A letter of credit is an assurance given by an importer's bank of the financial standing of the customer undertaking to make the payment required in due course. The letter of credit is in fact the letter sent from the importer's bank confirming this arrangement.

Other documents

Bill of lading

The bill of lading is used in the shipping of goods and it represents the title to ownership of goods. It shows details of the goods, their destination and the terms under which the shipping company agrees to carry the goods. Three copies of the bill of lading are raised:

1. one is retained by the exporter
2. one is given to the ship's captain
3. one is given to the importer who has to produce her copy to take possession of the goods on arrival.

Air waybill

This is used in connection with air transport and it serves as a receipt for goods carried by an airline. It is a kind of bill of lading for air transport. But it is not a document of title, and the sender of the goods does not have to be given a copy. In fact, because air transport is so fast, the goods could arrive before any documentation, so often documentation accompanies the goods.

Manifest

A summary of all the bills of lading and cargo a ship is carrying.

Freight note

The bill or charge for shipping goods; it is sent to the exporter by the shipping company.

Certificate of origin

This is a document certifying the country of origin of goods. It is sometimes required by the importing country if it has been agreed that the goods of a particular country will be allowed to enter the country at a more favourable tariff rate.

Import licence

This is issued by the importing government giving permission to bring certain commodities into the country. It can be used to enforce quotas (government limits on particular goods allowed to be imported).

Export licence

An export licence is sometimes needed before certain goods are allowed to leave a country (e.g. works of art of historical value).

9.7 Stock records

The importance of stock

Stock is the goods or materials held by a business. The stock can be for internal use (e.g. stationery), or for external use, such as to supply customers.

Stock is part of the capital or **assets** of a firm. It is important because it is used to support internal operations, as well as to meet orders from customers. For these reasons a business must hold adequate stocks in order to continue its operations. However, holding stock can also adversely affect **cash flow**. If a business holds too much stock, it can be a drain on its resources.

INTERNAL STOCK
STATIONERY STOCK CARD

Item: A4 Headed Paper–981   Max. stock: 30 Reams
Location: Store Cupboard 5   Min. stock: 15 Reams

Date	Receipts			Issues			Balance in stock
2007	Supplier	Order no.	Quantity	Department	Req. no.	Quantity	
7 Jun							20
8 Jun				Pool	208	2	18
9 Jun				Sales	239	2	16
12 Jun				Export	241	1	15
14 Jun	Printwell	SS.143	15				30
16 Jun				Transport	300	4	26
18 Jun				Admin	302	10	16
18 Jun	Printwell	SS.143	12				28

Fig. 9.12 This is a simple handwritten stock record.

1 Explain the purpose of the 'receipts' and the 'issues' sections.   2 How is the 'balance in stock' figure calculated?

Stock levels

Minimum and maximum stock levels are often established to ensure that:

- sufficient stocks are available for internal operations
- stock is readily available to meet customers' orders
- too much stock is not held.

Minimum stock level

This is the lowest level to which stock is allowed to fall. It is used to safeguard against the possibility of running out of stock. When stock falls to the minimum level, further supplies are ordered to arrive before existing stock is completely used.

Maximum stock level

This is the greatest figure that the stock of a particular item will be allowed to rise to. It is used to ensure that stock does not rise above what is considered to be an economic level, and to avoid tying up capital unnecessarily.

Principles of Business – Profile 1

Stock records

The term 'stock records' refers to the ways in which additions and deductions from stock are recorded, together with the current overall balance. The basic principle of all stock recording systems involves *adding* new stock, *deducting* withdrawals, and maintaining a *cumulative balance*.

There are a variety of methods of recording stock movements and businesses will choose which method they feel suits them best. Two examples are given in figures 9.12 and 9.13, but there are many other ways of recording stock.

STOCK RECORD CARD

Item: Desert Crisps – Cat. No. 37 Max. Stock 7000
Stock Price: $8.50 per carton Min. Stock 2000
Location: Block 3 Room 35

Flavour	1	2	3	4	TOTAL
Stock carried forward	1500	2000	2000	1500	7000
Bastin 1/11/07	100 / 1400	100 / 1900	100 / 1900	100 / 1400	400 / 6600
Perry 17/11/07	300 / 1100	300 / 1600	250 / 1650	250 / 1150	1100 / 5500
Scattergood 4/12/07	800 / 300	800 / 800	800 / 850	800 / 350	3200 / 2300
New supplies 10/12/07	1200 / 1500	1200 / 2000	1150 / 2000	1150 / 1500	4700 / 7000

Fig. 9.13 *A computerised stock record*

1 What is the purpose of the minimum and maximum stock figures?
2 Why do you think a stock record may include a 'stock price'?

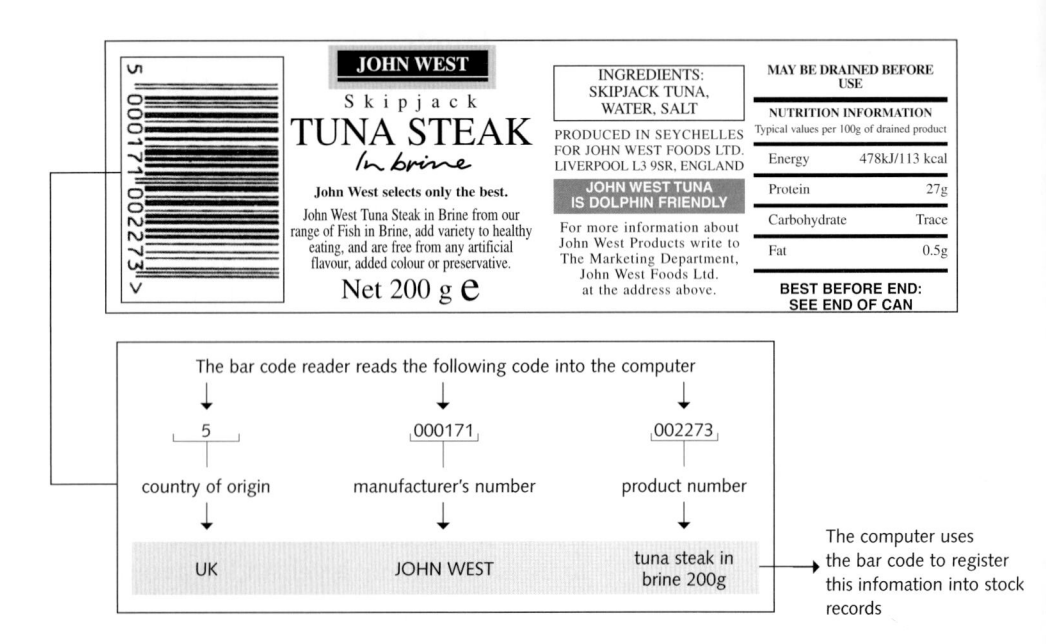

Fig. 9.14 *A bar code is sometimes used to assist stock recording. (Courtesy of John West Foods Ltd.)*

1 How is the information contained in a bar code passed to the main computer?

2 How do you think a 'product code' is used to update stock records?

Chapter 9 – **Business documentation**

Computerised stock records

In the case of a small, simple stock record system, it may be maintained on cards and may be handwritten. Larger stock records may be **computerised**. For example, a stock record system can be incorporated into a computer **spreadsheet**. This computer program automatically carries out all the calculations necessary in response to stock increases or decreases, and instantly calculates a new balance. It can even be programmed to signal when the minimum stock level has been reached.

A **bar code** system extends the computerised stock record system further. All stock items are labelled with a unique bar code, which is a pattern of thick and thin lines (see figure 9.14). This bar code incorporates the **product code number** (stock identification number).

As items are taken out of the stockroom, or as a customer presents items being purchased at the cash-point (**point of sale** (**POS**)), the bar code on each item of good is 'read' by a scanning device connected to the main computer. This enables stock records to be instantly updated. The computer can even be programmed to order replacement stock automatically when the minimum stock level is reached.

KEY WORDS

Find out the business-related meaning of each of the following terms. Write a separate sentence for each term to show your understanding.

- freight note
- documentary credit
- certificate of origin
- creditor manifest debtor
- bill of exchange
- bill of lading
- stock record

9.8 Things to do

This section contains a variety of exercises to help you create revision notes, to test your understanding and to prepare you for examinations.

Search and find

Write out the question and the answer by referring back through the text to form revision notes.

1. What is a transaction?
2. Why do businesses use trading documents?
3. What is the purpose of an enquiry?
4. Briefly describe the various forms that a quotation might take.
5. What is an estimate?
6. Describe the various discounts used in trading.
7. Why is it useful to use catalogue numbers as well as descriptions in price lists and other trading documents?
8. Explain the difference between an order and a requisition.
9. State four items of information contained in an order.

Principles of Business – Profile 1

10. What is the purpose of an advice note?
11. How does the function of a delivery note differ from that of a consignment note?
12. State four items of information found on an invoice and explain the purpose of this document.
13. How does a pro forma invoice differ from the standard invoice?
14. What is the difference in function between a debit note and a credit note?
15. What is the function of a statement of account, and what is the purpose of the debits and credits columns?
16. Describe the various arrangements for the payment of debts between sellers and buyers of goods.
17. Explain how a bill of exchange assists a business involved in foreign trade.
18. What is documentary credit? Explain how this assists foreign trade.
19. Explain the similarities and the differences between a bill of lading and an air waybill.
20. What is the difference between an import licence and an export licence?
21. What is stock and why is it important to businesses?
22. How can stock levels affect the cash flow of a business?
23. Describe the basic principles of stock recording.
24. How can a computer spreadsheet be used to maintain stock records?
25. What is a bar code and what kind of information can it contain?
26. In what ways can a bar code system be said to be an 'extension' of a computerised stock record system?

What do you know?

Write out the complete sentence and insert the missing word, which can be chosen from the list at the end of the test.

1. The ..... seeks out information about products a seller has to offer.
2. The ..... is a communication that says what a seller can offer.
3. To advise the seller what he wishes to buy the buyer will send an official ..... .
4. Where it is not possible to give a precise price the seller may give an ..... cost.
5. Firms may offer their customers a ..... to encourage prompt payment of debts.
6. The seller will ..... receipt of an order to confirm that he is willing to supply the goods or services requested.
7. An ..... note will be sent to tell the buyer when her goods have been despatched to her.
8. The ..... advises the buyer how much she is expected to pay for goods or services.
9. A statement of account ..... the trading position between the buyer and the seller.
10. A ..... note can be used to give a refund to the buyer.

Choose the missing words from the following

summarises   order   discount   enquiry   credit   quotation   invoice   estimated   advice   acknowledge

Chapter 9 – **Business documentation**

Structured questions

Q1 Refer to the invoice in figure 9.9 and answer the following questions related to it.

(a) Name the seller and the buyer involved in this transaction. **2**

(b) Most trading documents show a number similar to that shown in the top right-hand corner of this example. What is the purpose of this number? **2**

(c) On what date were the goods on this invoice ordered and on what date were they despatched? **2**

(d) The goods on this invoice were supplied 'carriage paid'. What does this mean? How does this differ from goods sold 'ex-works'? **4**

(e) How does the function of an invoice differ from that of a statement of account? **4**

(f) Explain the difference between a cash discount and a trade discount, using data from the invoice to illustrate your answer. **6**

Q2 All the following questions are related to the invoice in figure 9.9.

(a) Why do both the seller and the buyer need copies of this document? **1**

(b) Find the following numbers on this invoice and explain the purpose of each of them: 013448, 137892, 3498. **3**

(c) How does the function of a pro forma invoice differ from that of an invoice? **4**

(d) Under what circumstances might the information contained on this invoice result in the need to issue a credit note and a debit note. **4**

(e) Explain each of the following terms using data from this invoice to illustrate your answer:
   (i) gross invoice amount   (iii) trade discount
   (ii) net invoice amount   (iv) E & OE. **8**

Q3 Refer to the statement of account in figure 9.11 and answer the following questions related to it.

(a) How frequently are statements such as this sent out? **1**

(b) What purpose does this document serve? **2**

(c) Name the creditor and the debtor involved in these transactions. **2**

(d) Why does this document show three months: May, June and July? **3**

(e) Give possible reasons for the entries 'by credit' and 'by debit'. **4**

(f) Clearly explain the meaning of the details, debit, credit and amount columns, using data from the document to clarify your explanation. **8**

Q4 All the following questions are related to the documents and stages shown in the flow chart in figure 9.15.

(a) What is the name given to the complete chain of business shown in this illustration? **1**

(b) At what point in this chain would the customer be asked to pay their outstanding account? **1**

(c) Where in the chain would a debit note be most likely to appear? **1**

131

Principles of Business – Profile 1

(d) Give two reasons why a debit note might be issued. **2**

(e) Under what circumstances would this diagram show the words 'consignment note', and where would this appear in the diagram? **3**

(f) State three items of information likely to be found in a quotation. **3**

(g) The flow chart shows that the remittance is being paid by cheque. Assuming that the transaction involves foreign trade, clearly describe the functions of three documents that are likely to be involved in payment arrangements. **9**

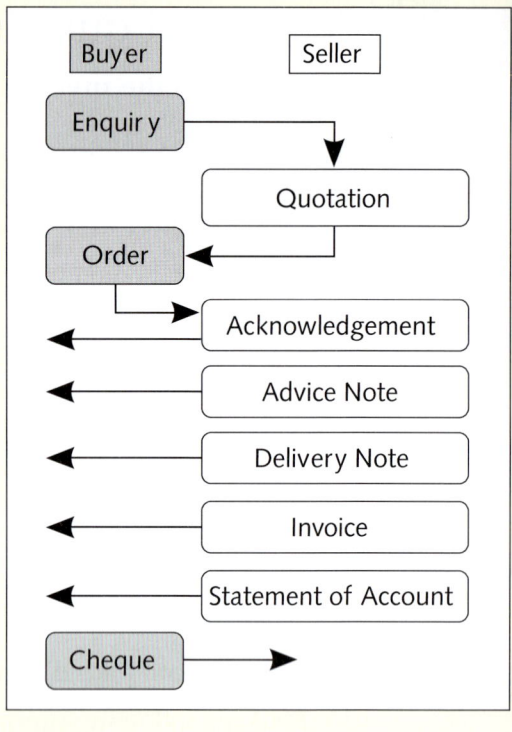

Fig. 9.15 *Flow chart for question 4*

Research assignments

1. You are the managing director of a medium-sized manufacturing company engaged in the production and sale of small items of farm equipment. Design five trading documents that you are likely to use in your business. For each document give a detailed explanation of the important functions of the various parts of it.

2. You work for a manufacturing company that is currently only engaged in home trade, but is considering expanding into overseas trade. Write a detailed report for your managing director explaining some of the ways in which documentation can support this development.

3. Visit local firms and collect samples of the documents used in local trade as well as foreign trade. Put the documents in a scrap book under the headings:
   a) documents used in local trade
   b) documents used in foreign trade.

   Display the documents collected on the bulletin board in your classroom or on a chart. Use appropriate headings.

4. Investigate a small and a medium-sized local business you have access to. Obtain permission to examine their stock record procedures. Formulate a few questions that will guide your search. Write a report on your findings, including examples of differences you have identified in the methods that each size of business employs.

Chapter 10
Instruments of payment

In Chapter 9 you learnt about the documentation that has to pass between the seller and the buyer during the process of trading. Some of those documents have implications for the payment of goods or services received. For example, the issue of an invoice implies that a payment must be made in response to the charge made. The company receiving the invoice must have a means of paying the charge.

The place where money, or wealth, is stored until it is required for making payments is generally in some form of a bank account. Banks and other financial institutions also provide a wide range of means of transferring money as payment. This chapter examines the main services that make payments possible.

10.1 Cash and near cash

The part of a country's **money supply** that is totally acceptable as payment or discharge of debt, such as coins and banknotes (**currency**) issued by the government is called **legal tender**. However, it is often not realistic to use 'legal tender' to pay for purchases. For example, can you imagine a business paying in cash for a delivery of a shipload of timber? However, there are many other instruments of payment that, whilst not *legal tender*, are generally more acceptable than others as methods of payment, and because of their acceptability they are sometimes referred to as 'near cash'.

Money order

A **money order** is an instrument of payment sold by banks (and in post offices in some countries). They are used to facilitate making payments to others, particularly in overseas countries, for example to pay for goods and services. The money order states the amount of money to be paid to the recipient (the **payee**) named on the order. Because the value of the money order (and a fee) has already been paid by the sender, payment is backed by the bank or post office, and payment is assured.

The money order:

- is an instrument for making payments
- payment is guaranteed
- can be negotiated by endorsement (signed by the payee and passed to someone else)
- can be exchanged for cash or paid into a bank account
- can be used by people who do not have a bank account.

A money order is normally sent via the postal system and sometimes the delay involved is not convenient. A **telegraphic money order** is a speedier method. The system is speeded up by a message being sent (in the past by telegraph/telegram) instructing the post office or some other financial institution to release the funds on demand. Today other methods of transfer of funds have become more frequently used (see later in this chapter).

Bank draft

A *bank draft* is in effect a cheque drawn on the bank itself, making it very trustworthy. It is generally used if businesses are unsure of the *credit worthiness* of the people or firms who owe them money. The firm that owes money pays their bank the sum they owe, and the bank will then make out a cheque made payable to the *creditor*.

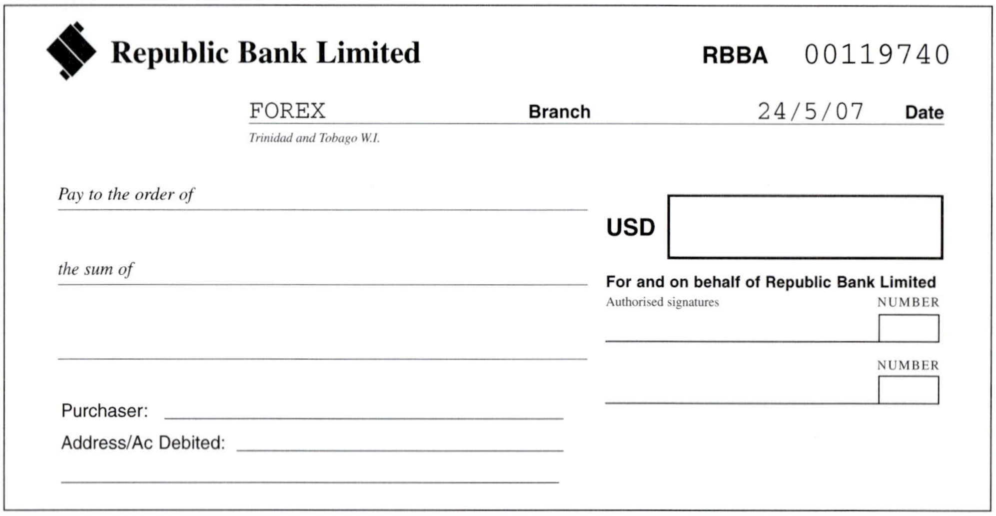

Republic Bank Limited RBBA 00119740
FOREX Branch 24/5/07 Date
Trinidad and Tobago W.I.

Pay to the order of _____

the sum of _____ USD [   ]

For and on behalf of Republic Bank Limited
Authorised signatures NUMBER

NUMBER

Purchaser: _____
Address/Ac Debited: _____

Fig. 10.1 *Example of a bank draft*

In Chapter 9 you learnt about several other instruments of payment used particularly in foreign trade, for example the *bill of exchange*, *documentary bill*, *documentary credit*, and the *letter of credit*. If you do not recall the purpose of each of these, now would be a good time to look at them again to refresh your memory.

10.2 Bank accounts

Deposit accounts

This type of account is used by individuals, businesses and associations wishing to keep in a safe place money not required for immediate use. With a deposit account:

- credit slips are used to pay money into the account
- withdrawal slips are used to take money out of the account.

No cheques are issued with this type of account, and therefore any transfer of money to another person can only be done by the use of cash.

The bank may require seven or more days' notice for the withdrawal of money from a deposit account, because they lend the money to others. Where small amounts are concerned this rule may not apply.

As a reward for lending their money to the banks, depositors are paid *interest*, which is calculated as a percentage of the money in the account.

The depositor cannot draw out of his or her deposit account more money than he or she has in the account.

The banks lend the money deposited with them to borrowers, and charge them interest. This is one of the main ways in which banks earn money.

KEY WORDS

Find out the business-related meaning of each of the following terms. Write a separate sentence for each term to show your understanding.

creditor   interest
deposit account
legal tender
joint account
bank draft
credit worthiness
current account
near cash

Current accounts

The bank current account makes the transfer of money from one person to another very simple. You can open a current account by paying in a nominal amount at a bank. You will be issued with the following.

- A *credit* or *paying-in book* to pay money into your account.
- A *cheque book* to enable you to transfer money from your account to someone else.

The current account (also called the cheque book account or checking account) is meant to provide a place for keeping money that needs to be available for immediate use.

The bank will send you a statement of account (also called a bank statement) from time to time to tell you how much you have paid out, how much you have put into the account, what charges the bank has deducted from your account, and what is the balance in your account.

Banks have sometimes experimented with paying interest on money left in the current account. When interest is paid, it is usually at a lower rate than the interest on a deposit account.

By agreement with the bank it is possible to overdraw on a current account, that is, to draw out more money than you have in the account. Interest is charged to the customer on the overdrawn balance.

A joint account may be shared by two or more persons. In the case of a joint account (a 'business account' is similar), the account holders can make a variety of arrangements for signing of cheques. For example, cheques can be signed by any one, or any two of a number of authorised signatories.

Cheques

A cheque is a written instruction to the bank (the drawee) to pay money to the account holder (the drawer) or to another person (the payee). Most cheques are order cheques, which means they must be signed (endorsed) on the reverse by the named payee if he or she wishes to pass them on to someone else. So the three parties to a cheque are the drawee, the drawer and the payee.

There are five entries written on a cheque by the drawer:

1. the date on which the cheque is written
2. the name of the payee
3. the amount to be paid, in words
4. the amount to be paid, in figures
5. the signature of the drawer.

Written entries on a cheque should be made in such a way that they cannot easily be altered. For this reason they should not be written in pencil or with a pen whose ink can be easily erased. Care should be taken to avoid leaving spaces where someone could write in something extra.

If a mistake is made when writing a cheque, the error should be neatly crossed through, and the correct entry written in and signed by the drawer to show that it is his/her alteration and not a forgery.

Cheques may be open or crossed.

Principles of Business – Profile 1

Open cheque

An open cheque does not have two parallel lines drawn across it. It is 'uncrossed'. The payee can do three things with the cheque:

- pay the cheque into his or her own bank
- exchange it for cash at the bank on which it was drawn
- pass it to someone else by signing the back of the cheque (endorsing it).

Although an open cheque can be useful, it does have drawbacks because if the cheque were to fall into the hands of someone dishonest they would also be able to cash it at the bank on which it is drawn. For this reason, banks prefer their customers to use crossed cheques.

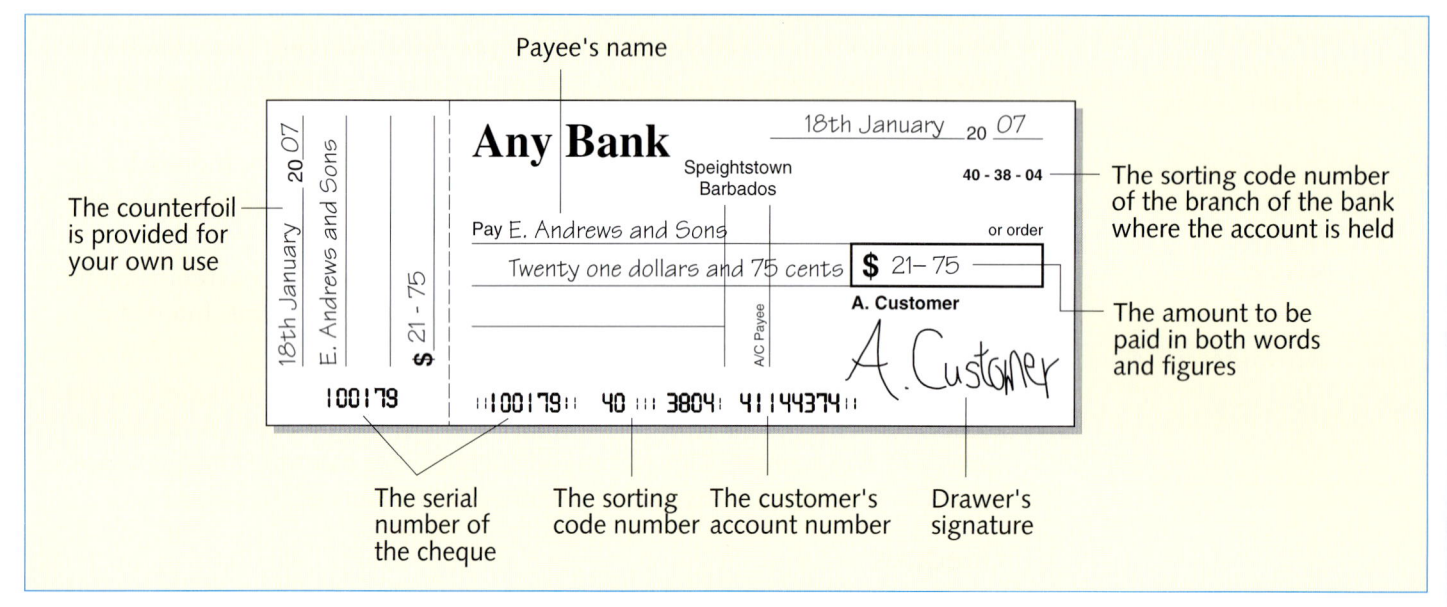

Fig. 10.2 *A cheque*

An image of a cheque is shown with the following labels:
- Payee's name
- The counterfoil is provided for your own use
- The serial number of the cheque
- The sorting code number
- The customer's account number
- Drawer's signature
- The sorting code number of the branch of the bank where the account is held
- The amount to be paid in both words and figures

Cheque details:
- Any Bank, Speightstown, Barbados
- 18th January 20 07
- 40 - 38 - 04
- Pay E. Andrews and Sons or order
- Twenty one dollars and 75 cents $ 21- 75
- A. Customer
- Signed: A. Customer
- 100179   ⑈100179⑈ 40 ⑈ 3804⑈ 41⑈44374⑈

Crossed cheques

Crossed cheques are safer than open cheques because they must be put through a bank account. In other words they cannot be exchanged for cash, unless the drawer is obtaining cash for himself or herself as will be explained later.

Open cheques can be crossed by drawing two parallel lines vertically across them, but banks provide cheques with the crossing already printed.

The crossing on a cheque is called a **general crossing** if nothing is written between the lines. But wording can be written between the lines of the crossing to make it a **special crossing**.

Post-dated cheques

An occasion could arise when you need to give someone a cheque that is dated some time in the future, and this is called **post dating** the cheque. The bank will not pass the cheque for payment until the date you have written on the cheque arrives.

Chapter 10 – **Instruments of payment**

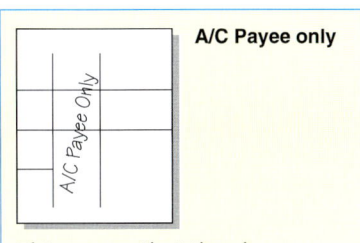

A/C Payee only

This means that the cheque can only be paid into the account of the payee, but he can pay it into his account via any bank he wishes.

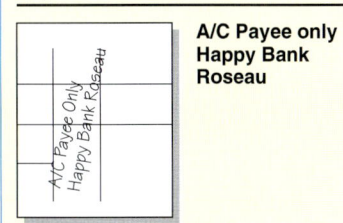

**A/C Payee only
Happy Bank
Roseau**

This means the same as the above, but further instructs that the cheque can only be paid in at a certain bank.

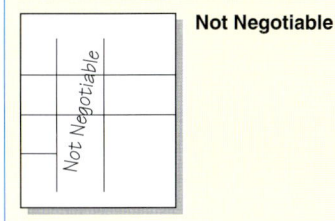

Not Negotiable

The crossing 'not negotiable' acts as a protection against loss or theft and is a warning to anyone receiving such a cheque that they should be careful when accepting it. The reason for the warning is that if someone accepts a cheque crossed 'Not Negotiable' and it has been stolen, then the person accepting it is liable to refund the rightful owner with the amount shown on the cheque.

Fig. 10.3 *Special cheque crossings*

Dishonoured cheques

Cheques which are not passed for payment by the drawer's bank are said to have been dishonoured or to have 'bounced'. The drawee bank will write 'Refer to Drawer' or R/D on the cheque and send it to the collecting bank, who will in turn send it back to their customer (the payee). It is then the payee's responsibility to find out from the drawer why the cheque has not been honoured.

Refer to figure 16.1 in Chapter 16 for how banks clear cheques for payment.

Reasons a cheque might 'bounce'

- The drawer may not have enough money in their account to cover the amount on the cheque.
- The cheque may be incorrectly completed, e.g. unsigned, or the figures and words differ.
- The cheque may be out of date ('stale'). The life of a cheque is six months.
- The signature of the drawer may differ from the example held by the bank.
- The cheque may have been altered and the alteration not signed.
- The cheque is post-dated.
- The cheque has been 'stopped' by the drawer, that is, the drawer has instructed the bank not to make the payment.

Cheque guarantee card

Cheque cards are issued by banks to trusted customers. The branch bank which has issued a cheque card to a customer undertakes to pay cheques supported by the card up to an amount which is displayed on the card.

The cheque card is mainly used to obtain cash from a bank other than that at which the customer's account is held, or to support a cheque offered to a trader in payment for goods or services. Having issued a cheque and used the cheque guarantee card it is not possible to stop payment of the cheque.

The bank statement

At regular intervals, or on request, the bank will send to a customer a bank statement which provides a record of all transactions that have taken place between the customer's account and the bank.

Amounts which reduce the balance in the account are shown in the payments column, and amounts which increase the balance are shown in the receipts column. As each payment or receipt is recorded a new balance figure is shown in a third column.

KEY WORDS

Find out the business-related meaning of each of the following terms. Write a separate sentence for each term to show your understanding.

crossed cheque   drawer   payee   cheque   drawee   order cheque

post dated   dishonoured cheque   open cheque   bank statement

Principles of Business – Profile 1

```
SPECIMEN ONLY issued by Bank Education Service

TITLE OF ACCOUNT   T. D. ILETT                    IN ACCOUNT WITH
                                                  BANK OF EDUCATION
                                                  HOMETOWN
ACCOUNT NUMBER   8793132                          STATEMENT NUMBER   3
```

DATE	PARTICULARS		PAYMENTS	RECEIPTS	BALANCE
	Balance Forward				250.55
21 May		99681	123.72		126.83
		99682	53.80		73.03
27 May		BGC		512.32	585.35
1 June	Trusty Ins.	DD	15.00		570.35
3 June	Newtown Bld. Soc.	DD	202.00		368.35
5 June		99683	14.98		353.37
8 June		99684	123.42		229.95
15 June		99685	31.25		198.70
16 June	Sundry Credit			25.38	224.08
18 June	S.A.Y.E.	SO	35.00		189.08

ABBREVIATIONS

BGC Bank Giro Credit   DIV Dividend   O/D or DR Overdrawn Balance
DD   Direct Debit   CHS Charges   SO   Standing Order
CD   Cash Dispenser   ADV Separately Advised   TFR   Inter-Account Transfer

Fig. 10.4 *A bank statement*

10.3 Electronic banking

There are a variety of services that banks provide that make it possible to transfer funds electronically from one account to another without the use of cheques.

The ones most frequently used are: standing order, direct debit, credit transfer and electronic funds transfer.

Standing order

Imagine that a business has purchased a piece of machinery on credit (i.e. paying for it by monthly instalments). This could mean that every month a member of the firm will have to remember to:

➤ write out a cheque
➤ produce a covering letter of explanation
➤ address an envelope and post it.

This obviously takes time and it is inconvenient. But more importantly, there is the danger that the payment may be forgotten. This can be damaging to the reputation of the company owing the money (the debtor). The commercial banks help businesses to avoid this problem by offering the **standing order** (SO) service.

The customer fills out a standing order form which instructs the bank to make regular payments on their behalf on a specific date of each month (or some other regular period of time), until further notice in writing is given. The bank will then make regular payments on behalf of their customer and will ensure that the payments arrive on time.

The standing order service is available to both business and private current account holders, but it can only be used if the regular amount to be paid does not vary. Where the amount to be paid varies a different service has to be used.

Direct debit

This is a variation of the standing order service. Instead of customers instructing the bank (the drawee) to make regular payments on their behalf, they complete and sign a form which gives permission for someone else (the

STANDING ORDER MANDATE

To: Any Bank

Address: High Street, Nassau, New Providence Island

Please Pay

Bank	Branch Title (not address)	Code Number
Other Bank	Hamilton	01-22-03

for the credit of

Beneficiary	Account Number
Highlife Finance Co. Ltd	3 2 3 1 1 1 5 6

the sum of

Amount in figures	Amount in words
$25.37	Twenty five dollars and 37 cents

commencing

Date and amount of 1st payment		and thereafter every	Date and frequency
1 May 2007 *now	$25.37		1st Monthly

*until

Date and amount of last payment	
1 April 2014	$25.37

quoting the reference: HP 2238   and debit my/our account accordingly

*This instruction cancels any previous order in favour of the beneficiary named above, under this reference
If the amount of the periodic payments vary they should be incorporated in a schedule overleaf

Special instructions: None

Signature(s): A. Moment   Date: 10/4/2007

Title and number of account to be debited: A. Moment   0 1 2 3 7 3 5 4

Fig. 10.5 *A standing order instructs a bank to make regular payments on the customer's behalf*

payee) to withdraw amounts from their account at regular intervals. The amount withdrawn can be varied by the payee and the variations notified to the account holder (the drawer) at some later time.

This service is suitable for repayments of credit where the repayment amount varies. For example, with some forms of credit the repayment amount will change as the interest rate changes. Under these circumstances the standing order system would not be suitable but the direct debit method is.

Both the standing order and the direct debit systems have dual benefits for businesses. They not only make it easier for the business to make regular payments, but also help the business to receive payments from its customers.

Credit transfer

This is a means of transferring money from one bank to another without the use of cheques. There are two basic methods of credit transfer that are generally used, the single transfer and the multiple transfer.

Single transfer method

A form is filled out with the details of the person to whom the payment is to be made and their bank. The bank where the money is paid in (or where the drawer's account is held) will then transfer the payment to the bank where the account to be credited is held.

Multiple transfer method

Using this method, a bank customer writes out a single cheque, or gives the bank permission to withdraw a single amount from his or her account, and then use this to make several payments. For example, a private individual might want to pay several bills, or a firm may want to pay the wages of each of its employees.

A list or schedule is passed to the bank by the account holder showing details of a number of different accounts to be credited by direct transfer. The bank uses the drawer's cheque made out in favour of the bank or withdraws the total amount from the account. The bank then credits each of the accounts listed in the schedule, thus saving the account holder the necessity of writing out many cheques.

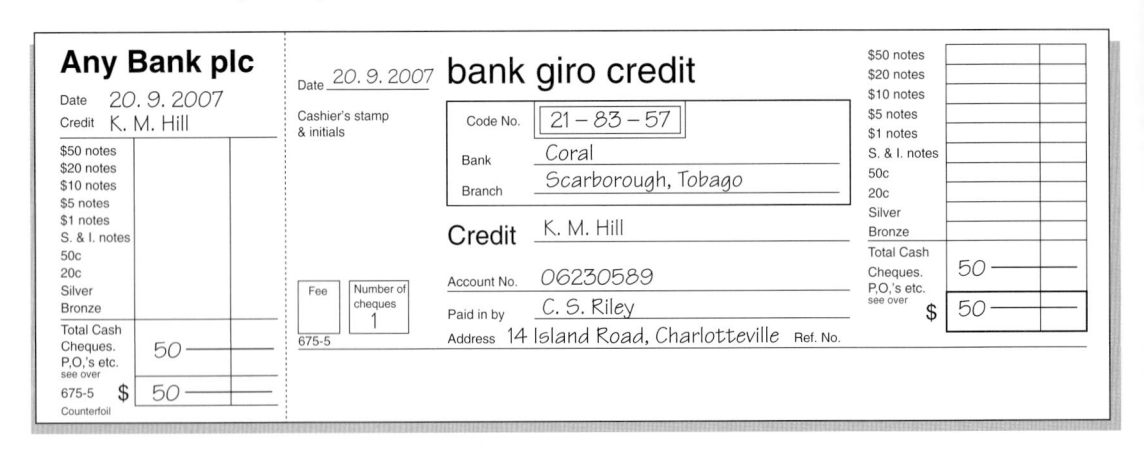

Fig. 10.6 *The credit transfer system saves the inconvenience of sending a cheque and a covering letter*

Electronic funds transfer

An important recent banking development is the movement towards an electronic payment system. This is known as **EFT (Electronic Funds Transfer)** and **EPOS (Electronic Point of Sale)**. These are computer-controlled payment systems, and represent a special form of co-operation between retailers and banks.

While a checkout till operator in a shop is totalling up the customer's purchases using a computer (EPOS), the customer inserts a bank card into a machine linked to his or her bank, building society or credit card company. The customer then keys in his or her **PIN (Personal Indentification Number)** and this is verified by the bank's computer. The computer authorises the payment immediately (by EFT) and debits the customer's account, assuming sufficient funds are available. The transaction may be rejected if sufficient funds are not available.

Tele-banking and Internet banking

Tele-banking refers to the modern method of managing a bank account over the telephone. It makes it possible to make payments and transfer money from one account to another whilst talking to the bank employee over the phone. For example, it is now possible to set up standing orders and direct debit accounts entirely over the phone. Details of bank balances and other information can also be accessed in this way. **Internet banking** allows similar arrangements, but with this system the account holder carries out the processes directly, without talking to anyone. In both cases there are stringent security devices (e.g. passwords, PIN and codes) to safeguard the account holder. (See also Chapter 16.)

With the explosion of **e-commerce**, whereby **on-line retailing** allows customers to view and buy products and services through **Internet sites**, the foregoing methods of banking have become increasingly popular. (See also Chapter 16.)

10.4 Bank cards

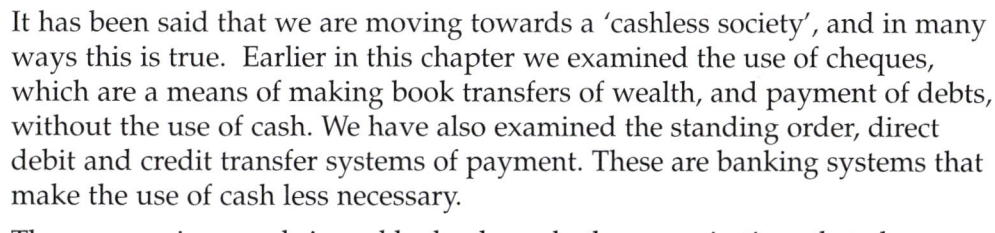

It has been said that we are moving towards a 'cashless society', and in many ways this is true. Earlier in this chapter we examined the use of cheques, which are a means of making book transfers of wealth, and payment of debts, without the use of cash. We have also examined the standing order, direct debit and credit transfer systems of payment. These are banking systems that make the use of cash less necessary.

There are various cards issued by banks and other organisations that also reduce the need to use cash. You should bear in mind that although we are going to be concerned with bank cards here, there are card systems in existence outside banking. For example, there are retailers' charge cards, telephone credit cards and others that are discussed elsewhere in this book. Together they all contribute to the view that we are developing a cashless society.

Credit card

This card enables the holder to buy goods or services from a trader without using cash or a cheque.

The purchaser presents the card and signs a voucher when making the

Fig. 10.7 *Using a cash dispenser*

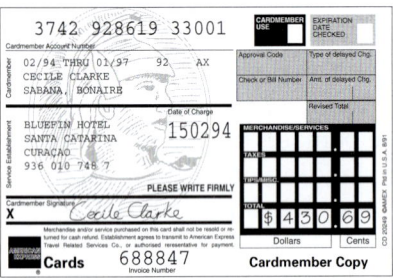

Principles of Business – Profile 1

purchase. Increasingly, the signing of a voucher is disappearing, and instead the cardholder keys their PIN into a device at the pay point. The trader claims the money from the issuers of the credit card and has the money credited to his or her account.

Eventually the holder of the credit card will receive an account from the issuers which he or she can settle by one payment, or alternatively pay monthly interest on any outstanding balance.

A bank customer might use a credit card to make many purchases in a month, and then settle the total debt by writing out one cheque or credit transfer, thus reducing both the number of entries on his or her account and his or her bank charges.

There are companies that specialise in credit cards, such as Access, American Express and Diners Club. Local banks also have their own credit card services.

Cash card

These cards are issued to account holders by the bank (and other financial institutions) to allow the holder to draw money out of an automatic teller machine (ATM). Although you may not consider these as 'instruments of payment', they do enable banks to make payments to their customers, and allow account holders to access their money when the bank is closed.

The card holder is given a PIN for use with the card. Keying in this number on the key pad at the cash dispenser gives the card holder access to his or her account; therefore it is important to keep the PIN a secret. It is best to memorise the number rather than write it down where it might be seen by others.

To operate the cash dispenser, the card holder inserts the card into the machine. The card shows the holder's account number, and this can be 'read' by the machine and relayed to the bank computer. When the customer keys in his or her PIN, the bank computer checks that it is correct for the account to which the card corresponds. If the entered PIN is correct, then the dispenser will issue the money requested (up to a daily individual limit). The customer's account is immediately automatically debited with the amount withdrawn. The machine will also provide information such as the current account balance.

Debit card

A debit card is issued by banks to their account holders. It allows the holder to make purchases at home or abroad and connect directly with their bank account to make instant payment to the trader, without using a cheque or cash. The debit card is inserted into a device at the 'point of sale'. Much like a credit card, the cardholder signs a receipt or keys in their PIN to allow the purchase amount to be deducted from their bank account and transferred to the account of the trader. However, unlike a credit card, this happens immediately. This is excellent for the trader because they have actually received payment before the customer leaves the store, and they do not have to wait for a credit card company to process their payment.

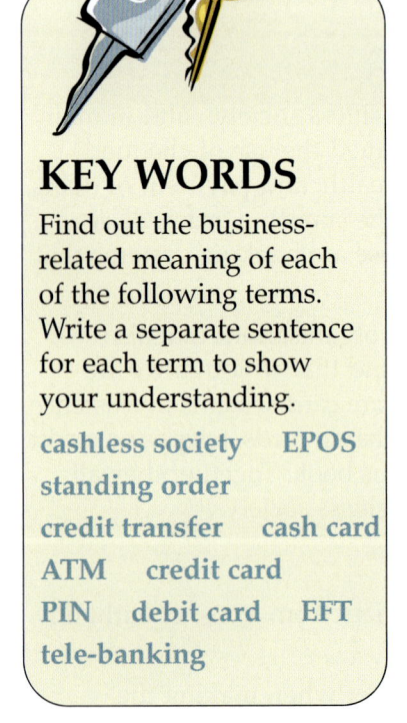

Fig. 10.8 *The credit card is presented and a voucher is signed by the card holder.*

KEY WORDS

Find out the business-related meaning of each of the following terms. Write a separate sentence for each term to show your understanding.

cashless society   EPOS
standing order
credit transfer   cash card
ATM   credit card
PIN   debit card   EFT
tele-banking

142

Chapter 10 – Instruments of payment

10.5 Things to do

This section contains a variety of exercises to help you create revision notes, to test your understanding and to prepare you for examinations.

Search and find

Write out the question and the answer by referring back through the text to form revision notes.

1. What is meant by the term 'legal tender'?
2. What is a money order and under what circumstances might it be used?
3. Why is a bank draft more acceptable than a normal cheque?
4. Briefly explain the difference between a deposit account and a current account.
5. How can tele-banking be said to be an instrument of payment?
6. Why would a business use a deposit account when most of their payments will be made by cheque?
7. Explain who are the drawer, the drawee and the payee of a cheque.
8. Why is the cheque system particularly useful to a business?
9. How does a crossed cheque differ from an open cheque?
10. Describe some of the precautions that one can take to make a cheque safer.
11. What is a dishonoured cheque and why might it have been dishonoured?
12. What is the purpose of a cheque guarantee card?
13. What are the functions of a bank statement?
14. The balance column of a bank statement is sometimes said to show the 'cumulative balance'. Explain this term.
15. Explain the similarities and the differences between the standing order and direct debit services.
16. Describe both the single and the multiple transfer system of credit transfer, including examples of when each would be used in preference to the other.
17. Why is it sometimes said we are moving towards a 'cashless society'?
18. Describe the process of using a credit card and say how the use of the card helps to promote trade.
19. What is the function of a cash card? How can this be said to be 'an instrument of payment'? What protection is there against fraud?
20. In what ways does the debit card system help both the trader and their customer?
21. Explain the terms EFT and EPOS.

Principles of Business – Profile 1

What do you know?

Write out the complete sentence and insert the missing word, which can be chosen from the list at the end of the test.

1. A ..... can be used for the safekeeping of money not required for immediate use.
2. The ..... account makes transferring money from one person to another very simple.
3. By agreement with the bank, it is possible to be ..... on a current account.
4. A ..... is a written instruction to a bank telling them to do something with the account holder's money.
5. A crossed cheque is ..... than an open cheque.
6. A cheque that has been ..... is said to have 'bounced'.
7. The standing order service is useful when the ..... amount is to be paid on each instalment.
8. The direct debit service is useful if the amount of a credit repayment .....
9. Credit transfer is a system for transferring money ..... from one account to another.
10. The ..... credit transfer can be used by a firm to pay the wages of many employees.

Choose the missing word from the following:

multiple   deposit   same   safer   varies   current   cheque
directly   dishonoured   overdrawn

Structured questions

Q1 Refer to the bank statement in figure 10.5 and answer the following related questions.

(a) Name the account holder. — 1
(b) What is the purpose of this document? — 2
(c) How much was brought forward from the previous statement, and how much will be taken forward to the next statement? — 2
(d) Why is it important for customers to receive bank statements regularly? — 2
(e) Explain the meaning of the following abbreviations shown on this statement: BGC, DD, SO. — 3
(f) Since this statement was issued, T. Ilett has written three cheques, for $133.66, $12.50, $7.80. In addition an inpayment has been made of $389.23. 'Reconcile' the bank statement to find out the present balance at the bank. — 4
(g) Give a clear explanation of the purpose of the payments, receipts and balance columns. — 6

Q2 Look at the cheque in figure 10.10.

(a) There are two reasons, other than the date, why the bank will refuse to pass this cheque for payment. What are these reasons? — 2
(b) The bank will write R/D on this cheque and return it to the payee. What do the letters R/D stand for, and what must the payee do when the cheque is given back to her? — 3
(c) Name the following parties to this cheque: the drawer, the payee, the drawee. — 3

Chapter 10 – Instruments of payment

d) The cheque below has a 'general' crossing. What is the effect of this? Describe and explain two other forms of cheque crossing. **6**

e) Why do banks offer more than one type of account to their customers? **6**

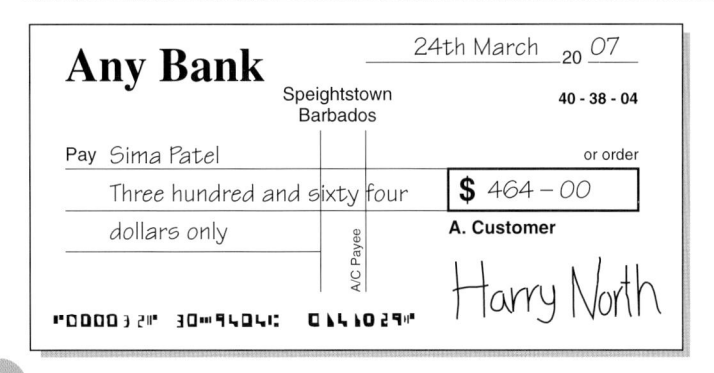

```
Any Bank                    24th March  20 07
        Speightstown                    40 - 38 - 04
        Barbados
Pay  Sima Patel                              or order
     Three hundred and sixty four   $ 464 – 00
     dollars only                   A. Customer
                                    Harry North
```

Fig. 10.9 *A refused cheque*

Q3

(a) What main advantage does a crossed cheque have over an open cheque? **2**

(b) If the named payee of a cheque wants to pass the cheque to someone else, what must they do? Why might someone want to do this? **3**

(c) Briefly state four reasons why cheques are sometimes dishonoured. **4**

(d) List the five entries that the account holder must write on a cheque. **5**

(e) Explain the importance of a bank current account to a trader, giving specific examples to illustrate your answer. **6**

Q4
Refer to the standing order mandate in figure 10.10 and answer the following questions related to it.

(a) What is the name of the person who has initiated this order, and who benefits from it? **2**

(b) Name the bank of (i) the drawer (ii) the payee. **2**

(c) Why do you think that the amount to be paid is written in both words and figures? **2**

(d) How many months is this order intended to operate for, and for how many payments in total? **4**

(e) This order refers to hire purchase repayments. What will be the total amount paid at the end of the order period? **4**

(f) Explain clearly the advantages that the standing order service has for both the individual initiating it and also for the beneficiary of it. **6**

Q5
The statement of account in figure 10.12 refers to the use of an Any Bank credit card by the account holder.

(a) Who is the holder of the Any Bank credit card to which this statement refers and what is their account number? **2**

(b) Why do you think that the use of a credit card is generally restricted to persons over the age of 18? **3**

(c) What is meant by the entry 'previous balance $165.27'? **3**

Principles of Business – Profile 1

    (d) Explain each of the following terms shown on this account:
        (i) new balance   2
        (ii) credit limit   2
        (iii) minimum payment.   2

    (e) Clearly explain the difference in function of a credit card when compared with a cheque card.   6

STANDING ORDER MANDATE

To: Any Bank PLC

Address: Enterprise, Barbados

Please Pay

Bank	Branch Title (not address)	Code Number
Other Bank	Westmoreland, Barbados	01-66-77

for the credit of

Beneficiary	Account Number
Goodtime Co. Ltd	6 6 6 7 7 4 2 1

the sum of

Amount in figures	Amount in words
$60.77	Sixty dollars seventy seven cents

commencing

Date and amount of 1st payment		and thereafter every	Date and frequency
6 May 2007 / *now	$60.77		6th Monthly

*until

Date and amount of last payment	
6 May 2024	$60.77

quoting the reference

HP	6600	and debit my/our account accordingly

*This instruction cancels any previous order in favour of the beneficiary named above, under this reference
If the amount of the periodic payments vary they should be incorporated in a schedule overleaf

Special instructions: None

Signature(s): Constance Credit   Date: 10/4/2007

Title and number of account to be debited: C. Credit   0 1 2 3 4 3 2 1

*Delete if not applicable

Fig. 10.10 *Standing order mandate*

Chapter 10 – **Instruments of payment**

Any Bank Credit

Any Bank PLC (Plastics Department)
Westwood House
Manzanilla
Trinidad

PO13269

Enquiries: Trinidad 7634
To report card lost/stolen 7635

STATEMENT OF ACCOUNT

Please quote your account number
5334 003062545318
in all correspondence

MR MICHAEL DAVIS
6 FERNANDO ROAD
SANGRE GRANDE
TRINIDAD

Statement Date
14/02/07

12345
A minus sign indicates a credit

Date	Reference Number	Description	Previous Balance
			165.27
17/01/07	HDY5XG	GOODBUY, GUANAPO	41.83
18/01/07	HDY6LJ	HERON SERVICE STATION, MANZANILLA	15.83
25/01/07	HDV623	BEST ELECTRICS, SANGRE GRANDE	27.99
01/02/07	HEP32X	PAYMENT THANKYOU	65.27−
05/02/07	HFNP37	HAPPY INN, CUMUTO	25.86
11/02/07	JKP83L	GOODBUY, GUANAPO	19.98
13/02/07	JL3SP9	HERON CAR REPAIRS, MANZANILLA	61.55
		INTEREST	2.00

New Balance
294.64
Your Credit Limit
$700.00

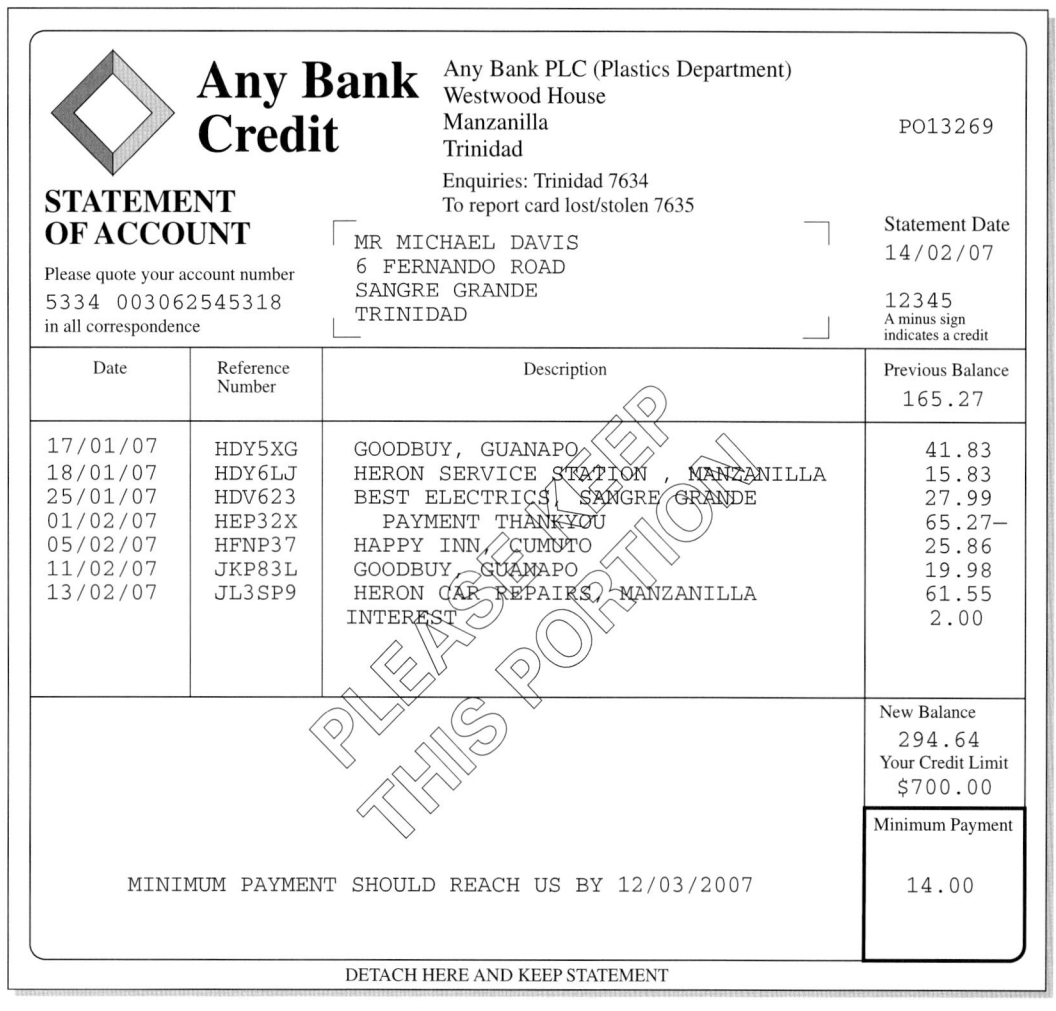

Minimum Payment
14.00

MINIMUM PAYMENT SHOULD REACH US BY 12/03/2007

DETACH HERE AND KEEP STATEMENT

Fig. 10.11 *Credit card statement*

Research assignments

1. Assume the role of one of the commercial banks in your locality. Explain to the owner of a local shop the advantages of having both a current account and a deposit account at your branch, using bank leaflets to support your claims. What other banking facilities do you feel would benefit the shop owner?

2. Carry out a survey of services, other than bank accounts, that are provided by banks to assist the entrepreneur. Describe the services you have researched within a report, including relevant literature you have collected.

3. What evidence can you find that banks assist local businesses, and how might the bank be influenced by the local economy?

4. To what extent would you consider that we have a 'cashless society' today? In what ways does this benefit business in particular? Support your views with data you have personally researched.

5. 'The services offered by commercial banks are essential to the efficient operation of both industry and commerce.' Discuss this statement from a basis of personally researched data.

6. What evidence can you present that proves that tele-banking and internet banking are expanding in both business and personal use?

Insurance

11.1 The insurance industry

The Superintendent of Insurance – Jamaica

The office of the Superintendent of Insurance was established by the Insurance Act of 1971 and pertinent regulations of 1972. Through these the Superintendent of Insurance is given the power to:

1. supervise the operations of the insurance industry
2. make decisions about the continuation or discontinuation of an insurance enterprise based on its operations as revealed in its annual report.

The aim is to protect consumers of insurance, who, prior to 1971, experienced difficulties as a result of the unscrupulous operations of some insurance businesses.

Insurance laws established prior to 1971 were included in the Companies Act and the Motor Vehicle Insurance (Third Party Risks) Act, which assisted in regulating some aspects of the insurance industry. These legal provisions were inadequate, and left insurance companies to operate largely as they wished, sometimes to the detriment of the consumer. Hence the regulatory laws and the accompanying government office were set up to ensure that procedures in the insurance industry are kept under surveillance.

Each Caribbean island has a regulatory authority with similar aims and objectives.

Insurance companies belong to various associations:

- Life Underwriters Association of Jamaica (LUAJ)
- Life Insurance Companies Association (LICA)
- Jamaica Insurance Advisory Council (JIAC)
- Brokers Association and General Agents Association.

Jamaican companies such as

- Life of Jamaica
- Mutual Life
- Insurance Company of the West Indies (ICWI)

have established offices in other Caribbean islands. Similarly, other Caribbean islands such as Trinidad and Tobago have established insurance businesses in neighbouring territories:

- Guyana and Trinidad Mutual Fire Insurance Co. Ltd.
- The Barbados Mutual Life Assurance Society.

11.2 The purpose of insurance

All individuals and organisations face a wide variety of risks, but only some of them actually suffer a loss during the course of a year. Insurance provides a system of providing compensation to those who suffer a loss.

Chapter 11 – **Insurance**

Simply put, insurance is an agreement between an insurance company (**the insurer**) and someone who wants financial protection (**the insured** – the proposer) that compensation (indemnity) will be paid if a particular loss occurs. Insurance companies are businesses, and therefore they charge for their services. The charge they make is called a **premium** and the contract drawn up between the insurer and the insured is known as the **policy**.

The purpose of insurance is to uphold the principle of indemnity, that is, to put someone who has suffered a loss back into the position they would have been in had the loss not been suffered.

Insurance companies are able to **compensate** people and organisations in this way in return for a relatively small charge. This is because insurance 'pools risks'.

Insurance is vital not only to individuals, but to all forms of business and the economy as a whole. If as individuals we had to face all the risks of life ourselves there are many things that we would not do, and at times we would even hesitate about leaving the safety of our homes. Similarly, many businesses would not be formed if individual entrepreneurs and their backers had to face all the risks of enterprise themselves. Insurance relieves individuals and business people from some of the risk they face. In this way it can be seen that insurance helps to promote trade.

Many businesses at risk contribute money to a pool

When one of the businesses suffers a loss

The insurance company will help with finance for repairs

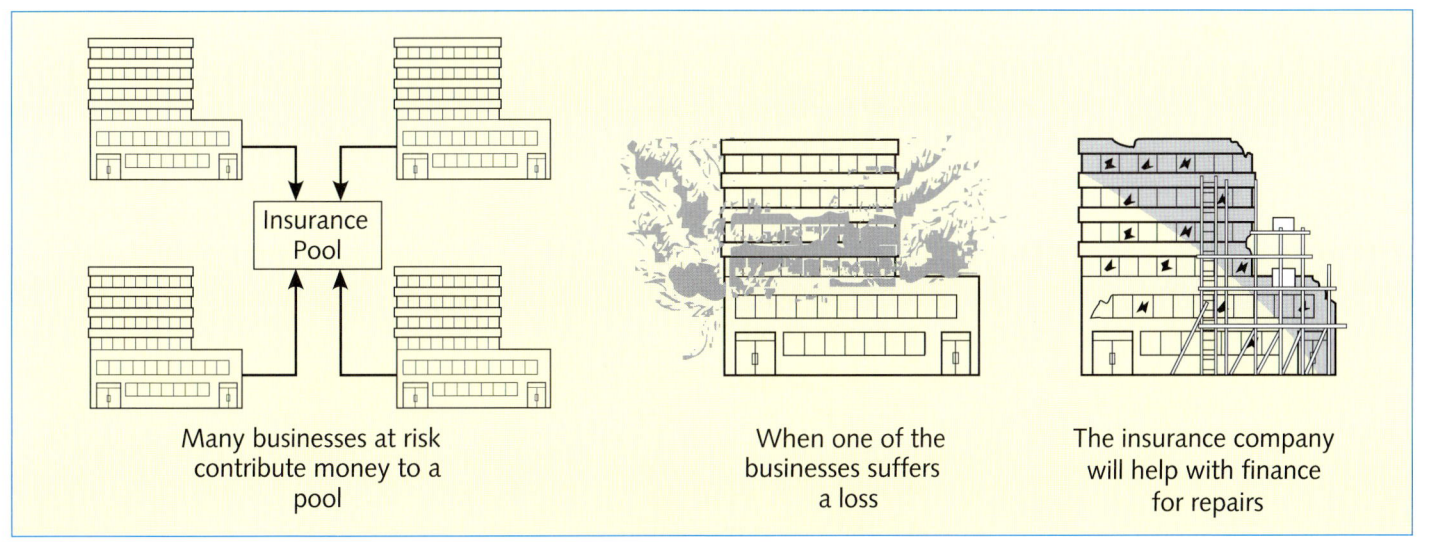

Fig. 11.1 *Pooling risks*

Pooling of risks

To offset the possible effect of a loss, all those at risk can contribute a relatively small sum of money (called a premium) to a fund ('pool') operated by an insurance company. The many small sums of money people pay in premiums form a large pool of money. When a contributor to the pool suffers a loss there is enough money in the pool to compensate (**'indemnify'**) them.

The result of co-operating with others in this way is that risks are 'spread' or 'shared' between the many people and organisations that have contributed to the insurance pool. For this reason insurance is sometimes said to be the **'pooling of risks'**.

Principles of Business – Profile 1

You cannot insure against wear and tear on equipment and property

You cannot insure that you will do well in exams

Fig. 11.2 *Uninsurable risks*

For example, if a trader owns a shop worth $100,000 and it burns down, it would cause considerable hardship to replace it and it could in fact be impossible to replace it if the owner could not raise the money.

However, if many shop owners agree to pay a regular, relatively small amount of money into a pool, then when one of the shops is burnt down, there will be enough money in the pool to compensate for the loss. What has happened in this example is that the risk has been spread between the many shop owners.

11.3 Uninsurable risks

The success of insurance is dependent upon the ability of insurance companies to meet a loss if it occurs. The companies are able to ensure that they can meet any claims that arise by using statistical analysis.

The people within insurance companies who accept the risks of insurance (**underwriters**) use their records of past claims to calculate the probability of the risk involved occurring.

If it can calculate the probability of an event taking place, an insurance company will be willing to take on the risk involved, and it will be able to calculate how much to charge the customer (the premium). But not all events are insurable. The following are typical examples of uninsurable risks:

- when the loss is inevitable
- where there is insufficient past experience to assess risk
- if the proposer does not have insurable interest
- against fair wear and tear such as rust and corrosion
- that a business will be successful.

KEY WORDS

Find out the business-related meaning of each of the following terms. Write a separate sentence for each term to show your understanding.

risks   underwriter   compensation   insurance   premium   uninsurable risks
pooling risks   policy

11.4 The principles of insurance

Insurance is successful and trusted because the parties to insurance honour four basic principles. They are the principles of:

➤ insurable interest ➤ indemnity
➤ utmost good faith ➤ proximate cause.

Insurable interest

With the exception of life assurance (where a husband and wife can insure the life of each other) it is not possible to insure against a risk unless you have an 'insurable interest'. In other words, the insured must be the one that would suffer financially if an event occurred. You can insure the house or car you own, but you cannot insure the car or house of your neighbour. If your neighbour's house burns down you have lost nothing (unless you have some property there, in which case you would have insurable interest).

Utmost good faith

This aspect of insurance means that the parties to an insurance contract must be truthful in the declaration they make. Obviously, this ruling affects the proposer more than it does the insurer, because it is the proposer (the insured person) who provides the information upon which the insurer decides the premium and issues a policy.

Indemnity

This is the insurance principle by which a policy-holder is compensated for the loss incurred. There are several important aspects to this principle.

- *No profiteering.* Although we take out insurance to receive some money in compensation should we experience a loss, we are not supposed to make a profit from our claim for compensation. The idea is that the insurance policy should indemnify the insured, in other words return him or her to the financial position before the event took place.
- *Overinsurance.* If the insured overinsures an item (more than its true value), in the event of a loss he or she will only be compensated for the true value.
- *Underinsurance.* If a loss occurs where the item is underinsured, the policy-holder will only receive a proportion of the loss.

    e.g. Shop value $100,000
         Insurance for $ 80,000
         Damage by fire $ 20,000 (i.e. one-fifth)
         Compensation (one-fifth) $ 16,000

- *Contribution.* It would be easy for a situation to arise in which a claim could occur where two insurance companies are liable to indemnify the insured for the same event, for example, where two policies overlap. In such a case, both insurance companies will contribute towards payment of the claim.

The proportion that each insurance company pays will depend upon the amount of insurance placed with each company in relation to the cover. For example, if a building valued at $160,000 (insured with A for $100,000 and with B for $60,000) is burnt down, A will pay 10/16ths and B 6/16ths of the loss.

Two companies each cover part of insurance of a building

Company A cover $100,000 → Premium → $1000
Company B cover $60,000 → Premium → $600

A fire damages the building. Total rebuild required

Company A Compensation $100,000
Company B Compensation $60,000

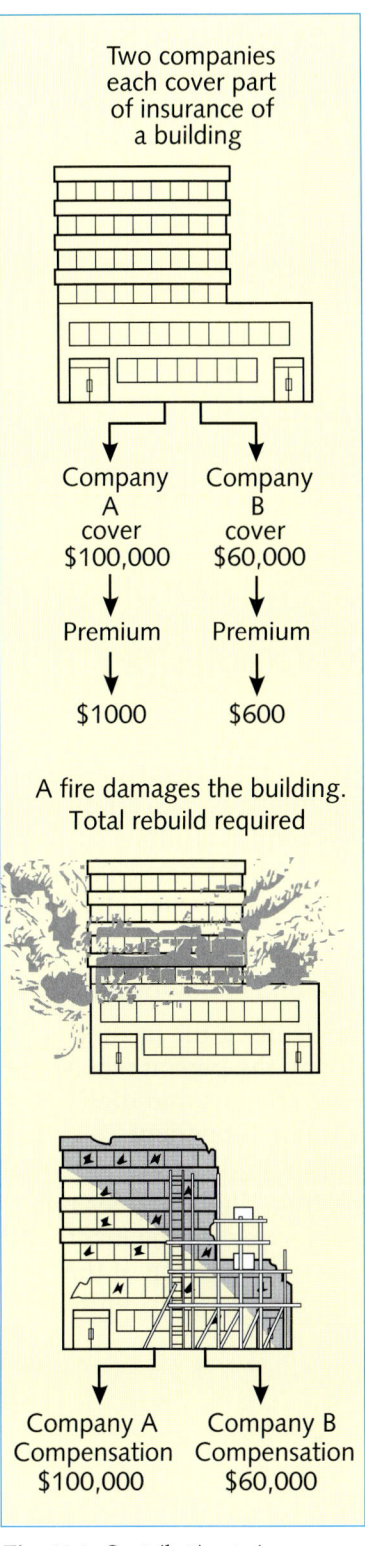

Fig. 11.3 *Contribution to insurance*

Principles of Business – Profile 1

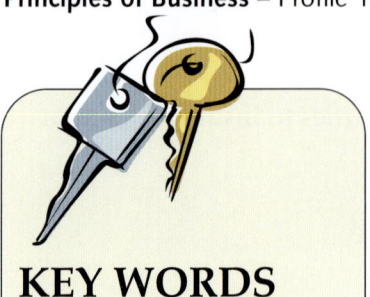

KEY WORDS

Find out the business-related meaning of each of the following terms. Write a separate sentence for each term to show your understanding.

subrogation   indemnity
under-insurance
insurable interest
proximate cause
utmost good faith
over-insurance
contribution

- *Subrogation.* To subrogate means 'to take the place of'. When an insurance company pays out compensation on a claim, the money they pay out takes the place of the article damaged. For instance, if my car is 'written off' (too badly damaged to be repaired), the insurance company will indemnify me for the value of the car. The money they pay me takes the place of the car and the damaged vehicle now becomes the property of the insurance company, who will sell it and retain the scrap value.
- *Proximate cause.* When an insurance policy covers a particular risk, it is quite possible that damage may be incurred which is not directly related to the terms of the policy, but which still may be indemnified by the insurance company. For example, your house may be covered by fire insurance and, of course, the insurance company would be expected to pay out compensation as a result of a fire; but they will also pay for damage to doors caused by the firemen having to break into the house to fight the fire. However, such a claim will only be allowed if the loss incurred is closely related to the original event. For example, if your car is damaged in an accident and you leave it unattended for a long period of time the insurance company would be expected to pay for repairs to the car, but would not necessarily be expected to pay for a travel rug stolen from the back seat.

11.5 Types of insurance

There are four broad types of insurance: life, marine, fire and accident.

Life assurance

This type of cover is often referred to as 'assurance' rather than 'insurance'. At one time 'insurance' and 'assurance' had different meanings. Insurance was against a risk which might or might not happen, whilst assurance concerned an event which was inevitable (death or reaching a particular age). Today this difference is less important, but the word 'assurance' is still often used in relation to life policies.

There are two main types of life assurance: whole life and endowment.

- *Whole life policies* provide for a payment after the death of the insured. Premiums are usually paid quarterly or annually by the person whose life is insured or by their spouse. The idea is that when the insured dies, someone will benefit from the policy, e.g. a spouse or dependent.
- *Endowment* policies provide for a payment of a basic sum at a certain age or on the death of the insured, whichever occurs first. This provides not only for the dependents, but also a useful sum of money for the insured if he or she survives the period covered by the policy. A variation of this type of policy is one 'with profits' which, for a higher premium, entitles the insured to a share in the profits of the insurance company.

Marine insurance

This covers loss and damage to ships and their cargoes. Today, aircraft insurance also falls within this category. There are four broad categories of marine insurance.

- *Hull insurance* covers damage to the vessel itself and all its machinery and fixtures.

- *Cargo insurance* covers the cargo the ship is carrying.
- *Freight insurance*: it is customary for an insurance policy to be taken out to cover the possibility that for some reason the shipper does not pay the transport (freight) charges to the shipowner.
- *Shipowner's liability*: the owner of a vessel has to insure himself or herself against a wide variety of events, for example collision with other vessels or a dock, injury to crew members or passengers, and pollution of beaches.

Fire insurance

Fire insurance, as the name suggests, primarily covers fire risks. But many policies combine cover with other risks such as theft, storm, flood and lightning.

This form of insurance can include cover for loss of earnings (e.g. by a business) or for rental of alternative property whilst a building damaged by fire is being repaired.

Fire policies exclude certain special conditions such as fire resulting from earthquake or riots. In addition, items of high value (paintings, jewellery, antiques, etc.) must be insured separately.

Accident insurance

All insurance not contained within the foregoing categories is included under accident insurance. This type of insurance covers a wide range of policies. The following are the main examples:

Motor

Any vehicle taken on public roads is required to have a certain minimum level (third party) of insurance to ensure that drivers can meet their liability for injury to others. The two commonest types of motor insurance are as follows.

- *Third party, fire and theft:* the motorist insures the liability for damage to other people and their property, plus the loss of damage to his or her own car through fire or theft.
- *Comprehensive* policies not only give the above third party, fire and theft cover, but also provide compensation for accidental damage to the vehicle of the insured.

Personal accident and sickness

These are policies which can be taken out against death or disability in special circumstances, for example during holidays, flights, etc.

Liability

This type of policy covers the risk of liability for the injury or death of someone else. There are two main forms.

- *Employer's liability* covers the employer's legal liability for the safety of each employee.
- *Public liability* covers the liability of individuals and businesses for members of the public visiting their premises.

Property

Property insurance covers a wide variety of items from goods in transit or in store to buildings or contents. It applies to both the business person and the private householder.

Credit
This covers against losses resulting from bad debts, for example the failure of customers to pay for goods obtained on credit.

Fidelity
Fidelity insurance is used particularly by businesses to protect against loss by fraud and stealing by employees.

Insurance for business
The types of insurance cover business people might consider taking out would be as follows:

- employer's liability
- public liability
- damage to premises
- stock damage
- theft, burglary
- motor fleet
- bad debts
- product liability
- consequential loss (earnings).

Business interruption
This is sometimes called '**consequential loss**' insurance. It provides insurance covering the loss of earnings of a business following a fire or some other specified damage. Business may have to be suspended for a time, resulting in a loss of earnings for both the owners of the firm and the employees. This insurance cover is available for such losses, and the cover can include loss of wages, rent and the cost of temporary alternative accommodation.

11.6 The insurance contract

Insurance is provided by insurance companies, friendly societies, underwriters and the government (national insurance). Non-government insurance may be taken out through agents working for a particular company or through brokers selling insurance for a number of different companies. Whichever approach is used a similar basic procedure is followed.

The prospectus
If you visit the offices of an insurance company to find out what insurance policies they have to sell, it would take them too long to explain all the different forms of cover they have available. To save time, the insurance companies produce a leaflet, called the prospectus, which explains each type of policy that can be taken out with them.

The proposal
To formulate an agreement between the **insured** (the person buying insurance) and the **insurer** (the person selling insurance), it must be made clear what is being insured, in other words what risk is being covered, and how much the cover is going to cost. The precise details of what is required are given initially by filling out a proposal form.

As its name suggests, the proposal form tells the insurance company what risk the person buying insurance proposes to insure against. In other words it is a suggestion by the insured that he or she would like the insurance company to agree with.

It is essential that the proposer (the one who wants to buy insurance) gives every detail which applies to the risk, and conceals nothing. If what insurers call a 'material fact' is concealed, the policy will be ineffective.

The premium

When the insurance company has received the proposal form from the person wishing to take out insurance, the underwriters of the insurance company will work out how much they will charge to cover the risk being insured. This charge is called the premium, and to put insurance cover into effect, the person buying insurance cover pays the premium.

In calculating the premium for the cover, there are many points to take into consideration, and one of them is obviously the value of the item being insured. Another is the risk: an insurance company might charge 10% for one risk (say the stock of a factory) and 5% for another risk (say the buildings of the factory) to the same customer, because one risk is greater than the other. In such a case the premium on a $20,000 risk at 10% would be $2,000 and the premium on a $100,000 risk at 5% would be $5,000.

The insurance specialist statistician who calculates the premium based on the degree of risk is called an actuary.

The policy

This is a document sent by the insurer to the insured which states what has been agreed between the two parties. It is like a contract agreement. Many people find policies confusing because of the 'small print', which refers to the 'rules', clauses and 'exceptions' to the agreement, but in spite of the confusion it is important that you read this part of the policy and question the person selling the insurance about any point you do not understand. Failure to read policies, or ask for explanations, is the biggest cause of misunderstanding about insurance.

The following documents may also be issued in association with the insurance policy.

- *Certificate of insurance:* for employer's liability and for motor insurance, the law requires evidence that the insurance has been put into effect. A certificate issued by the insurer acts as evidence.
- *Cover note:* this is a temporary document provided whilst the certificate of insurance is being prepared.
- *Endorsement:* this is a notice of an amendment to the policy, usually by the insurer. The endorsement is attached to the policy and from then on becomes a part of the policy.
- *Renewal notice:* this is issued by the insurer prior to the expiry date of the insurance cover, inviting the insured to renew the cover and advising of the renewal premium and the date on which it is due.

The claim

If the risk insured against takes place, the insured completes a claim form and submits this to the insurer for consideration. Loss adjusters are frequently engaged by insurers to ensure that claims are settled fairly from the point of view of both the insured and the insurer.

The insurance company will only compensate the insured if the loss has been truly accidental; for example one cannot expect an insurance company to pay out on a claim for damage to a car through accident if the accident occurred because the vehicle was not kept in good order.

In making a payment against a claim the insurance company will only compensate for the current value of the item which has been lost or damaged.

Principles of Business – Profile 1

For example, if a housewife claims for the replacement of a carpet purchased five years ago and now damaged by fire, she will receive the current replacement price less an amount calculated to represent the five years' use she has had of the carpet. A modern development is 'new for old' policies, which give the claimants the value of the goods as new. These policies do of course cost more in premiums.

KEY WORDS

Find out the business-related meaning of each of the following terms. Write a separate sentence for each term to show your understanding.

consequential loss   claim   insurer   liability   loss adjuster   actuary
prospectus   proposal   insured   renewal   certificate of insurance

11.7 Things to do

This section contains a variety of exercises to help you create revision notes, to test your understanding and to prepare you for examinations.

Search and find

Write out the question and the answer by referring back through the text to form revision notes.

1. What is the purpose of insurance?
2. Explain how insurance encourages business activity.
3. In what way does insurance 'pool risks'?
4. Why are some risks uninsurable? Give four examples.
5. In what way can insurance be said to have a statistical basis?
6. Explain, giving an example, the meaning of 'insurable interest'.
7. Why does the insurance principle 'utmost good faith' affect the insured more than the insurer?
8. Insurance is said to be a contract of indemnity. What does this mean?
9. What do the terms 'contribution' and 'subrogation' mean in relation to insurance?
10. Giving an example, explain the insurance principle of proximate cause.
11. Why is life insurance often referred to as 'assurance'?
12. Name the four broad categories of insurance.
13. In relation to insurance, explain the terms 'whole life', 'endowment' and 'with profits'.
14. The word 'freight' is often used to refer to the cargo a ship is carrying. So, what is the difference between freight insurance and cargo insurance?
15. What sort of special conditions are excluded from fire insurance?
16. Define accident insurance.

Chapter 11 – **Insurance**

17 Briefly explain the differences between third party; third party, fire and theft; and comprehensive motor insurance.

18 Why would the owner of a shop be likely to take out both employer's liability and public liability insurance?

19 Briefly describe four types of insurance not dealt with so far that you feel would be essential to a business. Give reasons for each of your choices.

20 Describe the process of putting an insurance contract into effect, including mention of the documents and any payments involved.

What do you know?

Write out the complete sentence and insert the missing word, which can be chosen from the list at the end of the test.

1. Cover for ships and their cargoes falls under the category of ..... insurance.
2. Insurance that covers against loss of life is sometimes referred to as ..... .
3. Motor vehicle insurance comes under the category of ..... insurance.
4. The purpose of insurance is to provide monetary ..... to someone who has suffered a loss.
5. Those that take out insurance cover contribute money to a ..... .
6. An insurance company will only agree to provide cover if it can ..... the frequency with which an event could occur.
7. You cannot insure against a risk unless you have an insurable ..... .
8. In the event of a loss, the insured will fill out a ..... form.
9. Before they pay out a against a claim the insurance company may send a ..... to verify that the amount claimed is fair.
10. When two insurance companies are liable to indemnify against the same claim they each ..... towards the payment.

Choose the missing words from the following:

interest   contribute   pool   claim   marine   assurance   loss adjuster   accident   predict   compensation

Structured questions

Q1 **Figure 11.5 shows typical questions that are asked when someone is completing a proposal for car insurance.**

(a) Why is the insurance company interested in the age of the proposer for motor insurance? **2**

(b) Explain the relevance of Questions 4 and 5 to the premium that will be charged. **4**

(c) Describe three types of motor insurance cover that it is possible to obtain. **6**

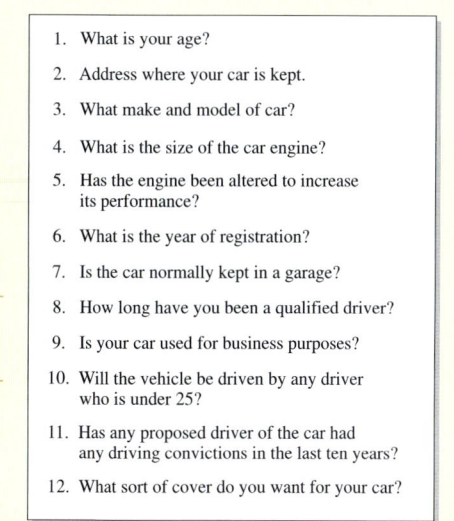

1. What is your age?
2. Address where your car is kept.
3. What make and model of car?
4. What is the size of the car engine?
5. Has the engine been altered to increase its performance?
6. What is the year of registration?
7. Is the car normally kept in a garage?
8. How long have you been a qualified driver?
9. Is your car used for business purposes?
10. Will the vehicle be driven by any driver who is under 25?
11. Has any proposed driver of the car had any driving convictions in the last ten years?
12. What sort of cover do you want for your car?

Fig. 11.5 *Proposal form questionnaire*

Principles of Business – Profile 1

    (d) Take any four questions from the list not considered so far, and explain the purpose of including them on a motor insurance proposal form. Try to choose questions that deal with different factors that influence the amount of premium to be charged. **8**

Q2 Look at the newspaper article in figure 11.6, and answer the questions that follow.

    (a) Give an example of how the insurance principle of 'proximate cause' might apply in relation to the above event. **2**

    (b) Explain the effect on the insured's claim:
        (i) if the building was overinsured
        (ii) if the building was underinsured. **4**

    (c) The manufacturer referred to in the newspaper article was covered by both fire insurance and business interruption insurance. Describe the kind of things the manufacturer might claim for against each of these forms of insurance cover. **6**

    (d) The owner of this business would be required by law to have employers' liability insurance and he may also have public liability insurance. Give a brief description of each of these types of cover. **8**

> **FACTORY BLAZE**
>
> Fire has wiped out the factory of Tower Toys Ltd. on the Barn Mills Industrial Estate just weeks before the Christmas rush. The Chief Fire Officer said that the fire was caused by an electrical fault in a storeroom and quickly spread throughout the factory.
>
> A spokesman for Tower Toys said that extensive damage to buildings, machinery and stock means that production will be suspended for at least two months. No one was hurt in the fire.

Fig. 11.6 *News of a factory fire*

Q3 Look at the article in figure 11.7, taken from the business section of a newspaper, and answer these questions.

> **BUSINESS NEWS**
>
> **THE DANGER OF BEING UNDERINSURED**
>
> In a recent case two workmen employed by a firm were removing a large boiler from a cheese-processing plant. The workmen secured a rope around one of the pillars supporting the factory. As a result the building collapsed causing $500,000 of damage, and the manufacturer had to close down the plant for several weeks.
>
> The company presented a claim to its insurers for the repairs to the plant, and for the cost of loss of business. But the insurers would only meet 80% of the value of the claim because the firm were underinsured. Although the firm took a variety of measures to find the shortfall, they could not make the balance from their resources. And financial institutions were unwilling to lend money to a business that was in fact standing idle.
>
> Within three months the firm was forced into bankruptcy, and what had been a thriving business employing 15 workers ceased to exist.

Fig. 11.7 *Danger of underinsurance*

    (a) What is the purpose of insurance? **2**

    (b) What is meant by underinsurance? **2**

    (c) Why is insurance unable to fulfil its main purpose in the example in this article? **3**

    (d) State at least three different categories of insurance which a business will generally need but which a private individual will not require. **3**

    (e) Briefly describe how the insurance company will have decided that it can only meet 80% of the cost of the claim of the dairy producer. Why not 85%? **4**

    (f) What led to the failure of the firm? How could this have been avoided? **6**

Chapter 11 – Insurance

Q4

(a) Explain what is meant by saying that insurance is based on 'pooling' of risks. **2**

(b) Name two types of insurance which are compulsory by law. Name two types of insurance which are voluntary. **4**

(c) Certain principles apply to all insurance contracts. Name three of these principles and explain fully what they mean for a person seeking insurance. Give an example in each case to show how these principles work. **6**

(d) Explain fully four of the following terms associated with obtaining insurance: proposal, premium, policy, cover note, agents, brokers. **8**

Q5 Table 11.1 is a simplified version of the type of table that an insurance company would issue to its agents to help them quote a premium for life assurance cover. The table shows that at 30 years of age a man is expected to live another 44.9 years, i.e. to 74.9 years of age.

Years of age	Further expectation of life	
NOW	MALE	FEMALE
20	54.6	58.3
25	49.9	53.6
30	44.9	48.8
35	40.1	44.0
40	35.3	39.1
45	30.6	34.3
50	26.1	29.7
55	21.9	25.3

Table 11.1 *Expectation of life table*

(a) What is the term for the insurance worker who calculates the statistics in a table such as this? **1**

(b) If a man has reached forty years of age, what is his expectation of further life and to what age can he expect to live? **2**

(c) To take out life assurance you are charged a premium. What factors other than age are considered in the calculation of this premium? **3**

(d) Explain the differences the table shows between male and female life expectancy, and say why you think this difference exists. **6**

(e) Give a clear explanation of the difference between insurance and assurance using examples to illustrate your explanation. **8**

Research assignments

1. 'Insurance is based on statistics.' Explain this statement, giving specific examples of the kind of information insurance companies use in calculating premiums.

2. How important is insurance to economies in the Caribbean region?

3. a) On the news the weather forecasters stated that recently installed computerised forecasting equipment will enable them to give reliable 24 hours' notice of weather conditions. In what ways could this help to reduce insurance claims?

   b) What evidence can you find of other specific factors that influence the number of insurance claims?

Production

12.1 The factors of production

Aims of production

Production refers to the creation of goods and services, i.e. the creation of utilities. The purpose of production is to provide people with the goods and services that they need or want to consume. **Needs** are things that are essential to human survival. There are three primary needs:

- food
- clothing
- shelter.

Production also provides the many things that people want to consume, but which are not necessary for survival. These things help to make the quality of life better: for example, televisions, cars and books.

The four factors

In Chapter 1 we learnt that there are only scarce resources to meet our unlimited wants. The scarce or limited resources which are used to produce the commodities people want to consume are collectively called the factors of production. They are:

- land
- labour
- capital
- enterprise.

Each of the factors receives payment or reward in return for the contribution it makes to production. Land receives rent, labour wages, capital interest, and entrepreneurship is rewarded with profit, although some factors actually receive more than one return.

Fig. 12.1 *The four factors of production: land, labour, capital and enterprise*

Natural resource	Country	Example usage
Bauxite	Jamaica, Guyana	Refined as aluminium, used in pots and pans, machines and parts (e.g. aircraft parts)
Clay	Throughout Caribbean	Bricks, earthenware pots
Diamonds	Guyana	Jewellery, industrial diamonds
Forestry	Guyana	Furniture
Gold	Guyana	Jewellery
Limestone	Barbados, Jamaica, Trinidad and Tobago	Cement products
Manganese	Guyana	Metal and glass production
Natural gas	Barbados, Trinidad and Tobago	Energy fuel
Oil	Trinidad and Tobago	Petrol and by-products such as plastics and paint
Pitch	Trinidad and Tobago	Asphalt, shingles
Sand and silica	Throughout Caribbean	Building materials, glass
Sun	Throughout Caribbean	Solar energy

Table 12.1 *A sample of the industries that have developed from the natural resources of the Caribbean region*

The factor of land

Land as a factor of production includes not only the land itself but all natural resources found in the earth and sea. Land includes mineral deposits such as bauxite, oil, iron ore, gold and diamonds. It embraces sunshine and rainfall, rivers, ponds and lakes, the seas and oceans, deserts and forests. Land in this sense includes:

- geographical surface area
- rivers, lakes and seas
- minerals and chemicals.

Land is fixed in supply. In other words, the supply cannot be increased, although the quality of the soil may be improved by the use of fertilisers, drainage, land reclamation, contouring and reafforestation. The search for minerals below the surface of the land and sea continues.

Production cannot take place without land. Primary, secondary and tertiary production and all economic activity involve the use of land.

The natural resources of the Caribbean region include minerals such as bauxite, oil, natural gas, gold, diamonds, clay, limestone, gypsum, manganese, sand, silica, marble and many others. Some of the physical forces which are harnessed for energy production include lakes, rivers and the wind. And of course the climate is a natural resource which helps to promote the tourist industry.

The factor of labour

Labour is the factor of production which is people's physical and mental contribution to the creation of goods and services. It is the factor that

Principles of Business – Profile 2

converts resources into goods and services that people want. This contribution to production is generally rewarded with wages, although sometimes profit or interest is the return received.

All production requires some labour. Even the automated factory requires workers to supervise machinery, program computers to operate equipment, and process paperwork. Therefore, it is important that there is an adequate supply of labour, with the required skills. In this respect, labour is often divided into three broad groups:

- *Semi-skilled and unskilled:* jobs which involve little or no special training and usually involve working with the hands – drivers, cleaners, street sellers and some factory production line workers, watchmen, etc.
- *Skilled:* engineers, mechanics, electricians, plumbers, trained machine operators, computer operators, clerks, junior supervisors, etc.
- *Managerial and professional:* business executives, teachers, doctors, nurses, solicitors, architects, pharmacists, senior supervisors, etc.

These groups generally reflect differing qualities and levels of training.

Many businesses improve the quality of their labour force through education and training. This results in efficient use of the capital goods the business employs, and therefore contributes to the growth and development of the firm. But there are many other factors which determine the supply and quality of labour.

Determinants of the labour supply

Labour supply is influenced by several factors.

- *The size and structure of the population:* a large population will give a greater supply of labour. But a high proportion of very young or very old people will tend to reduce the supply of labour. These proportions will be influenced by school-leaving age, retirement age and birth rate.
- *The number of women at work:* this is influenced by many factors such as economic conditions in the country, wages, and attitudes towards working mothers.
- *Hours of work:* if there is a general trend towards a shorter working week (which is the case in developed countries), this has the effect of reducing the supply of labour.
- *Quality of the labour force:* it is not enough to have sufficient numbers of people available for work. They must also have the appropriate skills that are needed. If the required skills are not available the effect will be to limit the supply of labour.
- *Adequacy of health services:* it is important that adequate and readily available health services exist to keep the population healthy.
- *Mobility of labour:* the ability and willingness of workers to move to new jobs in other areas affects labour supply.
- *Government policies:* government commitment to training and other policies that help to improve the labour force and make it more mobile can have the effect of increasing the supply of labour in appropriate areas, and with the skills required.

It is natural for people to want to move to another job to improve their way of life, and often in order to achieve this improvement it may be necessary to move to a new location. This is called **migration**. **Internal migration** occurs when a person moves from one place to another *within* their home country;

external migration occurs when a person leaves their homeland to move to *another* country. In Chapter 1 we looked at the difficulties this can cause and the ways that government help can help to alleviate these problems.

Mobility of labour refers to the ability or willingness of workers to move to new jobs in different places. Mobility of labour can have beneficial effects for a country, but it does have its down side. Whilst migration may improve the situation of the person moving from one place to another, the effect this has on the supply of labour is mixed. Those moving into a new location may benefit that area by increasing the labour availability there, and perhaps bring new skills to the area. But it also means that the place they have moved away from has a smaller labour force and perhaps fewer skills available.

The foregoing reflects one of the difficulties the Caribbean region has faced in the past. Whilst many of those who migrated to other countries were unskilled, untrained and poorly educated, a lot of them were skilled and well-educated, including teachers, engineers and others. This '**brain drain**' resulted in a shortage of labour in important skill areas. This has the effect of restricting economic development. However, the region has also been able to attract people from other countries to come to the region, thus bringing their skills to help development. It is achieving the balance that is the tricky problem, not only as a country but even when internal migration occurs.

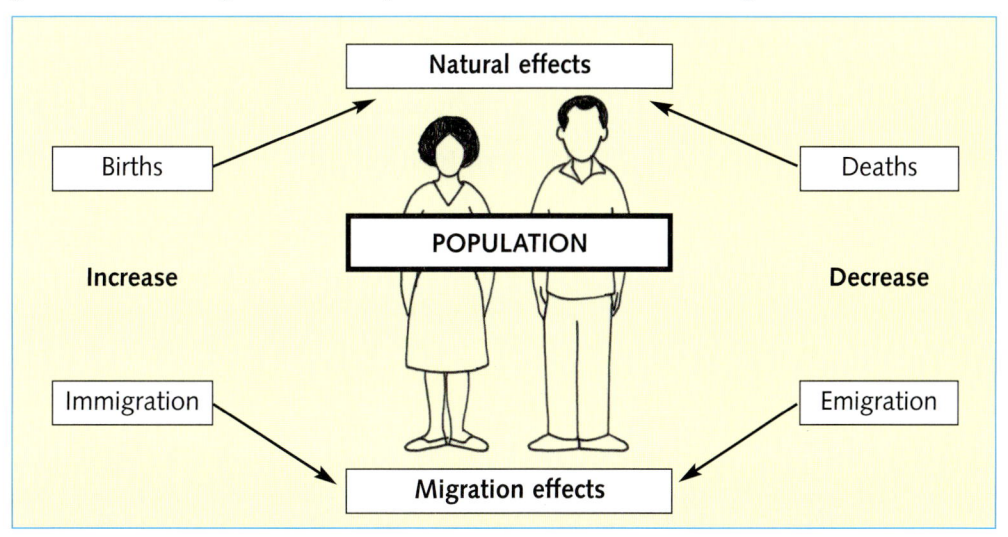

Fig. 12.2 *The working population in an area is affected by birth and death rates, and migration.*

Labour quality is influenced by the following factors.

- *Quality of education:* education plays an important part not only in producing a knowledgeable workforce, but it also contributes towards making people more mobile and adaptable to change.
- *Training facilities:* a shortage of workers with particular skills can be overcome by training more of these specialists through the education system or in-service occupational training.
- *Natural talent:* some skills are important but are natural talents and cannot be taught, although they may be increased by training; for example, acting, drawing or playing a musical instrument.
- *Health:* the standard of health of workers obviously affects their efficiency and productivity. Health is affected not only by living conditions, but also by working conditions.

Principles of Business – Profile 2

- *Self-help and community work:* these have become an important aspect of the economic contribution of labour in the Caribbean region. Examples are projects in which the government provides materials and the community provides the labour. Organisations (e.g. Red Cross Society, Lions Club) use the self-help approach to help the provision of social or cultural facilities which the State does not provide.

Self-help or community organisations such as trade unions often act as potent pressure groups which try to influence the government to the benefit of the whole community.

Labour makes an important contribution to the efficiency of production because it has a direct effect on **productivity**. Productivity refers to the relationship between the output of a product and the factor inputs. Productivity is generally measured in terms of *output per man hour*. An increase in productivity would be shown as an increase in output per man hour.

Productivity is important to any business because it helps the firm to establish a **competitive advantage** over its rivals. A firm can improve its productivity in a variety of ways, but particularly by adopting better **working practices**. For example, it might implement pay incentive schemes such as profit-related pay and profit sharing schemes.

An especially effective way of improving productivity is by the use of better **production methods**, e.g. changing from labour intensive production methods (e.g. batch production) to methods using latest technologies such as computer-aided manufacturing (CAM), which are examined later in this chapter.

Modern technology

Modern technology has resulted in increased automated methods and strategies being adopted by organisations involved in the production process. It is common today for machines to be programmed to receive, interpret and process information in the completion of a task. Take the **point of sale** in a supermarket as an example. Hand held and counter-top **scanners** read **barcodes** placed on packaging, transfer the information to the computer

Fig. 12.3 *How many of the factors of production are involved in the operation of a busy port?*

system, and once recognised, the prices are calculated and the customer is told how much to pay. For a cash payment the cashier receives the payment immediately. But if the customer chooses to pay by credit card, then another device comes into the process. The card is checked by the computer system to determine its validity before the transaction is completed by debiting the credit card company and crediting the shop (in due course). During all of this process, the computer system will be automatically updating the stock records of the shop, and even ordering replacement stock.

Human effort is needed to program, activate, monitor and maintain technological equipment and systems. However, less human effort is now needed to carry out the many routine tasks in organisations. Consequently, people need to be retrained to manage technological devices, strategies, methods, procedures and concepts in modern society. This has implications for the education of the population and the redistribution of employment.

The factor of capital

Capital, as a factor of production, is the money that is invested in a business in order to acquire the assets which the business needs to trade or produce. Venture capital refers to money subscribed to finance new firms and activities that are considered to be of a risky nature and, therefore, not usually financed through traditional methods. Capital includes the money and all other assets (possessions of value) that are employed in the process of production. Capital includes the buildings, machinery, equipment, stocks and many other things (producer goods) used in making the items we consume (consumer goods).

Capital, in this sense, takes two forms: fixed capital and working capital:

- Fixed capital is the items such as buildings, machinery and other equipment with a long life, which are used many times over in the production of goods and the creation of further wealth.
- Working capital is the firm's short term assets which are turned over fairly quickly in the course of business. They include cash, bank balances, stocks of raw materials, work in progress, finished goods and other items required for the day-to-day operation of the business and which are continually being used up.

Enterprise

Enterprise is similar to labour but is separated because it refers to the special skills (called entrepreneurship) that some people have to organise the other factors of production to produce goods or services and make a profit in the process. These people are called entrepreneurs. They are the owners of business enterprises who, by taking risks and making decisions, enable production to be carried out in anticipation of demand.

If entrepreneurs successfully predict future demand they are rewarded by a special form of income called profit. If, however, their judgement is incorrect they may get no reward or may even make a loss. For example, a shopkeeper may buy stocks of a new brand of confectionery, but has no guarantee of being able to sell them. There would be far fewer businesses in existence if there were not entrepreneurs around willing to take the risk involved.

In order to participate in entrepreneurship the entrepreneur must be willing to do a number of things.

Principles of Business – Profile 2

- To raise capital, from savings or by borrowing, for investment in the business.
- To organise the various levels of labour required.
- To define and clarify business policy decisions so that all levels of personnel can understand what the firm is trying to achieve.
- To make any change necessary in the interest of the growth and development of the business.

KEY WORDS

Find out the business-related meaning of each of the following terms. Write a separate sentence for each term to show your understanding.

external migration   mobility of labour   enterprise   land   brain drain
venture capital   labour   capital   internal migration
entrepreneur   fixed capital   working capital   productivity   assets

12.2 Production levels

In Chapter 1 we said that production can be divided into three main sectors: primary, secondary and tertiary. It can also be classified according to the levels of operation. These levels are dependent upon the resources available, and the extent to which the country has developed to exploit those resources. There are three basic levels of operation: subsistence, domestic and surplus.

Subsistence level

This level of production meets only the basic needs of the country in which it takes place. In other words, sufficient is produced only to enable the population to survive, but not enough to improve the way of life. This is the kind of problem faced by many of the underdeveloped communities of the world.

Subsistence economy is a term usually applied where agriculture is the main source of production. In other words, people live almost entirely by what can be obtained from natural resources, and this could lead to a very poor quality of life. Usually the subsistence level of production is inefficient and very dependent upon the climate and weather. Periods of drought or other climatic problems result in severe hardship. Fortunately, the subsistence level of production is not as common today as it has been in the past.

Domestic level

At the level of domestic production everything is produced locally, that is, in the home country. This level does not involve any imports from foreign countries. Both human and natural resources are employed and the whole economy is dependent upon what it can produce from these resources.

Some developed countries, such as the USA, try to grow all the food they need because they have the resources to do so. The governments of developing countries, including the Caribbean region, encourage domestic production in order to make full use of the resources available in their country, e.g. the promotion of self-sufficiency in agricultural produce.

Small farmers in Barbados and St Christopher, for example, grow a high proportion of the vegetables and fruits available locally. The Windward Islands and Jamaica produce bananas for the world market. However, because many small farmers also engage in banana farming, large amounts can be obtained on the local market. A number of other islands produce yams, potatoes and cassava which serve as staple foods. Animal rearing in Guyana, Trinidad and Tobago and Jamaica assists in the provision of protein and other dairy products for the local markets.

Surplus level

Developed countries, such as the USA, Britain and Germany, have a wide variety of resources and exploit these to the full. They also have advanced technology which enables them to take full advantage of their resources.

Such countries are able to achieve a level of production which not only satisfies domestic consumption, but also produces a *surplus* that can be *exported* to other countries. This results in a better quality of life for the population because there is access to a wider variety of products, prices are competitive, and more can be earned from production.

The various Caribbean territories are at different stages of development in their levels of production, although they have developed beyond the subsistence level. Their operations at domestic and surplus levels vary. CARICOM and the CBI (Caribbean Basin Initiative) are two organisations which aim to encourage industrialisation throughout the territories.

The Caribbean Community, usually known as CARICOM, consists of Trinidad and Tobago, Jamaica, Guyana, Barbados, Anguilla, Antigua, Barbuda, Belize, Dominica, Grenada, Montserrat, St Kitts and Nevis, St Vincent, St Lucia and The Bahamas.

CARICOM is a 'Common Market'. That is, it is a group arrangement whereby there are no import duties on trade between one member state and another, and no restrictions on the quantity that can be exported or imported between member states. In addition, member states have agreed to impose the same rate of import duty on goods from outside CARICOM. An important objective of CARICOM is co-ordinating industrialisation in the region and assisting development.

12.3 The chain of production

We have said that that businesses engaged in primary production are concerned with getting raw materials from the land or the sea, or using the earth to grow crops. We have also said that those engaged in secondary production process raw materials and turn them into some finished item. Businesses engaged in tertiary production provide a service either to other businesses or to consumers and assist in the change of ownership of goods and services that help promote the welfare of people.

From the foregoing you should be able to see that there are links between the three production levels we have examined. These links are sometimes said to show the chain of production. The links in the *chain of production* can be seen in figure 12.4 given here showing the stages in the production of carrots.

Principles of business – Profile 2

PRIMARY PRODUCTION	SECONDARY PRODUCTION	TERTIARY PRODUCTION
Farmer grows carrots	Manufacturer cans carrots	Retailer sells carrots

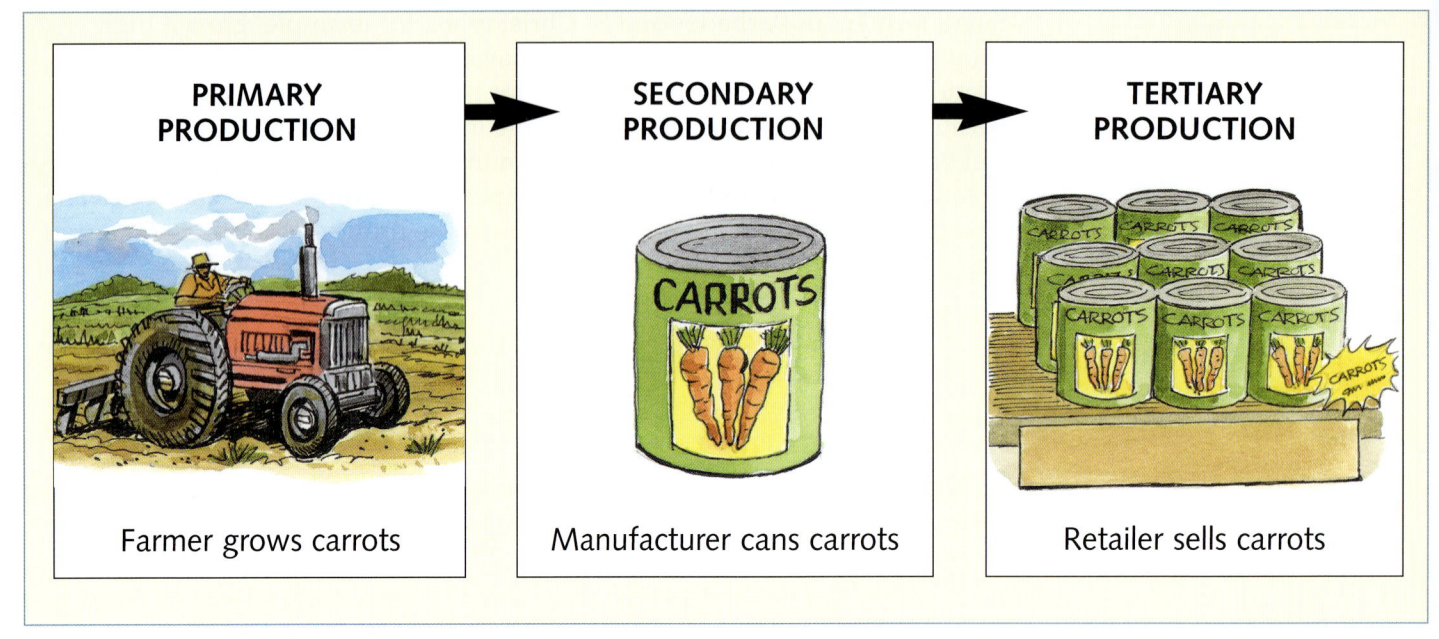

Fig. 12.4 *The chain of production for carrots*

The chain of production in practice

Traders such as retailers, wholesalers, importers and exporters support producers by carrying out the sale and distribution of goods and bridging the time gap between production and consumption. For example, retailers and wholesalers order goods from producers and hold them until they are required. Exporters are involved in the distribution of home-produced goods overseas. This not only provides work for producers but also raises foreign capital, which is needed to pay for the imports of raw materials that producers need. Importers buy from other countries the raw materials and finished goods that we cannot economically produce in our own country, thus allowing producers in the home market to specialise in manufacturing products for which they are best suited.

The services provided to traders by some businesses also play a major part in co-ordinating the activities of producers and promoting their enterprise. Financial services provide the money for the capital assets needed by businesses, and also for consumers and businesses who wish to buy on credit. Banking makes the transfer of payments between buyers and sellers of goods possible and also provides a variety of services that facilitate payment and encourage production and trade to take place. Insurance overcomes some of the risks involved in producing and trading, such as the danger of the loss or damage to capital assets or goods. Transport creates the physical links between producers, traders and consumers, and gets goods to the right place at the right time and in the right condition.

Communication through advertising, mail and telecommunications help to make potential customers aware of the commodities available, and enable businesses to communicate with each other and with their customers at the various stages of production and distribution.

From the foregoing you can see that the different elements of the chain of production are dependent on each other, which is why they are sometimes said to be interdependent.

12.4 Techniques of production

Types of production

In Chapter 1 we learnt that production can be divided into three types:

- *Primary production*, which is often seen as the first stage of the production process and is concerned with extracting raw materials (agriculture, mining, fishing).
- *Secondary production*, which consists of the manufacturing and construction industries (assembling, refining and building).
- *Tertiary production*, which is the sector that provides the services that are so important to the first two stages of production (marketing, transporting, communicating, tourism, etc.).

Methods of production

There are basically three methods of production used by firms engaged in the manufacturing industries:

- *Job production* (also called **unit production**) – this refers to the process of making a single item from start to finish, often in response to a specification from a customer.
- *Batch production* – this occurs where groups of similar products are made in batches on a production line. One batch is completed before commencing the next.
- *Flow production* – this refers to the continuous production of a large number of items on a production line. This method is also known by a number of other names such as, **mass** or **flow-line production**. Where the product is in liquid form (e.g. oil, plastic or chemicals), the mass production is sometimes referred to as **continuous-flow** or **process production**.

Job Production

Examples:

Furniture, bridges, ships, roads, houses, aircraft, tailored clothes, birhday cakes.

Batch Production

Examples:

Clothes, bread, cakes, biscuits, shoes.

Flow Production

Examples:

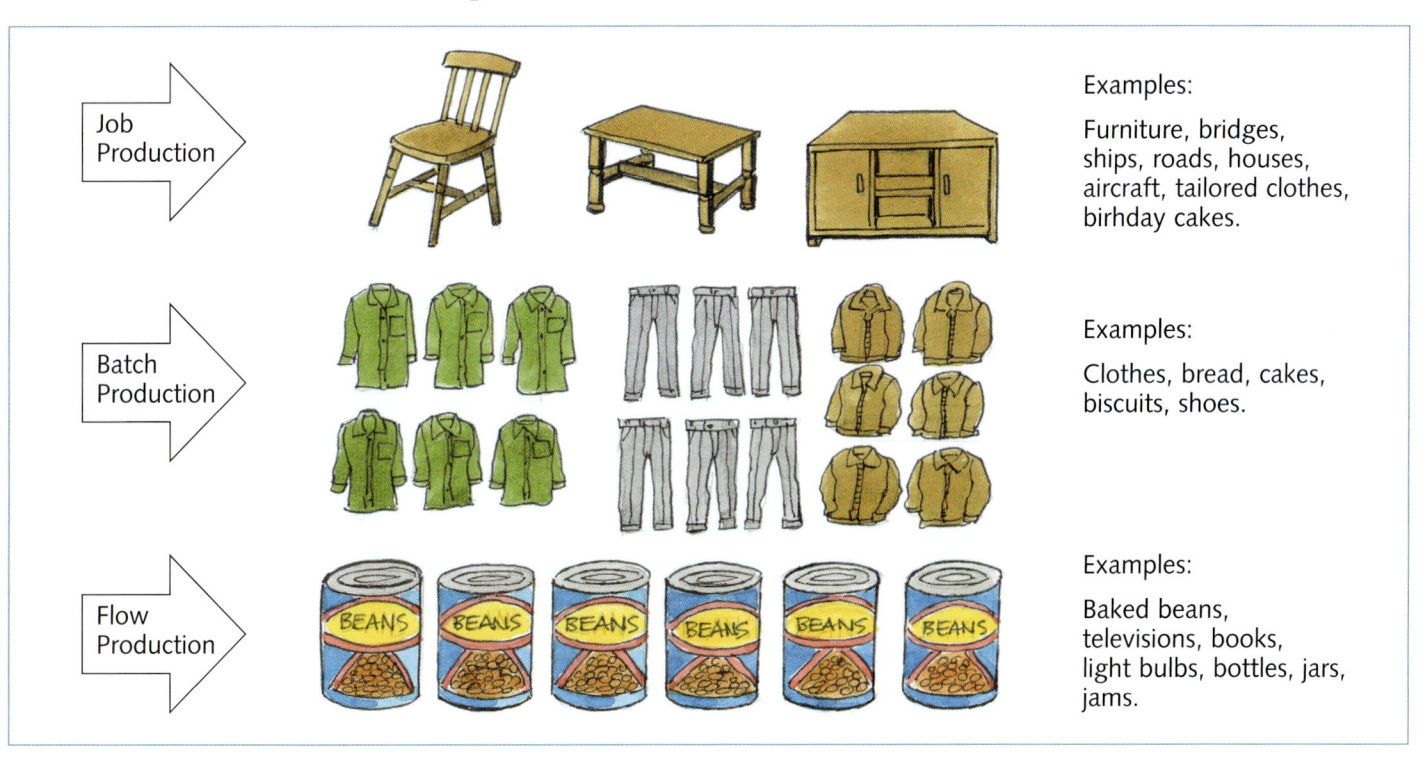

Baked beans, televisions, books, light bulbs, bottles, jars, jams.

Fig. 12.5 *Examples of products created by the different methods of production*

Principles of Business – Profile 2

Choice of production method

The method of production that a firm will choose will depend on the product or the way that orders are received from the customers. Where orders are for a single unique product based on the customer's specification (e.g. made to measure clothing or fitted furniture), the job method will be used. With orders for similar products (e.g. bread, cakes and biscuits) from different customers which are likely to be repeated, the batch method will be used. Mass production will be used when very large quantities are required continuously, for example with cars, books, televisions, jars and bottles, etc.

From the foregoing you will have gathered that job production tends to be labour-intensive and often requires skilled labour. Batch production requires smaller quantities than mass production (but still requires organising into economic runs). Mass production is capital-intensive, involves very large quantities, and gives the best opportunities for economies of scale and the use of specialist equipment (e.g. computer-aided design and computer-aided manufacture, which are dealt with later in this chapter).

Quality control

The process of ensuring that a company's products meet the standards that the firm has set, or the minimum legal requirements, is called quality control. Quality may be controlled by quality inspectors who are used to check on the quality of products as they leave the production line. They may check every item, or they may make spot checks of items at random. Sometimes a sample of the product will be tested to destruction to make sure it is as long-lasting as the company requires.

Alternative methods of quality control include using the statistical process control, where a machine operator checks that the machine is working correctly during every work shift. Some companies, for example car manufacturers, build in quality control through teamwork, with members of the team carrying out jobs in some rotation system. The wages of the team may be linked to the quality of output of the whole team, so that each person will watch the quality of work of other team members. A structured version of this team system is the concept of Total Quality Management (TQM). Each member of a team or group of workers is required to take a turn at doing the work of others in the team. This helps the business to provide a high-quality product or service.

Quality control is important as all goods have to fulfil a particular purpose. In some cases, the safety aspect is particularly important. Quality control is necessary to maintain both customer satisfaction and the firm's reputation. There is likely to be a decrease in sales if poor quality products are produced.

Work study

Work study is the scientific investigation of what a job involves, the way it is carried out, and how long it takes to complete. Work study is carried out by work study experts. The information they obtain is used to improve working methods. It can also be used to relate pay to productivity.

KEY WORDS

Find out the business-related meaning of each of the following terms. Write a separate sentence for each term to show your understanding.

economies of scale
tertiary production
domestic level
work study   TQM
job production
surplus level
subsistence level
batch production
flow production
primary production
chain of production
secondary production

12.5 Business size

Economies of scale

The producer has to decide how to use the factors of production to the best advantage, because the chances of making a good profit depend upon how effectively the factors are employed. The entrepreneur also has to decide on what scale to produce and what size of business to operate, because the size of the business and the scale of production can also influence profitability. These decisions have to be taken by all entrepreneurs. Obviously, the entrepreneur should aim for the scale of production which yields the greatest profit margin.

Large businesses tend to dominate certain industries because their size gives them advantages over smaller organisations. For example, by producing larger quantities they can reduce their production costs. These advantages of size are called **economies of scale**. Sometimes business growth results in disadvantages; when this occurs it is referred to as **diseconomies of scale**. You should realise that there can be advantages in a business remaining small as well as advantages in being large.

In addition to economies of large scale and small scale, there are external and internal economies of scale. **External economies of scale** refer to the benefits gained by the whole of a certain industry, or the whole of society. For example, a particular invention may result in benefits to all firms in an industry, or to the whole of society. Internal economies of scale refer to the benefits gained by one particular industry. **Internal economies of scale** can be grouped into four categories:

- technical
- managerial
- marketing
- financial.

Technical economies of scale

Greater size allows more opportunities for division of labour, the use of machinery and automation, and other methods of increasing efficiency. It also allows a company to allocate more resources to research and development, which can result in further economies through increased efficiency and effectiveness.

As a firm increases its output and employs more workers there are more opportunities to divide work into stages and, consequently, workers become more efficient in their work. Dividing the work into stages in this way also makes it easier to introduce machinery and other labour-saving equipment.

Managerial economies of scale

Larger firms are able to employ more highly skilled personnel. Such employees will be attracted to the company not only by the higher salaries offered but also by the prestige of a larger organisation, and greater scope for advancement.

The employment of skilled specialists in charge of functions such as design and production results in the advantages of the division of labour. Small firms often do not have sufficient work to enable them to form separate specialist departments and, therefore, managers have to undertake a variety of tasks which can make them less effective.

Principles of Business – Profile 2

Marketing economies of scale

Larger firms can purchase their supplies in bigger quantities than small firms. They can also engage in mass production and they save in advertising and distribution costs. The important result of these advantages is that such firms can market their goods more cheaply than smaller competitors, and obviously consumers will be more likely to give their custom to such firms.

Most firms see public relations as an important part of their marketing strategies, because if potential customers regard the reputation of the company as 'good' they will be more likely to want to give their custom to the firm. Large businesses are in a better position to sponsor sports and public events and offer attractive prize-giving competitions, thus promoting good public relations.

Financial economies of scale

A major advantage of being a large firm is that, because large firms own more assets, they find it easier to borrow money and they are more able to withstand financial pressures (e.g. of cash flow) than smaller businesses.

Banks and other lending institutions feel safer in lending money to large companies because they feel there is less risk involved. Similarly, creditors (e.g. suppliers) feel more confident in giving trade credit to larger firms than to smaller ones.

Large businesses

Both economies and diseconomies of scale can be examined by looking at the advantages and disadvantages of large-scale business.

Advantages of large businesses

- They find it easier to raise large amounts of capital.
- More capital is available for:
  - extensive advertising
  - research and development
  - employing specialist personnel
  - labour-saving machinery.
- Mass production allows greater possibilities of specialisation.
- They can obtain special prices and discounts.

The advantages of large businesses summarised in the foregoing list refer only to internal economies of scale, but there are also external economies of scale. Sometimes many related businesses in a particular industry are located in one place. This will encourage the provision of skilled maintenance and other backup services such as training facilities which benefit all members of the industry. In addition, all firms engaged in a particular industry may combine for the purpose of advertising, research, or technical developments. Groups of industries will also attract good transport facilities, or special treatment from banks and other financial institutions.

Disadvantages of large businesses

- They can become too complex to manage.
- Lines of internal communication and management become unwieldy.
- Customers may find the large organisation too impersonal.
- Mass production can lead to boredom for workers and reduce quality.
- Workers find it easier to organise restrictive working practices.

The Law of Diminishing Returns

A firm cannot continue to grow indefinitely unless some factors change. If you continue to blow up a balloon it will eventually burst because the fixed factor (the balloon) cannot contain the varying factor (the added air). The same principle applies to a growing business. If the fixed factor is factory space and if the firm continues to add more workers, initially there will be more production, but eventually additional workers will result in less output per person as too many workers in a restricted space get in each other's way.

Units of workers	Total output	Marginal output	Average output
1	5	5	5
2	18	13	9
3	30	12	10
4	36	6	9
5	35	−1	7

Table 12.2 *The Law of Diminishing Returns*

As a firm grows, it is subject to the Law of Diminishing Returns. When a firm is growing rapidly it experiences increased returns and rising profits. But there is a point in any productive organisation when diminishing returns will begin to operate. The additional output (marginal output) achieved as a result of the addition of a unit of labour begins to fall; therefore, the average output also falls. This is illustrated in table 12.2.

Small businesses

In spite of the benefits of large-scale operations, small firms continue to exist because they have their own special advantages, and in some cases (e.g. direct services such as hairdressing) do not lend themselves to large-scale operations.

Many persons in the Caribbean engage in small business operations. This is one way of alleviating the unemployment problem. Small business entrepreneurship training programmes and centres, as well as small business associations, have been established in the Caribbean islands to assist and encourage small business operators.

Generally there is only limited management structure in small businesses and often the only management will be the owner(s) of the firm. This has its advantages in that there is less need for consultation when making decisions because the manager or owner performs all the important functions. But this person also requires a wider range of management skills than his or her counterpart in a large organisation.

Advantages of small businesses

- Closer communication exists between employees.
- It is easier to have good working relationships.
- Employees feel a personal involvement in the business.
- There is more personal contact between employees and customers.

Value of small businesses to a country

- The small business provides employment, and thus utilises labour available.
- Small businesses can respond to customers' needs faster than a larger

Principles of Business – Profile 2

business. For example, if a customer desired a variation to a product, a small, locally based business can make adjustments to meet local market conditions. The ability to respond in this way to market conditions enables small businesses to continue to operate and provide employment.
- Small businesses contribute to the competitive spirit of the economic life of a country by competing with larger organisations, thus preventing them from having a monopolistic position.

Small business incubator

The idea of the small business incubator is relatively new, but centres have been established to provide:

- essential business services
- consultancy and training
- a flexible working space for the new businesses.

The incubator is seen as a tool that can be used to bring about economic growth in industrialising developing nations. A major objective of the incubator is to encourage innovations and the incubator will then provide some resources and training for the small to medium-sized businesses. The incubator will provide space, shared office facilities, advisory services, skills development in small business management, assistance and speed in securing office space, and access to 'seed money' through a loan scheme.

Small businesses are often born out of cottage industries (see below) or other community self-help projects. Many are family businesses with limited capital. These businesses often find it difficult to obtain a loan from the established financial institutions that tend to focus their attention on the larger, well-established businesses. However, small businesses have an important role in the economy.

- They contribute to the economic life of the country by providing employment.
- They provide a service that is needed by the population, especially in small communities that are not easily serviced by the businesses in the towns and cities.
- Because of the size of the business, customers' personal preferences are identified and met.

Cottage industries

A cottage industry is one of the extremes of small business. As the name suggests, cottage industries are carried on in the home, although increasingly they are to be found in community centres, parish halls or some other similar village facility. Frequently such businesses will involve handwork carried on at home but the term also applies to many other forms of employment, often where workers supplement their normal earnings in cottage industries after their day's work is completed.

Cottage industries originated as ways of increasing income without leaving home. They also satisfy the psychological need to use one's spare time productively. Today they are recognised as playing an essential part in the Caribbean economies.

People who have skills in handicrafts have for a long time successfully used free or relatively cheap local materials to produce a variety of goods, particularly to meet the demands of the tourist trade. This not only provides income for the producers of such items but also makes sensible use of their spare time. In some examples it can also provide employment for others who provide raw materials or who sell the finished product on behalf of the makers.

Cottage industries have continued to survive in the Caribbean because those involved have diversified and increased the range and scope of their products. Products produced by cottage industries include: pastries, straw hats, garments, embroidery, basketry, jams and jellies, string arts, flower arrangements, as well as direct services such as tailoring, beauty culture, catering, knitting, smocking and crocheting.

Throughout the Caribbean region various governments have tried to encourage production in this manner. For example, Caribbean governments may arrange major exhibitions and competitions, provide skills training, assist in the marketing of products, and may even make factory space available.

Apart from the aforementioned reasons for the continued existence of cottage industries, they have other important contributions to make to the economy of their countries. During a time of high unemployment they provide income and independence for many people. We also have to remember that the money earned by those engaged in the cottage industries is eventually spent – thus providing work for others.

Linkage industries

In Chapter 1 we said that there are three types of productive industries:

- *Primary:* the industries concerned with the extraction of basic materials provided by nature (farming, fishing and mining).
- *Secondary:* the industries that change raw materials and partly produced goods into a finished product (manufacturing and construction).
- *Tertiary:* the service industries (such as transport or tourism).

The linkages between these aspects of production are important because they facilitate a series of relationships between the productive sectors mentioned above. These linkages are of crucial importance to Caribbean development. For example, agriculture is an important economic base in many of the territories and the linkage industries make an agricultural–industrial drive possible.

A linkage industry is one that is linked with another. It is sometimes called a 'screw-driver' industry or a 'spin-off' because it has come about as a result of some other development. For example, canning and preservation of foods are 'spin-offs' of agriculture (forward linkage); one industry is producing the raw material for another industry. Conversely, manufacturers of farm machinery will supply to agriculture (backward linkage).

The linkage industries are important in the Caribbean at both national and regional levels because they:

- provide increased employment and an improved standard of living
- assist regional self-sufficiency (reduced dependence on imported goods)
- reduce wastage of the country's resources
- increase opportunities for combined research and development
- encourage more skills in the labour force
- forge closer Caribbean links at the social, economic and political levels
- promote earnings of foreign exchange.

Crude oil (refining)	Petroleum, plastics, asphalt
Sugar cane	Candy, rum
Fruit	Canning
Bamboo	Baskets
Asphalt	Road-building
Livestock	Hides, leather goods

Table 12.3 *Examples of industrial linkage in the Caribbean*

Benefits of local and regional linkages

The Caribbean Community (CARICOM) has been established to encourage economic development in the region. The organisation has been seeking ways and means of achieving its objectives and one of these is to establish linkages in terms of economic activity within the region. The argument is that if nations are to do well economically, then linkages between industries is a worthwhile alternative to current practices.

For example, Trinidad and Tobago is a major producer of pitch which is a by-product of oil – one of their major resources. Other islands could form linkages with this industry in order to obtain the raw materials for their own purposes. For example, with further processing, asphalt used in road construction can be obtained from the pitch.

Another example is the hospitality and tourism sector which is a major earner of foreign currency for most Caribbean islands. Because of the nature of the hospitality and tourism product, it is an area in which considerable co-operation and **linkages** are needed. For example, linkages can be established between the agricultural sector and the hospitality and tourism sector because large volumes of farm produce are consumed by this sector on an annual basis. Information about the quality, quantity and variety of the produce required by the sector is of importance to the farmers. Farmers would then be in a better position to produce to meet the product specifications of the hospitality and tourism sector.

The design and management of facilities are important aspects of the hospitality and tourism sector. Training of managers to develop these skills and competencies would complement their existing general management skills.

This type of training is best delivered by a building services engineer, allowing building services engineers and hospitality and tourism to work co-operatively.

Finally, craft items are produced by many local artisans for the hospitality and tourism sector. Yet, in the marketing of the tourist product, limited attention is given to this often small but important sector.

It is, therefore, clear that the opportunities for linkages at the local and regional levels exist, but a concerted effort must be made by the decision-makers to bring these sectors together so that they complement each other. In this way decisions can be made about how much of what is earned in one sector, for example, hospitality and tourism, should be ploughed back into other sectors such as craft and small farming, in order to improve the quality of their products. In other words, the backward sector could benefit from the modern or technologically advanced sector for their mutual benefit. This can only be achieved if a concerted effort is made by the decision-makers to forge the necessary linkages. This would help to reduce or prevent **economic dualism**.

Regional linkages can result in:
- providing outlets for raw materials (at the primary and secondary levels)
- assisting in the development of the region at a faster pace
- assisting in reducing unemployment
- providing opportunities for countries to develop their expertise in the production of specific products
- giving the opportunity for the region, in the long-run, to compete in the global market-place
- preventing scarce resources from being used to obtain products from outside the region which could, with greater co-operation, be produced within the region. This would then leave the savings free to obtain products that are necessary, but for which there would be no clear comparative advantage if attempts are made to produce them locally or regionally.

The role of governments in developing regional linkage

Governments can contribute to the ideal of regional linkage by:
- outlining the benefits to be gained by CARICOM countries from regional strategies. Through CARICOM, regional strategies and policies could be identified and pursued.
- educating business organisations about the benefits to be derived from regional linkages. Encouraging businesses to use the raw materials of the region, as well as buying locally produced goods. In this manner both local and regional businesses will be supported and helped to survive and develop.
- financing trade fairs at which both local and regional persons could be brought up-to-date on what is being produced in the region, and thus encourage businesses to obtain their supplies from both local and regional markets.
- ascertaining the skills and competencies needed for the industries and collaborating in providing the necessary training of the labour force to handle the tasks to be carried out.
- pooling resources in order to obtain the capital needed by various industries.

12.6 Location of business

A major decision that all firms have to take is where to site their premises. A variety of factors will influence this decision, including the size of the organisation and the expected scale of its operations, but most choices of site are a compromise between several advantages and disadvantages. The summary chart, figure 12.6, on the following page, shows the main influencing factors.

12.7 Business expansion

Business risk

Being in business is risky. Some of the risks involved can be insured, e.g. bad debts, damage or theft. However, some cannot. For example, it is not possible to insure against a business making a loss. The main risk a business faces is that it will fail to make a profit; and even worse, if this continues over a period of time, the business will be forced to cease trading.

Principles of Business – Profile 2

INFLUENCES ON LOCATION OF BUSINESS

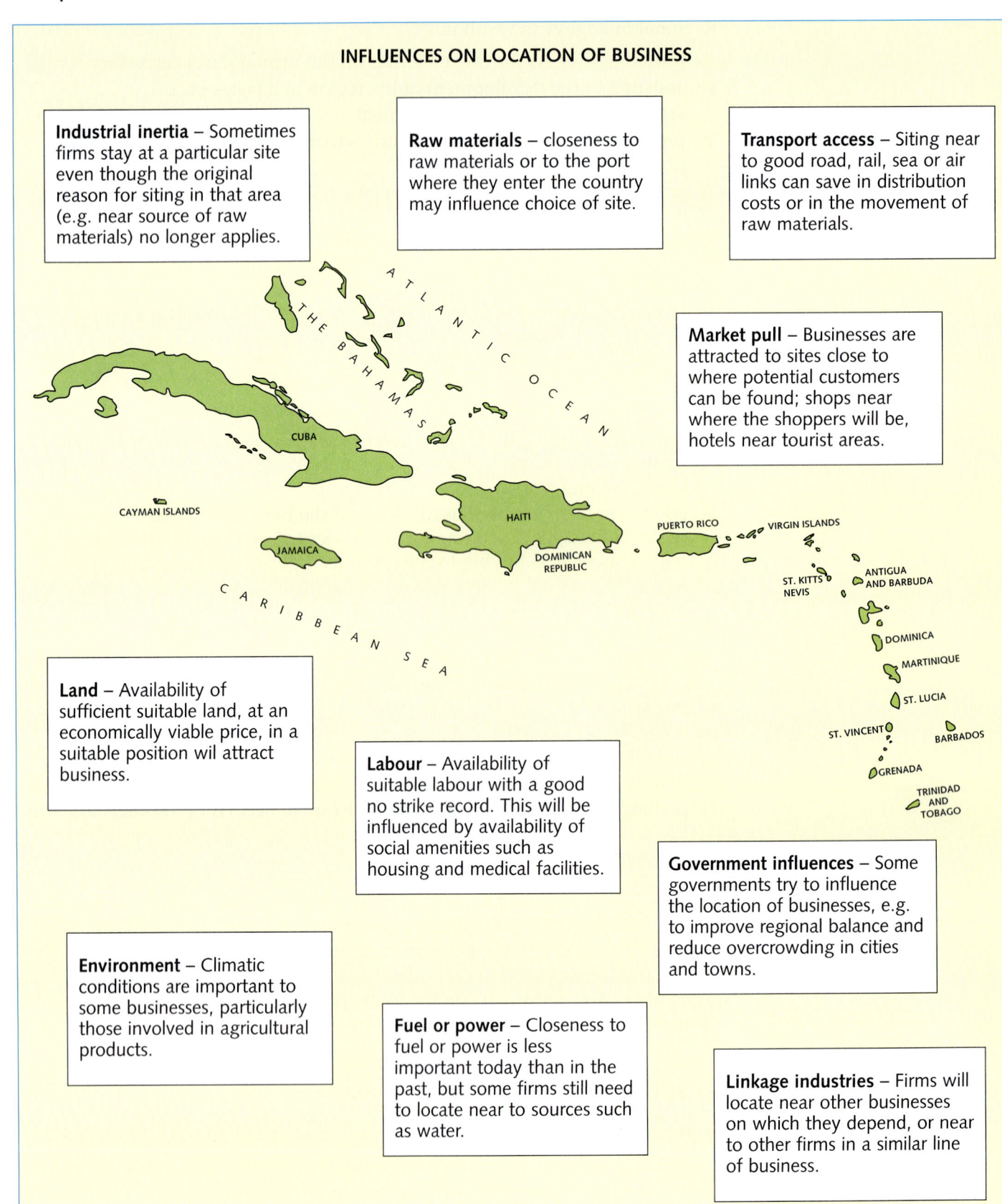

Industrial inertia – Sometimes firms stay at a particular site even though the original reason for siting in that area (e.g. near source of raw materials) no longer applies.

Raw materials – closeness to raw materials or to the port where they enter the country may influence choice of site.

Transport access – Siting near to good road, rail, sea or air links can save in distribution costs or in the movement of raw materials.

Market pull – Businesses are attracted to sites close to where potential customers can be found; shops near where the shoppers will be, hotels near tourist areas.

Land – Availability of sufficient suitable land, at an economically viable price, in a suitable position wil attract business.

Labour – Availability of suitable labour with a good no strike record. This will be influenced by availability of social amenities such as housing and medical facilities.

Government influences – Some governments try to influence the location of businesses, e.g. to improve regional balance and reduce overcrowding in cities and towns.

Environment – Climatic conditions are important to some businesses, particularly those involved in agricultural products.

Fuel or power – Closeness to fuel or power is less important today than in the past, but some firms still need to locate near to sources such as water.

Linkage industries – Firms will locate near other businesses on which they depend, or near to other firms in a similar line of business.

Fig. 12.6 *A business will take many factors into account when deciding where to locate its premises. Look at the examples given here. Where can you see examples of these influences on businesses in your locality?*

Chapter 12 – Production

One of the obvious ways a business can reduce risks is by being successful and increasing profitability. As a firm becomes more successful, it tends to grow in size. Through this growth, it usually creates further profitability and success and so increases its chances of surviving, and the growth continues. The most obvious way that this growth is seen is in the organisational structure of the firm. For example, the structure of a large business will be more complex and versatile than that of a small business (see figure 12.7 for comparison).

The benefits of business expansion

The main aim of a business is to create a profit for its owners. The larger the profit the greater capital is generated, and the more satisfied the owners will be because the chances of survival and continued growth will have increased. Profit is what remains after all the costs of running the business have been met. Costs include things such as wages paid to employees, rent of buildings, and payment for stock and equipment. Anything that reduces these costs increases profitability.

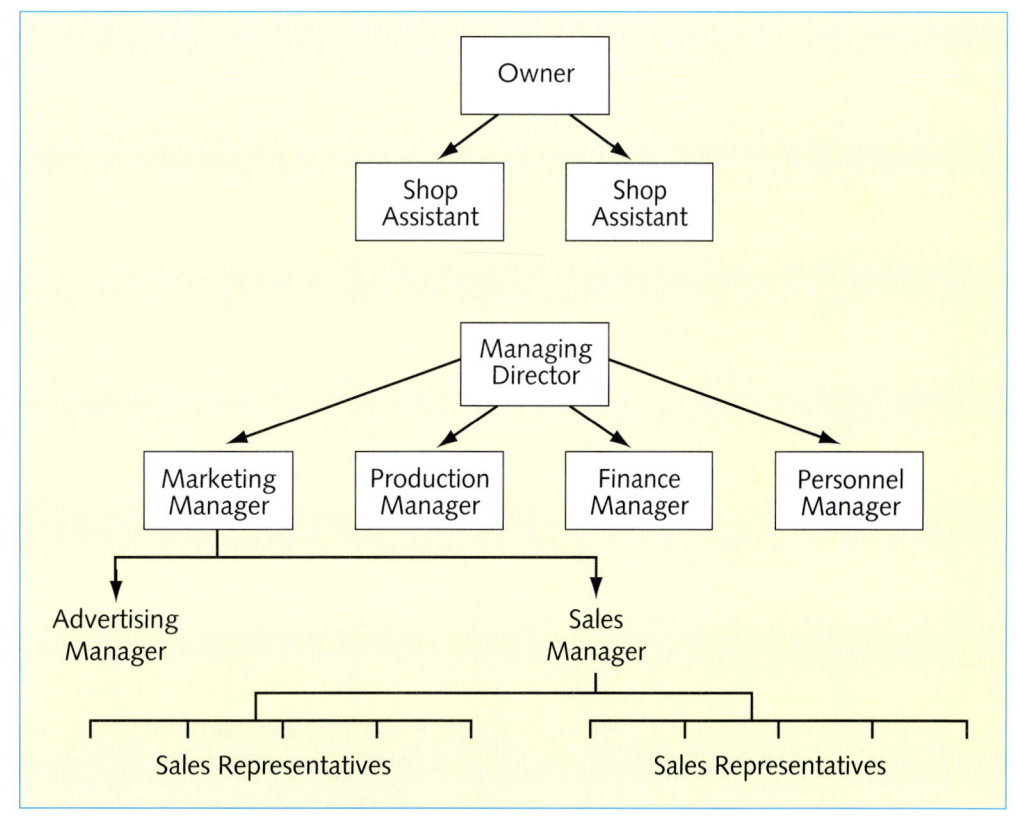

Fig.12.7 *The size of a business will influence its structure*

Growth can help to increase profitability in the following ways:

Economies of scale

As a business grows it usually generates economies of scale. This means that as the business size increases, its unit costs fall; the cost of each thing the business sells is reduced because unit costs are more widely spread. Thus, it is cheaper to produce goods on a larger scale.

Internal economies of scale occur as a result of various factors within the business, and these are related to its size. For example, a larger business can afford to use better technology, and this reduces its operational costs. This will enable it increase the scale of production, thus further increasing economies. Other internal economies of scale include being able to employ specialist labour, being able to buy in bulk and finding it easier to raise further capital.

External economies of scale refer to the benefits gained by all the businesses in a particular industry. Sometimes, for example, businesses with similar interests locate in a particular area. This can benefit all such related businesses because other supporting businesses (e.g. those providing support services) will locate in the region, making access to them easier. Similarly, skilled labour will move into the area to benefit all the businesses. In addition, such business may co-operate to create joint research facilities which benefit them all.

Increased share of the market

When a business is becoming more successful, it will be obtaining an increased share of the market, and it will be achieving this increase at the expense of its competitors. This increased market will, in many cases, include exporting potential. In order to satisfy the increased number of customers, the business will have to expand to meet the extra demand it creates.

Securing sources of supply

When a business has to rely on others to supply it with materials or services, it can be at a disadvantage. For example, if the supplier receives a better offer from other buyers, it may bargain for a better price. Similarly, when a supplier is finding that demand for its goods or services are particularly good, it will be more discerning about to whom it will provide them. A business may become large enough through expansion to create its own sources of supply and avoid having to rely on other businesses. For example, a tinned food manufacturer may extend into farming, thus becoming its own supplier.

Securing outlets

Growth can enable a business to create its own outlets for its products. For example, a clothes manufacturer could expand to set up its own retail outlets or a mail order company.

Methods of business expansion

There are four main ways a firm can grow:

1. Working existing plant and machinery harder and more efficiently, and as close to capacity as possible.
2. Extending existing capacity by moving to a new bigger site.
3. Merging with another company. A merger is where two or more companies join together to form a single business. A horizontal merger occurs where two or more businesses at the same stage of production join together, for example a producer of custom furniture joining with another in the same trade. A vertical merger is where two businesses at different stages of production join together, for example a cheese processing company buying a dairy farm.
4. The take-over of another business. This differs from a merger in that the company being taken over has not agreed to the development. This is achieved by buying a controlling interest in the other business. (See section 2.6 in Chapter 2.)

KEY WORDS

Find out the business-related meaning of each of the following terms. Write a separate sentence for each term to show your understanding.

exporting potential
cottage industry
market pull
linkage industry
internal economies of scale
external economies of scale
profit
specialist labour
industrial inertia

12.8 Labour versus technology

Some forms of production are said to be **labour-intensive**, that is, they are highly dependent on labour, e.g. farming. Where labour is relatively cheap and capital is expensive then firms will be inclined to use large amounts of labour in their production processes. In some cases firms have no choice but to depend on labour because of the nature of the business. For example, a hairdresser remains labour-intensive irrespective of the cost of capital.

Production is said to be **capital-intensive** when it uses a considerable amount of expensive plant, equipment, etc. Where capital is relatively cheap and labour is comparatively expensive, firms will be inclined to use large amounts of capital in their production processes and be more inclined to automate (see below).

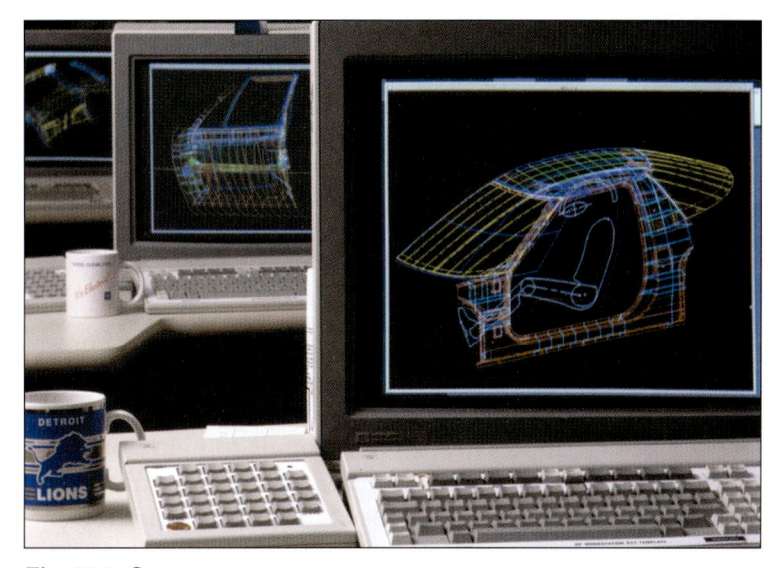

Fig. 12.8 *Computer system*

In developing countries there is a painful transition through which each country must pass in its movement towards international competitiveness. This means that fewer labour-intensive methods are used and modern technology increasingly becomes the norm. During the process there are many problems of adjustment for workers and businesses as the new technologies are embraced.

Throughout the world, each sector of industry has been transformed by new technology. **Lean production** is the name given to making the best use of technology and labour techniques in order to continuously improve the production methods of a business. In the forefront of lean production is automation, computer-aided design (CAD), computer-aided manufacture (CAM) and computer-aided instruction (CAI).

Automation

The term **automation** refers to changing a task so that it can be carried out by machines. Automation in the modern sense involves the use of sophisticated machinery, which is electronically or computer controlled, to carry out manufacture with minimal human intervention. Automation has been with us for a long time, but rapidly changing technology has led to automation being increasingly computer driven, as explained in the following sections.

Effects of automation

⬇

Increased technical innovation

⬇

Shorter working week

⬇

Need for retraining

⬇

Improved working conditions

⬇

Increased unemployment

⬇

More leisure

⬇

?

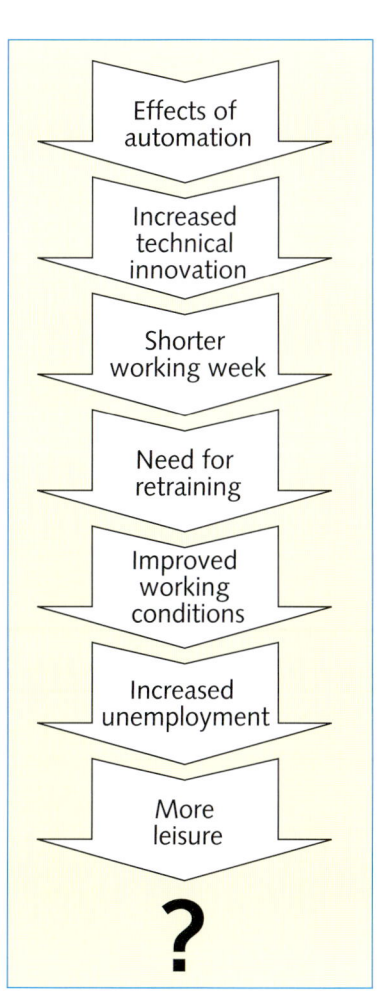

Fig. 12.9 *Some effects of automation. What next?*

Principles of Business – Profile 2

Computer-aided design (CAD)

CAD uses computer technology to design products on the screen of a *visual display unit* (VDU). The 'prototype' can be built up in picture form and rotated to show different angles. The design can even be submitted to on-screen tests, such as that for load limits, etc. Various alternative models can be compared and modified on screen, and then printed out as **hard copy**. The use of CAD in this manner saves the need to produce expensive models and prototypes of major items such as ships, bridges or aircraft. In addition, the whole design process is now much quicker and can be relatively easily modified when a new model is needed. For example, a CAD package developed to design fitted kitchens can readily be adapted to many rooms of different shapes and sizes.

Computer-aided manufacture (CAM)

CAM has become commonplace in modern manufacturing, where large quantities are being produced by mass or flow production. Robotics is also playing an increasingly important part. Industrial robotics has become a logical extension of computerised automation. Robotics is ideal for carrying out work that is repetitive and boring, or dangerous. They are used, for example, in car plants for weld body parts and spray paint, and even to fit windscreens. They are expensive to set up, but use minimum labour.

Computer-aided instruction (CAI)

Even the process of teaching people to use new technology has developed to the stage where the instruction is frequently carried out by computer. You can recognise this to be true if you are familiar with using a computer; few computers supply manuals to help you learn about your computer because the modern computer is 'user friendly' and teaches you much of the knowledge you need. Similar instruction programmes have been developed in the workplace to familiarise staff about the work they must do.

Fig. 12.10 *Robotics in a car plant*

The use of computers in production can have the following results:

- *The standardisation of products* results in more economical production, and lower prices.
- *Business risk can be increased* because sophisticated, expensive machinery must be purchased well in advance of the sale of products.
- *Fewer people will be employed*, and those displaced by automation need to find alternative forms of employment.
- *Leisure time* could theoretically be increased, e.g. by job sharing.
- *The need for tertiary services* is increased. Tertiary services are those businesses that are involved in the change of ownership of goods and the provision of services.

KEY WORDS

Find out the business-related meaning of each of the following terms. Write a separate sentence for each term to show your understanding.

hard copy   computer-aided design   labour intensive   automated   capital intensive
computer-aided manufacture   automation   computer-aided instruction

Chapter 12 – **Production**

12.9 Things to do

This section contains a variety of exercises to help you create revision notes, to test your understanding and to prepare you for examinations.

Search and find

Write out the question and the answer by referring back through the text to form revision notes.

1. What is meant by the term 'production'?
2. Name the three primary needs.
3. In what ways would you say that the aims of primary and secondary production differ from the aims of tertiary production?
4. Briefly describe the four factors of production.
5. How would all of the factors of production be involved in the creation of a new office block?
6. Briefly describe the three categories that land can be divided into as a factor of production.
7. Why does the factor of land include minerals?
8. Describe some of the ways that the supply and quality of labour are affected.
9. 'Mobility of labour can have good and bad influences on labour supply.' Explain this statement.
10. 'The factor of capital includes far more than money.' Explain this statement.
11. What is the particular significance of venture capital to a business and why can it be costly to obtain?
12. Explain the difference between fixed capital and working capital.
13. In what ways can entrepreneurs be said to 'co-ordinate' the factors of production?
14. Briefly describe the three levels of production.
15. Give examples of the levels of production in the Caribbean region.
16. What is meant by the term 'the chain of production'?
17. Describe the possible chain of production for a wooden chair.
18. How does the chain of production illustrate that the various levels of production are interdependent?
19. Give reasons why you think the 'primary', 'secondary' and 'tertiary' types of production are given these names.
20. Give examples of products that would be likely to be produced by each of the three methods of production, 'job', 'batch' and 'flow'.
21. What factors influence the choice of these methods of production?
22. Why does job production tend to be labour-intensive, but flow production particularly capital-intensive?
23. Why is quality control important in ensuring that customers get value for money?
24. Why do you think time is an important aspect of work study?
25. What do you understand by the term 'economies of scale'?

Principles of Business – Profile 2

26 What are the advantages enjoyed by large firms? Why do large firms also have disadvantages?

27 In what ways does the Law of Diminishing Returns show the limits of large-scale production?

28 Why do small firms continue to exist even though large businesses have so many advantages?

29 Why are cottage industries important to the Caribbean region?

30 What is a linkage industry? Why are they important?

31 Give an account of what you see as the most significant influences on the location of business.

32 How can business size affect the organisational structure of a business?

33 Give two examples each of internal and external economies of scale.

34 Describe the four main ways a firm can grow.

35 What factors influence the location of a business?

36 Explain the difference between the terms 'labour-intensive' and 'capital-intensive'?

37 Explain the similarities and the differences between CAD and CAM.

38 'CAI has taken the human element out of learning.' Briefly discuss this statement.

39 Explain how a business can benefit from computer technology. Are there any disadvantages from the point of view of the business?

40 'Technological developments are good for business, but many workers fear the changes they bring.' Discuss this statement.

What do you know?

Write out the complete sentence and insert the missing word, which can be chosen from the list at the end of the test.

1 The purpose of production is to provide people with the things they ….. or want to consume.
2 A major decision that a firm has to make is where to ….. its premises.
3 ….. occurs when a person leaves one area and moves to another.
4 The ….. of value that a firm owns is usually referred to as its capital.
5 The ….. level of production meets only the basic needs.
6 In order to be able to export a country needs to be producing a ….. .
7 ….. is the human contribution to production.
8 The chain of production shows the ….. between the three levels of production.
9 If an entrepreneur successfully predicts future demand they are usually rewarded with ….. .
10 Large firms achieve bigger profits because they enjoy ….. of scale.

Choose the missing words from the following:

surplus   need   subsistence   migration   economies   locate   links   profit   assets   labour

Chapter 12 – Production

Structured questions

Q1 The tables 12.4 and 12.5 relate to a small firm which specialises in the production of hand-made dolls. The firm has varied its workforce in order to assess the optimum size.

Labour force	Total output (per week)	Average output
4	200	
5	260	
6	324	
7	392	
8	456	
9	504	
10	540	
11	572	
12	576	

Table 12.4 *Varying the workforce*

Number of workers employed	10
Number of dolls produced	540
Weekly wages of each worker	$1100
Rent, rates, depreciation, etc.	$ 260
Power	$ 100
Raw materials	$ 500

Table 12.5 *The different costs incurred by the firm during a five day working week*

(a) Explain the difference between the terms 'output' and 'average output'. **2**

(b) What does the wording 'optimum size' mean? **2**

(c) What is the optimum sized labour force indicated by table 12.4? **2**

(d) Calculate the average output of dolls for each of the different sizes of labour force. **3**

(e) Using the given data draw curves on a graph to show average output. **3**

(f) Give a reason why the firm may not wish to produce its maximum output of 576 dolls per week. **3**

(g) If the dolls were selling for $10 each:
 (i) What would be the firm's weekly income? **2**
 (ii) Subtract the total production costs from the firm's weekly income to calculate the firm's weekly profit. **3**

Q2

(a) What do you understand by the term 'automation' in relation to production? **2**

(b) In what ways could automation improve working conditions in a factory? **2**

(c) Give three examples of ways that automation can 'increase technical innovation'. **3**

(d) Why does automation often result in a need for retraining? How can CAI assist in this? **3**

(e) What are CAD and CAM and how do they contribute to automated production? **5**

(f) Give examples of what makes some production defined as 'labour-intensive' and others 'capital-intensive'. **5**

Principles of Business – Profile 2

Q3

(a) Define the terms below.
  (i) economies of scale — *2*
  (ii) diseconomies of scale. — *2*

(b) Select one product being manufactured for the tourist industry in your country, and explain to a manufacturer who could, but does not currently benefit from large-scale business, four benefits to be derived from such an operation. — *8*

(c) Since you wish to provide some amount of balance in your discourse with the manufacturer in (b) above, highlight four disadvantages which could result from large-scale business operations. — *8*

Q4

(a) Primary production is sometimes referred to as the extractive industries. Why is it referred to in this way? — *1*

(b) How do the extractive industries support the other forms of production? — *2*

(c) What is secondary production? Name and define the two main categories into which this form of production can be divided. — *3*

(d) Wholesalers, retailers, exporters and importers are sometimes referred to as the 'distribution trades'. Explain why they are referred to in this way. — *3*

(e) 'Tertiary production is very different from the other forms of production but it is just as important.' Discuss this statement. — *5*

(f) Take a particular product and describe its development from primary through to the tertiary stage. Explain why each stage is important to the others. — *6*

Q5

(a) What is the 'chain of production'? — *2*

(b) Briefly describe the three types of production that are normally involved in the chain of production. — *3*

(c) Why does the chain of production result in interdependence in the economy? — *3*

(d) Draw a simple flow diagram to show comparisons of the contrasting chains of production of each of the following items: a woollen sweater, a china vase, cheese. — *6*

(e) Draw a simple table with three columns headed by the titles 'Primary', 'Secondary' and 'Tertiary' production. Enter six of the following occupations in the appropriate columns, with at least two in each column: farmer, shopkeeper, road maker, fisherman, builder, bank cashier, lorry driver, miner, oil driller, market trader, engineer, insurance agent, dressmaker, carpenter. — *6*

Q6

(a) Name two of the basic needs of people. — *1*

(b) State one way that secondary production helps to meet the basic needs of people. — *2*

(c) Describe three ways that tertiary production helps both producers and consumers. — *3*

Chapter 12 – **Production**

(d) State two contrasting examples of enterprises you would expect to find in each of the sectors of production (primary, secondary and tertiary). Give reasons why you have categorised them in the way you have. **6**

(e) Clearly explain why all three sectors of production are interdependent. **8**

Q7

(a) Define production in its broadest sense. **2**

(b) How does production provide help to meet human needs? **2**

(c) Define the four factors of production. **4**

(d) How can the four factors of production be linked to earnings? **4**

(e) List each of the following in a table under the appropriate factors of production: oil; computer; fish; farm; farmer; bakery; trees; lorry; factory; stock; supermarket; engineer; electrician; dairy; bricklayer. **8**

Research assignments

1 Describe the economic factors you would consider if you were an entrepreneur choosing a site in the Caribbean to locate a medium-sized manufacturing business. Include in your report information and evidence to support your views.

2 a) What is meant by 'economies of scale'. Use specific examples from businesses in your region to illustrate your answer.

   b) Using examples from your region, show why small firms are able to survive even though they do not benefit from economies of scale in the manner of large organisations.

3 Give an outline description of four firms within a 25-mile radius of your home, and offer explanations of the reasons they are situated where they are. Present copies of all correspondence between yourself and these firms.

4 What is meant by the term 'linkage industry'? Select one product from one sector and trace the linkages which result in its production. Provide evidence to show that you have personally researched a genuine linkage.

5 Consider the extent to which siting of any two businesses in your locality can be seen to be influenced by local or national government. Write a summary report containing evidence to support your findings.

6 Investigate the various types of cottage industry that are in operation in your local community. How do they benefit the economy?

7 Produce a report that contains evidence from local businesses that shows that the success of manufacturing industry is dependent on the effectiveness of those engaged in tertiary production.

8 Design and implement a survey of local firms that clearly shows the difference between the manufacturing and construction industries, and compares the percentage of each in your sample area. Write up a report that includes graphic illustrations of the data you have collected.

9 Research evidence that illustrates the types of production that have declined and those that have grown in your country. To what extent are these trends reflected in business in your area? Give possible reasons for the trends you have identified.

Chapter 13 Marketing

13.1 The market

The market

The term **market** can be broadly described as any situation which brings together the **sellers** and **buyers** of **goods** (tangible commodities) or **services** (work performed for reward). For example, the exchange may take place in a well-defined place such as a local street market, a wholesale market, or a retail store. Or the market-place may be less specifically defined, such as selling by post, telephone or via the internet.

The function of the market is to establish a link in the **chain of supply** between the producer, or the supplier, and the customer (see figure 13.1). Customers are sometimes referred to as **consumers** because they use up (consume) goods.

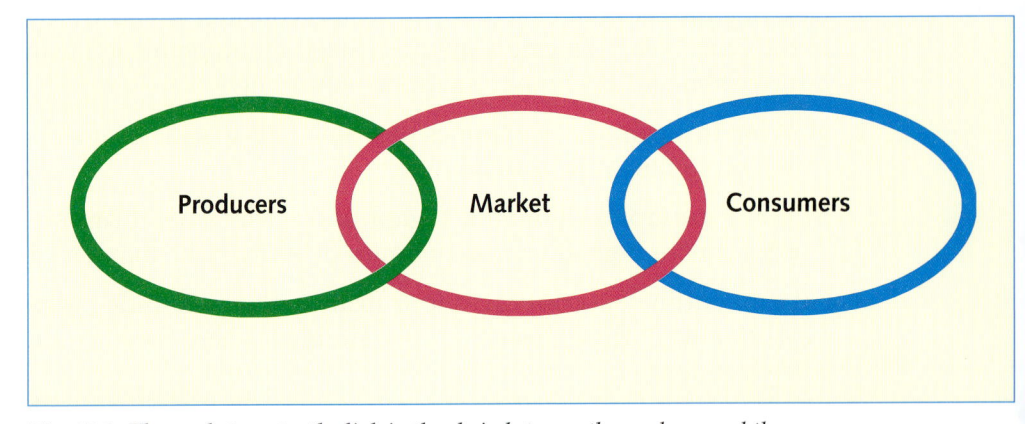

Fig. 13.1 *The market creates the link in the chain between the producer and the consumer*

Unlike the barter system that we touched on in Chapter 1 (*direct* trading), this buying and selling is *indirect* because it involves products being exchanged for money, and the money used later to buy other goods or services.

A market consists of four important elements:

1. Buyers
2. Sellers
3. Goods or services
4. Price

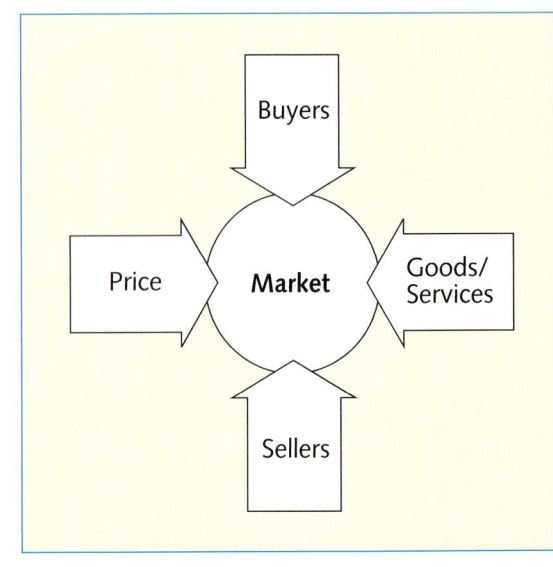

Fig. 13.2 *The market mechanism*

Chapter 13 – **Marketing**

It is the interconnection of these elements that makes it possible for a market to operate. Take away any one of these elements and it is difficult for the market to function effectively.

It is important to realise that not all markets are concerned with the sale of goods. Some markets provide specialist services, for example the stock market. A market can be divided into two clear types: the consumer market and the industrial market.

The consumer market refers to individuals and households who buy goods and services for their personal use. These purchases may be:

- durables – those goods which last a relatively long time and are not purchased frequently (e.g. cars, furniture, and electrical goods such as washing machines, etc.). Consumer durables are sometimes considered part of an individual's personal wealth.
- non-durables (*consumables*) – are bought frequently and used quite quickly, e.g. food and cosmetics.
- services – tasks provided, for a fee, to benefit the consumer in some way, e.g. hairdressing, entertainment, car repairs, plumbing, house repairs, window cleaning.

The industrial market refers to individuals or organisations who buy products or services that will be used in running their own business, or to be resold to other customers. These may be:

- capital goods – purchased infrequently and used over a relatively long period of time (e.g. new premises, vehicles, machinery, computer equipment).
- consumable products – bought frequently and used relatively quickly (e.g. raw materials, lubricants, goods for resale, office stationery, etc.).
- services – provided by specialists to carry out specific tasks for the business (e.g. transportation and distribution, advertising agencies, recruitment agencies, machinery and vehicle servicing, cleaning, etc.).

Market segmentation

A market segment is a part of a market that has its own distinct characteristics, for example where a group of consumers within the market have similar requirements (e.g. teenagers and pop music).

When a market segment can be identified, it can be targeted separately from other segments of the market. For example, sports equipment will be more likely to be bought by young people, and so suitable products can be targeted to this group.

There are some clearly identifiable factors that can be found influencing market segmentation:

- *Geographical factors* – where the potential consumer lives can influence the likely demand for a product. For example, the market for latest fashion clothes is greater in high-population areas than in less densely populated places.
- *Demographic (age) factors* – older people are more likely than younger persons to buy products purporting to make you look younger. Young people tend to have different leisure pursuits compared to older people.
- *Gender factors* – female demand for products are clearly different from the demand by the male population, e.g. clothes and cosmetics.

KEY WORDS

Find out the business-related meaning of each of the following terms. Write a separate sentence for each term to show your understanding.

market
consumer market
industrial market
durable
non-durable goods
services   capital goods
consumable products

Principles of Business – Profile 2

■ *Income factors* – working people have more money to spend than students, consequently, working people can afford to buy more extravagantly. A family with a low income will spend money very differently from the way of a high-income family.

Market orientation

Sometimes marketing is product orientated – it pursues a sales concept. This means that the product and its price is the most important concern, as opposed to what the consumer wants. Clearly this approach is not in the best interests of the consumer and, in today's international markets, few firms can afford to be too product orientated. Marketing is said to be market orientated when market research is carried out to find out what the customer wants, and how much they are prepared to pay, prior to commencing production. In following this approach the producer is more assured of success because the marketing concept is being pursued (as discussed later).

Market share

The proportion of total sales of a product accounted by an individual brand is known as its market share. A business's market share, when compared to the market share of its competitors, provides an indicator of its success in marketing its product over a given period of time. Generally, a firm will need to achieve sufficient sales to justify economic production, but beyond its minimum target the firm may aim to increase its market share to become a market leader in a particular product by increasing its market share. Market share is calculated by the following formula:

$$\text{Market share} = \frac{\text{Total sales of the business's product}}{\text{Total sales in the whole market}} \times 100$$

Market research

Market research (examined in detail in Chapter 14) is concerned with the collection and analysis of information about a specific market. It aims to identify customer needs. Market research involves the study of statistics and reports that already exist (secondary data), and gathering new data (primary data) first-hand through market research surveys of consumers.

From the data gathered, market researchers hope to find out what people want in quite specific terms, for example colours, shapes, packaging, quality and price, etc. This information is used to give direction to the production and marketing of goods, thus increasing the possibility of success.

KEY WORDS

Find out the business-related meaning of each of the following terms. Write a separate sentence for each term to show your understanding.

market segment
product orientated
market orientated
market share
market leader
market research
secondary data
primary data

13.2 What is marketing?

The previous section was concerned with what a market is and it summarised the various types of markets that exist. Some of these types of market have a direct influence on the distribution of goods, that is, how the goods reach the consumer. The marketing department of a large organisation is concerned with this: getting the products to the consumer.

Marketing refers to all the processes involved in selling goods or services in the most profitable and efficient manner. It begins with an examination of what people want from a product or service (market research). This is followed by **product development**: an assessment of how to produce a product or service that will satisfy people's requirements, and at the same time make a profit. The next stage is to develop a **marketing strategy** that will get the product to the appropriate market at a competitive price. This will involve creating an **advertising campaign** that is backed by selling and distribution procedures.

The flow chart in figure 13.3 shows the way that the marketing process is developed.

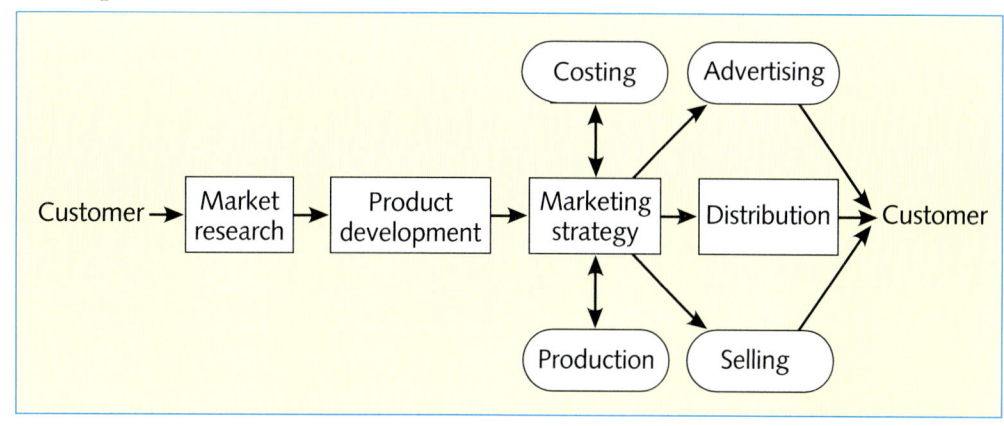

Fig. 13.3 *Marketing flow chart*

Marketing in this sense is a two-way process. It connects those who produce goods and services with potential buyers. It also finds out what products and services consumers want and relays this information to the producers. This enables them to make the right things available (see figure 13.4).

The way that a business finds out what the customer wants is by **market research**. This is the systematic and continuous evaluation of all the factors involved in the transfer of goods and services from the producer to the ultimate consumer. It is particularly concerned with the reactions of consumers.

Sales is a support system for marketing. In other words, sales is a marketing strategy which facilitates exchange. Therefore, a major part of the work of a marketeer is to choose the best possible methods of sales to match the products being marketed. For example, the sales strategies for a new flavour soft drink would differ from the sales strategies for a property. Market research plays an important role in the development of sales strategies.

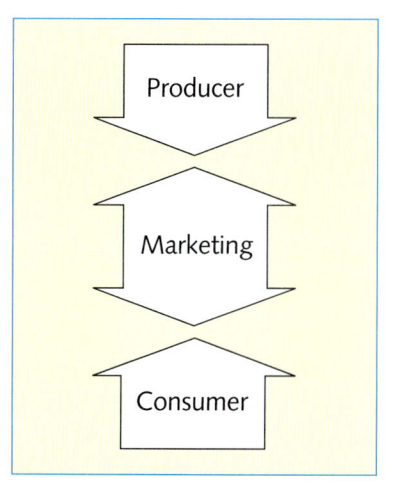

Fig. 13.4 *Marketing is a two-way process*

13.3 The marketing department

A firm's marketing department is concerned with selling its products or services. This can mean disposing of products the firm has produced, but more often it is a case of identifying what customers want (customer concept) and then arranging to meet the need that exists, hopefully making a profit in the process.

There are many ways to organise a marketing department, and its structure will be influenced by the size of the firm. In a large company it would be possible to split the department into several sub-divisions, each with a specific marketing function. In a small organisation a few members of staff may have to incorporate several of these functions into their duties.

Principles of Business – Profile 2

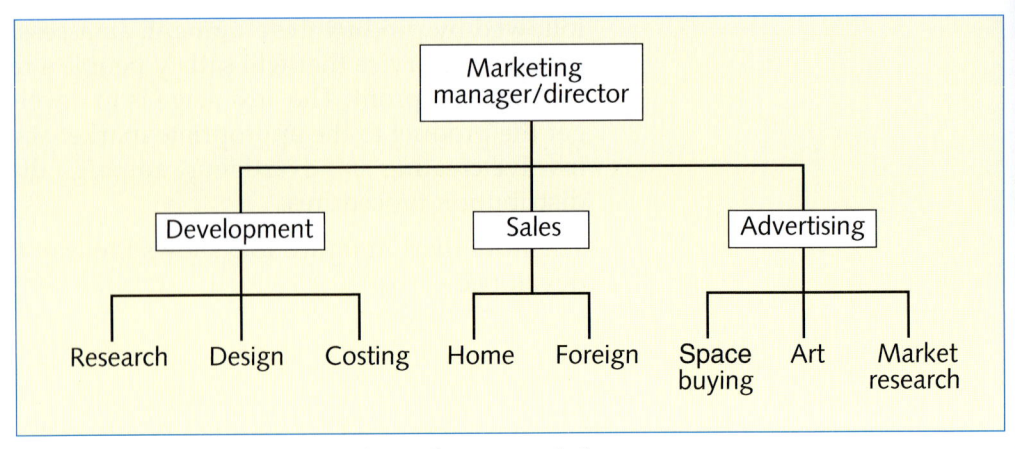

Fig. 13.5 *Typical structure of a marketing department of a large company*

The functions of a marketing department

The marketing department is controlled by the marketing director or a senior manager. This position entails carrying out sales policies decided by the board of directors, and supervising the work of all people employed in the department, including the company's *sales representatives*, whose job is to visit potential customers and obtain orders.

All documentation related to sales of the firm's products is dealt with either directly or indirectly by the marketing department. This includes sending out *mail shots* (sales leaflets), dealing with customers' enquiries and orders, arranging for the despatch of goods, and sending out invoices and statements of account.

A major part of the work of the marketing department is to choose the method of sales to be employed. This will vary according to the product or service being marketed. For example, the method of marketing a new chocolate bar will differ from that used to sell a valuable antique.

The way that products are to be distributed is given careful consideration. This involves decisions of which *channels of distribution* should be used, and whether trade will be directed through wholesalers, retailers, or by direct marketing.

The marketing department is obviously involved in advertising the firm's products. Where the firm is large, it may have a separate advertising department. This department will carry out the instructions of the marketing department, and will also offer advice on marketing strategies, including market research. These aspects of marketing are covered in more detail later in this book.

KEY WORDS

Find out the business-related meaning of each of the following terms. Write a separate sentence for each term to show your understanding.

- marketing concept
- sales concept
- customer concept
- mail shots
- marketing department
- sales representative
- distribution channels

13.4 Marketing mix

Those directly involved in marketing generally follow the customer concept defined earlier; that is, they try to see things from their customers' point of view. Where a business wants to influence a specific group of customers (e.g. teenagers), then they are its target market. A business often has many *target markets*, perhaps one for each of its products or services, and it may well approach each *target market* in a different way.

Chapter 13 – **Marketing**

Once a business has identified its target market it will select what it considers is the most appropriate **marketing mix**. The marketing mix is a collective term that is used to refer to the whole range of marketing activities, techniques and strategies that a firm uses to reach its target market. The variables of a marketing mix can easily be remembered by referring to the 'four P's': *product*, *price*, *place* and *promotion*.

Fig. 13.6 *The marketing mix*

Product

Clearly, the product, good or service (or even an idea to be sold) plays an important role in marketing. There is little point in trying to market something that the consumer does not want. For this reason, the needs of the consumer must be focused on.

Packaging is linked with the product. Packaging is the outer wrapping or container for goods. Packaging not only presents the product in an attractive way but it also gives details about the contents, any potential hazards, correct usage, etc. In this respect packaging:

- protects the product
- promotes the product
- preserves the life of the product
- prevents health hazards that could result from use of the product
- makes it more convenient for the consumer to handle the product
- enhances the general appearance of the product.

An old-established product in a new and improved package usually enhances the marketing potential of the product.

Branding is another important aspect of the product. Branding is giving a product a distinctive name, term, symbol or design to enable it to be recognised easily.

A **brand name** (or **trade mark**) is that part of branding which represents the actual letter, letters, word or group of words which make up the name of the product. The brand name differentiates one product from another similar or dissimilar product. Trade marks can be registered so that they can only be used by one firm.

In section 13.5 you will learn about the analysis of the product through an understanding of the **product life cycle** and the **Boston matrix**.

Fig. 13.7 *The 'four P's'; variables of the marketing mix enabling the seller to reach the target market*

Fig. 13.8 *A brand name has to be short, descriptive and easy to pronounce, and it must appeal to the target consumers*

Principles of Business – Profile 2

Price

No matter how attractive a product is, a crucial factor in the success of the marketing strategy will be the price. It is important to the seller because it incorporates profit, and it is important to consumers because it affects their ability to purchase what they want. Having decided on a product or service to sell, the business has to decide what price to charge. Most products have a *price plateau* that represents the price the customer expects to pay for a product or service. If the seller's price is too high, customers will not buy it. If the price is too far below the plateau, the customer may think the product is inferior, and still not buy it. In addition, if the price is too low, the seller might not cover their costs. Sometimes a firm may set a price that is deliberately low (called *penetration price*) in order to gain entry to a new market. In due course it would raise the price to a more profitable level.

Although it is the market that eventually determines the price (see later), it is initially fixed by the seller.

Cost-plus pricing: Many firms decide their price using this approach. It is the simplest method of deciding a price. It involves taking the unit cost (cost of producing a single item), adding overheads and a profit margin to arrive at the selling price. However, this method does not necessarily arrive at a price the market will accept. In this respect cost pricing could be seen as:

price = unit variable cost + fixed costs + mark up

Market-oriented pricing: With this method of deciding price, the seller surveys the market to find out what customers are willing to pay before setting their price. Following this strategy they can make their price more competitive than other firms. However, they must ensure they cover their costs. *Fixed costs* (e.g. rent for buildings, taxes, insurance, wages, etc.) are those that have to be paid whether or not a product or service is sold. *Variable costs* (e.g. raw materials, parts and packaging, etc.) are those which change depending on the quantity of a product made or a service provided.

Promotional pricing: This is a form of sales promotion used by producers and retailers that involves 'introductory-price' offers, 'money-off' packs, 'two-for-the-price-of-one' offers, etc. – sometimes referred to as 'below-the-line promotion'. In addition to increasing the sales of the product it is used to entice people into a shop with the lure of '*loss leader*' goods, tempting them to buy other products as *impulse buying*.

Market-skimming pricing: This is a pricing policy that involves charging a relatively high price for a product in order to secure a large profit margin. This could be used by a firm when targeting consumers who are not sensitive to price (e.g. consumers of luxury goods or services). The policy may be used during the early stages of the life cycle of a new product that has unique or novel features that enable it to command a high price.

Psychological pricing: With psychological pricing, firms will keep their prices just below certain levels so that they appear cheaper to the customer, for example charging 99 cents instead of $1, or $99.99 instead of $100.00. Firms may also operate a *differential pricing* policy. This is where the same product is sold at different prices to different market segments. For example, many transport facilities will offer lower prices at off-peak times.

Later in this chapter (in section 13.7) you will learn about the influence of *supply* and *demand* on price determination.

KEY WORDS

Find out the business-related meaning of each of the following terms. Write a separate sentence for each term to show your understanding.

brand name
target market
marketing mix
packaging
price plateau
loss leader
penetration price
cost-plus pricing
market-orientated price
promotional price
market-skimming price

Chapter 13 – **Marketing**

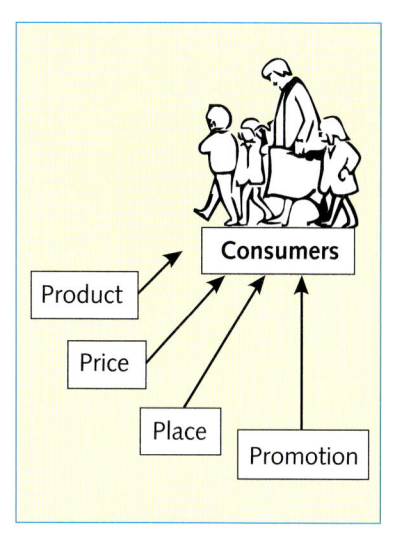

Fig. 13.9 *The strategies involved in the marketing mix are aimed at meeting the needs and desires of the consumer*

Place

Those involved in marketing a product have to ensure that it reaches a place where potential customers can conveniently make purchases. Getting them to this convenient place is called distribution. This requires wholesalers, retailers, importers, exporters and many other intermediaries, including transportation. This involves the business in selecting the best way to distribute a product from the producers or warehouses to a number of destinations so as to minimise transportation costs while meeting the customers' requirements. This topic is examined further in Chapter 15.

Promotion

This refers to the ways in which consumers are made aware of the availability of the product or service and the qualities it has. Advertising is the most important aspect of product promotion, and this is dealt with in Chapter 14.

Sales promotion is any activity that supplements advertising and other aspects of visual promotion. The following are just a few of the strategies used in sales promotion. You should look for examples of them.

- Trading stamps
- Free gifts/gift tokens
- Competitions.
- Product demonstrations
- Loss leaders
- Exhibitions
- Free samples

From the foregoing you can see that the marketing mix aims to get the right product to the consumer at the right price, and to a convenient place where it can be bought. The consumer is made aware of what is available through product promotion. All the strategies involved in the marketing mix are aimed at meeting the needs and desires of the consumer.

13.5 Product life cycle

In addition to deciding on the marketing mix, a firm must consider how sales might develop. All products move through identifiable stages, which are referred to as the product life cycle. Understanding this 'cycle' assists in the preparation of a sound marketing plan.

Pre-launch

This stage consists of all the developmental work undertaken before the product is put on the market. During the pre-launch phase, the decision has to be taken as to whether it is worthwhile to pursue the new development. Once it has been decided to proceed, a considerable amount of capital is consumed with no income being earned for some time. The time between the design of a product and its production is known as lead time.

Introduction

In the early stages of marketing, sales tend to be low, but large amounts of capital continue to be consumed. It is some time before the break-even stage (see Chapter 17) is reached and the product begins to show a profit.

Growth

If all goes well, sales and profits are steadily rising. Marketing becomes more economically viable as more cash comes in from customers. This is a time for vigorous advertising to promote maximum demand for the product.

Maturity

During this crucial period the rate of sales growth begins to slow down. The advent of maturity is often signalled by a falling off in profits. The product reaches its ceiling and begins to decline. This is a crucial period for the business because it is important to recognise the signal to improve the product or find a new one.

Decline

This is the period when sales volume shows a marked fall. Decline reveals that the product has lost its appeal or competitive edge. If steps have not already been taken to improve the product it will probably now have to be withdrawn in order to avoid making a loss.

Most products have a life cycle similar to that shown in the graph in figure 13.10, which plots a product from its introduction through to its decline. The production and marketing sections of the firm have to be aware of the position in their life cycle in order to maximise profits, and to plan the introduction of replacement products at the appropriate time.

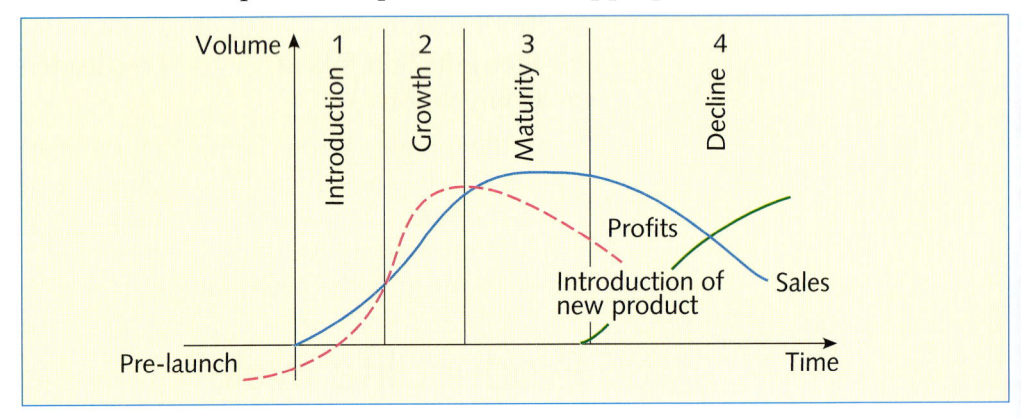

Fig. 13.10 *Product life cycle*

Product range and product mix

From the foregoing examination of product life cycle you will realise that if a firm markets only a single product it faces a considerable risk. In fact, most products are not marketed on their own but are part of a **range** of products. For example, a firm might produce a range of cake mixes, etc. Many small firms commence their business in this way. A large firm will have a product mix which consists of several different products, each with its own range, for example cake mixes, biscuits, chips, instant sauces, dessert toppings, etc.

The Boston growth and market share matrix

Product development is a strategy followed by a firm with the aim of increasing sales by developing *new* products which can be sold in *existing* markets, or new products which the firm uses to break into a new market (**diversifying**). Product development in a large organisation may be the responsibility of a Research and Development Department.

The **Boston matrix** (also referred to as the *Boston Box*) is a framework, used by larger companies with a wide product range, for highlighting and analysing product development. It identifies products that are **cash generators** and those that are **cash users**. The matrix depicts market growth rate on one axis

Chapter 13 – **Marketing**

	Market share	
	High	Low
High Market growth	Stars	Problem children
Low	Cash cows	Dogs

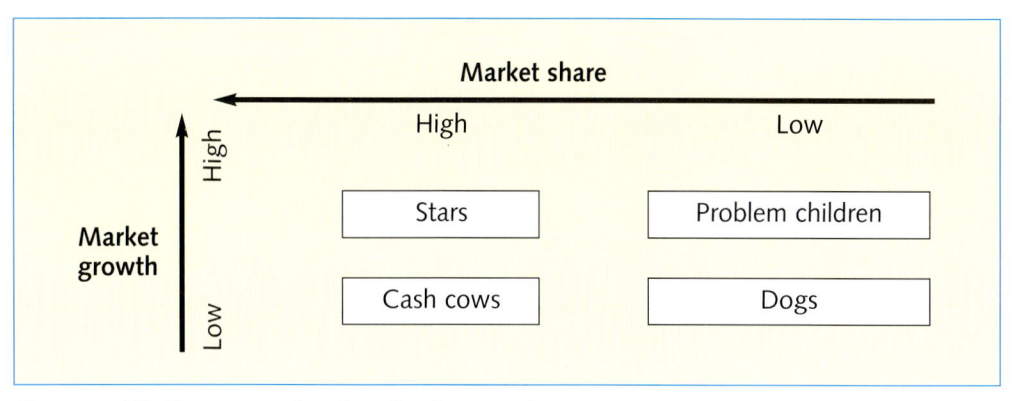

Fig. 13.11 *The Boston growth and market share matrix*

and the product's market share on the other (see figure 13.11). The matrix indicates that the higher the product's growth rate, the greater will be the capital investment required, while the greater the product's market share the greater will be the profit earned.

The four market growth/share segments relate to four product types:

- *'Cash cows'* are products in the mature phase of the product life cycle (see figure 13.10), which have a low growth rate (so they need little new investment to support them), and a high market share (yielding a high profit return). 'Cash cows' are the firm's main sources of internal funds for financing the introduction and development of new products.
- *'Stars'* are products which have a high growth rate (and need a considerable amount of new investment to keep up with market demand), and a high market share, often creating enough cash to make their operations self-financing. 'Star' products are normally relatively new products in the growth stage of the product life cycle. With careful management 'star' products can become the future 'cash cows' of the firm.
- *'Problem children'* are products which have a high growth rate and so demand large inputs of capital to support them, and have a low market share providing little or no profit. Such products are a drain on the firm's cash, but they can become 'stars' if their share of the market improves.
- *'Dogs'* are products which have a low growth rate and a small market share, and they appear to lack potential for future development. They are heavy users of resources, but remain unprofitable. 'Dogs' are clear candidates for abandonment, but the firm may retain them for strategic reasons (e.g. to maintain market share).

13.6 Merchandising

Packaging and display

Merchandising is an important marketing technique. It refers to the display of goods so that potential customers can conveniently see them and be influenced to buy. The following are just some of the methods of merchandising used by sellers of goods.

- Eye-catching window displays, including special offers.
- Use of in-house displays to reduce the number of employees needed to sell the goods.
- Careful layout of premises, allowing customers to get near to goods and move into other parts of the store.

KEY WORDS

Find out the business-related meaning of each of the following terms. Write a separate sentence for each term to show your understanding.

distribution
lead-time
cash generators
sales promotion
cash users
product mix
product life cycle
product development
product range
Boston matrix

- Packaging design that presents goods attractively.
- Opportunities for customers to inspect and perhaps touch goods.
- Clear labelling and price marking to reduce the need for customers to ask questions.
- Eye-level shelf displays for high priority goods.

Packaging and branding are important features of merchandising. Producers are required to comply with certain regulations related to the information that must be shown on their products (e.g. contents, weight, etc.), but they also want to put them in containers that will appeal to the customer.

Branding

Branding refers to giving a product a distinctive name that will be easily recognised and identified with the item in question. This is of considerable advantage in advertising a product, because if the brand name is easily recognised then less expense is involved in trying to make the public aware of the qualities of the product.

An example in which merchandising is particularly apparent is in self-service stores, but you should not think of merchandising as being confined to the retail trade. Merchandising is used by any business that displays goods rather than just keeping them inside their premises.

Protecting ideas

An entrepreneur may have created an idea or a product that he wants to protect or regulate other the use by others. There are four main ways of doing this:

1. **By patent** This gives the right to be the sole user of a completely new product to a person or a business.
2. **By registered design** A new design that has a distinctive visual appearance may be registered prior to its actual production.
3. **By trademark** Using a logo or symbol to distinguish a firm's brand (branding).
4. **By copyright** This gives legal protection by persons or businesses over certain kinds of intellectual material, e.g. artistic works, literary works, sound recordings, films, etc.

A franchise gives a person or a business (the franchisee) the right to sell a good or service that is owned by someone else (the franchisor). A franchise agreement usually involves the franchisor retaining an interest in the product in some way. For example, the franchisee may be required to follow merchandising rules set by the franchisor. Or, the franchisor may receive a percentage of the profits.

13.7 Price determination

All free markets involving many buyers and sellers operate according to the law of demand and supply. That is, if demand for goods and services increases faster than supply of them, then prices rise. If supply increases faster than demand, prices fall. In other words, the price of goods and services is determined by the interaction of the forces of demand and supply, and this of course has a direct influence on production.

Chapter 13 – **Marketing**

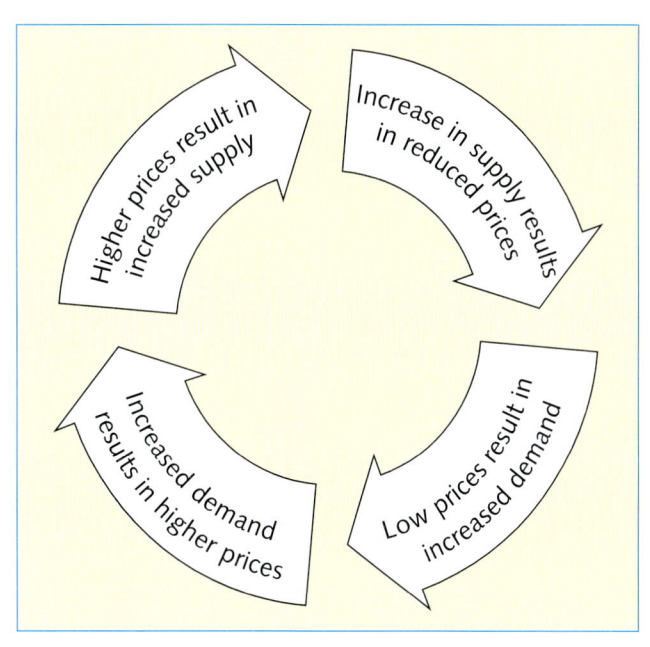

Fig. 13.12 *Interaction of demand and supply*

Demand

The demand for any commodity is the amount that consumers are prepared to purchase at a given price in a given period of time. For each price the demand is different. Usually, the lower the price the higher the quantity demanded, and vice versa, although there are exceptions. **Giffen goods** is a name given to those essential and relatively cheap goods for which demand is likely to increase following a rise in price. The term 'Giffen' is from a nineteenth-century economist of that name who noticed that when the price of bread increased, consumers bought more of it, being unable to afford to buy other more expensive alternatives such as meat and fruit.

The table in figure 13.13 shows an individual's possible demand schedule for candy bars at various prices. A demand schedule can also be shown graphically by plotting the data on a demand curve: the point X indicates that at a price of 30c, the person would be likely to buy three bars.

This demand schedule and demand curve only refer to an individual consumer, but market demand is created by many people. A market demand curve is obtained by summing the demand curves of all individuals, so we can expect the market demand to behave in a similar way to individual demand.

Both the individual demand curve and the market demand curve express a relationship between the demand for a commodity and the price of it, but there are other determinants of demand.

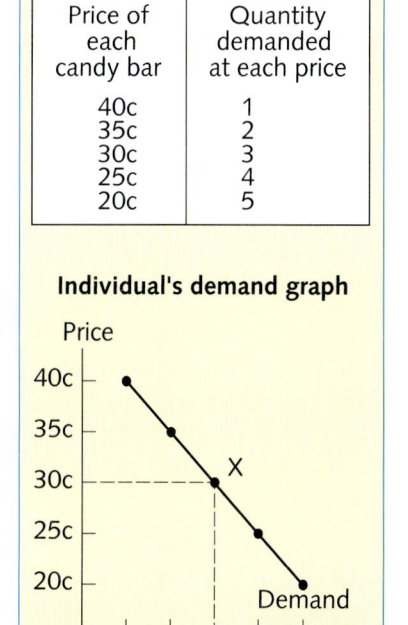

Individual's demand schedule

Price of each candy bar	Quantity demanded at each price
40c	1
35c	2
30c	3
25c	4
20c	5

Fig. 13.13 *Demand schedule and demand graph*

Determinants of demand

- The price of the commodity
- The price of other commodities
- The income of the buyers
- Population or number of buyers
- The buyer's scale of preferences, i.e. how much the buyer values or prefers the items he or she wants in comparison with other commodities.

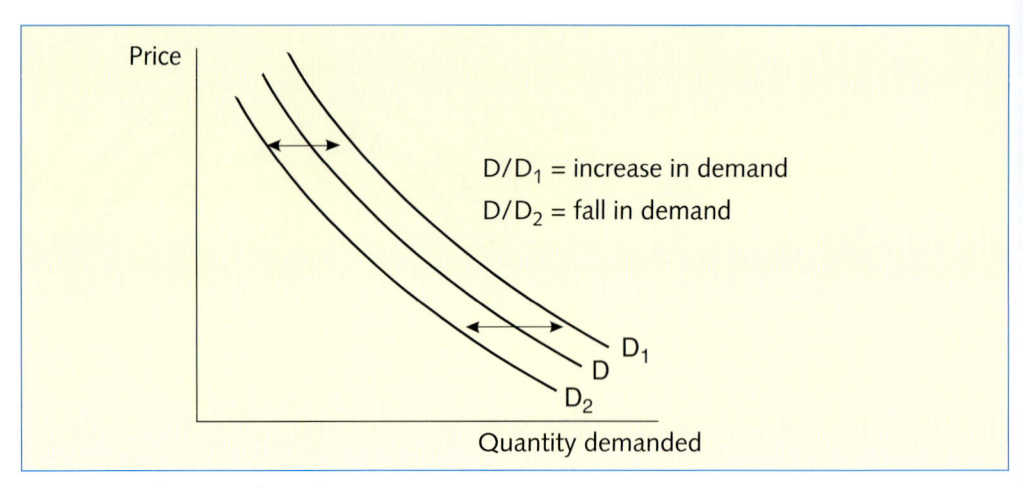

Fig. 13.14 *Changes in demand*

If one of the conditions of demand changes, the demand curve moves to a new position, as shown in figure 13.14. For example, a rise in income or purchasing power could increase market demand and shift the demand curve to the right (D to D1). On the other hand, if one of the determinants causes a fall in market demand, the curve moves to the left (D to D2).

Supply

Supply is the amount of a commodity that producers are willing to put on to the market at various prices in a given period of time. For each price the amount supplied is different. Alternatively, we could say that the supply curve shows the price that is necessary to persuade the producer to provide output. Usually, the higher the price the more of the commodity the producer will want to supply and vice versa, but as is the case with demand, there are some exceptions to this.

A supply schedule and graph can be constructed in a similar way to a demand schedule and graph. Unlike the demand curve, the supply curve usually slopes upwards to the right (see figure 13.15).

Equilibrium price

Price is the charge assigned to something, or the **exchange value** for a product or service. The demand for a product or service will be influenced by the price of it.

From our examination of supply and demand so far, it should be clear that buyers want to buy at the lowest price they can, whilst sellers want to obtain the highest price they can for their goods. Whilst these seem conflicting interests, it is a combination of demand and supply that determines price.

When any two forces balance each other they are said to be in **equilibrium**. Under the conditions of a perfect market, the price of a commodity is determined by the interaction of supply and demand. This can be made clearer by looking at a combined demand and supply schedule which is also expressed graphically for simple observation.

As shown in figure 13.16, it is only at the price of $3 that the number of teddy bears the consumers wish to buy is equal to the amount of teddy bears the producer is willing to supply. This is called the **equilibrium price**, the only price at which the amounts willingly demanded and supplied are equal.

Chapter 13 – **Marketing**

Market supply schedule	
Price	Quantity
10c	100
20c	200
30c	300
40c	400
50c	500

Price	Quantity demanded	Quantity supplied
$5	100	500
$4	200	400
$3	300	300
$2	400	200
$1	500	100

Fig. 13.15 *Supply schedule and supply graph*

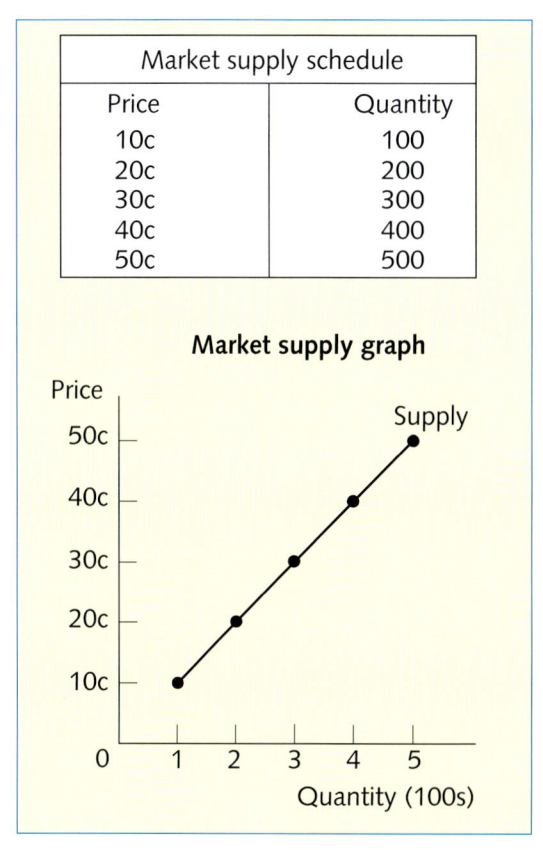

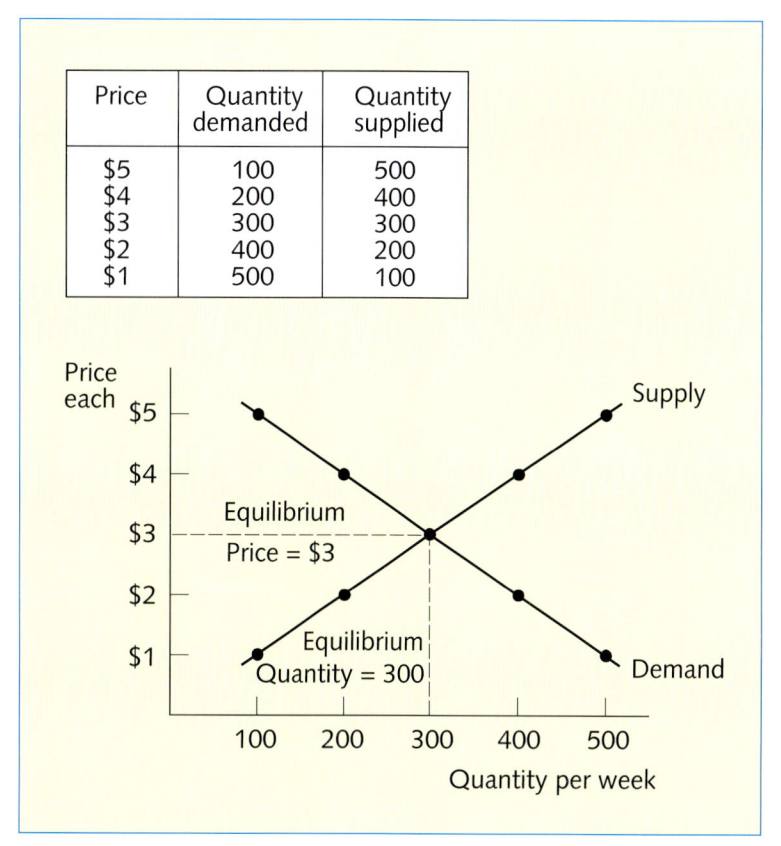

Fig. 13.16 *Market for teddy bears – amount demanded and supplied at various prices during one week*

In the diagram it can be seen that the equilibrium price is at the intersection of the demand and supply curves. We can also see that if the price is above the equilibrium price, there is an excess of supply and insufficient demand. The result of this is that the price falls towards the equilibrium price. Alternatively, if the price is below the equilibrium price there is insufficient supply and excess demand. This results in the price rising towards the equilibrium price.

13.8 Competition

Competition enhances the efficiency of the economic system. It is a major factor in the determination of price.

There are two main types of competition: perfect, pure or free competition, and imperfect competition.

Perfect competition

Perfect competition results from a market situation in which the products of the market-place are of the same kind, are well known to the participators in the market, and where 'breaking into' the market on the part of both buyers and sellers poses little or no problem. In other words, no one buyer or seller dominates. The competitiveness of the market eventually forces costs and prices to settle at the lowest possible levels, whilst production climbs to its peak.

Imperfect competition

When there are very few producers of goods and services in the market-place there is **imperfect competition**. In other words, there is less evidence of rivalry and excessive exchange in the market-place. In this atmosphere there is a **monopoly** or an **oligopoly**.

Monopoly

A monopolistic situation results when a single organisation controls an entire line of products, and is therefore able to determine the selling price. However, the seller is unable to fix both the price and the quantity supplied; the seller fixes prices at the highest level that the market is likely to tolerate. Cement production in Jamaica is a good example of this monopolistic situation. The price of the product is set by a single firm.

Oligopoly

Oligopolistic situations result when a few large suppliers dominate the market-place. There are many examples of oligopolies in the Caribbean. The products being marketed are generally the same in kind, for example soap powder. Prices are usually tightly structured. The aim is to reduce or even prevent competition.

Cartels

Cartels are also members of the imperfect market. A cartel consists of a number of firms within a particular industry, such as the Organization of Petroleum Exporting Countries (OPEC) in the petroleum industry. The firms agree on things such as pricing, production levels, sales and the division of the markets.

Government intervention

Governments are sometimes obliged to intervene and protect consumers from imperfections in the working of the price system. There are two basic methods of government intervention that are used.

- *The control of prices* through taxation or **subsidies**. Taxation increases production costs, whereas subsidies reduce them.
- *The control of demand* by **rationing**, which is an attempt to influence production and consumption by regulating effective demand.

Imperfect competition influences on market

It will have been obvious from the elements of imperfect competition we have looked at here, that they demonstrate how supply and price can be influenced by a powerful business or governments. They can set prices to whatever level they wish, even to the extent of charging unreasonably high prices. They can restrict output, which can ensure they will still sell their products, whatever price they charge. They can also influence what will exist within the market, for example fashion and other market trends.

Caribbean market structure

Monopolies in the Caribbean can be seen in the **public utilities** companies, where light, power and water supply are usually provided by a State Corporation or a nationalised industry. Telecommunications, telegraph and telephone services are provided by the Cable and Wireless Company.

Chapter 13 – **Marketing**

KEY WORDS

Find out the business-related meaning of each of the following terms. Write a separate sentence for each term to show your understanding.

merchandising
profit maximisation
demand supply price
equilibrium price
perfect competition
imperfect competition
monopoly patent
oligopoly
cartel copyright

Newspaper companies of Jamaica, Barbados, Trinidad and Tobago, among other nations, operate in an oligopolistic market structure. The oil companies operating within the region do so within an oligopoly market structure. However, oil prices are fairly stable throughout the region. This type of market structure is also seen in the electronic media whereby some media houses own television and radio stations. Radio Jamaica Limited is one such media house.

Multinational corporations control the production of bauxite and oil. These also operate within an oligopoly market structure. Their operations can be described in a global context rather than in a regional context.

The role of governments

From the foregoing it will be realised that governments have an important part to play in a free economy to ensure that, whilst imperfect competition may be impossible to avoid, it is not allowed to exploit the public. Governments attempt to restrict the development of non-competitive market structures such as those examined earlier. The major goal is to ensure consumers are protected from unfair practices. In some cases, because of the size of the countries involved, and the resources available, it is difficult to prevent monopolies from developing.

However, not all monopolies restrict the supply of essential products in order to gain the highest profits possible, or produce inferior goods. Some monopolies have been able to operate efficiently and thus produce large quantities of goods at reasonable cost to the consumer.

Governments, therefore, put policies in place by which such businesses are to be guided. They also intervene when situations arise that are untenable.

13.9 Things to do

This section contains a variety of exercises to help you create revision notes, to test your understanding and to prepare you for examinations.

Search and find

Write out the question and the answer by referring back through the text to form revision notes.

1. In what ways can a market be said to 'bring together the buyers and sellers of goods and services'?
2. How do goods differ from services?
3. Why are customers sometimes referred to as 'consumers'?
4. Briefly explain the difference between the consumer market and the industrial market.
5. Why is it useful to divide the market into segments?
6. Give one different example each of market segments for dishwashers, beauty products, vitamin pills, sports trainers, CAD/CAM equipment.

Principles of Business – Profile 2

7 Why is it generally better for a business to be market orientated?

8 Under what circumstances might a firm decide to be product orientated?

9 Calculate the percentage of market share for 'Filled Buns' of each of the following leading fast food companies for the last two years:

Company	Millions sold last year	%	Millions sold this year	%
The Runaway Chicken	65		68	
Sizzling Sausages Ltd.	117		119	
Flying Fish Bar	78		153	
Total sales	???		???	

10 Which company in the table above was the market leader last year, and which is the market leader this year? Which company has made the greatest improvement in the percentage of its market share in the last year?

11 A firm is surveying the potential market for a new type of energy drink. Give two examples of sources of secondary data that might help them, and two examples of ways they might collect primary data.

12 Why is marketing said to be a 'two-way process'?

13 Explain the difference between 'sales concept' and 'marketing concept'.

14 List the functions of a marketing department and briefly describe the work of two personnel that would work within it.

15 What kind of factors do you think help a business to identify its 'target market'?

16 Why does the marketing mix involve the business in making decisions?

17 Pair up some of the 'ingredients' of the marketing mix (e.g. price and product) and say why they are important to each other in the marketing of goods.

18 How do you think changes in the marketing mix could help a business to achieve the best possible sales?

19 Describe some of the factors that will influence the price the seller will charge.

20 Why can promotion be said to be 'about communicating'?

21 Describe at least four methods used in the 'promotional mix'.

22 Explain some of the ways a firm might decide the market price for its products.

23 What is the product life cycle and why do firms need to have knowledge of it?

24 Explain the difference between the terms 'product range' and 'product mix'.

25 The Boston matrix can be used to identify 'cash generators' and 'cash users'. Explain this statement.

26 List at least six merchandising techniques used by the seller of goods.

27 What is distinctive about brand names?

28 How does the use of brand names assist in the marketing of products?

29 What do you understand by 'demand'? What are the determinants of demand?

Chapter 13 – Marketing

30 Use the following information to produce a simple demand graph:

Price per unit (cents)	Quantity at each price (kilos)
45	1
40	1
35	3
30	4
25	5

31 With the aid of a simple diagram explain the effects of changes in demand on the demand graph.

32 What do we mean by the term 'supply'?

33 Why are there so many different ways of deciding what price to charge?

34 How does supply and demand help to identify the 'equilibrium price'?

35 How does monopoly differ from oligopoly?

36 Give examples of monopolistic situations in the Caribbean region.

37 'Not all monopolies are in conflict with public interest'. What is your view?

38 What is 'imperfect' about 'imperfect competition'?

What do you know?

Write out the complete sentence and insert the missing word, which can be chosen from the list at the end of the questions.

1. Marketing connects those who produce goods with potential ..... .
2. The ..... concept refers to the business goal of trying to satisfy customers and make a profit in doing so.
3. The way a business finds out what customers want is by market ..... .
4. A firm's marketing department is concerned with ..... its products.
5. In a large firm it is possible to ..... the marketing department into several sub-divisions.
6. Sales ..... visit potential customers and obtain orders.
7. A business will often have a number of ..... markets.
8. If supply increases faster than demand, prices ..... .
9. Usually, the lower the price the ..... the quantity demanded.
10. When any two forces balance each other they are said to be in ..... .

Choose the missing words from the following:

target   buyers   divide   fall   higher   marketing   selling   research   equilibrium   representatives

Structured questions

Q1 This question is related to the illustration of a product life cycle shown in figure 13.10.

(a) What is meant by 'product life cycle'? — 2

(b) At what stage in a product life cycle is marketing at its maximum level? — 2

(c) Why is it important for both the production and marketing departments to be aware of the position of their products in the life cycle? — 4

Principles of Business – Profile 2

(d) Compare the functions of the production and marketing sections of a large organisation. **4**

(e) When is the most appropriate time in a product life cycle:
(i) to begin new product development? **2**
(ii) to introduce the new product? **2**

(f) Why is it important that the production and marketing departments should co-operate with each other? **4**

Q2

(a) The advertisement in figure 13.17 refers to a 'product line' (i.e. product range). Name four different items that might be included in the range. **2**

(b) State four different appropriate places to sell this company's products. **2**

(c) How could branding assist the marketing of the product range? **3**

(d) Name three marketing occupations between completion of production and eventual purchase by the consumer. **3**

(e) Briefly describe four different ways in which the public might be made aware of this product range. **4**

(f) What factors would be likely to influence customers to purchase Lushlocks' products? **6**

> *Do you want to improve the condition of your hair?*
>
> *Do you suffer from hair loss or dandruff?*
>
> *We have the answer*
> **LUSHLOCKS**
> *is a completely new hair care product line from Vincent & Son Martinique Ltd*
> *PO Box 9 Bellefontaine*

Fig. 13.17 *Hair care advertisement*

Q3

Juicyfruit Ltd. is a major producer and distributor of fresh fruit and fresh vegetables. Juicyfruit's own fleet of delivery vehicles plays an important part in distributing its products throughout the Caribbean region. The figure 13.18 shows how Juicyfruit can quickly distribute its products in the Caribbean to reach the final consumer within 24 hours.

(a) Why is it important for Juicyfruit to distribute its products within 24 hours? **2**

(b) Explain the difference between an 'imported product' and a 'home-grown product'. **2**

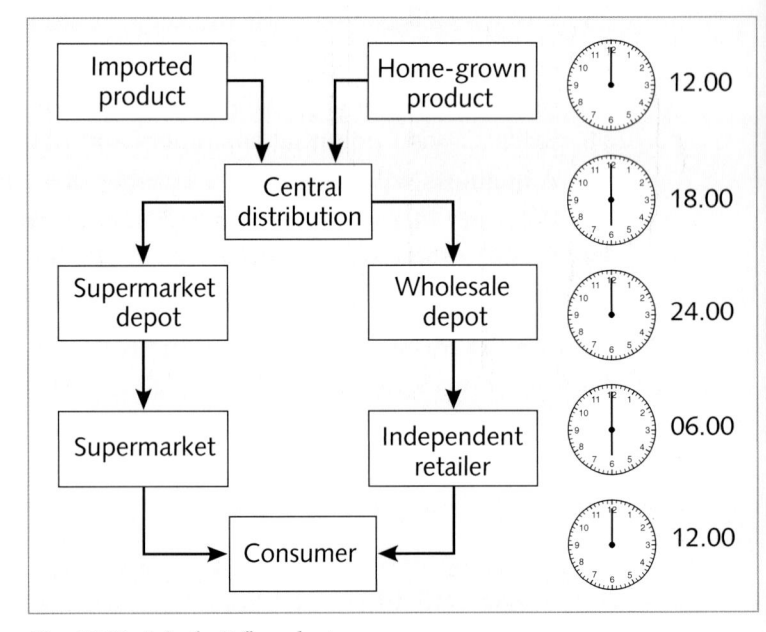

Fig. 13.18 *Juicyfruit flow chart*

(c) Why do Juicyfruit's own fleet of delivery vehicles play an important part in distributing its products? *4*

(d) Why would a supermarket chain be able to sell Juicyfruit's products at a lower price than an independent retailer? *4*

(e) Describe the difference in marketing techniques that a supermarket chain would be likely to employ in comparison with an independent retailer. *8*

Q4 Read the newspaper article in figure 13.19 and answer the questions that follow:

(a) What is meant by the following terms used in the newspaper article:
   (i) branded name products *1*
   (ii) turnover of $4 billion a year? *1*

(b) In what way is television shopping likely to be convenient for consumers? *2*

(c) What marketing techniques are likely to be used by the seller? *3*

(d) How will the producers of goods advertised on the 'Armchair Shopping Show' benefit? *3*

(e) What factors will determine whether or not the 'Armchair Shopping Show' is a success? *4*

(f) 'Armchair shopping has taken on a new meaning with the development of Internet shopping.' Discuss this statement, emphasising the development of marketing through the Internet. *6*

BUYING FROM YOUR OWN HOME

Television shopping has just arrived in the Caribbean. For one hour, every Saturday morning, families will be able to shop from their TV screens.

Each product will have a four minute slot. During this time viewers can telephone using one of 200 lines, free of charge. They will be able to order a product over the telephone and pay by quoting their credit card number.

The Armchair Shopping Show will follow the pattern of successful shopping shows running in the United States of America.

In the Caribbean, mostly branded name products will be sold, with nothing costing below $200, and presented in an interesting and informative way. Typical items will include clothes, washing machines, cameras, and other goods.

The idea began with the Homes Shopping Network, in the USA, a 24-hour show. The US show started from nothing in 1986 and by 1990 had a turnover of $4 billion a year.

Fig. 13.19 *Television shopping*

Q5

(a) Who is a consumer? *2*

(b) Name two middlemen between the producer and the consumer. *2*

(c) What do you understand by the term 'consumer market'? *4*

(d) Name the four elements of commerce that are directly involved in the marketing of a producer's goods. *4*

(e) Describe the importance to the marketing and distribution of goods of four aids to trade. *8*

Q6

(a) One example of a marketing decision a firm must make is what segment of the market it wants to influence. For example, it may want to influence a particular age group. Give two more contrasting examples of people-related marketing decisions that a firm might make. *2*

(b) What is market research, and what part does it play in helping a firm to decide on its marketing mix? *3*

(c) Describe the work of two jobs in different departments of a firm, and say why they play a major part in the marketing mix. *3*

Principles of Business – Profile 2

(d) Clearly describe three contrasting ways that a producer of toys might change the product mix of an established product to help revive falling sales. **6**

(e) 'One reason why a firm might change the product mix is because the product life cycle shows the item is in decline.' Explain this statement, and give other reasons why the business would change the product mix. **6**

Q7 Refer to the diagram shown earlier in this chapter as figure 13.5 and illustrating the possible structure of a marketing department and answer the following questions.

(a) Why is the diagram shown not likely to be typical of a small company? **2**

(b) How do home sales differ from foreign sales? **2**

(c) What work is carried out in the costing section of a marketing department? **3**

(d) Why is market research an essential feature of marketing? **3**

(e) In what way can the structure shown be said to be illustrative of the 'marketing mix'? **4**

(f) Explain how the market research, development and sales sections of this hypothetical marketing department are interrelated. **6**

Research assignments

1. Visit two different types of local business, such as a food store, clothing store, or furniture store. Compare the merchandising techniques that each uses, and comment on whether differences that exist arise from the nature of the products or from differences in techniques.

2. Choose a product or service that is of interest to you. Visit four different stores that sell the product or service. Make a comparison of the ways each store markets the product or service. What advice would you offer any of the stores?

3. Name a product or service that you purchased recently. Describe the marketing techniques that you know helped you to make your choice and purchase. Take three products you would not buy and frankly describe the marketing techniques that could help to change your attitude to these products.

4. Assume that a major company is planning to build a large sports complex and has asked for your help. You are required to identify different groups of people who would be likely to pay to use the complex, and indicate the features or facilities that should be included in the sports complex so that it will appeal in the fullest to each of these groups of people. Describe in detail how you would carry out this assignment.

5. Describe a promotional plan that could be used to market your school or college in order to make as many people as possible aware of the good features of it. How could you evaluate the effectiveness of your plan? In what ways would you motivate other students to participate in the plan.

6. Considering a particular product, such as a car, explain why deciding on the marketing price requires a knowledge of the product life cycle. What evidence can you present proving that product life cycles really exist?

7. What evidence can you find that monopolies exist in the Caribbean region? To what extent do you feel they operate adversely or otherwise to the best interests of the consumers?

Chapter 14

Market research and advertising

14.1 Aims of market research

In Chapter 13 we learnt that the marketing concept requires a firm to be aware of the customer's needs, to try to meet those needs, and to attempt to make a profit in the process. Market research assists the firm to meet the goal of the marketing concept by helping the process of finding out what the customer wants. In other words, market research identifies the marketing strategy that will reach the target audience.

Market research investigates what consumers are buying or are likely to buy in the future. The research is normally carried out before launching the advertising campaign. Thoroughly carried out, market research can help to direct advertisers to the most economic and effective way of running their campaign. Sometimes market research is carried out after the product is already well-established, in order to assess and improve advertising and evaluate product performance.

Market research has three broad aims.

- *To find out what the public wants* so that the business does not waste resources producing goods or services that are not required.
- *To assess likely volume of demand* to ensure that over-producing does not occur.
- *To discover what will influence consumers* – product name, style and colour of packaging, best target audience, price range, effective hidden persuaders.

In order to achieve these aims the marketeer needs to be aware of the following factors that influence consumer behaviour.

Choice. Where there are several competitors in the market consumers will have several alternatives to choose from. For this reason the marketeer is forced to be competitive.

Taste. People differ in their preference for goods and services, and therefore the marketeer has to identify these preferences.

Tradition. In some circumstances there may be a longstanding tradition that influences consumer behaviour. For example, products such as scent have traditionally been associated with members of only one of the sexes.

Income. The amount of money a person earns clearly affects his or her ability to purchase. Consequently, some highly priced products and services will only be purchased by the higher-paid wage earner.

Brand loyalty. Marketeers often try to create loyalty for their products with consumers. The hope is that customers will stay with their existing product because it has satisfied them for some time. Conversely, brand loyalty also makes it difficult for the marketeer to woo consumers away from a product that they are satisfied with.

Principles of Business – Profile 2

The importance of market research

Market research provides a marketeer with information which will help in making decisions about:

- where to sell a product or service
- how to sell it
- which customers need the product and exactly what they want
- how to price the product
- how to promote the product
- who are the competitors in the market-place
- what the size of the market is.

The person responsible for market research has to be able to answer a number of appropriate questions in order to come up with useful information which can aid marketing decision-making in the firm.

Those carrying out market research find out the information they seek by asking a cross-section of the public (from all age groups and social backgrounds) a number of carefully designed questions. The questioning is carried out in a variety of places.

In the street, shop or home

The researcher has a set of prepared questions. The answers to many of these questions can be recorded quickly by ticks in boxes marked Yes or No. The telephone is increasingly being used for research in the home.

Questionnaires circulated in shops or homes

A carefully constructed questionnaire must be:

- easy to understand
- simple to answer, perhaps by ticks
- capable of useful analysis (frequently by computer).

---

1 Why is a different marketing strategy likely to be required for each target market?

2 Form three columns with each headed by one of the following target markets: pensioners, businesses, teenagers. List the following items in what you feel is the appropriate column: vitamins, chewing gum, computer networks, gardening equipment, fashion clothes, retirement homes, stationery, sportswear, hot water bottles, a pop concert, conference catering, thermal underwear, roller skates, commercial vehicles, walking aids.

3 Which of the items included in your lists could have been included in more than one column? Give reasons for your answer.

Fig. 14.1 *The target market is the people the business wants to influence*

Please indicate your hobbies, sports and interests.

Hobbies and interests
- 1 Cooking
- 2 Eating out
- 3 Gardening
- 4 Crocheting
- 5 Photography
- 6 Dressmaking
- 7 Collecting
- 8 Home Computing
- 9 Listening to Music
- 10 Reading

How many magazines do you buy per month?
- 11 0
- 12 1–3
- 13 4–6
- 14 7+

Sports and Activities
- 15 Fishing
- 16 Tennis
- 17 Squash
- 18 Cycling
- 19 Horse Riding
- 20 Golf
- 21 Running
- 22 Swimming
- 23 Football
- 24 Sailing
- 25 Dancing
- 26 Please tick if you normally include your sports and activities as part of your holidays

Clothing and Fashion
- 27 Ladies' Fashion
- 28 Men's Fashion
- 29 Beachwear
- 30 Women's Clothes Size 16+
- 31 Please tick if you have ever bought anything for your leisure via mail order
- 32 Please tick if you were satisfied with the purchase

What do you drink?
- 1 Beer
- 2 Wine
- 3 Spirits

Are you interested in buying?
- 4 Wine from the brewery
- 5 Home Brewing Kits

Do you smoke?
- 6 Cigarettes/Cigars
- 7 A Pipe
- 8 Please tick if you would like to stop smoking

Fig. 14.2 *A market research questionnaire can be used to collect information about potential markets for goods and services*

Sampling

- Members of the public may be invited to try the product, or compare one or more samples and make constructive observations.
- Test marketing may be carried out by selling the product in a small sample area in order to assess likely demand prior to commencing full-scale production.

14.2 Types of market research

The following are some of the market research strategies used by marketeers.

Experiments

A product may be developed and marketed in one or two limited geographical areas. During this process, data are collected, tabulated and analysed. The findings are then used in deciding whether the 'pilot' experiment suggests that it would be worthwhile embarking on large-scale production and distribution.

Observations

Observation is perhaps the most widely used form of market research. The observations may be formal or informal.

Using the observation approach, the researcher watches how people behave or respond to certain situations. For example, does a change in packaging design have the effect of improving sales?

Guidelines to be followed during the observations are set out by the researcher, and appropriate notes are made during the period. The information collected is passed on to the researcher's firm for analysis and decision-making.

Surveys

Sometimes we encounter market research personnel in supermarkets, our communities, in airport buildings and other places. These people use questionnaires, personal interviews or telephone interviews based on carefully constructed questions to establish the views of consumers.

It is impossible to survey every consumer, and therefore a sample is used. This sample has to be representative of the whole population. So, the representative sample includes both sexes, a variety of age groups, country and town dwellers, and people who are poor as well as those who are not.

The main ways of conducting surveys are as follows.

- *By post.* This is by far the easiest method but it has its disadvantages in that many people will not bother to complete and return the questionnaires.
- *By personal interview.* This is the most common method, but it can be expensive because it is very labour-intensive.
- *By telephone.* This approach is becoming increasingly common, although it sometimes has the counter-effect on consumers that they are put off the product because they object to being disturbed in their home.

14.3 Market research in action

The market research team

Market research is carried out by specialists called **market researchers**. In a large organisation several such specialists will be used to form a team.

Sometimes, specialists called **research consultants** will be used to interview members of the public and record their responses to carefully formulated questions.

The market research team must ensure that their research is relevant to the needs of the firm as well as to the needs of the consumer. Research must be accurate, and also timely if it is to achieve the desired result. For example, if an organisation that produces clothing for teenagers learns from its research findings that certain types of T-shirt are popular among teenagers during the summer months, then, to meet the demands of the teenagers, the T-shirts must be produced to the required specifications. Decisions must be made on the right:

- styles
- colours needed
- quantity required
- sales timing for the summer
- places where the buyers can access them.

If a business is not large enough to employ its own market researchers, it can hire the services of a **market research agency**, which is a firm that specialises in this work.

Market research information is also collected by **employees** at all levels of the firm. The owner of a hairdressing salon that has suffered a decline in custom may ask staff to tactfully question customers to find out how they can improve their service. Or the owner might send a letter or questionnaire to all past customers aimed at finding out why they have taken their custom elsewhere. The cashier in the supermarket not only charges the customer for their purchases, but their modern till can also be used to provide information on what merchandise is selling well, and when stocks must be reordered.

Market research data collected can be either quantitative or qualitative:

- *Quantitative research* concentrates on factual information, e.g. figures, estimates of market potential, sales, % of market share.
- *Qualitative research* focuses on attitudes and opinions, e.g. consumer tastes, likes and dislikes.

Market segmentation

The potential market for a seller of goods or services can be individuals and also other businesses. Rather than trying to sell to everyone, it makes sense for a seller to identify specific parts of the total market and concentrate on trying to reach those parts. These parts of the market are called **market segments** and dividing the market in this way is called **market segmentation**. The following are a few examples of market segments, but there are others:

- *Geographic segmentation* – identifying people from a particular country, region, city, suburb or rural area.

Chapter 14 – Market research and advertising

> **KEY WORDS**
>
> Find out the business-related meaning of each of the following terms. Write a separate sentence for each term to show your understanding.
>
> qualitative research
> survey research
> consultant
> market researcher
> questionnaire
> market segment
> quantitative research
> sampling
> representative sample
> brand loyalty

- *Behavioural segmentation* – people with similar interests, e.g. those in a particular line of business.
- *Demographic segmentation* – targeting people from a population group such as that for age, gender, income or social class.

For demographic analysis potential buyers of a product are grouped together in terms of certain common personal and economic characteristics (see table 14.1). These groups are likely to differ in the level and pattern of their spending. Therefore, they can be used as the basis for identifying market segments. The segmentation can then be used by targeting specific products or services to meet the customer requirements of those segments.

Social class categories are often based on the occupation of the head of the household as follows, although there are variations of this:

Class A	Higher managerial, administrative, or professional.
Class B	Intermediate managerial, administrative, or professional.
Class C1	Supervisory or clerical, junior managerial, administrative or professional.
Class C2	Skilled manual workers.
Class D	Semi and unskilled manual workers.
Class E	State pensioners, casual workers, unemployed.

Table 14.1 *Example of social grades*

Sampling

Having identified a market segment for research, it is not realistic to approach everyone in the segment to find out information. Information is usually collected from a **sample** of the market segment. The methods of sampling most frequently used include *random, stratified, quota* and *cluster* sampling:

- *Random* – those to be surveyed (**interviewees**) are picked from some reliable official list or database such as the telephone directory or the electoral register, at fixed gaps of, say, every 50 or 100 names in the list.
- *Stratified* – researchers deliberately allow bias towards a particular category of persons, e.g. housewives, pensioners, teenagers, or people in a particular profession or type of business.
- *Quota* – this is the most common method of sampling. Here, interviewees are chosen randomly, but a certain number of people in specific categories (e.g. social grade or sex) must be chosen. The numbers interviewed are in proportion to the total population; for example, if the population contains 10% more males than females, then 10% more males will be sampled.
- *Cluster* – a cluster sample includes groups of people rather than individuals. For example, the researchers might choose the residents in several towns, randomly chosen, and in certain streets (also randomly chosen) in each town.

Sources of information

The sources of information from which a market researcher collects data can be classified as primary or secondary:

Primary data is usually drawn from original sources. In other words, none of the data has been collected previously by someone else. This type of data can be collected through experiments, observations and interviews, as described earlier.

Secondary data refers to information that is already in existence in a form different from the one the researcher intends to use, but which may be useful to managers in the decision-making process. In other words, secondary data has already been gathered previously by someone else, and the researcher's intention is to access the data and make use of it. Rich sources of secondary data for the market research team include a firm's files, annual reports, manuals and brochures.

Secondary data also includes items such as government statistics, reference books, newspaper articles and even the sales literature of competitors. Because the researcher does not actually have to go out into the field to collect this data first-hand, it is often referred to as desk research. The internet has become an important source of desk research.

Research procedures

The following are typical examples of procedures followed by professional researchers:

1. Identify the problem to be solved or the information to be obtained.
2. Set limits to the problem. Focus on one or a few manageable things.
3. Draw on current knowledge (of the product or of the market).
4. Seek out new knowledge (current knowledge might be inadequate, irrelevant, or just out of date).
5. Consider all possible solutions to the problem (careful examination of current and new knowledge).
6. Attempt to find alternative solutions to the problem.
7. Select the best solution to the problem. This should always be related to the target market.
8. Try out the identified solution, e.g. experiment with a sample or a trial run.
9. Evaluate, and adjust where necessary.

Research methods

Methods of research can be usefully grouped into those which are *desk-based* and those which are *field-based*.

Desk research refers to research that can be carried out without going outside the organisation. For example, the firm's own statistics, such as sales and accounts records, will reveal which products are in highest demand, or those that are in decline. Another source for desk research is government statistics which, for example, indicate the *extent* of a potential market. And, of course, the internet provides an almost unending source of information useful to the desk researcher.

Field research involves carrying out research and surveys outside the firm. There are many ways that this can be done, and some of the main ways are as follows:

- *Postal questionnaires.* This can be an economical method of collecting research data because it is less labour-intensive than other methods. A carefully worded questionnaire can be sent relatively cheaply to all, or a selection, of potential customers, and they can respond anonymously. The problem with this method is that the respondents cannot ask questions if they do not understand something. This is why the questionnaire must be carefully worded. Another weakness of this method is that often a great percentage of the questionnaires are not completed and returned.

KEY WORDS

Find out the business-related meaning of each of the following terms. Write a separate sentence for each term to show your understanding.

desk research
interviewer
stratified sampling
field research
interviewee
cluster sampling
primary data
quota sampling
random sampling
secondary data

Sometimes, reply-paid envelopes help, but the time it takes to complete the questionnaire is the main drawback. (See figure 14.2 for some examples of parts of questionnaires.)

- *Telephone surveys.* This is a convenient and quick way of carrying out field research without actually leaving the firm. However, one of the weaknesses of this method is that some people do not have a telephone, even though they are commonplace today. This may mean that people that are important to the survey are omitted.
- *Direct interviews.* This is a costly type of survey because it is labour-intensive, and interviewers need special skills to question people without influencing their answers. A skilful interviewer, however, can help overcome any reluctance on the part of the respondents to reply frankly to questions.
- *Test marketing.* With test marketing, a new product is tried out in a small area to gauge public response before full-scale production is undertaken. Testing a product in a relatively small region can give a producer and idea of how much to produce.
- *Observation.* This technique is applied by researchers who watch to see how consumers behave in the market-place, e.g. how they respond to shop layouts and displays. The information obtained can help store owners to design the organisation of their premises, and producers to package their goods in the most effective way.

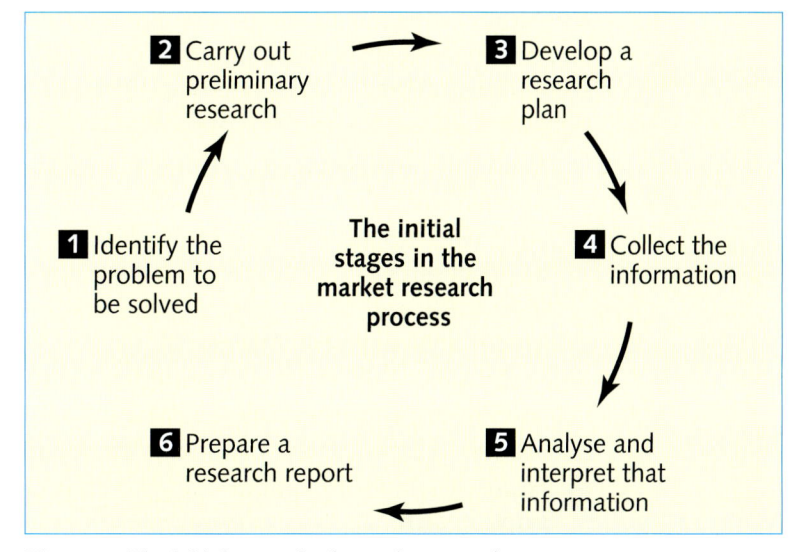

Fig. 14.3 *The initial stages in the market research process*

14.4 Functions of advertising

The main functions of advertising are as follows:

- To announce new products
- To highlight the unique features of a product
- To build a firm's image around its products
- To highlight special events, such as concessions, sales and late openings
- To increase market share by stimulating demand
- To educate consumers about the products.

Principles of Business – Profile 2

The purpose of advertising

It would be pointless for a business to develop a product or service if there were no way to tell consumers about it. Advertising is a means of communication: it is used to make consumers aware of the goods and services that producers and traders have to offer. An advertisement is a message that uses words, pictures or sound:

- to **inform** potential buyers of the availability of goods and services
- to **persuade** people to buy or to behave in a particular way.

Informative and persuasive advertising

Informative advertising gives detailed information about the goods or services available and leaves consumers to decide, without persuasion, whether or not they wish to purchase. An informative advertisement contains useful details such as specification, sizes, colour and material. This type of approach can also be employed in public relations and image creation.

Persuasive advertising uses a variety of techniques to persuade people to buy a product or service, irrespective of whether they need it or not.

Advertising's 'hidden persuaders'

One of the ways an advertiser may use an advertisement to promote sales is to persuade the consumer that the advertiser's product will make the consumer better off in some way. Some of the motives to which this type of advertisement appeals are far from obvious and, therefore, they are sometimes called 'hidden persuaders'. Some of the motives to which persuasive advertisements appeal are the following.

- *Sex appeal:* the product is claimed to make the user attractive to the opposite sex.
- *Ambition:* the advertisement implies that those who use the product will be successful.
- *Personality appeal:* famous personalities are shown using the product to give it an acceptable image.
- *Social acceptability:* the advertisement implies that by using the product the consumer becomes more acceptable to others.
- *Work simplification:* the product is claimed to make a task easier to carry out.
- *Health:* the advertisement suggests that use of the product contributes to good health.

RECESSION:
IS BUSINESS SLOW?
Ask us how the **Purple Advertiser** can boost your business or sevice

Purple Advertiser

The **Purple Advertiser** offers a comprehensive leaflet delivery service throughout the Kingston Metropolitan Area.
We can print and deliver leaflets and help publicise your comany or service.

Call at Acorn House, Great Oaks, Manor Park, or telephone: Rob, Elaine or Melanie 927-0007

MENSWEAR FOR THE LARGE AND TALL MAN

MEDIUM TO 76in CHEST & WAIST

Trousers 29in to 40in leg

INCLUDING WORKWEAR
MANSWORLD

Manhatton House   Tel: 981-5251
George Town
Grenada

Fig. 14.4 *Informative advertisements*

Fig. 14.5 *Persuasive advertising*

Chapter 14 – Market research and advertising

14.5 Forms of advertising

Advertising media

There is a wide variety of ways in which an advertisement may reach the public, but not all are suitable for every advertisement. There are many media through which advertising may take place, each of which has a varying degree of effectiveness and cost.

- *Television and radio:* very expensive, but it is the most effective method of reaching a large audience.
- *National press:* reaches a wide area, but is expensive and, therefore, mainly used by large companies.
- *Local newspapers:* offers cheaper advertising rates for cover of a limited area. Free local newspapers rely on advertising to meet costs.
- *Magazines or journals:* usually have a more limited circulation than newspapers, but reach a selected audience, offer greater scope for colour advertisements, and have a longer life.
- *Cinemas:* reach a relatively small audience but can be effective, particularly in advertising local shops, etc.
- *Posters and hoardings:* eye-catching, high impact signs, sited in public places or on public transport.
- *Point of sale:* use eye-catching shop counter or window displays to influence the consumer to buy on impulse.
- *Exhibitions:* attract large numbers of people who already have at least some interest in the product. Exhibitions also enable specialists in a field to meet and compare products and experience.
- *Circulation:* by leaflets can be an effective medium but if they are delivered by hand, it is very labour-intensive, and costly if they are posted (a 'mail shot').

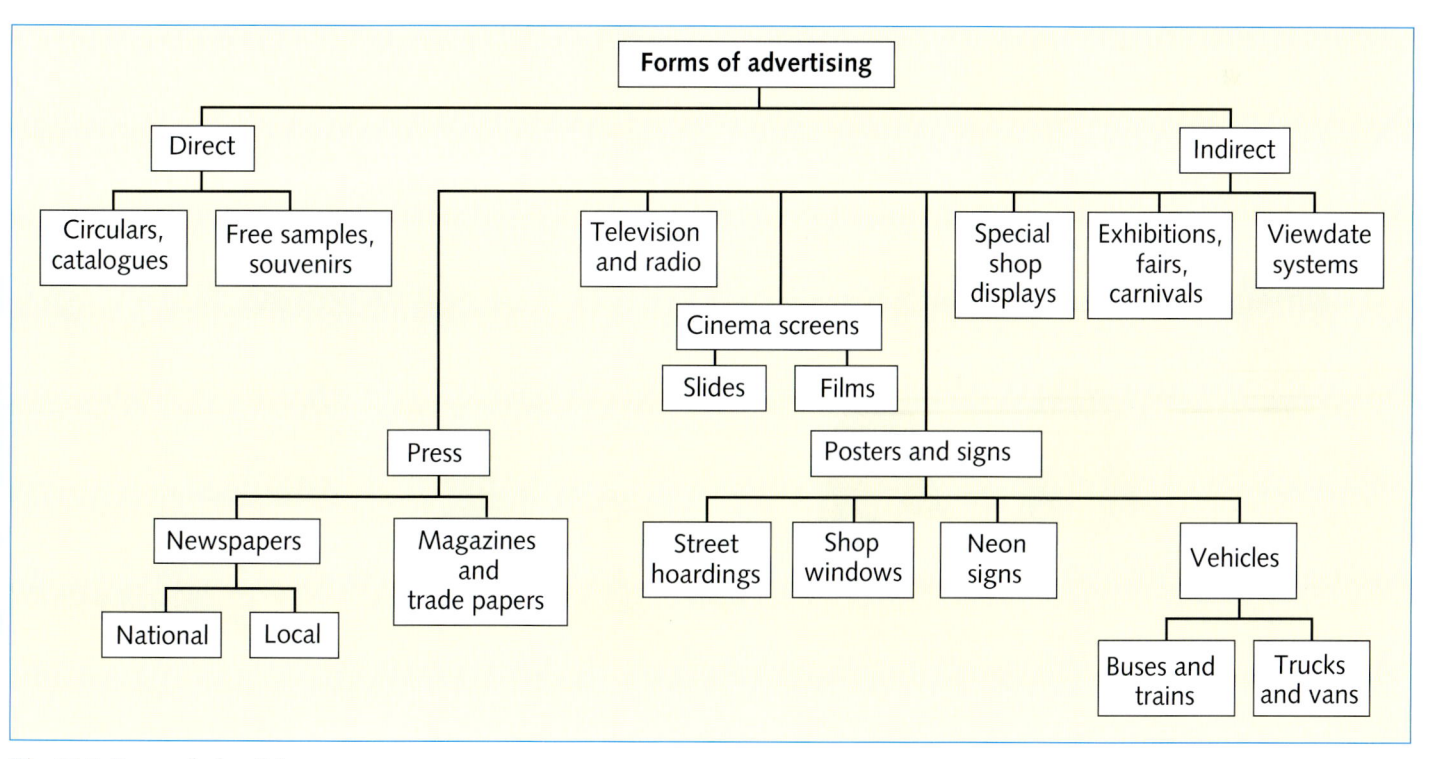

Fig. 14.6 *Forms of advertising*

Principles of Business – Profile 2

> *Word of mouth* (by recommendation): sometimes encouraged by firms carrying out a 'whispering campaign' by giving away free samples which they hope the users will talk about favourably.

The marketeer has to decide which medium is most appropriate for the product or service he or she is trying to sell. Often, a combination of the forms of advertising listed above will be incorporated into the seller's advertising campaign.

14.6 The advertising campaign

An **advertising campaign** consists of all of the processes a firm uses to sell its goods or services. A campaign is based on a clearly defined plan, much of which is formed as a result of market research (described earlier).

Some firms are large enough to have their own advertising department, others may decide it is preferable to employ an advertising agency to carry out an advertising campaign on their behalf. Whichever is the case, the advertiser or agency will have to take many factors into account. The following questions must certainly be answered if the campaign is to be effective.

➤ Which groups of the public ('target audience') is the campaign intended to reach?
➤ How much money is available to be spent on the campaign?
➤ How extensive is the campaign intended to be – countywide, countrywide or worldwide?
➤ Which techniques will catch the attention of buyers?

Fig. 14.7 *Key advertising agency personnel planning an advertising campaign*

Some of these questions, such as the amount of money to be put into the campaign, can only be answered by the advertiser. Others can be solved through market research.

Advertising agencies

Advertising agencies are businesses which specialise in assisting others with their advertising needs, a service for which they are paid.

The extent of the work that the agency undertakes for their client depends on how much the client wishes to spend on advertising a product. The agency may work in conjunction with the client's own advertising department, advising them how they might conduct their campaign, or alternatively it may be employed to organise the complete advertising campaign.

It takes the work of many skilled people to formulate a single advertisement, and the formulation of a complete campaign for a large national company is a vast undertaking. An agency handling such a campaign employs people with specialist skills associated with marketing.

Apart from market research, an advertising department or an advertising agency is concerned with artwork and space-buying.

Artwork

This involves the formation of the pictorial display of the advertisement, and includes the creation of the wording to go with the advertisement. In these aspects of advertising brainstorming gets good results. The team creating the advertisement brainstorm by freely expressing ideas until the most suitable wording and visual display is found.

Space buying

This is the process of hiring the most appropriate space in which to display the advertisement: not only the most effective but also the most economically appropriate. For example, although television is one of the most effective forms of advertising, it is far too expensive for selling a few inexpensive items.

14.7 Promotion

We saw in Chapter 13 that promotion is one of the important parts of the marketing mix. The term promotion refers to the means of bringing products or services to the attention of consumers, and persuading them to buy. The promotional mix is the methods that a firm can use to inform prospective customers of the nature and attributes of its products and to persuade them to buy them. The promotional mix includes: advertising, sales promotion, personal selling, merchandising, packaging and public relations.

Advertising was examined earlier in the book, as were some of the methods that advertisers use to promote products and services. These include: advertising through television, newspapers and magazines, etc.

Sales promotion refers to the measures used by businesses, alongside other promotional elements of the promotional mix, to increase the sales of their products. In the case of consumer goods, while advertising seeks to develop and sustain brand loyalty in the long term, sales promotions are mainly used

Principles of Business – Profile 2

KEY WORDS

Find out the business-related meaning of each of the following terms. Write a separate sentence for each term to show your understanding.

- advertising campaign
- industrial products
- informative advertising
- loss leader
- brain storming
- hidden persuaders
- space buying
- persuasive advertising
- sales promotion
- promotional mix

in short bursts. For example, it might be used to promote the introduction of a new product, or to renew interest in a product whose sales have fallen, or it may be used to stimulate sales of an established product.

The techniques used in sales promotion include: issue of trading stamps and coupons that can be exchanged for cash or goods; free gift with a purchase; free trial of a product; money-off packs; extra quantities for the same price, such as two for the price of one; coupons offering gifts; in-store demonstrations; point-of-sale displays; special cash offers on purchases; product competitions offering prizes; etc. One of the most powerful means of promotion is using a 'loss leader', which is where a retailer sells a manufacturer's branded product at a price below its bought-in cost.

In the case of industrial products, trade fairs, exhibitions and demonstrations are used to back-up the most commonly used promotion, personal selling.

Personal selling is a means of increasing a firm's sales by involving direct contact between the firm's sales representatives (persons employed to represent a company) and prospective customers. Unlike passive means of communicating (e.g. by literature and advertising), face-to-face meetings with customers involve a more active approach, with sales representatives being able to explain the details of the product, and to be able to answer questions.

From the foregoing you will realise that sales personnel play an important part in the direct selling of a firm's products or services. In the case of sales representatives, they are responsible for visiting customers at the buyers' premises, and they are often generally responsible for visiting customers within their designated sales territory. Other sales personnel will be employed in the sellers' own premises, attending visiting customers.

Whichever of these sales duties applies, sales personnel will be carefully recruited and then trained. The training they will be given can be divided into two broad areas: knowledge and skills. The knowledge a sales person requires are those related to the product or service they are selling, for example knowledge about the company and the products or services it sells. The skills required of a salesperson could be technical skills, for example how to operate a piece of equipment being sold. But a salesperson also needs behavioural skills. Behavioural skills are difficult to define, but they are concerned with the development of empathy between the buyer and the seller, e.g. knowing when to listen; being a good communicator; having an ability to engage the customer's attention.

Merchandising was examined in Chapter 13. Merchandising refers to the in-store promotional activity by producers or retailers at the point-of-sale, and designed to stimulate sales. Obviously, pricing is an important factor in merchandising, and sometimes the price of products will be adjusted for a variety of reasons, many of which you have already learnt about. Merchandising makes special use of point-of-sale display materials and the special buying incentives already mentioned such as free gifts, coupons, money-off packs, etc.

Packaging refers to the means of physically protecting and selling a product. Functionally, packaging protects a product while it is in transit and being stored. It also enables products to be sold in conveniently sized retail packs, in standard sizes or weights. In addition, packaging provides a means of identifying the contents through labelling.

Packaging can also play an important role in the marketing of a product. This is particularly so when the product is being marketed on a **self-service** basis, that is being chosen off the shelf. The **attractiveness** of the packaging is important in drawing the attention of the customer. In addition, the use of a **brand name** on the packaging facilitates rapid recognition, while reinforcing the perception of the brand at the point of sale.

Public relations (PR) refers to the general process of promoting a business's **company image** with a view to encouraging customers to buy its products, or investors to buy its shares. It can also be used in an attempt to influence the government on policies or issues related to the company.

In a large company it is possible to employ a specialist called the **public relations officer (PRO)**, who has the responsibility of promoting a good public image. In a smaller business this role has to be carried out by the owner or a responsible senior employee. But the promotion of public relations is really the responsibility of all employees.

Good public relations may be promoted in direct ways such as making donations to charities, giving away free samples and gifts, operating prize-giving competitions, using famous personalities to endorse the company's goods and so on. These and many other methods are deliberately used to encourage the public to look on the business in a favourable way.

Sponsorship of the arts and sport and other public events has become a common feature of indirect public relations activities. **Business entertainment** has become commonplace where a firm will meet the cost of the provision of entertainment for select customers, for example it will pay for seats and refreshments at major sporting events, or shows. Such events may also be used to reward key staff. In addition, **special awards** may be presented to staff or customers in recognition of the part they play in the success of the business.

There are also many indirect ways that companies use to promote their public image, and often these will draw on the help of all employees. For example, potential customers will be influenced by the manner in which employees talk to them on the telephone or at the shop counter. They will also be influenced by the way that their enquiries or complaints are dealt with.

Many companies take particular care with the way that they handle after-sales services, because they recognise that this is a vehicle for good public relations. They try to ensure that when a customer has a complaint about a purchase made, it is turned to the seller's advantage by showing courtesy and a willingness to put things right quickly.

Terms of sales

This refers to the way that payment for purchases are made. While most of your personal purchases will be paid for in **cash** you will be aware that there are many other ways of making purchases. We will now examine some of the main ways.

Credit is a financial facility which allows a person to borrow money to make purchases (i.e. take immediate possession of them). Obtaining money in this way takes a variety of forms including, overdrafts, instalment credit (see below), credit cards and trade credit. **Trade credit** occurs when a supplier allows a customer a certain period of time (typically one or two months) after receiving the products in which to pay for them.

Hire purchase (or instalment credit) is a contractual means of purchasing a product over a period of time. This facility may be provided by a financial institution, such as a **finance house** or the firm selling the product concerned. An initial 'down payment' is usually required followed by monthly fixed payments, including **interest charges**.

Cash and trade discounts A cash discount is a reduction in the total amount owed by a customer to a seller in return for **prompt payment**. They are used by sellers to encourage customers to pay quickly and improve the firm's **cash flow**. A trade discount (sometimes called a **quantity discount**) is a price reduction given by a seller to purchases in **bulk**, and calculated in accordance with the quantity bought. It is usually only extended to other traders.

KEY WORDS

Find out the business-related meaning of each of the following terms.
Write a separate sentence for each term to show your understanding.

cash discount   business entertainment   behavioural skills   packaging
sales representatives   company image   merchandising   public relations
hire purchase   trade discount

14.8 Consumerism

The term **consumerism** refers to an organised movement to protect the interests of consumers by forcing businesses to act in a socially responsible manner. The need for consumer protection arose as a result of the increasing complexity of products and the growth in the power of businesses and their marketing techniques. In many countries there are **legislative measures** that help to protect the consumer, and also **consumer associations** which provide product testing facilities and publish comparative information.

The need for consumer protection

All people, businesses and even governments are consumers, although we usually refer particularly to individuals when talking about consumers. We have seen elsewhere in this book that the aim of production is to make things that can be used by consumers. In fact it has been said that the sole end and purpose of all production is the consumer. We have also seen in this chapter that advertising aims not only to inform us about goods and services, but also to persuade us to buy them.

With the growth of large-scale production and the increased spending power of many people, the motivation for firms to obtain and maintain a larger share of the consumer market has risen considerably. This has been further encouraged by technological changes which have revolutionised not only products and the way they are manufactured, but also the manner in which they are marketed.

At one time, the attitude of the law in relation to the protection of consumers was **caveat emptor**, or 'let the buyer beware'. In other words, consumers were expected to protect themselves. Today, consumers are protected in a number of ways by legislation and government agencies, but it is still important for consumers to help protect themselves by shopping wisely.

Traders cannot go against consumers' rights without facing the risk of legal action. Traders need to know the rights of their customers and realise that they have a responsibility to treat them fairly in order to meet their legal obligations. In addition, traders have rights concerning their suppliers similar to those customers have against traders, so long as they have not agreed to give up those rights.

The Sale of Goods Act

This British law has been very influential in the Caribbean as a major legal standard for the protection of consumers. It has been amended several times since it was first established in 1893. Today, the act has several implications.

The act covers all goods (including food) bought from a trader through a shop, a doorstep seller, or sales by mail order. The seller has three main obligations.

- Goods must be of merchantable quality. This means that goods must be reasonably fit for their normal purpose, bearing in mind the price paid, the nature of the goods and how they were described. Thus a new item must not be damaged and must work properly.
- Goods must be as described. They must correspond with the description given by the seller, or with labels on the item or the packaging.
- Goods must be fit for any particular purpose made known to the seller by the customer. For example, if the customer asks for plates that are 'dishwasher safe', the seller has an obligation to ensure that the plates sold meet the requirement made known to him by the customer.

When things go wrong

Of course, things go wrong, and it may not always be the fault of the seller. Before you charge off to the shop to complain about faulty goods, ask yourself three simple questions:

- Was it a fault I should have noticed when buying?
- Was it something I was told about?
- Am I expecting too much from something cheap?

If the answer to all three questions is 'no', then go ahead and complain. Take along proof of purchase (e.g. the receipt), and remember to act in a reasonable manner. Most respectable traders will want to put things right.

If you have no success at the shop, write to the head office. Keep copies of all correspondence. Should you still not be satisfied you may well need support from some other agency, or you may decide to take legal action.

Supporting agencies

There are a variety of agencies that support the consumer; the following are just some of them.

Manufacturers' associations

A manufacturers' association has many similarities with a chamber of commerce, but in this case each association consists of people from a similar business. An example is the Citrus Growers Association. These organisations provide an ideal forum for the exchange of information between members, and on occasions a common body for carrying out wage negotiations with trade unions.

Such associations have a number of aims, but an important one is to create codes of practice that are to be followed by their members. In this respect the trade association acts as a focal point for dealing with consumer complaints, as well as promoting goodwill for all its members.

The Metrication Board of Trinidad and Tobago

This board was established to plan, co-ordinate and supervise the change-over from imperial units to metric. But the board also provides consumer protection by raising consumer awareness through lectures, seminars, leaflets, handbills and advertising pertaining to metric equivalents of the imperial system.

The bureaux of standards

Bureaux of standards institutions are government agencies which try to help to protect consumers by ensuring that goods produced meet certain minimum requirements with regard to quality and basic raw materials. Sometimes a bureau will try to encourage a producer to manufacture in a particular way to meet the bureau's standards.

Ministry of Consumer Affairs

In nearly all the countries in the region, overall government responsibility for consumer protection is administered by this ministry. The brief of the ministry includes the following:

- giving advice to consumers
- control and supervision of prices
- promotion and implementation of food policy legislation
- control of quality and weights and measures
- enforcing fair trading practices
- supervision of hire purchase and credit control.

The ombudsman

An ombudsman is a government-appointed person who is charged with investigating malpractices, maladministration and injustices brought to his notice by the public. It is often the case that an ombudsman specialises in particular areas of public concern, but many governments have such a person to investigate consumers' complaints.

KEY WORDS

Find out the business-related meaning of each of the following terms. Write a separate sentence for each term to show your understanding.

caveat emptor   bureaux of standards   consumer association
consumer legislation   manufacturers' associations   ombudsman
code of practice   consumerism

Chapter 14 – **Market research and advertising**

14.9 Things to do

This section contains a variety of exercises to help you create revision notes, to test your understanding and to prepare you for examinations.

Search and find

Write out the question and the answer by referring back through the text to form revision notes.

1. In what way does market research help a firm to achieve a marketing concept?
2. What kinds of decision do market researchers hope to be able to make from the data collected?
3. Briefly describe the factors that influence consumer behaviour.
4. Where is market research carried out?
5. Describe some of the strategies used by market researchers to gather information.
6. Why is it often important that a market researcher uses a 'representative sample'?
7. How can normal employees be used to collect market research data?
8. Explain the difference between quantitative and qualitative research.
9. Why is it useful to divide a potential market into segments?
10. What are social 'grades'?
11. Describe the four most frequently used forms of sampling.
12. Explain the difference between 'primary data' and 'secondary data'.
13. How does field research differ from desk research?
14. What is the aim of advertising?
15. How does 'informative' advertising differ from 'persuasive' advertising?
16. What are 'hidden persuaders'?
17. Briefly describe the various advertising media.
18. What do we mean by the term 'advertising campaign'?
19. What is the function of an advertising agency?
20. What is the 'promotional mix'?
21. Describe examples of sales promotion methods used in marketing.
22. How does 'passive' selling differ from 'active' selling?
23. What kinds of knowledge and skills do you see as essential in sales personnel?
24. 'Merchandising is more than selling.' Explain this statement.
25. Why is packaging an important aspect of promotion?
26. Why do businesses care about public relations?
27. Describe some of the forms that public relations can take.
28. Give examples of the terms of sales that are common practice.
29. What is consumerism?

Principles of Business – Profile 2

30 List the main forms of consumer protection that exist in your country.

31 In what way is self protection the best form of consumer protection?

What do you know?

Write out the complete sentence and insert the missing word, which can be chosen from the list at the end of the questions.

1. The marketing concept requires a firm to be aware of the customer's .....
2. Market research provides a marketeer with information which helps to make ..... about marketing goods or services.
3. Those carrying out market research find out the information they seek by ..... a cross-section of the public.
4. A ..... sample includes people from a variety of backgrounds.
5. ..... data refers to information that is collected from original sources.
6. ..... data refers to information that is already in existence.
7. The main aim of advertising is to make consumers ..... of the availability of goods and services.
8. .... advertising leaves consumers to decide, without persuasion, if they wish to purchase.
9. The ..... audience is the section of the public an advertising campaign is trying to reach.
10. Advertising ..... are businesses which specialise in assisting others with their advertising needs.

Choose the missing words from the following:

agencies   decisions   primary   target   questioning   representative   aware   needs   secondary   informative

Structured questions

Q1 Refer to figure 14.8.

(a) Define the term 'prototype'. — 2

(b) What is the purpose of a prototype? — 2

(c) What is a 'brainstorming session'? — 2

(d) Describe the kind of market research that would be carried out:
   (i) before the cleaner goes onto the market — 3
   (ii) after the cleaner goes on sale to the public. — 3

(e) List four contrasting questions that could be included in a market research questionnaire to help the development of an advertising campaign for this new product. — 4

(f) If the market research clearly shows that there is a need for the planned cleaner, why will there still be a need for an advertising campaign? — 4

Idle Hands Ltd is a manufacturer of household electrical goods. They have decided to produce a new product aimed at the busy working housewife: a remote-controlled vacuum cleaner. The head of the product development department has been instructed to produce a prototype with electronic sensors to prevent collisions with furniture, etc.

A name for the new cleaner has yet to be decided; this will be the subject of a brainstorming session. The advertising campaign will be decided following market research and pilot marketing.

Fig. 14.8 Remote-controlled vacuum cleaner

Chapter 14 – Market research and advertising

Q2

(a) State one of the main functions of advertising. *1*

(b) Briefly state two ways in which advertising benefits the community. *2*

(c) How does market research give direction to advertising? *3*

(d) Explain the difference between informative advertising and persuasive advertising. Give descriptive examples to illustrate your explanation. *6*

(e) Describe four of the main methods of advertising, and give examples showing when it is appropriate to use each method you have chosen to describe. *8*

Q3 Refer to the illustration of part of a market research questionnaire in figure 14.2, and answer these questions.

(a) Who would you consider are the target audience of this questionnaire? Give a reason for your answer. *2*

(b) A result of information obtained in this way could be the implementation of 'test marketing'. What do you understand by this? *2*

(c) Give at least two reasons why the company that has paid for this survey to be carried out would be interested in the hobbies and interests of the people surveyed? *4*

(d) How could the information collected by this questionnaire assist product development? *4*

(e) Describe how information collected by market research could be used to conduct an advertising campaign. *8*

Q4

(a) Advertising is often concerned with creating the right 'image' for products. What is meant by image in this context? *2*

(b) For what purpose might a manufacturer of a new soft drink use a hoarding for advertising? *2*

(c) How would the advertising methods of a small local business differ from those of a major manufacturer? *2*

(d) Explain, with an example, circumstances when it could be more appropriate to place an advertisement in a magazine rather than a newspaper. *6*

(e) Describe the work of an advertising agency. *6*

Q5

(a) Give two contrasting reasons why firms advertise their goods or services. *2*

(b) Advertising is generally directed at consumers, but consumers themselves also advertise. State three cheap ways that consumers might advertise items they have for sale. *3*

(c) (i) Briefly state *three* marketing techniques that a business may use in the selling of any product. *3*
   (ii) Show how you could use two of these techniques in the selling of a new portable cassette player. *4*

(d) In what ways can it be said that advertising is not always in the best interest of the consumer? *4*

(e) State, with reasons, why there are fewer criticisms of informative advertising than there are of persuasive advertising. *4*

Principles of Business – Profile 2

Q6 Read the information in figure 14.9 about marketing, and then answer the questions which ask you to relate market research to this information.

WHAT IS MARKETING?

'Marketing is the management process responsible for identifying, anticipating and satisfying customer requirements profitably'.

Don't think – as many people do – that marketing is just the smart 'in' word for selling. Selling is a vital indispensable component of marketing, but only one of several other activities. Marketing thinking and planning begins at or even before the drawing board and ends only when the company is really satisfied with the products or service provided. Because marketing affects so many of the company's resources and activities, it is essentially a team effort.

Good marketing is the end product of a well-led management team fully embracing the marketing concept.

The marketing manager is responsible for the marketing plan and the basic information and guidance about prospective markets, their behaviour, size and potential for each product or service supplied by the company.

The Marketing Spectrum
- RESEARCH: identifying, analysing and predicting customer needs.
- PLANNING AND DEVELOPMENT: deciding on who, what, when and how to meet these needs via new or existing product or service development.
- PRICING: setting an acceptable and profitable price level.
- PACKAGING: matching physical requirements with visual image.
- PROMOTION: generating product awareness and influencing customers' purchasing decisions, e.g. advertising, public relations.
- SALES: choosing the most efficient and effective sales approach.
- DISTRIBUTION: evaluating the most efficient way of getting the product to your customer, whether directly or indirectly.
- AFTER SALES: providing a comprehensive customer care service.

The Marketing Spectrum comprises a number of different functions, many of which are undertaken by specialists. It is the role of the Marketing Manager to co-ordinate the efforts and advice of these people and, based on a view of the situation overall, decide on future action.

Fig. 14.9 *What is marketing?*   Source: The Chartered Institute of Marketing (UK)

(a) What does market research tell a business? **1**

(b) In what way would you say that market research helps a firm to set an 'acceptable and profitable price level'? **2**

(c) How would market research help a producer to 'match physical requirements with visual image'? **3**

(d) Describe two examples of ways that market research can help a business to choose 'the most efficient and effective sales approach'. **4**

(e) 'Marketing thinking and planning begins at or even before the drawing board …' How does market research contribute at this early stage? **4**

(f) 'Good marketing is the end product of a well-led management team fully embracing the marketing concept.'
  (i) What do you understand by 'the marketing concept' in the sense in which it is used here? **3**
  (ii) Give examples of other wording included in this document that can be directly related to the marketing concept. **3**

Q7 A confectionery manufacturing company is considering launching a completely new high-energy snack bar. It is relying on market research to guide its marketing strategy.

(a) What is the main aim of market research? **1**

(b) Briefly describe two examples of market segments that would be relevant to this company's new product. **2**

Chapter 14 – **Market research and advertising**

(c) Give two examples of the sort of information that research consultants might usefully collect for this company. **2**

(d) How could market research consultants help this company decide its best target market? **2**

(e) The firm intends to draw on both desk research and field research. Explain the difference between these two ways of collecting information. Include examples of related information to illustrate your answer. **4**

(f) Describe three specific ways in which market researchers could collect information through field research. For each method, give a different example of the kind of data that could be gathered that would be of particular use to a supermarket chain or its suppliers. **9**

Q8 Refer to the part of a market research questionnaire shown as figure 14.2. This questionnaire is used to find out information about readers of a consumer magazine called *Home Market*. The magazine is given away free to the shoppers of a large supermarket chain as they pass through the checkout. Some of the information collected is given by the supermarket chain to other suppliers. All the following questions are related to this aspect of market research.

(a) Who is the target market for this questionnaire? **1**

(b) How could market research help a business to improve its sales? **2**

(c) Questionnaires are of no use if people are not willing to complete and return them. Briefly describe two ways that the supermarket chain could encourage customers to complete and return the questionnaire. **2**

(d) Give three examples of the use that the researchers might make of information about the hobbies and interests of shoppers in a food store. **3**

(e) Design a small additional section that could be incorporated into this questionnaire and would result in information that could help improve its customer relations. Briefly say why you feel your suggestion would be effective. **4**

(f) The magazine editors give some of the information collected from the survey free to firms who pay to advertise in the magazine. These advertisers are often the firms that sell to the market chain. Why would the information gathered be of particular interest to these advertisers? Use examples taken from the part of a questionnaire shown to illustrate your answer. **8**

Research assignments

1 At your school, develop a questionnaire that will enable you to obtain answers to the following market research question: What are the buying habits of pupils of your age at school? In carrying out your research, follow the six stages shown within figure 14.3 in this chapter. Formulate a report that summarises your findings. You may use a computer to analyse and present as much of your work as possible, if you have access to one. The following questions should help you in your research:

   a) What is the age of your sample? What can you say about the family background of the sample? On what grounds would you say your sample is 'representative'?

   b) On average, how much pocket money do the people in your sample receive each week? Is there any difference between males and females with regard to pocket money and spending patterns?

Principles of Business – Profile 2

    c)   What are the sources of the total money they receive?
    d)   In what way do they use their money? For example, how much is spent on clothes, entertainment, personal care products or saving? What other categories can you add here?
    e)   What percentage of their income is saved, and for what purpose do they save? For example, are they saving for personal purchases, presents for others, or for other reasons?
    f)   Do your findings differ from one age group to another?
    g)   What conclusions can you draw from the information you have collected? What recommendations could you make to a business in your location that sells to the age group of the people in your sample?

2 Design a market research questionnaire that will effectively answer the following questions if presented to a random sample of consumers. Visit a local retail business such as a supermarket, and carry out your survey on at least 20 customers as they leave the store.
    a)   What factors appear to have influenced the customers' purchasing decisions?
    b)   Did the customer spend time examining the information shown on product packaging or on display?
    c)   Did the customer compare the prices of competing brands of products?
    d)   Did the customer look for a specific item or a particular brand of product?
    e)   How long approximately did each customer spend in the store?

Present your findings in the form of a report. What observations can you make from your findings?

3 You are the advertising manager of a firm that is developing a new soft drink. Describe how you would formulate an advertising campaign to promote the launch of your product into a highly competitive market. Compare your planned campaign with the marketing strategies of an existing soft drink.

4 'Advertising is wasteful of resources and causes an increase in the cost of goods.' Discuss this statement, using appropriate data to support your arguments.

5 Sometimes market research takes the form of 'desk research', that is finding out information about a potential market by referring to reference sources readily available to anyone. Describe the application of some specific reference sources available to market researchers.

6 Using specific examples of marketing techniques employed by companies with which you are familiar, explain why advertising is important to industry, commerce and the consumer.

7 Using a selection of advertisements to assist you, explain why you consider that there is a case for consumers having some protection against the claims of advertisers. Describe the main forms of consumer protection and explain why you find some more relevant to you than others.

Chapter 15

Distribution

15.1 What is distribution?

In Chapter 13 we said that one of the elements of the marketing mix is 'place', the point where those involved in marketing want their product to reach. We also said that a market is any situation that enables trading to take place between sellers and buyers of goods or services. This trading may be carried out by direct selling, where the products reach the final consumer without passing through intermediary stages or middlemen. The most common ways of doing this are through factory shops or selling door to door. Mail order is another method of direct selling. Customers order their goods through a catalogue, or by telephone. Much of the selling on the internet is really a form of mail order, with the catalogue displayed on screen, although goods still have to be delivered by traditional methods. Indirect selling occurs where the buyer the seller actually meet such as through some form of intermediary such as a retail outlet. We shall look in more detail at indirect selling shortly.

A market may be local, national, regional or international in scope. A business involved in production or selling will decide in which of these potential markets it wishes to participate, and it may choose to operate in more than one of them. This decision will be influenced by many factors, including: transport costs (i.e. is it cost effective to send a low-value product on an expensive journey?), product characteristics (e.g. is it realistic to send perishable goods, such as lettuces, long distances?), and the suitability of the product to buyer tastes (e.g. there is little point in marketing automatic washing machines in a country where water and electricity are relatively scarce).

Chapters 13 and 14 explored the main ways that producers and sellers learn about the buyers' needs and wants through market research, and use the information gathered to form a production strategy and a marketing strategy. In this way the business increases its chances of being successful because it is recognising and satisfying customer needs.

Distribution refers to *storing* and *moving* products to customers, often through intermediaries such as wholesalers and retailers, and it also includes transportation, which involves the physical movement of goods. The task of distribution is getting specified quantities to places where customers can conveniently buy them, in time to replenish stocks, and in good condition. Distribution is part of one of the four Ps of the marketing mix examined in Chapter 13, as it is concerned with getting products to the correct place where they can be bought. Therefore, distribution will involve the selection of appropriate channels of distribution.

Principles of Business – Profile 2

15.2 The channels of distribution

The route used to physically get the product from the manufacturer to the actual buyer of that product is referred to as the **distribution channel**. A typical distribution channel consists of four interrelated operations:

- *Manufacturing* – producing the product.
- *Wholesaling* – holding large stocks and 'breaking bulk' into smaller packs for retailers.
- *Retailing* – the sale of the product in convenient quantities to the final buyer.
- *Consumers* – the final purchasers of the product.

These functions may be carried out by firms that specialise in particular stages in the chain of distribution (e.g. wholesalers and retailers), but sometimes they may be integrated by one firm (**vertical integration** – see Chapter 2) in order to gain control over distribution and to achieve various advantages over competitors.

The final destination of the distribution service is the customer or consumer of the products, making the fourth element in the **chain of distribution**. Thus the complete chain consists of:

Producer → Wholesaler → Retailer → Consumer

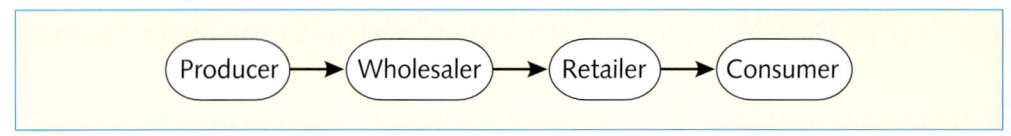

Fig. 15.1 *Chain of distribution*

Traditionally, the producers sell their output to a wholesaler, but other alternatives may be used. Sometimes a producer may bypass the wholesaler and sell direct to retailers as in figure 15.2, or perhaps the producer may supply directly to its own retail outlets. In other circumstances the producer may bypass both the wholesaler and the retailer and sell direct to the consumer, for example a producer of fitted furniture, bathroom suites (**job production**) may well sell to the consumer and even have their own team of fitters/installers.

Producer → Retailer (Wholesaler bypassed)

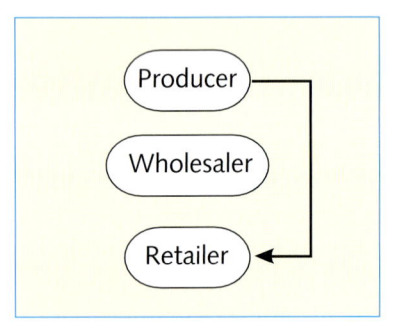

Fig. 15.2 *Bypassing the wholesaler*

15.3 Wholesalers

Producers need to sell their products in large quantities to enable them to carry out mass production and enjoy economies of scale. But many retailers cannot buy the large quantities that the producers and manufacturers want to sell. **Wholesalers** bridge the gap between producers and retailers by buying in large quantities and selling in smaller, more convenient lots to the retailer. The retailer in turn sells individual items to the consumer.

The wholesaler's premises are usually a large **warehouse** divided into sections dealing with specific commodities, and organised like a large supermarket.

Retailers may visit the wholesaler to choose their purchases, or orders may be telephoned in or passed to the wholesaler's representative on his or her periodic visits to retailers, and delivered in due course by the wholesaler's own delivery vehicles.

Chapter 15 – **Distribution**

Types of wholesaler

There are two basic forms of wholesaler.

- *General wholesalers* operate from large warehouses sited for convenient access from many local towns. They allow retailers credit, and deliver goods to retail shops.
- *Cash-and-carry wholesalers* do not allow credit and do not deliver goods. Retailers come to the warehouses, select goods, pay for them, and provide their own transport.

Sometimes wholesalers specialise in a particular aspect of trade. For example, one might specialise in supplies in hair care products, whilst another might specialise in clothing and footwear.

Functions of wholesalers

Acting as an intermediary

The wholesaler is positioned between the producer and the retailer. For this reason the wholesaler is sometimes referred to as a 'middleman' or 'intermediary'.

But there are exceptions where the producer will sell direct to the retailer, or even straight to the consumer, bypassing both the wholesaler and the retailer.

Breaking of bulk

The wholesaler buys in large quantities from the producer and sells in smaller lots, usually to the retailer.

Taking on risks

The wholesaler predicts market trends and buys ahead of demand.

Warehousing

By storing goods, the wholesaler saves space for both the producer and the retailer.

Offering credit

The wholesaler may supply goods and allow the retailer to pay at some later date (**trade credit**). This may give the retailer the opportunity to sell the goods before he or she has paid for them.

Fig. 15.3 *A wholesale warehouse*

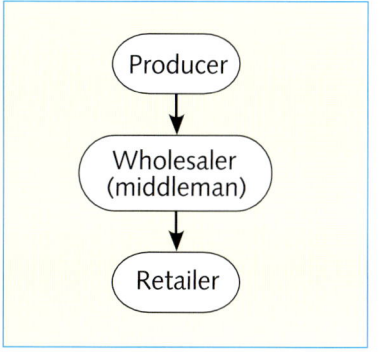

Fig. 15.4 *Wholesaler as middleman*

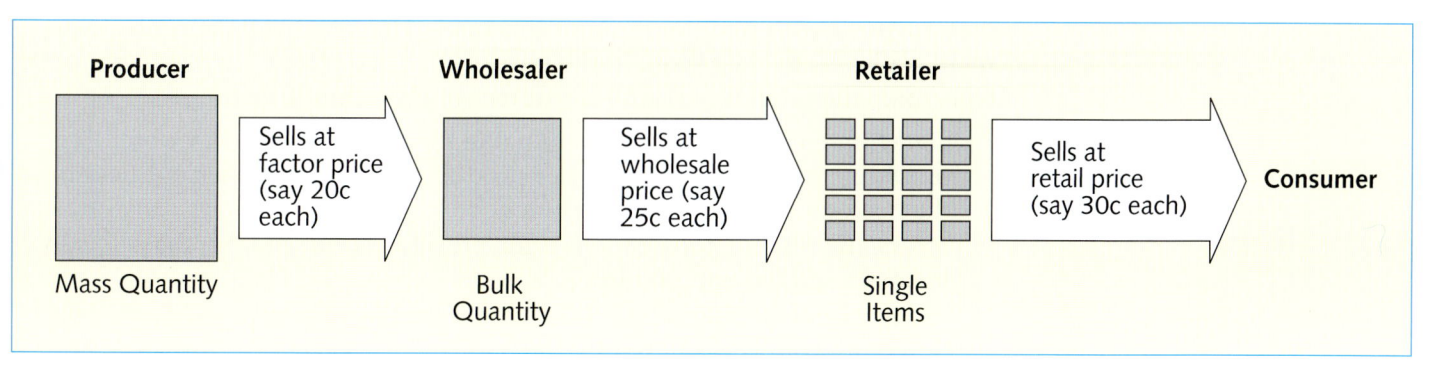

Fig. 15.5 *Wholesaler breaking bulk*

Principles of Business – Profile 2

KEY WORDS

Find out the business-related meaning of each of the following terms. Write a separate sentence for each term to show your understanding.

distribution intermediary
distribution channel
mail order   direct selling
indirect selling
chain of distribution
warehouse   wholesaler

Services provided by wholesalers

For the producer

- Reduces transport costs.
- Advises the producer of current market trends.
- Finishes goods by grading, packing and branding.
- Makes mass production possible by ordering in large quantities and therefore reducing production costs.

For the retailer

- Offers choice of products from many producers.
- Supplies small quantities to suit retailers' needs.
- Locally situated, providing quick access to goods, and open until late in the evening.
- Advises on latest trends and 'best buys'.
- Pre-packs goods ready for the retailers' shelves (graded, labelled, priced and weighed).

15.4 Retailers

Retailers are traders providing goods and services directly to the consumer. They are positioned either between producers and consumers, or between wholesalers and consumers. In other words, the retailer is the last link in the chain between the producer and the consumer.

The retailer buys in large quantities from the wholesaler and sells in small, convenient quantities to the consumer. If the retailer can order a great enough quantity he or she may buy direct from the producer.

The functions of retail trade

Today we live in a society in which specialisation plays a major part. Most of us concentrate on carrying out our particular specialisation and rely on others to satisfy most of our needs. For each of us to be able to specialise in this way requires an intricate pattern of distribution between producers and consumers. This involves a whole range of intermediaries such as banking, insurance, transport, advertising and the many other commercial activities that are dealt with in other parts of this book. Here we shall concentrate on retail trade. As the last stage in the passage of goods from the producer to the consumer, the retailer performs a number of important functions.

- *Outlet:* the retailer performs a valuable service to the producer by providing an outlet for his or her products, thus saving the producer from the need to market his or her own goods.
- *Stocks:* the retailer holds stocks which the consumer can purchase locally in small, convenient quantities.
- *Choice:* the consumer is able to choose from the variety of products from different producers offered by the retailer.
- *Information and advice:* retailers' expert knowledge and experience enable them to advise and inform customers on the quality and suitability of products.

- *Feedback:* the retailer provides a feedback of consumer responses to wholesalers and producers. This helps the producer to become aware of what the consumer market wants, and also helps to ensure that consumers' requirements are satisfied.

Types of retailer

Door-to-door

Door-to-door trades people generally deal in relatively minor goods and services.

- *Pedlars* carry goods from door to door on foot.
- *Hawkers* use some method of transport.
- *Mobile shops* are vehicles adapted to serve as travelling shops, for example the ice cream truck and soft drink truck.

Market traders

These operate from stalls in open or covered areas, sometimes along streets and sometimes in areas specially kept for markets. Market traders can often keep prices very low because they avoid expenses (overheads) such as electricity, high rent, shop fittings, etc.

Independent shops

This category of retailer is not attached to a large organisation, and for this reason is referred to by a variety of names, including 'sole trader', 'corner shop', 'unit shop' and 'convenience shop'.

An independent shop is owned by a sole trader or small partnership and is typically sited away from town centres. It often specialises in offering a single commodity or service, as does a baker, butcher or confectioner. There are advantages and disadvantages in this type of retailing.

Advantages

- Gives personal attention to customers.
- Saves customer from travelling into town.
- Owner has a thorough knowledge of the business.
- Sometimes allows customers credit.

Disadvantages

- Cannot buy in very large quantities.
- Prices often higher than larger shops.
- Carries a limited range of stock.
- Difficulties in running the shop if the owner is sick.

Small retailers such as the independent shop are facing considerable difficulties in larger towns where they have to face the competition of large organisations that tend to be more cost-effective.

Multiples (chain stores)

Multiples are chains of shops trading under a single name and all owned by one company. They are generally controlled from a central headquarters and tend to be sited in town centres and shopping precincts. Examples of multiples are Bata, Woolworths and Kirpalani.

Fig. 15.6 *Selling bananas*

Fig. 15.7 *Street market in Bridgetown, Barbados*

Fig. 15.8 *An independent retailer in Dominica*

Principles of Business – Profile 2

Fig. 15.9 A multiple

Multiples enjoy many advantages over smaller retailers.
- Their large size enables them to bypass wholesalers and buy in large quantities direct from the producer.
- A single national advertisement can cover all branches nationwide.
- They have the resources to rent or buy stores in prime central sites with large car parking space.
- They can afford to attract customers with loss leaders (goods sold at below cost price).

Supermarkets

A supermarket is a large self-service store. A self-service store is defined as a supermarket when it has more than 200 square metres of shopping area and three or more checkout points. Such stores are often organised as multiples.

Supermarkets deal particularly in prepacked, priced products. Loss leaders are frequently used to attract custom, and customers serve themselves. The provision of shopping trolleys reduces customers' awareness of the weight of their purchases and encourages impulse buying (unplanned purchases).

Because supermarkets are often organised in multiples, they usually enjoy the advantages mentioned earlier. They also benefit from economies of scale. For example they are able to employ specialist staff such as butchers, bakers and fishmongers. In addition, they save on staff because the customers do much of the work by serving themselves.

Although this type of shop has many advantages over other retailers it faces some disadvantages.
- Large premises in prime areas are expensive.
- Pilferage (stealing) levels are high.
- Customers receive little personal contact.
- Shopping trolleys are stolen.

Department store

This type of shop is sometimes called a 'shop of shops' because it is divided into commodity departments. Each department is operated like a single shop, and so is responsible for its own profitability.

Department stores tend to be comfortably equipped with carpets, lifts and a restaurant. **Merchandise** is attractively displayed, and credit facilities (sometimes interest-free) are given to suitable customers. Some have introduced their own charge cards.

Advantages
- Customers can shop in comfort.
- A wide variety of goods is available under one roof.
- Shop assistants give personal service.
- Sited in towns and convenient for public transport and car parks.

Disadvantages
- Large central sites are expensive.
- Cannot compete with prices of multiples.
- Comfortable surroundings can be a drain on profits.
- Labour-intensive compared with some retailers.

Fig. 15.10 A supermarket

Hypermarkets

These are a very large form of supermarket with a shopping area in excess of 5,500 square metres. They offer a very wide range of goods in many specialist departments similar to the divisions in a department store. Alternatively, parts of the hypermarket complex may be rented out to other approved traders.

Hypermarkets are usually organised in chains, like multiples. They are frequently sited on the outskirts of towns where land is cheaper. Good parking facilities are provided and some late night trading.

Mail order

Products are sold in a variety of ways through the mail-order method.

- Advertising in the press, on radio or on television which invites potential customers to buy by post.
- Direct selling, with customers choosing articles from a catalogue at home.
- Part-time agents selling to friends from catalogues in return for a commission.

Advantages

- Interest-free credit often given.
- Buying in the comfort of one's home.
- Goods chosen at leisure.

Disadvantages

- Prices often higher than in shops.
- Difficult to assess quality from a catalogue.
- Can be inconvenient to return unsuitable goods.

Vending machines (automats)

These retail outlets are open twenty-four hours a day, and provide a wide variety of products such as hot and cold snacks, confectionery, drinks, petrol, etc. Vending machines are sited in busy public places and they are sometimes the target of vandalism.

Catalogue shops

A catalogue shop publishes a comprehensive catalogue (like a mail-order catalogue) detailing all the products it has for sale. Catalogues are given away free to prospective customers.

Customers who see an item they are interested in buying visit the shop to see a sample of the item. If they like the product, they can then make the purchase on the spot.

Telephone order trading

Sales persons use the telephone to contact potential customers to try to persuade them to buy their company's products.

Sometimes the telephone canvasser knows about the person's interest, perhaps because he or she has replied to an advertisement. But sometimes the canvasser just selects the customer at random from the telephone directory. This is sometimes referred to as 'cold selling'.

Fig. 15.11 *Example of a bar code*

Patterns in retailing

The following are just some of the many growing trends in the retail trade.

Bar codes

A bar code consists of a pattern of vertical lines that a computer can read. Producers and large retailers are increasingly giving a bar code to each item on the shelves. As customers leave through the checkout, the bar-coded items are automatically totalled by the point-of-sale terminal (POS) computer link to produce an itemised bill for the customer. The same data transfer method can also be used to automatically update stock records and to decide when the retailer needs to order more stock.

Logos

Many large firms now use logos (symbols) with the company title on their products to assist recognition.

Branded goods

Producers and retail multiples use a distinctive trade or brand name to allow easy identification of their goods. Sometimes large retailers buy products from manufacturers and have their purchases 'branded' with their own names.

Credit facilities

Many retailers offer suitable customers credit facilities, sometimes without charging interest. Some of the larger retailers have introduced their own charge cards, which allow customers to pay for purchases later in instalments.

Shopping precincts

Sometimes called malls or shopping centres, these are shopping areas shut off from traffic, well served by public transport, road links and car parks, and often with an information centre.

Franchise shops

A franchise agreement is made between an entrepreneur (business person) and a franchise house. The agreement allows the entrepreneur to use the name of a well-known company and the exclusive right to market its products within a specified area. This form of business is particularly common in the fast food ('takeaway') trade.

Below-the-line promotion techniques

Below-the-line-promotion refers to techniques that encourage the consumer to buy, but are not a direct sale as such. For example, **point of sale displays** and in-store **demonstrations** make customers aware of products without actually selling to them. Giving away **free gifts** encourages customers to enter the store, and perhaps encourages **customer loyalty** when linked to a *'token system'*, where the customer receives tokens in relation to the amount spent that can be exchanged for gifts. This encourages the customer to return to the store in order to obtain more tokens.

Other below-the-line-promotions include free samples, which potential customers are given to test, hoping they will be convinced enough to make purchases. Buy one, get one free (or two-for-the-price-of-one) is another technique that draws on the consumer's natural desire to *get something for nothing*. Similarly, loss leaders (selling something at cost price, or below cost price), are used to entice people into the shop in the hope that they will buy other items also. A business could use a competition as a part of its below-the-line-promotion. For example, the customer could be given an entry to a draw for a major prize when purchasing certain items, or a making a stated value of purchases.

Below-the-line-promotion techniques are almost endless, and they are not restricted to retailing. They include personality promotions (using famous people to endorse products), off-price labels featuring so much off the normal price, or a label on the purchase offering an amount off a future purchase.

Below-the-line-promotions such as those summarised above have cost implications. Obviously when a firm gives away free gifts, prizes, price reductions, etc. there is an expense involved. This expense has to be met in addition to the cost of other promotional activities such as advertising. The firm embarking on below-the-line-promotions has to make the tricky decisions of deciding whether to use such promotional activities, and which of the many alternative methods of promotions to use, taking into consideration the costs involved.

Selling through the internet

Shopping via the internet (e-commerce) is a relatively new but fast growing method of trading. Customers can access a shopping channel through their internet service provider. This enables them to make purchases from companies participating and selling through the system. The potential customer can view data related to products sellers have on offer. Having compared the offers of competing sellers and made their choice of purchases, consumers can place their order and pay directly by credit or switch card.

A typical example of trading by the internet is shown by the company trading as eBay. This company was established in a very small way in 1995 by Pierre Omidyar and has since become the world's largest online market place – with 94.9 million users worldwide and some 9 million visitors to the site in just one month. At any given time there are more than 21 million items on the site worldwide and 3 million items are added each day. According to recent figures there are more than 430,000 registered sellers using eBay to trade goods full-time or part-time. Gross merchandise sales (the value of goods traded on eBay) exceeds US$24 billion a year.

On the eBay site you can buy anything from mobile phones to model trains, football shirts, cars and computers. The most expensive item sold at the time of writing was a Gulfstream jet for US$4.9 million.

Selling on credit

Selling on credit means allowing a buyer the use of goods which are paid for after the purchase, perhaps over a period of time by regular instalments. There are a variety of forms that selling on credit may take.

KEY WORDS

Find out the business-related meaning of each of the following terms. Write a separate sentence for each term to show your understanding.

retailer   market trader
mobile shop
independent shop
multiple   supermarket
department store
hypermarket
below the line
vending machine
bar code   franchise shop
mail order   e-commerce

Trade credit

Trade credit occurs where the seller allows the buyer to have goods and pay for them after an agreed period of time. For example, a producer or wholesaler may allow the retailer to have supplies and pay for them at the end of the month. This allows the seller the opportunity to resell the goods before he or she has even paid for them, thus increasing the scope of his or her business.

Hire purchase agreement (HP)

This is a contract for hiring goods for a fixed period with an option to purchase them for a nominal sum (e.g. $1) at the end of the period.

An initial **deposit** is paid, a percentage of the purchase price, and a number of equal weekly or monthly **instalments** are repaid over a given period. Interest is charged for the credit given.

The goods purchased do not become the property of the buyer until the last instalment has been paid. The item purchased must not be sold until the last repayment has been made because the seller or finance company remains the legal owner until the last instalment has been paid.

The seller can repossess the item if the buyer defaults on repayments.

Credit sale agreement

This is a deposit, instalment and interest system similar to an HP agreement, but the buyer becomes the owner of the goods immediately the agreement has been made.

In the case of a credit sale agreement, if the buyer defaults on the repayments the seller or finance company does not repossess the goods but can sue for repayment of the debt.

Note that most retailers do not finance HP and credit sales agreements themselves, but use companies that specialise in this kind of finance.

Interest-free credit

The buyer is allowed to pay for purchases by regular instalments but is not charged any interest.

Credit cards

The holder of a credit card can use it to make purchases up to a set amount without paying cash. The trader claims the money due for the purchases from the company that has issued the credit card.

The card holder is presented with an account from the issuer of the credit card. Payment of the outstanding amount can be made at once in full, or at some later time. Interest is charged on the outstanding balance.

Examples of credit cards are American Express, Diners Club and Visa.

Charge cards

Some retailers have introduced their own form of credit card for use in their stores. These allow approved customers to make purchases and charge these to their personal account, the money to be repaid later. The system is frequently linked to an instalment payment system operated by the firm, sometimes providing interest-free credit.

Chapter 15 – Distribution

Mark-up and profit margin

Both of these terms refer to ways of looking at the differences between a trader's cost price and his selling price.

- Mark-up refers to the percentage profit which is added to the cost price by a trader to establish the selling price. For example, if an article has a cost price of 80c and it is to be sold for $1, the mark-up is:

$$\frac{20}{80} \times 100\% = 25\%$$

- Profit margin is the percentage of the selling price which is the seller's profit. For example, on an article with a cost price of 80c which is sold for $1, the profit margin is:

$$\frac{20}{100} \times 100\% = 20\%$$

15.5 The international market

International marketing refers to the marketing of a firm's products in a number of overseas markets as opposed to selling only in the firm's domestic (home) market. Sometimes a large firm may be able to promote its products as a global brand across all its overseas markets. For example, the unique brand names Coca Cola and Microsoft are used in all the many countries where the products are marketed as opposed to a different brand name for each product in each country.

However, not all overseas marketing can be carried out using a single brand name. More frequently a firm will be required to adopt a more customised approach for its products. They may have to be adapted because of language differences, local regulations or technological variations (e.g. different levels of electricity voltage, and types of plug).

Because the trading referred to here takes place in an overseas market it is sometimes called 'foreign trade'. Traders involved in international trade make money by selling to or buying from other countries. Goods that are sold to another country are called exports. The exporter sells to a firm in an overseas country (the importer) and earns money in the process. Goods that are bought from another country are called imports and the firm bringing them into the country is now the importer. Frequently a firm acts as both exporter and importer and in each case makes a profit on the deals irrespective of which direction the goods are going.

15.6 Transportation

The importance of transportation

Transport is an important element to all parts of the chain of distribution involved in getting products to the consumer. Businesses often have a choice of the method of transportation they can use to get products from factories or warehouses to a number of destinations. They will want to use the method most appropriate for their products and will be under pressure to move the goods before any deterioration in quality occurs, or any depreciation in value. However, at the same time they will want to minimise transportation costs.

Principles of Business – Profile 2

KEY WORDS

Find out the business-related meaning of each of the following terms. Write a separate sentence for each term to show your understanding.

profit margin
trade credit   mark-up
credit card   pilferage
spoilage   insurance
deterioration
depreciation   charge card
misdirection
security measures
industrial conflicts
warehousing

The factors that determine the form of transport used are as follows:
- the nature of the goods
- how urgently the consignment is needed
- the value of each item and insurance costs
- cost of transportation
- handling and warehousing costs
- distance the consignment must be transported
- the size and weight of the load
- convenient position of terminals, e.g. docks, airport, railway station
- possibility of combining loads to reduce costs
- the reputation of the carrier.

In spite of taking into account all of these considerations involved in transportation, problems still occur. Shipments can be delayed for a variety of reasons, such as industrial conflicts or even something as simple as poor communication. Consignments of products can suffer from spoilage and pilferage, and of course goods may even be misdirected. All of the foregoing has implications on the profitability of the business.

The answer to these problems is to have effective processes in place to cover such contingencies. Whilst every eventuality cannot be offset by organisation, the effect of them can be reduced. For example, provision of adequate warehousing will help to reduce deterioration, security measures will reduce pilferage, and of course high quality insurance can compensate for losses incurred, but the cost of insurance will have to be offset against profits.

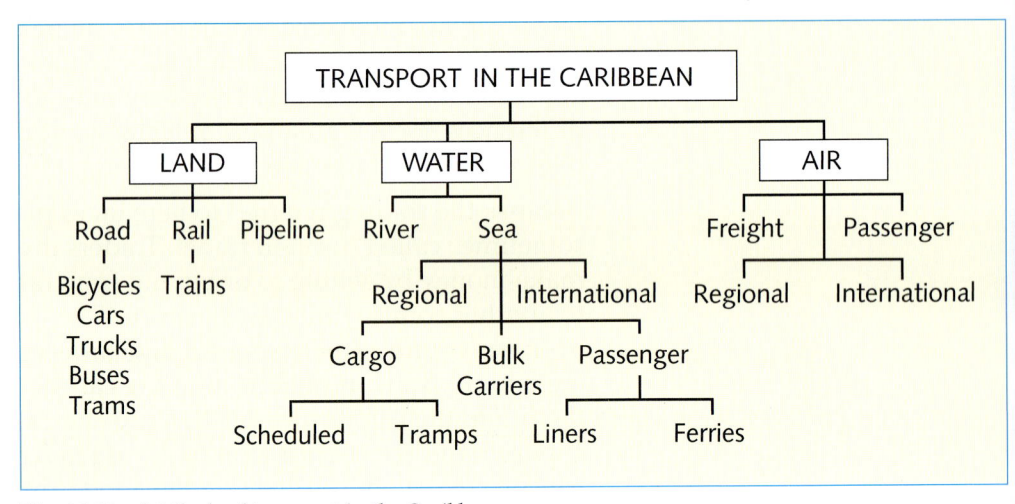

```
                    TRANSPORT IN THE CARIBBEAN
                    ┌───────────┬───────────┐
                   LAND        WATER        AIR
            ┌──────┼──────┐   ┌───┴───┐   ┌──┴──┐
           Road   Rail  Pipeline River  Sea  Freight Passenger
            │     │           ┌──┴──┐        │       │
        Bicycles Trains    Regional International Regional International
        Cars              ┌────┴────┐
        Trucks          Cargo   Bulk    Passenger
        Buses                  Carriers
        Trams          ┌────┴────┐   ┌────┴────┐
                    Scheduled Tramps Liners  Ferries
```

Fig. 15.12 *Methods of transport in the Caribbean*

Methods of transportation

As in most other areas of the world, there are five methods of transportation in the Caribbean region: rail, road, water, air and pipelines.

Rail

Rail transport is generally a lot more widely used in overseas countries than it is in the Caribbean. However, we need to be aware not only of our own limited use of railways but also of the importance of rail in other countries. This is because it is used by some of our businesses, particularly those engaged in the overseas market.

Advantages of rail transport
- More comfortable and easier for passenger travel than road transport.
- Faster than road on long distances.
- Less labour-intensive than road transport.
- Especially suited for container traffic.
- More economical in fuel-use than road transport.

Disadvantages of rail transport
- Routes determined by railway lines and stations.
- Equipment costs are very high.
- Relies on road transport for transshipment.
- Less economic than road movement for short journeys.

Road

One of the main reasons that rail transport has limited use in the Caribbean is that the length of journey is often not sufficient to offset the inconvenience of transporting cargo from road on to rail and later back on to road for local delivery. Conversely, road transport is by far the most important in the region because journeys between delivery points are relatively short.

Advantages of road transport
- Door-to-door service provides maximum flexibility.
- Fast over short distances.
- Risk of damage reduced by lack of need for transshipment.
- Can reach places inaccessible to other forms of transport.
- A good road network speeds up movement and reduces congestion.
- Less tied to a rigid timetable than railways.
- Suitable for speedy direct delivery of perishable goods.
- Other forms of transport rely on road transport to connect with terminals such as airport, station and docks.

Disadvantages of road transport
- Expensive to operate in large congested cities.
- Subject to mechanical breakdowns.
- Affected by adverse weather conditions (e.g. high winds, floods).
- Loads are limited in size and weight.
- Some roads are unsuitable for very large vehicles.
- Slower than railways over long distances.
- Wastes resources if truck returns empty.
- Tax on vehicles and fuel must be incorporated into costs.

Water

Water transport is important in the Caribbean not only because it helps in the transportation of goods and people between islands, but also because it provides an important link to other parts of the world. The majority of all our raw materials (e.g. bauxite and petroleum) sold to other countries are transported out of the region by water.

Two forms of water transportation are used in the region: river transport and sea transport.

River transport

Rivers provide a means of moving goods and people into inland areas, although they are only used to a limited extent in the region. For example, timber is floated down the Belize River, and in Guyana river transport is used for much heavy traffic. However, overall, river transport is not used to the extent that it is in many other parts of the world.

Sea transport

Sea transport is particularly important to the Caribbean region for the obvious reason that it is a group of islands surrounded by sea. The following are the main forms of sea transport used in the Caribbean.

Passenger liners
Passenger liners are built primarily for passenger travel, particularly cruising. They carry some cargo, and as they follow fixed routes and keep to a regular timetable, delivery dates can be guaranteed. However, high freight costs limit use to high-value cargoes.

Cargo liners
Cargo liners sometimes carry a few passengers, although their main purpose is to deliver cargo. They operate on fixed routes and to a regular timetable. A vessel always sails from a port on time, even if some of the scheduled cargo has not arrived.

Tramp ships
Tramps are ships that have no timetable or set route. They will carry any type of cargo to any part of the world. The vessels are chartered through a charter party agreement (see later).

Special freighters
For special cargoes there are a variety of purpose-built ships.
- *Container ships:* cellular design vessels for fast load/unload.
- *Bulk carriers:* for ore and grain.
- *Tankers:* for oil and other bulk liquids.
- *Ferries:* roll-on/roll-off ferries can carry vehicles. Hovercraft have proved particularly successful in this role in some parts of the world.

Advantages of sea transport
- The way is free and gives access to most parts of the world.
- A large ship can be propelled with a relatively small amount of power.
- The natural buoyancy of the water enables ships to carry very heavy loads, which gives economies of scale.

Disadvantages of sea transport
- The main disadvantages of sea transport is that it can only carry its cargo as far as the ports. Thereafter the cargo has to be transferred to some other form of transport to reach the final destination.
- Sea transport is a relatively slow method of moving freight.

Requirements of a sea port

Efficient sea transport operations require the provision of good terminal facilities which enables vessels to 'turn round' quickly. The following are the main requirements of a modern port.

Fig. 15.13 *The port of Kingstown, St Vincent*

- Clear access channel with deep water.
- Some protection from rough seas.
- Wharves with appropriate lifting gear and equipment such as that necessary for moving containers, etc.
- Warehouses, including specialist storage, such as refrigeration, bonded stores, hazardous cargo.
- Supplies of oil, water and other ship's requirements.
- Repair facilities such as dry docks.
- Customs and immigration facilities.
- Good links with road or rail network.
- Buildings for offices and commercial services such as banks and restaurants.

Air

This is the youngest but most highly technical form of transport. It is constantly expanding in the volume of passengers and freight it handles. It is by far the most important method of transportation of people, both within and to and from outside the region. Air transport makes a major contribution to the tourist industry, but it is becoming increasingly important also for carrying cargo.

Advantages of air transport
- It is the fastest form of transport.
- It operates to timetables, mostly on direct routes.
- It reduces the risk of damage or pilferage.
- Shorter transit time reduces insurance costs.
- Packaging costs reduced.
- Particularly effective over long distances.
- Containers are now being used to speed up cargo loading and unloading.

Disadvantages of air transport
- High operational costs result in high freight rates.
- Weight and size of cargo are limited.
- Sometimes affected by adverse weather conditions.
- Relies on other forms of transport to and from airport.
- Not suitable for short distances.

Fig. 15.14 *Grantley Adams International Airport, Barbados*

- Causes noise and pollution.
- Economic use is limited to certain cargoes, particularly light-weight, high value, urgently required commodities such as drugs, mail or high value perishable goods.

Requirements of an airport

In a similar way that a sea port demands facilities that enable it to operate efficiently, an airport also has requirements that must be met if it is to fulfil its functions.

Siting
The siting of an airport is very important. Whilst it would be convenient to site an airport in a country area where land costs are cheaper than in cities, most air travellers are heading for one of the world's major cities where they can link up with other forms of transport. For this reason, an airport has to be sited as near as possible to a major city, but avoiding high rise buildings and causing as little noise and pollution as possible.

Road and rail links
Road and rail links play an important part in providing easy access for travellers and freight. If the road and rail links are speedy and efficient, they can allow the airport to be sited further away from a city centre. The modern terminal also requires facilities for long- and short-term parking as well as freight storage areas such as a bonded warehouse.

Operational, repair and safety facilities
A wide range of equipment and repair services is necessary to keep aircraft flying. For example, sophisticated radio, radar, computer and other technical equipment (and the people to operate them) have become increasingly important at busy international airports. In addition, aircraft use vast quantities of highly inflammable fuel. This must be stored safely, and a fleet of tankers and other vehicles is needed to load fuel, luggage and freight on to aircraft. In addition, safety and medical services such as fire engines and ambulances must be permanently ready for action.

Customs and immigration officials
These are needed to regulate the import of goods on which duty must be paid, as well as to check for prohibited items such as drugs and firearms. Immigration officials are also necessary to ensure that those who enter the country have the right to do so.

Terminal buildings and personnel
Terminal buildings containing baggage and freight-handling equipment are required to ensure speedy movement of passengers and cargo. Within these buildings there may be hotel accommodation and commercial services such as banks, a post office, a duty free shop, and bars and restaurants. Airports require a variety of personnel to operate the terminal buildings. Security staff have become increasingly important.

Pipelines

Pipelines allow the transport of commodities without using a vehicle. Examples are gas, oil and water.

Fig. 15.15 *Containers on the dock at Fort de France, Martinique*

Containerisation

A container is a large pressed steel box available in two International Standards Organisation (ISO) sizes, capable of carrying twenty or thirty tonnes of cargo. The container is packed at the factory or inland pooling depot and delivered to the container terminal by rail (freightliner) or road, and deposited in the container parking area in the dock container terminal.

The containers are moved around the terminal by straddle carriers. The container is loaded precisely into position in the ship's hold by special gantry cranes.

Containerisation is also increasingly being used in air transport, to help speed up 'turn round'.

Advantages of containerisation

- Reduced staffing requirements lowers transport costs.
- Damage and pilferage is reduced.
- Packaging and insurance costs are reduced.
- Ship/aircraft 'turn round' is speeded up considerably.

Transportation terminology

- *Air waybill:* used in air transport as a receipt given to the consignor by the aircraft captain.
- *Bill of lading:* a document used in shipping which includes:
    a) a description of the cargo and its destination
    b) title of ownership of goods in transit
    c) a receipt for goods aboard ship.
- *Charter party:* a contract made between a shipowner and a consignor for the transport of cargo.
- *Consignment note:* accompanies goods being transported by land and is signed by consignee on delivery.

Principles of Business – Profile 2

KEY WORDS

Find out the business-related meaning of each of the following terms. Write a separate sentence for each term to show your understanding.

foreign market
global brand   pipeline
exports   imports
importer
containerisation
pilferage   exporter
transportation

- Delivery terms:
  a) *Carriage forward:* cost of transport to be paid by consignee.
  b) *Carriage paid:* cost of transport is paid by consignor.
  c) *Cost insurance, freight (CIF):* cost of goods includes freight and transit insurance.
  d) *Franco:* price of goods includes delivery to buyer.
  e) *Free alongside ship (FAS):* cost of goods includes delivery to side of ship.
  f) *Free on board (FOB):* cost includes freight as far as loading on to ship.
  g) *Free on rail (FOR):* transport costs are paid by the seller as far as railway.
- *Freight note:* a bill presented to the consignor by the shipping company for shipping goods.
- *Lloyd's List:* a daily newspaper published by Lloyd's of London listing ship movements.
- *Manifest:* a summary of all the bills of lading and cargo a ship is carrying.
- *Shipping agent* (freight forwarding agent): a company specialising in deciding the best form of transport and arranging necessary documentation.

15.7 Things to do

This section contains a variety of exercises to help you create revision notes, to test your understanding and to prepare you for examinations.

Search and find

Write out the question and the answer by referring back through the text to form revision notes.

1. Why is distribution important to both producers and consumers?
2. What are the common channels of distribution for consumer products?
3. How might the distribution chain for industrial products be different from that of consumer products?
4. List the functions of wholesalers.
5. Why is the wholesaler sometimes referred to as an intermediary?
6. In what way can the wholesaler be said to 'break bulk'?
7. Why is trade credit useful to the retailer?
8. Describe two circumstances in which the producer might sell direct to the retailer.
9. Give three examples in which the producer might bypass both the retailer and the wholesaler.

Chapter 15 – **Distribution**

10. What are the main ways in which general wholesalers and cash-and-carry wholesalers differ?
11. Describe the functions of the retail trade.
12. Explain the difference between a pedlar and a hawker.
13. What are 'overheads'?
14. List the advantages and disadvantages of being a sole trader.
15. What are chain stores, and how are they generally controlled?
16. Name four examples of multiples.
17. List the advantages the multiple store enjoys over smaller retailers.
18. Give three examples of the economies of scale gained by operating as a multiple shop.
19. What are the main disadvantages faced by supermarkets?
20. Why is a department store sometimes called a 'shop of shops'?
21. List the advantages and disadvantages of department stores.
22. What is a hypermarket?
23. List three methods of mail-order selling.
24. What are the advantages and disadvantages of buying by mail order from the point of view of the customer?
25. Make a list of ten items you can think of that are sold through vending machines.
26. What is a catalogue shop?
27. Describe telephone-order selling.
28. Briefly describe the features of a shopping precinct.
29. What are franchise shops?
30. Describe some of the techniques of 'below the line' promotions with which you are familiar.
31. Why do countries need to trade overseas?
32. Define the terms, 'imports' and 'exports', and 'importer' and 'exporter'.
33. What is meant by the term 'global trade'?
34. What difficulties exist in foreign trade that do not occur in the home market?
35. Briefly describe the use of the credit card system in the retail trade.
36. Give three examples of credit cards.
37. Explain the terms 'mark-up' and 'profit margin'.
38. Describe three factors it is necessary to take into account when setting up a retail business.
39. Why is the siting of a shop very important?
40. Describe two legal requirements that need to be observed by the shop owner.
41. Why is transportation particularly important to the Caribbean region?
42. List the factors that a business would take into account when deciding which form of transport to use.

Principles of Business – Profile 2

43 Give one reason why rail transport is not extensively used throughout the Caribbean region.

44 Give three advantages and three disadvantages of using road transport as part of the system of distribution of manufactured goods.

45 Why is sea transport particularly important to the Caribbean?

46 List the advantages and the disadvantages of sea transport.

47 List the requirements of a modern port.

48 What are the advantages and the disadvantages of air transport?

49 List three examples of cargo for which you think air transport is particularly suited.

50 Give a detailed description of the facilities needed for an airport to function efficiently and safely.

What do you know?

Write out the complete sentence and insert the missing word, which can be chosen from the list at the end of the questions.

1 The wholesaler is sometimes referred to as a …..
2 The wholesaler makes mass ….. possible by ordering in large quantities.
3 Sometimes producers ….. the wholesaler and sell direct to the retailer.
4 The retailer is usually the last ….. in the chain of distribution between the producer and the consumer.
5 A ….. is one of a chain of shops situated in several towns.
6 An efficient transport system reduces the amount of ….. needed to be tied up in stocks.
7 Some forms of transport are more suitable for particular ….. than others.
8 The ….. of an item will have some influence on the form of transport that is likely to be used.
9 A major advantage of ….. transport is that it provides door-to-door service.
10 ….. transport is the youngest but most highly technical form of transport.

Choose the missing words from the following

value   air   production   link   capital   tasks   middleman   road   multiple   bypass

Structured questions

Q1

(a) Why are supermarkets sometimes referred to as self-service stores? 1

(b) State one advantage that a supermarket has over a sole trader. 1

(c) Why is a supermarket able to operate with fewer staff than many other forms of retail outlet? 2

(d) Describe two ways in which goods are displayed in this type of shop. 2

(e) Name three other forms of retailing. 3

(f) Supermarkets are often part of a multiple chain. What is a multiple chain, and what economies of scale does it experience? 3

Chapter 15 – **Distribution**

(g) List four disadvantages supermarkets face. | 4

(h) Describe two specific ways in which supermarkets try to encourage 'impulse' buying. | 4

Q2

(a) Why does a small retailer tend to deal with a wholesaler instead of dealing direct with producers? | 2

(b) Give two examples of items that a consumer might buy direct from a producer. | 2

(c) State four ways in which a wholesaler might contact potential customers. | 4

(d) Give a brief comparison of the methods of the wholesaler and the retailer in the purchase and selling of goods. | 4

(e) Explain the difference between the general and cash-and-carry wholesaler. | 8

Q3 This question is all about types of retailer.

(a) What is a mobile shop? | 2

(b) Why is a market trader often able to sell goods at a price lower than a conventional shop? | 2

(c) State two ways in which a hypermarket differs from a supermarket. | 2

(d) Why are the majority of greengrocers independently owned, whereas supermarkets are usually part of a multiple organisation? | 3

(e) 'All supermarkets are self-service stores, but not all self-service stores are supermarkets'. Explain this statement. | 3

(f) State four special features that might attract customers to a department store. | 4

(g) In view of the competition from the larger forms of retailer, how are smaller types of retailer still able to exist? | 4

Q4 The following questions are all related to the things that an entrepreneur needs to take into account when setting up a retail business.

(a) What is a retail business? | 1

(b) What is an entrepreneur? | 1

(c) Name the type of business organisation that would be appropriate for two people setting up a small corner shop together. | 2

(d) State two possible ways by which the necessary capital could be raised. | 2

(e) Give two examples of the knowledge or skills that the owner or manager of a shop must have. | 2

(f) What considerations would be taken into account when choosing a site for a shop? | 6

(g) Describe two safeguards that the owners of a shop must observe in the interests of the staff or customers. | 6

Principles of Business – Profile 2

Q5 Look at the magazine advertisement in figure 15.16, and answer the questions which follow.

(a) Name the form of retailing this advertisement is related to. **1**

(b) Name the company that is trying to influence the sale of goods through this advertisement. **1**

(c) State two items of information likely to be contained within the catalogue mentioned. **2**

(d) What must the consumer do before receiving the 'free' personal stereo offered? **2**

(e) How can the seller afford to give away a personal stereo 'free'? **3**

(f) This form of retailing is called 'direct selling' under certain circumstances. Why is it sometimes referred to in this way? **3**

(g) The advertisement claims that the method of shopping being encouraged is 'better'. Give four advantages of this type of shopping. **8**

FREE Personal stereo! Sounds too good to miss!

We'll send you this fabulous gift **FREE** when you start shopping with the WISEBUY catalogue.

WISEBUY – the better way of shopping in the comfort of your home.

Post to WISEBUY, Vieux Fort, St. Lucia

Claim your free catalogue by completing this coupon
Mr/Mrs/Miss ....
Address ....

Fig. 15.16 *Free personal stereo*

Q6 This question is related to computer-based equipment used in retail marketing.

(a) What is the name given to the series of lines that many shop products have on their labels? **1**

(b) Where would a point-of-sale terminal be found in a shop and why would it be placed in this position? **2**

(c) How does the use of point-of-sale terminals help to reduce queues in supermarkets? **3**

(d) How do computers help to reduce staffing levels in the retail trade? **3**

Fig. 15.17 *Point-of-sale terminal with bar code reader*

(e) In spite of their many advantages, some shoppers are not happy about the introduction of point-of-sale terminals. Why do you think this is the case? **3**

(f) Explain how point-of-sale terminals help shops to improve their efficiency. **4**

(g) Although computerised stock records are automatically updated, periodic manual stocktaking is also necessary. Explain why manual stocktaking has to be done occasionally. **4**

Q7

(a) What is the name given to the computer terminal at the checkout point of a supermarket? **1**

(b) What advantages does an itemised till receipt have over conventional supermarket receipts? **1**

(c) What is the purpose of a bar code? **2**

(d) Why does a computerised checkout system result in fewer mistakes? **2**

Chapter 15 – Distribution

(e) Write out the following supermarket operations in the correct sequence:
- stock record updated
- itemised receipt produced
- bar code read by reader device
- products taken off shelf by customer. **2**

(f) The photograph in figure 15.17 shows a scanner being used to read a bar code. State one other method of reading a bar code. **2**

(g) Although point-of-sale terminals increase the efficiency of shops, many do not have this facility. Give two possible reasons why some shops do not have them. **2**

(h) Briefly describe two jobs that supermarket personnel do not have to do if computers are used in the store. **4**

(i) Details of a purchase can be input to the computer by keyboard or by a bar code reader. Briefly compare these two methods. **4**

Q8 The data in table 15.1 shows the volume of inland passenger transport for the imaginary country of Noland. Answer the questions related to the data.

Passenger transport in Noland: Estimated passenger kilometres (thousand million kilometres)	1989		1999	
		%		%
Air	2	0.50	3	0.60
Rail	36	9.11	35	6.97
Road				
Public service vehicles	54	13.68	42	8.37
Cars and taxis	297	75.19	410	81.67
Motorcycles	3	0.76	7	1.39
Pedal cycles	3	0.76	5	1.00
Total	395	100	502	100

Table 15.1 *Transporting bulky and heavy loads*

(a) Which type of inland transport, air, rail or road, carries the greatest volume of passenger transport? **1**

(b) The data shown here relates to domestic passenger traffic. What is meant by 'domestic' in this respect? **2**

(c) State the total percentage of passenger traffic carried by road in 1989 and in 1999. **2**

(d) Draw an appropriate graph to show a comparison between air, rail and road as a percentage of the volume of domestic passenger traffic carried in both 1989 and 1999. **3**

(e) Briefly state the general trend that can be seen between 1989 and 1999 in relation to each of the three categories of transport shown. **3**

(f) What trend can be observed if public transport is compared with private transport? **3**

(g) Explain some of the possible reasons for the trends that can be observed in this data. **6**

Q9 The graph in figure 15.18 shows the cost per kilometre of transporting bulky and heavy loads for various journeys up to 350 kilometres.

(a) (i) Which is the cheapest method of transport for a journey of 100 kilometres? **1**
(ii) Which is the cheapest method of journeys exceeding 300 kilometres? **1**
(iii) At what distance does it cost the same to transport goods by road as it does by rail? **1**

(b) Copy and complete table 15.2 which aims to show the difference in total costs between road and rail transport for various journeys. **3**

253

Principles of Business – Profile 2

(c) Why does road transport have an advantage over rail transport for shorter journeys, but is at a disadvantage for longer journeys? **4**

(d) Why does rail transport depend heavily on road transport? **4**

(e) Other than distance, what other factors will influence a business's choice between road and rail transport for delivering goods? **6**

Q10

(a) State two major factors that need to be taken into account when choosing a site for an airport. **2**

(b) Why do airports rely on other forms of transport? **2**

(c) What is the function of an air waybill? **2**

(d) What part does a freight forwarding agent play in the transportation of goods? **3**

(e) Describe examples of goods and circumstances for which air transport would be appropriate, and others for which air freight is impracticable. **5**

(f) What are the requirements for an efficient and safe airport? **6**

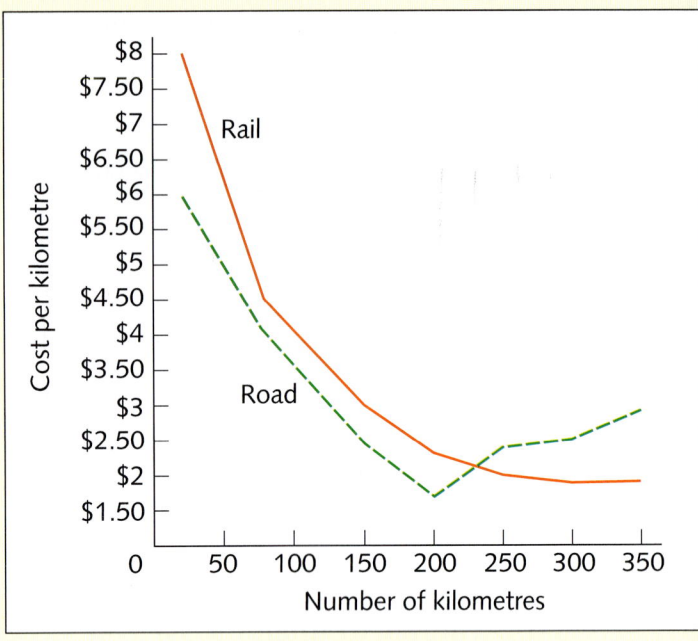

Fig. 15.18 *Transporting bulky and heavy loads*

Miles	Road	Rail
125		
200		
300		

Table 15.2

Q11

(a) Briefly explain each of the following delivery terms related to the carriage of goods:
- (i) carriage forward **1**
- (ii) carriage paid **1**
- (iii) franco **1**
- (iv) CIF **1**
- (v) FOB. **1**

(b) The following are documents used in freight transport. Explain the purpose of each of them:
- (i) consignment note **2**
- (ii) bill of lading **2**
- (iii) freight note. **2**

(c) Describe the function of each of the following people involved in the movement of goods:
- (i) consignee **3**
- (ii) consignor **3**
- (iii) shipping agent. **3**

Chapter 15 – **Distribution**

Q12 The graph in figure 15.19 shows the cost of various means of transport.

(a) Why is the line for water transport a relatively level line? **2**

(b) List the cheapest methods of transport at each of the distances shown as A, B, C and D. **4**

(c) Which of the points X, Y and Z would you consider to be related to air transport? Give reasons for your answer. **6**

(d) List the factors a business would take into account in deciding which method of transport to use. **8**

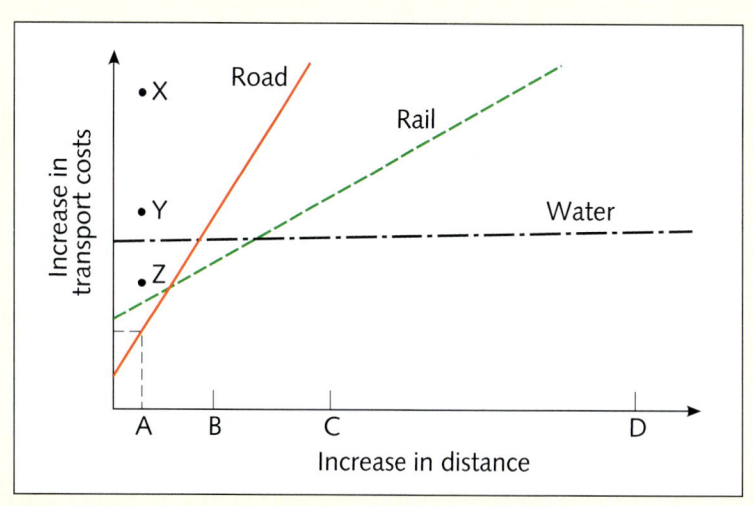

Fig. 15.19 *Cost of means of transport*

Q13 The data in figure 15.20 refers to the domestic transport of the imaginary country of Noland in 1989 and 1999.

(a) Which method of transport generally carries the greatest volume of goods? **1**

(b) Name two forms of goods that would be likely to be transported by pipelines. **2**

	1989		1999	
		%		%
Road	1537	84.54	1444	86.21
Rail	176	9.68	79	4.72
Water: seagoing	44	2.42	57	3.40
Water: internal	11	.61	7	.42
Pipelines	50	2.75	88	5.25
Total	1818	100	1675	100

Fig. 15.20 *Domestic goods transport of Noland*

(c) The data shown here refers to the 'domestic' transport of goods but it includes seagoing water transport. Why is it possible to include seagoing transport in domestic data? **2**

(d) Use an appropriate form of graph to compare the volume of freight carried by each of the categories of transport in 1989 and 1999. **3**

(e) Which category shows the greatest percentage increase in transported goods 1989–1999, and which shows the greatest percentage decline? **4**

(f) How important are the methods of transport shown in this data in the Caribbean region? **8**

Principles of Business – Profile 2

Research assignments

1. Discuss the view that wholesalers should be eliminated because they cause an increase in the cost of goods. What evidence can you present that supports your discussion?

2. Take any local retail business with which you are familiar and explain the sort of factors that the owner would have needed to take into account in setting it up. Include evidence that proves you have carried out personal research.

3. Collect personally researched data that addresses the question, 'To what extent would you say that there is genuine competition between retail outlets in your town?' Present your findings in report format.

4. Give a detailed explanation of the various forms of credit available to the consumer. To what extent do you feel that credit is a good thing? Carry out a survey of a cross-section of adults to identify which forms of credit are most frequently used.

5. Describe the features of four contrasting forms of sea transport, including an explanation of the types of freight for which each would be used. Obtain examples of four documents used in transport of freight by sea and clearly explain the function of each.

6. Discuss the importance of transportation to the CARICOM economy. Use examples from current newspapers to support your discussion.

7. Compare road, rail, water and air vehicles as means of transport for freight and passengers. What evidence exists to show that some of these are more important than the others to your country?

8. Carry out a survey of at least ten local businesses to establish the methods of transportation they use. Give reasons for any differences identified.

9. Study any firm which you know sends its goods to a number of different markets. Comment on the various delivery methods the firm uses.

10. If a new factory were established in your locality producing household utensils for sale throughout the Caribbean and overseas, what transport facilities would be likely to be used? Present evidence to support your research.

Chapter 16: The financial sector

16.1 Caribbean banking

Banking activities in the Caribbean are similar to those carried out in other parts of the world. Immigrants from the Caribbean who reside in the United Kingdom, the United States of America and Canada, for example, can transfer money to and from their relatives quite easily by utilising an appropriate banking service. In fact, **telegraphic money transfer**, a modern banking service made possible through the integration of telecommunications technology and computer technology, is very popular in the Caribbean today. Funds transferred from one location to another can reach the recipient less than half an hour after transmission. Naturally, businesses benefit from this service too.

Caribbean banking has a long history. The first commercial bank to operate in Jamaica was established in 1836 by merchants based in the United Kingdom who had business connections in the island. The Central Bank of Jamaica records reveal that by 1846 the bank had six agencies in operation throughout the island. The bank was named the *Bank of Jamaica* (no relation to the now existing Bank of Jamaica).

The *Colonial Bank* opened its doors in Jamaica in 1837. Later on, branches were established in other West Indian islands and in British Guyana. Services in 'trade and travel' were the major concern of the Colonial Bank. Later on, planters found it necessary to open the *Planters Bank*, mainly because the banks which were then in existence were not in a position to meet their need for 'easy credit'.

Today, a variety of banks can be found in the Caribbean islands. These include regular commercial banks, specialised banks such as merchant banks, agricultural credit banks, development banks, investment banks, other financial institutions which offer banking services, and central banks.

Many of the banks which operate in the Caribbean are branches of banks located in North America and the United Kingdom. A few national banks are also in operation.

16.2 Commercial banks

A **commercial bank** is a bank that accepts deposits of money from people and businesses and provides them with a payments transmission service (see Chapter 10) and various savings and loan facilities. Commercial banks are essential to businesses because so many of the services they provide are the backbone of commercial activities. You studied many of these services in Chapter 10 of this book, and you might like to read it again once you have worked through this chapter.

The main functions of the commercial banks are to:

➤ Provide a safe place for holding money while it is not being used, often in a current or deposit account.

Principles of Business – Profile 2

- Maintain customers' accounts, collect payments and make payments from and to others.
- Provide money and payments from the account when it is needed by the account holder.
- Provide loans.

These functions are met through the many services commercial banks provide, these include:

- Lending money to borrowers. This is mainly done through loans and overdrafts. Bank loans and overdrafts are examined shortly.
- Making it possible for customers to put their money in a safe place and spend it at a later time. This is achieved through the provision of current and deposit accounts.
- Provision of the cheque system. This makes it possible to make payments to others in an easy and safe manner.
- Operation of the standing order system that makes it easy for customers to pay an identical amount on the same day of each month.
- Offering the direct debit service whereby a varying amount (e.g. telephone bill) can be withdrawn from the customer's account by their creditors.
- Selling of travellers' cheques and foreign currency, assisting in foreign travel.
- Assisting businesses with raising letters of credit. This is an acceptable document used to effect payment for internationally traded goods.
- Buying and selling stocks and shares for their customers and collecting dividends on such investments for them.
- Provision of financial advice to customers.
- Providing help and guidance that encourages people to participate in entrepreneurship.
- Supplying banker's references for their customers. For example, when their customer wants to buy goods or services on credit when the vendor is not familiar with them.
- Discounting bills of exchange, which enable traders to have access to payment before goods are actually delivered to their customers.
- Providing a safe place for the storage of valuables, for example, the night safe facility removes the need for a trader to leave money on the premises overnight.
- Providing a credit card facility, which allows purchase of goods or services on credit.

The foregoing should not, of course, be seen as exhaustive because there are many other services that commercial banks provide. However, those listed here are particularly relevant to our studies here.

16.3 The central bank

A country's leading bank is its central bank, which acts as banker to the government and the banking system and acts as the authority responsible for implementing the government's monetary policy. The central bank is often referred to as The Bank in its home country.

KEY WORDS

Find out the business-related meaning of each of the following terms. Write a separate sentence for each term to show your understanding.

current account

night safe   direct debit

letter of credit

deposit account

commercial bank

banker's reference

standing order

bill of exchange

The functions of the central bank

A central bank, such as the Bank of Jamaica, has certain basic functions. These are summarised below.

It is the government's bank

Serving as the government's bank is a major function of a central bank. It manages the government's bank accounts, that is, the bank accounts of the various government departments.

The central bank also handles arrangements for government borrowing.

- *Short-term borrowing:* principally through the sale of treasury bills.
- *Long-term borrowing:* management of government stocks, which form the bulk of the national debt.

Management of the exchange equalisation account is carried out by the bank, and it is through this activity that the bank can influence the value of the dollar. It does so by selling or buying dollars to affect the foreign exchange market prices.

It acts as adviser to the government

The central bank advises the government on the formulation of monetary policy. Since regulations related to money and credit change from time to time as a result of a country's economic situation, the central bank ensures that the monetary policies adopted by government are in harmony with the real needs of the economy.

It executes the government's monetary policy

The central bank is responsible for carrying out the monetary policy of the government. This particularly involves the bank in exercising control of the money supply and the lending activities of the banks. It does this in a number of ways.

- *Open market operations.* The central bank can intervene in the financial market as both buyer and seller of bills, securities and certain other forms of credit instruments. The purpose of doing this is to influence the levels of money supply.
- *Bank rate.* This is the interest rate the central bank charges on its loans to the commercial bank as 'lender of last resort'. The bank can use this regulatory tool to influence the cost of borrowing.
- *Reserve and liquid asset requirements.* Commercial banks are required to place a percentage of the money they hold with the central bank, theoretically to ensure that they always have access to sufficient funds should there be a 'run of withdrawal requests'. In effect these deposits can be used as an instrument of monetary control when the central bank:
  - raises the percentage of deposits required
  - refuses to release the deposits to the commercial banks.

It is the 'lender of last resort'

If the commercial banks run short of cash they firstly recall deposits they have in the money market, thus reducing money in the market. If they still have insufficient funds, the commercial banks are forced to borrow. Where they cannot obtain sufficient funds from normal sources they are obliged to go to the central bank as a last resort.

Principles of Business – Profile 2

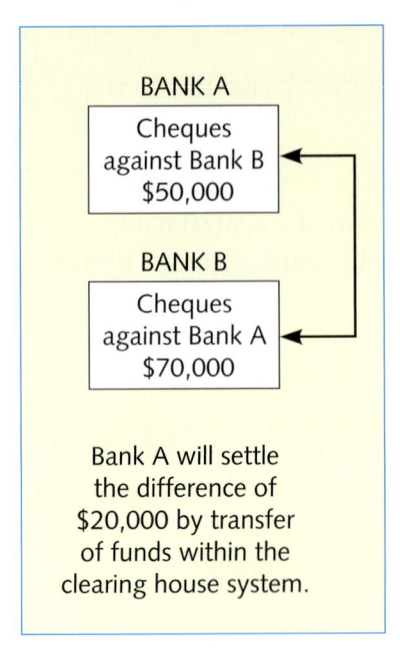

BANK A
Cheques against Bank B
$50,000

BANK B
Cheques against Bank A
$70,000

Bank A will settle the difference of $20,000 by transfer of funds within the clearing house system.

Fig. 16.1 *Cheque clearing*

It controls the issue of currency

The bank has the sole responsibility for the physical operations relating to the issue of currency.

It manages government borrowing

The central bank handles the arrangements for government borrowing. Here the bank issues 'treasury bills' which are used in short-term borrowing situations. From time to time, announcements inviting members of the public to invest in government treasury bills for a fixed period of time and at attractive rates, are published in newspapers.

It is the bankers' bank

Each of the clearing banks has an account with the bank, and during the process of cheque clearing, debits and credits are made to these accounts as a means of inter-bank settlement.

The clearing banks keep about a half of their liquid reserves (short-call money) deposited at the bank and use these for settling debts among themselves (e.g. in cheque clearing activities).

The commercial banks rely on the bank if they run short of money or require loans.

16.4 Specialist banks

Merchant banks

These are not banks in the commonly understood sense, but are private firms that offer highly specialised services almost exclusively for business customers. The main activities of merchant banks can be divided into accepting house activities, issuing house activities and capital market activities.

Acceptance house activities

The traditional activity of merchant banks is accepting (i.e. lending their name to) a bill of exchange issued by a less well-known trader, so that it becomes more acceptable because of the bank's good reputation in the financial world. By endorsing the bill, the accepting house guarantees payment of the bill should the drawer default (see Chapter 13 for application of bills of exchange in finance of international trade).

Issuing house activities

Merchant banks play a major role in assisting in raising company finance by sponsoring first issues of company shares on behalf of their clients, or acting as intermediaries between companies seeking capital and those willing to provide it. It should be noted that not all issuing houses are merchant banks.

Capital market activities

In addition to raising capital for companies by their issuing house activities, merchant banks are also involved in a wide range of other capital market operations, some of which are as follows:

- operating some current account services for businesses
- accepting larger deposits, generally for one year or more
- offering consultancy services to businesses wishing to become limited liability companies
- advising on company problems such as capital reorganisations, dividend policy, mergers and takeover bids
- providing finance for hire purchase to businesses
- assisting in the investment of trustee funds for large institutions
- acting as agents to companies establishing branches overseas
- dealing in the precious metals market.

Merchant banks are required to submit monthly returns to the central bank for scrutiny.

Agricultural credit banks

These are specialist banks which provide services to the agricultural sector. Small farmers who would not necessarily qualify for loans on the open market can be assisted through these financial institutions.

Development banks

As the name implies, development is the major concern of these banks. The Caribbean Development Bank (CDB), which has its headquarters in Barbados, is a prime example. The bank's aim is to provide financing to aid economic development, and to 'promote economic co-operation and integration' among its members (the English-speaking Caribbean). Other development banks exist. Their objectives are similar: to provide financing, technical assistance and management advice to support the productive sector.

Investment banks

These specialist banks deal mainly in investments. Their aim is to attract investors through the provision of attractive investment packages. The money is then re-invested in different types of securities, and interest is paid on investments.

Other non-banking financial intermediaries which contribute significantly to the economic development of a country are trust companies, credit unions and building societies.

16.5 Personal budgeting

The need to budget

Budgeting means having a plan for systematic saving and spending. This involves making sure that, over a given period of time, spending (expenditure) does not exceed income.

All people and organisations have to budget and to make sure that they do not spend more than they earn. Governments have to make sure that they strike a balance between what they collect through taxation and what they spend on the services they provide. And companies face the risk of bankruptcy if they allow their expenses continually to be higher than what the firm earns from its customers. Similarly, families and individuals have to budget to make sure that what they spend does not exceed what they earn.

Principles of Business – Profile 2

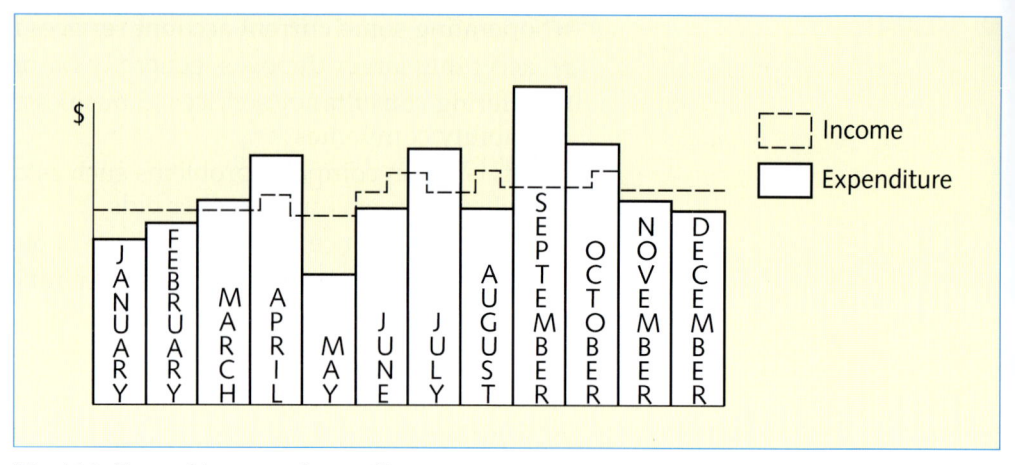

Fig. 16.2 *Personal income and expenditure*

Personal budgeting

We all differ in what we choose to do with the money we earn because we have different tastes. But we all face similar basic problems in making sure that we can meet bills when they come in and ensuring that we do not spend more than we can afford. This is why we need to budget.

Look at the graph in figure 16.2. This shows the monthly income and expenditure of one person over a period of one year. The pattern is typical of most working adults. Notice how generally speaking what the person earns does not alter very much. There may be occasions when they earn a little extra in the form of a bonus, commission or overtime (April, June, July, August, October), and they might get an annual rise (June), but overall their income does not change very much from one month to another. But when we look at expenditure, this varies considerably. Perhaps sometimes several bills come in together, or there is a holiday to pay for, or maybe there is just a need to buy a present for someone special.

The main problem is how to meet bills when they total more than has been earned in a particular month. The answer is to plan ahead, preferably for twelve months, to form a personal budget. This is done by working out your total expected annual expenses on things such as rent or mortgage, electricity, telephone, insurance, etc., and dividing the total by twelve. This amount must then be saved each month so that you can meet the cost of each bill when it arrives. The part of your wages that is left over after saving towards your budget can first be used for daily expenses such as food and travel. Any remainder can be used for luxuries or investment.

Budget accounts

Banks operate this type of account to help people who find it difficult to organise or stick to a budget. The account operates on a similar principle to the personal budget described earlier and it aims to help to even out annual household expenses.

The account holder pays an agreed weekly or monthly amount to the bank, and the bank agrees to meet the costs of any bill up to an agreed credit limit. Whilst the account is in credit it earns interest, and interest is charged when the account is overdrawn. There is also a charge for each cheque or other withdrawal (such as a standing order).

KEY WORDS

Find out the business-related meaning of each of the following terms. Write a separate sentence for each term to show your understanding.

cheque clearing
bankers' bank
merchant bank
capital market
central bank
issuing house
government bank
investment bank
expenditure
development bank
acceptance house
budget   income

16.6 Sources of finance

Finance is a business's most important resource because it is through finance that the business obtains all its other resources. Money (and the things bought with it) used in a business is known as capital. The things that the business owns that have a money value are known as assets and they are part of the capital of the business. Assets can be divided into two broad areas:

- *Fixed assets* are things that are intended for permanent or long-term use by the business (e.g. buildings, land, machinery, vehicles, etc.)
- *Current assets* (also called circulating assets), refers to things that are constantly changing and are easily turned into cash (e.g. raw materials, stocks of finished goods, debts owed by customers (debtors), money in the bank, etc.)

A business needs sufficient capital to get started (start-up capital), and once it is established, it needs further finance to keep trading or to meet the cost of expansion. Finance is needed to meet expenses, such as wages and raw materials, or to buy machinery or premises. Money is not as important to a business as the ability to use it to create revenue (income) for the business.

Start-up finance

Money has to be provided to start-up a business. The entrepreneur can use their own money or someone else's. It is often a case that the initial capital will come from both these sources. Using their own money the entrepreneur may call on their savings or perhaps those of their friends or family. The difficulty in the latter circumstances is that people other than the owner of the business are taking a risk. An alternative is to take in a partner (or several), which means giving up some of the ownership and sharing the profit.

By using someone else's money the business person gets to retain control of the business, and also keeps all the profit. The problem with using someone else's money is that it has to be repaid at some time, and interest will have to be paid while the loan is in effect. The interest paid has the effect of reducing the profit the business achieves.

Both central and local government want to encourage businesses to form and prosper because this provides employment and creates national wealth. The help provided by central and local government frequently changes but can include grants, loans, tax concessions, buildings at low rents, relocation grants, etc.

There are two main sources of finance for established businesses. They can use their own internal sources, such as money they have saved or retained from profits, or they can use money obtained from external sources.

Internal sources

- *Retained profits:* are the main source of finance for an established firm. These are net profits that are reinvested (ploughed back) into the business rather than being paid out to the owners in dividends. These retained earnings, when invested in additional fixed assets and current assets, serve to swell the value of the business and increase the capital employed.
- *Selling assets:* involves selling things it owns (e.g. part of its chain of shops) to raise finance to expand another division of the business (e.g. its

KEY WORDS

Find out the business-related meaning of each of the following terms. Write a separate sentence for each term to show your understanding.

capital   assets

fixed assets

current assets

start-up capital   revenue

partner   interest

debtors

production plant). This needs careful consideration to ensure it is not selling assets that are vital to the future prosperity of the firm.

External sources

There are a wide range of sources of finance from outside the business, and these can be divided into two broad categories, short-term and long-term sources. The most frequently used external sources are: overdrafts, loans, hire purchase, leasing, share issue, debentures, trade credit and factoring (as explored below).

Most businesses operate on borrowed money. A newly formed business may well need to engage in long-term borrowing to see it through until it is a well-established firm, and a business that has been operating for some time may need long-term finance in order to expand or modernise. Borrowing must be long-term if it is being invested into fixed assets (e.g. land, buildings or capital machinery). Whether a business is new or has been operating for some time it will at some time experience a need for short-term finance for an unexpected occurrence, e.g. to aid cash flow.

The cost of borrowing is generally a payment of interest, and this cost is based mainly on the amount borrowed and the length of time for which it is required. In times of declining and fluctuating sales and profits, heavy interest charges may lead to cash flow problems.

Short-term finance

Short-term finance is normally for a period of less than three years, and it is usually suitable for a business that needs cash for its working capital. The following are the most used sources of short-term capital:

- *Overdraft:* This is a banking credit facility that enables a business to spend more than it has in the bank, up to an agreed limit. Interest is charged on a daily basis on the amount overdrawn on the day. In the case of businesses, overdraft facilities tend to be provided on an ongoing arrangement, thus providing the borrower with a continuous credit arrangement. It tends to be used to finance working capital requirements and is a relatively cheap form of borrowing.
- *Short-term loans:* These are loans given for a fixed period of time at a fixed rate of interest. The loan and interest are usually repaid in regular monthly instalments. This kind of borrowing is more expensive than the overdraft and will be used for purchase of vehicles, equipment, etc. With a secured loan the borrower offers some form of collateral security (e.g. the deeds of property), which the lender can take if the loan is not repaid. In the case of an unsecured loan the borrower offers no collateral against the loan. Because of the risk the lender faces in this type of loan the interest rate tends to be higher.
- *Hire purchase:* In hire purchase a finance company pays for goods (e.g. equipment) that the firm needs. Ownership of the goods remains with the finance company until the end of the payment period. The cost of borrowing the money is added to the purchase price, and the debt is repaid in regular instalments. This an expensive form of finance and tends to be used mainly by small firms, usually when other forms of finance are not available.
- *Leasing:* This refers to the hiring out by one firm (the lessor) of an asset (e.g. a building, machinery, vehicle, etc.) to another firm (the lessee) under

a rental agreement (the lease) in return for an agreed rental payment. A leasing arrangement can be useful to a business in that it enables it to employ assets without having to tie up large amounts of capital for a long period of time.

- *Trade credit:* This is a deferred-payment arrangement whereby a supplier gives a business a certain amount of time (e.g. one or two months) after receiving products in which to pay for them. As there is usually no charge for trade credit, this is a good source of finance for a short period of time.
- *Factoring:* This is a financial service provided by one firm (the factor) to another firm (the client) by discounting unpaid invoices issued to customers. In other words, the client 'sells' the debts owed by its customers to the factoring firm, and the factor collects the payment due. This increases the client's cash flow.

Long-term finance

- *Shares:* Incorporated (limited liability) private or public companies can issue shares in order to raise large amounts of money. The purchase of shares gives the shareholder part ownership in the company, with voting rights. Because the shareholders are providing capital for the company, the company has a responsibility to earn enough money to pay a dividend (a share of the profits) to the shareholder. There are different types of share, and the size of the dividend is influenced by the type of share, and the risk involved.
- *Debentures* (loan stock): This is a method of financing companies through fixed interest long-term loans secured against company assets. Most debentures are redeemable by the borrower at a specified date (e.g. 10 or 15 years) from the date of issue. Failure to repay the loan gives the lender the right to seize the secured asset (e.g. building or machinery).
- *Mortgage:* The issuing of shares and debentures is a method that is only available to incorporated companies. Sole proprietor and partnership businesses need finance to provide finance for large capital outlays, such as the purchase of property. A mortgage is a long-term loan against which the property is offered as security. Failure to repay the capital and the interest means that the lender can exercise a legal charge against the property secured.

Choosing the method of finance

The length of time the finance is needed will have an influence on the method chosen. For example, as you read earlier, most businesses will use an overdraft regularly for short-term cash flow. In the case of long-term finance, businesses tend to not rely on just one source but often use several depending on certain factors. An obvious influence will be the cost of obtaining the finance. The firm will compare the alternatives and choose which it feels is most economical.

Sometimes the nature of the need for finance will determine the method chosen. For example, purchase of a building will direct the borrower towards a mortgage or the issue of shares. A temporary borrowing, say to aid cash flow for a few weeks, will probably influence the borrower to seek an overdraft facility.

Sometimes the degree of risk involved may mean that only certain sources are available. For example, if the business needs finance to expand into an area where there is a risk that it could make a lot of profit, but maybe none, it

---

KEY WORDS

Find out the business-related meaning of each of the following terms. Write a separate sentence for each term to show your understanding.

retained profit
overdraft   loan
hire purchase   leasing
dividend   shareholder
trade credit   factoring
debenture   mortgage

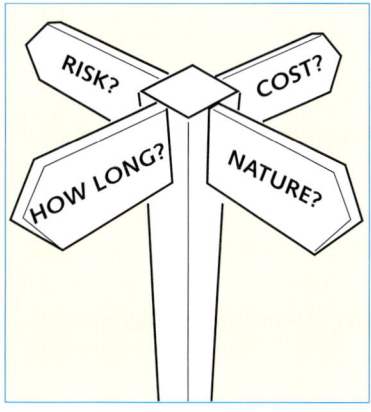

Fig. 16.3 *Choosing the method of finance*

will find that the sources of finance are very limited. In such a case the business may have to consider selling additional shares, or taking in some partners. Selling shares (or *more* shares), or taking in partners, involves giving up some of the ownership and control of the business, and the owners will need to consider if they want to give up this ownership, or give some of the profits to others.

16.7 Savings and investment

The term **savings** refers to that portion of the income of a person (personal savings) or a business (retained profits) that is not spent. Typically, such savings are placed in an account with a bank or building society, or some other financial institution. In the case of personal savings, the investor will be looking to receive **interest** as a reward for saving. In the case of business savings, it may be used to acquire financial and physical assets such as shares or machinery. By forgoing immediate spending on consumption, savers hope to improve their future income through dividends, interest, rent receipts, and through capital appreciation.

Savings are important, not only to the saver, but also to the economy. They finance the physical development of the country to increase its **capital stock** and in this way it helps the country to produce a greater volume of products.

The practice of **sou sou** (which refers to saving in turn) originated from Africa and was brought to the Caribbean by slaves. It is still a common method of saving among West Indian working-class people. In a sou sou, or Meeting Turn, a group of people agree to contribute a fixed sum to a common savings pool each week or month. The approximate value of the pool is given to a different member in turn each week or month until each member has had a turn. Then the sou sou begins all over again. In some sou sou arrangements, the person who is in charge of operating the sou sou receives a percentage of the pool. The sou sou benefits the members in that it encourages a form of **planned saving**. It also enables members to purchase some substantial item at some time in the future.

The **credit union** movement is a system of co-operation intended to help people, particularly with respect to saving, but also in the personal, social and cultural development of people. The control of the union lies with the members and follows the lines of co-operatives, with one vote per member. The members pool their savings into a common loan fund, from which loans are made to members at a low rate of interest. The loans are made for 'approved' purposes, such as house repairs or medical bills.

Investment can be financial expenditure on the purchase of financial securities such as stocks and bonds. A **financial portfolio** is undertaken by individuals, companies and financial institutions and will contain a spread of investments of varying degrees of risk. Investment can also refer to physical investment, such as plant, machinery and equipment (fixed capital assets) and stocks (working capital assets). Fixed capital investment is undertaken by firms to replace obsolete or worn out capital items. It is also used by firms to increase its total assets to enable it to increase its output. Investment tends to tie up capital for a longer period than savings and, in addition, is less quickly accessible than savings.

For individuals, some forms of **insurance** provide a method of investment. For example, **endowment policies** provide for a payment of a basic sum at a certain age or on the death of the insured, whichever occurs first. This provides not only for dependents, but a useful sum of money for the insured if he or she survives the period. A variation of this type of policy is one 'with profits' which, for a higher premium, entitles the insured to a share in the company's profits.

You will learn a lot more about investment in the next section of this chapter.

16.8 The stock market

Selling new shares

If a company wishes to raise capital, the methods it uses are the same whether it is a new company or an established one attempting to increase its capital. There are two broad choices. A company may either:

- raise the capital privately, or
- invite the public to subscribe to a share issue.

The sale of shares is an attractive option to a company because money raised in this way does not have to be repaid, whereas almost all other methods do involve repayment.

A new issue of shares may be made by:

- a new company forming
- a private company turning into a public company
- an existing public company trying to raise more capital.

The selling of new shares may be offered to the public in three main ways.

- *The company may issue a* **prospectus**. This is a leaflet or advertisement giving details of:
  - the history of the company
  - its plans for the future
  - the amount of capital it requires to raise
  - an invitation to the public to buy shares.

A closing date for applications to buy is set, and after that date the shares are allotted to those who have applied to buy.

If the issue is **over-subscribed**, in other words people wish to buy more shares than are available, the applicants receive a percentage of the shares they requested. If the issue is **under-subscribed** the company could end up in the position of not raising all the capital it needs. This is where it is an advantage to use an **issuing house** to sell shares on behalf of the company because they will often **underwrite** the complete issue. This means that if all the shares are not sold, the issuing house undertakes to buy all the remaining shares, thus guaranteeing that the company will raise the total capital it requires.

- *The company may offer the shares for sale:* that is, sell the shares outright to an issuing house who then dispose of them as best they can, ensuring that the company will receive all the capital it wishes to raise.
- *The company may 'place' the shares* with Stock Exchange brokers, who offer them to their clients, and to other brokers.

Principles of Business – Profile 2

Selling second-hand shares

Once a company has raised capital by the sale of shares it has given up part of the ownership of the business to shareholders, and at the same time it puts this capital to use and the shareholders cannot change their minds and take the money back. However, if a shareholder was expected to invest his or her money with no opportunity to sell his or her shareholding, few people would be willing to take the risk of investing in business. In this respect the Stock Exchange plays a vital role.

The Stock Exchange provides a market-place where buyers and sellers of securities (the name given to describe all stocks, shares, etc.) can meet to buy and sell. As the shares they deal with have already been sold once, to the first owner, we say that the Stock Exchange is a market-place for 'second-hand' securities. The wider market of share dealing, including deals outside of the Stock Exchange, is called the 'Stock Market'. 'Bidding' is the basis for carrying out deals. A sale is made when someone purchases a security at a price offered or as a result of their bid.

The Stock Exchange is responsible for making arrangements for the trading of shares and other securities. The exchange sets the rules of operation in the Stock Market and ensures that members adhere to the rules at all times.

The Caribbean Stock Exchange

The Caribbean Stock Exchange, also referred to as the CARICOM Stock Exchange, is a relatively recent phenomenon. The idea of establishing a regional stock exchange was first proposed in 1988 by Michael Manley, the then leader of the opposition in Jamaica.

However, the CARICOM Heads of Government found the idea of a single regional stock market difficult to handle, and agreed to 'cross-border' trading on the markets of three CARICOM member countries – Barbados, Jamaica, and Trinidad and Tobago – which already had established stock markets.

The broad purpose of the CARICOM exchange is to encourage Caribbean economic integration. 'Exchange controls' have been relaxed to permit cross-border trading in CARICOM shares. This will give rise to the 'free movement' of capital within CARICOM. Useful mergers resulting in larger companies will emerge eventually, and it is hoped that the Caribbean people will benefit greatly.

Securities traded

Ordinary shares

Ordinary shares are sometimes referred to as equities because each share has a claim to an equal division of the profit of the business. Equities carry the right to vote at shareholders' meetings, with each share carrying one vote. Therefore, the more shares held, the greater the voting power of the holder.

Each ordinary share is entitled to an equal share ('dividend') of the company's profit (if a profit has been made); the more shares that are held the greater will be the shareholder's dividend. The return that investors receive on their investment is dependent on the performance of the business over the period (six months or one year) since the last dividend was distributed. If the company has done well the reward for the shareholder will be good. If the company has not done well, the shares will be less profitable, and may even pay no dividend at all.

The general trend of ordinary share prices can be an indicator of the prosperity of the country in general and of industry in particular. The general trends (growth or contraction) are reflected all round the world in the stock exchange 'indices' – in the UK there is the Financial Times Index, in the US the trend is shown in the Dow Jones Index, and in the Caribbean the trend is reflected in daily newspapers and financial publications.

Ordinary shares and debenture stocks (see later notes) illustrate the extremes of risk undertaken by investors in public companies. The ordinary shareholder takes the greatest risk and therefore reaps the greatest reward if the firm is prosperous, whereas the debenture holder takes little risk and therefore tends to receive less return on his or her investment.

There is, however, a type of holding which to some extent combines the speculative nature of ordinary shares with the security of debentures, and this is the **preference share**.

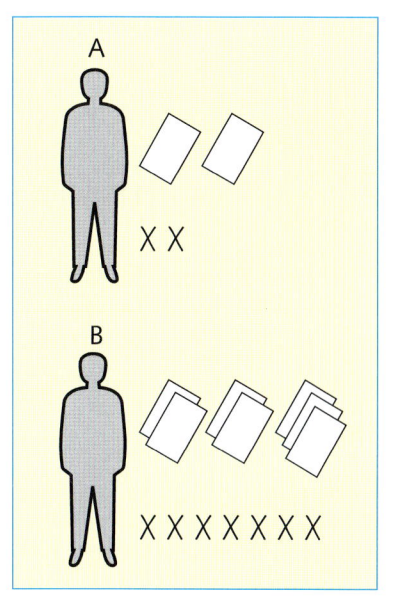

Fig. 16.4 *Equities and voting power*

Preference shares

There are three classes of preference shares.

- *Ordinary preference shares* carry a fixed rate of dividend which is payable (if sufficient profit is available) before any dividends are paid to ordinary shareholders, but after payment of interest to debenture holders.

  As their name suggests, preference shares receive preferential treatment over ordinary shares in the payment of dividends and in a share of the assets in the event of the business going bankrupt.

  Whilst preference shares are safer than ordinary shares, if the company is particularly profitable they are also less rewarding because of the fixed dividend. Normally preference shares do not carry any voting rights unless dividend payments by the company are in arrears.

- *Cumulative preference shares* are similar to ordinary preference shares except that if the business does not make enough profit to allow payment of the dividend due one year, the amount outstanding is carried forward and held outstanding until payment can be met. The outstanding amount is allowed to accumulate until payment is eventually made.

- *Participating preference shares*. It can be seen that, because of the relatively safe nature of preference shares and the fact that they pay a fixed rate of dividend, the preference shareholder does not reap any additional reward when the company's profits are good.

  To overcome this situation some companies create shares called 'participating preference shares'. These are the same as other preference shares but they award the normal fixed dividend, and if there is still any profit remaining after payment of other dividends, the participating preference shareholder may receive a further dividend additional to the fixed rate already paid.

Debenture stocks

Strictly speaking, debentures are not shares but long-term loans to a company, which are usually to be repaid at some future date. They carry a fixed rate of interest which is payable every year whether the company makes a profit or not.

Debenture holders:
- do not share in the ownership of the company
- have no voting rights
- have no say in the running of the business.

However, debentures are transferable and, therefore, the holders can sell them via the Stock Exchange for the highest price they are able to obtain.

Debentures are secured against specific fixed assets owned by the business or generally against all the assets of the business. If the debentures are secured against specific fixed assets, they are called mortgage debentures. If a company goes bankrupt, debenture holders have a right to repayment before any funds are distributed to shareholders.

Investment trusts and unit trusts

Investment trusts and unit trusts have become increasingly popular, especially with the small saver. These trusts invest the capital they receive over a wide range of securities, thus spreading the risk involved. After paying administrative expenses, the net yield from the various investments is distributed as a dividend.

The return on shares

The return, or reward, given to shareholders is called a **dividend**, because it is a division of the profit available for distribution. The dividend is usually expressed as a percentage of the nominal or **par value** of the share, that is, the issue price (the price the share was originally sold for), normally in units of one dollar.

If the dividend is said to be 8% then for every $1 share the shareholder owns, he or she will get 8c (8% of $1). However, the shareholder may have bought the share for a price above its par value. If this is the case he or she is really interested in the actual return on the money paid for the share. This is called the **yield**.

The yield on a share is worked out as follows:

$$\frac{\text{Par value of share}}{\text{Market value of share}} \times \text{Rate of dividend} = \text{Yield}$$

The market value of the share is the price paid for it on the Stock Exchange. In our example, if the shareholder had paid $2 for the share, the yield would have been 4%.

$$\frac{\$1}{\$2} \times 8\% = 4\%$$

When the par value and the market value are the same, the dividend and the yield are the same. If the market value is below the par value, the yield will be greater than the dividend.

Factors affecting share prices

If speculators could accurately predict share price movement they could guarantee to make a fortune several times in one week. However, investment in shares remains speculative because there are numerous factors that influence the rise or fall in share prices.

Some of these factors can be summarised as follows:

- supply and demand for the shares
- recent performance of the company (good or poor profits)
- political changes affecting the company, for example change of government
- changes in interest rates or taxation
- popularity or otherwise of the company's products
- changes in market trends
- takeover or merger being considered
- general national prosperity
- industrial disputes, or settlements of disputes.

Speculation

There is an important distinction between an investor and a speculator.
An investor buys shares in order to receive a share of the company's profits. A speculator on the other hand hopes to make a quick profit by anticipating changes in share prices. There are three types of speculator, and they are known by the colourful names of **bulls**, **bears** and **stags**.

- **Bulls** buy or hold shares anticipating a price rise, and make a profit by selling at a higher price. In a *'bullish'* market, prices are generally rising.
- **Bears** sell shares anticipating a fall in market prices, perhaps buying them back later at a lower price, for example if they need to fulfil a contract to supply the shares. In a *bearish* market, prices are generally falling.
- **Stags** buy new issues of shares expecting to resell them at a profit when second-hand dealing starts on the Stock Exchange.

It should be noted that when referring to bulls, bears and stags, we are talking about the way someone is behaving and not three different people. An individual may be a bull at one time or a bear at another. The terms may be used to describe someone even if he or she is not a Member of the Stock Exchange.

How a stock exchange works

A free market

A stock exchange is a 'free' market in that prices are allowed to rise and fall in accordance with supply and demand. Such freedom and variations can only exist if buyers and sellers are able to trade, and this could create a problem. If all the people who wanted to sell or buy shares want to meet at the same market-place the result would be chaos. For this reason, only Members of the Stock Exchange are allowed to trade in the market. Those who are not Members have to buy and sell through the Members.

It is the Members of the Stock Exchange who take the part of the buyers and sellers of securities and thereby maintain a free market. There are two classes of Members of the Stock Exchange, **brokers** and **jobbers**.

Stockbrokers (brokers)

It is the brokers' business to buy and sell shares on behalf of their clients, obtaining the best deal they can for them, for which service they are paid a fixed rate of commission.

The brokers come into the Stock Exchange and visit several jobbers, checking prices before buying to ensure that they obtain the best price for their clients,

Principles of Business – Profile 2

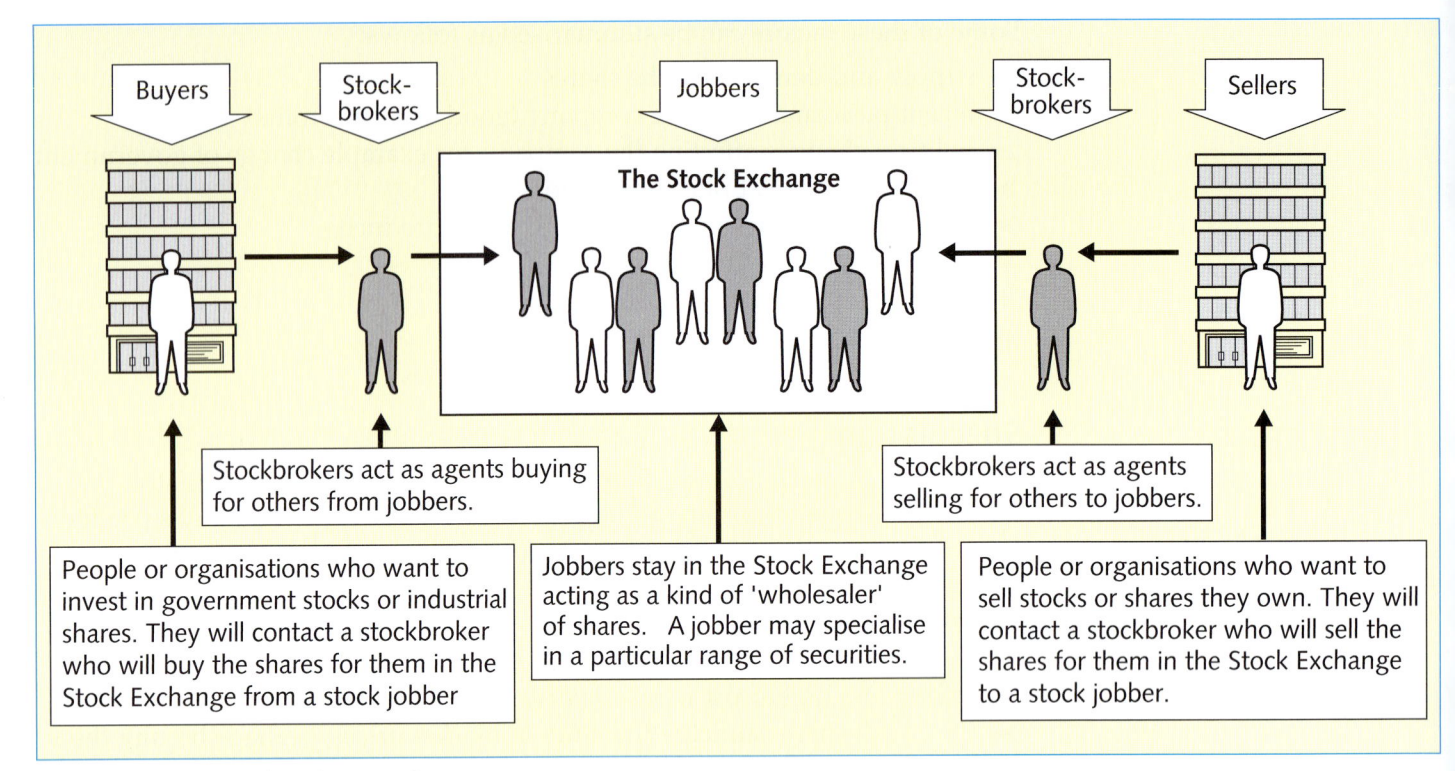

Fig. 16.5 *How the Stock Exchange works*

Buyers: People or organisations who want to invest in government stocks or industrial shares. They will contact a stockbroker who will buy the shares for them in the Stock Exchange from a stock jobber

Stockbrokers act as agents buying for others from jobbers.

Jobbers stay in the Stock Exchange acting as a kind of 'wholesaler' of shares. A jobber may specialise in a particular range of securities.

Stockbrokers act as agents selling for others to jobbers.

Sellers: People or organisations who want to sell stocks or shares they own. They will contact a stockbroker who will sell the shares for them in the Stock Exchange to a stock jobber.

who cannot approach the jobbers directly themselves. They will also offer advice to their clients, and such advice will be based on their knowledge and experience of the operations of the market.

Stockjobbers (jobbers)

Whereas brokers deal directly with people outside the Stock Exchange and bring their business into the market, jobbers stay in the Stock Exchange and only deal with brokers and other jobbers. Therefore they do not come into contact with the real sellers and buyers. Jobbers are in fact wholesalers of stocks and shares, hoping to make a profit (called the jobber's 'turn' or 'margin') by buying shares from brokers or other jobbers at one price and selling them for a higher one.

Jobbers tend to specialise in a particular range of securities. For example, some may specialise in government stocks whilst others specialise in oil or industrial shares. Other typical markets in which jobbers specialise are motors, aircraft, shipping, chemicals, rubber and mining property.

Striking a bargain

When you go shopping you will look around various shops trying to find the lowest price you can, and perhaps hoping to come across a bargain. If you discover your particular brand of chocolate is cheaper in one place than another, then you will buy in the cheaper shop. Brokers will also shop around different jobbers when buying or selling shares to try to obtain the best deal they can for their clients.

Eventually the shareholder will receive a 'contract' giving the details of their deal(s), and in due course they will receive a 'share certificate' signifying how many shares they own in a particular company.

Chapter 16 – **The financial sector**

KEY WORDS

Find out the business-related meaning of each of the following terms. Write a separate sentence for each term to show your understanding.

jobbers   par value
debenture stocks
ordinary share
securities   bears
prospectus   bulls
dividend   preference
share   broker
yield   stags

The importance of stock exchanges

Many large businesses need to appeal to the public for the vast sums of money they require to finance the purchase of new premises or new machinery, or to expand the business. People are not willing to invest money to finance this sort of development unless they can be sure that they can get the money back again. But, as we have observed earlier in this chapter, the business uses the money invested with it and it cannot be returned.

When an investor needs his or her money back he or she does not need to go to the company with whom it was originally invested. Instead, the investor sells his or her shares to some other investor through the Stock Exchange. In other words, although the Stock Exchange does not directly raise new capital for business, it encourages people to invest in companies because it provides facilities for the sale of second-hand securities.

The government also needs to borrow money from the public to help finance the many industries and services it provides through central or local government. These require a continuous supply of new capital to fund new equipment and development research. Local and central governments rely on the Stock Exchange to help raise the capital they need.

All stock exchanges have an international importance because they provide a market for the shares of foreign countries. For example, Caribbean-based investors can easily buy shares in companies in other countries, and investors in foreign countries can similarly easily put money into businesses in the Caribbean region.

16.9 Things to do

This section contains a variety of exercises to help you create revision notes, to test your understanding and to prepare you for examinations.

Search and find

Write out the question and the answer by referring back through the text to form revision notes.

1. Why are commercial banks sometimes referred to as 'clearing banks'?
2. What are the main functions of commercial banks?
3. Briefly describe six services commercial banks provide that particularly benefit businesses.
4. Take any three services that commercial banks provide and show how they benefit both businesses and individuals.
5. How does a central bank differ from a commercial bank?
6. A central bank is sometimes referred to as the 'bankers' bank'. Why is it referred to in this way?
7. Why is the central bank so important to the government of its country?

Principles of Business – Profile 2

8. Why is a merchant bank sometimes referred to as an 'acceptance house'?
9. In what way does a merchant bank help to raise money for businesses?
10. List six other services which are provided by merchant banks for businesses.
11. Why are agricultural credit banks particularly important to the small farmer?
12. In what ways do development banks aid economic development?
13. What is budgeting?
14. Why do organisations and businesses have to budget just as carefully as individuals?
15. Describe the way that someone might organise a personal budget.
16. How can a bank budget account help someone to manage their personal finances?
17. Why is finance so important to a business?
18. What do you understand by the term 'start-up capital'?
19. What are the main sources of finance for a sole proprietor business?
20. Many businesses suffer a 'start-up crisis'. Why do you think this occurs?
21. In what way is a large limited liability company in a stronger position than a sole proprietor with regard to raising finance?
22. Give one good reason for using 'internal' sources of finance, and one example where a business would need to think carefully before it used internal sources.
23. List the main sources of short-term finance available to businesses, and by each item in your list give a benefit and a drawback of the source listed.
24. Under what circumstances is it necessary for a business to seek long-term finance rather than short-term?
25. Briefly describe the main sources of long-term finance.
26. What are the main factors that will influence a business in its choice of sources of finance?
27. Explain the difference between the terms 'saving' and 'investment'.
28. Why does the government have an interest in people saving?
29. Describe at least three methods of saving that individuals might use.
30. 'Investment tends to be less flexible than saving, but potentially more rewarding.' Explain this statement.
31. What are the main choices open to a company wishing to raise capital?
32. Why is the sale of shares an attractive option for companies raising capital?
33. Briefly describe the three main ways a company might sell shares.
34. The term 'stock market' has a wider meaning than 'stock exchange'. Explain this statement.
35. What is the main function of a stock exchange?
36. A stock exchange is a market for 'second-hand' securities. Why is it described in this way?
37. In what ways are ordinary shares 'speculative'?
38. What is 'preferential' about preference shares?
39. Briefly describe each of the three categories of preference shares.

Chapter 16 – The financial sector

40 'Debentures are not really shares.' Explain this statement.

41 In what ways do unit trusts and investment trusts spread the risks faced by investors?

42 How do you work out the yield on a share? Why is yield the most important figure for an investor?

43 Clearly describe the activities of stock market speculators, including use of the terms 'bulls', 'bears' and 'stags'.

44 List the factors that influence share prices.

45 In what ways can the Stock Exchange be said to be a 'free market'?

46 Explain the difference in function between a stockbroker and a stockjobber.

47 Why are stock exchanges important?

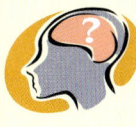

What do you know?

Write out the complete sentence and insert the missing word, which can be chosen from the list at the end of the questions.

1. A central bank advises the ….. on the formulation of monetary policy.
2. ….. bills are issued by the central bank to provide short-term borrowing by the government.
3. ….. in the form of notes and coins is issued through the central bank.
4. As the ….. bank, the central bank provides banking services for the commercial banks.
5. The ….. banks are those found in the high streets, providing banking facilities for individuals and businesses.
6. Development banks are primarily concerned with aiding ….. development.
7. By accepting a bill of exchange, a merchant bank backs it with its ….. .
8. The stock exchange is a ….. for the buyers and sellers of second-hand securities.
9. Ordinary shares are sometimes called ….. because they are entitled to an equal share of profits.
10. General market trends in share prices can provide an indicator of the ….. of industry.

Choose the missing words from the following:

market   bankers'   reputation   treasury   equities   currency   government   economic   prosperity   commercial

Structured questions

Q1 Your friend, Sybile, has regular employment and she earns $2,000 net basic wage each month. Sometimes she also earns $250 a month from overtime, although there are times when no overtime is available. The table on the right shows Sybile's basic expenses during her last twelve months of employment.

Rent	$640	per month
Fuel bills	$240	per year
Insurances	$240	per year
Fares	$240	per month
Food etc.	$320	per month
Holidays	$100	per month
Clothes	$ 80	per month
Telephone	$240	per year

(a) What does the word 'net' mean in relation to Sybile's earnings? How much can Sybile expect to earn as her basic net wage for a complete year?   **2**

(b) What was the total cost of all Sybile's basic expenses for the last year?   **3**

Principles of Business – Profile 2

(c) What is 'overtime'? Why is it best not to rely on overtime when making a personal budget? | **3**

(d) What is a personal budget and why is it important to be able to operate one? | **4**

(e) Sybile found that when her last telephone bill arrived she did not have enough money to pay it. But now Sybile says she will buy a new hi-fi system on credit. Explain how you would advise Sybile to handle her personal finances more sensibly, including mention of the ways in which a bank could assist her. | **8**

Q2 Look at the cycle of credit in figure 16.6.

(a) How much cash is there circulating in the system? | **1**

(b) How much money have the banks created? | **2**

(c) State two methods which Mr B could use to borrow the $800 from the bank. | **2**

(d) (i) State two functions of commercial banks illustrated in the diagram.
    (ii) State one function of commercial banks not illustrated in the diagram. | **3**

(e) Briefly describe what the bank would do with the remaining $200 of Mr A's deposit that was not advanced to Mr B. Give reasons for your answer. | **4**

(f) If the government wished to reduce the amount of credit in the economy, how could the central bank implement this policy? | **8**

Fig. 16.6 Credit creation cycle

Q3 Consider the two bills in figure 16.7.

(a) What is the maturity value of the treasury bill shown? | **1**

(b) Name (i) the drawer and (ii) the drawee of the bill of exchange. | **2**

(c) Assuming interest rates of 10%, what would be the appropriate market value of the bill of exchange immediately after it had been issued? | **2**

(d) Explain how the drawer of a bill of exchange may make use of a merchant bank and why he would be inclined to do so. | **4**

(e) Explain the difference in functions between a treasury bill and a bill of exchange. | **4**

(f) Describe some of the ways that a central bank can influence the economy, including reference to the use of treasury bills. | **7**

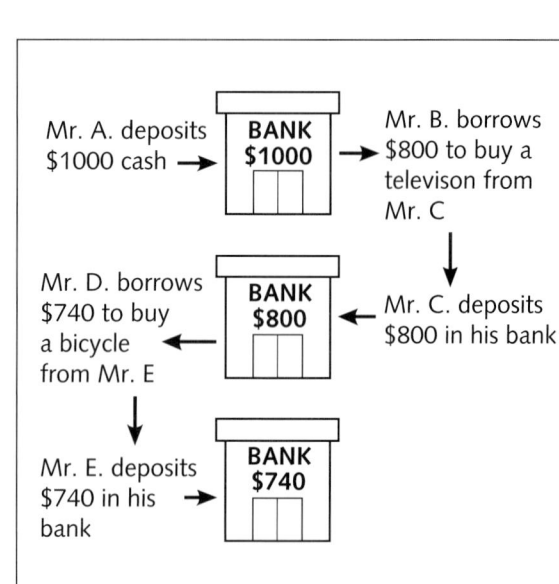

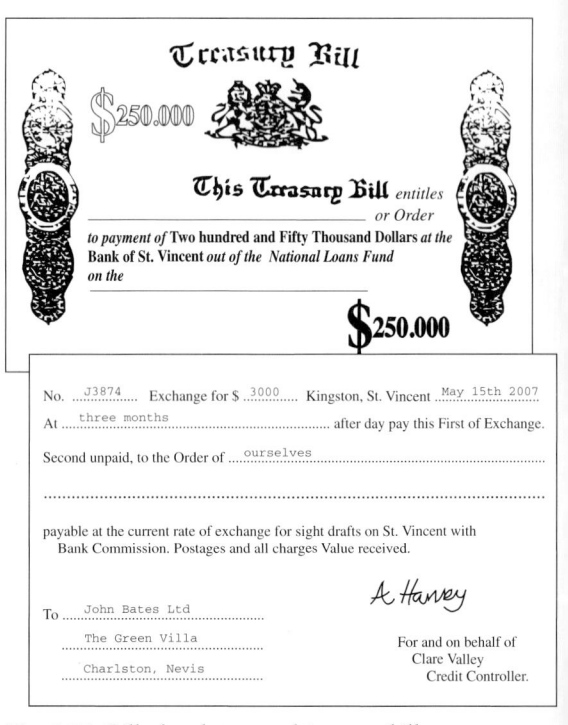

Fig. 16.7 Bill of exchange and treasury bill

Chapter 16 – The financial sector

Q4
(a) What is a treasury bill? *1*

(b) Who sells treasury bills on behalf of the government? *1*

(c) State two factors that would influence the price that someone would be prepared to pay for a treasury bill. *4*

(d) When a central bank acts as 'lender of last resort' (i) who is it lending to and (ii) why is it a 'last resort'? *3*

(e) Exporters who receive bills of exchange as a method of payment may get them 'accepted' by a merchant bank. Explain what this means and how it helps the exporter. *5*

(f) Apart from 'accepting' bills of exchange, describe the other work of a merchant bank. *8*

Q5 This question is related to figure 16.5.

(a) State two ways in which an individual could reap a reward through owning shares. *2*

(b) Name two different forms of organisations that might want to buy or sell shares. *2*

(c) In what way does the illustration show that the Stock Exchange is a 'market'? *4*

(d) Clearly explain the difference in function between a jobber and a broker. *6*

(e) 'A stock exchange performs an important function not only for individuals but also for businesses and the economy in general.' Discuss this statement. *6*

Q6 Jim Gray inherited $3,000 which he decided to divide into three equal parts for investment purposes. $1,000 was placed with a unit trust. Another $1,000 was invested in the ordinary shares of Company A, and the remaining $1,000 was invested in the ordinary shares of Company B. Jim recorded the current value of his three investments once a week over a six-month period. His records are reproduced in the graph in figure 16.8.

(a) Which of Jim's investments had the highest value at the end of the second month of the investment period? *1*

(b) Which investment reached the highest value over the six-month period? *1*

(c) The firm that purchased Jim's investments for him charged him 'commission'. What is commission in this respect? *2*

Fig. 16.8 *Jim Gray's investments*

(d) Company A is a company whose shares are consistently high in value. Give two reasons that could influence this high value. *2*

(e) State two ways that Jim could profit from his investment in ordinary shares. *2*

(f) What are unit trusts and how do they reduce the risk associated with investment? *3*

(g) Give a brief description of the process that would occur if Jim wished to sell his shares. *4*

(h) Jim's investment record shows widely differing rates of success and failure. Explain some of the possible reasons for this. *5*

Principles of Business – Profile 2

Q7

(a) Why is a stock exchange an important feature of a *laissez-faire* economy? **2**

(b) Explain how both public limited companies and 'institutional investors', such as pension funds, benefit from the existence of stock exchanges. **3**

(c) What do we mean when we say the stock market is 'bearish'? Who benefits from this sort of situation? **3**

(d) Discuss the view that speculation is not in the best interest of the investor. **6**

(e) 'When we talk about "bulls", "bears" and "stags", we are not talking about three individual types of person but about the way people are behaving.' Explain this statement, including a description of the function of these specialisations in the Stock Exchange. **6**

Q8

(a) With regard to the Stock Exchange, explain what is meant by 'equities'. **2**

(b) Why is the return on a debenture generally lower than that of an ordinary share? **3**

(c) Why is investing in unit trusts generally less risky than investing in ordinary shares? **3**

(d) Explain the difference between the dividend and the yield of a share. **4**

(e) Explain the way the Stock Exchange encourages investors to help finance industry. **8**

Research assignments

1. How do the functions of a central bank differ from those of other banks?

2. Private institutions in the money market both lend and borrow money, making a profit in the process. Choose two institutions from the money market and show how this happens.

3. Explain why bank deposits must be included in calculations of the money supply. Show how the central bank tries to regulate the money supply.

4. 'Today there is no difference between the facilities provided by the various commercial banks.' Discuss this statement using examples from bank literature to support your discussion.

5. Sophie Carter has inherited $10,000 which she has decided to invest in the ordinary shares of a major public limited company whose shares are listed on the Stock Exchange. Describe the process which would be followed in the purchase of these shares, and discuss the ways in which Sophie could profit from her investment.

6. Discuss the view that a stock exchange is only a place where speculators gamble. Present evidence to support your discussion.

7. Take any five companies of your choice that are listed on the Stock Exchange. Invest an imaginary $5,000, approximately $1,000 in each company. Record the weekly change in value of each of your holdings over a six-week period. At the end of the six weeks compare the total current value of your five holdings with the original amount invested.

8. Congratulations! You have won $60,000. Invest this money in three contrasting ways, including at least one non-stock exchange method. Record the progress of each $20,000 over a six-month period. Give reasons for any differences in return achieved for each of the chosen investments.

9. Why is it possible for $1,000 invested in government bonds to become worth, say, $1,500, whereas the same amount invested in a portfolio of ordinary shares could realise a market value of twice the original investment in just one year?

Chapter 17

Business finances

17.1 The balance sheet

We said in Chapter 12 that capital is one of the four factors of production. **Capital** is important because without it production would not take place.

The **initial capital** of a business comes from **investors** and **entrepreneurs**. The only reason that they take the risk of putting their money into a business is that they hope to make a profit. Achieving this profit is the aim of all business activity. Whether the business makes a profit, and the size of the profit, will depend on how efficiently the capital, or **assets** (things owned), of the business are used.

By looking at the financial facts and figures of a firm it is possible to get an idea of how 'healthy' it is, and what might be done if it is 'sick'. In other words, the facts and figures tell us how efficiently the assets are being used. A balance sheet provides a basis for understanding the financial position of a firm, but it is not the whole story.

A balance sheet is like a snapshot – it assumes that the firm has been *'frozen'* at that time, showing the financial position of the business at a particular moment in time. A firm's balance sheet is a summary of two things:

- liabilities/debts (things owed)
- assets (things owned).

If you look at the example of a balance sheet in figure 17.1, you will see that it basically consists of two lists.

- The list on the left shows who the business is responsible to for various debts (**liabilities**).
- The list on the right shows all sorts of property the business owns (**assets**).

```
          Balance Sheet FLORIDA TRADING COMPANY LTD.
                    as at 30 June 2007


     Liabilities          $             Assets                  $
     Capital        100,000.
                                        Fixed assets
                                        Land & Buildings   80,000.
     Long-term liabilities              Equipment/Fittings 20,000.
     Mortgage        44,000.            Vehicles           10,000.

                                        Current assets
     Current liabilities                Stock*             32,000.
     Tax to be paid   2,400.            Debtors            12,000.
     Bank overdraft   5,600.            Bank balance        5,400.
     Creditors        8,000.            Cash float            600.

                   $ 160,000.                           $ 160,000.

                                        * at cost price
```

Fig. 17.1 *Balance sheet*

Principles of Business – Profile 2

The items in both lists are placed in order of **liquidity**, i.e. how readily they can be converted into cash. The most **liquid items** (those easiest to turn into cash) are shown at the bottom of the list. The balance sheet shown here gives the financial position of the Florida Trading Company at a given time: 30 June.

There are other methods of presenting a balance sheet. For example, liabilities and assets can be shown vertically. The balance sheet for most banks shows the more liquid items at the top, the reverse of the balance sheet shown here.

From the 'lists' shown on a balance sheet we can classify the capital used by the firm in various ways. This helps us to understand how effectively the business is using its assets.

17.2 Cash flow

The flow of money into and out of a business is called **cash flow**. It is the difference between the receipts from sales and the amount spent on expenses such as raw materials, interest paid on loans, dividends paid to shareholders, etc. Money received into the firm adds to its capital reserves, money paid out reduces them.

If income from sales is equal to expenditure, the business can possibly survive. If income from sales is greater than expenses, the business makes a **profit**. If income is less than expenses, it makes a **loss**, and unless something is done to correct this the firm will eventually go bankrupt.

The foregoing is a relatively simple way of looking at cash flow. In reality it is more complex. We can understand this complexity if we look at a simple imaginary **cash flow forecast**, a statement or estimate of cash receipts and payments over a given period.

The Florida Trading Company produces ornamental pots for the tourist industry. Whatever it sells, fifty per cent of the income goes in expenses. Most customers take at least four weeks to pay for the goods supplied. Today, in the fourteenth week of this year's trading, Florida has received an order for $5,000 worth of pots. Should it accept the order? At first sight the answer to this might seem to be obviously 'Yes'. But look at the simple cash flow forecast in figure 17.2 and then see what you think.

From the cash flow forecast you can see that at the start of week 11 of this year's trading, Florida had $5,000 at the bank. It then received an order worth

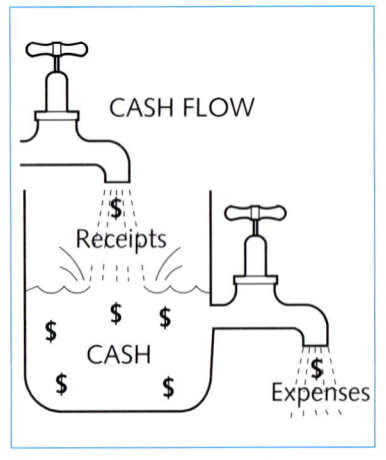

Fig. 17.3 *It is important that money going out of a business does not exceed the money it receives*

Cash flow forecast **FLORIDA TRADING COMPANY LTD.**

Week	11	12	13	14	15
Cash at bank	$5000	$3500	$3000	$1500	?
Order received	$5000	$5000	$5000	$5000	?
Cost of production	$2500	$2500	$2500	$2500	?
Cash receipt	$1000	$2000	$1000	Nil	?

Fig. 17.2 *Cash flow forecast*

Chapter 17 – **Business finances**

$5,000 which cost $2,500 to produce. In that same week one of its customers paid Florida $1,000. On this basis Florida started Week 12 with a cash balance of $3,500 ($5,000 minus $2,500 plus $1,000 = $3,500). Now follow this process through to weeks 14 and 15: you will see that Florida has a cash flow problem. This is sometimes called a '**liquidity problem**'.

The difficulty described here does not mean that Florida should not accept the new order, but it does mean that they have to decide how they will finance the cost of production if they do accept it. Should they borrow from the bank, which will take some of their profit? Should they pressurise some of their customers to pay outstanding debts, which may cause them to lose customers?

To achieve even cash flow is far from simple. It is important to recognise that payment for goods or services supplied will often not be received until some future date. This means that the business must budget with this possibility in mind. If the company's budgeting is unsound, the firm will have to request extended credit from its own suppliers, seek financial support from a bank or some other financial institution, or obtain capital from another source. These considerations have to be taken into account before Florida Trading accepts their most recently received order.

One way of solving a cash flow problem is by using a **factor**. A firm that is owed money can 'sell' its debts to a type of business called a factor. The factor collects all the payments due and pays the firm the amount owed, less the charges for the factoring service. A major part of the payments due may even be paid by the factor before they have been collected. Charges for a factoring service can be very high, but it can solve a cash flow problem and can also save a business the cost of employing its own staff for debt collection.

Many businesses enter their cash flow forecast into a computer **spreadsheet**. This allows the firm to see instantly how various changes might affect the business. The different situations presented to the computer are sometimes called 'what if' scenarios.

A cash flow forecast can be used by a firm to measure its progress against expectations. However, a forecast is no more than an estimate made at a given time, and there may be many reasons why actual cash flow differs from the forecast. For example, actual sales might be higher or lower than anticipated, or the cost of materials may have changed.

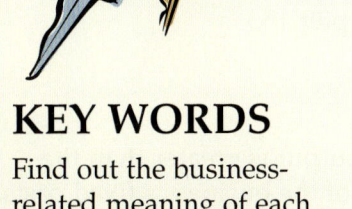

KEY WORDS

Find out the business-related meaning of each of the following terms. Write a separate sentence for each term to show your understanding.

**liabilities   cash flow
factor   liquidity problem
cash flow forecast
entrepreneurs   loss
initial capital   assets
spreadsheet   investors**

17.3 Costs and revenues

A business can be seen as a simple system: it buys things (**inputs**), it does something (**a process**) to the inputs and then sells the results of that process (**outputs**). The outputs could be goods or services (the enterprise's **product**). The product(s) could be made by the business, or they could be items bought for resale. The money that a business uses to pay for its inputs is called its costs. These costs can be divided into fixed costs and variable costs.

Fixed costs are those that have to be paid and do not alter (hence the term fixed), irrespective of what the level of output is. Examples are: rent on premises, insurance premiums, local government taxes and rates, office salaries and interest on loans.

Variable costs are related to output, and vary (go up and down) in line with the level of output, e.g. the amount of business done. Examples are raw

Principles of Business – Profile 2

materials and other stocks used, wages and electricity related to producing and selling, and transport.

It is useful to bear in mind that even fixed costs can change in the long term because, if output increases sufficiently, these may have to increase. For example, increased shop, office or factory space may be needed. By adding together fixed costs and variable costs, we arrive at the *total costs* of the business. The enterprise must cover these costs in order to make a *profit*. It is important that a business keeps control over its costs in order to *maximise* its profits (achieve the best possible return). For example, a producer will want to ensure it keeps raw materials wastage as low as possible, and a retailer will want to deter shoplifting.

The money a business receives from selling its products or services is its income or *revenue*. The revenue of a business is linked to the price and volume of its outputs. The greater the volume, the greater will be the revenue (but not necessarily a greater profitability). A business will want to sell each unit of output at a price greater than the total cost of the unit. This additional sum is called the *profit* or *mark-up*. (See also Chapter 15.)

17.4 Break-even

Provided the revenue received from each unit of output is greater than the unit's variable cost, each unit sold will cover part of the business's fixed costs. At some stage, as revenue rises, the total of the fixed costs will be covered. This is called *break-even point* – where total revenue equals total costs (i.e. both fixed and variable). At the break-even point, the business is making neither a profit nor a loss. This is shown in figure 17.4.

If a business does not sell the volume of output required to break-even, it will make a loss because it is not covering its total costs (also shown in figure 17.4). In such circumstances the business will eventually be forced to cease trading. The same situation will occur if a business does not sell its products at a price higher than the variable costs of those products.

A business has to calculate the break-even point for each of its products in order to:

- identify the level of sales required for total revenue to match total costs
- help set the selling price for the product
- show the effect of profit or loss at different levels of sales.

As with cash flow forecasts, computer *spreadsheets* enable businesses to see instantly how different selling prices or levels of output might affect the business.

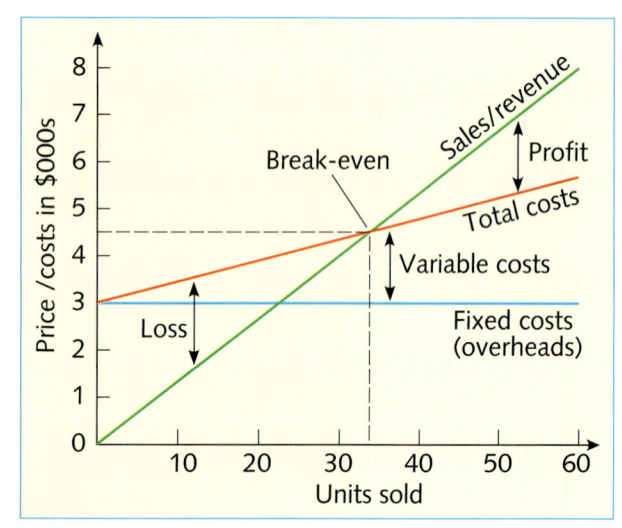

Fig. 17.4 *Break-even chart*

KEY WORDS

Find out the business-related meaning of each of the following terms. Write a separate sentence for each term to show your understanding.

maximise   mark-up
outputs   fixed costs
variable costs   inputs
revenue   total costs
break-even

17.5 Capital

Some people find the term 'capital' difficult to understand because it has so many meanings. In respect of business accounts capital refers to the value of the things owned by a business.

If you refer again to the balance sheet for Florida Trading in figure 17.1 you might be puzzled why capital is listed as a liability, when you perhaps would have considered it an asset. Capital is listed as a liability because it represents the money that the business owes to the owners or shareholders. It is the amount they might receive if the business were sold.

We said earlier that capital is the money, or the assets bought with money, used to run a business. The owner(s) of a business can use their own money, or somebody else's. In using their own money they will be limited in scope and rarely have enough. In using someone else's money they will either have to pay interest, or give up some part of the ownership of the business (e.g. to partners or shareholders). There are three main sources of capital.

Sources of capital

- *Share capital (equity):* money subscribed to the company by shareholders in return for a share of the company's profits ('dividend'). Share capital is not repayable.
- *Loan capital* (loan, debt or debenture): usually a long-term loan which must be repaid at some time.
- *Reserves* (retained earnings, undistributed profits, reinvestment): a percentage of gross profits being put back into the business.

You will observe that share capital involves giving up some of the ownership of the business. Obtaining capital from reserves results in less reward being given to the owner(s)/shareholders. Loan capital incurs a charge called interest, and is, therefore, a drain on the profits of the business.

There are many sources of loan capital, for example hire purchase, bank loans and overdrafts, trade credit (suppliers agreeing to wait for payment) and debentures. It is usual for those providing loan capital to insist on collateral being provided. This refers to the assets of the business that the lender will be able to take if the loan is not repaid. For example, a debenture is a special kind of loan to a business. It is often linked to specific assets (known as collateral) owned by the firm, such as particular items of machinery. Other forms of collateral include items such as deeds of property, insurance or endowment policies, land titles, etc.

Categories of capital

It is often useful to divide capital into categories, and use these in calculations to analyse and interpret a balance sheet. The following are typical of the categories and calculations commonly used.

Fixed capital + Circulating capital = Employed capital

Employed capital − Current liabilities = Capital owned

Circulating capital − Current liabilities = Net working capital

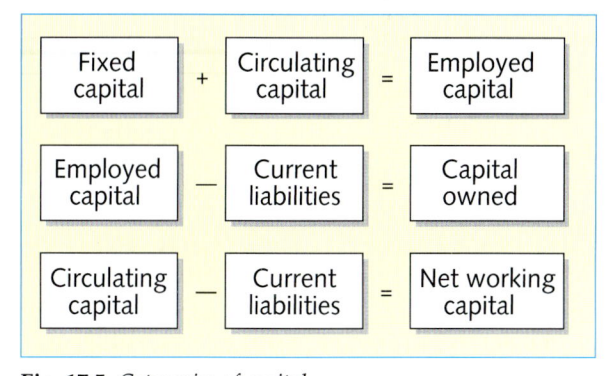

Fig. 17.5 *Categories of capital*

Principles of Business – Profile 2

- *Fixed capital/assets.* These are the durable (long-term) assets of a business which are used over a long period of time and are tied up in permanent use. Examples: land, buildings, machinery, furniture, vehicles, etc.
- *Circulating capital/current assets (working capital)* is capital which is continually changing in quantity, total value or nature. Examples include stocks, cash, bank balance and the amount of money owed to a firm by its customers (debtors).
- *Employed capital.* This is obtained by adding together the fixed and current assets of the firm. In other words, it is the total of all the assets being used by the business.
- *Current liabilities* are debts which will have to be repaid in the near future. Examples include bank overdraft, debts owed to suppliers (creditors) and taxes payable to the government.
- *Capital owned* is the net value of the assets owned by a business. In other words, it is employed capital minus current liabilities.
- *Liquid capital* consists of that part of the current assets which are cash or are easily changeable into cash without delay, for example bank balance, cash in tills and debts owed by others (debtors). Liquid capital is important because it can be used to pay creditors immediately, and therefore it should always be above the current liabilities figure.
- *Net working capital* is the current assets minus the current liabilities. Net working capital is particularly important because it takes into account the possibility of all the creditors to the business calling for payment. Therefore, it is important for a business to have sufficient working capital to exist as far as possible without borrowing from a bank.

Example

(CA – CL = NWC)

Current Assets	= 50,000 –
Current Liabilities	= 16,000
Net Working Capital	= 34,000

KEY WORDS

Find out the business-related meaning of each of the following terms. Write a separate sentence for each term to show your understanding.

working capital
interest   share capital
fixed capital   profit
capital   collateral
loan capital
employed capital
liquid capital

17.6 Turnover

Turnover refers to the total sales of the business over the previous year and can indicate how busy the firm has been. Generally, the greater the turnover the more business the firm is doing. (However, this is not always the case. For example, if the firm has increased its prices it might be that increased turnover in reality does not indicate a greater volume of sales.)

Net turnover

This is found by taking the value of total sales and deducting the value of goods returned or credits issued. For example, if a firm has total sales of $100,000 but has given refunds of $25,000 to customers, net turnover would be $75,000.

Rate of turnover

This is sometimes called 'rate of stock turn'. It is the figure which gives the number of times the average stock held has been sold during the year. It shows how many times the stock has been turned over. There are two methods of calculating the rate of stock turnover.

Chapter 17 – **Business finances**

1   $$\frac{\text{Cost of stock sold}}{\text{Average stock at cost price}} = \text{Rate of stock turnover}$$

2   $$\frac{\text{Net turnover}}{\text{Average stock at selling price}} = \text{Rate of stock turnover}$$

The 'value of average stock' in the above calculations is worked out by taking the stock value at the beginning and at the end of the trading period, adding them and dividing by two.

Example

	$
Stock at the beginning of the year	$ 4,000
Stock at the end of the year	$ 6,000
Average stock	$\frac{\$10,000}{2} = \$5,000$

Using method 2: if we assume that the average stock at selling price is $5,000 and the net turnover is $50,000, the calculation is as follows:

$$\frac{\$50,000}{\$5,000} = 10 = \text{Rate of stock turnover}$$

This means that the stock is turned over ten times in a year. Whether this is good or not would depend on the type of business the figure refers to. For a confectioner to turn over the stock only ten times a year would be acceptable, but for a greengrocer to do likewise would be unsatisfactory because it would mean that his or her stock would perish.

So the rate of stock turnover can also be seen as an indicator of how old the goods in stock are.

In making the calculations it is important to remember that the figures used must either both be at selling price or both at cost price.

Importance of rate of turnover

The rate of turnover indicates how busy a business is, and this is obviously a valuable indicator when a business is being bought, sold or valued because it allows comparison with other similar businesses.

▶ A low rate of turnover is associated with sellers of highly valued goods or consumer durables (long-lasting goods).

Examples:

	Normal rate of turnover
Jewellers	3
Electrical goods	6
Furniture and books	6
Confectioners	12

▶ A high rate of turnover is associated with businesses selling perishable goods.

Examples:

	Normal rate of turnover
Butchers	78
Dairies	67
Greengrocers	53
Bakers	42

> If the rate of turnover is increasing it would indicate that the firm is doing more and more business in real terms; it is selling more goods so profits should be increasing.

17.7 Profit

Profit is the reward the business person receives for taking the risk involved in business and for being able to combine all the factors required to produce and sell goods or services. In order to make a profit, the firm's turnover must be bigger than its operating expenses (the day-to-day costs of running the business).

The profitability of a business can be looked at from the point of view of either gross profit or net profit.

Gross profit

This is the revenue obtained from the sale of goods or services, minus their cost price. For example:

Sales − Cost of goods = Gross profit
($40,000) ($30,000)   ($10,000)

Gross profit can be expressed as a percentage of the cost or of the selling price.

Example

	$
Selling price	1.00
Cost price	0.75
Gross profit	0.25

Mark-up (on cost price) = $\dfrac{25}{75} \times 100 = 33\tfrac{1}{3}\%$

Profit margin (on selling price) = $\dfrac{25}{100} \times 100 = 25\%$

Gross profit takes no account of the **overheads** the business has to meet, for example, wages, advertising, lighting, etc.

As a plain monetary figure, gross profit tells us little about a firm, but if we turn it into a percentage it can be compared with previous years' figures and with the gross profit figures of other similar businesses, indicating how competitive the business is. The method for calculating the gross profit percentage is as follows.

$$\dfrac{\text{Gross profit}}{\text{Turnover}} \times 100 = \text{Gross profit percentage}$$

Example

	$
Turnover	80,000
Cost of goods	60,000
Gross profit	20,000

As a percentage $\dfrac{20{,}000}{80{,}000} \times 100 = 25\%$

Most businesses require a gross profit of between 20% and 40% to ensure that they are covering their overheads (expenses) easily, and to reward the owners sufficiently. Over the years, the gross profit percentage should remain relatively stable, since if it drops too much the business may fail to cover its overheads and start to make an overall loss. There are a number of reasons for a falling gross profit percentage.

- Possibly the staff of the business are stealing stock or takings.
- Stock may be getting damaged or allowed to perish.
- New stock may have been bought in at higher cost price and the increases may not have been passed on to customers.
- The business may be employing more staff than is necessary for the volume of business (overstaffing).
- Expenses are rising (e.g. wages, heating, lighting, etc.) and this is not being incorporated into prices.

Net profit

This is the real profit made by the business after having taken into account the expenses incurred in carrying on the business, such as wages, rent, rates, advertising and bills of all kinds.

Net profit = Gross profit minus all expenses

Example

Gross profit = $20,000, Expenses = $5,000
Net profit = $20,000 − $5,000 = $15,000

Again this figure is better expressed as a percentage so that it can be used in comparison.

$$\text{Net profit percentage} = \frac{\text{Net profit}}{\text{Turnover}} \times 100$$

$$= \frac{15,000}{80,000} \times 100 = 18.75\%$$

17.8 Return on capital invested

This is the figure that matters most to the owners of a business. It is a figure that shows how much profit has been made as a percentage of all the capital employed in the business. The return on investment must be sufficient to make it worthwhile for the owners of the business to face the risks involved in enterprise. If the return on the investment is not sufficient, the owner(s) may be tempted to place their money in other less risky forms of investment. The risks in business are high, therefore the return on capital invested must be higher than the return from a no-risk investment.

$$\frac{\text{Net profit}}{\text{Capital employed}} \times 100 = \text{Return on capital invested}$$

KEY WORDS

Find out the business-related meaning of each of the following terms. Write a separate sentence for each term to show your understanding.

turnover   profit
return on capital
rate of turnover
overheads
net profit   gross profit
net turnover

Principles of Business – Profile 2

17.9 Things to do

This section contains a variety of exercises to help you create revision notes, to test your understanding and to prepare you for examinations.

Search and find

Write out the question and the answer by referring back through the text to form revision notes.

1. What is the main aim of all businesses?
2. What is a balance sheet?
3. Explain the difference between assets and liabilities.
4. What is the meaning of the term 'cash flow'? Why is cash flow important to a business?
5. How can factoring help solve a cash flow problem? What other alternatives are there?
6. Explain the difference between fixed costs and variable costs.
7. Give three examples of 'overheads'.
8. Why does a business need to control its costs?
9. What do you understand by the term 'break-even'? How is break-even calculated?
10. Explain why the unit cost per item decreases when output increases.
11. Why would a business want to prepare a break-even forecast?
12. What is business capital and from where is it obtained?
13. Briefly describe each of the categories that capital can be divided into. Why is it useful to categorise capital in this way?
14. Why is it important that liquid capital should not fall below current liabilities?
15. A firm has fixed capital of $60,000, circulating capital of $6,000, and $7,000 current liabilities. What is its capital owned and its net working capital?
16. Define turnover. Explain the difference between gross turnover and net turnover.
17. What is rate of turnover, and why is this important to a firm?
18. The following figures relate to Florida Trading Company Ltd.:
    Jan. 1 $ 6,000
    Dec. 31 $ 9,000
    Net turnover $60,000

    Calculate the rate of stock turnover and comment whether the rate would be good for a butcher's shop. Give reasons for your answer.
19. Explain the relevance to the business person of 'high', 'low' and 'increasing' rates of turnover.
20. Explain the difference between mark-up and profit margin.
21. Define profit and explain the difference between gross profit and net profit.
22. Florida Trading Company Ltd. is experiencing falling gross profit. List some reasons why this might be happening.
23. Why is the figure referred to as 'return on capital invested' the most important figure to the owners of a business?

Chapter 17 – Business finances

What do you know?

Write out the complete sentence and insert the missing word, which can be chosen from the list at the end of the questions.

1. The initial capital of a business comes from investors and .....
2. A balance sheet is like a ..... of the financial position of a business at a particular moment in time.
3. Money received into a business adds to its ..... reserves and money paid out reduces them.
4. It is important to recognise that ..... for goods and services supplied may not be received until some later date.
5. If a company does not have enough ..... capital, it is said to have cash flow problems.
6. ..... refers to the total sales of a business the previous year.
7. Rate of stock turnover can be seen as an indicator of how ..... goods in stock are.
8. ..... is the reward the business person receives for taking the risk involved in business.
9. ..... costs are relatively constant figures.
10. ..... costs change with increases and decreases in output.

Choose the missing words from the following:

variable   snapshot   turnover   profit   working   entrepreneurs   payment   capital
old   fixed

Structured questions

Q1 This question is related to the balance sheet shown in table 17.1.

(a) What is a balance sheet? **1**

(b) Why is a balance sheet sometimes referred to as a 'snapshot'? **2**

(c) If a competitor were considering making a take-over bid for Florida Trading Company, why would the contents of the balance sheet be important to them? **3**

(d) Why is a balance sheet important to both the owners and the workforce of the business? **4**

(e) Refer to the balance sheet in figure 17.1 and complete the analysis in table 17.1 of the trading figures of the Florida Trading Company Ltd. **10**

	$	$	$	$	$
1 Fixed capital	80,000 +	?	+ 10,000		= 110,000
2 Circulating capital	?	+ 12,000 +	?	+ 600 =	?
3 Employed capital	110,000 +	?			= ?
4 Current liabilities	?	?	?		= 16,000
5 Capital owned	?	–	?		= 144,000
6 Liquid capital	12,000 +	?	+	?	= 18,000
7 Net working capital	?	– 16,000			= ?

Table 17.1 *Florida Trading Company trading figures*

Q2 Look at figure 17.6, and answer the following questions.

(a) List four examples of sources of business capital. **2**

(b) Briefly explain the difference between fixed assets and current assets. **2**

289

Principles of Business – Profile 2

(c) Explain the difference between gross profit and net profit. Why do you think it is important to distinguish between these two aspects of profit? **4**

(d) The illustration shows that the net profit might be used in three ways: for repayments, dividends and reinvestment. Briefly explain each of these. **6**

(e) A shop's capital is $50,000. It has stock which cost $30,000 that is turned over three times a year, making 20 per cent gross profit on sales. Expenses are $7,000 for the year. Find the percentage of the net profit to the capital. **6**

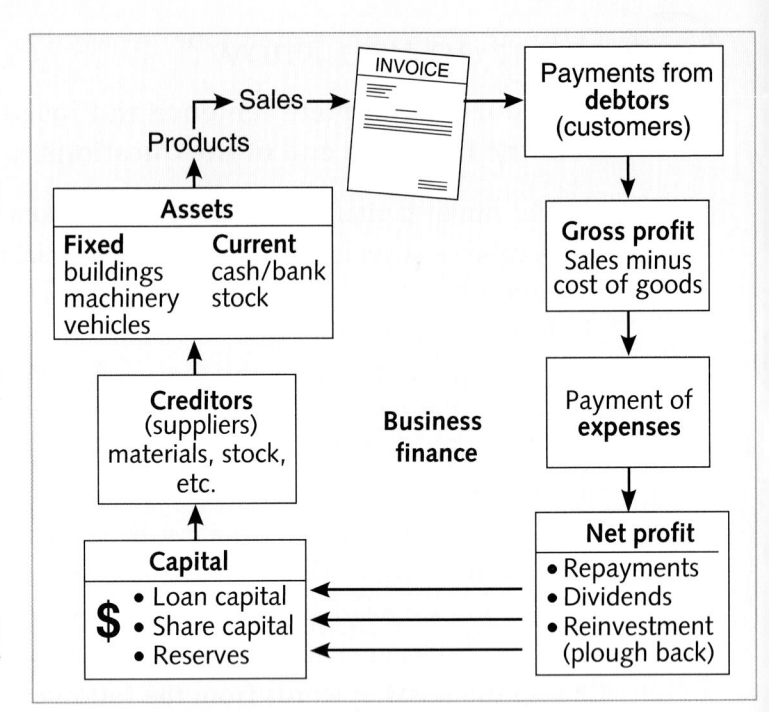

Fig. 17.6 *Business finance flow chart*

Q3 Two stores have recorded the trading figures in table 17.2.

(a) Which store has the greatest sales? **1**

(b) Name two expenses that both stores are likely to incur. **2**

(c) What is meant by profit margin? **3**

(d) What sort of goods in Store B are likely to be selling? Give reasons for your answer. **4**

(e) Explain the fact that both stores have a net profit of $4,000. **4**

(f) If you had $80,000 invested in Store A what would be your return on the capital invested? What could be done to increase your return? **6**

	Store A $	Store B $
Sales	100,000	16,000
Average stock at cost	5,000	4,000
Profit margin	8%	30%
Expenses	4,000	800
Net profit	4,000	4,000

Table 17.2 *Trading figures*

Q4 Table 17.3 shows various assets and liabilities of the Akela Trading Company Ltd.

(a) Name the company to which this data refers. **1**

(b) What are assets? **1**

(c) Write one sentence to define the following terms and calculate their values from the above figures:
  (i) fixed capital **2**
  (ii) circulating capital **2**

Assets	$	Liabilities	$
Factory	300,000	Trade debtors	10,000
Creditors	10,000	Reserves	100,000
Petty cash	500	Finished goods	18,000
Share capital	209,000	Tax due	4,000
Office typewriters	10,000	Overdraft	18,000
Typing paper	500	Machinery	100,000
Cash at bank	6,000	Raw materials	11,000
Debentures	87,000	Loans	105,000
Computer	10,000	Factory fittings	20,000
Unfinished goods	16,000	Trucks	40,000

Table 17.3 *Assets and liabilities of Akela Trading Co. Ltd.*

(iii) liquid capital		2
(iv) current assets		2
(v) net working capital.		2
(d) Draw up a balance sheet for the Akela Trading Company Ltd. using the data shown in the table.		8

Q5

(a) Using the information in table 17.4, and clearly showing all working, calculate for each store:

(i) gross profit		3
(ii) net profit		3
(iii) rate of turnover.		3

	Store A $	Store B $
Sales	100,000	16,000
Average stock at cost	5,000	4,000
Profit margin	8%	30%
Expenses	4,000	800

Table 17.4 *Comparison of two stores*

(b) Write a report comparing the finances and trading strategies of each store. Explain the differences and account for the similarities.   **11**

Research assignments

1. Make a comparison between the final accounts of two firms of similar size and comment upon the differences between them.

2. Explain the various ways by which a business might raise capital **(a)** for short-term and **(b)** for long-term use. Why does a firm need to make this distinction between sources of capital?

3. Why is cash flow forecasting important to all types of business? Use simple data to illustrate your answer using a small local manufacturing company as an example.

4. 'Break-even charts do not give a precise picture of when a business will begin to make a profit, but they do provide a useful guide.' Explain this statement including a simple but clearly labelled break-even chart to illustrate your answer.

5. Write to a major public company in your region and ask for a copy of its most recent annual report and accounts. From the accounts explain the following in your own words.

   a) How the net profit (or loss) figure is arrived at.

   b) What percentage of the company's profit is paid to the shareholders and what percentage is retained.

   c) Give your personal view of the prospects you see for the business and its shareholders in the year ahead.

6. a) Describe how a limited company may increase its capital employed:
      (i) temporarily
      (ii) permanently.

   b) What evidence can you obtain that shows how a business you have access to has taken these steps?

7. What is meant by a company's capital? How is it that a business might only have $1,000 in petty cash and at the bank, and yet have capital of $50,000? Use specimen figures to illustrate your answer.

Principles of Business – Profile 2

8 A large public company needs further capital for expansion. Describe three different ways in which it might try to raise this money, and give your views on what factors are likely to influence the method chosen.

9 Table 17.5 shows the balance sheet of a retailer. Obtain similar data from a retailer you have access to.

	$		$
Owner's savings	850	Fixed assets	8,225
Mortgage	8,000	Current assets	625
	8,850		8,850

Table 17.5 *Balance sheet*

a) What is meant by each of the following:
   (i) Mortgage
   (ii) Fixed assets
   (iii) Current assets.

b) Why distinguish between these different aspects of a balance sheet?

10 a) Ask a local retail trader to allow you to produce a specimen balance sheet which shows the value of its 'fixed' and its 'working' capital.

b) Explain what is meant by 'fixed' and 'working' capital using data from your balance sheet to clarify your explanation.

11 Make a study of one local private and one public company. Write a report on the finance-related differences you can observe between them.

12 Take two local businesses that you have access to. One should be a private limited company and the other a public limited company. Find out their sources of capital **(a)** in the shorter, and **(b)** in the long term. What similarities and differences exist? Give possible interpretations of your findings.

13 Obtain examples of a variety of financial documents used by companies. Explain why it is important for a company to maintain proper financial records, using examples from the data you have collected to illustrate your explanation.

Chapter 18: The role of governments

18.1 The responsibilities of governments

In all countries, the government plays a crucial role because it has such a wide-reaching effect on the community. The level of government involvement in the economy or in the life of the country is influenced by the type of economic system that the country has – free, planned or controlled, or mixed (see Chapter 1). Most Caribbean economies are based on the 'mixed' system, that is, a mixture of the free and controlled economic systems. In other words, there is some government involvement in the economy and in the life of the country.

As you can imagine, the responsibilities of any government are wide-ranging and they cannot all be included here. However, the following will certainly be included in the priorities of most governments.

Security of the State

The government is the protector of the people. The general aim is to ensure that all persons in the community receive 'just treatment'. **Law and order** are important in society because they promote economic stability. For example, tourists are not likely to want to visit a country where there is unrest and **instability**. Similarly, investors will be less likely to invest their money in a country where law and order are not evident.

In order to meet this responsibility, the government must promote appropriate **legislation** and provide police and courts of justice to administer law and order in the country. The government also has to make provision for **defence** (e.g. armed forces) against external dangers, and to provide **diplomatic representation** abroad.

Strategic planning

The government will develop plans for particular sectors of the economy. It may want to promote development in particular industries or in particular locations so that it encourages businesses to locate in zones where it serves the economy best. To support such plans, the government may provide **grants**, **subsidies** or **'soft' loans**, **advisory services** and other agencies to the industries or people it wants to influence.

As part of their strategic planning, the government may provide **public utilities**, such as water or telephone. Many aspects of public transport may also be provided or regulated by the government.

To support their strategic plans, the government will implement **legislation**, e.g. Acts to promote clean air and water, maintain public health, protect wildlife, limit pesticides, control quarrying, regulate litter, and many others.

Welfare of citizens

The government will provide services which private enterprise would be unable or unwilling to supply at a price that all people could afford to pay, including education, health, welfare, culture and sanitation. The provision of **social services** is examined in more detail later in this chapter.

Principles of Business – Profile 3

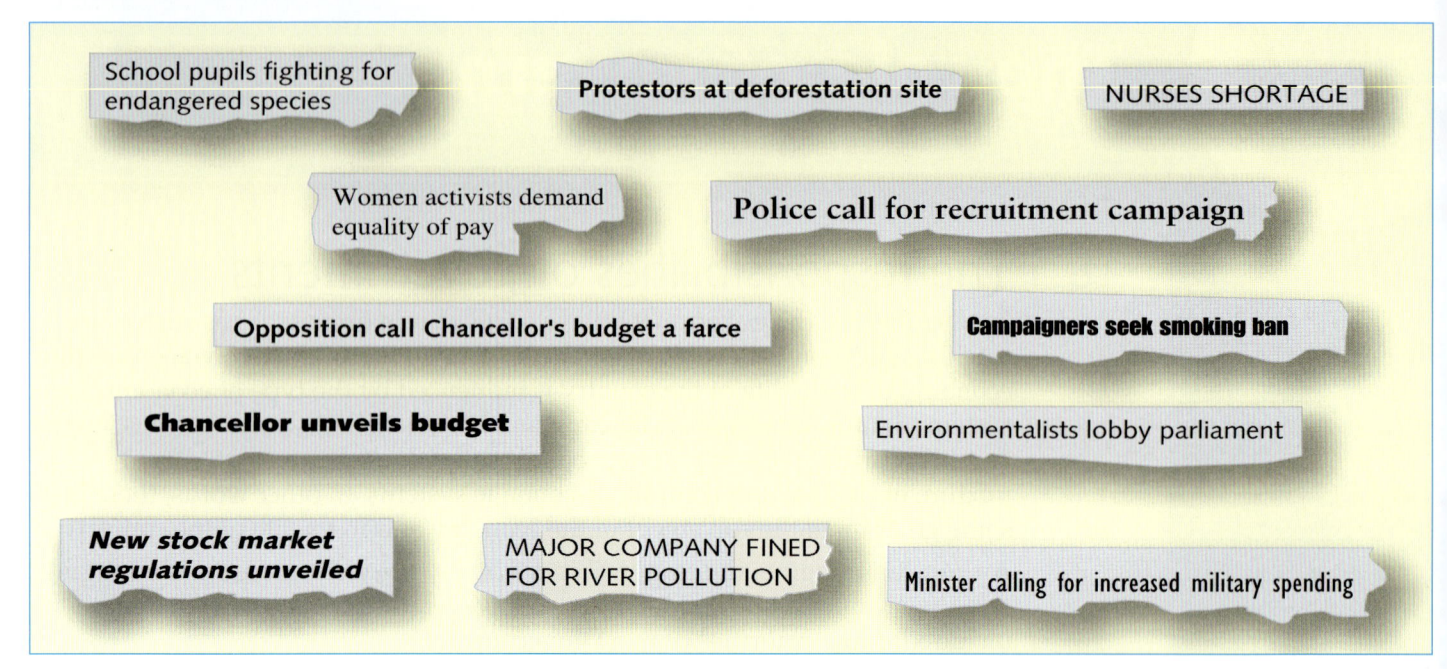

- School pupils fighting for endangered species
- Protestors at deforestation site
- NURSES SHORTAGE
- Women activists demand equality of pay
- Police call for recruitment campaign
- Opposition call Chancellor's budget a farce
- Campaigners seek smoking ban
- Chancellor unveils budget
- Environmentalists lobby parliament
- New stock market regulations unveiled
- MAJOR COMPANY FINED FOR RIVER POLLUTION
- Minister calling for increased military spending

Fig 18.1 *Look at these examples of newspaper headlines. Can you see how they reflect the responsibilities of governments?*

Job security

The government will want to help create the highest level of **employment** it can because the greater the number of people employed, the higher will be the **national income**, and the fewer unemployed people there are, the less will be the drain on the country's resources. Aspects of the strategic planning mentioned earlier could be directed at achieving this aim. The government will also be concerned with ensuring that **severance benefits** are available for workers who are made redundant or have to retire early. They may do this through a statutory directive that ensures employees are entitled to a redundancy or severance payment.

Environment protection

We regularly hear of environmental issues being highlighted in the media. This is because we have all become more 'environmentally aware', and our concerns and protests are good news items for the media.

In the past, business decisions have been made mainly on the basis of **private costs** (e.g. cost of land and building, interest charges, etc.), and **private benefits** (e.g. increased turnover, higher profits, reduced unit costs, etc.). But **environmentalists** have made us see the world in a different way. Now we consider **social costs** such as increased pollution, greater noise, increased congestion, etc., and **social benefits**, for example increased employment, greater choice of goods, reduced prices, etc.

Governments are not only aware of environmental issues, but they accept the responsibility for taking a lead in promoting **environmental awareness**. They will create and enforce laws that aim to protect the environment. Examples of issues that governments may address include: atmospheric contamination (e.g. global warming); destruction of forests (deforestation); land degradation; toxic waste disposal; water shortage. Waste disposal and recycling has become an important issue in most countries, and recycling processes have become part of a new breed of both State and private industry.

Chapter 18 – The role of governments

KEY WORDS

Find out the business-related meaning of each of the following terms. Write a separate sentence for each term to show your understanding.

social costs
social benefits
national income
legislation   soft loan
public utilities
severance benefits
grants   social services
defence

Secure investment environment

All economies require investors to take a healthy interest in business and investing money in companies. This interest depends on a secure investment environment, a situation where investors feel confident to take the risk involved in investing. This will be largely dependent on how well the government is managing the economy. But governments can also positively encourage investment through investment incentives, which are inducements given by the government to a firm as a means of encouraging new investment. Such inducements can include cash grants to defray part of the costs on relocation, new buildings, or installing new machines and equipment.

Management of the economy

The government is charged with overall control of the economy. It will aim to achieve a high level of employment and to encourage economic growth through sound productivity. It will want to manage the national debt and protect the country's balance of payments position, and maintain its foreign reserves.

The budget

In order to meet its responsibilities, the government needs to raise the necessary revenue and exercise control over the economy. The budget plays a key part in the government's strategies for managing the economy.

The budget is a statement of the government's financial position that is used for planning the government's economic and social welfare programmes as part of its fiscal policy for managing the level and distribution of spending in the economy.

A budget surplus occurs when a government takes more in taxation than it spends. This has the effect of taking money out of the economy and making less available for expenditure and has the effect of curbing inflation. However, it can also have other effects, for example, when there is less money in circulation it can result in unemployment. A budget deficit occurs when the government spends more than it takes in taxation, which may result in borrowing from the country's savings. This has the effect of increasing spending and can cause output and employment to grow, possibly causing inflation.

When the government makes public its budget at the beginning of each financial year, it summarises what services the government intends to provide for its citizens, how much money is needed, and how it intends to raise the necessary revenue. The budget may also set out the measures that are going to be taken to stimulate or depress key areas of the economy and to encourage saving and investment.

KEY WORDS

Find out the business-related meaning of each of the following terms. Write a separate sentence for each term to show your understanding.

inflation   budget   fiscal policy   budget deficit   productivity
investment incentives   investment environment   social costs
private costs   environmental awareness   revenue   social benefits

18.2 Government assistance to entrepreneurs

It is in the interest of all governments to help businesses to achieve their full potential, because in doing so businesses contribute to the ideal of full employment and add to national prosperity. Most governments will try to support businesses in the following ways.

- By providing an environment that is conducive to **economic growth**. They will do this by setting rules for business operations, and providing utilities and other facilities which support business activities.
- By the promotion and maintenance of **competitive markets**. Governments will prevent companies from abusing their power by taking action against monopolistic activities. This benefits businesses that are not in a monopolistic position, as well as safeguarding the consumer.

Trade promotion

The governments of CARICOM countries provide various forms of assistance to encourage trade, particularly in respect of the export sector. The latter is recognised as of special importance in contributing to the balance of payments (see Chapters 21 and 22).

The following are typical examples of government assistance in promoting trade.

- Tax-free loans given to manufacturers involved in export trade, to help them buy imported machinery.
- Technical and professional training, e.g. in management and in information technology developments such as CAD/CAM (computer-aided design and computer-aided manufacture).
- Favourable low-cost ('soft') loans to manufacturers and farmers through institutions such as the Industrial Development Corporation.
- Subsidies and grants (see later in this chapter).

Foreign market intelligence

The government provides information about foreign markets and trading opportunities. For example, it will advise on the market potential of an exporter's goods, and provide details of regulations and other specific local requirements in the target market. The government will also assist in the process of advertising and marketing the country's products abroad, for example co-ordinating participation in overseas trade fairs.

Many foreign market intelligence operations are carried out by governments through their embassies and diplomats abroad. These officials also register protests on behalf of their country if free trade is unduly threatened by the import controls of foreign governments.

Export Credits Guarantee Department

Some territories in the Caribbean region have set up departments such as this to provide a special form of insurance against the possibility of non-payment of debts by overseas traders. This facility encourages exporters to participate in foreign markets confident in the knowledge that they will receive payment for their exports.

Industrial development areas

Governments set aside large areas specifically reserved for industrial development, sometimes accompanied by subsidies and grants. An example of such a development area is Point Lisas, Trinidad.

The government may even build factories and then lease them to businesses that could not have undertaken such developments alone, thus encouraging productivity and employment.

Technical assistance

Caribbean governments recognise the need to attract investment, and they take an active part in encouraging investment from sources which are locally based or regionally based, or from international sources.

Caribbean governments will provide a variety of technical assistance to these sources of investment to encourage them to participate. The form this assistance takes could include the following:

- infrastructure support (e.g. road networks and public utilities)
- tax concessions (e.g. tax exemption for a limited period)
- supporting agencies to encourage exporting
- bureaux of standards to promote and develop standardisation
- tourism development boards to promote the tourist industry
- co-ordination facilities through government agencies (see later)
- provision of factory spaces
- advice on investment opportunities.

18.3 Government intervention in business

Governments throughout the world intervene in business activities for a variety of reasons and to different degrees. Sometimes they might do so in order to support enterprises. In other circumstances governments might be motivated by a need to control or regulate enterprises.

Consumer protection

Consumer protection refers to the range of facilities that exist to help consumers to make a wide range of purchases and to protect them from exploitation.

Governments accept some of the responsibility for consumer protection, and demonstrate this in a variety of ways, including the following:

- contributing to consumer education and advice
- establishing and enforcing appropriate legislation
- control of quality, and weights and measures
- monitoring and control of prices
- promotion of fair trading practices
- supervision of credit facilities.

Consumer protection is examined in detail in Chapter 14.

Price controls

The government may pass laws which give them the power to limit the price that can be charged for certain goods or services. It may wish to do this where the items are in short supply, or are seen as essential to ensure supply at an economic price to poorer sections of the community (e.g. rice and bread).

Principles of Business – Profile 3

Price controls are difficult to enforce because they often result in less incentive to produce the items, because the profit margin is reduced. Price controls also encourage the development of 'informal markets' – unofficial or illegal sales at uncontrolled prices.

Subsidies

Subsidies provide a way of solving the problem of reduced incentive to produce, which is a difficulty with price controls.

Subsidies are cash grants given by governments to entrepreneurs to encourage them to provide goods or services at a price below that normally recognised as economic. For example, a grant might be given to farmers to encourage them to grow certain crops and sell them at a price lower than they would normally expect to receive. Such grants are administered in the Caribbean by officers of the Ministry of Agriculture, who ensure that the system is applied correctly.

Subsidies are not restricted to agriculture. Sometimes they may be given to industries during a difficult period (e.g. to avoid the need to shed their workforce), and to infant (newly formed) industries to help them to get established. Subsidies may also be given to importers to enable certain urgently needed products to be brought into the country at a more favourable price.

Import controls

Sometimes governments may feel it necessary to place controls on goods being brought into the country in order to protect industries in the home market, or to secure a favourable balance of payments position (see Chapter 21). There are two basic methods of import controls – quotas and tariffs.

- *Quotas* are a limit on the quantity of a product that is allowed to enter the country in a given period of time. Sometimes the government may implement an embargo, which is a complete ban on the import of certain goods (or goods from a specific country).
- *Tariffs* are a tax on imports which has the effect of raising the cost price of the import. The tax may be specific or ad valorem (for an explanation of these terms see Chapter 21).

Taxation

Taxation of income, goods and property can also be used to influence and to encourage industry and commerce. For example, increasing taxation on certain products can depress demand and discourage production, and vice versa. Taxation is dealt with in depth in Chapter 19.

Nationalisation

We have seen in Chapter 2 that sometimes the state will take over the ownership of certain industries. When a business is taken into public ownership in this way, it is said to have been nationalised. Sometimes enterprises are in state ownership but have not been nationalised, in other words, they are enterprises that were originally established by the government. State ownership of industries has become a prominent feature in the Caribbean region. State control of industries allows the government to ensure that certain goods and services are made available at an economic price, and it also makes it possible to plan for particular sectors of the economy. You should refer again to Chapter 2 for wider examination of the state ownership of industries. Look particularly at the arguments for and against state ownership.

KEY WORDS

Find out the business-related meaning of each of the following terms. Write a separate sentence for each term to show your understanding.

nationalisation
price control
economic growth
import control
quota   tariff
market intelligence
competitive market
subsidies   embargo
consumer protection
industrial development area

18.4 Social services

In modern society, the responsibilities of governments are now seen to include the provision of social services at a national and personal level, including social security, medical and health care, education, housing, roads and transportation, and welfare facilities including sanitation.

It is generally recognised that governments have an obligation to provide their citizens with social services, because without government intervention many in the community would be denied their basic material needs. In this regard the government takes a political decision to provide services either free or at a cost subsidised by funds obtained from taxation.

Education

The Caribbean region has a strong tradition of education. Governments fund nurseries for infants, basic schools, primary and secondary schools. At the post-secondary and tertiary levels, many institutions are sponsored by the governments. The University of the West Indies has campuses in Barbados, Tobago, Trinidad and Jamaica, and there are affiliate centres in many of the other islands in the region. Guyana has its own university.

In addition, there are other important institutions providing tertiary education, such as the College of Arts, Science and Technology in Jamaica, the Imperial College of Agriculture in Trinidad, and the College of Agriculture in Jamaica. There are also a number of teacher training colleges, and technical training is provided at youth camps, technical colleges and trade centres throughout the region.

The foregoing are just a sample of the many educational initiatives and institutions that exist as a direct result of the influence of governments in the Caribbean.

Health

A healthy population is important to all countries, and therefore promotion of healthy living and provision of medical care is an important responsibility of government. This will include not only the provision of medical facilities such as hospitals, but also broadcasting information on health-related matters, such as sensible diet, hygiene and contraception.

National insurance (NI)

National insurance, which is a system contributing to health care, is operated by many countries as a social service. It should be noted that national insurance is not only concerned with health care, although this is one of its main aims.

National insurance is an example of the way that some governments ensure that medical and health care and other support services are available for all members of the community. National insurance is a scheme which aims to raise money through premiums deducted from wages, with contributions (approximately two-thirds) from employers. The funds raised in this way are used to provide the following benefits.

- sickness
- maternity
- invalidity
- old age
- funeral grant
- survivors benefit
- employment injury benefit
- unemployment.

Recreational facilities

Recreation also plays an important part in the health, education and leisure of both citizens and tourists. Governments provide libraries, botanical gardens and recreational parks for the use of both local residents and visitors. Sport is also encouraged by the government, often with a sports minister to oversee it. In addition, there are national galleries of art, museums and zoos, all considerably influenced by government.

Summary

The foregoing are just some of the many social services that countries provide for their citizens. It would be impossible to include all of them here. But the importance of social services is demonstrated by the fact that most governments establish ministries with responsibilities for various areas of social services. For example, there may be a ministry of education, of transport, of health and so on.

18.5 The role of government agencies

Government agencies are sub-sections of the government which assist it in running its affairs. Some of these agencies may be created by legislature and charged with specific functions, others may be less formally organised but still exist as a part of the government machinery. We have chosen a selection of these agencies to examine here, but there are many more than could be contained here.

The Industrial Development Corporation (IDC)

The IDC in Jamaica, Trinidad and Tobago, and Barbados is an example of the way that governments can assist commerce and industry. The IDC has operated for a number of years to assist the general development of industries in the following ways.

- Publicise the local industrial and business climate to overseas clients.
- Provide factory accommodation.
- Administer fiscal (taxation) incentives legislation.
- Assist in training workers through grants to employers.

The Management Development Centre (MDC)

This government agency offers advice, provides facilities for lectures, and operates seminars for business executives and managers and those being prepared for management positions. Although the MDC is based in Trinidad, it draws participants from throughout the Caribbean region. The centre publishes bulletins and newsletters which are distributed to interested parties. These publications often contain summaries of management studies carried out in other parts of the world (e.g. the United States and Europe) that are of interest to our own industries, managers and executives.

Both the IDC and the MDC will sometimes co-operate to the benefit of businesses. For example, the IDC might provide a business with a loan to help it set up a manufacturing plant, and the MDC will advise the firm on the best ways to carry out its operations.

Tourism Development Board (TDB)

Tourism is a major industry in the Caribbean region and most of the islands have established a TDB to monitor, co-ordinate and develop tourism. The TDBs will provide technical assistance to those involved in the tourist industry, such as hotel owners, travel agents, tour operators and airlines.

Government Statistical Office

All of the Caribbean islands have a need for the provision of statistical information. Governments need statistics such as those referred to in Chapter 20, to show how the economy is performing. Census statistics are also needed to show any changes in population, for example growth or decline of population, and employment statistics. Data such as these are important to governments because they contribute to strategic planning, but they are also of interest to business people both locally and overseas.

Various statistical reports are published annually by the Government Statistical Office, although businesses also compile their own data banks from a wide variety of sources.

Export consolidation and investment

We have acknowledged earlier in this chapter and elsewhere in this book that governments are keen to encourage export trade, and there are a variety of agencies that support this. State corporations such as the Jamaica National Export Corporation have done much to promote the acceptance of some of Jamaica's products in the United States, Europe and Japan.

Agreements such as the Caribbean Basin Initiative which provides tax concessions and other incentives to encourage United States companies to invest in the Caribbean Basin, and also made it possible for certain Caribbean products to be exported into the U.S. duty-free for a period of 12 years (1983–95), have been influenced by governments. So have trade agreements such as the Lome Convention with the European Union. All these initiatives provide important support for industrial development and investment in the Caribbean.

18.6 Governments and the labour force

Unemployment

One of the biggest problems of the Caribbean region is unemployment. In Chapter 1 we saw that there are many types of unemployment, and many reasons why unemployment persists.

The obvious solution to the problem of unemployment is to create more jobs (employment). Whilst the majority of the opportunities to create jobs lies in the private sector, governments also have an important role to play. The government can create more jobs by directly employing more people to deliver the services it is responsible for. However, a better long-term strategy is to take steps which will make the labour force more employable. This is done through making workers more efficient and thereby more mobile.

Raising the efficiency of the labour force

An obvious way to raise the efficiency of labour is through education and training, and this is clearly an area where the government has a major role to play. Education must embrace the technology needed by commerce and industry. It must not only be able to provide the initial skills training that are needed by industry, but also play a part in re-training people as the need arises for them to change jobs or update their skills. By raising the efficiency of the workforce the government can contribute to the reduction of unemployment as well as make the workforce more effective.

Mobilisation of the labour force

Self-help and community groups do much to organise labour for productive activity. Community self-help organisations such as the Red Cross, Kiwanis, Jaycees, Lions and Leo clubs, Business Women's Associations, and church-based organisations engage communities in productive work. Often the persons being served are persons who lack the skills required for jobs, or who are unemployed. These self-help and community groups are non-governmental organisations (NGOs) that raise funds and establish skills training programmes combined with productivity for people who are in need, especially the young. By providing people with greater skills, we are making them more mobile in terms of employment.

Although the organisations we have examined here are independent of the government, there is an important role for governments to play. The government can encourage such organisations in their endeavours by providing community centres, perhaps in schools and other public places, that can be used by self-help groups. Governments can make a further contribution by providing tutors to train people directly or raise the skills of other tutors so that they can help others. The government also has an important part to play in funding such organisations through funding agencies, and encouraging the private sector to also provide funding. Businesses can be encouraged by the government to provide 'on the job' training for people.

Migration and the labour force

Migration refers to the movement of people from one geographic area to another on a permanent basis. Some people migrate from one part of the country to another, whilst others go to another country. If the person is moving from one country to another, then the person is referred to as an emigrant. When that person arrives in the recipient country, the person is referred to as an immigrant. Migration is a term used to represent both immigration and emigration.

Migration affects a country's labour force, because the country loses persons who would have been available for employment or would have been gainfully employed. Therefore, economic growth is affected by migration. Where skilled and competent persons as well as professionals migrate, then a 'brain drain' is the result.

Persons may migrate:

- to find a better or more prosperous life
- in order to find or change employment
- to study and work
- for political reasons.

Chapter 18 – **The role of governments**

The effects of internal migration on the labour force:

- Communities lose qualified people who could have participated in the development and economic growth of the community, and could have helped to raise the standard of living of the community.
- The labour supply in the community is reduced. A sector such as agriculture may suffer from a shortage of labour which could have been solved by those who have migrated.
- The community or area to which persons migrate is often overcrowded, since many persons gravitate to the same economic centres seeking work. This brings pressure on the local amenities. This has the effect of causing funds to be diverted from economic development in order to take care of social developments and social welfare demands (e.g. overcrowding, unemployment, social disorder, inadequate housing and insufficient supply of utilities services).

The effects of external migration on the labour force:

- Skilled and competent persons emigrate and so the country experiences problems in achieving its goals of economic growth and development.
- The labour force is reduced, often considerably.
- The country is required to continually put resources into training and re-training. If a community lacks the resources to do this, then a shortage of skilled and competent persons occurs. This leaves countries/governments with a need to recruit people from overseas with the skills required, often at considerable costs.

The effects of migration on the recipient country

- The recipient country receives skilled as well as unskilled persons who are added to the labour force.
- If the migrants move to overcrowded areas, then the country will have to divert funds from other targeted areas for development of social services needed to meet the demands caused by internal migration.
- Cultural differences could lead to many social, political and economic problems.

Although migration can have a serious social and economic effect on a country or a region, there are major benefits to be derived. For example, in the Caribbean where unemployment is a major problem, migration provides an avenue through which the unemployment problem can be eased. Persons who migrate support their families who are left behind, and so inflows of foreign currency classified as gifts from abroad add to Gross National Product and thus, National Income.

KEY WORDS

Find out the business-related meaning of each of the following terms. Write a separate sentence for each term to show your understanding.

migration   recreation
export trade
national insurance
emigrant   census
immigrant   health care
Tourism Development Board

Principles of Business – Profile 3

18.7 Things to do

This section contains a variety of exercises to help you create revision notes, to test your understanding and to prepare you for examinations.

Search and find

Write out the question and the answer by referring back through the text to form revision notes.

1. Describe the four main areas of responsibility of governments.
2. How can 'soft loans' help businesses and why would the government want to make these available?
3. Why is it in the government's interest to promote the fullest employment it can achieve?
4. The world has generally become more environmentally aware. What contribution can governments make towards this ideal?
5. What is the purpose of the government budget?
6. What is inflation and how can the government use its budget to control it?
7. How can a government assist the promotion of trade?
8. Why should a government be keen for a business involved in exporting to be successful? How could it help such a business?
9. How does an Export Credits Guarantee Department encourage foreign trade?
10. What is an industrial development area?
11. How does technical assistance provided by government encourage investment in the Caribbean region?
12. Why do governments intervene in business activities?
13. What are price controls and what kind of problems can they create?
14. How might subsidies be more effective than price controls?
15. Why would a government impose controls on imports and what form might these controls take?
16. For what reasons might a government want to own certain industries?
17. Describe some of the social services that your government provides.
18. How do government agencies assist business?
19. Why is it better to make the workforce more 'employable' than just providing them with employment?
20. What is the main effect of raising the efficiency of the workforce?
21. Explain the difference between the terms 'emigrant' and 'immigrant'.
22. Give reasons why people migrate.
23. What are the effects of migration on the workforce?
24. How might migration affect the recipient country?

Chapter 18 – **The role of governments**

What do you know?

Write out the complete sentence and insert the missing word, which can be chosen from the list at the end of the questions.

1. As protector of the people, the government must promote appropriate .....
2. A government might want to promote ..... in particular industries or locations.
3. Governments often provide ..... that private enterprise would be unwilling to supply at a price everyone can afford.
4. The government is charged with overall control of the .....
5. The ..... summarises the government's expected income and expenditure for the year ahead.
6. Successful businesses contribute to the ideal of full employment and add to national .....
7. ..... trade is seen as of special importance in contributing to the balance of payments.
8. The government will advise on the market ..... for an exporter's goods.
9. The government may build factories and ..... them to businesses to encourage industrial development.
10. Consumer ..... refers to the range of facilities that exist to help people to make wise purchases.

Choose the missing word from the following:

export   economy   lease   legislation   services   potential   protection   prosperity   development   budget

Structured questions

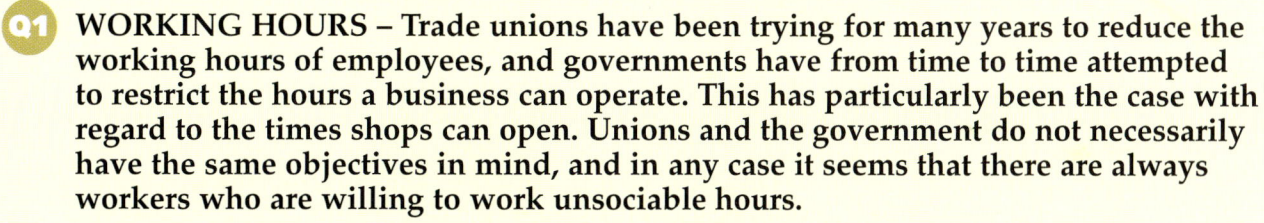

Q1 **WORKING HOURS** – Trade unions have been trying for many years to reduce the working hours of employees, and governments have from time to time attempted to restrict the hours a business can operate. This has particularly been the case with regard to the times shops can open. Unions and the government do not necessarily have the same objectives in mind, and in any case it seems that there are always workers who are willing to work unsociable hours.

(a) What do you consider as 'unsociable working hours'? **1**

(b) Give two examples of ways that the government might try to restrict business operational hours. **2**

(c) State two reasons why the government might want to influence the hours a business can operate. **2**

(d) State two ways in which the reasons why unions try to influence working hours might differ from the reasons of the government. **2**

(e) Give three economic or social reasons why some workers would be more willing than others to work unsociable hours. **3**

(f) Allowing all businesses to operate unrestricted hours can affect different groups of people in varied ways. Describe the ways in which it could affect each of the following:
  (i) the employee   (iii) the government
  (ii) the employer   (iv) religious groups   **4**

(g) Write a report that argues against allowing businesses to operate unrestricted hours. **6**

Principles of Business – Profile 3

Q2 **THE BUDGET** – The Chancellor of the Exchequer presents the main Budget once a year, and occasionally mini-budgets in between. Sometimes a budget surplus is achieved and sometimes a deficit. The Chancellor may prefer a deficit at a time of high unemployment but a surplus to check inflation.

(a) What is 'the Budget'? — *1*

(b) Explain the terms 'surplus' and 'deficit' used here. — *2*

(c) State two examples of sources of government income as a result of measures contained in the Budget. — *2*

(d) List three major elements of central government expenditure. — *3*

(e) If there was high inflation because consumers were spending too much money, the government could create a budget surplus by increasing taxation and lowering its own spending. What could be the effect of this on business? — *3*

(f) Describe four circumstances where business organisations would want to influence government budgetary measures. — *4*

(g) Describe two examples of ways that individuals, and three examples where businesses, are affected by government fiscal policies. — *5*

Q3 **MONOPOLIES** – Throughout the world there are many examples of industries that are dominated by a few very large firms. Even where there are a lot of firms the competition between them may not be particular effective.

When the supply of a product is controlled by one or a group of firms acting together we say that a monopoly exists.

Monopolies can be granted by law. For example, if you invented something you would be given the right (by patents) to have complete control of the production and sale over a given period of time.

Sometimes the advantages of a monopoly outweigh its disadvantages and for this reason governments have sometimes not interfered, and may even encourage it. But the disadvantages of monopoly, particularly from the point of view of the consumer, have generally caused governments to exercise some control over it.

(a) Define the term 'monopoly'. — *1*

(b) Why do monopolies occur? — *2*

(c) Give three examples of how a monopoly can occur. — *3*

(d) Explain how a monopoly can bring advantages and disadvantages for the public. — *4*

(e) In what ways might the government try to restrict mergers and monopolies? — *4*

(f) What are the reasons for saying that monopolies should be the subject of state control? — *6*

Q4 **NOLAND NEEDS NEW LIFE** – Business activities in the country of Noland are slowing down. Many people are being laid off work and each week reveals substantial numbers of businesses going bankrupt. There are over-populated areas where unemployment is abnormally high and there is insufficient industry. The government has an important part to play in reviving economic activity.

Chapter 18 – **The role of governments**

(a) State two reasons why business activities in a country might be 'slowing down'. **2**

(b) What could the government do to influence consumer behaviour particularly in order to help increase economic activity? **2**

(c) In what ways could a government relieve the pressure of industry and population in congested areas? **3**

(d) Describe two social problems and two economic problems that could result from the situation described above if the government did not intervene. **4**

(e) What strategies could the government use to increase employment in areas in which unemployment is abnormally high? **4**

(f) Governments sometimes give tax relief and other incentives to small firms. Describe how such a policy could help to solve the situation described above. To what extent do you agree that the government is justified in interfering in business activities in this way. **5**

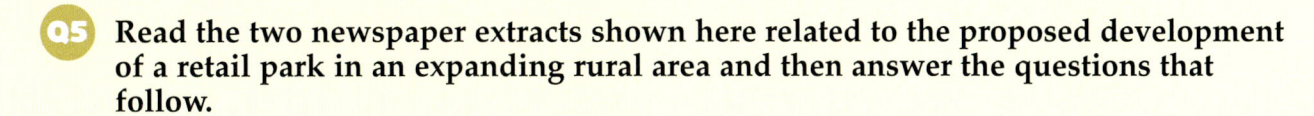

Q5 Read the two newspaper extracts shown here related to the proposed development of a retail park in an expanding rural area and then answer the questions that follow.

RETAIL PARK DEVELOPERS SEEK SUPPORT

Jenny Davidson, Planning Director of the planned new retail park, talked today of the 'wonderful opportunities that will be brought to the local community by the proposed development incorporating many retail outlets'.

Mrs Davidson highlighted the many new jobs that would be created, both during the construction period and after the stores are up and running. She emphasised the increased prosperity the development will bring to the locality and asked for support of the local community.

RETAIL PARK – PUBLIC MEETING PLANNED

At last night's council meeting Councillor Howard brought to the attention of the members the many concerns he had received from local residents about the proposed developments of a retail park on the recreation ground to the west of the town. He warned councillors that public objections to the development were growing.

The council decided that a public meeting should be called with an open invitation to all parties involved.

(a) What is a retail park? **1**

(b) State one possible private cost and one private benefit of the development referred to in these two articles. **2**

(c) On what social cost grounds might the local community object to the proposed development? **2**

(d) Why is it more difficult to measure social costs and benefits than private ones? **3**

(e) Briefly describe how you would organise a group of residents with the aim of trying to stop the development with sound arguments. **3**

(f) Describe three different ways the group you have organised could use to gain publicity and political support for their cause? **4**

(g) Outline a possible cost benefit analysis that could be put to a public meeting, fairly putting arguments for and against the proposed development. **5**

Principles of Business – Profile 3

Research assignments

1. To what extent do you agree or disagree with the view that the provision of social services by the State is too generous in your country and, therefore, taxation is higher than necessary? Provide examples to support your views.

2. Design a questionnaire which concisely states the social welfare services provided by the State, and then present a series of questions aimed at identifying the social services which residents in your locality use most frequently. Present your findings using tables and charts and present a summary.

3. 'Cigarette smoking has a private cost to the individual and social cost to the economy.' Investigate this statement including data obtained by personal survey to establish private costs and data from government departments to identify social costs. Present your discussion of the statement in the form of a report that aims to raise awareness of the real cost of smoking to the economy.

4. What evidence can you find to support the view that there is a difference in living standards between the various parts of the Caribbean region? What influence can the government have on this?

5. Make a collection of newspaper articles from your local press related to matters of local concern, and related to business activities. Divide your articles into issues that you feel could be solved by local government and those that are central government responsibility. Write a summary report, in two parts, to say how you feel the issues should be tackled:

    a) by local government
    b) by central government.

Chapter 19 Taxation

We all pay tax in some form or other, either directly or indirectly. The government does not take this money from us without reason. The money taken is used to control and direct the economy as well as to fund government expenditure and redistribute wealth.

19.1 Principles of taxation

A tax is a compulsory money payment to the State by businesses and individuals levied on property, income and the use of goods and services.

The following four principles of taxation were stated by an economist, Adam Smith, over 200 years ago, but they are still sound concepts that are applied in economies around the world today.

- *Equality* Taxes should be based on the ability to pay. Those with higher incomes should pay a higher proportion of their income in tax than those with low incomes. In this way people bear a fair burden rather than all paying the same amount.
- *Certainty* The easier it is to understand a tax system, the less incentive there is to evade paying the amount levied. The form and manner of payment and the quantity to be paid should be clear and unambiguous to the contributor and to everyone else. In other words, the tax system should be clear enough so that those liable for tax are certain of what is expected of them.
- *Convenience* A tax should be convenient for the taxpayer to pay and for the tax collector to collect. The pay as you earn (PAYE) method of payment and collection of income tax is convenient because it is collected by employers before the employees receive their pay. PAYE is also a convenient system because it fits in with the normal activity of regular payment of wages.
- *Economic* Taxes should be collected as economically as possible because there is little to be gained if the cost of collection is more than the money received.

A tax may take one of three forms.

- *Proportional* Every taxpayer pays the same proportion of his or her income in tax.
- *Progressive* A taxpayer with a higher income not only pays a larger amount of taxes but also a larger proportion. Income tax takes this form in Caribbean countries.
- *Regressive* This refers to a situation where the tax represents a smaller proportion of a wealthier person's income than that of a poorer person as with a purchase tax.

19.2 Functions of taxation

There are five functions of taxation: to raise revenue, to maintain economic stability, to influence expenditure, to redistribute income, and to satisfy specific objectives.

To raise revenue

The main function of taxation is to raise **revenue** (money raised by taxation) to pay for things provided by the State which private enterprise would be unable or unwilling to provide at prices the majority of the population are generally able to pay. Police, medical care, education and roads are examples of where provision is largely met through taxation.

To maintain economic stability

Governments use taxation to exercise overall control of the economy in a manner that attempts to level out the 'highs' and 'lows' in economic activity, to promote economic growth and to try to achieve full employment. A major factor involved here is the control of inflation.

To influence expenditure

Taxation can be used to influence the level of total expenditure. The higher the level of taxation the lower the level of real expenditure is likely to be, and vice versa. This principle can be used to deflate or reflate the economy. Inflation is examined later in this chapter.

To redistribute income

Taxation can be used to effectively redistribute income and capital ownership in the community, by taxing some members of the community more than others, for example redistributing in favour of poorer members of the community. Redistribution of income will, in the long term, influence the distribution of wealth.

To satisfy specific objectives

Taxation can be used to achieve specific objectives such as the following:
- Discouraging habits like smoking, drinking and gambling.
- Encouraging activities such as healthy eating and safe driving.
- Stimulating production, exporting and the improvement of the balance of payments.
- Encouraging movement of industry into depressed areas.
- Promoting mobility of labour.
- Protecting particular industries, e.g. from foreign competition.
- Helping to re-organise, re-equip and expand key sectors of the economy.

19.3 Methods of taxation

No single method of taxation is ideal, and consequently governments use a variety of methods, which spread the burden over the population in what the government thinks is a fair way.

Generally there are two classes of taxes – **direct** and **indirect**.

Direct taxation

A direct tax is one that is levied directly on individuals or on companies. They are taxed 'at source'. Income tax, corporation tax, capital gains tax and capital transfer tax are examples of direct taxes.

Income tax

Income tax is both a direct tax and a progressive tax, and it is the most important and largest source of revenue for most governments. It is a tax on personal earned income. Wage earners are allowed a certain amount in tax-free allowances, and the rest of their income is taxed. It is normally collected by a system called 'pay as you earn' (PAYE). Through the PAYE system, the tax is deducted by the employer before wages are given to the employee.

Corporation tax

Corporation tax is levied on the profit of companies. As with individuals and income tax, companies are allowed to deduct certain expenditures as tax-free allowances from their gross profit. The remaining net profit is liable for tax.

Capital gains tax

Capital gains are the profits obtained from the sale of capital items such as business enterprises, property, land, machines, etc. A percentage of the profits from these sales has to be paid to the government as capital gains tax.

Capital transfer tax

Capital transfer tax is a tax on gifts or gratuitous transfers of personal wealth from one person to another, whether they take place during a person's lifetime, or at death.

Indirect taxation

An indirect tax is paid by the taxpayer indirectly to the tax authority. It is levied on one person but is collected and ultimately paid by someone else such as a retailer. Indirect taxes can either be specific or ad valorem.

- *Specific* This means that a specific sum of money will be levied irrespective of the value of the product – a set amount per item.
- *Ad valorem* In this case the amount of tax levied is a percentage of the value of the product. The higher the product value, the higher will be the amount of the tax paid.

Purchase tax, customs and excise duties, stamp duties, rates and property taxes are examples of indirect taxation.

Purchase tax

This is a tax applied to a wide range of consumer goods, and the tax rate varies depending on the type of goods in question. The tax is paid by the original seller (e.g. the manufacturer) and passed on to the consumer in the form of higher prices.

General consumption tax (GCT)

This is a variation of the purchase tax that has been adopted by some Caribbean countries. A percentage (currently 10%) tax is levied on many items and services. Such a tax has the effect of raising prices and bringing in revenue for the government.

Customs and excise duties

These taxes are charged in addition to purchase tax or GCT – on a variety of important goods such as motor vehicles, alcohol and tobacco. Customs duties are taxes levied on imports; excise duties are levied on home-produced goods. These taxes are intended to raise revenue for the government, but are also used to protect home industries from foreign competition.

Stamp duties

This method of taxation is payable on certain monetary instruments such as cheques, commercial documents and contracts.

Rates and property taxes

These taxes are usually raised by local government authorities, and the revenue is used to help provide localised services.

19.4 Economic effects of taxation

Effective taxation should achieve the functions stated earlier, but at the same time meet the longstanding principles of taxation (equality, certainty, convenience, economic). No single tax can meet all of these requirements and raise all the revenue governments need. Consequently, governments use a variety of methods of taxation, which tends to even out some of the inadequacies of some of them. A key source of debate is whether direct or indirect taxation is more appropriate.

The main advantage of direct taxes is that the rate charged can easily be changed or varied for different circumstances. For example, the overall rate of income tax can be simply changed centrally by the government, and it is possible to have varied rates: income tax is generally charged at a progressively higher rate to the rich and, conversely, at a lower rate to the poor. The PAYE system ensures that income tax is not only relatively easily collected (employers do much of the work) but it also allows the taxpayer to make contributions in small regular payments.

The main disadvantage of direct taxes is that they are expensive to administer and collect; many civil servants are involved and complicated rules and paperwork persist. Direct taxation often results in disputes between taxpayers and tax officials over the amount of tax due. In addition, those who do not pay their income tax by the PAYE method can fall into the trap of not saving sufficient money to pay one or two large payments a year.

Indirect taxes have the advantage that they are relatively easy and cheap to collect, the amount to be paid is generally clear and unambiguous, and it is difficult to evade paying them. In addition, indirect taxation collects money from foreigners (e.g. tourists) whereas they do not pay direct taxes.

The main disadvantage of indirect taxes is that they are regressive, in that poorer people tend to pay a higher proportion of their income in tax than those on higher incomes do. For example, payment of purchase tax or GCT is at the same rate whether one is a high earner, a low earner, or even a non-earner.

19.5 Inflation

Earlier in this chapter we saw that one of the functions of taxation is to maintain economic stability. One of the main threats to this stability is inflation, and governments throughout the world are continually striving to offset the effects of it.

Inflation describes a situation when prices are persistently rising and the real value of money is declining, which means that the cost of living has increased. If people's incomes do not improve, then the money they earn will purchase less. Under such circumstances we say that **real income** has fallen, and this results in a fall in the standard of living unless some other factor changes.

The **retail price index** (RPI) shows the average of prices of a general 'basket' of goods, and is used to indicate the rate of inflation.

Cost–push inflation

This form of inflation is caused by rises in the cost of factors of production such as raw materials or labour, e.g. oil prices and wages. For example, wage increases may not be matched by increased productivity. When such increased costs are passed on to the consumer in the form of increased prices, this results in cost–push inflation. The resultant increase in the cost of living encourages workers to press for further wage increases, causing a continuing inflationary spiral with rising wages chased by rising prices, or vice versa.

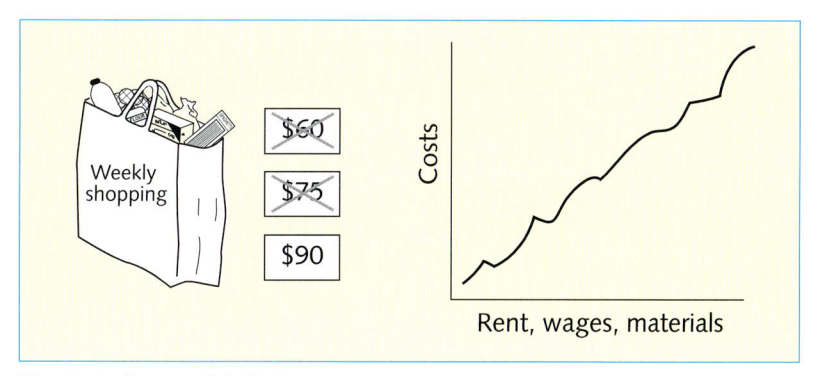

Fig. 19.1 *Cost–push inflation*

Demand–pull inflation

This type of inflation involves 'too much money chasing too few goods', that is, an excessive supply of money relative to the goods and services available for purchase. Upward movement of wages can be an explanation of this, but 'too much money' usually refers to excessive credit expansions, for example easier bank loans and other borrowing facilities, which encourage people to spend money that they do not immediately have available.

The effects of inflation

Inflation has the effect of making us all worse off. If your country has more inflation than other countries this will mean that your prices will rise faster. Consequently, your exporters will find it harder to sell their products. Consumers both in your country and abroad will be less inclined to buy the more expensive home-produced goods, preferring the less expensive foreign

Principles of Business – Profile 3

> **SUMMARY**
> **Inflation** Persistent rise in the general level of prices of consumer goods and services.
> **Cost–push inflation** Inflation caused by increases in costs to producers (e.g. higher wages or material costs).
> **Demand–pull inflation** Inflation caused by more demand in the whole economy than can be supplied at existing prices.
> **Deflation** Where the value of money is rising while prices are falling.
> **Deflationary measures** Strategies used by the government in an attempt to reduce spending in the economy (usually through monetary or fiscal policies).
> **Reflationary measures** Strategies used by the government to increase demand and encourage growth.
> **Hyperinflation** When prices are rising so fast that generally people prefer to spend their money rather than hold on to it.

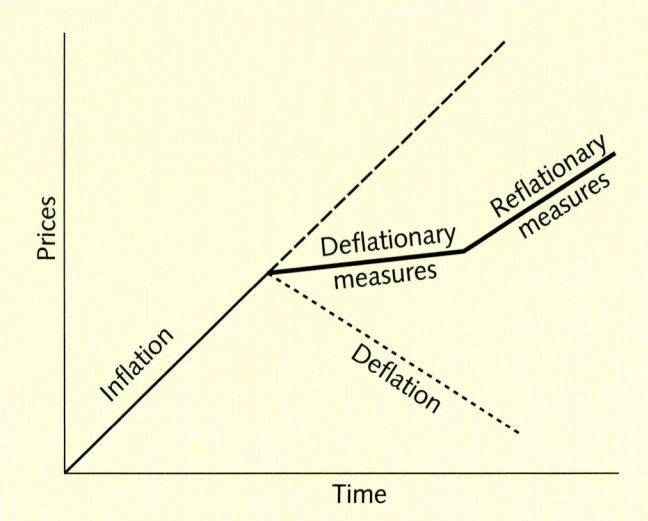

The dashed line shows what would be the trend if inflation remained unchecked. The thicker line shows the possible effect of deflationary or reflationary measures.

Fig. 19.2 *Government intervention*

KEY WORDS

Find out the business-related meaning of each of the following terms. Write a separate sentence for each term to show your understanding.

inflation   revenue
general consumption tax
direct taxation
income   taxation
economic stability
expenditure   income tax
corporation tax
indirect taxation
capital gains tax

products. This will lead to reduced output at home and job losses, further adding to the rate of inflation. The following summarises the main effects of inflation.

- Prices are persistently rising, resulting in a decline in the standard of living, especially for those on fixed incomes.
- Saving is discouraged because people recognise that money saved will buy less in the future.
- Exports become more expensive because of increased production costs. Consequently, there is a tendency to import more goods, since they are relatively cheaper than domestic production.
- People who owe money to others (debtors) gain from inflation, whereas those who are owed money (creditors) lose.

Controlling inflation

If a government believes that demand–pull is the cause of inflation it can put a number of measures into effect. The government can:

- reduce its own demand for goods and services
- encourage increased productivity
- try to reduce demand by consumers and producers
- make credit more expensive and more difficult to obtain
- take more in taxes than the government spends
- introduce controls, for example of wages, prices, imports.

Where cost–push inflation is thought to be the cause, the remedies are more complex, and often open to political argument. For example, the price of imported goods and raw materials is outside the control of the government. However, some control can be exercised over wage increases and the cost of home-produced goods through a firm prices and incomes policy, although the desirability of this is subject to political debate and there is no clear evidence that such a policy works.

19.6 Things to do

This section contains a variety of exercises to help you create revision notes, to test your understanding and to prepare you for examinations.

Search and find

Write out the question and the answer by referring back through the text to form revision notes.

1. Describe the principles upon which taxation should be based.
2. Explain the differences between the proportional, progressive and regressive forms of taxation.
3. Explain the five functions of taxation.
4. Define direct taxation and describe the forms it can take.
5. How does indirect taxation differ from direct taxation?
6. Explain the difference between the terms 'specific' and 'ad valorem' in relation to indirect taxation.
7. Describe the forms of indirect taxation commonly used.
8. Do you feel direct or indirect taxation to be the more appropriate form? Give reasons for your answer.
9. What is inflation? How does 'cost–push' inflation differ from 'demand–pull' inflation?
10. What steps might a government take in order to control inflation?

What do you know?

Write out the complete sentence and insert the missing word, which can be chosen from the list at the end of the questions.

1. Money taken in taxation is used to control and direct the .....
2. A tax is a ..... money payment to the State.
3. Taxes should be based on the ability to .....
4. The easier it is to understand a tax system the less incentive there is to ..... paying the amount levied.
5. A tax should be ..... for the taxpayer to pay and the tax collector to collect.
6. Taxes should be collected as ..... as possible.
7. Taxation can be used to influence the level of total .....
8. Taxation can effectively ..... income.
9. ..... taxation is levied at source.
10. ..... taxes can be 'specific' or 'ad valorem'.

Choose the missing words from the following:

indirect   economically   redistribute   pay   evade   convenient   compulsory   direct   expenditure   economy

Principles of Business – Profile 3

Structured questions

Q1 Ms Wiltshire earns $92,455 a year as a managing director of a large multi-national company. Ms Wiltshire resides in the country of Noland which operates a system of income tax 'banding'. Taxpayers are charged different rates for various levels of income. A breakdown of Ms Wiltshire's income tax paid for the last year is given in figure 19.3. Answer the questions related to this data.

Income		%	Tax paid
$49 800	at	60%	$29 880
$7 900	at	55%	$4 345
$7 900	at	50%	$3 950
$5 200	at	45%	$2 340
$16 200	at	29%	$4 698
$3 000	at	40%	$1 200
$3 455	Tax Free		
Total $92 455			$46 413

Fig. 19.3 *Ms Wiltshire's income tax breakdown*

(a) What is income tax? **1**

(b) What was the total amount of income tax paid by Ms Wiltshire? **1**

(c) What is meant by taxable income? Calculate Ms Wiltshire's taxable income. **3**

(d) Ms Wiltshire pays income tax by the PAYE system. Describe this system of tax payment. **3**

(e) Use the data shown here to help you explain whether income tax is 'progressive' or 'regressive'. **4**

(f) Bearing in mind the 'principles of taxation', explain fully whether or not you think income tax is a good tax. **8**

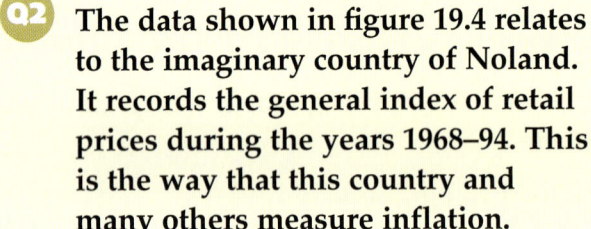

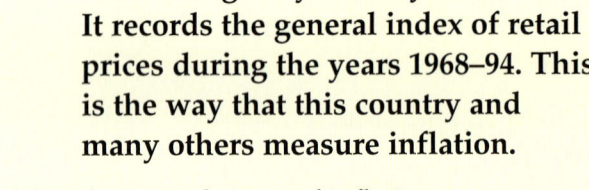

Q2 The data shown in figure 19.4 relates to the imaginary country of Noland. It records the general index of retail prices during the years 1968–94. This is the way that this country and many others measure inflation.

Fig. 19.4 *Retail price index for Noland*

(a) What was the rate of inflation in 1973? **1**

(b) What was the highest rate of inflation between 1968 and 1994, and in which year did it occur? **2**

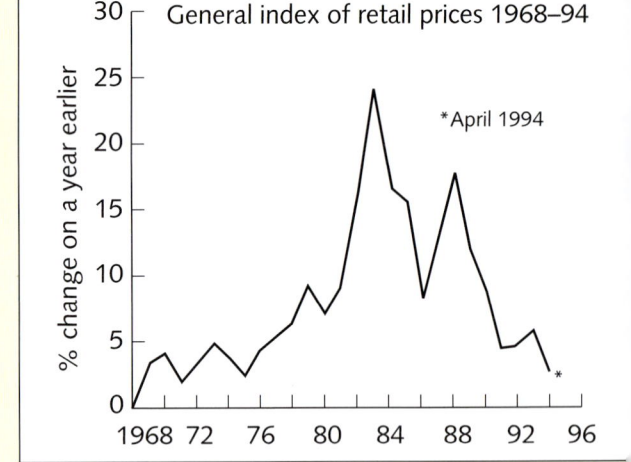

(c) The rate of inflation in 1994 was 3%. What does this mean? **2**

(d) Average earnings in 1978 were $29.30 per week; in 1992 the figure was $178.80 per week. Does this mean that the people were six times better off in 1992 than in 1978? **4**

(e) In a period of inflation, which of the following in your opinion would be the best and which the worst forms of personal investment. Give your reasons.
   (i) Bank deposit accounts
   (ii) Solid gold coins
   (iii) House purchase **4**

316

Chapter 19 – Taxation

(f) 'The high rate of inflation shown in this data in the 1980s was the result of cost–push inflation, partly caused by imports. It was not a result of demand–pull inflation.' Explain this statement. **7**

Q3

(a) Explain any situation where you would pay two taxes in making a single purchase. **2**

(b) Explain the difference between capital gains tax and capital transfer tax. **4**

(c) Describe how the government might use taxation as a method of redistributing income and wealth within the country. **6**

(d) Explain the working of either income tax or general consumption tax in your country, and describe its merits as a form of taxation. **8**

Q4 Look at figure 19.5, and answer these questions.

(a) Name the government department that collects GCT. **1**

(b) Why is general consumption tax so called? **2**

(c) How can one tell whether GCT is a direct or an indirect tax? **2**

(d) State one advantage of GCT from the point of view of the government and one disadvantage for the consumer. **4**

(e) A wholesaler sells 16 items at $25 each to a retailer, to whom he allows a 25% trade discount. GCT at a rate of 15% must be added to the transaction. Produce a breakdown similar to that in the data in figure 19.5 to show the way in which the eventual charge will be calculated. **5**

General Consumption Tax (GCT)

GCT is a tax levied by central government on general expenditure. It is a tax added to many goods and services at every stage of production. When several traders are involved in the movement of goods from the producer to the consumer, each will charge GCT to the person to whom they sell. Each trader, however, only pays to the Customs and Excise Department the amount of GCT they have charged their customers less the amount of tax paid to their own suppliers.

Example GCT		
10 items at $20 =	$200.00	Gross invoice value
Less 25%	50.00	Trade Discount
	$150.00	Net goods value
Plus 15%	22.50	GCT
Total	$172.50	Invoice value

Fig. 19.5 *General consumption tax (GCT)*

(f) Explain the difference between an ad valorem tax and a specific tax, using examples to illustrate your answer. **6**

Q5 Refer to the data in figure 19.6. It compares the weekly expenditure of old age pensioners (OAPs) and a high-income family with the Retail Price Index.

(a) What is the OAPs' total weekly expenditure? **1**

(b) What percentage of the high-income married couple's income is spent on clothing and footwear? **2**

(c) If food prices rose by 10%, how much extra would the two families quoted in this data have to spend to maintain their real standard of living, assuming no other price increases? Express your answer:
 (i) in $s. **1**
 (ii) as a percentage of their total expenditure (i.e. their personal rate of inflation). **2**

Principles of Business – Profile 3

(d) Why are the rates of inflation worked out in (c)(ii) both below 10%? **2**

(e) If food prices rose by 20% and housing costs rose by 10%:
  (i) calculate the rate of inflation for each household. **2**
  (ii) account for the difference in the rate of inflation between the households. **2**

(f) Describe and analyse the construction of the Retail Price Index and explain its use for measuring inflation. Explain clearly why it may not be a true reflection of individual households' personal rates of inflation. **8**

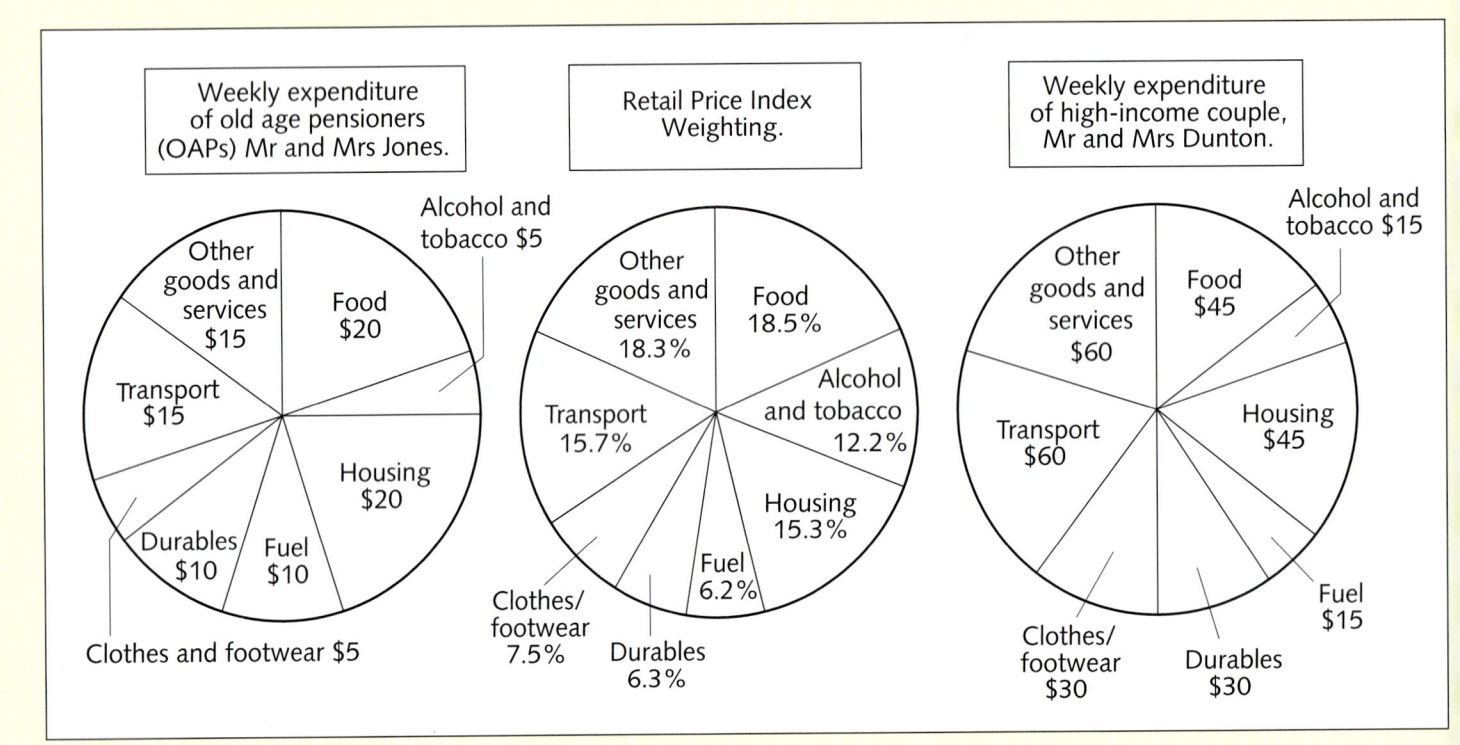

Weekly expenditure of old age pensioners (OAPs) Mr and Mrs Jones.
- Food $20
- Alcohol and tobacco $5
- Housing $20
- Fuel $10
- Durables $10
- Clothes and footwear $5
- Transport $15
- Other goods and services $15

Retail Price Index Weighting.
- Food 18.5%
- Alcohol and tobacco 12.2%
- Housing 15.3%
- Fuel 6.2%
- Durables 6.3%
- Clothes/footwear 7.5%
- Transport 15.7%
- Other goods and services 18.3%

Weekly expenditure of high-income couple, Mr and Mrs Dunton.
- Food $45
- Alcohol and tobacco $15
- Housing $45
- Fuel $15
- Durables $30
- Clothes/footwear $30
- Transport $60
- Other goods and services $60

Fig. 19.6 *Comparison of expenditure of two households with Retail Price Index*

Research assignments

1. Why does any government need to redistribute incomes? To what extent do you feel taxation achieves this aim? Give specific examples to illustrate your answer.

2. Using data quoted from any reliable source, describe the effect of inflation on your country and explain how the government is attempting to control it.

3. Describe four taxes levied on individuals by your government. How far do you consider them to be either progressive or regressive? To what extent do you consider them fair?

4. Explain the difference between direct and indirect taxation. How, if at all, do they affect the rate of inflation as measured by the Retail Price Index? Use official data to support your observations.

5. Use a collection of newspaper articles and headlines, together with your own explanations, to show the difference between demand–pull and cost–push inflation. What policies might a government adopt to reduce inflation?

6. Investigate the following question over a six-month period. To what extent is your family's personal rate of inflation the same as the official government rate?

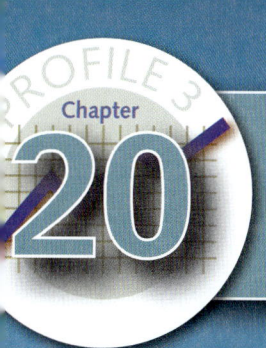

Social accounting

20.1 The standard of living

What is the standard of living?

The term **standard of living** refers to the quality of life that the people of a country have: the types of house they live in, the quality of food they eat, the clothes they wear and so on. Obviously, the standard of living is dependent upon the work people do and the wages they receive. Even the methods that workers use to travel are seen as contributing to the standard of living, as are methods of communication used and the entertainment that they have ready access to. The level of education the population receives is also seen as important.

The standard of living is often reflected in the average lifespan of the people of a country. It is likely that people who live where there is a high standard of living will generally live longer than those who have a poor standard of living.

Country	Male	Female
Afghanistan	43	42
Barbados	73	77
Great Britain	72	78
Grenada	69	74
Jamaica	75	78
Libya	64	69
Madagascar	50	53
Nigeria	47	49

Table 20.1 *Average life expectancy*

Look at the table 20.1, which contains data relating to the average life expectancy of people in a number of countries. What reasons can you give to explain the differences that exist between countries and between the sexes?

It is generally the case that countries with a poorer standard of living are located in the tropics, whilst countries which have higher living standards are found in the colder areas. This does not mean that standard of living is a result of temperature: it is very much to do with the stage of development that the country has reached, and the resources it has available. And, of course, the way that these resources are developed affects the standard of living.

Factors affecting the standard of living

You will learn later that something called the National Income has influences on the standard of living, but here we will look at some other things that affect the standard of living.

Population

The size and make up of the population has an influence on the standard of living in obvious ways; the more working people in the population, the greater will be the contribution they can make to the wealth of the country and the standard of living.

The size of the population is influenced by factors like life expectancy rate and infant mortality, and these are also affected by the quality of life of people and the influence of negative factors such as pollution.

If the working population is supporting an increasing number of non-working people, for example the unemployed, the elderly, or the very young, the standard of living will be declining. The quality of the working population will also have an influence on the standard of living. For example, the more educated or skilled the population is, the more productive they are likely to be.

Income

The wages or salaries that people receive govern what they can buy. Theoretically, the higher the wages of the population, the better should be their standard of living. Conversely, generally low or falling wage levels imply a falling standard of living. However, no matter what the levels of wages being received, they can only be as effective as the price of goods allow them to be.

Inflation

Inflation is a general rise in the prices over a period, which means that the value of money is falling. Poor people and those on fixed incomes (such as pensioners) find their standard of living more adversely affected by inflation than those whose income keeps up with it.

Government

The government can influence the standard of living of the population in many ways. The way that the government manages and administers its budget will have an affect on the quality of life of the people. The government may take deliberate measures to improve the standard of living by increasing the output per head of the population, or it may reduce taxes to increase spending power.

Exporting

If a country is exporting a greater value of goods that it is importing, it is generally growing richer. Conversely, if it is importing more than it is exporting, the country will become poorer. The standard of living will be favourably or adversely affected.

Devaluation

Devaluation refers to the decrease in the value of a country's currency compared with the value of other currencies. This has the effect of making the country's exports cheaper (increasing sales to other countries). It also has the effect of making imports more expensive, thus discouraging imports and increasing the wealth of the country. Devaluation can occur naturally, but it can also be implemented by the government. Either way, it affects the standard of living.

Cost of living

As you can imagine, measuring the standard of living is a formidable task because there are so many factors involved, and some of these are difficult to quantify. Some of the main methods of measuring national prosperity will be examined shortly, but the cost of living gives some indication of the quality of life of people, and how it is changing from one year to another.

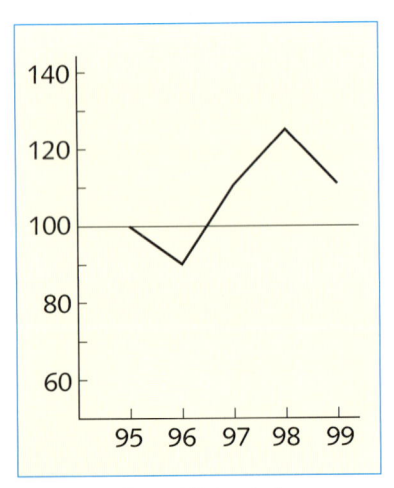

Fig. 20.1 *Cost of living index*

Chapter 20 – **Social accounting**

The cost of living refers to how much can be bought with a person's net income (after deduction of income tax). Measuring the cost of living is important because it is continually changing, and therefore it shows whether 'real' income is changing. In other words, are people better or worse off, taking into consideration rising costs and income increases? Measurement of the cost of living is achieved by constructing a 'price index'. There is more than one type of price index, but the most popular and more generally well known is the 'consumer price index' (CPI).

The CPI is made up of the prices of goods and services purchased by consumers. It is often used in the Caribbean and other parts of the world as a basis for negotiating wage increases. The object of this is to ensure that workers' wages maintain a constant or increasing value in 'real' terms.

A 'cost of living index' is constructed by taking the total value of a collection of items purchased by consumers in a particular year, which is referred to as the 'base year'. We say that the index figure for that year, say 1995, is 100. The same items are subsequently valued periodically (usually annually) and general price movements can be plotted on a graph similar to the imaginary one shown in figure 20.1.

Depending upon whether each new plotted position is above or below the base line, it is possible not only to know whether prices have generally risen or fallen, but also to establish an approximation of the percentage change. The change can then be checked against wage rises, in order to establish whether workers end up better off in real terms.

Useful though it is, a cost of living index gives only a limited indication of the state of the economy of a country. Statistics included in the national accounts are a more revealing indication of the state of the economy.

KEY WORDS

Find out the business-related meaning of each of the following terms. Write a separate sentence for each term to show your understanding.

inflation   exports
cost of living   income
population   imports
standard of living
income   devaluation
cost of living index

20.2 National income

Economic growth refers to an increase in the output of all things we consume, use, invest in or otherwise produce. Economic growth is important because it usually means that the country is increasing its wealth, and probably improving its living standards. One way to assess economic growth is through measurement of the national income.

What is national income?

Imagine you were asked to calculate the total income of your family for the year: how would you go about doing so? You would probably add together the total yearly income of each member of the household, including any return received from savings or investments. But there are other ways of reaching the same figure. For example, it can also be obtained by adding together the total amount spent and the total amount saved by each member of the family in the year. You should understand that both methods reach the same answer because both look at the same amount of money, but in a different way. The national income of a country can also be assessed in a similar way.

If you were asked to assess your income, you would refer to wages and other returns which add to your wealth. You would not count money you invested in the building society last year, but you would include the interest you received this year. Income is a *flow*, and not a stock of money or equipment.

Principles of Business – Profile 3

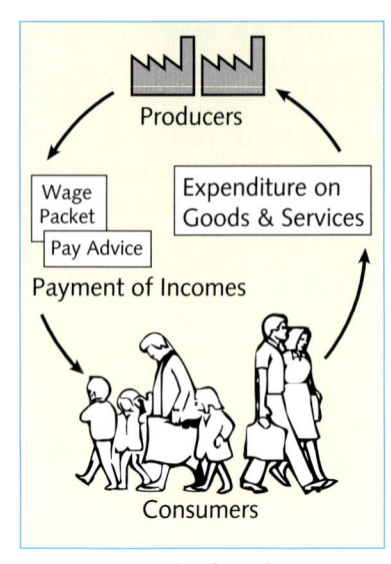

Fig. 20.2 Circular flow of income

National income is concerned with new additions to the wealth of the country for a specific period (normally a year).

There are three approaches that can be used to measure the national income, and all the methods should reach the same answer because (in a way) they are all measuring the same thing.

- *Income method:* the aggregate value of all forms of income, including personal incomes, profits of firms, rents, etc.
- *Output method:* the total net output of every form of production, taking care not to count any output twice. 'Net' in this case implies subtracting an allowance for capital consumption (depreciation – fall in value due to wear and tear) on all buildings and machinery.
- *Expenditure method:* the total value of all expenditure by consumers, firms and the government.

National income accounting problems

Quite apart from the obvious difficulty of data collection, there are a variety of problems associated with the foregoing methods of national income measurement. The following are some of these problems.

Money terms

It is not possible to add together things such as tons of fish, bottles of wine and thousands of tractors. To evaluate items such as these we have to express them in money terms. But the value of money is constantly changing, and inflation can cause it incorrectly to appear that national income is increasing. What is important is the real increase in national income, and to establish this requires allowances to be made for the changing value of money.

Double-counting

Double-counting can occur when output is considered. If timber is included in output measurement, should furniture made from timber also be included? The answer to this difficulty is that each firm should only count the value added to products by its activities. Theoretically this avoids counting output more than once, but in effect the result is still not a very precise measurement.

The 'informal' economy

Babysitting, bartending, taxi driving and car repairs are typical examples of jobs that are sometimes being done 'on the side', that is, without the Inland Revenue knowing about them, because the income is not declared for tax purposes. The work is usually done for cash rather than cheque payment, and for a charge lower than for 'official' work. Activities such as these are sometimes called the 'hidden' or 'underground' economy, but most commonly they are referred to as part of the informal economy.

Probably every developed country has its own informal economy, and in some countries it is so substantial that it props up the official economy. It has been estimated that the informal economy adds almost a third to the gross national product.

The informal economy is to be condemned because tax evasion by some in this way increases the tax burden of others. However, more important here is the fact that the informal economy creates a problem for recording domestic statistics. The main source of information for the income method is the Inland Revenue, but we have seen that the informal economy means that a large proportion of income is not recorded.

Uses of national income statistics

The final national income figure is only an estimate, because of the foregoing and other accounting difficulties which result in discrepancies. However, in spite of all the difficulties in measuring national income, the figures have several uses.

- *Change in living standards.* Most governments use national income statistics to indicate changes in living standards.
- *Comparison with other countries.* National income figures enable comparisons to be made between one country and another.
- *Economic growth.* A comparison can be made between one year and another in respect of economic growth.
- *Instrument of economic planning.* The figures provide the government with information which can be used to assess the effectiveness or otherwise of its past policies. This information can then be used in the planning of the economy, and implementation of the redistribution of wealth.

National income and standard of living

In order to get a general idea of the standard of living of a country, we divide the national income by the population, and the resulting figure is called **per capita income**. This figure allows us to make comparisons, for example, between the standard of living of one country and that of another. But such comparisons must be treated with caution.

Whilst national income is of vital importance in determining our standard of living, a high national income does not necessarily mean a high standard of living exists generally. It does not show how the income is distributed.

To illustrate this point, let us imagine that there is a Middle Eastern country called Hullabahoo, and that that country has experienced dramatic economic growth because of the discovery of vast deposits of oil five years ago. If Sheik Shinpad, ruler of the state of Hullabahoo, receives the vast majority of the national income, the country may be earning more, but its people will see little improvement in their living standards. Therefore, the way that the wealth is **distributed** is just as important to the population as the national income.

Although per capita income provides a useful indicator of the standard of living of a country, apart from ignoring the distribution of income, it has the following shortcomings. These have to be taken into account when making comparisons using per capita income.

- There are variances in prices from one year to another, and between one country and another.
- It does not take into account the effect government spending (e.g. on defence) has on national income.
- It is possible that increased national income has resulted from increased working hours.

Factors influencing national income

Economic growth is important for increased national prosperity, but this is influenced by many factors, the following of which are particularly crucial.

- *National resources:* the availability of resources such as fertile land and good climate, and how effectively these are used.
- *Industrial development:* how well-equipped and technically advanced industry and commerce is.
- *Quality of the labour force:* the size and health of the working population and the skills it has.
- *Economic stability:* the extent to which economic activity is spread over a wide range of industries.
- *Political stability:* political unrest will adversely affect investment and the achievement of economic objectives.

20.3 Gross national product (GNP)

When we looked at the output method of measuring national income earlier, we said that an allowance was made for 'capital consumption' or loss in value (depreciation) of buildings and machinery. In other words, in the case of national income measurement we only know the total production output after taking away that allowance. But in national accounting, it is useful to be able to measure the total value of all things actually produced in a country, that is, a figure which does not include a reduction for capital consumption.

In most countries, the principle measure of the total output of the country is called **gross national product** (GNP). The word 'gross' indicates that no deduction has been made for capital consumption.

National income of Noland	Simple imaginary analysis by expenditure method
	$ billions
Consumer expenditure	168.2
Public authorities expenditure	60.1
Gross domestic fixed capital investment	43.5
Value of physical increase in stocks	2.1
Exports of goods and services	73.3
Total final expenditure	347.2
less imports of goods and services	− 67.1
less taxes	− 38.3
plus sudsidies	+ 4.1
Gross domestic product	245.9
Net property income from abroad	+ 2.2
Gross national product	248.1
less capital consumption	− 36.9
National income	211.2

Table 20.2

The word 'national' in this instance does not imply that GNP is the total output produced within the borders of a particular country. The GNP measure includes some output taking place and produced by resources owned by people from other countries. Clearly, this outflow cannot be counted as part of our national income. At the same time, some sources of output are situated in other countries but owned by the citizens of the country in question. Therefore, the GNP can be defined as the total output of

Chapter 20 – Social accounting

all the resources owned by residents of the country, wherever the resources themselves are situated.

The total output actually produced within the borders of a country is called the **gross domestic product** (GDP). GDP can be defined as the output of all resources located within the country, wherever the owners of the resources happen to live. In a similar manner to GNP, the GDP becomes net domestic product when an allowance for depreciation is deducted from it. In many ways, GDP is the more important measure.

The national cake

The amount of wealth or gross national product a country generates each year is sometimes referred to as the **national cake**. The national wealth 'cake' is made up of contributions from various parts of the economy, including commercial activities such as services, distributive trades and transport, together with important contributions from industrial production and agriculture, fishing, etc.

Wealth in this sense is more than a stock of money and possessions. Wealth is the total of what the economy produces each year in the form of goods such as clothing and food, and services such as those of doctors or teachers. We normally find it convenient to measure wealth in money terms, but this can create problems, because not all wealth can be counted in money terms. For example, how do we put a precise value on the quality of education, medical care or environment? And yet sometimes the effect of things such as these can be greater and more important than the production of goods, to which we normally attribute wealth.

The well-known saying 'you cannot have your cake and eat it' is undoubtedly true, and yet many people want to do just this. As a country we cannot have what we have not earned; we cannot eat more cake than we have. Consequently, the bigger the slice of the cake one person or group takes, the less there is left to distribute to others. Clearly, we must make a bigger cake before we can distribute bigger slices from it. This is often the source of a continual wrangle between governments, employers and workers over demands for wage increases.

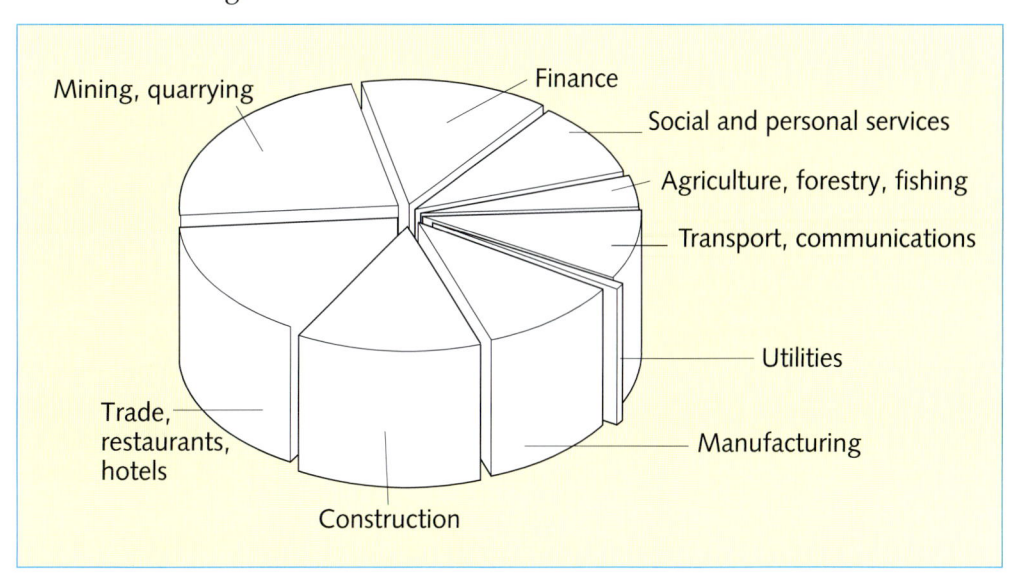

Fig. 20.3 *Where the national wealth comes from*

Principles of Business – Profile 3

20.4 National expenditure

Whilst the gross national product tells us what was produced in a country, national expenditure tells us who bought what was produced. We can say that national expenditure is the sum of the following.

- *Private expenditure:* this includes every kind of consumption spending by the population, from food and clothing to cars and entertainment (but excluding the purchase of homes).
- *Public expenditure:* central and local government spending on goods and services, for example salaries of teachers and soldiers, provision of pensions and family benefits, etc. (but excluding capital expenditure on durable assets such as buildings).
- *Gross domestic capital formation* (GDCF): this refers to the total investment by business firms, public enterprises and public authorities in new fixed capital such as new plant and equipment, buildings, ships and other durable means of production. The purchase of new dwelling houses is also included in GDCF.
- *Overseas trading:* the effect of the net differences between the value of a country's exports and imports of goods and services (balance of payments).

From the foregoing it can be seen that national expenditure is necessarily identical in value with the national product, because it is merely another way of classifying the same information.

Public expenditure

This term refers to government spending. Some of this spending is carried out by local government, but by far the greatest expenditure is carried out by central government. In fact, so great is government expenditure that any cutbacks it implements can have a serious effect on employment statistics.

The following are typical of just some of the needs of a country that are met from public expenditure.

- *Defence:* maintenance of defence systems, army, navy and air force.
- *Medical care:* provision of hospitals, doctors, dentists, etc.
- *Education:* the provision of basic, primary, secondary and further education.
- *Law, order and protective services:* the courts, police and fire services are the major items.
- *Environmental services:* water, sanitation, etc.
- *Roads and transport:* government is almost the sole provider of roads and makes contributions to other transport facilities.
- *Grants and subsidies:* given to help develop or support key sectors of the economy.
- *Social services:* provision of many facilities such as benefits for the elderly, unemployed, sick, etc.
- *Debt interest:* when the government spends more than it obtains through taxation it has to borrow. The total amount owed is known as the **national debt**. The government has to pay interest on this debt.

20.5 National debt

If you spend more than you earn you will end up in debt. There are two ways you can put the matter right. You can earn more, or you can borrow to pay off the debt. In the latter case you are creating another debt, but delaying ultimate payment. The government faces a similar problem.

Each year the government prepares the budget, in which it plans the next year's government revenue and expenditure. If expenditure equals revenue the budget is in balance. When income exceeds expenditure a surplus has been created, and a deficit results when expenditure exceeds income.

The **public sector borrowing requirement** (PSBR) indicates the extent to which the government borrows from other sectors of the economy and from overseas to balance its deficit on the expenditure and revenue accounts. The PSBR is an important indicator of how the government's policies are affecting the economy.

In many countries, the PSBR is partly satisfied through public sale of government stocks (see Chapter 16) at home and overseas, but much has to come from other sources. The national debt is the total amount owed by the government to people both in the home country and in other countries.

Wherever there is a budget deficit, the PSBR bridges the gap and results in an increase in the national debt. For most countries the national debt has accumulated over many years and today the total is so huge that it is no longer possible for it to be repaid, although it is important to restrict growth of the debt as far as possible.

20.6 Growth and development

Growth refers to an all-round expansion of the economy. It is concerned with the quantitative increases in the country's output. It is concerned with the rate of economic change, for example increase in tourism, increase in sugar production, increased construction of roads, building of more schools, etc.

Growth can be measured by changes in GNP, which reflects general increases in total net output. Negative growth means that the country is doing less well than in the previous year, zero growth indicates that there has been no change when compared with previous years. All governments are keen to see their countries achieve growth, because it generally results in an improved standard of living and greater economic and political stability.

Development is not the same as growth. It is a qualitative concept and is more concerned with the *pattern* of economic change. Development refers to the provision of facilities that enable growth to take place, for instance the availability of resources such as machinery and of a workforce with appropriate education and skills. Often development takes place in just some sectors of the economy, but provides thrust for other sectors. In order to have development, there must be growth. However, there may be growth but no development. Highly developed countries are better able to exploit their natural resources than underdeveloped countries, and consequently more advanced economies have a better standard of living.

An underdeveloped country tends to have the following features:

- Poor economic performance

- High rate of population growth
- Low standard of living
- Relatively short life expectancy
- High unemployment
- Considerable dependency upon agricultural employment
- Poor educational opportunities.

Many (but not all) European countries, the United States, Japan and Australia are examples of highly developed economies. By contrast, most underdeveloped countries are situated in Asia and Africa. The Caribbean countries are part way between the two extremes. They are sometimes referred to as 'developing countries'.

Economic growth

Economic growth is the goal of all governments, and it is affected by the following factors.

- *Investment.* Capital accumulation and the use of capital to create further wealth through the provision of capital or equipment is essential to economic growth. For this reason, the government is keen to encourage saving and investment, and will also allocate a large share of its resources to development.
- *Technical progress.* Economic growth is promoted by the exploitation of technical development so that increased productivity can be achieved with the same resources. For this to take place the workforce must have the skills to take full advantage of new technology. Consequently, there must be adequate investment in education as well as technology.
- *Balance of payments.* A persistent adverse balance of payments will hinder growth and development. A continued unfavourable balance will 'bleed' the country of the capital that it needs to direct towards development and growth. It will also have the effect of discouraging capital inflows from overseas investors, who will be more interested in investing in more stable economies with healthy balance of payments positions.
- *Government expenditure.* Government spending is so extensive that it has the power to stimulate particular sectors of the economy when carefully directed. Public expenditure should be used, at least in part, to stimulate those sectors of the economy that will assist future output.

The role of education

Education plays an important role in the economic growth and development of all countries. The following are the main contributions that education makes to the growth and development of an economy, but the list is really unending, which only emphasises the importance of education.

- It helps to improve the knowledge and skills of the workforce. This not only makes them more effective in the workplace, but it also enables them to move to other areas where there are shortages of labour (mobility of labour).
- Better educated people are more able to adapt to changes that are necessary in a developing economy. For example, new technologies require workers that are willing and able to embrace technological change.
- Education makes people more literate, which is important in the modern world where communication skills have become increasingly important.

> Entrepreneurs are an essential factor in economic development. Entrepreneurs tend to come from the better educated sectors of society.

Development in the Caribbean

Caribbean economies are developing at a slow and uneven pace. This is due to problems of economic dualism referred to earlier in this book (see Chapter 2). Economic dualism results from a situation in which the economy is divided into two distinct sectors – one that can be said to be advanced, and one that is backward.

The advanced sector usually employs modern technological means, concepts, methods and procedures. This is seen in areas such as mining, manufacturing, hospitality and tourism, the financial sector including insurance and building societies, among other areas; while the backward sector continues to use old or out-dated technology and other modes of operation that give rise to inefficiency. Backwardness in terms of productive activity can be seen in small farming and the craft industry, among other areas. Yet, these sectors coexist and somehow need each other.

The hospitality and tourism sector and the agricultural sector are two examples of this idea of economic dualism. The hospitality and tourism sector boasts modern methods of operation and thus produces a high quality product and service. The agricultural sector, on the other hand, especially in the area of small farming, does not enjoy the quality of technology and services employed by the hospitality and tourism sector. As a result, the needs of the hospitality and tourism sector are not adequately addressed by the agricultural sector, and this causes the sector to rely on businesses outside the region to provide the goods and services it needs. Where this happens, the small farmers and eventually the agricultural sector as a whole suffer, and economic dualism, which is undesirable, will continue to exist.

Therefore, clear linkage between the hospitality and tourism sector and the agricultural sector as a whole should be established. These sectors should be appropriately linked so that they each depend on the other for economic support.

The characteristics of underdevelopment in the Caribbean

> Rapid population growth and high levels of unemployment due to the inability of countries to provide jobs in the quantity needed at any one time.
> Low rates of income as a result of poor economic returns.
> Low standards of living.
> Inadequate educational facilities to provide people with the skills and competencies needed to support modern economic activities.
> Worsening terms of trade in traditional agricultural areas such as banana and sugar in which large numbers of persons have invested, and areas on which many persons depend for employment, whether seasonal or not.

KEY WORDS

Find out the business-related meaning of each of the following terms. Write a separate sentence for each term to show your understanding.

per capita income
public expenditure
gross national product
informal economy
national expenditure
national income   growth
development
gross domestic product
national debt   budget

Principles of Business – Profile 3

20.7 Things to do

This section contains a variety of exercises to help you create revision notes, to test your understanding and to prepare you for examinations.

Search and find

Write out the question and the answer by referring back through the text to form revision notes.

1. 'The cost of living is just one aspect of the standard of living.' Explain this statement.
2. 'The population is one of the factors that affects the standard of living and is also affected by it.' Explain this statement.
3. What is the consumer price index?
4. How is a consumer price index constructed?
5. Define national income.
6. What do we mean when we say that income is a 'flow' and not a 'stock' of wealth?
7. Describe the three methods of measuring national income.
8. What are the problems of measuring national income?
9. What useful purpose is there in measuring national income?
10. Define the term 'per capita income'.
11. 'Rising national income does not necessarily imply a rising standard of living.' Discuss this statement.
12. List the factors that influence national income.
13. Define gross national product and say how this figure differs from national income.
14. The gross national product is sometimes referred to as the national 'cake'. What makes up the national cake? Why is it true to say that we cannot 'have our cake and eat it'?
15. What is 'national expenditure'?
16. What is the national debt and why does it exist? To whom is the debt owed?
17. In what way is growth different from development?
18. How does 'zero' growth differ from 'negative' growth?
19. Give simple definitions to show the difference between an underdeveloped country, a developing country and a highly developed country.
20. Why are all governments keen to see economic growth?
21. Simply state the main factors that affect economic growth.
22. Why is education an important part of economic growth and development?
23. What do you understand by the term 'economic dualism' in respect of the Caribbean region?

Chapter 20 – Social accounting

What do you know?

Write out the complete sentence and insert the missing word, which can be chosen from the list at the end of the questions.

1. The standard of living refers to the ..... of life that the people of a country have.
2. The cost of living refers to how much can be bought with a person's net .....
3. Economic growth is important because it usually means that the country is increasing its .....
4. Work that is done unofficially is sometimes referred to as part of the ..... economy.
5. Whilst national income is important, it does not necessarily mean a high standard of ..... exists.
6. Gross national product is the total ..... of all the resources owned by the residents of a country.
7. The total amount a government owes is known as the national .....
8. The public sector borrowing requirement indicates the extent to which the ..... borrows from other sources.
9. More ..... economies tend to have a good standard of living.
10. Economic growth is promoted by the exploitation of ..... developments to increase productivity.

Choose the missing words from the following:

technical   quality   output   informal   debt   advanced   living   government   income   wealth

Structured questions

Q1 Refer to the data in table 20.3 showing the national income accounts of the country Noland for last year.

(a) What was the value of public expenditure last year? *[1]*

(b) Name two goods which would be considered part of consumer expenditure. *[1]*

(c) Calculate the value of 'taxes on expenditure' which are marked '?' in the accounts. *[1]*

(d) Refer to the data 'Total final expenditure'. Why is it necessary to add subsidies in the calculation? *[2]*

(e) Calculate Noland's balance of payments on current account from the data given. *[2]*

(f) State another method, besides aggregate expenditure, which can be used to assess the national income. What problems are encountered using this method? *[3]*

(g) Explain the difference between GNP and national income. Why is the distinction between them important? *[4]*

(h) 'During the last five years, the national income of Noland doubled from $84.9 billion to $171.1 billion, but the standard of living in Noland did not double over this period.' Discuss this statement giving reasons to support your observations. *[6]*

Analysis by expenditure method

	$ billions
Consumer expenditure	137.0
Public authorities expenditure	48.9
Gross domestic fixed capital investment	41.6
Value of physical increase in stocks	– 2.9
Exports of goods and services	63.1
Total final expenditure	**287.7**
less imports of goods and services	– 57.8
less taxes on expenditure	– ?
plus subsidies	5.6
Gross Domestic Product	**199.2**
Net property income from abroad	0.2
Gross National Product	**199.4**
less capital consumption	– 27.9
National Income	**171.5**

Table 20.3 *National income of Noland*

Principles of Business – Profile 3

Q2

(a) Define national income. — *1*

(b) Explain the difference between consumption and investment. Why is investment necessary to an economy? — *4*

(c) With the use of examples, explain what 'injections' and 'withdrawals' are with reference to the circular flow of income. State how each affects the level of national income. — *6*

(d) Show with the aid of a simple diagram that national income = national expenditure = national output. — *9*

Q3

(a) What is meant by the 'standard of living' of a country? — *2*

(b) Why do some countries have a higher standard of living than others? — *3*

(c) Describe four factors that influence the standard of living. — *4*

(d) What is 'per capita income'? To what extent would you say that this can be seen as an indication of the standard of living of a country? — *5*

(e) In what way could we measure the standard of living of any Caribbean country? — *6*

Q4

(a) What is economic growth? — *2*

(b) Explain the difference between a 'boom' and a 'recession' in the economy. — *4*

(c) Describe four factors that may lead to economic growth. — *6*

(d) Economic growth does not always mean a better standard of living. Why is this? — *8*

Q5

(a) What is the purpose of a government's budget? — *2*

(b) Explain the difference between a budget surplus and a budget deficit. — *2*

(c) State three services that governments provide which private enterprise would be unwilling to supply at an economic price. — *3*

(d) List three methods governments use to influence business activities. — *3*

(e) To what extent would you argue that governments interfere too much in business activities. — *4*

(f) One type of business that all governments try to influence is importing and exporting.
 (i) Why is this of such importance?
 (ii) How do governments try to influence this aspect of business? — *6*

Chapter 20 – **Social accounting**

Q6 Study the chart in figure 20.4, which shows a breakdown of Florida Trading's expenditure, and answer the questions that follow.

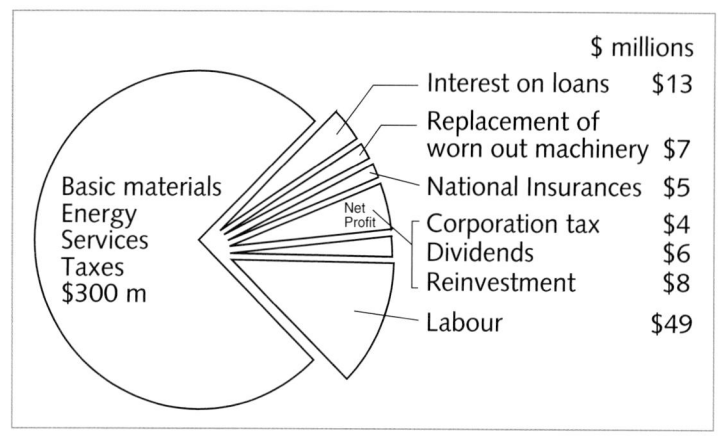

```
                                                    $ millions
                                Interest on loans    $13
                                Replacement of
                                worn out machinery   $7
    Basic materials             National Insurances  $5
    Energy          Net Profit  Corporation tax      $4
    Services                    Dividends            $6
    Taxes                       Reinvestment         $8
    $300 m
                                Labour               $49
```

Fig. 20.4 *Florida Trading expenditure*

(a) By the efficient use of the factors of production, businesses are able to create wealth. Name two such factors of production which are included in the data shown here. **1**

(b) What was the total output of Florida Trading Ltd.? **1**

(c) What was this company's net output? **2**

(d) Explain why net output and not total output is used in the compilation of national income accounts. **3**

(e) Explain the difference between depreciation and reinvestment. How much does Florida Trading spend on each. **4**

(f) By making a net profit, Florida Trading created $18 million of wealth. If all other companies in the economy did the same, the result would be economic growth for the country. By analysis of the breakdown of Florida Trading's net profit, show that economic growth may not always lead to a general rise in living standards. **9**

Research assignments

1 Find out the amounts your government spends on each of the main components of its expenditure. Present the data researched in some appropriate graphical form. Write a summary report which includes explanation of the ways your government raises the revenue it needs.

2 **a)** Give a detailed description of five contrasting services provided by the government of your country.
   b) In what ways would you say that there is a need for your government to improve the social services it provides? Give reasons for your answer.

3 **a)** Why is it difficult to use national income statistics to compare the standard of living in different countries? What other statistics might you consider using in order to make a realistic comparison?
   b) Make a comparison between the standard of living of your country and one other outside the Caribbean region.

4 Using real data, explain the way that your government attempts to redistribute incomes. Quote the source of your data.

5 **a)** A major priority of most governments is the provision of welfare for their citizens. To what extent would you say that this is dependent upon growth and development?
   b) In what ways would you consider your country is restricted in the welfare provisions it makes available to the population?

6 **a)** By examination of your household or a local firm, show that national income can be measured in terms of output, income or expenditure.
   b) Present data to show how your country's national income can be measured in these three ways.

Global trade

21.1 The importance of international trade

The reasons countries trade

The overseas market is important to businesses and to countries as a whole. It is important to businesses because it provides potential additional income from the sale of goods and services. It is important to countries because it is by selling overseas that the home country can earn money to buy things from other countries. By doing this the quality of life of all the countries involved can be improved.

Because the trading referred to here takes place in an overseas market it is often called 'foreign trade'. Foreign trade is the buying and selling of goods and services between different countries of the world.

- *Imports* are bought from other countries and result in an outflow of funds.
- *Exports* are sold to other countries and result in an inflow of funds.
- *Visible trade* refers to the import and export of goods (e.g. food, machinery, vehicles).
- *Invisible trade* is the importing and exporting of services (e.g. tourism, transport, insurance and banking).

A country is in many ways like a big family or a household. Both have to earn money in order to purchase things they need (e.g. food, shelter and clothing) and things they want (luxuries). Countries earn money by selling their products and services overseas (exporting) and they spend their money

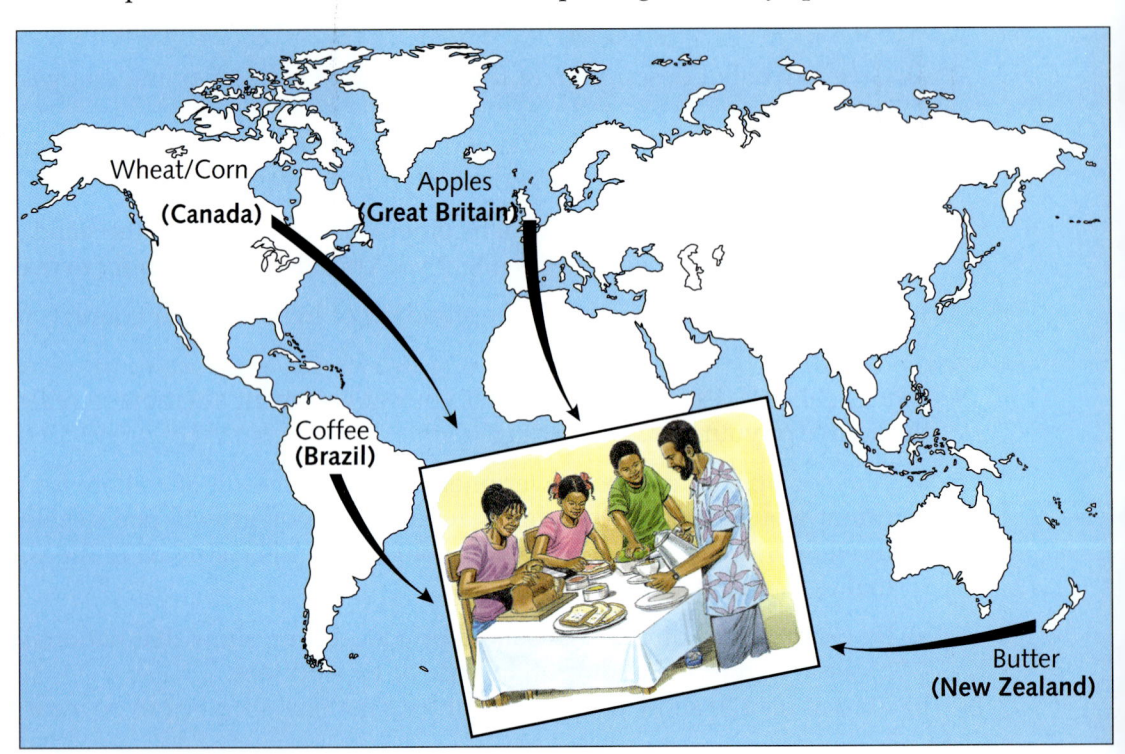

Fig. 21.1 *Examples of imported foodstuffs*

buying from other countries (importing). The result of this can be a better way of life for the population.

If people in a household, or country, earn more than they spend, they can build up a surplus, become wealthy, and generally have a better standard of living. If people or countries spend more than they earn, they get into debt, and generally this leads to a poorer standard of living.

Differences between countries in climate or natural resources mean that they have to trade in order to obtain goods which they cannot produce themselves, or do not find it economic to produce. One country may have natural deposits of oil or gas while another may have metal deposits not found in many other countries. By each country concentrating on producing those goods for which it has the comparative advantage, greater output is achieved more cheaply, which is in the best interest of all people. This is an extension of specialisation or the division of labour, and economists refer to it as following the principle of comparative costs.

Comparative cost

The principle of comparative-cost advantage, simply put, states that when a country is able to produce a variety of products, it will concentrate on those with a lower comparative cost of production.

	Costs per unit	
	computers	sugar
Country A	600	80
Country B	500	100

Table 21.1 *Comparative costs of two products (i)*

Table 21.1 uses a hypothetical situation in which the two countries involved trade only in two goods, computers and sugar. Country A is more efficient at producing sugar than country B, because it can produce it more cheaply than country B. Country A is said to have an absolute advantage in sugar, and country B in computers. If the two countries trade freely with each other, country A will specialise in the production of sugar and export it. Country B will specialise in the production and export of computers. This is to the mutual advantage of both countries.

It can also be mutually advantageous to trade even if a country does not have an absolute advantage in any commodity. Table 21.2 helps to clarify this.

	Costs per unit	
	computers	sugar
Country C	600	200
Country B	500	100

Table 21.2 *Comparative costs of two products (ii)*

In this second table it can be seen that country B has an absolute advantage in the production of both computers and sugar. However, country B has a comparative advantage only in the production of sugar. A unit of sugar in country B costs one fifth of a computer. So, sugar is relatively cheaper in Country B. Country C, on the other hand, has a comparative advantage in the production of computers.

From the foregoing it can be seen that it is to the mutual advantage of countries to specialise in producing and exporting commodities where they have comparative advantage, and import commodities from other countries where production is comparatively cheaper.

Sometimes the comparative advantage one country has over another is not the result of natural resources, but of advantages that have been developed.

Principles of Business – Profile 3

For example, a country may have developed the expertise to produce a particular commodity that other countries require, such as micro-electronic components. Countries will participate in international trade in order to use the specialisation of others, and obtain a wider variety of goods. Thus, by participating in foreign trade, each country enhances the way of life of its people. For example, although wheat is not grown in the Caribbean region, there is a considerable demand for flour (a by-product of wheat) and so this is imported. Similarly, we also import many technical products (e.g. TVs).

21.2 Balance of trade

In the same way that every family has to budget to ensure it spends only what it can afford, so every country must also keep its spending within the limits of its income.

The family may keep a record of its income and expenditure, and countries also record the difference in value between imports and exports. The difference between the value of goods a country imports and exports is recorded in the balance of trade. Because goods can be seen they are collectively called visibles.

When exports exceed imports, the balance, or trade gap, is said to be favourable because a surplus has been created resulting in a net flow of funds into the country.

When imports exceed exports, the balance is said to be adverse (unfavourable). A deficit (loss) has been created which has resulted in a net outflow of funds.

		($ million)	
1	Visible exports	+48,440	
	Visible imports	−47,322	
	Balance of trade	+ 1,118	surplus
2.	Visible exports	+47,322	
	Visible imports	−48,440	
	Balance of trade	− 1,118	deficit

Table 21.3 *Examples of balance of trade figures*

KEY WORDS

Find out the business-related meaning of each of the following terms. Write a separate sentence for each term to show your understanding.

visible trade   exports   adverse   deficit   comparative cost   imports
invisible trade   comparative advantage   favourable   visibles
absolute advantage   balance of trade

21.3 Balance of payments

In their trade with other countries, Caribbean countries buy and sell a number of services. Because these services, unlike goods, cannot be 'seen', they are collectively called invisibles. For example, the Caribbean region earns considerable income from tourists visiting our islands.

The balance of payments is a statement of the difference in total value of all payments made to other countries and the total payments received from them. This balance includes both visible and invisible trade, and it shows whether the country is making a profit or a loss in its dealings with other countries.

	($ million)	
1. Visible exports	+48,440	
Visible imports	−47,322	
Balance of trade		+1,118 surplus
Invisible exports	+25,650	
Invisible imports	−23,120	
		+2,530 surplus
Balance of payments on current account	+3,648	
2. Visible exports	+47,322	
Visible imports	−48,440	
Balance of trade		−1,118 deficit
Invisible exports	+25,650	
Invisible imports	−23,120	
		+2,530 surplus
Balance of payments on current account		+1,412 surplus
3. Visible exports	+48,440	
Visible imports	−47,322	
Balance of trade		+1,118 surplus
Invisible exports	+23,120	
Invisible imports	−25,650	
		−2,530 deficit
Balance of payments on current account		−1,412 deficit

Table 21.4 *Balance of payments figures*

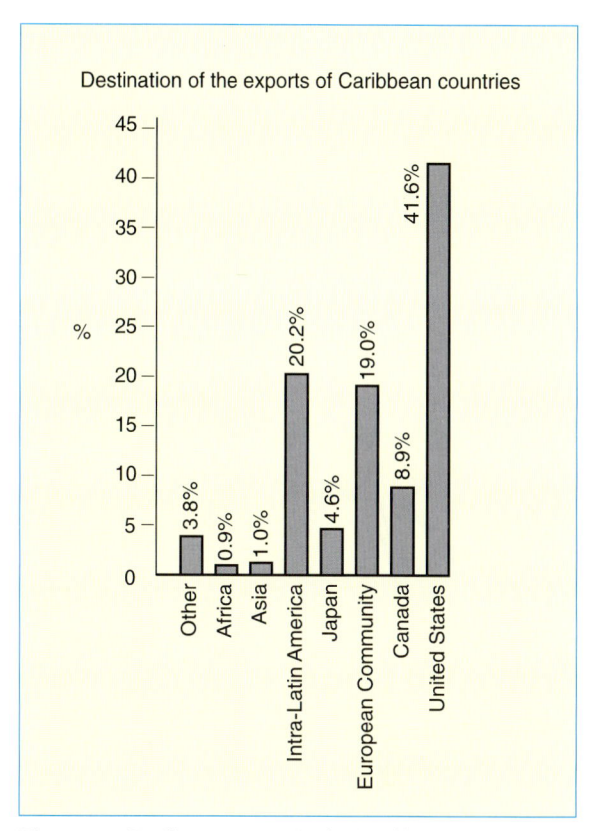

Fig. 21.2 *Trading partners in the Caribbean*

Destination of the exports of Caribbean countries:
- Other: 3.8%
- Africa: 0.9%
- Asia: 1.0%
- Intra-Latin America: 20.2%
- Japan: 4.6%
- European Community: 19.0%
- Canada: 8.9%
- United States: 41.6%

- A *favourable* balance of payments exists when there is net inflow of capital. The country has earned more than it has spent.
- An *adverse* balance exists when there is a net currency outflow. The country has spent more than it has earned.

The balance of payments comprises the **current account** and the **capital account**. The current account records trade in goods and services. The capital account records flows for investment and saving purposes. Table 21.4 shows three examples of imaginary balance of payments figures.

Correcting a balance of payments deficit

A recurring balance of payments deficit situation is worrying for any country because it means that there is a sustained outflow of funds – the country is spending more than it earns.

A current account deficit can only be tolerated in the short term. A persistent current account deficit must be dealt with eventually, because other countries are effectively having to lend to the deficit country; they will not permit this to continue indefinitely.

The following are temporary measures that a country can take to correct an adverse balance of payments problem, but these are not satisfactory in the long term because often they only delay tackling a more deep-seated problem.

➤ Borrowing from the International Monetary Fund.
➤ Obtaining loans from abroad.
➤ Drawing on gold and currency reserves.
➤ Selling off foreign assets.

The best way to solve a deficit problem is to increase exports. Governments can help to achieve this by offering incentives to firms involved in exporting goods. These incentives may take the form of tax relief and extended or special credit facilities, or subsidies on home produced goods to make them cheaper.

There are a variety of other strategies that a country may use in an attempt to combat a persistent balance of payments deficit. These include devaluation, deflation, exchange control and import control.

Devaluation

Devaluation means lowering the value of a currency in relation to other currencies. This makes imported goods more expensive and exports cheaper. For example, if your country's dollar is devalued by 10%, overseas buyers will now only have to pay 90 cents for items that previously cost them $1. Conversely, you will have to pay $1.10 for imported goods which prior to devaluation cost $1.

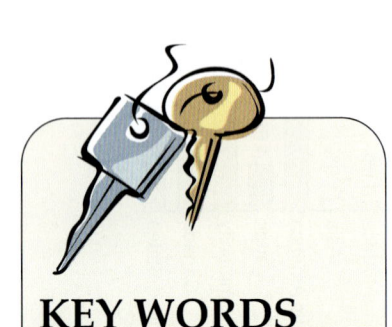

Deflation

If people's income (or its spending power) is reduced, this can lead to a reduction in imports because people will buy fewer goods, including imports. Deflation can be achieved by wage-rise controls, restricting credit and hire purchase, increasing interest rates and increasing taxes.

Exchange control

The central bank may take direct action to reduce outward flows of currency by **exchange control**: placing limits on the amount of foreign currency that can be bought. By refusing requests for foreign currency, the central bank reduces the supply of domestic currency on the market, thus raising the price of the currency.

Import control

The two main methods of restricting imports are by the use of **tariffs** and **quotas**. A tariff is a duty or tax imposed on imports to increase their cost and discourage purchase. A quota is a numerical limit put on the quantity of a commodity permitted to be imported. Both of these methods are dealt with later in this chapter.

KEY WORDS

Find out the business-related meaning of each of the following terms. Write a separate sentence for each term to show your understanding.

devaluation   invisibles
current account
import control
deflation
balance of payments
exchange control
capital account

21.4 Methods of selling abroad

The channels for selling abroad can be grouped into two broad categories: (1) selling from the home base, and (2) selling from an overseas base.

Selling from the home base

There are several ways in which an exporter can sell abroad without going overseas. Advertising in foreign journals or circulating catalogues, brochures and other sales literature can be effective, although some items are not easy to describe and more direct contact is necessary. This can be achieved through contact with the agents of overseas buyers visiting the home country.

Where a firm is not large enough to operate its own export department, it may use an **export house**, which is a firm that specialises in securing orders from abroad. The export house may act as a merchant or an agent.

Chapter 21 – **Global trade**

- *Merchant:* the export house actually buys the goods from the producer and then markets the goods overseas, accepting the risk of loss.
- *Agent:* the export house may market the goods on behalf of the seller, from whom it receives a commission.

Selling from an overseas base

The firm may send its own representatives overseas to make direct contact with potential customers. Alternatively, the exporter might employ an agent already based overseas and willing to seek contracts for sales in return for a commission.

Whichever of the foregoing approaches is employed, the representative or agent is helped by trade fairs and exhibitions, which provide a useful meeting place for buyers and sellers involved in international trade.

21.5 Difficulties faced by exporters

We have already recognised that it is important for a country to export in order to pay for its imports; but companies that engage in foreign trade face a number of difficulties. Some of these are also experienced in home trade, others are particularly evident in overseas trade. The main problems can be summarised as follows.

- *Language:* the exporter needs to be conversant with the language of the country to which he or she intends to export.
- *Differences in measurements, weights and sizes* have to be taken into account by the exporter.
- *Suitability* of products needs to be considered due to differing regulations, safety standards, etc. in some foreign countries.
- *Import regulations:* the exporter must observe and be familiar with the import regulations of other countries.
- *Damage* to goods during their long journey to the customer.
- *Packaging* may need to be stronger than that used for home trade.
- *Transport* will be more difficult to organise than for home trade, and the method chosen must be efficient and economic.
- *Documentation* and payment arrangements can be complicated in overseas trading.
- *Agent:* it may be necessary to find a suitable agent to act on behalf of the exporters to make contracts for the sale of goods.
- *Payment* defaults by overseas customers are more difficult to sort out than those in home trade.
- *Exchange rate fluctuations* can adversely affect the market price of exports:
    a) a *rise* in the value of the dollar results in a fall in the cost of imports, and a rise in the price of exports.
    b) a *fall* in the value of the dollar results in a fall in the cost of exports and a rise in the price of imports.

21.6 Free trade restrictions

If every country specialised in the things it does best, and then its products were freely traded anywhere in the world, all countries would gain maximum benefit. In fact, free trade between countries is difficult to organise.

Principles of Business – Profile 3

Countries sometimes use a variety of techniques in order to restrict free trade, sometimes in an attempt to correct an adverse balance of payments.

Subsidies

A government may give finance – a subsidy – towards the cost of the home-produced product to enable it to be sold at a lower price abroad.

Tariffs

These are a tax or custom duty imposed on imported goods to raise the price of foreign goods to the home consumer and thus protect the home market. There are two types of tariffs, which are collected by the customs department.

- **Specific duties** are a set price for each item imported.
- **Ad valorem duties** are calculated as a percentage of the value of the imports.

Note The importer can place goods in a 'bonded warehouse' under customs supervision until they are able to pay the duty due, or until the goods are re-exported.

Import and export licences

Many traders and manufacturers will import raw materials or finished goods as part of their production and trading activities. In order to import goods and materials, the **importer** requires an **import licence** provided by the government. Sometimes the government may put restrictions (through **quotas**) on the issue of licences. They may do this to restrict imports to protect home producers, or to stop an outflow of currency. Similarly, an **exporter** may require an **export licence** to send goods out of the country. Although governments usually want firms to export in order to bring currency into the economy, they may refuse granting of an export licence. For example, the government may want to stop the export of 'sensitive' products such as national treasures, works of art, armaments, or products related to endangered species.

Quotas

A quota is a limit on the quantity of a product allowed to enter the country during the year. An 'import licence' must be obtained before goods subject to quota restrictions can be imported.

Exchange controls

Sometimes a country will restrict the availability to importers of foreign currency, thus restricting their ability to pay for imports.

Embargo

This is a straightforward government ban on trading between one country and another.

Reasons countries have trade restrictions

There are four main reasons why a country may decide to impose trade restrictions.

- *To protect home producers.* Infant (newly formed) industries may need protection until they have become sufficiently established to be able to

KEY WORDS

Find out the business-related meaning of each of the following terms. Write a separate sentence for each term to show your understanding.

import licence
free trade   ad valorem
duty   dumping   tariff
subsidies   export house
quota   export licence
specific duties

compete fairly. Other industries may require protection because they are important to future national security.

- *To resist dumping.* Dumping means selling goods at a loss abroad. Some countries dump goods abroad either to reduce supplies at home or to increase their share of the market overseas. This kind of action can be very damaging to some industries in the country where the goods are being dumped.
- *To safeguard jobs.* Even when goods are brought into a country fairly and competitively, their import may threaten a particular industry. Under such circumstances the importing country may feel it necessary to introduce trade restrictions.
- *To correct a balance of payments deficit.* A continuous balance of payments deficit cannot be ignored. One way in which a deficit can be rectified is by reducing imports by the imposition of import control.

21.7 Seeking assistance

Borrowing from another country

Sometimes Caribbean countries seek assistance from their neighbours, or from other stronger economies, to curb some of their balance of payments problems. The money borrowed has to be repaid in due course and, usually, with some interest payment involved. In other words, the loan may solve a temporary problem, but eventually it has to be faced and the economic problem remains but has been delayed until another time.

Accepting gifts from another country

Caribbean countries accept gifts from other countries at times. For example, China and Japan have helped to alleviate some of the technical problems associated with their balance of payments. During the 1980s, the USA provided Jamaica with US$1 billion. Most of the funding went to balance of payments support. By the mid-1980s funding was typically transferred in the form of grants rather than concessional loans. AIDS assistance to Caribbean countries has also been accepted, which supported the policies of the IMF and the World Bank. Where such gifts do not compromise the governments of the recipient countries, they are of course most welcome, especially if they are truly gifts and do carry any 'hidden' penalties.

Importing on credit

Importing refers to the sale of a product which is produced in a foreign country. When importing on credit the importer gains access to the goods and pays for them at some later date. The fact that the debt eventually has to be paid does not mean to say there is no benefit from this arrangement. For example, the importer has the opportunity to sell the item before payment has to be made. However, from the point of view of the country's economy as a whole, the situation is somewhat different. Some countries may import goods on credit using this facility, especially if they are suffering from a balance of payments problem. Although the relief is only temporary as the debt must eventually be repaid, this will give the country time to recuperate from financial strain over a period of time.

Principles of Business – Profile 3

Borrowing from the IMF

You will have read elsewhere in this book that the International Monetary Fund (IMF) is an international organisation of some 184 countries that was conceived as a financial institution to assist member countries who are experiencing balance of payments problems. The IMF will lend to these countries the money to assist them, at a relatively favourable rate of interest. In return, the borrowing countries are required to implement a set of economic reforms aimed at overcoming their balance of payments difficulties. Loans are disbursed in instalments and payments are tied to the countries' compliance with structural adjustment policies imposed by the IMF. These policies are geared towards reducing inflation and public debt, or strengthening the financial system.

Borrowing from the IMF is not without its encumbrances. From the foregoing you will have observed that by borrowing from the fund, there is some loss of State authority to govern its own economy. There are also possible ethical repercussions. For example, infrastructural projects financed by the IMF may have environmental implications for the populations in the affected area. Similarly, if the IMF granted money to support deregulation of State-owned industries, this may undermine the role of the State as the primary provider of essential services, such as education and health care, resulting in a shortfall of such services in the region.

The difficulty involved in borrowing from the IMF, or the several other international financial institutions that exist (e.g. the World Bank), is that in due course the debt has to be repaid, so eventually the country borrowing has meet the debt and the additional charge for the loan. However, in desperate times such institutions give countries a bit of 'breathing space' within which they have time to possibly recover from a difficult situation. But invariably, having to resort to such measures places some form of restriction on the government and the economy it manages.

KEY WORDS

Find out the business-related meaning of each of the following terms. Write a separate sentence for each term to show your understanding.

- interest
- economic problem
- inflation   credit
- essential services
- infrastructure
- public debt
- deregulation

21.8 Things to do

This section contains a variety of exercises to help you create revision notes, to test your understanding and to prepare you for examinations.

Search and find

Write out the question and the answer by referring back through the text to form revision notes.

1. Why do countries need to trade?
2. Define the terms 'imports' and 'exports'.
3. Explain the term 'principle of comparative costs'.
4. Give one result of following the above principle.
5. Why is foreign trade particularly important to the Caribbean region?
6. Define 'balance of trade'.

Chapter 21 – **Global trade**

7. What are 'visibles'? Give three examples.
8. Explain each of the following terms: a) trade gap b) surplus c) deficit.
9. What are 'invisibles'? Give three examples.
10. Explain the following statement. 'Balance of trade is related to visible trade, but balance of payments includes both visible and invisible trade.'
11. Why is it important to try to achieve a favourable balance of payments?
12. Briefly describe ways in which an exporter can sell abroad without actually going overseas.
13. Explain the difference between the work of merchants and agents.
14. Briefly describe eight problems, other than fluctuation in exchange rates, that are faced by exporters.
15. Clearly explain how fluctuation in exchange rates can affect the price of both imports and exports.
16. What are tariffs? Describe the two ways by which tariffs are collected.
17. What is the function of a bonded warehouse?
18. What is a quota?
19. When is it necessary to obtain an import licence?
20. Why might a government subsidise home-produced goods?
21. What is an embargo?
22. Summarise the four main reasons countries impose trade restrictions.
23. Briefly describe some of the external assistance that exists to help the economies of a country.
24. In what ways can the acceptance of assistance from external sources be not only helpful to a country, but can also have adverse effects?

What do you know?

Write out the complete sentence and insert the missing word, which can be chosen from the list at the end of the questions.

1. The overseas market can provide additional ..... for a business.
2. ..... are goods brought into the country.
3. Goods sent out of a country are called ..... .
4. Every country must keep its ..... within the limits of its income.
5. When exports exceed imports, the balance of trade is said to be ..... .
6. If a country imports more than it exports, the balance of trade is said to be ..... .
7. An export ..... is a firm that specialises in securing orders from abroad.
8. A government might impose trade ..... to protect home producers.
9. Sometimes a country restricts the availability of foreign ....., which makes it difficult to pay for imports.
10. When importing goods on ..... the importer gains access to the goods and pays later.

Choose the missing words from the following:

adverse   credit   income   currency   house   exports   favourable   restrictions   imports   spending

Principles of Business – Profile 3

Structured questions

Q1 Consider figure 21.3.

(a) What do the letters CARTIS and CEDP stand for? **1**

(b) What is a 'profile'? **2**

(c) Why might a business not involved in foreign trade be interested in obtaining 'profiles' of exporters, importers, manufacturers or producers? **3**

(d) What 'trade' opportunities might a business obtain through the services of CARTIS and CEDP? **4**

(e) What are 'non-tariff barriers'? **4**

(f) Explain the sort of 'market research data' that a firm interested in breaking into overseas trade would find useful. **6**

NEED TRADE INFORMATION?

OUR TRADE INFORMATION NETWORK CAN PROVIDE THE FOLLOWING SERVICES
- Profiles of exporters/importers/manufacturers/producers
- Trade opportunities
- Market research data, including import/export regulations, non-tariff barriers
- Trade statistics

Contact our head office in Barbados
Tel: (809) 436-0578 Fax: (809) 436-9999/436-2820
Or your National Trade Promotion Office

CARTIS The Caribbean Trade Information Service
CEDP Caricom Export Development Project
A Project of the Caribbean Community Secretariat

Fig. 21.3 *Trade information advertisement*

Q2 Look at the imaginary balance of payments figures for three countries in table 21.5, and answer the following questions.

(a) Which country has the poorest trade balance? **1**

(b) Which country has the most favourable balance of payments? **1**

(c) Explain clearly the difference between exports and imports. **2**

(d) Explain the terms 'visible' and 'invisible' and give three examples in each case. **4**

(e) Use examples from the figures shown in the table to assist you to explain the difference between the balance of trade and the balance of payments. **6**

(f) Describe the likely effect on your country's balance of payments if there was:
   (i) a decline in the number of tourists visiting your country
   (ii) a devaluation of the dollar in relation to other countries.
   Give reasons for your answers. **6**

Balance of payments figures ($ million)

Country 1
Visible exports	+48,440	
Visible imports	−47,322	
Balance of trade		+1,118 surplus
Invisible exports	+25,650	
Invisible imports	−23,120	
		+2,530 surplus
Balance of payments on current account		+3,648 surplus

Country 2
Visible exports	+40,288	
Visible imports	−42,366	
Balance of trade		−2,078 deficit
Invisible exports	+25,650	
Invisible imports	−20,972	
		+4,678 surplus
Balance of payments on current account		+2,600 surplus

Country 3
Visible exports	+48,440	
Visible imports	−47,322	
Balance of trade		+1,118 surplus
Invisible exports	+23,120	
Invisible imports	−25,650	
		−2,530 deficit
Balance of payments on current account		−1,412 deficit

Table 21.5 *Trade figures for three countries*

Chapter 21 – Global trade

Q3

(a) State two sources of help for exporters. **2**

(b) Why is it important for all countries to try to sell overseas? **2**

(c) Describe briefly the likely effect on your country of each of the following:
   (i) increased expenditure by the residents of your country on holidays overseas
   (ii) a foreign country is 'dumping' goods on your market that are already being produced in factories in your country. **6**

(d) Explain the significance of each of the following to overseas trade:
   (i) tariff   (ii) quota   (iii) embargo   (iv) exchange control   (v) subsidies. **10**

Q4 Study the information in figure 21.4 and answer the questions related to it.

(a) Give two examples of specialisation that are evident in international trade. **2**

(b) In what way can international trade provide opportunities for greater economies of scale? **2**

(c) How does competition from abroad encourage home-based producers to become more efficient? **3**

(d) List three items which consumers in your country could not buy without foreign trade. **3**

(e) Why is it more difficult for businesses to trade overseas than at home? **4**

(f) Suggest three ways that your country could encourage more overseas tourists to visit it. **6**

THE BENEFITS OF FOREIGN TRADE

All countries gain advantages from trade with other countries. These advantages benefit both industry and consumers. Businesses can benefit from the opportunities they gain for increased specialisation and greater economies of scale. Another advantage of foreign trade is that the increased competition that comes from abroad encourages home-based producers to become more efficient. However, a major benefit for consumers is that they are able to choose from a wider range of goods and services.

Fig. 21.4

Research assignments

1. Describe some of the difficulties faced by exporters and say how these problems may be overcome. What evidence can you provide that shows the problems do exist, and that they can be overcome?

2. Describe the various methods a manufacturer from your country might employ to sell his or her products overseas, including mention of the various agencies that can be used. To what extent do you feel your government helps exporters?

3. 'Overseas trade is important to every member of our country.' Discuss this statement using specific examples related to your country to justify your answer.

4. 'Imports threaten home producers and can ruin national prosperity.' Discuss this statement, incorporating the views of others obtained through your own first-hand research.

Regional and global business environment

22.1 Caribbean economic institutions

Regional co-operation

There is hardly a country on this planet, whether rich or poor, large or small, which does not need to co-operate with at least one other country in order to meet its needs. But why do countries need to co-operate? Countries need to co-operate because the world's resources are not evenly distributed. In other words, no one country has all the resources it needs. For example, the peoples of the Caribbean are heavy consumers of bread, but the region does not produce the wheat that is needed to make bread. Therefore, the region has to import wheat from wheat-producing countries that can supply the product in the quantities needed. Likewise, countries of the Caribbean produce sugar, spices, bauxite, rice, citrus, oil, and timber among other products, for regional as well as international trade. To facilitate the necessary trade agreements, countries need to agree on trade policies related to import and export quotas, financing, transportation, foreign exchange, terms of trade and so on. Therefore, co-operation is almost mandatory if nations are to survive.

Regional trade

Regional trade has been a major feature of the Caribbean and is being facilitated through **regional strategies**. One such strategy is the Caribbean Community or CARICOM. International trade has also been seen as important among Caribbean nations for centuries. Caribbean countries rely on other countries buying their products such as coffee, spices, banana, sugar, bauxite, oil, rubber and other products. It is by selling products such as these that Caribbean countries are able to buy the many other items they need.

Local organisations

Chambers of commerce

Chambers of commerce are comprised of businesses involved in commercial activities. The major concerns of such businesses are addressed and are represented at the highest level possible.

Caribbean Association of Industry and Commerce (CAIC)

In this association, individual chambers of commerce are represented. Members focus on the problems of trade in the region, and how they can co-operate in fostering the growth and development of commerce. Issues of trade are addressed at their forum.

Manufacturers' associations

These are local associations of manufacturers. Their main concern is how to maximise manufacturing; a most important contributor to economic activity in a country. The concerns of manufacturing are also concerns of the governments since production is at the heart of economic development.

Economic institutions

The Caribbean Community (CARICOM)

The Caribbean Community and Common Market was established by the Treaty of Chaguaramas, and was put into effect on August 1, 1973. From its inception, the Community has concentrated on the promotion of the integration of the economies of Member States, by co-ordinating the foreign policies of the Independent Member States and by functional co-operation, particularly in relation to various areas of social and human endeavour.

CARICOM is the region's premier economic institution. It was established to encourage the region's development. It is in effect a movement towards *regional integration*, fostering economic co-operation in the region. CARICOM comprises the countries of the English-speaking Caribbean. Other countries have become members since the initial formation, because they are neighbours, even though their language may be different. A major focus of CARICOM has been the Caribbean Common Market (CCM). The CCM involves a group arrangement whereby the aim is that:

- Member countries do not impose duties on goods traded between them.
- Members do not restrict the quantity of goods to be traded among themselves.
- There is a common agreement among member states on the rate at which duty should be charged on goods imported from countries outside the Community.

The structure of CARICOM

The main body of CARICOM is *The Heads of Government Conference*, which is responsible for policy-making and direction. It has the ultimate authority on issues associated with CARICOM. The *ministers of government* comprise the *Common Market*, and they have the overall responsibility for its functions. The body that is charged with the responsibility of carrying out the decisions of the Heads of Government Conference is the CARICOM *Secretariat*.

Caribbean Single Market and Economy (CSME)

The CARICOM Single Market and Economy (CSME) has now become a reality through the Revised Treaty of Chaguaramas, which provides the legal

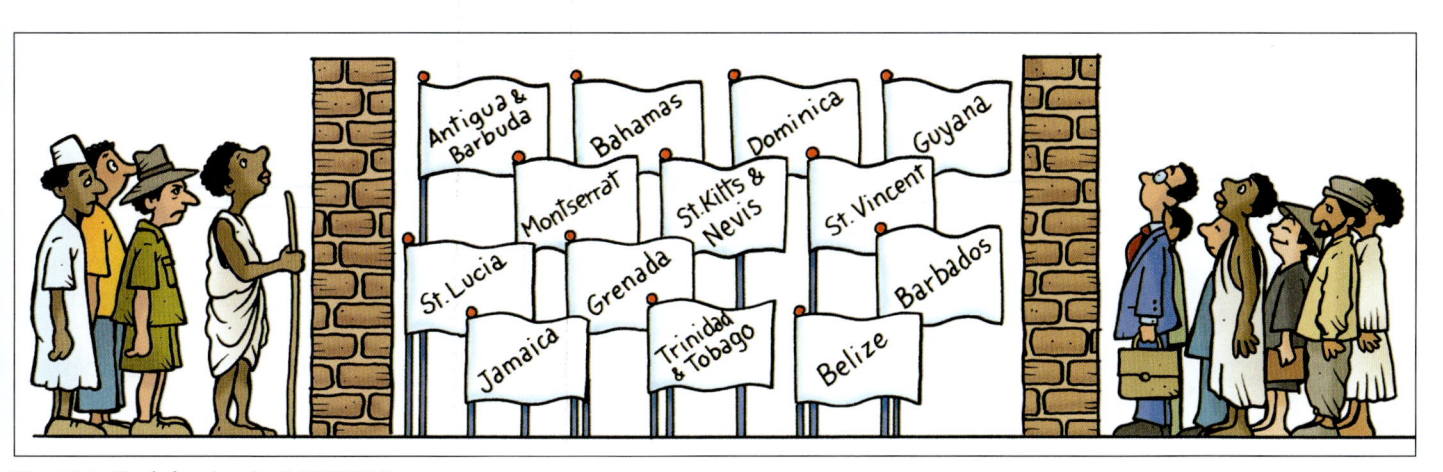

Fig. 22.1 *Trade barriers in CARICOM*

Principles of Business – Profile 3

status for the operation of the CSME. The CSME is designed to represent a single 'economic space' where people, goods, services and capital can move freely. This also requires the harmonisation and co-ordination of social, economic and trade policies by participating member states. Many of the required changes have already been made gradually by the participating territories, and others will be brought into effect in due course.

The CSME effectively means that there are no longer borders that prevent companies from selling in CARICOM markets or protect them from competition from other CARICOM firms. The single market enlarges the space for both sales and competition. It also allows for mergers and acquisitions within the CARICOM area, permitting companies to become larger and enjoy greater economies of scale, such as attracting more capital and investing in new technology. This will go some way to overcome the 'smallness' that has restricted the economic growth of Caribbean states.

Overall, it can be said that the CSME is intended to benefit the people and businesses of the region by providing more opportunities to produce and sell goods and services and to attract investment. It will create one large market among participating member states. It will also allow free movement of labour. Some of the eventual full effects of CSME can be summarised as follows:

- *Free movement of goods and services.* The elimination of all barriers to intra-regional movement and harmonising standards to ensure acceptability of goods and services traded.
- *Right of establishment.* To permit the establishment of CARICOM-owned businesses in any member state without restrictions.
- *A common external tariff.* A rate of duty applied by all members of the market to a country that is not a member of the market.
- *Free circulation.* Free movement of goods imported from extra-regional sources that would require collection of taxes at first point of entry into the region and the provision for sharing of collected customs revenue.
- *Free movement of capital.* Through measures such as eliminating foreign exchange controls, convertibility of currencies (or a common currency) and an integrated capital market, such as regional stock exchange.
- *A common trade policy.* Agreement among the members on matters related to internal and international trade and an external trade policy negotiated on a joint basis.
- *Free movement of labour.* Removal of all obstacles to intra-regional movement of skills, labour and travel, harmonising social services (education, health, etc.), providing for the transfer of social security benefits and establishing standards for accreditation and equivalency.

The International Monetary Fund (IMF)

The IMF was established in 1944 at a 'monetary conference' in Bretton Woods in the United States of America. Its major purpose is to provide short-term lending to countries that are experiencing balance of payments problems by providing foreign currency needed to pay for goods and services. Member countries contribute to the fund. Amounts contributed are set aside to be drawn upon in time of need. In this way, members have special drawing rights. Draw down from the IMF funds are based upon how much a country has contributed.

The IMF provision can be summarised as follows:

KEY WORDS

Find out the business-related meaning of each of the following terms. Write a separate sentence for each term to show your understanding.

- mergers
- economies of scale
- social policies
- regional integration
- acquisitions
- economic space
- economic policies
- trade policies

Chapter 22 – **Regional and global business environment**

> It provides short-term loans or temporary loans to countries.
> It helps countries in need and sets economic targets for them.
> It sets tough or stringent guidelines for economic management.

Unfortunately, many countries experience social and political hardships and consequently they are often not able to meet the IMF targets.

The Caribbean Development Bank (CDB)

This is a financial institution that has been established by Caribbean nations. The major aim of the bank is to provide funding for economic activities in the region. Additionally, the bank administers loans programmes for funding agencies. The CDB loans assist member states with activities associated with tourism, health and education, and agriculture, among other areas. Interest rates are low compared with those charged by other financial institutions. Member states also enjoy a 'period of grace' on the loan repayment plans. This means that the loan repayments do not begin as the contract would normally have dictated, but at a later date worked out between the member state and the bank, hence the loans are termed 'soft loans'. The International Bank for Reconstruction and Development (IBRD) provides financial services to the CDB.

World Bank

The World Bank (formerly The International Bank for Reconstruction and Development – IBRD) is an international institution established in 1947 to provide aid for developing countries to develop their economies through loans and technical assistance. The World Bank supports a wide range of projects in the less developed countries including the establishment of infrastructure (roads, gas and water supplies, schools and hospitals), the modernisation of traditional industries such as farm mechanisation and cultivation techniques, and the setting up of new industries, for example steel and textiles.

The Bank's resources come largely from subscriptions from the advanced countries, although it also issues its own securities to raise additional funds. Generally, the bank lends on a commercial basis (i.e. loans are repaid with market-related interest charges), but it also provides low interest ('soft') loans through an affiliate association.

The Inter-American Development Bank (IADB)

The services provided by this bank are similar to those provided by the World Bank. However, the beneficiaries of funding are the Latin American, Caribbean and North American countries. The major providers of funding are the United States of America and Canada.

The Organisation of Eastern Caribbean States (OECS)

This body comprises of the *less developed* countries of CARICOM. These countries include Antigua and Barbuda, Dominica, Grenada, Montserrat, St. Kitts and Nevis, St. Lucia, St. Vincent and the Grenadines, and Grenada. The OECS Treaty was signed in 1981, and the headquarters is located in St. Lucia.

The OECS aims to bring about:

> reasonable and workable trading arrangements among members, their CARICOM sister states and the international community
> economic and political integration

- common policies in areas such as agriculture and hospitality and tourism
- common practices and procedures in industrial policies to prevent unfair competition among countries
- establishment of a single central bank
- a single currency – the Eastern Caribbean dollar (EC dollar).

The Organisation of American States (OAS)

This organisation was established in 1948 and its major objective is to foster good relations among countries of the Americas. Membership of the OAS is drawn from North America, Latin America and the Caribbean. The body is governed by a Charter that sets out the general purposes and principles, the nature of the organisation, and the rights and obligations of members. The major concerns of the OAS are:

- the fostering of good relations among members
- settling disputes when they arise between members
- assisting with the maintenance of cultural heritage of the members
- assisting with obtaining and monitoring aid programmes
- providing training through scholarship programmes.

Economic Commission for Latin American Countries (ECLAC)

This is one of the five regional commissions of the United Nations, each of which is concerned with assisting and promoting economic and social development in a major region of the world. Created in 1948, ECLAC currently serves 33 governments from the Latin American and Caribbean region, together with several nations of Northern America and Europe that maintain historical, cultural and economic ties with the region. The Commission, therefore, has 41 member states and seven non-independent Caribbean territories hold the status of associate members.

ECLAC serves as a centre of excellence in the region. It collaborates with its member states and, with a variety of local and international institutions, in undertaking a comprehensive analysis of development processes based on an examination of the design, follow-up and research tasks. It also provides technical assistance, training and information services in selected cases.

Association of Caribbean States (ACS)

The convention establishing the ACS was signed on 24th July 1994 in Cartagena de Indies, Columbia, with the aim of promoting consultation, co-operation and concerted action among all the countries of the Caribbean, comprising 25 member states and three associate members.

The functions of the ACS can be summarised as:

- the strengthening of regional co-operation and the integration process, with a view to creating an enhanced economic space in the region
- preserving the environmental integrity of the Caribbean Sea on behalf of the peoples of the region
- promoting the sustainable development of the greater Caribbean.

The main organs of the association are the Ministerial Council, which is the principal body for policy making and direction of the Association and the Secretariat. The functions of the Secretariat are:

Chapter 22 – Regional and global business environment

> daily interactions with member states, social partners, Founding Observer organisations, regional and international organisations, donor agencies and countries on activities and fund raising related to the plan of action
> to execute the budget and work programmed
> strategic planning
> promotion of the ACS.

At present the ACS is:

> working on the sustainable tourism zone of the Caribbean
> facilitating language training
> working on the Caribbean Sea initiative
> co-ordinating an annual business forum of the Caribbean
> defending the interest and treatment of small economies
> updating building codes
> strengthening disaster contingencies.

22.2 International organisations involved in trade

European Union (EU)

A free trade bloc is a territorial grouping of countries that have dismantled all restrictions on cross frontier trade between themselves. The European Union (EU) and NAFTA (see below) are examples of this kind of development.

The European Union (formerly called the European Community) is a European regional bloc that was established to promote free trade between member countries, and the development of unification of economic, social and political systems of the member countries. The EU has expanded the number of its member states considerably since its inception and today it is a massive trading and economic bloc.

There is a wide range of rules and regulations that are applied to all firms trading in the EU, and in particular the free trade agreement that means that there are no customs duties on goods and services traded in the area. A common external tariff is placed on all imports into EU member states.

Many regulations that affect businesses of member states are monitored by the European Parliament rather than the governments of the member states. These include:

> Legislation supporting free competition between firms, thus banning practices such as price fixing and other activities that inhibit competition.
> A guaranteed fixed price to farmers for most agricultural products.
> Loans through a Regional Development Fund to influence the location of businesses.
> Regulations to make transparent the ingredients and additives in food, and appropriate packaging standards.

A single currency (the Euro –) has been introduced to become the official currency of the EU members, although some EU countries have decided not to adopt the Euro.

World Trade Organisation (WTO)

The WTO is a body established to perform a similar role to the GATT. Its

351

responsibility is for the administration of multilateral trade agreements that are negotiated by its members. It provides a forum through which rounds of negotiations can take place. It maintains a very tight dispute settlement procedure and a new trade policy review mechanism. In other words, members of trade agreements who believe strongly that unfair practices are being pursued by other members, can take their cases to the WTO.

The banana trade provides an example of the effect of the WTO. Banana is a major earner of foreign currency for the Caribbean. The banana industry also provides employment for a large number of persons. However, the 1990s have seen political changes in Europe leading to the establishment of a Single Market. The market adopted an open market system. This incorporates co-operation on economic and monetary policy, joint research and technological development, employment and environmental protection and a charter to promote social cohesion and thus reduction of regional disparities. This means the Caribbean banana industry can no longer continue to receive special treatment from the United Kingdom, which is a member of the European Union.

The United States, on behalf of one of its companies that are involved in the banana trade in Latin America, complained to the WTO about the preferential treatment of some countries in the banana trade – the Caribbean countries were the main targets. The USA argued and lobbied for the removal of the preferential treatment to allow for an open market. The WTO eventually accepted the USA proposal, and the result is that the Caribbean banana industry has come under severe economic pressure.

Caribbean Basin Initiative (CBI)

The CBI is a trade agreement between the USA and countries of the Caribbean Basin which allows 'preferential trading opportunities' for a wide range of Caribbean goods, such as garments, foods and a wide range of 'new' export products. This has enabled a range of non-traditional products from the Caribbean to enter the US market on preferential terms.

Organisation of Petroleum Exporting Countries (OPEC)

The term cartel is a form of collusion between a group of suppliers who make arrangements to limit output in order to keep prices artificially high. In order to do this the cartel must be in control of a large percentage of the output. OPEC is one of the world's major cartels.

This organisation was founded in 1960 by a group of the world's oil exporting countries, particularly those in the Middle East. The member countries co-operate to fix oil prices and control competition with the aim of protecting their interests, although they have also from time to time provided financial assistance to developing countries that are not members of OPEC.

The Eastern Caribbean Common Market (ECCM)

The ECCM is an outcome of the OECS Agreement. The establishment of the ECCM was a major objective of the OECS.

Major trade agreements

North American Free Trade Agreement (NAFTA)

NAFTA is a regional free trade area established by the USA and Canada and Mexico. NAFTA aimed to remove trade barriers for most manufactured

Chapter 22 – Regional and global business environment

goods, raw materials and agricultural produce, as well as restrictions on cross-border investment, banking and financial services. It is intended that there will also be freer movement of labour between the countries.

Free Trade Areas of the Americas (FTAA)

FTAA is a proposed agreement to eliminate or reduce trade barriers among all nations in the American Continents (except Cuba). Negotiations have been going on between some 34 nations. The proposed agreement is modelled after the above North American Free Trade Agreement (NAFTA). FTAA aims are summarised as follows:

- Trade laws that reduce poverty.
- Trade policies that create employment and protect workers' rights.
- Democratic trade negotiations that involve citizen consultation and participation.
- Trade policies that protect environmental and public interests.
- Trade policies that support family farmers and food security.
- Trade policies that encourage investment in sustainable development.

Although the foregoing aims are creditable, FTAA has not escaped criticism. Some political activists have expressed concern with the FTAA's plans to:

- Expand corporate rights (giving corporations the right to sue governments directly).
- Increase power to overturn national, state and local laws, particularly those seen as a 'barrier' to free trade.
- Privatise essential public services (e.g. water, health care and education).
- The 'locking' of some 34 countries into a corporate dominated legal system that would be difficult to reverse.

The Caribbean Canadian Agreement (CARIBCAN)

This agreement exists between Canada and the English-speaking Caribbean. The initiative allows for 98% duty-free concession on non-traditional products from the Caribbean entering the Canadian market.

General Agreement on Tariffs and Trade (GATT)

GATT was implemented in 1948. The major aim of the agreement is to promote free trade among its members. GATT supports the principle that no discrimination in tariff agreements should be levied against any member state. Therefore, the agreement aims to achieve free trade agreements among members through the reduction of tariffs and quotas.

The Caribbean, as well as other developing countries, have been able to arrive at an agreement called the Generalised Trade Preference. This permits developing countries to receive duty-free concessions on manufactured goods that they sell on the world market to developed countries.

The Association of African, Caribbean and Pacific Countries (ACP–LOME)

The LOME Convention, established in 1975, is another international trade agreement designed to foster international trade. Over 60 former British and French colonies were signatories to the LOME agreement. The agreement has been reviewed a number of times since its inception with the aim of making it

KEY WORDS

Find out the business-related meaning of each of the following terms. Write a separate sentence for each term to show your understanding.

regional cooperation
economic activities
free competition
cartel   free trade
infrastructure
drawing rights
external tariff

as reasonable as possible. It allows 94% of the agricultural products of ACP–LOME countries to enter the European Union duty-free. Countries are assigned quotas specifying the quantity they are allowed to trade in this manner. Caribbean countries trade mainly in sugar and bananas.

The LOME agreement includes an aid programme administered by the European Development Fund. Countries can obtain funding for road construction, the building of schools and for training.

The agreement also provides an Export Earnings Stabilisation facility to aid countries that experience adverse effects on their products as a result of natural disasters.

As a result of the closer linking together of the countries in the European Union, a number of these arrangements have changed and, therefore, Caribbean countries have had to seek other ways and means of marketing their products competitively.

22.3 Caribbean economic problems

The economic problem

Caribbean countries, like many other developing countries, face a number of difficulties. These include overpopulation, unemployment, limited natural resources, a largely unskilled labour force, and technical and scientific knowledge that is inadequate to meet the demands of modern society. Some areas of the region are at an advanced stage of development, whilst others are backward (economic dualism). These weaknesses are perpetuated by an inadequate infrastructure. A major result of this is insufficient inflow of foreign currency, thus making economic development difficult to sustain.

Because Caribbean economies are closely linked to and dependent upon the economies of developed countries, any economic difficulties experienced by those economies tend to be felt in the region's economies also.

Industrialisation

Industrialisation refers to business activities such as production or manufacturing. Thus we speak of the clothing industry, and the motor industry. Machine technology plays a major part in the transformation of raw materials into finished or semi-finished goods. This technology has to be financed through carefully planned investment and government support, sometimes through pooled resources. The major heavy industrial activities undertaken in the Caribbean region are in the areas of oil drilling and oil refinement, natural gas extraction, bauxite mining, production of petrochemicals and electronics.

Industrialisation has several consequences:

- The creation of jobs for both skilled and unskilled workers.
- Pressure is put on governments to ensure foreign currency is available to buy manufacturing materials and equipment.
- Goods are produced for the local as well as the overseas market.
- Governments earn revenue through taxation.
- More people are employed in manufacturing, which can mean fewer people being available in agriculture.

> There are possible adverse environmental effects such as pollution and contamination.

Industrialisation results in a number of problems for the region. These are now summarised, together with examples of possible solutions.

Disposal of industrial waste

Governments and companies need to develop policies that are implemented and carefully monitored to dispose of industrial waste acceptably. Additionally they have to consider where the residue from one industry could be used in another, and ensure that capital is available to implement such a process. For example, perhaps the clay left over from bauxite production could be used to make bricks for the construction industry.

Primary production dominance

Many Caribbean countries find it difficult to be more than primary producers, mainly because of lack of capital, technical knowledge and the availability of people with the necessary technical skills. Consequently, the region tends to be heavily dependent on the import of raw materials. Governments need to invest greater resources into research directed towards establishing how their primary resources could be utilised in other ways. Petro-chemicals are a typical example that countries could continue to investigate.

Economic and social conflicts

The capital-intensive nature of productive activity, especially in the modern industries, results in high levels of efficiency but it does not contribute to alleviation of the high level of unemployment and other regional problems. Governments and companies need to find ways whereby both economic and social issues are addressed.

Opportunity costs

Heavy industrial activities use much energy. Consequently, Caribbean countries face large energy bills if productive activity is to be fostered. The cost of this energy means that other much-needed goods and services must be foregone. Governments need to determine whether or not the opportunity cost involved is justified.

Plough back

Industries need to be encouraged to plough back a greater proportion of their profits into the business sector to generate more employment.

Light industrial activities are also important to the Caribbean region. These include:

> craft production, especially for the tourist industry
> garment production
> sugar production, flour milling
> food processing.

Problems encountered in the light industrial area are particularly related to distribution. For example, countries find it difficult to break into the international market. Although the region boasts a number of free zones, from which a number of manufacturing companies operate, these are mainly dominated by foreign-operated companies that produce goods especially for particular developed countries. For example, particular lines of clothing are produced for well-known designers for the international and other markets. Governments, therefore, need to continue their lobbying for participation in non-traditional markets.

Governments need to help these light industries to improve their products. For example, the craft industry needs not only funds, but also training for those involved in order to improve the quality of the products. This will increase their chances of participating successfully in the international market.

Unemployment

A large proportion of labour in the Caribbean is tied to agriculture and, because of the seasonal nature of some agricultural products, there are times when people are left unemployed. For example, sugar cane planting and harvesting is seasonal, and a large amount of labour is employed at these times. When the season is over, the workers return to their small-scale farming activities, or to casual work, or no work at all.

Perhaps governments could provide incentives for hoteliers who are willing to develop and market a tourism package for locals to encourage them to take their vacation in the local resorts rather than go overseas on trips which requires the use of much foreign currency.

Much of the local farm products could be produced by the farmers and sold to the tourism sector.

The population growth rate also has an effect on employment. Rapid population growth rate results in rapid growth in the labour force and, with the lack of availability of jobs, this poses many social problems. In this sense, unemployment can be said to create major social costs and also wastes economic resources. There are several types of unemployment in the Caribbean region:

Seasonal unemployment

This occurs in industries such as tourism and agriculture where the seasonal nature of the service or work leads to people being made unemployed at the end of the season's activities.

Casual unemployment

This occurs where persons only work occasionally. They have no set jobs and work mainly doing 'odd jobs'. Such people are classified as casual workers. Persons in this situation could be employed by governments to brush the streets and clean drains and gullies.

Cyclical unemployment

This is sometimes referred to as demand deficient unemployment, because it arises from a general lack of demand for goods and services. Governments could create special works programmes, thus providing employment. From the payments received these workers will demand goods and services. Thus, they bring life back into the economy.

Structural unemployment

This type of unemployment occurs where industries face structural decline through lack of competitiveness. For example, when a product, skill or process becomes out of date or unfashionable, the resulting fall in demand leads to a fall-off in jobs in the industry. Governments could provide incentives such as having no duty on raw materials purchased by these firms enabling them to produce goods competitively, and thus keeping persons employed.

Frictional unemployment

This form of unemployment is temporary and voluntary. The lapse of time between a person leaving one job and finding another is referred to as frictional unemployment.

Residual unemployment

This is associated with persons who only work to achieve a particular goal and then leave the work scene. It also refers to persons in the potential workforce who suffer from some disability that prevents them from being gainfully employed.

Migration

Migration refers to the difference between the total of people entering a country (immigration) and the total of those leaving (emigration). It is not just the number of people who enter or leave the country that is important: the skills they bring with them or take from the country is a significant factor. The knowledge and skills taken out of a country is sometimes referred to as a 'brain drain'. This is a major problem for the Caribbean region. The 'brain drain' has an important effect on economic growth and development.

Governments can help to alleviate the problems of unemployment and migration by:

- encouraging families to observe family planning, and to recognise it as a means of survival
- developing and pursuing policies regarding the location of industries. This could include providing incentives to businesses to locate in areas other than urban areas
- improving social amenities in 'relocation areas' to encourage people to live in such areas
- encouraging more self-help programmes, including training in skills as well as in entrepreneurial skills
- providing loans for small business ventures.

Urbanisation

The term urbanisation refers to the movement of people from rural areas to live in towns and cities. This is sometimes referred to as 'urban drift'. The effect of this movement is often adverse if it is not a controlled development. It can affect both the area the people are moving from, and the area they move to. The area people have moved away from is left with a shortfall in labour and local income. The area they have moved into may find their social amenities overstretched.

Whilst governments want mobility of labour, they also have to restrict the adverse effects of such movement. For example, they may develop policies that ensure business location is evenly spread: providing incentives to encourage businesses to locate in rural areas; ensuring that rural amenities encourage people to live and work in their communities; providing loans to encourage the formation of businesses in rural areas.

Education and economic development

The quality of the workforce of any country depends upon the quality of the education it has received. As Caribbean countries have moved away from their concentration on primary production towards the secondary and tertiary production referred to earlier in this chapter, there has been a need to raise the level of scientific and technological education in order to match the thrust for economic development. Particular attention has been given to technical-vocational education and the raising of industrial awareness.

A variety of educational initiatives have contributed to the aim of making education address the needs of modern industrial society. Skills training programmes have been designed to assist young people to achieve skills relevant to the work situation. A number of these training programmes were funded by the Canadian International Development Agency (CIDA), and the United States Agency for International Development (US AID). In addition, local chambers of commerce have also played a part in helping young people to gain an understanding of how businesses work.

Many other programmes exist, providing entry-, middle- and high-level skilled personnel to meet the needs of the public and private sectors in the Caribbean.

Education makes an important contribution to production because it helps to provide:

- a productive workforce
- skilled personnel required by employers
- economic growth through the training of people
- development of a creative, innovative workforce.

In addition, it is generally recognised that there is a relationship between education and population growth. Education assists in the regulation of family size and therefore assists in the long-term objective of reducing inequalities in our societies.

Caribbean governments have been investing in education. The University of the West Indies and the Caribbean Examinations Council are examples of the commitment of the governments of the region to education collectively. Individually, countries have been investing a large proportion of their budgets in education. More recently, CARICOM addressed the matter of human resource development as a strategy for economic development. Thus, much effort is being made to develop the human resource of the region.

However, governments need to ensure that education programmes are not only designed to take care of today's problems of the region, but that they also address the need to prepare their people for life in the new millennium.

Tourism

Tourism plays a crucial part in the economic life of some of the islands of the Caribbean. Visitors come mainly from Europe and North America, and also from Japan. Tourists are drawn by the natural environment – nice weather, good beaches, attractive mountains, springs, rivers and beautiful gardens.

Caribbean countries earn large amounts of foreign currency from tourism. This is needed by governments to pay for imports and to meet foreign debts. Tourism also provides employment for a large number of local people, such as producing local craft items for tourists.

Infrastructural developments that are put into effect to meet the needs of the tourist industry (e.g. road networks) also benefit the local community.

Whilst tourism brings its benefits, such as foreign exchange, employment and markets for some locally produced goods, it also has its negative effects. For example, land tends to be lost for structural developments, and agricultural workers leave the land to join the tourist trade labour force. Some critics argue that tourism contributes adversely to the spread of prostitution and drug problems. A less obvious adverse effect of tourism is that it can add to the imports bill, because goods are imported to suit the tastes of the tourists.

22.4 The impact of local and foreign investment

Economic development requires investment. This is necessary because economic growth is fuelled by the input of capital. This is particularly so where a nation wants to raise the standard of technology it employs. Attracting investment in industry:

- brings foreign capital into the country
- allows the purchase of capital equipment that would not otherwise be available
- increases employment possibilities
- provides extra income for governments through taxation.

CARICOM has done much to encourage the attraction of investment in industry from both local and foreign sources. The evolvement of the CSME has made this important requirement easier to achieve.

One of the disadvantages of attracting foreign investment is that profits tend to be taken out of the region by foreign investors. But foreign investment is often necessary to 'kick start' economic growth and development. However, governments have a duty to promote local investment, and to encourage foreign investors to plough money back into the economy rather than spend it elsewhere.

Individually, CARICOM member states represent a relatively insignificant share of global trade. CARICOM markets tend to be small and fragmented. In other words, individually the member states have limited access to global trade, and are often heavily reliant on imports and tourism.

The establishment of CSME will enable CARICOM to implement more liberal trade and investment arrangements by operating in an integrated market with countries within the Caribbean region. CSME gives the region of small states the benefit of a greater physical mass, pooled resources, improved ability to use skilled workers where needed, and increased economies of scale.

Principles of Business – Profile 3

KEY WORDS

Find out the business-related meaning of each of the following terms. Write a separate sentence for each term to show your understanding.

economic dualism
immigration
opportunity cost
emigration   brain drain
foreign investment
industrialisation
plough back   dominance
population growth rate
urbanisation
primary production

The expansion of CSME to encompass many more countries will give the CSME greater strength. Once businesses realise that the borders that used to prohibit them from selling in CARICOM markets, or protect them from competition from other CARICOM firms have been removed, they will become sharper and more competitive in the global market.

The evolution of CSME into maturity will enable the implementation of decisions through a central body, rather than through many heads of countries. For example, the EU established a European Commission with Commissioners appointed by the member countries to implement the decisions of a Council of Ministers, and to initiate policy actions on behalf of their countries.

A CARICOM Commission could help rationalise the administration of CARICOM and make policies more effective. With this kind of development, CARICOM could speak with one collective voice to the rest of the world, in a similar way to the EU.

One of the prerequisites of the free movement of goods within the CSME is the need for *harmonisation of standards*. This is already being implemented by the Caribbean Regional Organisation on Standards and Quality (CROSQ). Whilst this is essentially internal within the CSME, it also sends a clear message to other countries with which CARICOM wishes to trade; it says that CARICOM is serious about quality and standards, which will encourage foreign trade.

22.5 Things to do

This section contains a variety of exercises to help you create revision notes, to test your understanding and to prepare you for examinations.

Search and find

Write out the question and the answer by referring back through the text to form revision notes.

1. Why do countries need to co-operate with others?
2. In what ways do chambers of commerce and manufacturers' associations support businesses?
3. What are the aims of CARICOM?
4. Why is the CSME changing the region?
5. What is the aim of the IMF and what are the regulations governing the provision of loans from the IMF?
6. How does the Caribbean Development Bank differ from commercial banks?
7. What is the main purpose of the World Bank and from where does it obtain its funds?
8. 'Both CARICOM and the EU are referred to as *common markets*.' Explain this statement.

Chapter 22 – **Regional and global business environment**

9. 'The World Trade Organisation has both a beneficial and a detrimental effect on the Caribbean region.' Briefly discuss this statement.
10. What is the Caribbean Initiative?
11. OPEC is sometimes referred to as the world's largest 'cartel'. What does this mean, and what is OPEC most well known for?
12. 'NAFTA and FTAA have some similar aims.' Explain this statement.
13. How do you think the main aims of GATT help to improve international trade?
14. In what ways does the LOME agreement benefit the Caribbean region?
15. What is 'economic dualism'? What is the relevance of this to the Caribbean region?
16. Describe some of the industrial problems that exist in the Caribbean region.
17. Industrialisation has yet to realise its full potential in the Caribbean region. What reasons can you put forward for this?
18. Why do you think light industries are important to the Caribbean region?
19. Describe the different types of unemployment.
20. What is migration? Why can this have both a beneficial and an adverse effect?
21. What do you see as a connection between the term urbanisation and migration?
22. How can governments help to overcome unemployment?
23. Why is education important to economic development?
24. 'Tourism has benefits and costs to Caribbean society.' Explain this statement.
25. Why is the Caribbean region dependent on foreign investment as well as local input?
26. How can investment accepted from overseas have an adverse effect?
27. Suggest some possible solutions to Caribbean economic problems.

What do you know?

Write out the complete sentence and insert the missing word, which can be chosen from the list at the end of the questions.

1. CARICOM is in effect a movement towards regional ……
2. CSME is an economic space where goods, ….. and services can move freely.
3. The World Bank provides ….. and technical assistance for developing countries.
4. The free movement of goods in a region are characteristic of ….. .
5. A country's complaints of ….. practices by another country can be taken to the World Trade Organisation.
6. The Caribbean Basin Initiative enables some Caribbean goods to enter the US market on ….. terms.
7. World ….. prices tend to be fixed by OPEC.
8. FTAA is a proposed agreement to eliminate or reduce trade ….. in the American Continents.
9. The knowledge and skills taken out of a country is sometimes referred to as a ….. .
10. A major problem of ….. investment is that profits tend to be taken out of the country.

Choose the missing words from the following:

oil labour preferential brain drain unfair integration loans foreign barriers free trade

Principles of Business – Profile 3

Structured questions

Q1

(a) Why is investment from foreign investors important to the Caribbean? — 2

(b) How has foreign investment affected the region? — 4

(c) What is the major method used by your government to make the best use of investment attracted from overseas? — 4

(d) What assistance can be given to local investors to encourage them to invest in their own country? — 4

(e) Describe the work of two international organisations that encourage economic development in developing countries. — 6

Q2

(a) What is meant by the term 'industrialisation'? — 2

(b) List three of the main problems the Caribbean region has in increasing industrial development. — 3

(c) Discuss some of the factors that have created these problems. — 3

(d) What is 'economic dualism' and why does this exist in the region? — 4

(e) What are the measures that can be introduced by regional governments to overcome these problems? — 4

(f) Describe the ways in which other agencies can assist in increasing industrialisation. — 4

Q3

(a) What do the letters IMF stand for? — 1

(b) What is the purpose of the IMF? — 2

(c) Describe two ways in which countries can benefit from the support of the IMF? — 2

(d) Briefly describe three of the requirements the IMF impose in return for their help. — 3

(e) How can these requirements overshadow the government's sovereignty? — 3

f) Discuss the potential beneficial impact of the IMF on a developing country. — 4

g) Explain ways in which the IMF could help to solve some of the Caribbean economic problems. — 5

Q4

(a) What does CARICOM stand for? — 1

(b) What do the letters CSME stand for? — 1

(c) What was the main reason that CARICOM was formed? — 2

(d) Name the policy-making body of CARICOM. — 2

(e) What are the advantages of a country belonging to CARICOM? — 3

(f) State three objectives of CARICOM. — 3

(g) What benefits has CSME brought to the region? — 4

(h) In what ways can CSME be said to be a reflection on the success of CARICOM? — 4

Chapter 22 – **Regional and global business environment**

Q5

(a) Why are human resources so important to Caribbean countries? **2**

(b) Give two reasons why a high rate of unemployment exists in the region? **2**

(c) What is meant by the term 'brain drain'? **2**

(d) Why is the 'brain drain' a particular problem for Caribbean countries? **3**

What specific action could a government take to limit the effects of a 'brain drain'? **3**

(e) How could Caribbean governments increase the technological skills of their workforce? **4**

(f) Although Caribbean countries suffer from unemployment, labour is still recruited from overseas. Why is this so? **4**

Research assignments

1 The IMF has created restrictions on countries borrowing from their organisation. Research what these restrictions are, and explain some of the changes that a country must follow in order to adhere to the requirements set by this lending institution.

2 What evidence can you find that your country suffers from a 'brain drain'? What suggestions can you make to prevent this from happening?

3 Find out the original aims of CARICOM. To what extent do you feel these aims have been realised? Support your response with personally researched evidence.

4 Industrialisation has resulted in creating new avenues in the lives of Caribbean nationals. Find out the problems associated with industrialisation in your country and explain the measures your government is using to curtail these problems.

5 'The Caribbean needs to attract investment from foreign countries, but this too often results in a drain of capital out of the region.' Research data that proves or refutes this statement.

6 What evidence can you find that the government of your country is tackling the problems of attracting investment, and also taking steps to encourage investors to keep their profits in the country rather than repatriate them?

7 a) What business preparations have to be implemented to ensure the success of a major sporting event?
b) Describe the beneficial impact of events of this kind of scale on the local economy.

8 CSME, CARICOM and ASC have several things in common:
a) Investigate these similarities and briefly explain them.
b) In your opinion, which of these trade agreements is more effective? Give reasons for your views.

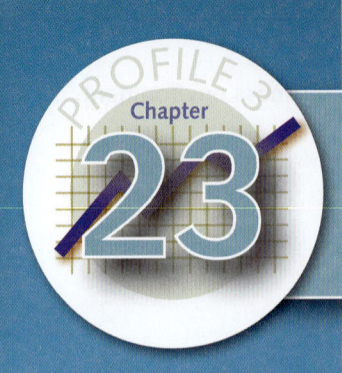

The school-based assessment

23.1 The basis of the assessment

The Principles of Business syllabus consists of three profiles:

Profile 1: Organisational Principles
Profile 2: Production, Marketing and Finance
Profile 3: The Business Environment

The following components comprise the assessment of the subject:

- **Paper 1** (1 hour 15 minutes). Value 30% of overall assessment: Multiple choice paper consisting of 60 items testing the three above profile dimensions.
- **Paper 2** (2 hours). Value 50% of overall assessment: An essay paper consisting of seven structured questions divided into two sections:
  Section One: three compulsory questions from the *core* areas of the syllabus (Profile 2).
  Section Two: four questions: two from Profile 1, and two from Profile 3.

  You are required to answer one question from each profile pair. Each question is worth 20 marks. Profiles 1 and 2 each contribute 40 marks and Profile 3 contributes 20 marks.
- **Paper 3.** A School-Based Assessment (SBA) component based on Profile 2 of the syllabus (Production, Marketing and Finance). Value 20% of overall assessment.

There are separate arrangements of a case study for private candidates.

23.2 The SBA requirements

From the foregoing you will have realised that the SBA component is a very important part of your assessment. It is intended to help you acquire certain knowledge, skills and attitudes that are associated with the Principles of Business. The activities for the SBA are linked to the syllabus and will form a part of your learning activities. Your teacher will guide you so that your research work will help you to achieve the objectives of the syllabus.

During your course of study for the subject, you will receive marks for the competence you develop and demonstrate in undertaking SBA assignments negotiated with your teacher. The marks you are awarded contribute to the final marks awarded to you for your performance in the examination. For this reason it is important that you follow your teacher's guidance, and that you complete any work assigned to you thoroughly and carefully. Your teacher's assessment marks will be moderated by the examiners.

The SBA component of the Principles of Business syllabus is a single research project guided by your teacher. The project is based on the theme, **Establishing a Business**, and should demonstrate your ability to apply knowledge and skills incorporated into ONE aspect of Profile 2: Production, Marketing or Finance, but drawing on all three of the profiles.

Chapter 23 – **The school-based assessment**

You are required to choose ONE aspect of establishment of a business, EITHER, Production, Marketing OR Finance. Each aspect has its own criteria and mark scheme and the relevant one will be used by your teacher to allocate marks. The project will be marked out of 40, weighted as follows:

- *Organisational Principles* (Profile 1) 10 marks
- *Production, Marketing and Finance* (Profile 2) 20 marks
- *The Business Environment (Profile 3)* 10 marks.

Every candidate who enters for the CSEC Principles of Business examination must submit a report on the theme 'Establishing a Business'. You may work individually or in a group to carry out your research. However, you must produce a complete report yourself. No two reports from the same group should be identical – your project presentation must be your own work.

Your project should be restricted to 1,000 to 1,200 words (not including appendices). If you exceed this length your assessment marks will be reduced.

23.3 Starting off the project

1. Choose the type of organisation you want to make the focus of your study. Earlier you were told that you are required to choose one aspect of the establishment of a business, EITHER, Production, Marketing or Finance. If you are also studying Accounts, or if you have some knowledge about accounts, you might feel that the finance option will particularly suit you because you will be familiar with some of the concepts involved.

   You might decide that you will develop an imaginary business, since this may be one of your aims when you leave school. In this case, it would be wise to visit the Small Businesses Association office in your community, or a related non-governmental organisation (NGO) that handles small business affairs to get some information on the subject of establishing a business.

2. Read through the syllabus sections 1–10 to ensure that the structure of the organisation or business idea you have chosen to investigate is sufficiently broad to cover the profile.

3. Clearly state why you have chosen the type of business organisation that is your topic, or, if you want to develop your own ideas for a business, why you have chosen to do that.

   What have you observed or learnt about the organisation/business idea that interests you? Why has this made you want to focus on your chosen type of business?

4. Then discuss your topic with your teacher. She/he will be supervising your SBA and will therefore confirm whether or not the ideas you have are suitable for the SBA.

5. Once the topic is confirmed, formulate purpose/problem statements – what are you going to investigate and why? You must formulate statements to cover each of the three profiles.

Example (area of investigation: Marketing)

- *Purpose statement:* The purpose of this part of research is to determine whether there is a relationship between the advertising medium(s) used by a firm, and its income.

Principles of Business – Profile 3

- *Problem statement:* What is the difference, if any, between income generated from the electronic media advertising, and the income generated from other forms of advertising used by a firm?
- *Hypothesis:* A greater amount of revenue is generated by a firm from advertising through the electronic media, that by a firm using other advertising media.

Once you have completed the above exercises of creating your purpose statement, problem statement and hypothesis related to your topic, you are ready to begin your research.

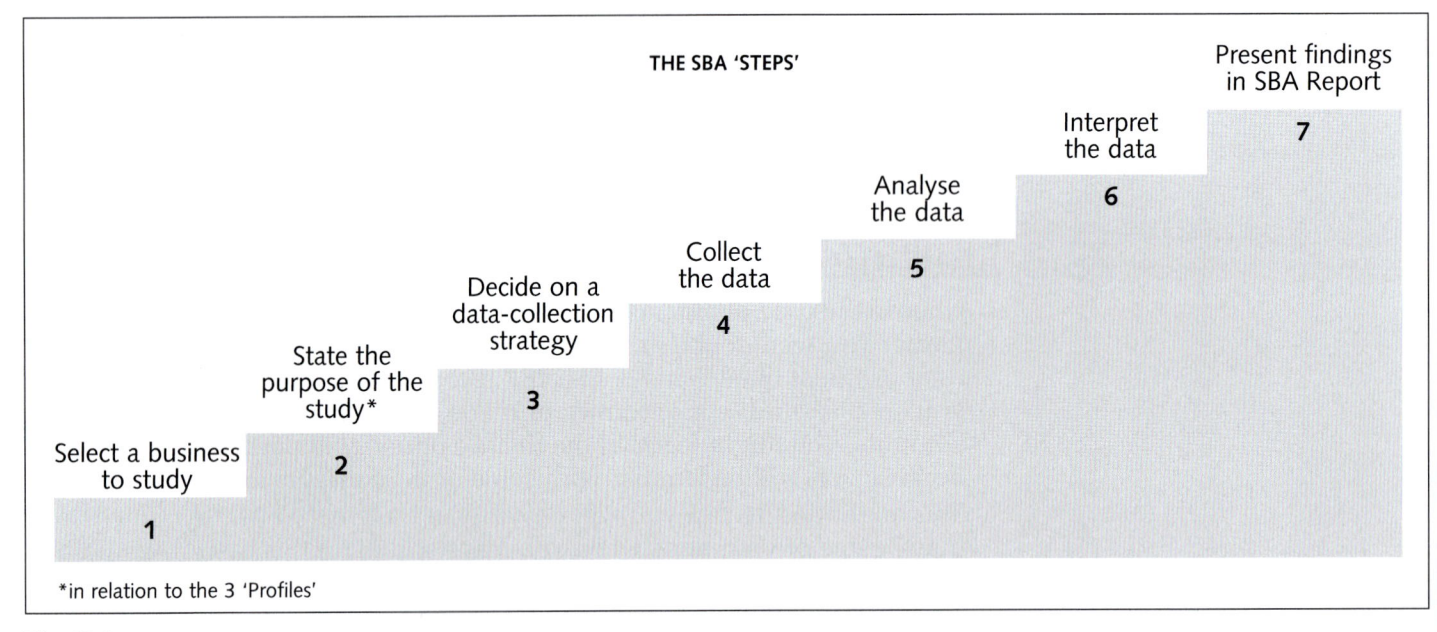

THE SBA 'STEPS'

1. Select a business to study
2. State the purpose of the study*
3. Decide on a data-collection strategy
4. Collect the data
5. Analyse the data
6. Interpret the data
7. Present findings in SBA Report

*in relation to the 3 'Profiles'

Fig. 23.1

23.4 Carrying out your research

The essential tasks you will need to undertake to complete your research are:

1. Decide what your data collection strategy will be.
2. Collect the data.
3. Analyse the data.
4. Draw conclusions based on the data.
5. Plan the report.
6. Write the report.

To help with your project, these six important steps are described in more detail below.

23.5 Data collection

This is a fundamental part of the project. If data is not collected, then your research questions and hypotheses cannot be adequately answered and confirmed.

Data can basically be defined as:

- *Primary data:* meaning that no other researcher has collected this data before you
- *Secondary data:* meaning that in the past a researcher collected and used

data for some purpose, but that the data can still be reused (by you) in a different way. In other words, you can examine the data from a different perspective.

Data consists of such things as:

- responses to a questionnaire or an interview, or both
- reporting on events observed or experiments observed
- documents or records or physical materials.

In your study of the organisation, you may use a combination of the various data-collection methods outlined above. However, it is important to ensure that the data is relevant to your study. Never collect data for the sake of collecting data.

Let us now examine in more detail some of the data-collection methods just described. It is up to you to decide (possibly with guidance from your teacher) which of the following instruments will be useful to your particular research.

Questionnaire

This is one of the most common instruments used in the collection of data for research projects. A questionnaire is a method of collecting data and information from a sample of people. These people are often representative of a particular segment or group in society.

For example, a sample of shoppers in a supermarket could be questioned to determine their opinion of its products and service. The questions to be posed must be pre-formulated, put into a certain order, and written down, so that each shopper is faced with exactly the same questionnaire. This makes your analysis of their responses easier.

You need to be clear in advance about what you are trying to find out. Target your questions to obtain the information you want. Avoid leading questions. These are questions that suggest answers, an example being, 'This is a good supermarket, isn't it?'.

The questions you ask may be either 'open-ended' or 'closed'. If they are closed, the person responding gives a simple answer without making comments. Thus, the answer could be a straightforward 'yes' or 'no' (to a question like, 'Do you think the service in this supermarket is good?'). The answer could also be given by ticking a box (for example, if you are rating the service of the supermarket as 'good', 'fair' or 'poor'). Closed questions invite a limited response, but they make the questionnaire easier to complete. If, on the other hand, the question is open-ended (for example, 'What aspects of the service in this supermarket appeal to you?'), then the person is being asked to give a full answer. This allows them to explain themselves more, but at the same time it makes your analysis of their response less straightforward.

A questionnaire is easy to use if carefully formulated. People can complete it themselves, or the researcher can ask questions and fill in the appropriate sections him/herself. However, you may find that some people do not like to answer questionnaires that are too long. For this reason, you must ensure that the instructions and questions are clear, simple and precise. They should only have one possible meaning. Also, make the questionnaire itself as short as possible.

Principles of Business – Profile 3

Often the questionnaire has to be left for the respondent to fill out, so you may need to visit them or call them by phone in order to retrieve it.

Once you have developed your questionnaire, ask your teacher or supervisor to check it.

The following ideas are given to help you in the formation of a questionnaire for each of the themes. However, they are offered as starting points and you should be aware that there are many other questions you could include. For example, within your chosen theme you should include acknowledgement of the need of businesses to take into account ethical issues, such as environmental and moral obligations. You should also ensure that the presentation of your findings follow a logical pattern using correct grammar.

Examples of questions for the theme: Establishing a business: Production

1. What is the official/legal name of the organisation?
2. What type of business is your company presently involved in?
3. What are the reasons for the location of your business?
4. Is your company run by a board of directors or a manager? How do you see the function of these key personnel in your business?
5. What form of organisational structure has been adopted by your firm?
6. What specially trained staff does your business employ? How are they recruited?
7. Which information recording methods are used in the organisation?
8. Is there a special department for dealing with this type of information?
9. How does this department interact with the others in the firm?
10. Do you manufacture finished products or items that are used by other producers?
11. Which markets does your firm produce for?
12. What levels of production do you operate, e.g. mass production or smaller?
13. To what extent do you use technology in your production processes?
14. What forms of quality control are your products submitted to?
15. What measures are put in place financially for the growth of your organisation?
16. What steps are put in place financially for the growth of the organisation?
17. Are there any government regulations that affect your business with regards to the production of your products?
18. What ethical issues (e.g. environmental considerations) does your firm try to observe?
19. How effective do you feel your business is?
20. What plans have you to develop or improve your business?

Examples of questions for the theme: Establishing a business: Marketing

1. What is the official/legal name of the business?
2. How long has your organisation been in operation?
3. What types of products are marketed by your firm?
4. To whom do you market these products?
5. What type of organisational structures exists in the marketing department?

6. How does your marketing department interact with the others in the firm?
7. What market research is undertaken by your firm and what market research methods are used?
8. What are the main aims of the market research?
9. What specific questions are asked by the researchers?
10. What marketing strategy has been adopted by the organisation?
11. What are some of the new technology used today by your firm to market your products?
12. How do you decide the price of your products?
13. What competition exists for your products?
14. How do your packaging and branding strategies relate to your marketing strategy?
15. How has technology affected your business?
16. What type of activities do you adopt when you want to introduce a new product to the market?
17. What type of promotion is used for exports?
18. What procedures are used when importing or exporting your products as part of adherence to government regulations?
19. How does your organisation deal with complaints from customers, and is there a special department for dealing with complaints?
20. What impact has the marketing department had on the success of the whole organisation?
21. What ethical issues (e.g. environmental considerations) does your firm try to observe?

Examples of questions for the theme: Establishing a business: Finance

1. What is the official/legal name of the business?
2. What type of business is your company presently engaged in its operation?
3. How extensive or limited is the scope of your business's operations?
4. Is your company run by a board of directors or a manager?
5. What kind of organisational chart can be used to depict your company?
6. What type of staff presently exists in your firm? Is there a need to change the staffing format?
7. What are the procedures required for recruiting staff in your organisation?
8. What are the main reasons for your firm's need for operating expenses?
9. What are some of the forms of collateral used by your company to generate additional cash?
10. The organisation of the finance department requires new technology in managing the business. What are some of the methods or equipment used by your firm to manage the operation effectively?
11. The funds raised by organisations are used for various activities. What are the main uses for these funds in your organisation?
12. The finance department is responsible for allocation of funds to all other departments within the firm. How does your finance department blend the cost of producing a product using prime and overhead expenditure as part of its pricing structure?
13. What are the main capital goods of your business? How are they valued?

14. What form of share issue does your firm employ, or other methods of raising finance?
15. What are some of the methods used by the finance department to monitor the payment of loans and the collection of payments from debtors?
16. What level of profitability has your business been able to achieve over the past five years?
17. What projection has your company got for future financial performance?
18. The finance department is responsible for carrying out certain government regulations. What are some of these that you have to observe?
19. How beneficial is the finance department to the whole of your organisation?
20. What ethical issues (e.g. environmental considerations) does your firm try to observe?

Interview

An interview is another common method used to collect data. This involves questioning people about their opinions of certain topics or issues. In this sense, it is very similar to a questionnaire.

But there is a subtle difference – an interview is less formally structured than a questionnaire, taking the form of questions *and* discussion with the person being interviewed. This allows the interviewee to respond in a more natural way. The interviewer, in turn, may ask a more varied range of questions. The questions asked need not necessarily be the same for all interviewees, but instead can be formulated to suit the person being interviewed. This allows the interviewer to investigate more deeply the interviewee's particular views. The questions asked will also probably change as the interview goes on, for example if the interviewee raises an interesting point and the interviewer decides that she/he would like to investigate that point further.

The interviewer may need to tape record the interview in order to transcribe and analyse the responses later. Before any attempt is made to tape record an interview, always seek the permission of the interviewee. In the absence of a tape recorder, the interviewer will need to make full notes of the interviewee's responses.

Interviews may be conducted face-to-face or via the telephone.

Observation and participation

Some researchers find that observing an event taking place, or actually participating in an event, is also a useful way of collecting data.

Observation is designed to help the observer get information about an organisation, or a group of people, by simply watching how they go about their business and listening to their conversations and interactions. The observer records what she/he sees and hears by positioning him/herself in a particular location in order to monitor events. Tape-recording and video-taping are therefore useful observational tools, if available. The essence of observation is that the observer does not interfere in events – she/he watches and listens from the sidelines.

The advantages of observation are that you can make judgements about how an organisation or group works based on what you see. The conclusions you draw will be entirely your own – whereas with an interview or a questionnaire your conclusions are based on what other people said to you.

Participation is another way of observing, but this time you observe the actions and behaviour of a group/organisation from within. In other words, the observer assumes a role inside the group or organisation being observed. Participation gives the researcher the opportunity to learn, from practical experience and a 'hands-on' approach, the working methods and behaviour of those being studied.

Points to remember when undertaking an observation or participation:

- Record as much as possible of what you see and hear.
- If you do not clearly understand what you have observed or participated in, seek clarification from someone within the group or organisation.
- In participatory observation, the observer could become so involved that she/he forgets the aim of the exercise. Be on the alert if you choose to gather data in this way.

Documents and reports

Gathering data from documents is common to all types of research studies. Documents may be able to answer some of the questions you want to ask, without the need for you to deal with people in the organisation directly. In the study of an organisation the following documents can all be useful sources of information:

Company year books; manuals used in the organisation (such as procedures manuals, policy manuals, staff manuals); reports of all types, e.g. financial, sales and marketing, and production reports; company journals and magazines; minutes of meetings.

Additionally, library resources and computer-based information can also be useful.

If a government department, ministry or agency is being studied, you may also be able to consult government statistical reports and policy documents.

Documents are secondary sources of data, i.e. the researcher has not collected the information within the documents him/herself. However, they are still useful for SBA-type projects, especially if you are finding it difficult to collect primary (original) data.

There are certain documents that are required to be included in your SBA, depending on which aspect you have chosen to investigate. The following are the main exemplar documents required, but you may include others:

For Establishing a Business: Production

- Articles of Association
- Invoices
- Legal documents (e.g. blank job application forms, etc.)
- Work permits
- Stamp duties forms, etc.

For Establishing a Business: Marketing

- Delivery slips
- Shipping documents (e.g. air waybill, bill of lading)
- Customs forms
- Purchase orders

Principles of Business – Profile 3

> Receipts of purchase
> VAT certificates
> Health certificates, etc.

For Establishing a Business: Finance

> A balance sheet
> An income statement
> An application form for a loan
> Insurance documents
> National insurance forms
> PAYE slips, etc.

23.6 Accounting for the '3 Profiles'

Once you have decided on the data-collection methods you are going to use, you will need to think how these can be applied to discover information about the three Profiles for the organisation you are going to study.

You will find the exemplar questions listed below useful in the preparation of your data-collection methods. Some of these questions can be 'built in' to your research, i.e. put directly into questionnaires, interviews, etc. Otherwise, they can be used as 'background thinking' for you to decide on the approach you are going to take in collecting your data (for example, the type of questions that will be in your mind during an observation).

You need to be aware that the exemplar questions are just a few examples to get you going. The questions you formulate for your particular research should be carefully thought out in relation to the overall aims of your investigation. You can get ideas for questions by looking at the syllabus, and from what you have learnt in class during the year.

Exemplar Questions for Profile 1: Organisational Principles

Basic structure and rationale for the organisation

1. What is the official/legal name of the organisation?
2. How long has the organisation been in operation?
3. In what line of product or service is the organisation involved?
4. Has the organisation formulated a Mission Statement?
5. What is the mission of the organisation?
6. Does the organisation have a structure?
7. What organisational structure has been adopted by the organisation (Line, Line and Staff, Committee structure)?
8. Why has the organisation adopted this structure?
9. What is the size of the management team?
10. What categories of managers are employed in the organisation?
11. How many employees are employed in the organisation?
12. What is the span of control of managers to employees?

Working conditions

1. Are all managers provided with job descriptions?
2. Are all employees provided with job descriptions?
3. Do all managers sign employment contracts?
4. Do all other employees sign employment contracts?

Chapter 23 – The school-based assessment

5 Are job specifications provided for all categories of employees?
6 Indicate the hours of work adopted by the organisation:
   a) shift work
   b) flexible working time
   c) fixed hours of work.
7 Have workers been provided with a copy of the health and safety regulations of the organisation?
8 Are health and safety regulations displayed in a prominent place in each department or office?
9 Are all workers covered under a health scheme?
10 Do workers in 'high risk' areas have insurance coverage?

Exemplar Questions for Profile 2: Production, Marketing and Finance

Production

1 Where is the organisation located?
2 What factors influenced this location?
3 What product is being produced?
4 What is the scale/size of production?
5 How do products reach the consumers?
6 Products' packaging:
   a) Is labelling appropriate?
   b) Is the product appropriately packaged?
   c) Is information provided on weights?
   d) Is information provided on measure?
   e) Is information provided on product usage date?

Marketing

1 What market research is undertaken by the organisation, and what market research methods are used?
2 What is the purpose of the research?
3 What specific questions are asked by the researchers?
4 How often is market research undertaken?
5 What marketing strategy has been adopted by the organisation?
6 How do branding and packaging relate to the marketing strategy?
7 How have the outlets for distribution of the organisation's product(s) helped to determine the marketing strategy (e.g. point-of-sale displays, etc.)?

Finance

1 How is the organisation financed?
2 Is the organisation insured, and what are the implications if it is not?
3 What level of profitability has the business been able to achieve over the past five years?
4 To what would you attribute the level(s) of profitability the organisation has been experiencing?
5 If the organisation is experiencing difficulty in its operations, what factors might be contributing to this difficulty?
6 Suggest ways the business could improve profitability.

7. What measures would you use to indicate whether or not the organisation is contributing to the social and economic development of a country, e.g. trade or exports?

Exemplar questions for Profile 3: Business Environment

1. What are some of the methods that the company must adhere to as part of government regulations?
2. What kinds of restrictions are used by the government to protect consumers in regards to the business?
3. What types of taxes does the business have to pay to the government?
4. If some of your workers fell ill, what steps are taken by the government to protect the workers as part of the social services?
5. What are some of the reasons for the high costs of some of your products?
6. What steps are imposed by your government to correct these high costs?
7. It is important to trade among CARICOM states. Do you think that the Caribbean Single Market Economy will benefit your business? Give reasons for your views.
8. In what ways can problems that affect the Caribbean region generally influence the growth, or otherwise, of your business?

23.7 Analysing the data collected

Once you have completed all your data collection, it is time to analyse the data. This will involve presenting the data in easily readable and easily interpretable form, which will make it easier for you to draw conclusions based on the data.

The data from **questionnaires** can sometimes be presented in graphic form (such as a pie chart or a bar graph), or as a table. For example, if you have asked 'closed' questions where only a 'yes' or 'no' answer is possible, or questions where the respondent is asked to tick one of three boxes, you can easily show this kind of data in a table or graph. You could show how many people replied 'yes' and how many replied 'no', or you could show how many people ticked each of the three boxes.

You should then be able to arrive at conclusions based on the graphic presentation of your questionnaire data. The data presented in graphic form will 'tell you' what you have found overall.

Data from **'open-ended' questionnaires**, or **interviews**, or **observation** and **participation**, is likely to be a little harder to analyse. This is because the answers/results recorded will be very descriptive. They will not be a simple 'yes' or 'no' answer – instead, they will be more in-depth, because individuals will have had more of a chance to express to you their own very particular views.

When analysing this type of data to draw conclusions, you need to look for overall patterns – did several individuals give the same kind of answers? It may be that no pattern emerges, and you should acknowledge this in your conclusion if that is the case (for example, every person interviewed may have given a completely different answer).

Based on all your research and the conclusions that have come out of it, you should now be able to give an indication of whether your original hypotheses or expected outcomes were correct. You may also like to make some recommendations. Remember, the conclusions you draw and the recommendations you make are not a place to include personal opinions about the organisation you are studying. Everything you say must be supported by the data from your research.

23.8 The report

Finally, having analysed the data and drawn your conclusions, you will be in a position to plan, and then write your report. It should be presented in an inexpensive folder in the following order, and you should ensure that the presentation of your findings follow a logical pattern using correct grammar.

I – Introductory section

It is important to keep this as clear but as precise as possible, bearing in mind the need to keep within the prescribed overall word limit.

A Title page

This page consists of your name, registration number, name of the subject, and the date presented, and of course the title of your chosen theme.

B Abstract

This is a brief summary of the report. It gives the busy reader information on what was investigated, and how the study was carried out, and the main findings, conclusions and recommendations.

C Acknowledgements

This is statement where you say 'thank you' to those who provided assistance with the research.

D Table of Contents

This gives clear and straightforward information on what the report contains, rather similar to the contents section of this book.

Contents	
	Page
Abstract	i
Acknowledgements	ii
Table of Contents	iii
List of Tables and Figures	iv
Description of the organisation investigated	1
Purpose of research/hypotheses	2
Description/justification of data-collection methods	3
Presentation of data collected (graphically where possible)	4–10
Analysis of data collected	11–14
Overall conclusions and recommendations	15–16
Bibliography	17
Appendix	18 onwards

E List of tables and figures

II – Main body

The main body of your report will of course be influenced by the theme you have chosen to follow. But the following will give you an idea of the format your report might take.

A Description of the organisation investigated

The type of organisation, its name, size, basic history and its reason for existing.

B Purpose of the research and hypotheses investigated

Example – area of investigation: Organisational Principles, Production, Marketing and Finance, Business Environment.

C Description/justification of data-collection methods

Outline the methods used. How do those methods relate to the purpose of your research, and the hypotheses you investigated. Show how you made sure your research was broad-ranging and as thorough as possible.

D Presentation of data collected

Present the data gathered. Wherever possible make the data interesting and easy to read by presenting it as graphs, pie charts or tables. Where you are reporting on interviews, observations or participations, you want to summarise what people said and what you saw in a few short, clear paragraphs. This is *not* the time to say what your data *means* – it is the place where you report, accurately, the evidence and facts you discovered in your research. Bearing in mind the word limitation allocated for your work, it will be useful to commit as much data as possible to the Appendices.

You may want to present your data in sections relating to each of the profiles. You may also decide to indicate how a particular piece of data relates to a purpose/problem you set out to investigate.

E Analysis of data collected

What does the data you have set out in the previous section tell you? Does it confirm or deny your original hypotheses? Write a few short paragraphs to say what you think each of the pieces of data you have collected means. You are now *explaining* what you think your data means, which is called analysis.

Note that in some instances the data you have collected may be inconclusive – neither confirming nor denying your original hypotheses. If some of your data seems to be like this, you should be honest about that fact. Your recognition of this will add credibility to your work.

III – Final section

A Overall conclusions and recommendations

Present some final conclusions and recommendations based on your presentation and analysis of the data you have gathered. These should be short, two- or three-line paragraphs that sum up the essence of what you have discovered. Set these out logically in your report – they should relate to the hypotheses you originally started out with, and to the three Profiles.

All your conclusions must be based on the research you have carried out. Have the findings helped you to confirm or reject your original ideas or hypotheses?

B Bibliography

From what sources did you draw information for your research?

These may have been company reports, staff manuals, yearbooks, books, journals, magazines, government reports (e.g. economic surveys) and policy documents. Prepare a list of these in alphabetical order, following an accepted format.

Example
1 Adams, Stephen, *Economic Principles for CXC* (pp. 30–40). Publishers of the Caribbean, Castries, St Lucia (1996).
2 Doublas, Robert, *Principles of Business for the Millennium*. SWIFT Publishers, Port Maria, St Mary, Jamaica (1997).
3 *Economic Survey* (pp. 16–20). Planning Institute of Jamaica, Government Printing Office, Kingston, Jamaica (1966).
4 Fyffe, Marcus, *Marketing Strategies for the Small Business*. Journal of Marketing, 2nd Edition, The Association of Marketers, Bridgetown Headquarters, Barbados (1977).

C Appendix

Place in this section of the report copies of documents such as employment contracts, job descriptions, memorandum of association, your completed questionnaires and interviews, observational notes and any other relevant documents you used in your research project.

23.9 Alternative to the SBA

Paper 3/2 is the Alternative to the School Based Assessment for the examination of the Principles of Business for private candidates. The alternative to the SBA takes the form of a written examination in lieu of internal teacher's assessment for school candidates. This paper is based on the same area of the syllabus as the SBA component defined in the syllabus and weighted in the same way as the SBA. The SBA is based on a case study. Candidates are required to answer 14 compulsory questions, which are marked out of 40. The total marks will account for 20% of the overall mark. Candidates are allocated one hour for the exam. N.B. Such candidates are not required to submit a project.

We wish you every success with your research and in your examinations.

Alan Whitcomb and Macpherson Barnes

Index

accident insurance 153–4
ACS see Association of Caribbean States
advertising 61, 215–22
advice notes 119–20
agencies
    advertising 218–19
    consumerism 223–4
    governments 28–31, 300–1
air transportation 245–6
applications, jobs 61–3
Articles of Association 97
artwork 219
Association of Caribbean States (ACS) 350–1
automation 181

balance of payments 336–8
balance sheets 279–80
balance of trade 337
banking 257–61, 349
    accounts 134–8
    bank drafts 125, 134
    cards 137, 141–2
    electronic banking 138–41
    statements 137–8
    see also finance
bar codes 238
barter 1–2
below-the-line promotions 238–9
Boston growth and market share matrix 196–7
branding 193, 198, 238
break-even point 94, 282
brokers 271–2
budgeting 261–2, 295
building societies 23
business
    background 1–14
    organisation 37–60
    types 15–36

capacity, contracts 108–9
capital 283–4, 287
    production 165
    raising 93–4, 97–8
Caribbean
    banking 257
    development 329
    economic aspects 346–51, 354–9
Caribbean Basin Initiative (CBI) 352
Caribbean Community (CARICOM) 167, 176, 296, 347–8, 359–60
Caribbean Congress of Labour (CCL) 82–3
Caribbean Development Bank (CDB) 349
Caribbean Single Market and Economy (CSME) 347–8, 359–60
Caribbean Stock Exchange 268
CARICOM see Caribbean Community
case law 109–10
cash cards 142
cash flow 94, 280–1
cash payments 133–4
catalogue shops 237
CBI see Caribbean Basin Initiative
CCL see Caribbean Congress of Labour
CDB see Caribbean Development Bank
central banks 258–60, 338
central government 29–30
chain stores 235–6
chains of command 44–5
charging, goods 119–25

charts, organisation 49–50
cheques 135–7
choices, modern society 4–5
claims, insurance 155–6
closed shops 85
co-operatives 20–2
collective bargaining 83
commercial banks 257–8
committee organisation 48
communication 43
comparative advantage 335–6
comparative costs 335–6
competition 164, 201–3
competitive advantage 164
computer-aided processes 182
consideration, contracts 108–9
consumers 189, 222–4, 297
containerisation 247
contracts 104–11
control 7, 44–7, 297–8
cost of living 320–1
cost-push inflation 313–14
costs 281–2, 335–6
cottage industries 174–5
credit
    cards 141–2, 165, 240
    notes 122
    promotions 221
    retailers 238–40
    transfers 140
CSME see Caribbean Single Market and Economy
current accounts 135
curriculum vitae 62
customs and excise duties 312

data collection 366–72, 374–5
debenture stocks 269–70
debit cards 142
debit notes 122
debts 124
deductions, wages 72
deflation 314, 338
delivery notes 119–20
demand 198–200, 313–14
demarcation disputes 84
department stores 236
departments 51–2, 63–4, 191–2
deposit accounts 134–5
despatching goods 119
devaluation 320, 338
development 300–1, 327–9, 358
differentials, wages 71
direct debits 139–40
direct production 1, 8, 11
direct taxation 311–12
discharge, contracts 110
discounts 222
dismissal, employees 65–6
displaying goods 197–8
distribution 231–56
    channels 232
    marketing 195, 241
    retailers 234–41
    transportation 241–8
    wholesalers 232–4
documentation 115–32, 371–2
    see also reports
door-to-door traders 235

Eastern Caribbean Common Market (ECCM) 352
ECLAC see Economic Commission for Latin American Countries
economic aspects
    activity 1–4
    Caribbean 346–51, 354–9
    development 358
    growth 328
    systems 6–8
    taxation 312
Economic Commission for Latin American Countries (ECLAC) 350
economies of scale 50–1, 171–2, 179–80, 348
education 299, 328–9, 358
efficiency, labour 301–2
electronic banking 138–41
Electronic Point of Sale (EPOS) 141, 164
employees 61–6, 70–81
    dismissal 65–6
    motivation 70–81
    organisation 46–7
    personnel 38, 63–4
    production 161–5, 181
    records 65
    recruitment 61–3
    redundancy 65–6
    stakeholders 98
    training 64
    welfare 65
    see also jobs; labour
enquiries 115–17
enterprise 165–6
entrepreneurs 90–1, 165–6, 296–7
environmental issues 294, 346–63
EPOS see Electronic Point of Sale
equilibrium prices 200–1
equipment purchase 94–5
European Union (EU) 351
exchange controls 338, 340
expenditure 326
experiments 211
exports 168, 301, 320, 339–40

finance 38, 257–92
    assistance 341–2
    balance sheets 279–80
    break-even point 94, 282
    budgeting 261–2, 295
    business plans 93–4
    capital 93–4, 97–8, 165, 283–4, 287
    cash flow 280–1
    costs 281–2, 335–6
    equipment purchase 94–5
    interest 95, 135
    investment 266–7, 270, 295, 359–60
    money 2–3, 133–4
    production 165
    profit 27–8, 165, 179, 241, 286–7
    questionnaires 369–70
    return on capital invested 287
    revenue 281–2
    savings 266–7
    sources 263–6
    stock market 267–73
    turnover 284–6
    see also banking; payments
fire insurance 153
flexitime 75
foreign trade 125–6, 241, 334–6
franchises 22–3, 238
free markets 6–7, 189, 271

free trade 339–41
fringe benefits 73
functional organisation 47–8

GDP see gross domestic product
global environment 346–63
global trade 334–45
globalisation 7–8
GNP see gross national product
going slow 85
Government Statistical Office 301
governments 293–308
    agencies 28–31, 300–1
    business interventions 297–8
    central banks 259–60
    competition 203
    departments 28–9
    entrepreneurs 296–7
    expenditure 326
    government-owned business 26–8
    labour force 301–3
    regional linkage 177
    responsibilities 293–5
    social services 292, 299–300
grievance procedures 66
gross domestic product (GDP) 325
gross national product (GNP) 324–5
group behaviour 41–2
growth
    Boston matrix 196–7
    business growth 23–6
    national growth 327–9
    small/large businesses 50–3

health 75–6, 299
Hertzberg, Frederick 54
hierarchy of needs theory 54, 70
hire purchase (HP) 222, 240, 264
holding companies 23
hours of employment 75
HP see hire purchase
human resources department 63–4
    see also employees
hygiene-motivation theory 54–5
hypermarkets 237

IADB see Inter-American Development Bank
IMF see International Monetary Fund
imperfect competition 202
imports 168, 298, 338, 340
income 71–3, 311, 320–4
indemnity 151–2
independent shops 235
indirect production 3–4, 8, 11
indirect taxation 311–12
industrial markets 189
industrial relations 53, 82–9
industrialisation 354–6
industry interdependence 11–12
inflation 313–14, 320
informal organisation 49
information 55–7, 213–14
insurance 148–59
Inter-American Development Bank (IADB) 349
interest 95, 135
international marketing 241
International Monetary Fund (IMF) 342, 348–9
international trade 334–6, 351–4
Internet 141, 239
interviews 63–4, 370
investment 266–7, 270, 295, 359–60
invoices 119, 121–2

jobbers 272
jobs
    applications 61–3
    satisfaction 70
    security 294
    unemployment 301, 356–7
    wages 71–3, 320
    working conditions 74–6
    see also employees

labour
    governments 301–3
    migration 162–3, 302–3, 357
    production 161–5
    technology 181–2
    trade unions 82–3
    see also employees
land 161
large businesses 50–3, 172
Law of Diminishing Returns 173
leadership 41–2
legal aspects 104–14
    consumerism 222–4
    contracts 104–11
    industrial relations 84
    insurance 148
letters
    applications 62
    enquiries 115–16
life assurance 152
limited companies 16, 18–20, 95–8
line organisation 46–7
linkage industries 175–7
local government 30–1
local organisations 176–7, 346
location of business 177–8
lock-outs 85
long-term finance 265

mail order 237
management 39–44, 55–7, 295
management information systems (MIS) 55–7
marine insurance 152–3
mark-up 241
marketing 38, 188–215
    competition 201–3
    departments 191–2
    free markets 6–7, 189, 271
    international marketing 241
    merchandising 197–8, 220
    mix 192–5
    orientation 190
    prices 198–201
    product life-cycles 195–7
    protecting ideas 198
    questionnaires 368–9
    research 190–1, 209–15
    segmentation 189–90
    share 190, 196–7
    traders 235
Maslow, Abraham 54, 70
media 217–18
Memorandum of Association 95–6
merchandising 197–8, 220
merchant banks 260
migration 162–3, 302–3, 357
MIS see management information systems
mistakes, contracts 110–11
mixed economies 7, 15
mobility of labour 163, 302
money 2–3, 133–4
monopolies 26, 202

motivation 53–5, 70–81
multinationals 25–6
multiples (chain stores) 235–6
municipal authorities 30–1

national cake 325
national debt 327
national expenditure 326
national income 321–4
National Insurance (NI) 299
nationalised industries 27, 298
natural resources 161
near cash payments 133–4
needs 54–5, 70
net profit 287
NI see National Insurance

OAS see Organisation of American States
observations, research 211
OECS see Organisation of Eastern Caribbean States
offers, contracts 106–8, 110
oligopolies 202–3
OPEC see Organisation of Petroleum Exporting Countries
ordinary shares 268–9
organisation, business 37–60
Organisation of American States (OAS) 350
Organisation of Eastern Caribbean States (OECS) 349–50
Organisation of Petroleum Exporting Countries (OPEC) 352
organisations
    international trade 351–4
    local organisations 176–7, 346
    structures 44–50
overtime bans 84
ownership 16–20, 26–8

packaging 193, 197–8, 220–1
parties, contracts 105
partnerships 16–17
patents 198
payments 123–6, 133–47
    balance of payments 336–8
    bank accounts 134–8
    bank cards 137, 141–2
    cash/near cash 133–4
    debts 124
    documentation 123–6
    electronic banking 138–41
    foreign trade 125–6
    goods 123–4
    promotions 221–2
    rates of pay 71–2
    wages 71–3, 320
perfect competition 201
personnel 38, 63–4
    see also employees
picketing 85
planning 91–4, 293
policies, insurance 155
pooling risks 149–59
PR see Public Relations
preference shares 269
premiums 155
pressure groups 85–6, 99
prices
    control 297–8
    determining prices 198–201
    marketing 194
    shares 270–1

primary production 8–10, 167–8
Principles of Business syllabus 364–5
private sector 15–20, 27–8
production 37–8, 160–87
    business location 177–8
    business size 171–7
    chains 167–8
    direct production 1, 8, 11
    expansion 177, 179–80
    factors 160–6
    indirect production 3–4, 8, 11
    levels 16–17
    methods 169–70
    questionnaires 368
    techniques 169–70
    technology 164–5, 181–2
    types 8–10, 169
products 193, 195–7
profit 27–8, 241, 286–7
promotions 195, 219–22, 238–9, 296–7
Public Relations (PR) 221
public sector
    companies 18–20, 50
    enterprise 15
    expenditure 326
    profit motive 27–8
purchasing 117–19, 122–3, 311

quality control 163–4, 170, 360
questionnaires 210, 213, 367–70, 374
quotas 338, 340
quotations 116–17

rail transport 242–3
rates, taxes 312
rates of pay 71–2
records 65, 127–9, 165
recreation 300
recruitment 61–9
redundancy 65–6
references 63
regional aspects 176–7, 346–63
regulatory practices 28
reports 371–2, 375–7
research 190–1, 209–15, 366
restrictions, free trade 339–41
restrictive practices 84–5
retailers 234–41
return on capital invested 287
return on shares 270
revenue 281–2
risk 149–50, 177, 179
river transportation 244
road transportation 243

safety 75–6
salaries 71–3, 320
Sale of Goods Act 223
sales 219–23, 238–40, 267–8, 338–9
sampling 211, 213
satisfaction, jobs 70
savings 266–7
SBA see school-based assessment
scarcity, modern society 4–5

school-based assessment (SBA) 364–77
    alternative to SBA 377
    data collection 366–72, 374–5
    Principles of Business syllabus 364–5
    report writing 375–7
    requirements 364–5
    research 366
    starting the project 365–6
    three profiles 364, 372–4
sea transportation 244–5
secondary production 8–10, 167–8
securities trading 268–70
security 293–4
segmentation, markets 189–90, 212–13
shareholders 17, 19, 98
shares 267–73
short-term finance 264–5
sit-ins 85
small businesses 50–3, 171–2
social accounting 319–33
social services 292, 299–300
sole proprietors 16
space buying 219
specialists 4, 11, 47–8, 171, 260–1
speculation 271
sponsorship 221
staff see employees
stakeholders 12, 98–9
stamp duties 312
standard of living 319–21, 323
standing orders 138–9
start-up finance 263–4
state corporations 26–7
state security 293
statements of account 123–4
stock market 267–73
stock records 127–9, 165
stockbrokers 271–2
strikes 84
subsidies 298, 340
subsistence economies 1, 6
Superintendent of Insurance, Jamaica 148
supermarkets 236
supply 200–1

tariffs 338, 340, 351
taxation 122–3, 298, 309–18
teamwork 43–4
technology
    Internet 141, 239
    MIS 55–7
    production 164–5, 181–2
tele-banking 141
telephone trading 237
termination, offers 110
terms of sales 221–2
tertiary production 8, 10–11, 167–8
tourism 301, 359
trade 296–7, 334–46, 351–4
trade unions 82–6
training 61–9
transactions 115–25
transportation 241–8
turnover 284–6
Two Factor Theory of Motivation 54–5

underdeveloped economies 329
unemployment 301, 356–7
uninsurable risks 150
union busting 85
unions see trade unions
unit trusts 270
urbanisation 357–8
utmost good faith 151

vacancies 61
vending machines 237

wages 71–3, 320
water transportation 243–5
welfare services 65, 292, 299–300
wholesalers 232–4
working conditions 74–6
working-to-rule 85
World Bank 349
World Trade Organisation (WTO) 351–2